THE WORD DOES EVERYTHING

Kenneth Hagen

THE WORD DOES EVERYTHING

KEY CONCEPTS OF LUTHER ON TESTAMENT, SCRIPTURE, VOCATION, CROSS, AND WORM.

ALSO ON METHOD AND ON CATHOLICISM

COLLECTION OF ESSAYS

MARQUETTE
UNIVERSITY
PRESS

MARQUETTE STUDIES IN THEOLOGY
NO. 87
ANDREW TALLON, SERIES EDITOR

© 2016 Marquette University Press
Milwaukee, Wisconsin 53201-3141
All rights reserved.
www.marquette.edu/mupress/

Library of Congress Cataloging-in-Publication Data

Names: Hagen, Kenneth, author.
Title: The word does everything : key concepts of Luther on testament,
 scripture, vocation, cross, and worm : also on method and on Catholicism :
 collection of essays / Kenneth Hagen.
Description: First [edition]. | Milwaukee, Wisconsin : Marquette University
 Press, 2016. | Series: Marquette studies in theology ; No. 87 | Includes
 bibliographical references and index.
Identifiers: LCCN 2016034157 | ISBN 9781626007123 (hardcover : alk. paper)
Subjects: LCSH: Luther, Martin, 1483-1546.
Classification: LCC BR333.3 .H34 2016 | DDC 230/.41--dc23
LC record available at https://urldefense.proofpoint.com/v2/url?u=https-
3A__lccn.loc.gov_2016034157&d=CwIFAg&c=S1d2Gs1Y1NQV8Lx35_
Qi5FnTH2uYWyh_OhOS94IqYCo&r=RDLTynvHMHORDX10ihnhDfYn3T
ge-JUP_TILOYVEj7s&m=Unt8x-lI9yMCFd-UU-46IBLEYlRBmm9nhUWYzY
OfmCE&s=QBppGijRIonm0AGejLO9b5VS_2U2Kt-p9RpYMqQAMGY&e=

Cover art: Freehand by Zora Ruen after traditional Luther rose.

♾ The paper used in this publication meets the minimum requirements of the
American National Standard for Information Sciences—
Permanence of Paper for Printed Library Materials, ANSI Z39.48-1992.

MARQUETTE UNIVERSITY PRESS
MILWAUKEE

The Association of Jesuit University Presses

CONTENTS

ACKNOWLEDGMENTS[1]

I acknowledge and thank the following persons, editors, and publishers for their permission to reprint the items included in this volume.

Michael J Albrecht, Senior Editor, *LOGIA* (I.0)

David Schultenover, S.J., *Theological Studies*, Editor (I.1)

Max Engammare, Directeur, Librairie Droz S.A. (II.2)

Tom DeVries, International Sales I Rights Manager, Wm. B. Eerdmans Publishing Company (II.3)

Paul Rorem, editor, and Virgil Thompson, Managing Editor, *Lutheran Quarterly* (III.2)

Charles Gieschen, Associate Editor, *Concordia Theological Quarterly* (IV.3)

Diane Grosse, Copyrights & Permissions Manager, Duke University Press (V.3)

---

1 The numbers in parentheses here in the Acknowledgments refer to the numbers in brackets in the Table of Contents [Series Editor's note].

PREFACE[2]

T he articles and chapters contained herein are well worth bringing to the public again. People still call Luther a "monk," people still try to pinpoint a time for Luther's "evangelical breakthrough," and charges of anti-Semitism are still current. I offer solutions to these problems (I.0, I.1, V.2).

I offer further evidence for Luther's early success with students (I.2, often cited in literature). A friend who encouraged me to go public with these publications made sure I included my study on Christ as "worm" (I.4).

My presentation before an international audience is II.2. One lecture at Marquette that the coeds loved was Luther's repeating Psalm 116: "Every man is a liar." I propose an end to the customary phrase "medieval quadriga" (II.6).

My critique of Wingren on vocation is well known (III.2). Would that my work on Luther's kingdoms (four instead of two) were well known (III.3).

One reason for this collection is that some of my writings appeared in confessional Lutheran publications, not well known outside Lutheran-confessional circles (III.1. III.3, III.4, IV.2).

I make my own statement about Bible and method. In the last section I come forward with my observations about Catholicism from my years at Marquette University.

I owe many thanks to my proofreader, Aldemar Hagen, and to Marquette University Press and Dr. Andy Tallon, director, for making this publication possible.

Kenneth Hagen
Lake Mills, Wisconsin
November 6, 2010

---

2   The numbers in parentheses here in the Preface refer to the numbers in brackets in the Table of Contents [Editor's note].

INTRODUCTION

Trained under Heiko Oberman at Harvard Divinity School in the History of Christian Thought, we were taught to view everything during the Reformation in the light of the (late) Middle Ages. Teaching at Marquette University brought me into the tradition that sprang from the late Middle Ages. One of my successors asked me if I learned anything about the Middle Ages by teaching there; I said definitely. In fact I found that I had to learn to think like a Catholic in order to be fair in my presentation of Catholic positions to the students, medieval thought and especially the Catholic Reformation(s).

After teaching for two years at a Lutheran college just out of Harvard, I was invited to come to Marquette University, initially as a visiting (assistant) professor. The rest is history, as they say.

What is not (recorded) history is that in the course of my work there I had something of a conversion in my thinking—from a typical Harvard liberal (everything is relative) to something akin to Luther's theology (relativism is relative). Many years later I became intrigued as to when this happened. I went back and checked my publications and could not see any changes in my thinking. Perhaps it was a coincidence that I was invited to give lectures at confessional Lutheran programs in the later years. My notes indicate that I had this turnaround in thinking around 1975.

The reason I know there was something of a conversion is that I and a Jesuit/student were on a program at a Lutheran pastors' retreat. He said to me: "I have not heard you talking like this before."

The focus on the Middle Ages was that of my dissertation: *Luther's Lectures on Hebrews in the Light of Medieval Commentaries on Hebrews*. Out of these years came my focus on testament and Scripture. I came to see that Luther's reworking of the relation of the New Testament to the Old was as nuanced and complicated as Augustine's was. Working on the "Young Luther" which included his lectures on Hebrews of 1517–18 led me to his unique view of Christ on the cross—as worm! Until my dying day, I suspect that I will ponder to what extent Luther is 'unique' (the German problem of *Eigentümlichkeit*) in relation to medieval theology. Of my students, Franz Posset is at one end of the possibilities (it is all in Bernard) and Burnell Eckhardt at the other end (Luther is a confessional Lutheran). If I were younger, I would research the Christology of the early church because I have a suspicion that the reception of Chalcedon holds a clue to Luther's Christology in context.

What I said at my retirement was that two things sustained me at Marquette University (I was the only Lutheran who survived at Catholic faculties): I did not emphasize Luther's view of the papacy and Norwegian stubbornness.

BIBLIOGRAPHIC INFORMATION

"Luther, Martin (1483–1546)." In *Dictionary of Major Biblical Interpreters*, edited by Donald K. McKim, 687–94. Downers Grove, Ill.: InterVarsity Press, 2007.

I

I.0 "So You Think Luther Was a Monk? Stop It! *Logia* 19 (Eastertide 2010) 35–37.

I.1. "Changes in the Understanding of Luther: The Development of the Young Luther," *Theological Studies* 29 (September 1968) 472–96.

I.2. "An Addition to the Letters of John Lang. Introduction and Translation," *Archiv für Reformationsgeschichte* 60/1 (1969) 27–32.

I.3. "From Testament to Covenant in the Early Sixteenth Century," *The Sixteenth Century Journal* 3 (April 1972) 1–24.

I.4. "The Testament of a Worm: Luther on Testament and Covenant to 1525," *Consensus. A Canadian Lutheran Journal of Theology* 8/1 (January 1982) 12–20.

I.5. "The Historical Context of the Smalcald Articles," *Concordia Theological Quarterly* 51 (October 1987) 245–53.

II

II.1. "The History of Scripture in the Church." In *The Bible in the Churches*, edited by Kenneth Hagen, revised for the 3rd ed., 1–28. Milwaukee, Wisc.: Marquette University Press, 1998.

II.2. "What did the term *Commentarius* mean to sixteenth-century theologians?" In *Théorie et pratique de l'exégèse*. Actes du troisième colloque international sur l'histoire de l'exégèse biblique au XVIe siècle (Genève, 31 août – 2 septembre 1988), edited by Irena Backus and Francis Higman. "Etudes de Philologie et d'Histoire," vol. 43, 13–38. Geneva: Libraire Droz, 1990.

II.3. "*Omnis homo mendax:* Luther on Psalm 116." In *Biblical Interpretation in the Era of the Reformation.* Essays Presented to David C. Steinmetz in Honor of His Sixtieth Birthday, edited by Richard A. Muller and John L. Thompson, 85–102. Grand Rapids, Mich.: William B. Eerdmans Publishing Company, 1996.

II.4. "Did Peter Err? The Text Is the Best Judge. *Luther on Galatians* (1519–1538)." In *Augustine, the Harvest, and Theology (1300–1650).* Essays Dedicated to Heiko Augustinus Oberman in Honor of his Sixtieth Birthday, edited by Kenneth Hagen, 110–126. Leiden: E. J. Brill, 1990.

II.5. "It Is All in the Et Cetera. Luther and the Elliptical Reference," *Luther-Bulletin. Tidschrift voor interconfessioneel Lutheronderzoek* 3 (November 1994) 57–67.

II.6. "A Ride on the *Quadriga* with Luther," *Luther-Bulletin. Tidschrift voor interconfessioneel Lutheronderzoek* 13 (November 2004) 5–24.

III

III.1. "Luther's Preaching to the Hometown Folks." In *Preaching through the Ages,* The Pieper Lectures, vol. 8, edited by John A. Maxfield, 64–87. St. Louis, Mo.: Concordia Historical Institute & The Luther Academy, 2004.

III.2. "*A Critique of Wingren on Luther on Vocation,*" *Lutheran Quarterly* 16 (Autumn 2002) 249–73.

III.3. "Luther's Doctrine of the Two Kingdoms." In *God and Caesar Revisited,* edited by John R. Stephenson, 15–29. "Luther Academy Conference Papers No. 1." Shorewood, Minn.: Luther Academy [USA], 1995. Reprinted in *Reformation & Revival, A Quarterly Journal for Church Leadership* 7 (Fall 1998) 103–27.

III.4. "The Doctrines of Vocation and Ethics and Martin Luther." In *Confessional Lutheran Ethics,* edited by Jennifer H. Maxfield and Bethany Preus, 47–63. "Papers presented at the Congress on the Lutheran Confessions, Itasca, Illinois, April 16–18, 1998." St. Louis, Mo.: The Luther Academy, 2009,

IV

IV.1. "Luthers Korsteologi." In *Theologi på tidens torg: Festskrift til Peter Wilhelm Bøckman*, edited by Peder Borgen, et al. "Publikasjoner utgitt av Religionsvitenskapelig institutt Universitetet i Trondheim," vol. 23, 71–81. Trondheim: Tapir, 1987.

IV.2. "Dr. Robert D. Preus. Confessional Systematician and Teacher of the Confessions." In *The Theology and Life of Robert D. Preus*, edited by Jennifer H. Maxfield and Bethany Preus. 1–19. "Papers presented at the Congress on the Lutheran Confessions, Itasca, Illinois, April 8–10, 1999," St. Louis, Mo.: The Luther Academy, 2009.

IV.3. "Luther on Atonement—Reconfigured. *Dedicated to the Memory of Dr. Robert Preus, Concordia Theological Quarterly* 61 (1997) 251–76.

V

V.1. "Does Method Drive Biblical Study?" *Logia, A Journal of Lutheran Theology* 10 (Epiphany 2001) 37–40.

V.2. "Luther's So-Called *Judenschriften*: A Genre Approach," *Archiv für Reformationsgeschichte* 90 (1999) 130–58.

V.3. "'De Exegetica Methodo,' Niels Hemmingsen's *De Methodis* (1555)." In *The Bible in the Sixteenth Century*, edited by David Steinmetz. "Duke Monographs in Medieval and Renaissance Studies," vol. 11, 181–96, 252–55. Durham, N.C.: Duke University Press, 1990.

VI

VI.1. "Observing Catholicism, 'What I observed about the Catholic Church while teaching with the Jesuits for 33 years at Marquette University,'" *Logia* 17/3 (Holy Trinity 2008) 57–59.

VI.2. "The Decline of Christianity in Europe," *Logia* 13 (Reformation 2004) 27–33.

MARTIN LUTHER (1483–1546)

L ife. Martin Luther, son of Hans Luther, a miner, and Margrete Lindermann, was born November 10, 1483, in Eisleben, Saxony. After early schooling he attended Erfurt University, 1501–1505, earning his bachelor's and master's degrees. While he was returning to Erfurt in July 1505, Luther was thrown to the ground in a thunderstorm; frightened, he declared "I will become a monk," a promise he honored by entering the Black Cloister of the Augustinian Hermits in Erfurt (July 7, 1505). Ordained February 27, 1507, he was assigned to study theology and was transferred to Wittenberg to study and lecture on moral philosophy in the arts faculty. He received the degree of bachelor of biblical studies in March 1509 from the theological faculty of Wittenberg; he also became a lecturer on Peter Lombard's *Sentences* that year (his notes from 1509 to 1511 on the *Sentences* are extant). In 1512 Luther received his doctorate in theology and was appointed professor of Bible. In 1513 Luther began lecturing in Wittenberg on the Bible and did so for more than thirty years.

Context. Luther's reformation was theological and pastoral. A basic presupposition of his reformation program is the conviction that external behavior reflects internal attitude. A favorite image for Luther is that a good tree bears good fruit and, conversely, a bad tree, bad fruit. The bad fruits in Christendom could be reformed only by rooting out the bad tree that produced them. Too many reformers had come no further than attacking the bad fruit. A good tree can only grow in the soil of the one, holy, catholic and apostolic faith expressed in the Scriptures, and therefore a reform of the church's life (fruit) could effectively come about only through a reformation of the church's faith (tree).

Luther's theological effort for reformation could be described as his effort to catholicize the church, feeling as he did that the church had ceased to be that one, holy, catholic and apostolic church it confessed to be. The church that Luther sought to bring about by his theological efforts was a church unified by the universal faith of the forebears, rooted in the holy gospel of Jesus Christ.

Luther's self-understanding revolved around his being a doctor of the church, a theologian responsible for the church's faith. Throughout his life, his professorial, pastoral and personal activities reflected his training as a doctor of sacred Scripture and the effort on his part to allow the Word of God to interact with faith and life. Theology must be biblical and vernacular.

The historical context for Luther's thought included his reaction to late medieval currents of thought. His response was both negative and positive.

First, Luther was negative toward nominalism, the philosophy that reality (universals) exists in name only. He had experience with nominalist currents of thought through his education. Because he was antagonistic towards nominalism does not mean that he favored scholasticism (academic theology), nominalism's opponent. Luther rejected scholasticism in general because of its speculative bent (theology of glory), seeking to penetrate into the nature and necessity of divine essence; for the same reason nominalism also rejected scholasticism. Luther was negative toward nominalism because of its optimistic and nonbiblical view of human, natural powers—that one is able and responsible to initiate and build up good works for salvation. The covenantal model of nominalism placed responsibility on both parties to carry out the obligations of their pact.

Luther later accused humanism of the same anthropological optimism. Humanism and nominalism held to the dignity and freedom of human will and reason. By opposing these two movements Luther was really being critical of human, natural abilities to initiate and cooperate with God. In his response to these movements Luther emphasized that human will and reason are in bondage until they are liberated by God's grace.

Second, Luther was positive towards certain late medieval movements. For example, he was impressed with the genuine piety of various mystical treatises, so much so that he edited and published some of them. Luther was a part of the movement of spiritual renewal. He was also inclined to mysticism because of its strong emphasis on the personal (noninstitutional, nonacademic) relationship with God. Like many mystics, Luther felt that pilgrims had been beset with too many roadblocks on their way up the mountain, whereas Christ had come to clear away the many roadblocks of legalism and speculation.

Luther also favored Augustinianism, the revival of Augustinian thought, because he held to the authority of the doctor of the church, Augustine. Luther often appealed to the great doctor in his quarrels with scholasticism and nominalism and in his opposition to late medieval Pelagianism (works righteousness). What attracted Luther in Augustine was the theology of grace that made humans incapable of earning it and God totally able to give it. Luther was impressed with Augustine's christological interpretation of Scripture: the unity of Scripture in Jesus Christ expressed in one testament of justification. Humans are concupiscent; God is grace.

Luther inclined towards conciliarism, at least through the 1520s, because like other (pre)reformers he felt that Christendom was encumbered with corrupted and corrupting power that would not bring about the necessary reformation. Politically and ecclesiastically Luther felt the best chances for the reform of Christendom lay with a council; but as his and other calls for a council were aborted, he became disillusioned with conciliar possibilities as the 1520s wore on.

The historical context of Luther's thought was to carry on in the doctoral tradition of Augustine and the Fathers, monasticism and mysticism (Benedictinism to Bernard), seeking theological renewal of his one, holy, catholic and apostolic church based on Scripture.

Major Writings. Early exegetical writings were *Lectures on the Psalms* (1513-1515), preceded by the *Preface of Jesus Christ,* and lectures on Romans (1515-1516), Galatians (1516-1517) and Hebrews (1517-1518). The first writing in German was *The Seven Penitential Psalms* (1517). Here the major Augustinian themes are present throughout as in all of his work: grace, faith, Christ, the testament of Christ, Scripture interpreting itself and the centrality of the Word.

The *Heidelberg Disputation* (1518) is the major source for Luther's theology of the cross. He issued several polemics on Indulgences (1517-1518), including the Ninety-five Theses (October 31, 1517). Important instructional treatises appeared in 1519 and 1520: penance, baptism, Lord's Supper, death, good works and the Lord's Prayer. Famous Reformation treatises were issued in 1520: *To the Christian Nobility* (on social reform), *Babylonian Captivity* (on sacraments) and *Freedom of the Christian* (Christian life). The *Magnificat* (1521) shows

Luther as a medieval theologian whose Mariology, typical of the age, was lost in later Lutheranism.

Luther's *Bondage of the Will* (1525), which along with his commentary on Galatians he regarded as his two most important works, is a fierce appeal for the freedom of God to save without any interference from will, reason or good intent. His sharp rhetoric sought to establish that before God we come with nothing; if we were to come with something, then God would not be totally free to save and totally Savior. It is a positive treatise on the power of the electing will of God to save.

Beginning in 1519 Luther published more commentaries on Galatians and the Psalms. He had a lifelong attachment to the Psalms, Paul and John. The prefaces to the Old Testament (1523) and New Testament (1522), continuing into the 1530s and 1540s, provide excellent entry into Luther's view of individual books of the Bible. An excellent overview of Luther's theology for church and home are his Small and Large Catechisms of 1529. Luther's major writing on the history of the church and the marks of the church is his 1539 treatise *On the Councils and the Church*. Luther's last major exegetical course was on Genesis (1535-1545).

Approaches and Methods of Biblical Interpretation. From early times through the Reformation, theology was practiced as the discipline of the sacred page (*sacra pagina*). The monastery became the place and the monks' daily liturgy was the context for the practice of theology. Holy Writ was the sacred page; the canon of Scripture was the rule of faith. The goal of life for the medieval pilgrim (*viator*) as well as the final goal of theology was to go home, home to God, home to the Trinity (in Augustine's words).

The sacred page was seen as coming directly from God, about God and for the pilgrim's journey to God. Theology, whether expressed in doctrine, liturgy or catechesis, was the discipline of the sacred page. The sacred page was the record of God's creation and redemption. Theology, Scripture, commentary and God were bound up in one world and were focused on the sacred page.

The rise of scholastic theology in the twelfth century was linked to the discipline of dialectic and its use of the question. The discipline of scholastic theology practiced in the schools (universities) was the discipline of faith seeking understanding. In the universities in the twelfth century, theology shifted to sacred doctrine (*sacra doctrina*).

The schoolmen wrote Bible commentaries, and they wrote sacred theology.

Scholastic theology was based on the method of *quaestio* (question) and dialectic. By the later Middle Ages, a caricature of the scholastic question was, How many Angels can dance on the head of a pin? Such a question cannot be found in scholastic sources themselves, although scholasticism, described as decadent by sixteenth-century Reformers, may have become too abstract by the eve of the Reformation. In the twelfth and thirteenth centuries the final goal of theology was still the Beatific Vision. The shift from sacred page to sacred doctrine was the shift from locating the substance of theology in Scripture to locating the substance in doctrine.

The scholarship of the Christian humanists and the invention of the printing press and in the latter part of the fifteenth century contributed to the shift within theology: the sacred letter as literature. Theology was seen not as the monk's work of prayer and praise or as the professor's academic questions and propositions but as the educative task of reviving the pagan and Christian classics. The study of the sacred letter of Scripture was intended to lead men and women not so much to God as to a better society, church, education and government. Theology as the study of the philosophy of Christ (Desiderius Erasmus) was to lead to piety, morality and justice.

The goal of the historical-critical method beginning with the sixteenth century is to understand the letter of the original text. The goal of sacred doctrine is to understand the faith of the Church. The goal of the sacred page is to understand and reach God (the Trinity).

These approaches to the sacred page (monastery), sacred doctrine (university) and sacred letter (printing press) continued in the early and late Reformation. Luther continued the monastic discipline of the sacred page minus monastic rules. The Council of Trent and Lutheran orthodoxy continued the discipline of sacred doctrine. Philipp Melanchthon approached Scripture as sacred letter (literature).

It is often assumed that Luther ended the medieval approach to the Bible and started the modern methods, but Luther approached Scripture in a manner appropriate to what the document is (*sacra pagina*). Luther did not superimpose his agenda onto Scripture; he took out and applied the message of Scripture as he claimed to do and thus was consistent with the grammar and vocabulary of Scripture.

Major Themes. Several major themes emerged in Luther's works.

Bible and Theology. Luther was very concerned to place the Bible in the center of everything: church, theology and especially preaching. The main point of the Reformation was that the gospel must be proclaimed. Along with the important pamphlets, the pulpits of the evangelical cities (Wittenberg, Zurich, Geneva) were the media for information. The Reformation was a movement of the Word: Christ, Scripture and preaching—in that order. They all are the Word of God. The Reformers used the printed Word, studied the Word, prayed the Word; but their concern was to bring preaching back into the Mass, preaching in the vernacular and preaching on the text of Scripture. When Luther said that the church is not a pen-house but a mouth-house, he meant that the good news cannot properly be put in (dead) letters but is to be proclaimed loudly (in German).

What the scholastics separated—theology and commentary on Scripture—Luther sought to bring together again along the lines of *sacra pagina.* Scripture alone is the sole authority for the church, the discipline of theology and the life of faith. Luther continued the call for the reform of the church on the basis of Scripture. Every office and activity in the Church falls under the judgment of Scripture. All of theology is contained in Scripture. God has revealed all that we need to know about God in Christ. Theology must be biblical theology; any other kind is human invention.

Scripture is its own authority because it is clear. No other authority is needed to see through its meaning. Luther was not concerned about some theory of inspiration. That came later. In his view the Bible is the Word. The Reformers were aware of the critical discussions among the humanists about the text, authorship and language, and Luther engaged in some of this. The point of the Word is the presence of the Word in Scripture, church and preaching. The humanist sense of the distance of Scripture from the present was not accepted. The scholastic separation of theology from Scripture was attacked. The purpose of theology is to serve preaching, the main task of the church.

Interpretation of the Bible. Luther was premodern; he continued the general medieval understanding of interpretation as commentary, annotation and exposition. The modern interpreter continues to develop the humanist perspective of the historical past; thus interpretation in modern time is bridging the gulf between ancient literature and modern thinking. The early Reformers continued the monastic approach of total immersion into the thinking and language of Scripture so that there is only one language, one biblical theology.

Luther emphasized that Scripture is its own interpreter. He argued that the papacy had built a wall of authoritative interpretation around itself so that Scripture could be read only as the papacy interpreted it. One late medieval synthesis maintained that Scripture is to tradition as foundation is to interpretation (Ockham). Strong in the sixteenth century was the question of an authoritative interpretation of Scripture. Summarizing the Roman position, the Council of Trent decreed later in the century: No one, relying on his or her own skill in matters of faith and morals, "wresting" the sacred Scriptures to his or her own senses, should presume to interpret the said sacred Scripture contrary to that sense which holy mother church, whose it is to judge of the true sense and interpretation of the holy Scripture, has held and does hold.

For Luther, Scripture itself attests to its message and meaning. Christ and the Spirit are at work in the Word. The Reformers insisted that postapostolic claims of authoritative interpretation were precisely the reason why the Word of God lost its central place in the life of the church.

The Reformation interpretation of Scripture was engaged in theological polemics. The humanists used Scripture to attack the church, but they were not so much interested in the pure doctrines of Scripture as they were in exposing the corruption and folly of the present situation in the light of the piety of Scripture. The early Reformers fought for pure doctrine on the basis of Scripture and the Fathers. The doctrine of justification by faith alone, by grace alone, by Christ alone was seen as the central doctrine of Scripture. The doctrine of justification by faith is the criterion by which all other doctrines, offices and practices in the church are judged. The criteriological priority of justification by faith is established in Scripture. The church stands or falls, said Luther, on the scriptural teaching of justification. There were other issues, other polemics, but the procedure was the same. Doctrinal reform was forged and pleaded on the basis of Scripture.

Law and Gospel. Basic for Luther's understanding of Scripture was his distinction between law and gospel. The gospel of Jesus Christ is the fulfillment and end of the Mosaic law. Law and gospel are in all books of the Bible. The gospel is the good news that salvation is in Christ alone. Abraham and others saw that gospel in the promises;

they believed and were justified. Luther transposes Augustine's distinction between Old Testament and New Testament as ways of salvation to law and gospel. The way of the law is do this, and do not do that. The way of the gospel is believe, and it has already been done for a person in Christ. The law is command; the gospel is gift, the gift of forgiveness. When the law commands, failure results because one cannot fulfill the law on one's own power ("The good I would, I do not"). The law humbles; the gospel picks up. One cannot be picked up unless one is put down to size. Being brought low (law) and being raised up (gospel) are the downs and ups of the Christian life, the experience of sin (brought by the law) and the experience of forgiveness (brought by Christ). The distinction between law and gospel, the doctrine of justification by faith apart from works and the understanding of the core of Scripture are all the same for Luther.

Christ the center of Scripture. The center of Scripture for Luther is Christ, present in both the Old and the New Testament. Christ is the eternal Word of God, present in Old Testament times in the form of promise, present in New Testament times in the person of Jesus and present in the church through Word and sacrament. In all cases, Christ the Word is the effective means of grace. The center or core of Scripture is "what drives Christ" (*was Christum treibet*), that is, what preaches Christ, what promotes or points to Christ. Christ is at the core of God's plan of salvation. God promises through prophets; God delivers in person. All of Scripture leads to Christ, and Christ leads to salvation.

The simple sense. Luther's response to the various senses of meaning in the Middle Ages (fourfold, double-literal) was that Scripture has one simple sense (most often, Christ). Or Luther will talk about the grammatical sense as the meaning of the text, that the grammatical meaning and theological meaning are the same. Luther availed himself of humanist scholarship and was a part of a late medieval trend to highlight (once again) the christological meaning of a text. Luther also used allegory, not to establish a doctrine but to embellish it. He also used the other spiritual senses. Luther on Scripture is often presented as a total break from the medieval world. That came later. In the area of the senses of meaning, Luther is a part of the medieval trend to call for a return to the letter of the text and then in practice to go on and find other senses of meaning. After all, and all the medievals knew this, the New Testament itself uses allegory.

Theology of testament. Luther's distinction is his construction of Scripture as containing a single testament (will, promise) of Christ. God's last and only will and testament is that he would die for our salvation. The promise is the declaration of the will and testament. The death of the God-man validates his testament. The inheritance is the forgiveness of sins and eternal life. The (new) testament of Christ is eternal. It is played out in time, but there is no development in the eternal. Augustine and the medieval theologians generally saw a development and transformation within and between the Old and New Testament. Luther held that the New Testament is older than the Old because it is the oldest (eternal). The Old Testament begins and ends in time.

Luther's response to his contemporary situation was the response of a theology of testament. Testament or will is the model that accounts for most of the pieces in Luther's supposedly nonsystematic theology. The word *testament* is a short summary of all God's grace fulfilled in Christ. Testament or will is the testament of God promised throughout the Old Testament era and books that he would send a testator (Christ) to bring the inheritance of forgiveness of sins and eternal life, which is received in faith. The death and resurrection of the testator, God in flesh, validates the testament.

Promise, one ingredient in the category of testament, is God's announcement of redemption. Redemption as well as creation is *ex nihilo.* The totality of the testament from promise through inheritance is a reality present from the beginning to the end of time. The New Testament is the eternal testament of Christ.

The second ingredient in testament is Luther's theology of Word. The Word is the dynamic manifestation of the person of God. Important for Luther is the passage in Isaiah that God's Word will not return void, which means the Word will accomplish that which it sets out to do. The Word accomplishes a faithful response which brings about the forgiveness of sins and eternal life. The promise is God's Word that he will one day die and rise and validate his testament.

The third part of Luther's testament theology is a theology of the cross. The theology of the cross has an antispeculative force to it which is directed against a theology of glory. The theology of the cross is contextual, working within what God did in Christ on the cross. Rather than using philosophical terms, Luther talks about the wounds of

Christ on the cross and Christ as a worm on the cross, thus emphasizing the total humiliation of the God-man. The humiliation of the cross is God's total identification with the human situation in order to redeem that situation so that we can live by faith.

The fourth aspect of Luther's theology of testament is grace. Grace for Luther is unilateral gift. One of the primary functions of testament is that the testator makes out his will without the recipient having done anything to deserve the inheritance. Testament, at least God's way, is gratuitous. The heir in no way merits the inheritance. Testament for Luther stands in contrast with covenant. Often Luther will use covenant as a synonym for testament and understand it as unilateral gift. In late medieval covenant theologies, the covenant is a bilateral, twoway pact, bond or agreement. These various covenant theologians were at least semiPelagian because they called for some human action as a necessary part of the pact. The grace of the unilateral testament, however, is the cross and resurrection. A covenant does not require death. The unilateral act of grace proves that God's promise is true. The cross is final proof that God's testament is valid. The resurrection completes God's action. For Luther, then, grace is God's selfactualizing Word that accomplishes its purpose without requiring any act on our part.

The fifth aspect of testament is faith or trust in the inheritance. One receives faith through the Word accomplishing its purpose. Faith is a gift of grace. Trust is confidence that Christ not only died for the sins of humankind but also he died for me. Trust is intimately bound up with Luther's notion of the certitude of salvation. Christians are certain of their salvation because their salvation is in Christ, and Christ is for me and for us. If salvation were dependent on something that we were to do, free will, free reason, then Luther in no way could have any confidence. Confidence rests in Christ alone.

Principles of Biblical Interpretation. Technically, Luther did not have a hermeneutic because hermeneutics is a nineteenth-century discipline that presupposes the distance of the biblical text and the need for the interpreter to bridge the gap and make any interpretative moves necessary to bring the text into modern linguistic jargon understandable in post-Enlightenment philosophy.

To be a theologian, the three rules (1539) of prayer (*oratio*), meditation (*meditatio*) and temptation or experience (*tentatio*), need to be practiced every day. These show Luther indebted to the sacred reading (*lectio divina*) of Scripture deep in the theological tradition of the Church.

The core of Scripture is what drives, teaches and pronounces Christ (*was Christum treibet*). *Treiben* has to do with transportation; so that in Scripture, the important thing is to see that the sacred page drives us and brings us to Christ.

Canon within the Canon is a principle often associated with Luther. The danger of this dictum for Luther would be that some subjective principle of selectivity would choose the inner canon and force everything into that mold. And yet several scholars feel that Luther did exactly that with his insistence that the first article, justification by faith, interprets the whole. Christ, not a doctrine or principle, is at the center of Scripture; Luther consistently maintains that Christ is the babe in the manger and Scripture is the manger that supports him.

Scripture alone means Scripture as the sole authority as opposed to the human traditions of the papacy. Scripture alone means Christ alone.

Scripture has a single, christological meaning. Luther recognized and used the biblical and medieval fourfold sense (literal, allegorical, tropological, anagogical) where it embellished the single simplest, that is, the grammatical sense.

Scripture is the living voice of the gospel (*viva vox evangelii*); it can never be contained in a writing, much less a law; nor can an interpretation take the place of the text itself (himself).

Scripture is it own interpreter (*scriptura sacra sui ipsius interpres*) means Scripture is to be used to interpret itself based on the echo of Scripture within Scripture. The Old Testament is ruminating over the Psalter, exodus, covenant and law, as the New Testament interprets the Old Testament and its own articles of faith.

Scripture confirms (authenticates) itself (*Die Schrift verbügt sich selbst*) means no outside authority is needed to bring credibility to Scripture. Scripture attests to its own veracity.

Scripture is clear because the message of salvation delivered by the Holy Spirit is overwhelmingly clear and persuasive.

Significance. Luther's understanding of his discipline of theology was that it was the discipline of the sacred page (*sacra pagina*). The linkage of Luther with the tradition of *sacra pagina* goes counter to much of modern effort to see Luther as the first Enlightenment figure, the first rationalist, nationalist, romantic, liberal, historical critic or hermeneutician. The distinctive feature of this discipline is that it sees sacred matters as a page, which is a more logical approach to Holy Writ than are the efforts of the eighteenth- and nineteenth-century Enlightenment to interpret the Bible as ancient literature because it is consistent with the text of Scripture. The sacred page is the work of God directly and immediately; it bears the imprint of God, God's will, God's action, God's Word.

The discipline of the sacred page, not new to Luther, assumes the unity of God's Word. The view of God is thoroughly trinitarian. The Christian confession of faith is based on the sacred page. The form that the confession or creed or rule of faith takes is trinitarian. The unity of Scripture thus is trinitarian. The action of God as recorded from beginning to end is the action of Three-in-One.

Scripture has a unique grammar. Luther was concerned to promote that grammar, that faith. Faith is the shape or form that the words take. It is true that Luther clung only to the grammatical meaning (*sensus*) of the words. He did so to preserve the single and simple sense, which most often is Christ. But Christ is not a meaning or sense. Christ is the *res*, the very thing itself of God.

Luther frequently urged the reader to pay special attention to the peculiar phrase, idiom, example or expression that Scripture employed. The grammatical sense points to Christ. The vocabulary of the sacred page takes the form of the creed. The faith of the church based on the grammar of faith is trinitarian. Thus the unity of the grammar of faith is the unity of God the Father, God the Son, and God the Holy Spirit. Luther was the doctor of faith.

When Luther used the word *interpret*, he attacked the idea and argued instead that Scripture is to be promoted and applied to the present age but not interpreted. Luther's work of commenting on Scripture continued the medieval genre of *enarratio*, which means to narrate and apply the message of Scripture in public. The use of Scripture is not to provide evidence or proof for an interpretation. Rather, Scripture is used to promote God.

To work with Scripture as Luther did is to employ the discipline of the sacred page. Theology for Luther employs the discipline of prayer, meditation and temptation. Such a discipline comes from the Psalter.

Luther was consistent to follow Scripture's lead for the discipline of theology. The goal of this discipline is God. Medieval commentators have been described as walking concordances. The same must be said for Luther. For Luther it was necessary that God's Word be consistent in its grammar, rhetoric and theology. The importance of Luther for our time is his clear perception and practice of theology in the tradition of *enarratio* and *sacra pagina*.

BIBLIOGRAPHY

Works. *Kritische Gesamtausgabe* (104 vols.; Weimar: Herman Bohlau, 1883-); *Luther's Works*, ed. J. Pelikan and H. Lehmann (55 vols.; St. Louis: Concordia; Philadelphia: Muhlenberg, 1955–). **Studies.** H. Bornkamm, *Luther and the Old Testament* (Philadelphia: Fortress, 1969); K. Hagen, *Luther's Approach to Scripture as seen in his 'Commentaries' on Galatians* (Tübingen: J. C. B. Mohr [Paul Siebeck], 1993). B. Hall, "Biblical Scholarship: Editions and Commentaries," *CHB* 3:38-93; W. J. Kooiman, *Luther and the Bible* (Philadelphia: Muhlenberg, 1961); B. Lohse, *Martin Luther: An Introduction to His Life and Work* (Philadelphia: Fortress, 1986); idem, *Martin Luther's Theology: Its Historical and Systematic Development*, trans. and ed. R. A. Harrisville (Minneapolis: Fortress, 1999); H. de Lubac, *The Sources of Revelation* (New York: Herder & Herder, 1968); D. H. McKim, ed., *The Cambridge Companion to Martin Luther* (Cambridge: Cambridge University Press, 2003); J. Pelikan, *Luther the Expositor* (St. Louis: Concordia, 1959); Luther Academy, *Luther Digest. An Annual Abridgment of Luther Studies*, ed. K. Hagen (St. Louis: Luther Academy, 1993-); J. Reumann, ed., in collaboration with S. H. Nafzger and H. H. Ditmanson, *Studies in Lutheran Hermeneutics* (Philadelphia: Fortress, 1979); D. C. Steinmetz, *Luther in Context* (Bloomington: Indiana University Press, 1986; idem, "Luther, Martin (1483-1546," *DBI* 2:96-98; E. Vogelsang, *Die Anfänge von Luther's Christologie nach der ersten Psalmenvorlesung* (Berlin: W. de Gruyter, 1929; J. W. Zophy "Martin Luther, 1483-1546," in *Research Guide to European Historical Biography*, ed. J. Moncure (Washington, DC: Beacham Publishing, 1993) 8: 3705-19.

SO YOU THINK LUTHER WAS A MONK? STOP IT!

How many times have you read in English the stereotypical line, "Martin Luther became an Augustinian monk in 1505 and was ordained a priest two years later"?[1] However, in the same issue of Calliope Mary Morton Cowan wrote, "Actually he became a friar."[2] Here is a sample of the cliché "Luther the monk" from the Internet and even from a published book:

> Although he would forever change Christianity, Martin Luther was a German monk who rose in his own rank to become a theologian, a reformer, and most importantly, a prominent figure who began asking deeper questions about the Bible and society.[3]

> Martin Luther (November 10, 1483 – February 18, 1546) was a German monk, priest, professor, theologian, and church reformer.[4]

> "How a Monk and a Mallet Changed the World."[5]

Even such a respected and established scholar as Scott Hendrix has Luther as "monk" plastered all over his book: "He was a sixteenth-century monk, priest, and professor in Wittenberg."[6] Confusion? Yes. Consider this: "Luther addressed his Latin treatise to his brother monks of the Augustinian order in Wittenberg" (AE 36:130). "Brother monks"? Talk about an oxymoron.

---

1 Lowell Green, "Seeds of Doubt: The Early Luther," in Calliope 9, no. 9 (May, 2009): 10.

2 Mary Morton Cowan, "I Will Become a Monk!" in Calliope 9. no. 9 (May, 2009): 7.

3 http://www. biographyshelf.com/martin_luther_biography.html.

4 http://www. ulike.net/Martin_Luther.

5 Stephen J. Nichols, The Reformation: How a Monk and a Mallet Changed the World (Wheaton, IL: Crossway/Good News Publishers, 2007).

6 Scott Hendrix, Recultivating the Vineyard: The Reformation Agendas of Christianization (Louisville: Westminister John Know Press, 2004), 42 and passim. He also mistakenly refers to Franciscans and Dominicans as monks.

monk—the same thing, right? Wrong. As editor of *Luther* ₀‑‑‑, ₁ do not know how many times I have had to correct the references to Luther as "monk." Monks were cloistered and were attached to a place (abbey) for life. Friars were attached not to a place but to an order and served their vocation in the secular world. Friar and monk are not synonymous terms, even though in popular usage monk is often used as a generic term for all members of religious orders. Thus the confusion and imprecision. But consider:

> Mendicant Friars (Latin *mendicare*, "to beg") are members of religious orders in the Roman Catholic Church, who take a vow of poverty by which they renounce all personal and communal property. They live chiefly by charity. After overcoming the initial opposition of the established clergy, the chief societies were authorized in the thirteenth century. They include: Friars Minor, or Franciscans (received papal approval in 1209); Friars Preachers, or Dominicans (1216); Carmelites (1245); and Augustinians (1256).

> The Augustinians, or Hermits of St. Augustine (Austin Friars), trace their origin to the illustrious Bishop of Hippo. The various branches which subsequently developed were united and constituted from various bodies of hermits a mendicant order by Alexander IV. (Const. "Iis, quæ", 31 July, 1255, and Const. "Licet", 4 May, 1256: *Ordo Eremitarum S. Augustini*).[7]

I used to tell my students that monks never went home for Christmas. Friars could leave at will, carrying out their professions outside the abbey walls. In the case of Martin Luther, who worked in the world preaching and teaching, the classroom and pulpit were where Professor Luther and Friar Martin served his vocations.

The distinction is clear in Latin and English: *frater* means friar, *monachus* means monk. Mönch in German is either monk or friar. In1518, Luther refers to himself as *Frater* (or F): "I, Friar Martin Luther Augustinian, Professor of sacred theology and of the same in Wittenberg" (WA 2:28.26–27).[8] He used *Frater* in titles of his writings, such as his 1518 letter to Pope Leo x (WA 1:527.17).[9] Also

---

7   http://www.mb-soft.com/believe/txh/friars.htm.

8   *Frater (or F) Martinus Lutherus: ego frater Martinus Lutherus Augustinensis, sacrae Theologiae professor eiusdemque in Vuittenbergensi.*

9   *Beatissimo patri Leoni Decimo Pontifici Maximo Frater Martinvs Lvther Avgvstinianvs aeternam salvtem.*

in 1518, in slightly different wording: "I, Friar Martin Luther, of the Order of the Hermits of St. Augustine, Master of sacred theology in Wittenberg" (WA 2:36.33–34).[10] He used almost identical language in 1520 (WA 7:76.18–19)[11] This is the last ascription I found in *Luthers Werke im WWW* in which Luther refers to himself as Friar Martin Luther. He also continued to name himself "Augustinian," for example, in his sermons on the Magnificat[12] and in his 1523 revision of his 1516/19 lectures on Galatians.[13] In 1545 Luther did say he lived as a monk: "Though I lived as a monk without reproach, I felt that before God I was a sinner with an extremely disturbed conscience" (WA 54.185).[14] Note that he says "as" (*uncunque*) a monk, not that he was a monk—which he couldn't say, since he was not a monk. He meant that he lived the rigorous disciplines that all the religious (*religious*) practiced—"beyond reproach"! Along the same line, earlier in 1531, he said, "I studied with the greatest dilengence to live the monastic life according to the prescribed rules (of the Augustinian order)."[15] **The same testimony he wrote in German in 1533:** "It is true that I was a pious friar (*Muench*), and I held so strictly to my order that I can say, if any friar (*Muench*) should get to heaven by his monkery (*Muencherey*), I would have done so. All of my brothers who knew me in the monastery (*Klostergesellen*) will testify for me."[16] Later in the same German treatise Luther again speaks of the promise of his *Muencherey* (WA

---

10 *ego Frater Martinus Luther Ordinis Eremitarum sancti Augustini, Vuittenbergensis Sacrae theologiae Magister.*

11 *ego frater Martinus Luther ordinis Eremitarum sancti Augustini, Vuittembergensis sacrae Theologiae Magister.*

12 *Das Magnificat vorteutschet und auszgelegt durch D. Martinum Luther Aug.* 1521 (WA 7:538–604; cf. AE 21:295ff.).

13 *In epistolam Pauli ad Galatas, D. Martini Lutheri Augustiniani commentarius,* Basel, 1523 (WA 2:439."G").

14 Ego autem, qui me, utcunque irreprehensibilis monachus vivebam, sentirem coram Deo esse peccatorem inquietissimae conscientiae

15 Ego Monachus studebam summa diligentia vivere iuxta praescriptum Regulae (WA 44,2:2.15b.

16 War ists, Ein fromer Muench bin ich gewest, Und so gestrenge meinen Orden gehalten, das ichs sagen thar: ist jhe ein Muench gen himel komen durch Muencherey, so wolt ich auch hinein komen sein. Das werden mir zeugen alle meine Klostergesellen, die mich gekennet haben. (WA 38:143.25–27.

38:152.30–31). He is referring to his life as an Austin (Augustinian) friar.

Luther refers to himself as F(f)rater in the present tense (1518, 1520) and as *monachus* in the past tense (1531, 1545). His use of *monachus* later in his life suggests to me that he is reflecting on his diligence as a religious *viator*, as a faithful member of the Augustinian order. Nothing changes the fact that he was what he was, namely, a friar, a mendicant. In writing Luther distinguished between *mona-chus* and *mendicus*. The American Edition of *Luther's Works* correctly translates the terms for Luther's "Explanations of the Ninety-five Theses" (1518):

> Christ must teach a repentance, I say, which can be done in every walk of life, a repentance which the king in purple robes, the priest in his purity, and the princes in their dignity can do just as well as the monk in his rituals and the mendicant in his poverty, just as Daniel and his companions did in Babylon [Dan. 1 and 3]. For the teaching of Christ must apply to all men, that is, to men in every walk of life (AE 31:85; see also 185, 207).

He elsewhere makes reference to "the mendicant friars" (AE 27:124) and "mendicant orders" (AE 9:147; 32:98; 36:219, 228).

Every so often *Luther Digest* publishes an abridgment of an article that uses the distinction between monk and friar correctly and explains the historical origin of the terminology. One such is Jared Wicks's evaluation of the famous Luther biography by Richard Marius, who was a Professor at Harvard:

> When Luther made his "flight to the monastery," to become a "monk" in Erfurt, Marius wonders why Luther did not act with the radicality shown later and become a Carthusian (46). Still, his life as an Augustinian is qualified, and this at a key moment in the interpretation, as a setting of solitude in which Luther's inner struggles were compounded by his "monastic" isolation.

> Here, however, little or no research was done in the Harvard libraries, celebrated by Marius as a scholar's paradise. The primary trait of the Augustinian Order's spirituality was not solitude but brotherhood in community. It was not a monastic order, but a mendicant group like the friars who followed the rules of Francis

or Dominic. The fraternal common life was to set an example for town-dwellers.[17]

Luther as "monk" is so firmly fixed in the popular mindset, as well as in a good deal of scholarly writing, that nothing I say will change the myth. As myth it is a wonderful legend along with the others—the lightning, the nailing, the inkwell, the Apple Tree, Emperor Karl at Luther's grave, and other legends.[18] The Luther drama-films, the popular biography of Bainton,[19] all paint Luther as the faithful monk of the Roman Catholic Church, who then rebelled.

Besides, friar is not a common or known commodity except for fryer chickens, the Providence Friars, the deep fryer, and of course, Friar Tuck. To Protestants all Catholic priests are the same—they wear black; few Lutherans could distinguish between religious and secular priests, let alone differentiate among the religious orders. Similarly, to Roman Catholics all Protestant churches are the same whether Lutheran or Methodist—they don't accept the authority of the pope; few Catholics could distinguish between Lutheran and Reformed, let alone name the Reformed churches. I asked my sister-in-law and her daughter what friar meant; I got "fryer chicken" and, "coming from you it means something Catholic." These are educated people!

I think the real reason monk is so cherished is that it evokes the quintessential Roman Catholic ascetic, fleeing the nasty thunderstorm, black robe, black cloister, black and bleek, coming into light and joy, being lifted out of gloom and doom, leaving behind penance and finding forgiveness. "Friar" does not come close to ringing the mournful bells of the destitute "monk." Isn't the point of the Reformation that Luther left the miseries of monkdom behind and was converted to a whole new way of salvation? Stop it!

One reason for the myth of Luther as monk is the widely reported thunderstorm experience, during which he is reported to have said (in translation) "St. Anne help me! I will become a monk."[20] The accounts, which became the basis for the reports, were recorded long after the

---

17 Jared Wicks, S.J. "Facts and Fears In and Around Martin Luther," *Moreana* 37 (March 2000) in *Luther Digest*, An Annual Abridgment of Luther Studies 10 (2002), 230.

18 See http://www.luther.de/legenden/.

19 Roland H. Bainton, *Here I Stand* (Markham, Ontario: Penguin Books, 1977).

20 Ibid.,15.

fact.[21] Further, the word used is German *munch* or *mönch*. Remember that in German there is no distinction between monk and friar; they are considered *religiosus*.

So, what's the big deal? Is this just a matter of terminological niceties? Just rhetoric? Hardly. *First* visit a monastery such as the monks at St. John's abbey in Collegeville, Minnesota, and witness the number of hours the monks are in prayer, in liturgy, in worship; see the discipline, the routine; breath the clean air; walk in the monastic gardens. *Then* visit the Jesuits (Regular Clerics) on 13th and Wisconsin Avenue in Milwaukee, Wisconsin, and smell the buses; see the bustle of students, the professor in class; breathe the ozone and hear the fire engines; walk the streets in the inner city. NOW tell me it's just of matter of a technicality of terminology.

In the late Middle Ages—Luther's day— monks and friars had two radically different ways of life, two different callings: a life of contemplation versus a life of action; living in secluded monasteries versus preaching in the villages; synchronized *ora et labora* versus work in hospitals; prayer versus reason; singing versus arguing.

"Luther the monk" is a cliché right up there with "Luther the spiritual predecessor of Adolf Hitler."[22] A "cliché" produces the likeness of a given object over and over, "and even the best cliché is never more than a rough approximation of the real thing."[23] The real thing is that Luther was a friar, but lived like a *monachus* in his theological discipline of *oratio, meditatio, tentatio* (prayer, meditation, temptation); he read Scripture in the monastic mode of *lectio divina* (sacred reading). But his calling was that of a friar, a mendicant of the Augustinian order.

So stop using the cliché, "Luther the monk"!

21   Otto Scheel, *Dokumente zu Luthers Entwicklung,* 2nd ed. (Tübingen: Mohr,1929), numbers 412, 423, 425.

22   Uwe Siemon-Netto, *The Fabricated Luther, Refuting Nazi Connections and Other Modern Myths,* 2nd ed. (St. Louis: Concordia, 2007), 23.

23   Ibid., 22.

CHANGES IN THE UNDERSTANDING OF LUTHER:

THE DEVELOPMENT OF THE YOUNG LUTHER

Is Luther a Lutheran? Is there such a thing as *a* Lutheran theology or *a* Lutheran interpretation of Luther? The evaluation and re-evaluation of Martin Luther is an old yet current and urgent problem.

It has always been urgent for Protestants to know the Reformers in order to know their tradition. Today it is especially important for both Protestants and Roman Catholics to understand the Reformation. On the Protestant side, contemporary theology has been influenced extensively by the Reformers. Thus one must be sure historically that the sixteenth century has not been distorted by contemporary interests, and systematically that the riches and relevance of Reformation theology have been fully realized. Traditionally, Roman Catholics have been interested in the Reformation more to attack it than to understand it. This is changing. Today Roman Catholics seek to understand the Reformation in order to achieve a theological *rapprochement* with its heirs. Christian theologians of all traditions must understand the Reformation in order to understand theology. Theology as the many splendored experience of the Church must appropriate the decisive product and critique of the Middle Ages.

Actually, the task of understanding the Reformers is very complex. The search for the historical Luther has never yielded many permanent conclusions. The interpretation of the "real" Luther has changed from generation to generation. Today there is a re-evaluation of Luther going on—but historically this has always been the case, in varying degrees.

One of the critical questions of modern Luther studies is the development of the young Luther. When did he "break" with Rome? Why? When does Luther become Protestant? When does he cease theologically to be Roman Catholic? At the heart of the youngLuther research is a theological and ecumenical effort to determine what is genuinely and distinctly Lutheran, what is Protestant, what is catholic, what is

Roman Catholic.[1] By studying the origins of Luther's theology one deals with the roots of the difference between Rome and Reformation.

The very specific problem that has occupied the majority of contemporary Luther scholars is Luther's reported "conversion" experience—his evangelical discovery of justification by faith. This breakthrough of Luther's is generally referred to as Luther's *Turmerlebnis* (tower experience), because it supposedly took place in the tower of the Wittenberg monastery. This problem will give us a good example of the evaluation and re-evaluation of Luther in our century. But first we must look at the general changes in the understanding of Luther from the sixteenth century to the early twentieth.

SIXTEENTH CENTURY TO WORLD WAR I

Luther has been variously interpreted throughout the past 450 years. He has been studied from almost every possible angle. He has been put into the framework of political science, economics, sociology, psychology, intellectual history, and theology. Every generation has been compelled to deal with Luther—which only testifies to his greatness. In fact, the history of Protestantism could be read as a history of Luther research.

The first generation of Luther interpreters saw him as a *Wundermann*, as one standing in a long tradition of great men sent by God. With fresh memories of his personality, Luther was regarded as a prophet who had ushered in a new evangelical age.[2]

The next generation of Lutherans, fighting for their ecclesiastical existence, underwent something of an identity crisis. Under pressure from without and torn by theological controversy from within, the followers of Luther concerned themselves with defining and defending Lutheran doctrine. And so the age of Lutheran orthodoxy arrived, also called Lutheran Scholasticism, concerned with confessional formulations and pure doctrine.

The orthodoxists of the late sixteenth and seventeenth centuries saw Luther as a professor of dogmatic theology. Neglecting his writings in general, they pictured Luther systematically spinning out pure

---

1   Gottfried Edel, Das *gemeinkatholische mittelalterliche Erbe beim jungen Luther* (Oekumenische Texte und Studien 21; Marburg, 1962) pp. 1–6.

2   Ernst Zeeden, *The Legacy of Luther* (tr. Ruth Bethell; London, 1954) pp. 10–17.

doctrine.[3] Justification, for example, was considered to be a doctrine that had a proper and logical "place" in the dogmatic system—actually, a rather belated position in the system.[4] Luther was seen by the orthodox theologians through their own rational and confessional eyeglasses.

In reaction to orthodoxy, with its rationalism, dogmatism, and confessionalism, the movement of pietism developed in the latter part of the seventeenth century. The pietists emphasized personal experience and holiness, pure faith and Bible study. Concerned for a subjective encounter with the Scriptures, the pietists had little regard for tradition, Roman Catholic or Lutheran.

The pietists regarded Luther as one evangelical among many, important only because of his witness to the Scriptures. Seen as human, Luther was commended and criticized as the pietists saw fit. They had empathy with Luther's preoccupation with the Word and *Anfechtung*. Among other things, they were critical of his boldness, occasional violence and cursing, and his concern about doctrine.[5] All postbiblical theologizing was considered by the pietists to be unimportant. Most important for the history of Luther research is, I think, the pietists' distinction between the "young" and "old" Luther, a distinction now commonplace in Luther studies. They were generally attracted to the young Luther, regarded as a warm evangelical, but were critical of the "old" Luther, seen as a dogmatician and encrusted institutionalist.[6]

The rationalists of the eighteenth century shared the generally negative attitude of the pietists toward tradition, but for entirely different reasons. Whereas the pietists desired a direct biblicism, the rationalists sought truth in the present, convinced that man had come of age. Reason was considered to be the judge of all revelation.

Luther was seen by the rationalists as the one who brought not the gospel of forgiveness but the gospel of pure reason. Luther was the

3 Theodore Tappert, "Orthodoxism, Pietism and Rationalism, 1580–1830," *The Lutheran Heritage* 2 (ed. Harold Letts; Philadelphia, 1957) pp. 47–48.

4 Carl E. Braaten, "The Correlation between Justification and Faith in Classical Lutheran Dogmatics," *The Symposium on Seventeenth Century Lutheranism* 1 (St. Louis, 1962) p. 85.

5 Tappert, p. 68.

6 Zeeden, pp. 56, 90–91.

hero of freedom from dogma and ecclesiastical traditionalism.[7] He was commended for his humanity and enjoyment of life as well as his critical attitude towards parts of Scripture. But he was criticized by the rationalists for his conservative and polemical doctrinal position.[8] The architect of liberty, Luther was an individual who thought for himself.

In the nineteenth century we have many philosophical, historical, and theological pictures of Luther, and through it all one can discover the rise and the fall of Luther research.[9] Of the idealists, Hegel, in the first half of the nineteenth century, mapped out a new way to understand Luther. The essence of Luther's thought, for Hegel, is the freedom of the spirit from any human mediation in man's relation to God. The romantics sympathized with Luther's emphasis on the individual, his freedom and integrity.

The picture of Luther in the second half of the nineteenth century is formed by a clash and mixing of the idealist and romantic traditions, particularly in the work of von Ranke. Von Ranke combines a romantic empathy with Luther's inner struggles with an idealist faith in the "inner life of the spirit." Rather than superimpose a philosophical structure on Luther's thought, he sought the roots of the Reformation in Luther's new experience of God.

The leading historian after von Ranke, i.e., von Treitschke, at the end of the nineteenth century, produced a very naturalistic and nationalistic picture of Luther. For von Treitschke, Luther is the German Luther who embodied and "unleashed the native power of German defiance." This is the Luther of German nationalism.

In addition to the philosophical and historical interest in Luther, the second half of the nineteenth century is marked by significant theological studies of Luther.[10] The first is that of Theodosius Harnack, who read Luther's theology with an eye to the doctrine of atonement and dealt with an important distinction in Luther research. Against J. C. K. von Hofmann, Harnack defended the orthodox interpretation of Luther. For Harnack, the traditional Lutheran interpretation

---

7   Zeeden, pp. 136–37.

8   Tappert, p. 82.

9   Heinrich Bornkamm, "Zum Lutherbild des 19. Jahrhunderts," *Theologische Literaturzeitung* 79 (1954) 425–30; Walter von Löwenich, *Luther und der Neuprotestantismus* (Witten, 1963) pp. 42–143.

10   Cf. Walter von Löwenich, "Zehn Jahr Lutherforschung in Deutschland, 1938–48," *Von Augustin zu Luther* (Witten, 1959) pp. 337–39.

of Luther's atonement theory had been correct, i.e., an Anselmian theory of forensic satisfaction. Von Hofmann had argued that one must distinguish between Luther and Lutheranism on the matter of atonement. For von Hofmann, Luther taught a dynamic, dramatic, salvationhistory theory, whereas Lutheranism taught an Anselmian theory.[11]

The distinction between Luther and Lutheranism, as well as the one between the young and old Luther, are current and critical questions in Luther research. A third figure entered the debate between Harnack and von Hofmann, using the distinction between the young and old Luther. He is the second significant Luther scholar in the nineteenth century, Albrecht Ritschl.[12] Ritschl argued that Harnack's interpretation of Luther is true only for the old Luther, whereas the young Luther emphasizes love and gives an ethical interpretation of justification by grace. For Ritschl, the kernel of Luther's theology is to be found in its early expression, and that is that man is a free moral person who is superior to the mechanistic process of nature.

The interest in Luther and the positive evaluation of him by the idealists and romantics, by von Ranke and von Treitschke, gradually declined in the latter part of the nineteenth century. The historian Jacob Burckhardt and the philosopher Friedrich Nietzsche hated Luther.[13] So also the positive theological evaluation of Theodosius Harnack and Ritschl was qualified by the negative criticisms of Adolf von Harnack, Wilhelm Dilthey, and Ernst Troeltsch at the turn of the century.

Adolf, the son of Theodosius Harnack, presented Luther as the end of the history of dogma, the end of the Hellenization of Christianity. He criticized Luther because he found many outdated medieval notions in his theology. Although Dilthey and Troeltsch differed on the relation of the Reformation to the Renaissance and their influence on the rise of modern culture, both affirmed the medieval element in Luther's theology, Troeltsch more than Dilthey.

---

11   Robert C. Schultz, Gesetz und Evangelium in der lutherischen Theologie des 19. Jahrhunderts (Arbeiten zur Geschichte und Theologie des Luthertums 4; Berlin, 1958) pp. 133–48. Cf. Gerhard 0. Forde, The LawlGospel Debate in German Theology from Hofmann to Ebeling (Dissertation, Harvard University, 1966).

12   Schultz, pp. 168–78.

13   Bornkamm, "Zurn Lutherbild des 19. Jahrhunderts," p. 428.

Thus by the beginning of World War I the Luther image of the nineteenth century had been destroyed. Interest in Luther had waned and judgment of him was generally negative. Luther was dead.

THE LUTHER RENAISSANCE

The state of Luther research, however, changed radically after World War I; for then interest in Luther became so intense and extensive that our century enjoys what is called a "Luther renaissance."

There are at least four causes of this revival of Luther studies: (1) Heinrich Denifle and Hartmann Grisar, (2) Troeltsch, (3) Karl Holl, and (4) dialectical theology. Troeltsch has already been mentioned as one who placed Luther back in the Middle Ages, both theologically and in respect to the cultural effect of the Reformation. This negative critique of Luther challenged the common assumption that Wittenberg and Rome were polar opposites and thus forced a reexamination of the Reformation.

An even more devastating attack on Luther came at the hands of two Roman Catholic Luther scholars. At the turn of the century, Denifle[14] and Grisar[15] leveled a character assassination at Luther that thoroughly undermined his integrity. Actually, this approach to Luther had been standard in Catholic Luther studies since the time of John Cochlaeus in the midsixteenth century.[16] Cochlaeus imputed the basest motives to Luther's actions, arguing that Luther had all the immoral prerequisites for a heretic. The reason Denifle and Grisar caused such a stir is that their attack on Luther was scholarly, based on Luther's writings. Denifle, the Vatican archivist, even had the advantage of using the unpublished lectures of Luther on Romans. The upshot of Denifle's arguments is that Luther's attack on the Church was a projection of his own diseased, oversexed soul. Grisar, while qualifying some of Denifle's character assassination, argued that Luther's heresy was due to his hatred of good works and that his Reformation discovery of justification by faith took place on the toilet. The effect of Denifle and Grisar's attacks was explosive and sent Protestants scurrying back to the sources to find the "real" Luther.

14   Heinrich Denifle, O.P., *Luther und Luthertum in der ersten Entwicklung* (2nd ed.; Mainz, 1904).

15   Hartmann Grisar, S.J., *Luther* 1 (Freiburg, 1911).

16   Adolf Herte, *Das katholische Lutherbild im Bann der Lutherkommentare des Cochlaeus* 1 (Münster, 1943) pp. ix–x.

Karl Holl was the single most important impetus to the rise of the Luther renaissance. His fresh analysis of Luther in 1921 became the focus of modern Luther research.[17] He, first of all, researched the newlydiscovered writings of the young Luther and showed what new insights they yielded in understanding the development of Luther's theology. Furthermore, he offered a systematic interpretation of Luther's theology, with the important result that Luther has been taken seriously by contemporary theologians. Against Troeltsch, he argued for the uniqueness of Luther and his creative influence on modern culture. Against Denifle and Grisar, he stressed the ethical motives in Luther's search for a gracious God.

The positive appreciation of Luther in the Protestant camp has been echoed in the Catholic camp. The Luther renaissance has reached ecumenical proportions. Beginning with Joseph Lortz,[18] Catholics have generally upheld the moral integrity of Luther and tried to discover the genius and originality of his thought.

A fourth cause of the Luther renaissance is the rise of dialectical theology; vice versa, the revival of Reformation studies contributed to the development of dialectical theology. Theology after World War I, frustrated with Liberal theology, turned to the sources of classical Protestantism in search for new directions and thus discovered the relevance of the Reformers. Dialectical theology became a revival of Reformation theology, creeds, and orthodoxy.

The revival of Luther studies in our century has produced a great quantity of work. The general approach has varied according to "school." The Holl school has concentrated on the young Luther and the "new" elements in his theology and has minimized the continuity of Luther with Lutheran orthodoxy. The older Lutheran school, in reaction to Holl and the young/old distinction, has minimized the development of Luther and emphasized the consistency of the whole Luther as well as the continuity of Luther and Lutheran orthodoxy. The dialectical school concurs with the method of the older Lutheran school, with the addition of emphasizing the effect of Luther on contemporary theology and the continuity of the two.

---

17 Karl Holl, *Gesammelte Aufsätze zur Kirchengeschichie 1: Luther* (6th ed.; Tübingen, 1932).

18 Joseph Lortz, *Die Reformation in Deutschland* 1 (4th ed.; Freiburg, 1962).

The study of Luther's theology has become increasingly specialized and concentrated. Many areas have been researched, such as Luther's theology of the cross, Christology, ecclesiology, law/gospel, two kingdoms, hermeneutics, and sacraments. Perhaps the most important issue in contemporary Luther research is the question of Luther's *Turmerlebnis* and the origins of his doctrine of justification.

THE "TURMERLEBNIS" PROBLEM

The occasion for all the discussion and controversy about Luther's theological development is his autobiographical statement in 1545. Here he gives a résumé of his early activities and describes how and when he arrived at a new evangelical understanding of justification. The occasion for all the speculation about the place of this discovery is the Table Talk. It is reported to have been a "tower experience" (*Turmerlebnis*)—in the tower of the Black Augustinian monastery in Wittenberg. Though this aspect of the youngLuther research is of minor importance, the term *Turmerlebnis* is generally used to designate the whole problem of Luther's development.

The Table Talk does not mention or infer a date for Luther's *Turmerlebnis*. The information concerning the place is confusing. There are different versions of what Luther said. The reports from two, Cordatus and Lauterbach, refer to the place as a "warm room" (*hypocaustum*) or "secret place" (*secrefus locus*).[19] However, Schlaginhaufen reports that Luther said that it occurred in or on a "Cl." (*auff diss Cl.*).[20]

The abbreviation "Cl.," as the place where the Holy Spirit revealed to Luther a new understanding of Rom 1:17, has caused much speculation and some embarrassment. Some later editors of the Table Talk have suggested that "Cl." means *cloaca* (toilet). Hartmann Grisar argues

---

19   *Dokumente zu Luthers Entwicklung* (ed. Otto Scheel; 2nd ed.; Tübingen, 1929) p. 91.

20   *Ibid.*, p. 94: "Vocabula Justus et Misericordia.' Haec vocabula Iustus et Misericordia erant mihi fulmen in conscientia. Mox reddebar pavidus auditis: Iustus, ergo puniet. 'Iustus ex fide.' Iustus ex fide vivit, iustitia Dei revelatur sine lege [Hb 2:4; Rom 1:17]. Mox cogitabam: Si vivere debemus ex fide, et si iustitia Dei debet esse ad salutem omni credenti [Rom 3:21 f.], mox erigebatur mihi animus: Ergo iustitia Dei est, qua nos iustificat et salvat. Et facta sunt mihi haec verba iucundiora. Dise kunst hatt mir der Spiritus Sanctus auff diss C1 eingeben."

that *cloaca* is the only possible reading.[21] Other suggestions have been that "Cl." means *cella* (chamber), *claustrum* (a confined place), *capitulum* (chapter), *c(apite)* 1 (chapter one) or *clarissimum* (very clear).[22] The last three suggestions refer to Scripture. According to Gordon Rupp, "Most scholars now believe it to have been a warmed room in which Luther studied."[23]

The Table Talk itself gives no conclusive evidence for the date or exact place of Luther's discovery. Furthermore, the details of the Table Talk must always be questioned, because the authenticity of the "reports" is always a matter of dispute. The main thrust of the Table Talk regarding Luther's *Turmerlebnis* is that it involved Rom 1: 17 and the understanding of "righteousness" (*iustitia*).

The principal source from Luther concerning the date and nature of his evangelical discovery is the *Preface to the Complete Edition of Luther's Latin Writings* (1545).[24] In this autobiographical "Preface" Luther discusses some of his thoughts and activities up to the year 1521. The *textus classicus* for the *Turmerlebnis* problem is Luther's account of his discovery of the true meaning of Rom 1:17. After rehearsing the events in his life up to 1519, he writes:

> Meanwhile, I had already during that year returned to interpret the Psalter anew. I had confidence in the fact that I was more skilful, after I had lectured in the university on St. Paul's epistles to the Romans, to the Galatians, and the one to the Hebrews. I had indeed been captivated with an extraordinary ardor for understanding Paul in the Epistle to the Romans. But up till then it was not the cold blood about the heart, but a single word in Chapter 1:17, "In it the righteousness of God is revealed," that had stood in my way. For I hated that word "righteousness of God," which, according to the use and custom of all the teachers, I had been taught to understand philosophically regarding the formal or active righteousness, as they called it, with which God is righteous and punishes the unrighteous sinner.
>
> Though I lived as a monk without reproach, I felt that I was a sinner before God with an extremely disturbed conscience. I could not

---

21   Luther 1, 323.

22   Ernst Stracke, *Luthers grosses Selbstzeugnis 1545 über seine Entwicklung zum Reformator* (Leipzig, 1926) p. 121.

23   *The Righteousness of God* (New York, 1953) p. 129.

24   *Luther's Works* 34 (ed. Lewis Spitz; Philadelphia, 1960) 327–38.

believe that he was placated by my satisfaction. I did not love, yes, I hated the righteous God who punishes sinners, and secretly, if not blasphemously, certainly murmuring greatly, I was angry with God, and said, "As if, indeed, it is not enough, that miserable sinners, eternally lost through original sin, are crushed by every kind of calamity by the law of the decalogue, without having God add pain to pain by the gospel and also by the general gospel threatening us with his righteousness and wrath!" Thus I raged with a fierce and troubled conscience. Nevertheless, I beat importunately upon Paul at that place, most ardently desiring to know what St. Paul wanted.

At last, by the mercy of God, meditating day and night, I gave heed to the context of the words, "In it the righteousness of God is revealed, as it is written, He who through faith is righteous shall live." There I began to understand that the righteousness of God is that by which the righteous lives by the gift of God, namely, by faith. And this is the meaning: the righteousness of God is revealed by the gospel, namely, the passive righteousness with which merciful God justifies us by faith, as it is written, "He who through faith is righteous shall live." Here I felt that I was altogether born again and had entered paradise itself through open gates. There a totally other face of the entire Scripture showed itself to me. Thereupon I ran through the Scriptures from memory. I also found in other terms an analogy, as, the work of God, that is, what God does in us, the wisdom of God, with which he makes us wise, the strength of God, the salvation of God, the glory of God.[25]

---

25   *Ibid.*, pp. 336–37. Scheel, *Dokumente,* pp. 191–92: "Interim eo anno iam redieram ad psalterium denuo interpretandum, fretus co, quod exercitatior essem, postquam S. Pauli epistolas ad Romanos, ad Galatas, et cam, quae est ad Ebraeos, tractassem in scholis. Miro certe ardore captus fuerarn cognoscendi Pauli in epistola ad Rom., sed obstiterat hactenus non frigidus circum praecordia sanguis, sed unicum vocabulum, quod est cap. 1: 'Iustitia Dei revelatur in illo' [Rom 1:17]. Oderam enim, vocabulum istud 'Iustitia Dei,' quod usu et consuetudine omnium doctorum doctus erarn philosophice intelligere de iustitia (ut vocant) formali seu activa, qua Deus est iustus, et peccatores iniustosque punit.

"Ego autem, qui me, utcunque irreprehensibilis monachus vivebam, sentirem coram Deo, esse peccatorem inquictissimae conscientiae, nec mea satisfactione placatum confidere possem, non amabam, imo odiebam iustum et punientem peccatores Deum, tacitaque si non blasphemia, certe ingenti murmuratione indignabar Deo dicens: quasi vero non satis sit, miseros peccatores et aeternaliter perditos peccato originali omni genere

The problematic of this passage as evidence for a particular date of Luther's discovery is threefold. The first question is whether Luther in his old age, some twentyfive to thirtyfive years after the event, had an accurate recollection of the exact time and sequence of events. Ficker, Loofs, Scheel, and Holl hold that Luther's dating (of 1519) in 1545 is erroneous and his memory faulty.[26] Grisar, however, thinks that Luther's dating and memory are accurate.[27] Some think that Luther confused his first and second lectures on the Psalms, and that he really meant the *Dictata* (151315) rather than the *Operationes* (1518–21).[28]

The second question is whether Luther is in fact referring to 1519. Ritschl, von Schubert, and Seeberg hold that he is not.[29] The key phrase is "captus fueram," a double pluperfect. Again the context:

---

calamitatis oppressos esse per legem decalogi, nisi Deus per evangelium dolorem dolori adderet, et etiam per evangelium nobis iustitiam et iram suam intentaret. Furebam ita saeva et perturbata conscientia, pulsabam tamen importunus eo loco Paulum, ardentissime sitiens scire, quid S. Paulus vellet.

"Donec miserente Deo meditabundus dies et noctes connexionem verborum attenderem, nempe:'Iustitia Dei revelatur in illo, sicut scriptum est: Iustus ex vide vivit,' ibi iustitiam Dei coepi intelligere cam, qua iustus dono Dei vivit, nempe ex fide, et esse hanc sententiam, revelari per evangelium iustitiam Dei, scilicet passivam, qua nos Deus misericors justificat per fidem, sicut scriptum est:'Justus ex fide vivit.' Hic me prorsus renatum esse sensi et apertis portis in ipsam paradisum intrasse. Ibi continuo alia mihi facies totius scripturae apparuit. Discurrebam deinde per scripturas, ut habebat memoria, et colligebam etiam in aliis vocabulis analogiam, ut opus Dei, i.e., quod operatur in nobis Deus, virtus Dei, qua nos potentes facit, sapientia Dei, qua nos sapientes facit, fortitudo Dei, salus Dei, gloria Dei."

26 Johannes Ficker, *Luthers Vorlesung über den Römerbrief 1515–16* (*Anfänge reformatorischer Bibelauslegung* 1; Leipzig, 1908) lxxilxxii; Friedrich Loofs, *Leitfaden zum Studium der Dogmengeschichte* (4th ed.; Halle, 1906) pp. 688–89; Otto Scheel, *Martin Luther: Vom Katholizismus zur Reformation* 2 (3rd–4th ed.; Tübingen, 1930) 664; Karl Holl, "Der Neubau der Sittlichkeit," *Gesammelte Aufsätze zur Kirchengeschichte* 1 (6th ed.; Tübingen, 1932) 195–96.

27 Luther 1, 320.

28 For example, Loofs, p. 689, and Ficker, p. lxxi.

29 Stracke, p. 122.

Meanwhile, I had already during that year [1519] returned (*redieram*) to interpret the Psalter anew. I had confidence in the fact that I was more skilful, after I had lectured in the university on St. Paul's epistles to the Romans, to the Galatians, and the one to the Hebrews. I had indeed been captivated (*captus fueram*) with an extraordinary ardor for understanding Paul in the Epistle to the Romans.

The question is whether "captus fueram" changes the time sequence and thus refers to a date earlier than 1519, or whether the double pluperfect was the usual late medieval form of the imperfect. Ernst Stracke claims that Luther's use of the double pluperfect shows that he has gone back in his reflection to an earlier, yet unspecified time.[30]

The third question and really the crux of the whole problem is the meaning of Luther's new understanding of justification. Luther says that everything became clear to him once he understood that the "righteousness of God" is "passive" (*iustitia Dei passiva*) and is "faith." The problem is that Luther does not actually use the phrase "the passive righteousness of God" until 1525 (in his *De servo arbitrio*).[31] And so scholars have been forced to interpret the meaning of the phrase in connection with Luther's early theological development. Once interpretation enters the picture, so does much discussion and disagreement among the interpreters.

DEVELOPMENT THESES

The question of Luther's evangelical discovery has occupied many Luther scholars since the beginning of the Luther renaissance. Luther scholars have defended datings anywhere from 1508 to 1519. Eleven years may seem inconsequential, but Luther produced a great deal of work and controversy in this span of time. If Luther is not "Lutheran" by Oct. 31, 1517, we are perhaps inappropriately celebrating the 450th anniversary of the Reformation.

One way to deal with the mass of literature is to ask a methodological question: Is there any pattern in the approach of contemporary scholars? Is there any trend or general consensus? A helpful way to categorize the various theories might be to group the Luther scholars

---

30   *Ibid.*, pp. 122–23.

31   *WA* 18:768.36 ff.

according to the conclusion they reach regarding the date of Luther's breakthrough. Five such groups are discernible.

1508–12

Luther scholars in the early part of the century tended to think that Luther's *Turmerlebnis* occurred at the beginning of his theological career, 1508–12. During this time Luther glossed some of the works of Augustine, Anselm, and Lombard. Those who argued for this earliest possible dating include (in order of publication) O. Ritschl,[32] Holl, R. Seeberg, and Böhmer (in the earlier editions of his work).[33] The positions of Holl and Seeberg are the most important in this group, in so far as they have received the most attention and been the most influential.

For Karl Holl, Luther's theological development is a new understanding of justification by faith. This new doctrine is sanative in character. Justification for the young Luther is not as Melanchthon and orthodox Lutheranism would have it—the forensic imputation of righteousness—but rather the healing impartation of righteousness. For Holl, justification in Luther's theology means renewal. God makes the sinner righteous and he becomes righteous.[34] Holl holds that there were two stages in Luther's development.[35] The first was an inner "ethical" struggle, occurring between 1509 and 1511. The second was a "religious" theological breakthrough, whereby he came to his "sanative

---

32 Otto Ritschl, *Dogmengeschichte des Protestantismus* 2 (Leipzig, 1912) 11 ff.

33 Heinrich Böhmer, *Luthers erste Vorlesung* (Leipzig, 1924) p. 52; *Der junge Luther* (Gotha, 1925) pp. 110–11.

34 Karl Holl, "Die Rechtfertigungslehre in Luthers Vorlesung über den Römerbrief mit besonderer Rücksicht auf die Frage der Heilsgewissheit," *Gesammelte Aufsätze 1*, 122–29.

35 "Der Neubau der Sittlichkeit," *Gesammelte Aufsätze 1*, 187: "Es ist ohne weiteres klar, dass das Auftauchen der neuen sittlichen Erkenntnis und die Wiederentdeckung der Rechtfertigungslehre nicht gleichzeitig bei Luther erfolgt sein können. Die Rechtfertigungsfrage konnte für Luther ihre volle Schärfe erst gewinnen, *nachdem* ihm die Höhe der sittlichen Forderung aufgegangen war. Darnach heben sich *zwei Stufen* der inneren Entwicklung Luthers voneinander ab; die eine, auf der er zu der neuen *sittlichen*, die andere, auf der er zu der neuen *religiösen* Erkenntnis vordringt."

doctrine" of justification. His new theological development took place between the summer of 1511 and early 1513.[36]

Reinhold Seeberg holds that the "starting point" for all of Luther's Reformation theology is a new discovery of "evangelical repentance":

Luther's decisive religious experiences were gained in connection with the sacrament of repentance, under the stress of a false conception of repentance for which he struggled to find a substitute. This was the starting point from which his fundamental religious ideas were developed. The latter may, therefore, be comprehended under the conception of *Evangelical Repentance, constituting a Substitute for the observance of the Sacrament of Repentance.* This is the point of view from which the work of Luther must be considered in the History of Doctrines. All his ideas in regard to penitence and faith, faith and works, sin and grace, law and gospel, God and Christ, together with his new ideal of life, constitute a complex of religious conceptions which were developed under the pressure of and in opposition to the sacrament of repentance.[37]

Seeberg explains that the influence of Johann von Staupitz, head of Luther's order, was decisive for Luther's development during the winter of 1508–1509.[38] Staupitz taught Luther that repentance begins with love towards God, that one comes to such repentance by turning to the work of Christ, and that his own temptations concerning predestination could be solved by turning to the wounds of Christ.[39] The date of Luther's evangelical discovery, according to Seeberg, is the summer of 1509.[40]

1512–13

Some Luther scholars around the second quarter of the century claimed that Luther's *Turmerlebnis* occurred during the time that he was preparing for his first lectures on the Psalms, late 1512 to the summer of 1513. Luther became a doctor of theology on October 19, 1512, and a member of the theological faculty at Wittenberg on Oct.

---

36   *Ibid.,* p. 193.

37   Reinhold Seeberg, *Lehrbuch der Dogmengeschichte* 4,1 (4th ed.; Darmstadt, 1959) 78; tr. Charles Hay, *TextBook of the History of Doctrines* 2 (Grand Rapids, 1958) 224–25.

38   *Ibid.,* p. 63.

39   *Ibid., p.* 66.

40   *Ibid.,* p. 71.

22, 1512.[41] He assumed the chair of biblical theology at Wittenberg previously occupied by Staupitz, and began his *lectura in Biblia* in August, 1513.

Those who pinpoint Luther's breakthrough somewhere between late 1512 and mid1513 include (in order of publication) Scheel (in the first edition of his *Martin Luther*[42]), Loofs,[43] Mackinnon,[44] Wendorf,[45] Böhmer (in the later editions of his work), Hamel,[46] Pauck,[47] Lortz, Prenter,[48] and Lilje.[49] The arguments of Böhmer and Lortz have received much attention.

Heinrich Böhmer argues that Luther's development is really Luther's search for the certainty of forgiveness.[50] The crux of Luther's *Turmerlebnis* was his struggle with understanding Psalm 30 ("in iustitia tua libera me").[51] His breakthrough meant a new insight and a new feeling for life[52]—the "Dawn of the Reformation Consciousness."[53] It occurred in AprilMay, 1513, while he was working on Psalm 30.[54]

41   Karl Bauer, *Die Wittenberger Universitästheologie und die Anfänge der deutschen Reformation* (Tübingen, 1928) p. 14.

42   Otto Scheel, *Martin Luther* 2 (Tübingen, 1917) 321.

43   Friedrich Loofs, "Luthers Rechtfertigungslehre," *Luther*, 1924, p. 84.

44   James Mackinnon, *Luther and the Reformation* 1 (London, 1925) 151.

45   Herman Wendorf, "Der Durchbruch der neuen Erkenntnis Luthers im Lichte der handschriftlichen Überlieferung," *Historische Vierteljahrschrift* 27 (1932) 315–16.

46   Adolf Hamel, *Der junge Luther und Augustin* 1 (Gütersloh, 1934) 197.

47   Wilhelm Pauck, "The Historiography of the German Reformation during the Last Twenty Years," *Church History*, 1940, p. 325; "General Introduction," *Luther: Lectures on Romans* (Library of Christian Classics 15; Philadelphia, 1961) pp. xxiv–lxi.

48   Regin Prenter, *Der barmherzige Richter* (Aarhus, 1961) p. 48.

49   Harms Lilje, *Martin Luther in Selbsizeugnissen und Bilddokumenten* (Hamburg, 1965) pp. 69–70.

50   Heinrich Böhmer, *Der junge Luther* (ed. Heinrich Bornkamm; 4th ed.; Stuttgart, 1951) pp. 86, 100.

51   *Ibid.*, p. 99.

52   *Ibid.*, p. 100.

53   *Martin Luther: Road to Reformation* (tr. Doberstein and Tappert; New York, 1957) p. 87.

54   *Der junge Luther*, p. 99.

The clue to Luther's development, for Joseph Lortz, is Luther's own experience, his subjectivism.[55] All of Luther's theology developed from his personal understanding of righteousness. The exegetical discovery of Luther's *Turmerlebnis* was really nothing new in comparison with medieval exegesis. It was only new for Luther. "Er entdeckte die heilende Gerechtigkeit Gottes als neu. Neu für sich."[56] The *Turmerlebnis* occurred in 1512, between his return from Rome and the beginning of his lectures.[57]

1513–15

The majority of Luther scholars from the twenties to *ca.* 1950 held that Luther's *Turmerlebnis* happened during the period of his first lectures on the Psalms (*Dictata super Psalterium*). Luther's first exegetical course as professor of biblical theology began on August 16, 1513, and ended before Easter, 1515.[58] In the thirties and forties there was almost a consensus among scholars that Luther's evangelical breakthrough took place in connection with his *Dictata*, either during their preparation or the period of their delivery. This early dating was seriously challenged in the fifties (see below). Now once again, with the reediting of the *Dictata*, scholars are interested in the uniqueness of Luther's first exegetical endeavor.

---

55   Lortz, p. 171: "Vorher wollen wir nochmals dies ganz klar festellen: nicht die Erringung einer neuen Lehre gibt Luthers Entwicklung die weltgeschichtliche Bedeutung. Die lieft vielmehr darin, dass er einen innern Vernichtungskampf bestand. Luther hätte immerhin auf irgend einem Wege zu theologischen Erkenntnissen kommen können, die denen, die wir als reformatorisch bezeichnen nahegekommen wären; manche Theologen vor ihm waren zu ähnlichen Resultaten gelangt. Ohne jenen innern Kampf und die allein in ihm entbundene Kraft wäre Luther nie der Reformator geworden. Erst die geheimnisvolle Einheit der reformatorischen *Persönlichkeit* mit den aus ihr entspringenden theologischen Erkenntnissen gab die Möglichkeit weltweiten Wirkens."

56   *Ibid., p.* 183.

57   *Ibid., pp.* 185, 171.

58   Böhmer, pp. 105–8.

Those who belong to this third group include Denifle,[59] Ficker,[60] Hirsch, von Walter,[61] Fife,[62] Vogelsang, Scheel (in the later editions of his *Martin Luther*), Reu,[63] Bornkamm, Pinomaa,[64] Watson,[65] Bainton,[66] Schwiebert,[67] Rupp,[68] Ebeling, Pfeiffer,[69] Green,[70] Lohse,[71] Todd,[72] and Boendermaker.[73] The work of Hirsch, Vogelsang, Scheel, Bornkamm, and Ebeling has figured most prominently in the discussion of Luther's development.

The title of Hirsch's famous article on the young Luther is telling: "The Beginning of Luther's Theology.[74] The "beginning," according to Hirsch, occurred when Luther reached a new understanding of the

59 Denifle, p. 397.

60 Ficker, p. lxxi.

61 Johannes von Walter, "Der Abschluss der Entwicklung des jungen Luther," *Zeitschrift für systematische Theologie* 1 (1923) 423–44.

62 Robert Fife, *Young Luther: The Intellectual and Religious Development of Martin Luther to 1518* (New York, 1928) p. 202.

63 J. M. Reu, *Luther's German Bible* (Columbus, 1934) pp. 106 ff.

64 Lennart Pinomaa, *Der existentielle Charakter der Theologie Luthers* (Helsinki, 1940) p. 134.

65 Philip Watson, *Let God be God!* (London, 1947) p. 28, n. 19.

66 Roland Bainton, *Here I Stand* (New York, 1950) p. 68.

67 E. G. Schwiebert, *Luther and His Times* (St. Louis, 1950) p. 288.

68 Gordon Rupp, *Luther's Progress to the Diet of Worms, 1521* (London, 1951) p. 38; *The Righteousness of God* (New York, 1953) pp. 136–37. Cf. his review of Ernst Bizer's *Fides ex auditu* in *Zeitschrift für Kirchengeschichte* 71 (1960) 353.

69 Gerhard Pfeiffer, "Das Ringen des jungen Luther um die Gerechtigkeit Gottes," *LutherJahrbuch* 26 (1959) 45–51.

70 Lowell Green, "Luther and Melanchthon," *The Mature Luther* (Decorah, 1959) p. 114.

71 Bernhard Lohse, *Mönchtum und Reformation: Luthers Auseinandersehung mit dem Mönchsideal des Mittelalters* (Forschungen zur Kirchen und Dogmengeschichte 12; Göttingen, 1963) p. 378; "Die Bedeutung Augustins für den jungen Luther," *Kerygma und Dogma* 11 (1965) 132.

72 John M. Todd, *Martin Luther: A Biographical Study* (New York, 1964) pp. 87–88.

73 J. P. Boendermaker, *Luthers Commentaar op de Brief aan de Hebreeën 1517–1518* (Assen, 1965) p. 14.

74 Emanuel Hirsch, "Initium theologiae Lutheri," *Festgabe für Julius Kaftan* (Tübingen, 1920) p. 150.

distinction between the law and the gospel—essentially a new understanding of Rom 1:17. There are three aspects to Luther's new discovery: the "righteousness of God" is not a retributory but a donated
righteousness; it is a righteousness of faith; and it is righteousness before God, not before man.[75] Hirsch specified the moment of Luther's
Turmerlebnis to be while Luther was working on Ps 31:2.[76]

Eric Vogelsang holds that Luther's evangelical discovery came about
through a tropological exegesis of the work of Christ.[77] Luther's
Turmerlebnis was a hermeneutical discovery of tropological exegesis.
Tropological exegesis is the application and appropriation of the work
of Christ for the individual believer—as in Christ, so in me (*wie* ...
so).[78] The work of Christ was that He achieved the most profound
humility on the cross—for me. Luther's theology is a theology of the
cross.[79] According to Vogelsang, Luther shows in his exegesis of Ps
71:2 (fall of 1514) that he had made his discovery.[80]

Otto Scheel distinguishes between Luther's *Turmerlebnis*, which
was a personalreligious experience, and his subsequent theological development.[81] Both involve justification. Both are evident in the *Dictata*.
The heart of Luther's experience and doctrine of justification is the
sanative renewal of the believer.[82] According to the first and second
editions of Scheel's *Martin Luther*, the *Turmerlebnis* occurred during
the winter of 1512, whereas according to the third and fourth editions
it occurred between the fall of 1513 and the fall of 1514.[83]

---

75   *Ibid., p.* 166.

76   *Ibid., p.* 165.

77   Erich Vogelsang, *Die Anfänge von Luthers Christologie nach der ersten
     Psalmenvorlesungen* (Berlin, 1929) p. 55. "Ich formuliere zusammenfassend
     den Vollsinn der Entdeckung Luthers: Opus *dei: iustitia dei, iudicium dei*,
     etc. est *Christus* (literaliter) id est fides Christi (tropologice), *qua—indi-
     cate—iustificamur, pacificamur, per quam in nobis regnat.*"

78   *Ibid.*, pp. 63–64.

79   *Ibid.*, pp. 48 ff.

80   *Ibid.*, pp. 57–61.

81   Otto Scheel, *Die Entwicklung Luthers bis zum Abschluss der Vorlesung
     über den Römerbrief* (*Schriften des Vereins für Reformationsgeschickte 100*;
     Halle, 1910) p. 93.

82   *Ibid.*, pp. 18182.

83   *Martin Luther* (3rd–4th ed.; Tübingen, 1930) pp. 572, 664.

Heinrich Bornkamm argues that the essence of Luther's theological development is his Christological interpretation of the "righteousness of God" (*iustitia Dei*). The *iustitia Dei* is bound up with the *fides Christi*. Bornkamm accepts Vogelsang's thesis about Psalm 71.[84] In opposition to Ernst Bizer,[85] who has presented a most serious challenge to an early dating, Bornkamm holds that Luther does not equate and confuse "righteousness" (*iustitia*) and "judgment" (*iudicium*) in the *Dictata*, as Bizer claims. At one point particularly, argues Bornkamm, Luther clearly distinguishes between "humility" (*iudicium*) and "faith" (*iustitia*).[86] Since at least 1940, Bornkamm has claimed that Luther's evangelical insight can be seen in the *Dictata*.[87]

The clue to Luther's development, according to Gerhard Ebeling, is hermeneutics.[88] Luther's discovery is a methodological revolution in biblical exegesis. In his *Dictata* Luther still employs the medieval *quadriga*, the fourfold sense of Scripture (literalhistorical, spiritualallegorical, moral-tropological, eschatologicalanagogical). However, he uses the *quadriga* and the distinction between the letter and the spirit in a very new way. He does not understand the literal and spiritual to be formal principles and methods of exegesis, but rather to be principles of existence.[89] One lives according to either the spirit or the flesh (letter). The literal and the spiritual is an existentialanthropological alternative confronting each and every man.[90] Luther's existential hermeneutic, holds Ebeling, is already operative in the *Dictata*.[91]

84   Heinrich Bornkamm, "*Iustitia Dei* in der Scholastik und bei Luther," *Archiv für Reformationsgeschichte* 39 (1942) 38 ff.

85   See below for a discussion of Bizer's *Fides ex auditu*.

86   In *Blätter* 103 and 104: "Zur Frage der *Iustitia Dei* beim jungen Luther. Teil I," *Archiv für Reformationsgeschichte* 52 (1961) 23.

87   "Luthers Bericht Uber seine Entdeckung der *iustitia dei*," *Archiv für Reformationsgeschichte* 37 (1940) 127–28.

88   Gerhard Ebeling, "Die Anfänge von Luthers Hermeneutik," *Zeitschrift für Theologie und Kirche* 48 (1951) 72 ff.

89   *Ibid.*, p. 187.

90   *Ibid.*, p. 195: "Ein *Gegensatz zweier Existenzmöglichkeiten* ein und desselben ganzen Menschen gemeint ist."

91   *Ibid.*, pp. 216, 230.

1515–16

A small group of Luther scholars holds that Luther's *Turmerlebnis* occurred during the period immediately following the *Dictata*. After lecturing on the Psalms, Luther turned to Paul and his letter to the Romans. He lectured on Romans from the summer of 1515 to September, 1516. Those who hold that Luther's new understanding of Rom 1: 17 came during this time are definitely in the minority and without much influence. They include Buchwald,[92] Müller,[93] Smith,[94] Rossi,[95] Kurz,[96] and Bellucci.[97]

1517–19

Several important Luther scholars have recently challenged an early dating of the *Turmerlebnis*. In the fifties and sixties many voices were raised, in Finland, Denmark, Germany, and America, to oppose the dominant opinion of the thirties and forties that the mature Luther is evident in the *Dictata*. The relevant documents for those who argue for a later dating are Luther's work on the Seven Penitential Psalms, 1517, his lectures on Hebrews, April 21, 1517 to March 26, 1518, his sermons on Twofold and Threefold Righteousness, 1518, the *Acta Augustana*, 1518, and the first part of Luther's second lectures on the Psalms (*Operationes in Psalmos*), 1518–21.

Those who hold that Luther's *Turmerlebnis* occurred sometime between 1517 and 1519 include (in order of publication) Grisar,[98]

---

92   Georg Buchwald, *Doctor Martin Luther* (Berlin, 1902) *pp.* 73 ff.

93   Alphons Victor Müller, *Luthers Werdegang bis zum Turmerlebnis* (Gotha, 1920) *pp.* 122, 136.

94   Preserved Smith, "A Decade of Luther Study," *Harvard Theological Review* 14 (1921) 112.

95   Mario Rossi, *Lutero e Roma* (Rome, 1923), noted by Gerhard Pfeiffer, "Das Ringen des jungen Luther um die Gerechtigkeit Gottes," *LutherJahrbuch* 26 (1959) 32.

96   Alfred Kurz, *Die Heilsgewissheit bei Luther* (Gütersloh, 1933) pp. 172, 180.

97   Dino Bellucci, S.J., *Fede e giustificazione in Lutero* (*Analecta Gregoriana* 135; Rome, 1963), noted by Francis Clark, *Heythrop Journal* 6 (1963) 93–96.

98   Grisar, *Luther 1,* 50.

Reiter,[99] Saarnivaara, Gyllenkrok, Stange,[100] Bizer, Jedin,[101] Wolf,[102] Cranz, Pohlmann,[103] Peters,[104] Dillenberger,[105] Seils,[106] Nembach,[107] Aland,[108] Pesch,[109] Bluhm,[110] and Hacker.[111] The studies of Saarnivaara, Gyllenkrok, Bizer, and Cranz have received extensive and critical evaluation from the world of Luther scholarship.

According to Uuras Saarnivaara, a Finnish scholar, the turning point in Luther's theological development is a forensic concept of justification.[112] He argues that Luther is "Augustinian" from 1513–18 and "Lutheran" only after 1518. Justification for the "Augustinian" Luther means, first of all, sanative renewal, and secondly, the nonimputation of sins. But for the "Lutheran" Luther, justification means,

99   Paul J. Reiter, *Martin Luthers Umwelt, Charakter und Psychose* 2 (Copenhagen, 1941) 316.

100   Carl Stange, *Die Anfänge der Theologie Luthers* (Berlin, 1957) pp. 10 ff.

101   Hubert Jedin, "Luthers Turmerlebnis in neuer Sicht: Bericht über Ernst Bizer, 'Fides ex auditu' (1958)," *Catholica* 12 (1958) 136.

102   Ernst Wolf, "Luther, Martin," *Evangelisches Kirchenlexikon* 2 (Göttingen, 1959) 1166.

103   Hans Pohlmann, *Hat Luther Paulus enideckt?* (Berlin, 1959) p. 146.

104   Albrecht Peters, "Luthers Turmerlebnis," *Neue Zeitschrift für systematische Theologie* 3 (1961) 211.

105   John Dillenberger, "Major Volumes and Selected Periodical Literature in Luther Studies, 1956–59," *Church History* 30 (1961) 72.

106   Martin Seils, *Der Gedanke vom Zusammenwirken Gottes und des Menschen in Luthers Theologie* (Gütersloh, 1962) pp. 26–27. Seils's book was written in 1959 and received as "Habilitationsarbeit" by the Martin Luther University, HalleWittenberg; it was published three years later.

107   Ulrich Nembach, "Zur Problematik von Luthers Turmerlebnis," *Theologische Zeitschrift* 19 (1963) 111–12.

108   Kurt Aland, *Der Weg zur Reformation: Zeitpunkt und Charakter des reformatorischen Erlebnisses Martin Luthers* (*Theologische Existenz heute* 123; Munich, 1965) p. 104.

109   Otto Pesch, O.P., "Zur Frage nach Luthers reformatorischer Wende," *Catholica* 20 (1966) 276.

110   Heinz Bluhm, "The Idea of Justice in Luther's First Publication," *Concordia Theological Monthly* 37 (1966) 565–66.

111   Paul Hacker, *Das Ich im Glauben bei Martin Luther* (Graz, 1966) pp. 345–46.

112   Uuras Saarnivaara, *Luther Discovers the Gospel* (St. Louis, 1951; first published in Finnish, 1947) p. 46.

first of all, the nonimputation of sins and the forensic imputation of righteousness, and secondly, renewal.[113] Luther's theological reversal, for Saarnivaara, occurred in the autumn or winter of 1518, while he was preparing for his second lectures on the Psalms.[114]

Luther's discovery, for Axel Gyllenkrok, a Danish scholar, is the discovery of the certitude of salvation (*Heilsgewissheit*)[115]. Gyllenkrok argues that in the lectures on the Psalms and Romans Luther is working with a humility-theology which is Augustinian.[116] In his comment on Rom 8:16, a beginning of a break between his humilitytheology and an evangelical theology is evident.[117] Luther works out the problem of *Heilsgewissheit*, according to Gyllenkrok, in his lectures on Hebrews and in a sermon preached during the Leipzig disputation.[118] Luther comes to see that certitude is possible only when the promise and the gospel are identical, only when faith comes by hearing and the Word brings salvation.[119]

Ernst Bizer is usually credited with reopening the whole *Turmerlebnis* problem in 1958 with the first edition of his *Fides ex auditu*. There were others who preceded Bizer, notably Gyllenkrok, but Bizer has received most of the attention.[120] Bizer's position is that Luther's discovery is a theology of the Word that teaches that the Word itself is the means of grace.[121] Luther's Reformation theology is that faith as a direct response to the Word and as a substitute for

---

113   *Ibid., p.* 14.

114   *Ibid., p.* 108.

115   Axel Gyllenkrok, *Rechtfertigung und Heiligung in der frühen evangelischen Theologie Luthers* (Uppsala, 1952) p. 72.

116   *Ibid., p.* 4.

117   *Ibid., pp.* 66–67.

118   *Ibid., pp.* 72–74.

119   *Ibid., p.* 75.

120   *Fides ex auditu* (2nd ed.; Neukirchen, 1961; 1st ed., 1958). It has received extensive review—e.g., Jedin, *Catholica* 12 (1958) 129; Bainton, *JTS* 10 (1959) 191; Lau, *LuJ* 26 (1959) 154–56; Weijenborg, *RHE* 54 (1959) 228; Kinder, *TZ* 15 (1959) 66; Löfgren, *LR* 8 (1958–59) 494–97; Rupp, *ZKG* 71 (1960) 351; Walty, *RSPT* 45 (1961) 337; Rost, *Luth Rdblick* 9 (1961) 52–54; Nembach, *TZ* 19 (1963) 105; Beintker, *TLZ* 88 (1963) 52.

121   *Ibid., p.* 7.

humility justifies.[122] The Word is not a moral, legal encouragement to appropriate Christ's humility, but is the means of grace whereby man is justified.[123] Faith which comes from hearing the Word brings the certitude of salvation.[124]

Bizer's argument is that in his lectures on the Psalms and Romans Luther is immersed in the humilitytheology of the Middle Ages whereby faith is the basis for humility.[125] Humility justifies. However, in his comments on Heb 5:1, 7:1, 7:12, 9:17, and 9:24, Luther has come to a new understanding of law and gospel, faith, certitude of salvation, and the sacraments.[126] In the *Acta Augustana* and parallel literature of 1518–19 there are selfconscious and clear theological statements about the understanding and implications of *fides ex auditu*.[127] The date of Luther's *Turmerlebnis*, therefore, according to Bizer, is the spring or summer of 1518.[128]

F. Edward Cranz, an American scholar, holds that the "crucial turningpoint in Luther's general development" involves basically a doctrine of the two kingdoms.[129] His argument is that Luther's "reorientation" occurs when he begins to recognize two realms of Christian existence which are simultaneous and yet distinct: existence in Christ and in the world. The Christian is totally just in Christ and simultaneously only partially just in the world where he is in the process of sanctification. Total justification is primary and antecedent; gradual sanctification is secondary and subsequent.[130] Luther's distinction between the two kingdoms provides the basis for rethinking his old ideas of justice, law, and society. The "reorientation" period is 1518–19.[131]

---

122 *Ibid.*, pp. 77, 80–81.
123 *Ibid.*, pp. 164, 167.
124 *Ibid.*, p. 91.
125 *Ibid.*, pp. 22, 51.
126 *Ibid.*, pp. 80–92.
127 *Ibid.*, pp. 115 ff.
128 *Ibid.*, p. 7.
129 F. Edward Cranz, An *Essay* on *the Development of Luther's Thought on Justice, Law* and *Society* (Cambridge, 1959) pp. 41 ff.
130 *Ibid.*, pp. xvi ff.
131 *Ibid.*, p. xvi.

CONCLUSION

On the basis of the foregoing analysis of development theses, I think three conclusions can be drawn. One is that there has been a trend in our century to date the *Turmerlebnis* progressively later and later. Scholars in the first quarter of the century (group 1) generally defended a very early dating (1508–12). Then, in the second quarter, some (group 2) argued for the time when Luther was preparing, but not formally giving, his *Dictata* (1512–13). Perhaps the largest group of scholars (group 3), perpetuating something of a consensus in the thirties and forties, dated the *Turmerlebnis* during the period of the *Dictata* (1513–15). In the fifties and sixties there has been a considerable effort (group 5) to update the *Turmerlebnis* to around 1517–19.

There is no consensus in the sixties among those who try to date the *Turmerlebnis*. While the majority of those who have published in the sixties seem to argue for a later dating (Peters, Dillenberger, Seils, Nembach, Aland, Pesch, Bluhm, Hacker), some argue for the 1512–13 dating (Prenter, Lilje), some for 1513–15 (Lohse, Todd, Boendermaker), and some for 1515–16 (Bellucci). In August, 1966, at the seminar on the development of the young Luther held during the Third International Congress for Luther Research in Järvenpää, Finland, the majority of participants who spoke out did so in favor of an early dating. Yet, called upon for a summary of the seminar, Gerhard Ebeling concluded that there was nothing to conclude.[132]

A second conclusion I would draw is that Luther scholars who have dealt with the *Turmerlebnis* problem have generally used a "key" method. Their method has been to operate with a single key doctrine or aspect of Luther's thought. They have generally approached the young Luther with some formulation of the essence of his evangelical theology. For Holl and Scheel, the "key" is a sanative theory of justification; for Böhmer, the certainty of forgiveness; for Lortz, subjectivism; for Hirsch, the distinction between law and gospel; for Vogelsang, tropological exegesis; for Bornkamm, a Christological interpretation of the *iustitia Dei*; for Ebeling, hermeneutics; for Saarnivaara, a forensic theory of justification; for Gyllenkrok, the certitude of salvation; for Bizer, a theology of the Word; and for Cranz, a doctrine of the two kingdoms.

---

132   Pesch, "Zur Frage nach Luthers reformatorischer Wende," p. 264.

With their key to the mature Luther, scholars read the young Luther to find the first evidence of his mature theology. When these are found, they figure that a revolutionary change has taken place in Luther's development: everything that was written before is considered medieval, everything after is Reformation. The concern in all the *Turmerlebnis* theses has been to specify the date Luther ceases to be Roman Catholic and becomes Lutheran. This is in part based on the assumption that there is such a neat category as Catholic doctrine and Lutheran doctrine and that by a conversion experience one changes his theological baggage completely. First of all, there are no standards for Catholic doctrine in the Late Middle Ages prior to Trent, but only several late medieval theologies. Secondly, the definition of Lutheran theology or Luther's "mature" theology has varied considerably through the centuries. Various definitions of Catholicity and mature Luther(an) theology have yielded various results. Different keys have opened up different doors to the later Luther. The world of Luther scholarship has reached no agreement or come to any decisive conclusions as to the date of Luther's so-called *Turmerlebnis*.

A final conclusion I would draw is that the onelevel, "key" approach to the early Luther has led to complete frustration and, hopefully, the death of the *Turmerlebnis* problem. Although some continue with the onelevel approach to date the *Turmerlebnis*, several have recently studied the development of the young Luther without reference to the *Turmerlebnis* problem (Oberman,[133] Schwartz,[134] Grane,[135] Rogge,[136]

---

133 Heiko A. Oberman, "Facientibus quod in se est Deus non denegat gratiam: Robert Holcot, O.P., and the Beginnings of Luther's Theology," *Harvard Theological Review* 55 (1962) 317–42.

134 Reinhard Schwarz, *Fides, Spes und Charitas beim jungen Luther* (Arbeiten zur Kirchengeschichte 34; Berlin, 1962).

135 Leif Grane, *Contra Gabrielem: Luther Auseinandersetzung mit Gabriel Bid in der Disputatio contra scholasticam theologiam 1517* (Acta theologica Danica; 4; Gyldendal, 1962).

136 Joachim Rogge, "Die Initia Zwinglis und Luthers," *LutherJahrbuch* 30 (1963) 107–30.

Metzger,[137] Tüchle,[138] Kantzenbach,[139] and Hagen[140]). Oberman, for example, treats the relation of Luther to nominalism. He concludes that Luther broke with the nominalist tradition on the relation of faith and reason in 1509 and on the relation of will and grace in 1515–16. However, Oberman does not claim to have solved the *Turmerlebnis* problem, but only to have "led us to a decisive transition between two stages in Luther's development." Hopefully, scholars have come to see that a single key to the later Luther opens up only a single door. Scholars have come up with different datings depending on what doctrine is used. Different keys open different doors.

A more fruitful approach to the young Luther would be to see Luther as developing on many levels concerning several theological doctrines and religious issues. Rather than trying to find in Luther an abrupt reversal from a "Catholic" position to a "Lutheran" one, it would be better to say that Luther develops in a more organic way on particular issues as the occasion and his exegetical work demand. There is always a complex interrelation between one's faith and one's theology, and between the various elements of theological understanding. These are perhaps many keys to Luther, but they are on the same chain; they open many doors, but doors of the same house.

And so the search for the real Luther continues as it has for 450 years. Luther has served in various capacities and has been used in various movements through the centuries. The developments and changes in Luther studies in general parallel the historical and theological development of Lutheranism. The history of Luther research as an index to the history of Lutheran theology shows that there is no single Lutheran theology or Lutheran interpretation of Luther. As there is a plurality of Luther images, so there is a plurality of Lutheran theologies. By virtue of the development and diversity in Lutheran theology, the ecumenical stance of Lutheran theology is not so much

---

137   Günther Metzger, *Gelebter Glaube: Die Formierung reformatorischen Denkens in Luthers erster Psalmenvorlesung (Forschungen zur Kirchen und Dogmengeschichle 14*; Göttingen, 1964).

138   Hermann Tüchle, *Reformation und Gegenreformation (Geschichte der Kirche*, ed. Rogier et al., 3; Einsiedeln, 1965).

139   Friedrich W. Kantzenbach, *Martin Luther und die Anfänge der Reformation (Evangelische Enzyklopädie 7/8*; Gütersloh, 1965).

140   Kenneth G. Hagen, *Luther's Lectures on Hebrews in the Light of Medieval Commentaries on Hebrews* (Dissertation, Harvard University, 1966).

one that stands over against other traditions as one that stands within the Christian tradition offering many of the same alternatives and presenting many of the same differences that one finds in other traditions. Using the history, for example, of Calvin studies and Trent studies as an index to the historical and theological development in the Reformed tradition and Roman Catholic tradition, one would find that there is no such thing as a Reformed theology or a Roman Catholic theology. Many divergent theological positions, past and present, are not so much differences between traditions as among traditions. While there always have been and, hopefully, always will be theological differences among the various traditions, perhaps the man who precipitated the division of Western Christendom can be a guide to the establishment of the real goal of the Reformation: the one, holy, catholic, and apostolic Church.

APPENDIX: GUIDES TO LUTHER STUDIES

ALTHAUS, Paul. "Luther in der Gegenwart," Luther 22 (1940) 1–6.

BAINTON, Roland. Bibliography of the Continental Reformation (Chicago, 1935).

_____."

Survey of Periodical Literature in the United States, 1945–51," Archiv für Reformationsgeschichte 43 (1952) 88–106.

BENZ, Ernst. "Das Lutherbild des französischen Katholizismus," Zeitschrift für Religions und Geistesgeschichte 4 (1952) 1–19.

Bibliographie de la Réforme 1450–1648: Ouvrages parus de 1940 à 1955: Vol. 1: Germany, the Netherlands (3rd ed.; Leiden, 1964). Vol. 2: Belgium, Sweden, Norway, Denmark, Ireland, USA (Leiden, 1960). Vol. 3: Italy, Spain, Portugal (Leiden, 1961). Vol. 4: France, England, Switzerland (Leiden, 1963). Vol. 5: Finland, Hungary, Czechoslovakia, Poland (n.d.).

BIZER, Ernst. "Neue Darstellungen der Theologie Luthers," Theologische Rundschau 31 (1966) 316–49.

Böhmer, Heinrich. Luther in the Light of Recent Research, tr. Carl F. Huth, Jr. (New York, 1916).

BORNKAMM, Heinrich. Luther im Spiegel der deutschen Geistesgeschichte. Mit ausgewählten Texten von Lessing bis zur Gegenwart (Heidelberg, 1955).

_____. "Luther zwischen den Konfessionen: Vierhundert Jahre katholischer Lutherforschung," *Festschrift für Gerhard Ritter* (Tübingen, 1950) pp. 210–31.

_____. "Zum Lutherbild des19.Jahrhunderts," *Theologische Literaturzeitung* 79 (1954) 425–30.

BRING, Ragnar. "Einige Blätter aus der schwedischen Lutherforschung," *Zeitschrift für systematische Theologie* 8 (1930–31) 615–70.

CARLSON, Edgar. *The Reinterpretation of Luther* (Philadelphia, 1948).

CONGAR, Y. M. J. "Luther in katholischer Sicht," *EvangelischLutherische Kirchenzeitung* 5 (1951) 261–64.

DILLENBERGER, John. *God Hidden and Revealed* (Philadelphia, 1953).

_____. "Literature in Luther Studies, 195055," *Church History* 25 (1956) 160–77.

_____. "Major Volumes and Selected Periodical Literature in the U.S.A., 1956–59," *Church History* 30 (1961) 61–87.

FUCHS, Walther Peter. "Forschungen und Darstellungen zur Geschichte des Reformationszeitalters (194555)," *Die Welt als Geschichte* 16 (1956) 124–53, 218–49.

GRIMM, Harold. "Luther Research since 1920," *Journal of Modern History* 32 (1960) 105–18.

HASHAGEN, Justus. "Die apologetische Tendenz der Lutherforschung und die sogenannte Lutherrenaissance," *Historische Vierteljahrschrift* 31 (1937–39) 625–50.

HERMELINK, Heinrich. "Das katholische Lutherbild von Cochlaeus bis zur Gegenwart," *Theologische Literaturzeitung* 69 (1944) 193–202.

_____. "Die neuere Lutherforschung," *Theologische Rundschau* 7 (1935) 63–85, 131–56.

HERTE, Adolf. *Das katholische Lutherbild im Bann der Lutherkommentare des Cochlaeus* (3 vols.; Münster, 1943).

HESSE, Johannes. *Luther in katholischer Sicht* (2d ed.; Bonn, 1949).

KANTZENBACH, Friedrich Wilhelm. "Lutherverständnis zwischen Erweckung und Idealismus," *Luther* 36 (1965) 9–30.

KNOLLE, Th. "Neuzeitliche Lutherforschung," *Luther* 22 (1940) 22–36.

Köhler, Walter. *Das katholische Lutherbild der Gegenwart* (Bern, 1922).

_____. "Der gegenwärtige Stand der Lutherforschung," *Zeitschrift für Kirchengeschichte* 37 (1917–18) 1–60.

Lienhard, Marc. "La place de Luther dans le dialogue protestant-catholique actuel," *Positions luthériennes* (Paris, 1965) pp. 65–87.

Lindroth, Hjalmar. *Recent Theological Research in Sweden: A Luther Renaissance*, tr. Gustav Carlberg (Hong Kong, 1950).

Link, Wilhelm. *Das Ringen Luthers um die Freiheit der Theologie von der Philosophie*, ed. Ernst Wolf and Manfred Mezger (2d ed.; Munich, 1955).

Lofgren, David. "Verschiedene Tendenzen in der neueren Lutherforschung," *Kerygma und Dogma* 5 (1959) 146–64.

Löwenich, Walter von. "Zehn Jahre Lutherforschung in Deutschland, 1938–48," *Von Augustin zu Luther* (Witten, 1959) pp. 307–78.

Lutheran World 13 (1966) 257–316: articles on "Luther Research since 1945" by Kantzenbach, Prenter, Haikola, Lindberg, and Pesch.

Lutherforschung heute: Referate und Berickle des I. Internationalen Lutherforschungkongress, Aarhus, 18–23. August, 1956, ed. Vilmos Vajta (Berlin, 1958).

Luther and Melanchthon in the History and Theology of the Reformation, ed. Vilmos Vajta. A Report of the Second International Congress for Luther Research, Münster, August 8–13, 1960 (Philadelphia, 1961).

Müller, Gerhard. "Neuere Literatur zur Theologie des jungen Luther," *Kerygma und Dogma* 11 (1965) 325–57.

Muralt, Leonhard von. "Zur LutherForschung und zum LutherVerständnis," *Zwingliana* 9 (1953) 576–96.

Pauck, Wilhelm. "Historiography of the German Reformation during the Last Twenty Years," *Church History* 9 (1940) 305–40.

Pesch, Otto H., O.P. "Zur Frage nach Luthers reformatorischer Wende: Ergebnisse und Probleme der Diskussion um Ernst Bizer, Fides ex auditu," *Catholica*; 20 (1966) 216–43, 264–80.

Reu, J. M. *Thirtyfive Years of Luther Research* (Chicago, 1917).

Roth, Erich. "Neuere britische Reformationsliteratur," *Archiv für Reformationsgeschichte* 43 (1952) 235–54.

Rupp, E. Gordon. *The Righteousness of God: Luther Studies* (New York, 1953).

_____. "Luther: The Contemporary Image," *The Church, Mysticism, Sanctification and the Natural in Luther's Thought*. Lectures Presented to the Third International Congress on Luther Research,

Järvenpää, Finland, August 11–16, 1966, ed. Ivar Asheim (Philadelphia, 1967) pp. 9–19.

SCHOTTENLOHER, Karl. *Bibliographie zur deutschen Geschichte im Zeitalter der Glaubensspaltung: 1517–1585.* 6 vols. (Leipzig, 1933–40).

SCHREY, HeinzHorst. "Die LutherRenaissance in der neueren schwedischen Theologie," *Theologische Literaturzeitung* 74 (1949) 513–28.

SPITZ, Lewis. *The Reformation: Material or Spiritual?* (Boston, 1962).

————. "Current Accents in Luther Study: 1960–67," *Theological Studies* 28 (1967) 549–73.

STAUFFER, Richard. "La théologie de Luther d'après les recherches récentes," *Revue de théologie et philosophie* 7 (1957) 7–44.

————. *Luther as Seen by Catholics*, tr. Mary Parker and T. H. L. Parker (London, 1967).

STEPHAN, Horst. *Luther in den Wandlungen seiner Kirche* (2d ed.; Berlin, 1951).

STORCK, Hans. "Die schwedische Lutherforschung in den letzten drei Jahrzehnten," *Luther* 28 (1957) 75–84.

STUPPERICH, Robert. "Lutherforschung und Reformationsgeschichte," *Archiv für Kulturgeschichte* 43 (1961) 377–92.

SWIDLER, Leonard. "Catholic Reformation Scholarship in Germany," *Journal of Ecumenical Studies* 2 (1965) 189–204.

WINGREN, Gustaf. "Swedish Theology since 1900," *Scottish Journal of Theology* 9 (1965) 113–34.

WOLF, ERNST. "Über neuere LutherLiteratur und den Gang der Lutherforschung," *Christentum und Wissenschaft* 9 (1933) 201–26; 10 (1934) 6–21, 203–19, 259–73, 437–57.

WOLFF, Otto. *Haupttypen der neueren Lutherdeutung* (Stuttgart, 1938).

ZEEDEN, Ernst Walter. *The Legacy of Luther*, tr. Ruth Bethell (London, 1954).

AN ADDITION TO THE LETTERS OF JOHN LANG

INTRODUCTION AND TRANSLATION

An item which has never been included in collections of correspondence by the Reformers[1] is a letter from the Wittenberg Professor of Greek and moral philosophy, John Lang.[2] It was addressed to George Spalatin,[3] and bears the inscription, "Wittenberg, from the Augustinian monastery, the 10th of March, Year of Salvation, 1516." It appears to be merely a friendly letter in which Lang calls Spalatin's attention to the work of an obscure fifth century monk. A careful examination of the letter, however, reveals something about the sequence of events in Lang's life, Luther's popularity, and the interest of the Wittenberg circle in the Church Fathers.

Early in 1516 Lang received a printed translation of Nilus' *Morales Sententiae* from Wolfgang[4] of the Nuremberg monastery. Impressed

---

1   My research has led me to the conclusion that this letter has not been used in studies on Lang, Spalatin or Luther. Nor has it ever been edited, as far as I know. It is not in Hermann Hering: *Epistolae Langianae* ("Programm der Universität Halle Wittenberg," Halle, 1886). While advising my doctoral dissertation, Heiko A. Oberman, then Professor at Harvard University, handed me this letter for critical evaluation.

2   John Lang (1488–1548), entered the Augustinian monastery at Erfurt in 1506. He pursued his academic career with Luther at Erfurt, where he taught him Greek and Hebrew, and at Wittenberg. Lang left Erfurt in 1511 to matriculate at Wittenberg, where he became Master of Arts in 1512. Sometime in 1516 he was transferred to the Erfurt monastery, where he became prior.

3   Georg Burkhardt of Spalt (1484–1545), always known as Spalatin, was ordained priest in 1508. In 1509 he was appointed to the Electoral Saxon court to educate the sons of Frederick the Wise. He soon won the Elector's confidence and became his librarian, court chaplain, secretary, and trusted confidant. One of the more influential people surrounding Frederick, Spalatin was the liason man ("Rectorum Studiorum") between the University of Wittenberg and the Electoral court.

4   Probably Wolfgang Stromer of Nuremberg, reported by Luther in his Table Talk from 1538 to be an old man who was extremely well trained

with the treatise, Lang requested the reprinting of the work and sent it to the printer Grunenberg, together with a preface addressed to Spalatin. The reprint was published by Grunenberg in 1516 in the monastery at Wittenberg.[5] Lang sent a copy of the Wittenberg edition to Spalatin.

Lang wrote his letter "from the Augustinian monastery," which suggests that Lang was still in Wittenberg on March 10. This contradicts the chronology of Reynold Weijenborg. The question is when did Lang return to Erfurt. Weijenborg says that Lang was transferred to Erfurt by Luther already in February of 1516.[6] This letter indicates that Lang was transferred from Wittenberg sometime after the date of this letter.

The Lang letter is also important for Reformation studies because of an implied reference to Luther which it contains. Lang says that the lectures on the Bible and the Fathers were being well received by many students and that the lectures on the scholastics were very poorly attended: "These are such studies which we are glad to see are now coming alive. Very many students are all excited and enthusiastic about the lectures on the Bible and the early Fathers, whereas the study of the scholastic doctors (as they are called) attracts maybe two or three students."

Lang must be referring to the situation in Wittenberg, because he speaks with firsthand knowledge, and to Luther's lectures on the Bible, which contained many references to the Church Fathers. Luther was solely responsible for the *Lectura in Biblia*. He had become a member of the theological faculty on October 22, 1512, succeeding Johann von Staupitz.[7]

---

in many languages (*WA Tr* 4, 384, 2–3). He is mentioned in Justus Jonas' correspondence (Gustav Kawerau: *Der Briefwechsel des Justus Jonas* [Hildesheim, 1964], Part 1, pp. 162, 178, 319).

5   "Wittenberg in aedibus Ioannis Grunenbergi. Anno MDCXVI. Apud Aurelianos."

6   "Luther et les cinquante et un Augustin d'Erfurt d'aprés une lettre d'indulgences inédite du 18 avril 1508," *Revue d'Histoire Ecclésiastique*, 55 (1960), p. 849.

7   Karl Baur: *Die Wittenberger Universitätstheologie und die Anfänge der Deutschen Reformation* (Tübingen, 1928), p. 14; Heinrich Böhmer: *Der junge Luther*, ed. Heinrich Bornkamm, 4th ed. (Stuttgart, 1951), p. 81.

This statement by Lang in 1516 gives us earlier and additional in-formation about the initial success of Luther's lectures. Previously, the only reliable information we had about the early reception of Luther's lectures was Luther's letter to Lang of May 18, 1517: "Theologia nostra et S. Augustimis prospere procedunt et regnant in nostra universitate Deo operante. Aristoteles descendit paulatim inclinatus ad ruinam prope futuram sempiternam. Mire fastidiuntur lectiones sententiariae, nec est, ut quis sibi auditores spearare possit, nisi theologiam hanc, id est bibliam aut S. Augustinum aliumve ecclesiasticae autoritatis doc-torern velit profiteri."[8]

Luther's claim is corroborated by Spalatin in his letter to Guy Bild *ca.* Dec. 10, 1518, in which he says: "Luther and Carlstadt have full lecture rooms."[9] In addition to the evidence from Luther and Spalatin, we had the report from the "somewhat unreliable" John Oldekop of Hildesheim, who matriculated at Wittenberg on April 16, 1515, that in 1513 Luther had many auditors; nothing is said about the relative success of Luther's lectures: "To dusser sulven tit hof an Martinus Luther den psalter Davidis to lesen, und was dar flitich bi und hadde vele tohorers."[10]

From the evaluation of Lang in Wittenberg we can conclude that Luther's lectures were well received by the overwhelming majority of students already in early 1516.

Another contribution which the Lang letter makes is the evidence it gives to how much appeal the early Church Fathers had for the Reformers. Lang cites approvingly the success which Biblical and Patristic studies, as well as Greek and Latin studies in general, had enjoyed among the students. But enthusiasm extends also to the facul-ty as well, for the purpose of Lang's letter is to acquaint Spalatin with the *Morales Sententiae* of Nilus. Lang "cannot imagine that there can be anything more erudite, more wonderful, or more holy than these *Sayings.*"

---

8   *WA BR* 1, 99, 8–13.

9   *Luther's Correspondence and Other Contemporary Letters,* ed. Preserved Smith, Vol. I: *1507–1521* (Philadelphia, 1913), p. 138.

10 *Chronik,* ed. Karl Euling ("Bibliothek des Litterarischen Vereins in Stuttgart," 190; Tübingen, 1891), p. 40. Concerning Oldecop's unreliability cf. A. Herte: "Johann Oldecop," *Lexicon für Theologie und Kirche,* 2nd ed. (Freiburg i. Br., 1935), p. 699.

The author of the *Ethical Sayings* was a monk, Nilus the Ascetic (d. 426), who was the founder and superior of a monastery near Ancyra. A minor figure, Nilus was neither bishop nor martyr as Pirckheimer believed. His *Sententiae* are short moral sayings which teach that one should continually imitate the virtues of Christ because the final judgment is near at hand.

Lang enthusiastically endorses the work of the translator of Nilus, Willibald Pirckheimer[11]: "Another indication of the complete dedication of this man to the right kind of studies is that fact that he has recently translated from Greek the *Ethical Sayings* of the Holy Father Nilus, bishop and martyr." Pirckheimer devoted himself at the turn of the sixteenth century to the translation of the Greek classics and Church Fathers into Latin. He discovered Nilus' work in a Greek codex and translated it during the Christmas holidays of 1515. His translation together with a preface addressed to his sister Clara was printed in Nuremberg by Fridericus Peypus and entitled: "Beatissimi Patris Nili, Episcopi et Martyris Theologi antiquis Sententiae Morales e graeco in latinum versa." Pirckheimer sent a copy as a Christmas gift to his sister Clara, who was an instructor of young nuns in Nuremberg, with a prefatory letter entitled: "Bilibaldus Pirckheymer sorori suae Clarae apud divam Claram Nurembergae moniall. S. D." The letter is dated January 4, 1516. However, Pirckheimer presumably reckoned the beginning of the new year from the first day of Christmas, as was the custom in Nuremberg at that time. Thus the date of his letter is actually December 29, 1515.[12]

---

11   Willibald Pirckheimer (1470–1530), member of Nuremberg's upper bourgeoisie, became town councilor in 1497. His patrician house soon became the center of learning. At his table dined Luther, Melanchthon, Celtis, Hutten, and many other leading figures of the day. A list of his correspondents includes Erasmus and Spalatin.

12   *Willibald Pirckheimers Briefwechsel*, ed. Emil Reicke, vol. II (Munich, 1956), 596–97. Lewis W. Spitz: *The Religious Renaissance of the German Humanists* (Cambridge, 1963), pp. 168–69. Karl Schottenloher: *Die Widmungsvorrede im Buch des 16. Jahrhunderts* ("Reformationsgeschichtliche Studien und Texte," 76/77; Munster i. W., 1953),p. 15. For other editions of Pirckheimer's translation see Georg Andreas Will: *Nürnbergisches GelehrtenLexicon*, cont. Christian Conrad Nopitsch (Altdorf, 1806), VII, 167.

In addition to Pirckheimer, Lang praises the contributions of Reuchlin, Erasmus, and Mutianus Rufus to Biblical and Patristic studies. In conclusion it can be said that, when carefully analysed, Lang's letter to Spalatin makes three contributions to Reformation studies: it helps to establish a more accurate chronology of Lang's life; it offers the earliest reliable evidence testifying to the early success of Luther's lectures; and it further indicates the extent of the Reformers' interest in even obscure Patristic figures.

GEORGIO SPALATINE RECTORUM STUDIORUM ADSERTORI AMICOQUE SINGULARI SUO IOANNES LANGUS ER. AUGUSTINIANUS S. P.

Symmystes[13] mihi est in coenobio Nurnbergensis, Spalatine frater suavissime, qui non minus eruditus quarn integer sit. Cui Wolfgango nomenclatura, Bilibaldo Pirckhaimero illi doctissimo non ignotus, quippe quo graecis in literis ut oraculo familiariter utitur. Is simul et Pirckhaimeri et mei tam est amantissimus ut nihil latinitati praeceptor donet, quod Lango discipulus non mittat. Nam et Luciani gloriosi subsannatoris, et Plutarchi philosophi quaedam, et Xenophontis τὰ Θουκυδίδου παραλειπόμενα τῆς συγγραφῆς (quod te non praeterit) in latinum e graeco tam proprie quarn eleganter vertit.

Huius hominis in bona studia propensam operam id quoque declarat, quod his diebus sancti patris Episcopi et Martyris Nili *Morales Sententias* e graeco traduxerit. Quibus profecto quid cruditius, quid melius, quid sanctius esse possit non video; cum tam breves ut cito perlegi, tam iucundae ut delectare, tam denique sanctae sint ut docere et vitam instituere valeant.

Talia sunt studia, quae iam reviviscere cum gaudio cernimus, dum sacram bibliam antiquosque scriptores complures et anhelant et laetanter audiunt, dum scholastici doctores (quod appellant) vix aut duos aut treis habent auditores. Dabit deus iis molestis perplexis et multo plus quam praebeant promittentibus studiis finem.

Quod ut fiat maximo sunt adiutorio Ioannes Reuchlinus, vir doctissimus pariter et integerrimus, et Erasmus Roterodamus ultra quern dicere possum et eruditus et frugi. De quibus studiis tam graecis quam latinis commentario mihi iucundissima solet esse dum vel apud Mutianum Rufum nostrum, non tantum amicum sed et patrem, cuius ab

---

13 *Symmystes* is a transliteration of σύμμυστης.

ore melle dulcior oratio fluit, quae non delecter modo verum et semper erudiat, vel apud te colloquor.

Hunc igitur Nili martyris libellum quern chalcographo excudendum tradidi tibi mitto; quem tu ita nunc excipias ut omnia nostra soles.

Valeto quam ocissime.

Wittenbergi ex Augustiniano coenobio. V. Idus Martiae, Anno salutis MDXVI.

To George Spalatin, Rector of Studies
My Illustrious Defender and Friend

Dear Spalatin, my dearest brother,
There is a fellow priest of mine in the monastery at Nuremberg, who is as erudite as he is upright. You are not unacquainted with that man, Wolfgang by name, nor with Willibald Pirckheimer, that most learned man, since he deals accurately with Greek literature as though it were oracular. The former is very close to both Pirckheimer and myself, so much so that his teacher, Pirckheimer, contributes nothing to Latin studies that the pupil does not send on to Lang. He (Pirckheimer) has translated from Greek into Latin with great accuracy and fine style certain works of Lucian,[14] that glorious wit, of Plutarch,[15] the philosopher, and the work of Xenophon entitled, τὰ Θουκυδίδου παραλειπόμενα τῆς συγγραφῆς (which will not have escaped your attention).

Another indication of the complete dedication of this man to the right kind of studies is the fact that he has recently translated from Greek the *Ethical Sayings* of the Holy Father Nilus, bishop and martyr. I cannot imagine that there can be anything more erudite, more wonderful, or more holy than these *Sayings*, because they are so concise that one reads through them quickly, so delightful that they have the power to please, and, finally, so holy that they have the power to instruct and govern life.

These are such studies which we are glad to see are now coming alive. Very many students are all excited and enthusiastic about the lectures on the Bible and the early Fathers, whereas the study of the scholastic doctors (as they are called) attracts maybe two or three students. God

14   E. g. *De conscribenda historia*. Nuremberg, 1515.
15   E. g. *De his qui tarde a numine corripiuntur*. Nuremberg, 1513.

will put an end to these taxing and confusing studies which promise more than they can give.

Of great help in bringing this about are Johann Reuchlin, a man who is equally learned and upright, and Erasmus of Rotterdam, who is both erudite and honest beyond anyone I am able to describe. I have very pleasant memories of these studies, both in Greek and Latin, whenever I discuss them with you or with our Mutianus Rufus,[16] who is not only a friend but also a father from whose mouth flow words sweeter than honey, not only delightful but always instructive.

Hence I am sending you this treatise of Nilus the Martyr, which I have handed over to be engraved on copper. May you accept it now as you always accept things from us.

Get well as speedily as possible.

Wittenberg, from the Augustinian monastery,
the 10th of March,
Year of Salvation, 1516.
John Lang, O.E.S.A.

---

16 Conrad Mutianus Rufus (1470–1526), key figure in the human-ist movement of central Germany, held undisputed leadership of the Humanist circle in Erfurt. In 1503 he entered the Chapter of Mary in Gotha as a canon and spent the rest of his life there. In 1516 Luther and Mutianus became friends through Lang and Spalatin, but the friendship was of short duration.

FROM TESTAMENT TO COVENANT
IN THE EARLY SIXTEENTH CENTURY

The Question of testament and covenant, whether old or new, one or two, for the reformers in the first quarter of the sixteenth century concerns the relationship of God and man, man and man. A "testament relationship" will be compared to a "covenant relationship." The question is hermeneutical, soteriological, sacramental, and political, because God touches man with His left and right hand. Word, sacrament and life are interrelated in various ways for the early reformers. Therefore, I will attempt to discern the relationship between their concepts of testament and covenant. The study involves: first, the hermeneutical question of the relation of the books of the Old and New Testament; secondly, the sacramental or soteriologlcal question of the reality of testament and covenant described in the two books; thirdly, the historical question of the relationship of their biblical and sacramental views to the political (legal and social) realities of their day. Here I will consider only the first two questions.[1] While many reformers not discussed below merit further consideration, I will examine the developments in Erasmus, Luther, Melanchthon, Zwingli, and Bucer, up to 1527.

The context for this discussion is theological and historical (what God has joined together let not man rent asunder). By way of contributing to the current interest in Old Testament hermeneutic and covenant theology I will examine the early sixteenth century on the basis of a judgment that it has not received an adequate treatment *de testamento seu foedere*. Historical interest in *de testamento seu foedere* has produced some work on the patristic (fourth century and following), medieval, and late medieval periods as well as on the modern period beginning with the seventeenth century. The sixteenth century, however, has been approached by scholars more interested in general backgrounds to the seventeenth century and following. They have

1   I would like to express my appreciation to the Newberry Library for its Grant-in-Aid and to Marquette University for its Summer Faculty Fellowship for making research possible for this article, which appeared in *Sixteenth Century Journal*, III, 1 (April 1972), 124.

not, therefore, studied the sixteenth century in terms of its own backgrounds in the Late Middle Ages or more immediately in Erasmus and the young Luther. Within this group are those interested in backgrounds to seventeenth century Reformed theology (Korff, Schrenk, Ritschl, and McCoy), Puritanism (Trinterud, Moeller, and Marsden) and Scottish covenant ideas (Burrell and Torrance).[2] Other general surveys of the sixteenth century can be set aside because of their utter superficiality and/or errors (Burrage, Schöffler, and Noltensmeier)[3]

---

2   Emanuel Graf von Korff, *Die Anfänge der Föderaltheologie und ihre erste Ausgestaltung in Zürich und Holland* (Bonn: Emil Eisele, 1908). Gottlob Schrenk, *Gottesreich und Bund im älteren Protestantismus: Vornehmlich bei Johannes Coccejus* (Gütersloh: Gerd Mohn, 1923; Darmstadt, 1967). Otto Ritschl, "Die Entwicklung des Bundesgedankens in der reformierten Theologie des 16. und des 17. Jahrhunderts," *Dogmengeschichte des Protestantismus*, (Göttingen: Vandenhoeck & Ruprecht, 1926), III, 412–58. Charles S. McCoy, "The Covenant Theology of Johannes Cocceius," Yale University, Ph. D. dissertation, 1957, unpublished. Leonard J. Trinterud, "The Origins of Puritanism," *Church History*, XX, 1 (March 1951), 37–57. Jens G. Moeller, "The Beginnings of Puritan Covenant Theology," *Journal of Ecclesiastical History*, XIV, 1 (1963), 46–67. George M. Marsden, "Perry Miller's Rehabilitation of the Puritans: A Critique," *Church History*, XLI, 1 (March 1970), 91–105. S. A. Burrell, "The Covenant Idea as a Revolutionary Symbol: Scotland, 1596–1637," *Church History*, XXIX, 4 (December 1958), 338–50. James B. Torrance, "Covenant or Contract? A study of the Theological Background of Worship in SeventeenthCentury Scotland," *Scottish Journal of Theology*, XXIII, 1 (February 1970), 51–76.

3   Champlin Burrage, *The Church Covenant Idea: Its Origin and Development* (Philadelphia: American Baptist Publication House, 1904), chapter one, is dependent only on secondary (19th century) sources. Trinterud, p. 56, n. 28, attacks Burrage's thesis that English Puritan covenant ideas come from the Anabaptists. Herbert Schöffler, "Abendland und Altes Testament: Untersuchung zur Kulturmorphologie Europas, Insbesondere Englands," *Kölner Anglistische Arbeiten* (BochumLangendreer: Verlag H. Pöppinghaus, 1937), XXX, has a few references which are mostly to secondary sources, misinterprets Luther's view of the Old Testament, pp. 17–20, and is brief and theologically poor in his interpretation of the Continental Reformation. Hermann Noltensmeier, *Reformatorische Einheit: Das Schriftverständnis bei Luther und Calvin* (Cologne: Böhlau, 1953) is simply superficial.

or because they see the beginnings of testamentcovenant discussions only later in the sixteenth century (Heppe, Diestel, and Lindsay).[4] Individual sixteenth century figures have been studied, though most often without relating them to other figures of the same century. Erasmus has received some attention. Aldridge, in his treatment of *The Hermeneutic of Erasmus*, surveys Erasmus' understanding of the "barbarians" of the Old Testament particularly with reference to the problem of authority and the *philosophia Christi* in Erasmus' thought.[5] Kohls, who makes Erasmus' theology sound very "Lutheran," portrays Erasmus as being more positive about the relationship of the Old Testament to the New.[6]

Two important works on Luther's understanding of the Old Testament have recently appeared in English, one by Preus, *From Shadow to Promise: Old Testament Interpretation from Augustine to the Young Luther*,[7] and the other a translation of Bornkamm's 1948 *Luther und das Alte Testament*.[8] In his treatment of the young Luther, Preus, *contra* Ebeling, attempts to work out a developmental thesis according to which the hermeneutical divide between the testaments shifts in the *Dictata* to a distinction within the Old Testament itself.

4   Heinrich L. J. Heppe, *Dogmatik des deutschen Protestantismus im 16. Jahrhundert* (Gotha: F. A. Perthes, 1857), I, 144. Idem, *Geschichte des Pietismus und der Mystik in der reformierte Kirche namentlich der Niederlande* (Leiden: Brill, 1879), pp. 205–16. Ludwig Diestel, "Studien zur Föderaltheologie," *Jahrbücher für deutsche Theologie*, X (1865), 209–76; see p. 212. Idem, *Geschichte des Alten Testaments in der christlichen Kirche* (Jena: Mauk, 1869), pp. 278–306. T. M. Lindsay, "The Covenant Theology," *British and Foreign Evangelical Review*, XXVIII (July 1879), 521–38.

5   John W. Aldridge, *The Hermeneutic of Erasmus* (Richmond, Va.: John Knox Press, 1966), pp. 44–56. An earlier and general treatment of Erasmus' exegesis also interprets Erasmus as being very critical of the Old Testament vis-à-vis the New. See Hermann Schlingensiepen. "Erasmus als Exeget: Auf Grund seiner Schriften zu Matthäus," *Zeitschrift für Kirchengeschichte*, XLVIII, 1 (1929), 16–57. in his recent work Roland Bainton mentions the problematic, *Erasmus of Christendom* (New York: Scribners, 1969), p. 143.

6   ErnstWilhelm Kohls, *Die Theologie des Erasmus* (Basel: Friedrich Reinhardt Verlag, 1966), I, 1–2.

7   Cambridge: Harvard University Press, 1969. Cf. John Pilch, "Luther's Hermeneutical 'Shift,'" *Harvard Theological Review*, LXIII, 3 (July 1970), 445–48.

8   *Luther and the Old Testament*, tr. Eric and Ruth Gritsch (Philadelphia: Fortress Press, 1969).

Bornkamm's description of the uniqueness of Luther and Preus' account of the un-"medieval Luther" will have to be reexamined in the light of patristicearly medieval theology.

The revival of Zwingli studies has brought some discussion of Zwingli's understanding of the two testaments and of his contribution to federal theology. Locher, who sees Zwingli's federal theology as a fruitful contribution to Protestantism,[9] says that for Zwingli the unity of God is grounded on the unity of the Old and New Testament.[10] Künzli has done a major study of Zwlingli›s understanding of the Old Testament.[11]

Neuser, Bizer and Sick have recently worked on Melanchthon but only in a limited way have treated the problem of the two testaments.[12] Sick's monograph has a few pages on the *Einheit* and *Unterschiedenheit* of the Old and New Testaments.

Bucer's understanding of the two testaments and covenants has received attention. Lang's old and important work on Bucer's *Enarrationum in evangelia* treats the problematic in terms of Bucer's understanding of law/gospel and the sacraments in the Old and New Testaments.[13] Müller›s more recent work on *Martin Bucers*

---

9   Gottfried W. Locher, "Das Geschichtsbild Huldrych Zwinglis," *Theologische Zeitschrift*, IX, 4 (July and August 1953), 296.

10   *Die Theologie Huldrych Zwinglis im Lichte seiner Christologie*, Part I: *Die Gotteslehre* (Zürich: Zwingli Verlag, 1952), pp. 96–98.

11   Edwin Künzli, "Zwingli als Ausleger des Alten Testamentes," *Corpus Reformatorum*, Vol. XIV of *Zwinglis Werke* (Zürich, 1959), CI, 869–99. Cf. Künzli, "Zwinglis theologische Wertung des Alten Testaments," *Der Kirchenfreund*, LXXXIII (1949), 244–48, 276–84.

12   Wilhelm H. Neuser, *Melanchthon-Studien Part I: Der Ansatz der Theologie Philipp Melanchthons. Part II: Die Abendmahlslehre Melanchthons in ihrer geschichtlichen Entwicklung (1519–30)*, Vol. IX of *Beiträge zur Geschichte und Lehre der Reformierten Kirche* (Neukirchen: Verlag der Buchhandlung des Erziehungsvereins Neukirchen Kreis Moers, 1957, 1968), I, 120–33; *ibid.*, II, 41–48. Ernst Bizer, *Theologie der Verheissung: Studien zur theologischen Entwicklung des jungen Melanchthon (1519–24)* (Neukirchen: Neukirchener Verlag des Erziehungsvereins, 1964), pp. 56–66. Hansjörg Sick, *Melanchthon als Ausleger des Alten Testaments*, Vol. II of *Beiträge zur Geschichte der biblischen Hermeneutik* (Tübingen: J. C. B. Mohr [Paul Siebeck], 1959), pp. 56–59.

13   August Lang, *Der Evangelienkommentar Martin Butzers und die Grundzüge seiner Theologie*, Vol. II, pt. 2 of *Studien zur Geschichte der*

Hermeneutik examines Bucer's Old Testament hermeneutic in terms of revelation, election, and typology.[14]

Given the limited and piecemeal treatment of the early sixteenth century, I will attempt to relate developmentally and chronologically the discussions of the specified early reformers as their works are relevant to the hermeneutical, soteriological, and sacramental aspects of the problematic. By tracing here the developments of the problematic more specifically in Luther from 1518 to 1527, and more generally in other reformers of this given time span, I propose to fill in a gap between Luther and the seventeenth century and to illumine an important period for the current interest in the hermeneutic of covenant.

LUTHER AND ERASMUS TO 1518

For the young Luther up to 151718,[15] only one Word comes forth from God. That Word is constant and the same. It is variously called testament, promise, law, gospel. In this context the designation of old and new testament does not refer to two different testaments of God; rather during the time covered by the books of both the Old and New Testaments the one testament of God is the *testamentum Christi*. The testament of God becomes old when it is received by man as law; just as it becomes new when it is received by man as spirit. The difference between old and new testament is with man, not with God. The two testaments refer to two different types of men; there are old testament men and new testament men during the time covered by the books of the Old and New Testament. The difference between the testaments is the difference between receiving the *testamentum dei et Christi* as letter or spirit, as old or new.

With reference to God there is one testament; with reference to man there are two. In order to understand what Luther means it is necessary, methodologically, to study his earlier works, particularly the

---

Theologie und der Kirche (Leipzig: Dietrich, 1900), pp. 140–47, 259–61, 329–39.

14 *Quellen und Forschungen zur Reformationsgeschichte* (Gütersloh: Gerd Mohn, 1965), XXXII, 200–26. In his general treatment of Bucer W. P. Stephens has a section, "The Relation of the Old Testament to the New Testament," in *The Holy Spirit in the Theology of Martin Bucer* (London: Cambridge University Press, 1970) pp. 109–21.

15 Kenneth Hagen, "The Problem of Testament in Luther's Lectures on Hebrews," *Harvard Theological Review*, LXIII (January 1970), 61–90.

Dictata and his *Lectures on Hebrews*, in the light of medieval exegesis. The argument has been that over against the medieval exegetical tradition, the fundamental force of Luther's interpretation of Hebrews (1517/18) is the absolute contrast between the two testaments. However, in the light of Luther's earlier exegetical work, this understanding of Luther in the "Lectures on Hebrews" is only one aspect of his understanding of the two testaments. Luther's more complete understanding of the two testaments is that their relationship is dialectical. The contrast is a continuous struggle within each and every man.

Luther's *theologia crucis*, in his "Lectures on Hebrews," is that revelation comes under opposites.[16] As Christ is lifted between earth and heaven, the Christian exists between the two testaments. Here God is *simul absconditus et revelatus* and man is old, yet new; sinner, yet justified; spirit, yet flesh. In a phrase, we might suggest that the relationship for Luther is *simul vetus et novum testamentum*.

For the young Luther the relationship between the two testaments is not a hermeneutical question of the relation of the books of the Old and New Testament, that is, a "senses" question. For him it is a question of hearing the Word of testament or covenant in any period of time, that is, it is a soteriological question of covenant as testament. The soteriological reality described in the books is dialectical, *simul vetus et novum testamentum*.

In our customary and comfortable way of slicing up the sixteenth century into several unrelated disciplines, Erasmus has been completely overlooked in terms of the development of sixteenth century concepts of covenant-testament. Aldridge only briefly observes that Luther and Calvin differ from Erasmus in their understanding of the authority of Scripture.[17] Beginning in his *Adagia* (1500) and *Enchiridion* (1503) Erasmus' discussion of testament is in terms of Old Testament hermeneutic which is determined by his *Weltanschauung*.[18] To educate his generation in the *bonis litteris* Erasmus considered the ancient civilizations of Greece and Rome to be the best of antiquity and by comparison those of Egypt, Babylon, and Syria to be uncultured. The people of the Old Testament were for him superstitious, cruel, and barbaric. The principle of the *philosophia Christi* relegates

---

16   D. *Martin Luthers Werke: Kritische Gesammtausgabe* (Weimar, 1883 ff.), LVII, iii, 79/16–80/11. Hereafter cited as WA.

17   Aldridge, pp. 54–56.

18   *Ibid.*, pp. 44ff.

the Old Testament to the status of preNew Testament background.[19]
On 3 November 1517 Erasmus writes to John Caesarius about the
PfefferkornReuchlin controversy:

> For my own part, provided that the New Testament remain intact,
> I had rather that the Old Testament should be altogether abolished,
> than that the peace of Christiandom should be destroyed for sake
> of the books of the Jews.[20]

Willing to give up the Old Testament Erasmus locates the *philosophia
Christi* in the New Testament. This "occupies the central place in the
hermeneutic of Erasmus."[21]

So far our treatment of early sixteenth century developments up
to 1517/18 has considered on the one hand, the Wittenberg profes-
sor of Bible. From 1517 to 1518 Luther lectured on the epistle to the
Hebrews as a commentary and guide to the Old Testament. In 1518
Erasmus, on the other hand, wrote to Capito, "I wish the Christian
Church did not rely so much on the Old Testament."[22]

LUTHER AND MELANCHTHON, 1519–1522

In 1519 we see Luther continuing and advancing his discussion of
testament. God, the testator, made a promise to Abraham and his
offspring, the heirs, that through Christ they receive the grace and
righteousness of faith, the inheritance.[23] Important to observe is that
Luther describes this testament of God as a publicly announced

---

19   *Ibid.*, pp. 44–46. ErnstWilhelm Kohls, who speaks of the *doctrina Christi*
as the central content of the entire Scriptures for Erasmus, puts Erasmus'
hermeneutic in terms of *Heilsgeschichte*. In so doing, drawing heavily on the
Enchiridion (!), Kohls cites Erasmus out of context at least once and thus
misinterprets him (I, 148). The context is the sins and sexual perversions
of people in the Old Testament. Then the text: "Audeo dicere *ne* in prophe-
tis *quidem* aut apostolis imitandum Christianis, si quid a Christi doctrina
divaricetur." Hajo and Annemarie Holborn, ed., "Enchiridion militis chris-
tiani," *Desiderius Erasmus Roterdamus Ausgewählte Werke* (Munich: C. H.
Beck, 1933),I, 108/27–29 (emphasis added).

20   Cited by Aldridge, p. 48.

21   *Ibid.*, p. 50.

22   Cited by Aldridge, p. 49.

23   "Lectures on Galatians," published 3 Sept. 1519; WA, 11, 519/3–17.
LW, XXVII, 264.

testament, *tanquam in nuncupato testamento.*[24] *Testamentum nuncupativum* is a special kind of will that is orally proclaimed before witnesses.[25] The publicly proclaimed testament of God can also be called a covenant. Through Jerome Luther is aware that the Hebrew term is covenant rather than testament, Luther remarks, "He who stays alive makes a covenant; he who is about to die makes a testament.[26] With his *theologia crucis* Luther lines up covenant with testament, just as in his earlier work he identifies *promissio* and *pactum* with *testamentum.*[27]

> Thus Jesus Christ, the immortal God, made a covenant. At the same time He made a testament, because He was going to become mortal. Just as He is both God and man, so He made both a covenant and a testament.[28]

Two months later Luther discusses baptism as a covenant.[29] In the covenant of baptism God promises the nonimputation of sins, and man pledges to die to sin through the grace of the Holy Spirit.[30] This covenant is a cause for comfort for the Christian because "God has there pledged himself to slay his sin for him...."[31]

Luther's understanding of testament — *pactum, promissio* — is beginning to have more and more a sacramental character. In his "Lectures on Hebrews" (9:17), for the first time, Luther understands the Eucharist to be primarily a testament rather than a sacrifice.[32] In 1520 it is very clear, in his two sermons on the Testament of Christ and in the *Babylonian Captivity,* that the question of testament is a

---

24   *WA,* II, 521/27–28.

25   Charles Du Cange, *Glossarium mediae et infimae latinitatis...* (New ed.; Niort, L. Favre, 1883–87), VI, 564–65; Charlton T. Lewis and Charles Short, *A Latin Dictionary* (Oxford: Clarendon Press, n.d.), p. 1228.

26   Galatians," 1519, *LW,* XXVII, 268. *WA,* II, 521/34–35.

27   Hagen, "The Problem of Testament," pp. 80–90.

28   "Galatians," 1519, *LW,* XXVII, 268; *WA,* II, 521/35–37. Cf. "The Misuse of the Mass" (1521), *WA,* VIII, 521; *LW,* XXXVI, 179.

29   The Holy and Blessed Sacrament of Baptism," *LW,* XXXV, 29–43; *WA,* II, 727–37.

30   *WA,* II, 730–33; *LW,* XXXV, 33–37.

31   *LW,* XXXV, 35; *WA,* II, 731/31–32.

32   *WA,* LVII, iii, 211/14–213/21.

Eucharistic question. "Quaeramus ergo quid sit testamentum, et simul habebimus quid sit missa ..."[33]

In July 1520 Luther published his sermon on the New Testament translated "A Treatise on the New Testament, That Is, The Holy Mass," which was an expansion of his 1520 Easter Sermon. In it he says that "'testament' is a short summary" of God's dealing with man, that is, that the whole gospel is an explanation of Christ's testament.[34] This testament was given to the people of the Old Testament.

> Just as certainly, then, as Abraham, Noah, and David accepted and believed God's promises to them, so certainly must we also accept and believe this testament and promise.[35]

The "old" testament is the testament of Moses, which involved land and lambs, and contains a *figur Christi*," whose testament is eternal.[36] Also in the "Babylonian Captivity" he says that while "This testament of Christ is foreshadowed in all the promises of God from the beginning of the world," God "at last made clear [to David] what the promise to the men of old really was," namely, the promise of Christ. "Hence the words 'compact,' 'covenant,' and 'testament of the Lord' occur so frequently in the Scriptures. These words signified that God would one day die."[37] He distinguishes between signs of the sacraments of the Old and New Testament, which are the same in their "effectiveness," and "legal symbols" of the Old Testament which did not have any word of promise requiring faith.

> The same God who now saves us by baptism and the bread, saved Abel by his sacrifice, Noah by the rainbow, Abraham by circumcision, and all the others by their respective signs.... Therefore the new sacraments cannot differ from the old sacraments, for both alike have the divine promises and the same spirit of faith, although they do differ vastly from the old symbols—on account of the word of promise, which is the sole effective means of distinguishing them.[38]

---

33   *WA*, VI, 513/22–23 ("Babylonian Captivity").
34   *LW*, XXXV, 84,106; *WA*, VI, 357/26–27, 374/3–5.
35   *LW*, XXXV, 89; *WA*, VI, 361/19–21.
36   *WA*, VI, 357/28358/13; *LW*, XXXV, 8485.
37   *LW*, XXXVI, 38–39; *WA*, VI, 513–15.
38   *LW*, XXXVI, 65–66; *WA*, VI, 532/6–8, 533/2–5.

Important for Luther in both works is that Christ's testament be living, spoken and sung. "Christ did not put it in dead writing."[39] Christ's notarization must come on loud and clear: "But would to God that we Germans could say mass in German and sing these 'most secret' words loudest of all!"[40] The *testamentum* is *nuncupandum*.[41] The word of Christ is the testament, the elements the sacrament. "And as there is greater power in the word than in the sign, so there is greater power in the testament than in the sacrament...."[42] Most important in this sermon, for our purposes, is Luther's clear indication that testament—sacrament, covenant, promise—denotes a unilateral gift on God's part.

> For a testament is not *beneficium acceptum, sed datum*; it does not take benefit from us, but brings benefit to us.... Just as in baptism, in which there is also a divine testament and sacrament, no one gives God anything or does him a service, but instead takes something, so it is in all other sacraments and in the sermon as well.[43]

Further in "The Misuse of the Mass" (1521), Luther asks,

> How can we then, out of this pledge and seal of God given to us as a gift, make a sacrifice and work of our own? Who among men would be so foolish as to sacrifice the seal on a letter, in which something is promised to him, to the one who makes the promise ?[44]

Both the old and new testament are given, not brought about by any work of man.[45]

Melanchthon copied and translated Luther's 1520 Easter Sermon (8 April), which clearly deals with *Quid testamentum, Quid novum testamentum*. Melanchthon begins to deal with the question of testament

---

39   *LW*, XXXV, 86; *WA*, VI, 359/20–21.

40   *LW*, XXXV, 90; *WA*, VI, 362/28–29.

41   "Testamentum absque dubio est promissio morituri, qua nuncupat haereditatem suam et instituit haeredes. Involvit itaque testamentum primo mortem testatoris, deinde haereditatis promissionem et haeredis nuncupationem." *WA*, VI, 513/24–26. Cf. "The Misuse of the Mass," 1521, *WA*, VIII, 444/17–24, 447/21–24.

42   *LW*, XXXVI, 44; *WA*, VI, 518/17–19. Cf. "The Misuse of the Mass," *WA*, VIII, 452/37–38.

43   *LW*, XXXV, 93; *WA*, VI, 364/19–28. Cf. "The Misuse of the Mass," *WA*, VIII, 522/9–13.

44   *LW*, XXXVI, 174; *WA*, VIII, 517/1–4.

45   *WA*, VIII, 446/24–29, "The Misuse of the Mass."

and covenant in his first work, *Lucubratiuncula*, written prior to 1520. He handles the question differently depending on whether his perspective is hermeneutical or soteriological and sacramental. His hermeneutical perspective is that the whole Scripture is divided into the law and the promise.[46] Since Christ is the author of the new testament, he antiquates the whole old law, including the moral law. Those who do not believe in Christ are still subject to the law, but those in Christ are free. The reason for this freedom is that Christ forgives sin and confers the Holy Spirit on Christians, who moves them to right acts. Christians do not need the law to prompt them to right deeds. They do what the law asks under the Spirit's guidance.[47]

The Old Testament book is law and *iubet Evange*, whereas the New Testament is promise by which we are filled with the Spirit.[48] "There are many places in the Old Testament about the promise, but they are most obscurely placed and understood by a very few."[49] A hermeneutical divide, then, is placed by Melanchthon between the books of Old and New Testament, though the few and obscure promise references are *semper clarior*.[50]

Melanchthon sees a soteriological and sacramental continuity of Old and New Testament in *promissio*, a synonym for *testamentum, pactum* and *foedus*.[51] In regard to the promise, Melanchthon says that God promises salvation through Christ. The proper response to the promise is faith. This was also the way of salvation in the Old Testament. The promise was made to Abraham, and the prophets proclaimed the promise to Israel. In fact, "The prophets can be read in place of the gospels; they are truly gospels."[52] Humans need external signs to aid them in their faith in the promise, so various signs were given in the Old Testament. Nevertheless, there was always only "one faith" in the

---

46   *Corpus Reformatorum* (Halle, et al., 1834ff.) XXI, 38. Hereafter cited as CR.

47   CR, XXI, 29, 31.

48   CR, XXI, 39: "Et omnis script: aut iubet aut: promittit. Lex et vetus testamentum: lubet Evange: et novum testamentum: promittit nobis spiritum quo compleamur."

49   CR, XXI, 37.

50   *Ibid.*

51   CR, XXI, 37–41.

52   CR, XXI, 36: "Prophetae possunt legi evangelij vice et sunt vere Evange."

coming Christ. In the New Testament, there are also signs of the promise. They are baptism, penance, and the eucharist.[53]

In Melanchthon's translation of Luther's Easter Sermon (1520) Luther is reported to be "melanchthonized."[54] On a soteriological level the sermon says succinctly that in the *testamentum (pactum, foedus, promissio)*, described in the Old and New Testament, God contracts with man because man by his reason, will or good works is not able to contract with God.[55] The response of man, however, "believing in the divine promise," is a necessary, though not equal part, in the contract. God has always acted through promises with man. He made promises with Adam and Eve, Noah, Abraham, Moses, the judges and David.[56] It is always by their response, however, that they are justified. The importance of faith as man's response was also stressed in the *Lucubratiuncula.*

Melanchthon again deals with the question of testament and covenant in his lectures on Matthew, 15:1920. He describes the Godman relationship in both books of the Bible in terms of promise and faith, which are "correlative." Terms which describe *promissio* are *testamentum, foedus*, and *pactum.*[57] God, then, promises something to man, as

53   CR, XXI, 36–38.

54   Neuser, II, 43: "Die Predigtnachschrift ist 'melanchthonisiert.'"

55   "Quid testamentum. Quando deus cum homine contrahit, fit hoc deo promittente et homine promissioni divine credente: per nostram rationem, per nostrum arbitrium aut nostra bona opera non contrahemus cum deo.... Ex his colligo, generalem significationem vocabuli 'testamentum' esse, cum deus per promissionem cum homine contrahit. Immo hae voces ferme rem eandem significant: pactum, foedus, testamentum, promissio.... Fuit ergo vetus testamentum promissio temporalium, sed cur testamentum? Quia deus testatus est." *WA*, IX, 446/6–447/4.

56   *WA*, IX, 446.

57   "Primum satis constat: fidem esse caput iustificationis nostrae. Est autem fides ascensus, quo humanus animus complectitur divinam promissionem. Ergo in theologia praecipue sunt observanda promissionum vocabula: testamentum, foedus, pactum, promissio, quibus vocibus divinae promissiones significantur.... Fidei vocabulum est correlativum ad promissiones Christi sive de Christo, ut patris ad filium, Domini ad servum. Signum sacramentale est, quo admonemur promissionum divinarum. Usus sacramenti est contemplatio signorum, per quam credimus et arripimus promissionem divinam." *Annotationes in Evangelium Matthaei*, published against Melanchthon's will from student notes in Basel, 1523; R. Stupperich, ed., *Melanchthons Werke* (Gütersloh: Gerd Mohn, 1953ff.), IV, 206–7.

if he were making a will. The human spirit receives this promise and believes. Faith is defined as *ascensus* and referred to as "laying hold" (*arripio*) of the promise.[58] The Old Testament figures Abraham and Noah received promises and believed.[59]

The shift from testament to covenant seems to begin in the young Melanchthon in his emphasis on the "correlative" necessity of faith in the promise, faith as accepting and assenting to God's action.

God confirms his promises through visible signs. Thus, circumcision was the sign of Abraham's promise. The New Testament signs are the same as in the *Lucubratiuncula*. Each of them has a promise attached to it. The sacraments, then in both Testaments are signs of the promise. Again, as in the *Lucubratiuncula*, the two books of the Bible are distinguished, the Old Testament promises temporal things, the New Testament gives the spiritual realities of justice and grace. By faith, however, in the promise, testament, covenant, pact, during the time of both Testaments, one is justified.[60]

Beginning with his 1521 *Loci communes* Melanchthon has a locus on "The Difference between the Old and New Testaments."[61] His interest is hermeneutical. The freedom of New Testament Christianity means the complete annulment of the law—ceremonial, judicial and moral. In his 1522 *Loci* the *abrogatio* of the law is defined more in terms of *mutatio*.[62] On a soteriological level, however, *testamentum* is still *promissio*. Those who believe the second covenant (the gospel) have the Spirit of Christ and are free from every law, irrespective of time period or Testament:

> In this way the fathers who had the Spirit of Christ were also free even before his incarnation.... It has been abrogated, however, only in the case of those who have believed in the later covenant, namely, the gospel.... You will say, however, that if those who have the Spirit of Christ are free, were both David and Moses free? Absolutely![63]

---

58 *Ibid.*

59 *Ibid*, IV, 206.

60 *Ibid.*, IV, 207.

61 CR, XXI, 192–206; W. Pauck, ed., *Melanchthon and Bucer* in *Library of Christian Classics* (Philadelphia: Westminster Press, 1969), XIX, 120–30. Hereafter cited as *LCC*.

62 CR, XXI, 202–3.

63 LCC, XIX, 124–29; CR, XXI, 196–205.

There is soteriological unity in the Testaments.

Melanchthon specifies three hermeneutical "differences." The Old Testament is "a promise of material things linked up with the demands of the law." God demands righteousness under the law and promises rewards for it, for example, the land of Canaan and wealth. On the other hand, "the New Testament is nothing else than the promise of all good things without regard to the law."[64] Another distinction between the Testaments is that the Old Testament merely promised Christ, while the New Testament witnesses that Christ is already revealed. Melanchthon adds that the promises of grace, righteousness, and eternal life are "more clearly" explained by the New Testament than the Old.[65] A final difference which Melanchthon sees is that the Old Testament is merely a type of the New, and "was in reality not a real testament because the testator did not die. In the New Testament the Testator dies."[66] Each of these hermeneutical distinctions, however, seems considerably less important than the basic soteriological—and sacramental[67]—unity of the testament. The concept of the promise still holds them together.

For Luther up through 1522 *testamentum* describes the God-man relationship from paradise to the eschaton.[68] *Foedus, pactum, promis-*

---

64   *LCC*, XIX, 120; *CR*, XXI, 192–93.

65   *LCC*, XIX, 74; *CR*, XXI, 143.

66   *LCC*, XIX, 133; *CR*, XXI, 208.

67   *CR*, XXI, 208–9; *LCC*, XIX, 133.

68   Luther discusses the relationship between the two Testaments in "A Brief Instruction on What to Look for and Expect in the Gospels" (1521). The gospels and epistles are hermeneutic of the Old Testament: "It is there that people like us should read and study, drill ourselves, and see what Christ is, for what purpose he has been given, how he was promised, and how all Scripture tends toward him." *LW*, XXXV, 122; *WA*, X, i (1), 15/5–7. Cf. "Prefaces to the New Testament" (1522), *LW*, XXXV, 380, 395. *WA DB*, VII, 27, 344. The Old Testament alone is Holy Scripture because "the gospel should really not be something written, but a spoken word which brought forth the Scriptures, as Christ and the apostles have done." *LW*, XXXV, 123; *WA*, X, i (1), 17/7–9. Christ did not publish anything but only spoke a gospel that is spread not by pen but by word of mouth. *WA*, X, i (1), 17/9–12. *LW*, XXXV, 123. "Darumb ist die kirch eyn mundhawss nit eyn fedderhawss," *WA*, X, i (2), 48/5, "*Adventspostille*," 1522. There is law and promise in each book of the Bible. The new testament is gospel. Luther emphasizes that the distinction between the old

sio are read as a gratuitous and unilateral *testamentum*. On a hermeneutical level there is one Word sounded in the books, Old and New Testament. To make it a letter is to kill it and make it a law. *Testamentum Christi nuncupandum*, as it is in each book of the Bible. On a soteriological level the relation of the testaments is *simul vetus et novum testamentum*. The sacraments, before and after Christ, show clearly the *testamentum Del*.

For Melanchthon up through 1522 there is a hermeneutical distinction made about "the difference" between the two books of the Bible. There is a hermeneutical development between the 1521 and 1522 *Loci* concerning the *abrogatio* of the moral law by the New Testament law, defined in 1522 as "change" rather than complete annulment.[69] The soteriological and sacramental reality is the same for the people described in both books. Faith is given a "co" responsibility for justification. *Testamentum* is lined up with *foedus* and *pactum* as synonyms for *promissio*, which shifts the emphasis in the Godman relationship from a unilateral testament to a correlative contract.

A brief comparison of Erasmus, Luther, and Melanchthon on their understanding of the relationship between the Testaments, books and covenants, could be made as follows: for Erasmus, *philosophia Christi* (*bonae litterae*),[70] for Luther, *testamentum Christi* (sacrament), for Melanchthon, *promissio Christi* (Word).

ZWINGLI, LUTHER, AND BUCER TO 1527

Zwingli and Zürich begin to play an important part in the development of testament covenant theology in the early sixteenth century.

---

and new testament must be made certain: what is promise is gospelbook, what is command is lawbook. *WA*, X, i (2), 159/5–20, "Adventspostille, 1522. The old testament is a "testamentbrieff Christi" *WA*, X, i (1), 182/1, "Kirchenpostille," 25 Dec. 1522.

69   Bizer's development thesis, accepted by Neuser, is that in connection with his lectures on Matthew (1519–20!) c. 26, Melanchthon discovers that promise is "means of grace" from Luther's Easter Sermon (1520). The difficulty with the thesis, apart from the chronological and textual problem, is, it seems to me, that Bizer reads the young Melanchthon much like he reads the young Luther, namely, to date a *Turmerlebnis* on the basis of discovering the Word as *Gnadenmittel*. Bizer, pp. 123–28; Neuser, II, 47.

70   Hermann Schlingensiepen, "Erasmus als Exeget," p. 24: In comparison to Erasmus' devaluation of the Old Testament in the *Enchiridion*, "in der Vorrede zur Matthäus Paraphrase [1522] geht er noch weiter."

Zwingli is frequently credited with the beginning of federal theology.[71] However, one must be careful about "beginning" and "federal theology." Contrary to Schrenk, who holds that Zwingli took over his covenant theology from the *Täufer*,[72] Locher argues that portions of Zwingli's early preaching in 1522/23 produced especially strong after effects with the *Täufer*.[73] Neither Schrenk nor Locher, however, deal with Zwingli in terms of his understanding of Old and New *Testamentum*, which is the problematic in the development of Zwingli's thought on covenant: *testamentum suum … instauraret.*[74]

An early indication of Zwingli's understanding of testament and covenant is contained in his work "On the Clarity and Certainty of the Word of God" (1522). The discussion is hermeneutical, presupposing a difference between the two books of the Bible. In each section on "The Certainty" and "The Clarity" of the Word, particularly in the former, the treatment of the Old Testament is considerably shorter and by far more negative than the examples from the New. The Old Testament is used generally as an example of disobedience. The Word of God in the Old Testament brings "toil and death."[75]

In his "Commentary on the Sixty-two Articles" (1523) Zwingli clarifies his understanding of *Testamentum*. While Scripture uses *testamentum, pactum,* and *foedus* interchangeably, *testamentum* is used most and means *Gemächd*.[76] In Swiss legal usage *Gemächd* is a special kind

71   Korff, p. 10; Schrenk, p. 36; Ritschl, p. 412; Locher, "Das Geschichtsbild Zwinglis," p. 296; J. Moltmann, "Föderaltheologie," *Lexikon für Theologie und Kirche* (Freiburg: Herder, 1960), IV, 190–92; Müller, p. 47; Torrance, p. 62.

72   Schrenk, p. 37.

73   Locher, "Das Geschichtsbild H. Zwinglis," p. 296. *CR*, LXXXVIII, 200/2–8: "Hinc quandoquidem, ut praefati sumus, deus, velut olim per prophetas suos aliis atque aliis temporibus Israel admonere solitus est, nostra nos tempestate evangelio suo illustrare dignatur, ut testamentum suum, quod aboleri non potest, instauraret, occasionem hanc duximus minime negligendam esse, quin perpetuo conatu laborandum potius, ut quam plurimi salutis huius et splendoris participes fiant" (*Supplicatio … ad Hugonem episcopum Constantiensem*, 2 July 1522).

74   *CR*, LXXXVIII, 200/5–6.

75   *LCC*, XXIV, 68–69, 72–78. *CR*, LXXXVIII, 353–54, 358–65. Cf. "Apologeticus Archeteles" (Sept., 1522): "Novum testamentum prestantissimum…. *CR*, LXXXVIII, 304/25.

76   *CR*, LXXXIX, 98, 101.

of *testamentum*, one different from Roman law where the *testamentum* rests ultimately on the free will of the testator. The *Gemächde* contain a genuine Germanic element—the necessity for an inheritance to be brought before a court of law to determine if there are any discrepancies. The inheritance will be denied if the rights of the original bequest are not to be maintained.[77] *Testamentum* also means *pundt oder verstand* whereby one with free will enters into a relationship with another.[78] The testatee does not automatically receive the inheritance. He must demonstrate that he has fulfilled his part. *Testamentum* has shifted to a two-sided covenant.

Also in his "Commentary" Zwingli highlights the contrast between the *testamentum, pactum,* and *foedus* in the Old and New Testament. *Testamentum* (*pundt, verstand und pflicht*) specifies God's encounter with the "old fathers" or with the "whole world through Christ." There is only contrast—blood of animals vs. blood of Christ—no unity.[79]

In his "Commentary on True and False Religion" (March 1525), Zwingli speaks of covenant. In his discussion of marriage, "a most holy covenant," he discusses Christ's relationship to his bride the church, as an example. This covenant relationship is "a covenant for life, a sharing of all possessions and a common risk (*communis alea*)."[80] A common "risk" or "venture" gives to *foedus* a strong bilateral connotation. Marriage is not a sacrament; it is a *foedus*, which is an enduring relationship between two people. Sacraments are *initiationes*.[81] A sacrament is an initiation ceremony or a pledge to a covenant. It is

---

77   J. K. Bluntschli, *Staats und Rechtsgeschichte der Stadt und Landschaft Zürich, Part I: Die Zeit des Mittelalters* (2nd ed.; Zürich: Orell Füssli, 1856), pp. 309ff. J. J. Blumer, *Staats und Rechtsgeschichte der Schweiz. Demokratien* (St. Gallen: Schleitlin und Zollikofer, 1850), I, 522–24.

78   CR, LXXXIX, 131/5–9. "Testamentum, pactum und foedus wirdt in der geschrifft offt für einandren gebrucht, doch würt testamentum aller meist gebruchet, der mass es uns hie dienet, und heisst ein erbgemächt; wirt aber ouch gebrucht für ein pundt oder verstand, so man pfligt mit einandren ze machen umb frydens willen."

79   "Usslegen und gründ der schlussreden oder artickeln durch Huldrychen Zuingli, Zürich uff den 29. tag jenners im 1523, jar ussgangen," CR, LXXXIX, 131.

80   CR, XC, 762/24.

81   CR, XC, 763/3–5: "Sacramenta ergo initiationes qum sint et nihil aliud, matrimonium veto qurn foedus sit, quod inter duos modo constat, hac voce obscurari non patiamur."

like, Zwingli says, when people begin litigation they deposit earnest money to ratify the contract. A sacrament is an *arrabo*, downpayment or pledge that one will not withdraw from his commitment.[82] *Foedus*, then, means bilateral commitment.

In his work "On Baptism" (May 1525), Zwingli continues to emphasize, against the Anabaptists, that the sacraments of the Old and New Testament are initiatory signs of the covenant, a pledge to a process of development.[83] "Baptism is an initiatory sign or pledge with which we bind ourselves to God...."[84] The covenant sign (circumcision and baptism) does not confirm faith but is a pledge to a life of faith and discipleship—"God calls it a contract [*pactum*]."[85] Just as one in Switzerland, who sews on a white cross, indicates that he is a Confederate and in accordance therewith pledges his life.[86] Bromiley criticizes Zwingli for an excessive emphasis on the bilateral character of the covenant.[87]

Zwingli remains critical of the Old Testament—its sacraments are carnal and external—and is concerned to show the dichotomy between the Testaments.[88] John the Baptist initiated the gospel as well as baptism. The "Anabaptists and papists" hold that John is a type and shadow of Christ and thus "reckon him with the Old Testament."[89]

Later in the year there is a noticeable shift in Zwingli's evaluation of the Old Testament and the New Testament's relationship to

---

82   *CR*, XCI, 759/5–20: "Unde adducimur, ut sacramentum nihil aliud esse videamus, quam initiationem aut oppignorationem. Sicut enim, qui litigaturi erant, certum pecuniae pondus deponebant, quod auferri non licebat, nisi vincenti, sic, qui sacramentis initiantur, esse adstringunt, oppignorant, ac velut arrabonem accipiunt, ut referre pedem non liceat.... Sacramentum ergo, qum aliud porro nequeat esse quam initiatio aut publica consignatio, vim nullam habere potest ad conscientiam iiberandam."

83   "Of Baptism," *CR*, XCI, 231, 238–41; G. W. Bromiley, ed., *Zwingli and Bullinger* in the *Library of Christian Classics* (Philadelphia: Westminster Press, 1963), XXIV, 141, 146–48.

84   *LCC*, XXIV, 148; *CR*, XCI, 241/28–29.

85   *CR*, XCI, 227–28; *LCC*, XXIV, 138–39. The quotation is from *LCC*, XXIV, 138; *CR* XCI, 227/21.

86   *CR*, XCI, 218; *LCC*, XXIV, 131.

87   Bromiley, ed., "Of Baptism," *LCC*, XXIV, 127.

88   *CR*, XCI, 217–19; *LCC*, XXIV, 130–32.

89   *LCC*, XXIV, 162; *CR*, XCI, 259/20, 260/1–2.

it (*"Antwort über Balthasar Hubmaiers Taufbüchlein,"* 5 Nov. 1525). There is a positive treatment of the Old Testament, and the continuity of the testaments is emphasized.[90] The Christian covenant or new testament is the old covenant of Abraham: "Abrahams testament der Christen testament."[91] We do not have a new faith or covenant but the faith and covenant of Abraham.[92] The difference between the testaments is promise and fulfillment.[93]

Before 1525 Zwingli is similar to Erasmus in his Old Testament hermeneutic. In his "Answer to Hubmaier" (late 1525) rather than the preliminary, carnal and temporal character of the old testament, Zwingli emphasizes the unity of the two testaments. Also Zwingli reads testament as covenant and sacrament as public initiatory ceremony, which entails for man the responsibility to fulfill the terms of the contract.

In four treatises from 1526-27 Zwingli develops his understanding of the unity of the two testaments along the line suggested in his "Answer to Hubmaier." In "De peccato originali," 1526, Zwingli says, "una est fides Abrahami et nostra … una est amborum ecclesia."[94] *Foedus, pactum, testamentum* are synonyms that apply to Abraham and his seed and to Christ and Christians.[95] Zwingli's "Amica exegesis"

---

90   CR, XCI, 629–39. Künzli refers only generally to 1525 as approximately the time Zwingli shifts his attack from Rome to the Anabaptists and, thus, his emphasis from the differences to the unity of the testaments. Künzli, however, draws on two works from 1527, "Against the Anabaptists" and "Commentary on Genesis" in "Zwingli als Ausleger des Alten Testamentes," CR, Cl, 897; "Zwinglis theologische Wertung des Alten Testamentes," p. 276.

91   CR, XCI, 635 ("A Marginal" to line 2).

92   CR, XCI, 636/9–10.

93   CR, XCI, 637/15–19: "Sprichst: 'Was underscheyds ist dann zwüschend dem alten und nüwen testament?' der, das per pundt Abrahams mit eim nüwen volck ist gmachet: mit den heyden; und das Christus yetz geleystet ist, der im noch nun (nur[!]) verheissen was, der uns vom gsatzt Moses erlösst hat."

94   CR, XCII, 385/18–21. Cf. "Farrago annotationum in Genesim ex ore Huldryci Zuinglii per Leonem Iudae et Casparem Megandrum exceptarum" (March, 1527), CR, C, 67/13–14, 22–23; 105/37–106/13.

95   CR, XCII, 387, 394/24–29: "In Christo autem sunt non modo parentes, quos misericordia divina in fidei lucem ac gratiam induxit, sed eorum quoque liberi non minus, quam qui ex Abraham secundum promissionem nati

(February 1527) appeared along with Luther's treatise, "This is my Body" at the Frankfurt spring book fair of 1527. Zwingli emphasizes that there is the one and same church, testament, and faith for those before and after Christ.[96] "Against the Anabaptists" (1527) Zwingli says that the two testaments are not two different testaments, because then there would have to be two different peoples and two gods.[97] "Unum atque idem" is the *testamentum Christi*, from the beginning to the end of the world.[98] What then "discrimenis inter vetus ac novum testamentum?" Now Christ is given as a model to pass from death to life; then *umbra*, now *lux clarius lucet*.[99] The difference then is not in terms of content. The content of God's covenanttestament to man is singular—He is our God and we His people. With reference to man's response, however, salvation has become progressively more clear.[100] In Zwingli's "Commentary on Genesis" (1527) the singular *foedus, pactum, testamentum* is a bilateral treaty between God and his people.[101] From 1522 to 1525 Luther amplifies familiar themes of his testament theology. The Eucharist is a testament and not a sacrifice.[102] The New Testament is distinctly a public proclamation of Christ.[103]

---

sunt. Eadem enim est fides, ac idem testamentum sive foedus, quantum ad interiorem hominem attinet."

96   CR, XCII, 649/9–15 ("Amica Exegesis, id est, expositio eucharistiae negocii ad Martinum Lutherum).

97   CR, XCIII, 164/2–4.

98   CR, XCIII, 169/6–11; 163/8–10: "Idem ergo foedus, quod olim cum populo Israelitico, in novissimis temporibus nobiscurn pepigit, ut unus essemus cum eis populus, una ecclesia, et unum foedus quoque haberemus."

99   CR, XCIII, 169/19–170/11.

100   Locher, *Die Theologie Huldrych Zwinglis*, p. 51; Künzli, "Zwingli als Ausleger des Alten Testamentes," CR, Cl, 898.

101   *In Genesim*, CR, C, 101–8.

102   WA, XII, 208/8–13; ("An Order of Mass and Communion for the Church at Wittenberg," 1523), LW, LIII, 22.

103   WA DB, VIII, 10/18–20. ("Preface to the Old Testament," 1523. WA, XII, 275/8–15, "Epistel S. Petri gepredigt," 1523): "Denn wie wol beydes dem buchstaben nach ist auff papyr geschrieben, so soll doch das Evangelion odder das new Testament eygentlich nicht geschrieben, sondern ynn die lebendige styrn gefasset werden, die da erschalle und uberal gehört werde ynn der wellt. Das es aber auch geschrieben ist, ist auss uberfluss geschehen. Aber das alte Testament ist nur ynn die schrifft verfasset, und drumb heysst es 'ein buchstab,' und also nennens die Apostel 'die

The Old Testament is a testamentcovenant of works.[104] The Old
Testament is most important because the New Testament and the
Christian faith are grounded in it.[105] Luther wants to keep Moses because of the promises about Christ. He wants to keep Moses' book
open—"nicht unter den banck stecken," not lay it in a lower shelf in
the pulpit.[106] The New Testament is eternal, *vetustissimum*, the Old
however began and ended in time.[107]

Luther's Eucharistic treatise of 1527[108] allows a simple but basic
contrast with Zwingli's "Commentary on True and False Religion" and
"On Baptism" (both of 1525). Their different notions of the Eucharist
reflect different notions of testament/covenant. For Zwingli the sacrament as covenant sign is an initiation ceremony, a downpayment
for future negotiations. It is a *Gemeindemahl*.[109] In his understanding of sacramenttestament as covenant Zwingli is a confederate. God

schrifft,' denn es hatt alleyn gedeuttet auff den zukunfftigen Christum. Das
Evangelion aber ist eyn lebendige predig von Christo, der da kommen ist."

104   *WA*, XIV, 602/13–18 ("Lectures on Deuteronomy," 1523–24): "Sed
absolute distinguere novum testamentum a veteri in hoc consistit, quod in
novo testamento absolute promissa nobis est gratia sine conditione et citra
respectum omnium operum nostrorum, sine meritis, in veteri autem testamento exigit opera, addidit conditionem, ut urgeret promissionem suam
per legem i. e. ut conscientias pressas lege sitire gratiam inciperent." Luther
lectured on Deuteronomy to a small group of close friends in his house,
beginning February, 1523. Bugenhagen was there. There are several tran-
scripts extant, including Bugenhagen's, *LW*, IX, ix–x. In Basel, September
1524, Bugenhagen published his *Annotationes in Deuteronomium, in duos
libros Regum.*

105   *WA DB*, VIll, 10/12–15 ("Preface to the Old Testament"). *WA*, XII,
274/34–35 ("Epistel S. Petri gepredigt").

106   *WA*, XVI, 376/6–7 ("How Christians Should Regard Moses," 1525);
mistranslated in *LW*, XXXV, 166.

107   *WA*, XIV, 602/34–37 ("Lectures on Deuteronomy," 1525): "Indicat
hic Moses differentiam testamenti novi et veteris. Testamentum novum est
vetustissimum [mistranslated in *LW*, IX, 63: "The New Testament is older...."] ab initio mundi promissum, imo ante tempora saecularia, ut Paulus
ad Titum loquitur, sed tantum sub Christo impletum. Vetus testamentum
sub Mose promissum, sub Iosue impletum est." Cf. *WA DB*, VIll, 28/1–11.

108   *WA*, XXIII, 64–283; "That These Words of Christ 'This is my Body,'
etc. Still Stand Firm Against the Fanatics," *LW*, XXXVII 13–150.

109   D. G. Schrenk, "Zwinglis Hauptmotive in der Abendmahlslehre und
das Neue Testament," *Zwingliana*, V (1930), 184.

is the initiator, but man must say yes by his actions. For Luther in the Eucharist one drinks to remember the fair and just purchase of forgiveness already completed in the testament or Christ's blood, just as one drinks wine after a transaction to celebrate a good purchase.[110]

For Luther and for Zwingli after 1525, there is no hermeneutical hassel about the two Testaments. On soteriologicalsacramental grounds, however, the reformers differ. For Luther, man's response is not a condition for God's unilateral testament, because man's response is contained in the gift (the *ex opere operato* efficacy of the Word). Man's historical (political, ethical, etc.) life is secularized and relieved of any ulterior soteriological motivations. Because of the *testamentum Christi* man is free.

For Zwingli, with perhaps a different political model, the discussion of *testamentum* develops in terms of covenant. Man's historical life, inspired by the Holy Spirit, is lived in "pact" with God. Man's response to the *foedus* must show that he is a confederate.

Bucer in 1527 in his *Enarrationum in evangelia* discusses the topic, "Discrimen inter vetus et novum testamentum.[111] He emphasizes that

---

110   *WA*, XXIII, 113/20–22: "gleich wie man wein trinckt zum gleichkauff, das da ein billicher und gleicher kauff sey, des man gedencken und fest halten sol."

111   *Enarrationum in evangelia Matthaei, Marci, et Lucae, libri duo* Strasbourg, 1527 [1530 and Basel, 1536], I, 150v–156v.

In 1520 (20 Jan.) Bucer sent Luther's *Lectures on Galatians*, 1519, with high praise to Rhenanus and requested that a reprint be arranged. Müller, p. 12.

In his *Summary* of 1523 Bucer says that the mass, an eternal testament, is a "pfand und worzeichen" — "er dir ein ring, sigel oder brieff geben.'"Martin Butzers an ein christlichen Rath und Gemeyn der statt Weissenburg Summary seiner Predig daselbst gethon" (Strasbourg, 1523), in *Martin Bucers Deutsche Schriften*, ed. R. Stupperich (Gütersloh: Gerd Mohn, 1960), I, 118/16–18. The old testament, given to Moses, is carnal and for land. To us, however, the new testament is the eternal testament in the blood of Christ. *Ibid.*, I, 119/2–12.

In 1524 Bucer translated Luther's "Epistel S. Petri gepredigt," 1523, *Ennarationes Martini Lutheri in Epistolas D. Petri duas, et Judae unam* (Strasbourg, 1524[1], 1525,[2,3]) and sent a letter the same year to his brethren in France giving Luther's work high praise particularly for his understanding of law/gospel ("Martin Bucer aux Frères disperses en France. De Strasbourg, 13 janvier 1525," *Correspondance des Réformateurs dans les Pays de Langue Francaise*, A. L. Herminjard (Geneva, 1866), I, 318–20).

the old and new *pactum, foedus, testamentum* are *idem in substantia*.[112] There is no other *discrimen* between the old and new than that the former was given as a promise to the land with ceremonies and external observances, whereas in the new God has promised to be our God and nothing is demanded of us except that we know and worship Him.[113] Both testaments are given through Christ. The difference is rather between the *verum et aeternum Dei foedus*, which is the same with all the elect, and the ceremonies of the covenant with the Hebrews, which are *umbras veri testamenti et beneficii Christi*.[114] For Bucer, then, the *foedus* with the elect is the same for all ages, but the Old Testament of Moses is a shadow of tile new.

By 1527 others in the Rhineland were developing covenant theology, Oecolampadius in Basel, Capito and Cellarius in Strasbourg.[115] Already in 1525 Heinrich Bullinger is considered a covenant

---

In 1524, Bucer says that Abraham was a true Christian: "Abraarn hat eüsserlich vil und war doch ein worer Christ, hatt allen dingen uffgesagt, war ein warer jünger Christi, wiewol der im fleysch noch künfftig was." "Ein kurtzer wahrhafftiger bericht, von Disputationem und gantzem handel, so zwischen Cunrat Treger, Provincial der Augustiner, und den predigern des Evangelii zü Strassburg sich begeben hat" (Strasbourg, 1524), in *Deutsche Schriften*, II, 62/3–5).

In "Grund und ursach auss gotlicher schrifft der neüwerungen ... zü Strassburg fürgenomen" (Strasbourg, 1524), Bucer is very critical of Old Testament customs and contrasts their carnal character with the New Testament. *Deutsche Schriften*, I, 234–35. He is critical of Rome and the Old Testament in the same breath because Rome patterns its priestly activities and adornments on the Old Testament. R. Stupperich in his "Einleitung," *ibid.*, I, 193. Bucer refers to the Pope and Moses simultaneously, *Ibid.*, I, 220/29. Müller overlooks Bucer's negative attitudes towards the Old Testament.

112   *Ibid.*, I, 150v, 151v.

113   *Ibid.*, I 151v.

114   *Ibid.*, By contrast Servetus, who came to Strasbourg in the early 1530s argues against confusing the two testaments by any sort of comparison— there are only sharp contrasts between the carnal Old Testament and the spiritual New Testament. "On the Righteousness of Christ's Kingdom," *Servetus*, ed. Earl Wilbur, Vol. XVI of *Harvard Theological Studies* (Cambridge: Harvard University Press, 1932), pp. 241–44.

115   Oecolampadius, *In lesiam* (1525) and *In post tres prophetas* (1527); Cellarius, *De operibus Dei* (1527). Cf. Trinterud, pp. 40–41.

theologian.[116] In the next decade it is his *De testamento seu foedere* which clearly defines his covenant position.[117] Also at this time the "covenantal ecclesiology" of the Anabaptists (*Bundgenossen*) was being developed by Hubmaier, by Denck (d. 1527), and a little later by Hofmann.[118] And so by 1527 the major figures in the beginning of testamentcovenant theology have spoken.

CONCLUSION

The thesis here presented on the basis of my investigation is that there is a development from testament to covenant theology in the first quarter of the sixteenth century. The various hermeneutical, soteriological, and sacramental aspects of the problematic show that the development is basically a shift from emphasizing the sole divine initiative in the Godman relationship to giving the manman relationship a bilateral component in the Godman relationship. The development away from Luther's more magisterial testament theology begins with Melanchthon's emphasis on faith as "co" responsible. Melanchthon reads *testamentum* more as *foedus*. Zwingli's covenant position can be seen in 1523. In 1525 we find a hermeneutical shift in Zwingli's position towards the unity of the Testaments.[119]

While the unity of the testaments, variously defined by the reformers, sounds trite today and in need of much refinement, it at least raises the question again of the Christian's posture towards the "other." The Old Testament lives on in various histories and traditions. The "branch" needs vital roots to grow.

---

116   Joachim Staedtke, *Die Theologie des jungen Bullinger*, Vol. XVI of *Studien zur Dogmengeschichte und systematischen Theologie Ger*, (Zürich: Zwingli Verlag, 1962), pp. 57–71. Antonius J. van't Hooft, *De Theologie van Heinrich Bullinger in betrekking tot de Nederlandsche Reformatie* (Amsterdam: Academisch Proefschrift, Rijksuniversiteit de Leiden, 1888), pp. 42–95.

117   *De testamento seu foedere dei unico et aeterno Heinrychi Bullingeri brevis expositio* (Zürich, 1534).

118   George H. Williams, *The Radical Reformation* (Philadelphia: Westminster Press. 1962), p. 154. Schrenk, *Gottesreich*, p. 37. Cf. Balthasar Hubmaier, *On Free Will*, 1527 (*LCC*, XXV, 114–35). Melchior Hofmann, *The Ordinance of God*, 1530 (*LCC*, XXV, 184–203).

119   The influence of Erasmus' negative attitude towards the Old Testament remains to be determined as does the more precise character of other discussions of testament and covenant around 1527 and following.

THE TESTAMENT OF A WORM:

LUTHER ON TESTAMENT AND COVENANT TO 1525

The theology of the young Luther has been described as a theology of testament.[1] What happened to the testament theology of the young Luther? Given the current interest in late medieval and early reformation developments of covenant theology, what was Luther's position on covenant?[2] This study is intended to answer these questions and, thus broaden the basis for evaluating the development "From Testament to Covenant in the Early 16th Century." In pursuit of the answer to these questions, every place has been chronologically researched where Luther used testament, covenant, and cognates through 1525. The material has been systematized around six main points, which constitute Luther's theology of testament. In this process I have become fascinated with Luther's curious designation of the testator (Christ) as "worm."

THE TESTAMENT[3]

The various aspects of the category of testament provided Luther with a frame of reference to handle the disparate, polemical issues he confronted. "Testament" was a means or model for theologizing about the Christian faith. The promise to Abraham was given *"per modum testamenti."*[4] Testament is also the message. "And so that little word

1 Kenneth Hagen, *A Theology of Testament in the Young Luther: The Lectures on Hebrews* ("Studies in Medieval and Reformation Thought," Vol. 12; Leiden: Brill, 1974).

2 Heiko A. Oberman, "Wir sein pettler: Hoc est verum: Bund und Gnade in der Theologie des Mit telalters und der Reformation," *Zeitschrift für Kirchengeschichte* 78 (1967), 232-52.

3 I wish to thank Marquette University and Prof. Heinz Bluhm and associates for allowing me and associates to use Prof. Bluhm's *Index verborum* of Luther's German works from 1517-25. We were able to note the places where Luther used *Testament(um)*, *Bund*, and *ca.* 20 cognates and words associated with testament and covenant.

4 *Ad Galathas* (1516), WA 57.II.24.9-10.

'testament' is a short summary of all God's wonders and grace, ful-filled in Christ."[5] The "whole gospel" is summarized in the testament of Christ.[6] The mode and message of testament comes from the New Testament and was read by Luther back into the Old Testament. It was important hermeneutically for Luther that the New Testament illumine the Old Testament; otherwise the latter remains obscure.[7] The Jews of the Old Testament had the same Christian faith that New Testament Christians did.[8] Luther first read the Old Testament as the Christian's book; then read the New Testament in the light of the Old Testament: "The books of Moses and the prophets are also the Gospel"[9]; the Old Testament is "the ground of our faith."[10] "*Nam vetus testamentum est fons novi, novum est lux veteris.*"[11]

1. PROMISE. Testament or will is initiated by God through the promise(s) to send the testator (God in Christ) to validate by his death the inheritance of the forgiveness of sins and eternal life.

The promise was given at the beginning. "It must happen in this manner ... that God alone without any entreaty or desire of man must first come and give him a promise." The promise is "the beginning, the foundation, the rock."[12] The one who makes out a testament is the testator. "God is the testator, for it is he himself who promises and bequeaths."[13]

The testament is the promise,[14] and the promise is in both Old Testament and New Testament: "all the fathers in the Old Testament, together with all the holy prophets, had the same faith and Gospel as we have," because, "it is all the one truth of the promise."[15] Properly

---

5   *Ein Sermon von dem neuen Testament* (1520), *LW* 35.84; *WA* 6.357.25-27.

6   *Ibid., WA* 6.374.3-9.

7   *Evangelium in der Christmesse, Luk. 2,1-14* (1522), *WA*10,1,1.79-84; cf. *Ein Klein Unterricht was man in den Evangeliis suchen und gewarten soll* (1522), *WA* 10,1,1.14.16-15.9.

8   *Von weltlicher Obrigkeit, wie weit man ihr Gehorsam schuldig sei* (1523), *WA* 11.255.35-256.1.

9   *Epistel S. Petri gepredigt* (1523), *WA* 12.275.5.

10   *Ibid., WA* 12.274.34-35.

11   *WA Tr* 5.378.25-26 (# 5841).

12   *Ein Sermon von dem neuen Testament, LW* 35.82; *WA* 6.356.3-8.

13   *Ad Galatas* (1519), *LW* 27.264; *WA* 2.519.5.

14   *Ibid., WA* 2.519.6-7.

15   *Das Magnificat* (1521), *LW* 7.354; *WA* 7.600.1-9.

speaking (*"proprie"*) the New Testament is primarily promise with some law, and the Old Testament is primarily law with genuine promises.[16] Really for Luther there is no book in the Bible which does not contain both law and promise.[17]

The testament is eternal, the promise is constant and continuous, and there is no development of testament within or between the Old Testament and New Testament. Some would say that the prophets and the New Testament add something to the books of Moses. "No," said Luther regarding all books of Scripture, "throughout them all there is one and the same teaching and thought."[18] Moses is the primary source. Moses pointed out that the New Testament, the testament consisting of the promise of Christ, is the oldest, promised from the beginning of the world.[19]

In every promise there is a word and a sign, just as notaries affix their seal or mark to make a will binding and authentic.[20] The signs were the rainbow, circumcision, rain on the ground; in baptism the sign is the water, in the eucharist (the testament of Christ), bread and wine. "The words are the divine vow, promise and testament. The signs are the sacraments, that is, sacred signs. Now as the testament is much more important than the sacrament, so the words are much more important than the signs...."[21]

2. WORD. The more one works on testament and covenant in the later Middle Ages and Reformation, the more one is struck how verbally oriented Luther's theology was. Luther often bemoaned the fact that we have the New Testament in written form.

The Word is the living, eternal promise of the testament of Christ. The gospel of Christ is not a writing but a word of the mouth.[22] "This report and encouraging tidings, or evangelical and divine news, is also called a New Testament. For it is a testament when a dying man bequeaths his property, after his death, to his legally defined heirs. And Christ, before his death, commanded and ordained that his gospel

---

16   *De servo arbitrio* (1525), WA 18.692.19-20; WA Tr 6.140.26-31 (# 6714).

17   *Adventspostille* (1522) WA 10,1,2.159.7-8; cf. *Ein Sermon von dem neuen Testament*, WA 6.356-57.

18   *Von Menschenlehre zu meiden* (1522), LW 35.132; WA 10,2.73.7-18.

19   *Deuteronomion Mosi* (1525), WA 14.602.34-603.36.

20   *Ein Sermon von dem neuen Testament*, WA 6.358.35-359.3.

21   *Ibid.*, LW 35.91; WA 6.363.4-7.

22   *Ein klein Unterricht*, WA 10,1,1.17.4-11.

be preached after his death in all the world."[23] Luther preferred tile gospel of John over the synoptics, because John is much more about the preaching of Christ than about his works. "If I had to do without one or the other—either the works or the preaching of Jesus—I would rather do without the works than without his preaching. For the works do not help me, but his words give life."[24] Christ did not write anything; the New Testament is a "living Word."[25] The church is a "mouth house" and not a "pen house."[26]

The testament itself is the word of Christ, "'his is my body'.... In like manner he says over the cup, 'Take it and all of you drink of it: this is a new everlasting testament in my blood'.... In proof and evidence of this he has left his own body and blood under bread and wine, instead of letter and seal."[27] Everything depends on the words of Christ's testament: "You would have to spend a long time polishing your shoes, preening and primping to attain an inheritance, if you had no letter and seal with which you could prove your right to it. But if you have a letter and seal, and believe, desire, and seek it, it must be given to you, even though you were scaly, scabby, stinking, and most filthy. So if you would receive this sacrament and testament worthily, see to it that you give emphasis to these living words of Christ...."[28] The Word is the promise. The Word is the testament. The Word is Christ. Christ's testament is the eucharist. "Let this stand, therefore, as our first and infallible proposition—the Mass or Sacrament of the Altar is Christ's testament."[29]

3. CROSS. Luther's theology of the cross was a part of a larger picture—it is not the whole story of Luther's thought. The whole picture is a theology of testament with many aspects, the cross being one. Luther's theology of death, Christ's, was more than a theological construct. As much of his theology was, it was a strategy to deal with an every day, existential dread: death, physical and imminent. Christ's

---

23　*Vorrede auf das Neue Testament* (1522), *LW* 35.358; *WA DB* 6.4.12-17.

24　*Ibid.*, *LW* 35.362; *WA DB* 6.10.20-22.

25　*Adventspostille* (1522), *WA* 10,1,2.35.1-2.

26　*Ibid.*, *WA* 10,1,2.48.5.

27　*Von den guten Werken* (1520), *LW* 44.55-56; *WA* 6.230.10-25.

28　*Ein Sermon von dem neuen Testament*, *LW* 35.88; *WA* 6.360.29-361.9.

29　*De captivitate Babylonica ecclesiae praeludium* (1520), *LW* 36.37; *WA* 6.513.14-15.

death was a *sacramentum* and an *exemplum*. The example of Christ shows us how to die confidently in the "passing over of our flesh."[30]

The sacramental effect of Christ's death is the validation of the eternal testament.[31] "So you have the Testator, the testament, the substance of the testament, and those for whom it was made. Now it remains that it be ratified ... that is, made valid through the death of Christ."[32] Heb. 9.16 was often cited by Luther, "'For where there is a testament, the death of the testator must of necessity occur.' Now God made a testament; therefore, it was necessary that he should die. But God could not die unless he became man. Thus the incarnation and the death of Christ are both comprehended most concisely in this one word, 'testament.'"[33] Testament is not a vow to be altered or recalled by the living; it is an irrevocable will of one about to die. The cross then is in the context of the promise of the testament, "that God would become man and die and rise again, in order that his word, in which he promises such a testament might be fulfilled and confirmed."[34]

The cross for Luther meant suffering and humiliation: the wounds of Christ, the blood of Christ, Christ as worm on the cross. Christ as worm meant, in part, total humiliation: "I am a worm and no man," (Ps. 22.6), said Christ on the cross, according to Luther.[35] "We find him [Christ] dying a shameful death."[36] The real holy relic of which

---

30 Hagen, *A Theology of Testament*, pp. 114-15.

31 *Dominica Iudica Sermo M. Lutheri* (probably 1516), WA 4.618.20-30: "A testament is the last will over a legal thing and is finished by the death of the testator. Thus the Old Testament was the land flowing with milk and honey (Ex. 24; Heb. 9), containing earthly and external things. God did not die there as testator, but cattle died instead, in order that the testament might be ratified. Since the Old Testament was earthly and transitory and, indeed, out of date, it was fitting that it be ratified with the blood of cattle, to affirm temporal possession, in which all the commandments of the law grew strong. In the New Testament, however, the remission of sins is promised, eternal life, and a heavenly inheritance, in the following words: 'This is the cup of the New Testament, which is poured out for you and for many,' etc. And, in order that this testament might stand, the testator himself died."

32 *Ad Galatas* (1519), LW 27.265; WA 2.519.38-520.6.

33 *De captivitate Babylonica*, LW 36.38; WA 6.514.6-10.

34 *Ein Sermon von dem neuen Testament*, LW 35.84; WA 6.357.22-24.

35 Cf. Part Two: THE WORM; below.

36 *Zei deutsche Fastenpredigten* (1518), LW 51.40; WA 1.270.26.

the Psalmist speaks, "*In reliquiis tuis praeparabis vultum eorum,*" (Ps. 20.13), is the testament which consists of cross and humility.[37]
4. INHERITANCE. The cross ratifies the legacy bequeathed. The inheritance bequeathed is the "grace of the new testament."[38] Whether seen as promise, Word, cross, inheritance or faith, the testament is grace. Luther defined the inheritance in slightly different ways. Sometimes it is "righteousness,"[39] sometimes it is "the grace and righteousness of faith."[40] Sometimes the inheritance is given as the forgiveness of sins,[41] sometimes as the grace for eternal life.[42] Most often the inheritance is defined as the combination of the forgiveness of sins and eternal life. Grace is promised for the forgiveness of sins so that the heirs might obtain the eternal inheritance.[43] "What is bequeathed to us by Christ in his testament? Truly a great, eternal and ineffable treasure: ... the forgiveness of all our sins and life eternal."[44] Testament, at least God's style, is totally gratuitous.

The testament is unilateral gift. One of the primary functions of the testament model is that the testator made out his will (the promise) without the heir having to do anything to deserve the inheritance. In the testament of the mass God does not receive a benefit but confers a benefit. By definition, a testament is "*beneficium ... datum.*"[45] "Christ has set up the mass as a sacrament and testament, which no one can buy, initiate or give, but like baptism one must receive it for himself."[46]

The unilateral testament is not a bilateral covenant. Whenever Luther thought positively about covenant, he was thinking about the covenant of grace as a synonym of testament. "This testament of Christ is foreshadowed in all the promises of God from the beginning of the world.... Hence the words '*pactum, foedus, testamentum domini,*' occur

---

37   *Ibid.,* WA 1.270.38-39.
38   *Sermo de triplici iustitia* (1518), WA 2.45.26-27.
39   *Ibid.*
40   *Ad Galatas* (1519), WA 2.519.7-8.
41   *De abroganda missa privata* (1521), WA 8.444.22-23.
42   *Sermon von der wurdigen Empfahung des heiligen wahren Leichnams Christi* (1521), WA 7.696.2-3.
43   *De captivitate Babylonica,* WA 6.515.5-16.
44   *Ein Sermon von dem neuen Testament,* WA 6.358.14-20.
45   *Ibid.,* WA 6.364.20.
46   *Adventspostille* (1522), WA 10,1,2.79.29-32.

so frequently in the Scriptures. These words signified that God would one day die. For where there is a testament, the death of the testator must of necessity occur (Heb. 9)."[47] In the Old Testament there was an old covenant which began and ended in time. Faithfulness to that covenant depended on works.[48]

Research on Luther's use of testament, covenant, and cognates to 1525 shows that, except where Luther sees covenant as a synonym for the testament of Christ, he uses *Pactum* and *Bund* pejoratively and in negative contexts. For example, there is a covenant between the Pope and the German people to raise money to fight the Turks; the context is deceit. Rome never intends to keep the *Bund*—it keeps the money in its "bottomless bag."[49] An example of disobeying the first commandment is a covenant with the devil.[50] For God to covenant with a person and place is to delimit God; to tie him down is contrary to Ps. 67.[51] Or, "Don't let yourselves be fooled" into making "oaths, vows, covenants, and adamantine or ironclad pledges ... that you will not produce seed and multiply," unless you are a eunuch.[52] Those merchants who buy up certain goods to control supply and raise prices engage in selfish profiteering—"when they have cornered the supply, they draw up a *Bund*."[53] The peasants force good people to join their "devilish *Bund*" against their wills."[54]

Luther's understanding and experience of covenants, historical and contemporary, seem to be consistently negative because they circumscribe freedom—theologically, the freedom of God. This is consistent with Luther's view of the bondage of the will. The freedom of the will to enter into a covenant of works with God destroys the freedom and authority of God. "If" type soteriologies are the way of the law. The freedom of the Christian man depends on the sovereign freedom of God to give the promise of the New Testament.[55]

47 *De captivitate Babylonica*, WA 6.514.4-7.

48 *Deuteronomion Mosi*, WA 14.627.7-8; 668.7 & 15; 721.19 & 22.

49 *An den christlichen Adel deutscher Nation* (1520), WA 6.419.5-6; cf. 424.8.

50 *Eine kurze Form der zehn Gebote* (1520), WA 7.207.19.

51 *Deutsche Auslegung des 67. (68.) Psalmes* (1521), WA 8.34.6-7.

52 *Vom ehelichen Leben* (1522), LW 45.19; WA 10,2.277.11.

53 *Von Kaufshandlung und Wucher* (1524), WA 15.308.25.

54 *Wider die rauberischen und morderischen Rotten der Bauern* (1525), WA 18.361.10.

55 *De servo arbitrio*, WA 18.690.31-693.5.

The testament is unilateral sacrifice. "In the New Testament there is no sacrifice other than the sacrifice of the cross and of praise."[56] Deceptive priests, papists and sophists want to change the testament into a sacrifice: "There is, they say, a single God and a single church, between which only the testament mediates from above and the sacrifice from below." Luther opposed a bilateral notion of sacrifice because the "sacrifice from below" meant "works."[57] Christ is the only testator in the mass, the beneficent giver of the inheritance. "How can we then, out of this pledge and seal of God given to us as a gift, make a sacrifice and work of our own? Who among men would be so foolish as to sacrifice the seal on a letter, in which something is promised to him, to the one who makes the promise?"[58]

The mass is a unilateral testament and sacrifice. The sacrifice is the sacrifice of prayer and praise offered by every Christian as spiritual priest through Christ as mediator. "We do not offer Christ as a sacrifice, but Christ offers us.... That is, we lay ourselves on Christ by a firm faith in his testament..."[59]

The legacy is the free gift of the forgiveness of sins and eternal life. The Christian cannot and does not offer a benefit, but he receives the benefit of the sacrifice on the cross.

5. FAITH. Faith is a part of the inheritance: "the grace and righteousness of faith." One receives faith through the Word accomplishing its purpose. The free gift of grace is unilateral. The heirs are those who believe.[60] "The Word of God is decisive for you; it determines when and how far you may believe." Faith builds on the Word and where there is no Word there is no faith. "That is why the words of God in Scripture are referred to as testament, *testimonia, pacta, federa,* because they demand faith."[61]

Faith is trust in the promise. God deals with his creatures through a Word of promise, and they with him through faith in the "Word of his promise.... For anyone can easily see that these two, promise and faith, must necessarily go together. For without the promise there is nothing

---

56   *Vom Missbrauch der Messe,* WA 8.506.11-12.

57   *Ibid.,* LW 36.180; WA 8.522.3-13.

58   *Ibid.,* LW 36.174; WA 8.517.1-2.

59   *Ein Sermon von dem neuen Testament,* LW 35.99; WA 6.369.3-7.

60   *De abroganda missa private,* WA 8.444.23-24.

61   *Kirchenpostille* (1522), LW 52.199; WA 10,1,1.616.2-7.

to be believed; while without faith the promise is useless, since it is established and fulfilled through faith."[62] The certitude of trust (*"cum fidutia"*) is based on the unworthiness of the heir and the magnitude of the inheritance.[63] We are *"debitores"* in the *"pactum fidei."*[64] Trust is confidence that God will keep his Word and provide; it is the same in both Old Testament and New Testament.[65]

Trust in the Word and promise is the foundation for life and death. Christ on the cross overcame sin, death and hell; his victory gives comfort and confidence for death. "What will it profit you to assume and to believe that sin, death, and hell are overcome in Christ for others, but not to believe that your sin, your death, and your hell are also vanquished and wiped out and that you are thus redeemed?"[66] Personal certitude of faith is based on God's promise, the validation of that promise in the death of the testator, and the fact that there is absolutely nothing the heir can do to deserve the promised inheritance.

6. LUTHER'S THEOLOGY OF TESTAMENT IS SOTERIOLOGICAL—SACRAMENTAL. It is a mode or model for explaining a theory of salvation, and it is the message of salvation. Luther, like other medieval theologians, discusses testament in terms of the books of the Old and New Testament and their hermeneutical relationship.[67] The two books cover the two great eras of salvation, the old and new eras of divine providence. Luther's principal interest in the category of testament, however, is not in terms of books or eras but ways of salvation. Like St. Augustine, Luther sees Old and New Testament as an old and new way of salvation, both ways being present in both books (Old Testament, New Testament) and eras.[68] When Luther and Augustine discussed old and new, they often meant old man and new man, letter and spirit, flesh and spirit. The man of faith is a New Testament man, that is, he has received the testament of

---

62 *De captivitate Babylonica LW* 36.42; *WA* 6.516.30-32 & 517.8-10.

63 *Ibid., WA* 6.519.29 & 520.4.

64 *Operationes in Psalmos* (1519-21), *WA* 5.663.27-29.

65 *Predigten über das 2. Buch Mose* (1525), *WA* 16.457.29-458.11.

66 *Ein Sermon von der Bereitung zum Sterben* (1519), *LW* 42.109; 2.691.12-21; 693.21-24; 695.12.

67 *Von dem Papsttum zu Rom wider den hochberuhmten Romanisten zu Leipzig* (1520), *WA* 6.302.21 & 303.10,12,26; cf. 314.5,7. "Von der figur und deutung," *Evangelium von den zehn Aussätzigen* (1521), *WA* 8.386.15-397.17.

68 *Grund und Ursach aller Artikel D. M. Luthers* (1521), *WA* 7.327.5-328.4.

Christ in faith and trust. Because the testament of God is eternal and his Word eternally effective, those men of faith who lived during the old era covered by the Old Testament belong to the New Testament. Luther does not conceive of salvation in terms of progressive providence, developing from old Testament to New Testament to church, but in terms of the everpresent promise, Word of God, inheritance, faith, all grounded in the death of Christ.

THE WORM

Luther's theology of testament (to 1525) was primarily a testamental soteriology. Some have suggested that all of Luther's theology was really a spirituality or all soteriology, or that Luther lacked a Christology. Most of these problems depend on the definitions of these terms. This research on testament and covenant has revealed something of a Christology: the nature of the person of Christ on the cross is worm. "I am a worm and no man" (Ps. 22.6). For research on worm, I have gone beyond 1525.

In reference to Heb. 2.7, "Thou didst make him a little lower than the angels," Luther first discounted those who understood "him" to be human nature close to the angels in dignity. Then he opposed those who understood "him" to be Christ but had an inadequate Christology. "Others understand this verse to refer to Christ as being lower than the angels, not according to his soul but according to his body which is capable of suffering. But even this interpretation is not precise enough, since he was not only made lower than the angels, but as he himself says: 'I am a worm, and not a man' (Ps. 22.6)."[69] Being made "lower than the angels" meant for Luther the time of total humiliation between the cross and the resurrection, the three days when, forsaken and deserted by God, "Thou didst hand Him over into the hands of sinners."[70] The meaning of Christ as worn on the cross carried the connotations of Christ being abject, the object of contempt, forsaken, nauseating, abominable, rotten stench, scandal, offensive or, simply, rotting worm.[71] "The prophets have a special way of speaking, but they mean exactly what the apostles preach; for both have said much about the suffering and glory of Christ and of those who believe in him. Thus David says of Christ in Ps. 22.6: 'I am a worm and no man.'

---

69   *Ad Hebraeos* (1517-18), WA 57,III.117.4-10.

70   *Ibid.*, WA 57,III.119.1-5.

71   *Operationes in Psalmos*, WA 5.614.4-24.

With these words He shows the depth of His abject humiliation in His suffering."[72]

Christ as worm refers to "the mode of his passion as pure man."[73] The state of *purus homo* is that he is a bag of worms. The first enemy that tempts the Christian away from the Word of God and faith is "our own flesh," a rotten old bag of worms hanging heavy around our neck.[74] "We are nothing other than filth, corruption and worms." In death the flesh turns to dust and the worms consume it. Faith looks beyond death and the consumption by worms, and believes that the body will rise.[75] "For thus it has pleased God to raise up from worms, from corruption, from the earth, which is totally putrid and full of stench, a body more beautiful than any flower, than balsam, than the sun itself and the stars."[76] The inheritance for the worm of faith is eternal life.[77]

Christ destroyed the devil's tyranny over death. God chose not to use heavenly spirits and princes, Gabriel, Michael and others, but "He degrades himself so profoundly and becomes a man, yes, even degrades himself below all men, as it is written in Ps. 22.6: 'I am a worm and no man; scorned by men, and despised by the people.' In such physical weakness and poverty he attacks the enemy, lets Himself be put on the cross and killed, and by His cross and death He destroys the enemy and the avenger."[78]

How is it that a worm on a cross destroys the enemy's tyranny over death? The force of the image of worm is illumined by an examination of some early Christian literature. In *I Clement* (16.15) Ps. 22.6 is used to describe the humiliation of Christ, and later (25.3) the worm is used as a resurrection symbol—the worm comes forth from the decaying flesh of the phoenix bird. The resurrection of the mythical phoenix is used as an illustration of the Christian doctrine

---

72 *Epistel S. Petri gepredigt und ausgelegt* (1522), LW 30.24; WA 12.279.23-27.

73 *Operationes in Psalmos*, WA 5.614.8-9.

74 *Das fünfte, sechste und siebente Kapitel Matthaei gepredigt und ausgelegt* (1532), WA 32.308.13-14 & 489.34-38. Cf. LW 12.105 & 230; LW 24.44.

75 *Lectures on Genesis* (1535-45), WA 43.318.22-23 & 303.36-304.6.

76 *Ibid.*, LW 4.190; WA 43.272.37-39.

77 *Das 16. Kapitel S. Johannes gepredigt und ausgelegt* (1537), WA 46.54.36-55.8.

78 *Der 8. Psalm Davids, gepredigt und ausgelegt* (1537), LW 12.110; WA 45.220.14-22.

of resurrection. "Now, from the corruption of its flesh there springs a worm, which is nourished by the juices of the dead bird, and puts forth wing." In Origen the worm as Christ's humanity is used as bait to catch the devil and his angels.[79] In Cyril of Jerusalem new life comes from worms, as evidenced by the bees and the birds. The transformation of the phoenix from a worm is proof of Christian resurrection.[80] In Gregory of Nyssa the gluttonous fish is lured by the flesh of Christ as bait; the divinity of Christ is the hook.[81] Luther refers to Gregory[82]: God took a sharp fishhook, put an angleworm on it and threw it into the sea. The worm is the humanity of Christ, the hook the divinity. On the hook the worm is *"gebunden."* The devil says, "Should I not swallow the little worm?" He did not see the hook.[83]

For Luther the testator on the cross is pure man, a worm. The testator is also the one who made the promise of the eternal inheritance. "The humanity did not conquer sin and death; but the hook that was concealed under the worm, at which the devil struck, conquered and devoured the devil, who was attempting to devour the worm."[84]

---

79   *Selecta in Ps.* 21.7, PG 12.1254C.

80   *Catechesis* 18.8, PG 33.1026-27.

81   *Oratio Catechetica* 24, PG 45.66A.

82   Probably, Gregory the Great; cf. *Moralium in Job,* lib. 33, PL 76.682C,D.

83   *Predigt am Ostersonntag* (1530), WA 32.41.12-26.

84   *Ad Galatas* (1531/35), LW 26.267; WA 40.I.417.31-33.

THE HISTORICAL CONTEXT OF THE
SMALCALD ARTICLES

The Smalcald Articles of four hundred and fifty years ago were to serve two purposes. First, they were to provide a Lutheran confessional identity in the face of impending political and religious warfare. In the face of the Augsburg Confession and Melanchthon's Apology and the current crisis, the concern of the Elector John Frederick was to have Luther, and not Melanchthon, express the truth concerning Lutheran identity. The second purpose of Luther's authorship was that the Articles were to be his "testament." Luther, who at the time thought that his end was near, says in the preface:

> I have determined to publish these articles in plain print, so that, should I die before there will be a council (as I fully expect and hope ...), those who live and remain after my demise may be able to produce my testimony and confession.

There is some concern in the scholarly literature, indeed, importantly expressed by Hans Volz and Ernst Bizer, that the Smalcald Articles be seen as Luther's testament and not as a confessional writing. While there was initial confusion about the acceptance and confessional standing of the Articles, they appear in the Book of Concord as Luther's vigorous "testimony."

I. THE POLITICAL CONTEXT

The literature that I have seen on the historical context of the Smalcald Articles has concentrated on the ecclesiastical-political maneuvering of the emperor, pope, and elector, as well as the theologians assigned to describe and defend the Lutheran position. The discussions about where a papal council was to be held were politically explosive. Much was at stake in the deliberations over Placentia, Bologna, and Mantua. The general background for the ecclesiastical-political maneuvering of the 1530s was the papal decision one more time to call a council in the face of the imperial and ecclesiastical demands for reform. To read the history of the events that led finally to the Council of Trent, beginning in 1545, makes one dizzy—dizzy not so much from the massive detail, but from the roller-coaster character of Vatican politics. The demands for reform would rise only to drop down in defeat. A major Roman Catholic thesis has been that, if a Council of Trent had materialized at the end of the Middle Ages, there would have been no Lutheran movement. The decision of Pope Paul III to convoke a general council to meet at Mantua on May 8, 1537, set in motion the events that led to the Smalcald Articles. The political context for the Articles will now be reviewed as it is generally presented in the literature.

Much of the maneuvering on the part of the elector and the theologians was occasioned by the fact that the papal bull expressly declared that the purpose of the council would be "the utter extirpation of the poisonous, pestilential Lutheran heresy." The elector was opposed to even hearing the papal invitation. The Lutheran concern throughout the mid-1530s was whether the council would be free and under the authority of Scripture or whether it would be under papal authority. Except for Luther, the Lutheran strategy was to avoid a papal council, where the Lutherans feared adverse judgment and defeat might ensue. Luther's attitude was consistently rather flamboyant. He was prepared to go anywhere, even to papal Bologna, with neck, head, and fist.

The Lutheran theologians were concerned to avoid the reproach of having prevented a council by turning down the legate. So they made distinctions between a citation and an invitation and between two kinds of citation, one whereby they could defend themselves openly in contrast to one whereby they would be declared as public heretics. The elector did not like these distinctions of the theologians. The elector was concerned that the theological authority for the council be Scripture while the theologians engaged in politics.

Luther was not concerned about the place or the politics but about his "testimony." Luther had been instructed to prepare articles that were necessary for Lutheran confessional identity, articles that could not be yielded without becoming guilty of treason against God. He was also instructed to prepare articles, expected to be few in number, that were not necessary and that could be yielded in good conscience. Toward the end of 1536 Luther was ready with the articles for the approval of his colleagues, and early in the new year with their subscription he sent them to the elector, who again supported Luther all the way. Luther did not provide any points that might be yielded. In fact, Luther was adamant about the necessity of all his articles in their entirety. Luther's articles were adopted by the theologians at the Smalcald meeting early in 1537 and endorsed privately by the Lutheran princes and estates.

These events, then, provided the political-historical context for the Smalcald Articles. The Smalcald Articles, however, are, as stated above, a theological testimony of Luther. The historical context necessarily involves the theology of Luther in the middle and late 1530s. The concern here is that this material and its author be approached in a manner appropriate to its intent, that is, that it be approached as theology in its historical, catholic, and medieval context. In the scholarly literature there is an abundant amount of material on Luther's soteriology, sacramentology, Christology, attitude toward the Jews, contribution to feminism and education, and the like. There is little if any attention paid to Luther's theology—his doctrine of God. At heart and head Luther was a theologian, and at the center of his theology is his doctrine of God. The following pages will look at the theological context of the Smalcald Articles by first looking at Luther's writings at the time and then defining and describing his foundational theological orientation as the grammar of faith based on the Trinity. With such a theological context the final focus will be on the Trinitarian and creedal form of the *prima pars* of the Smalcald Articles.

II. THE THEOLOGICAL CONTEXT

In the middle and late 1530s, as throughout his life, Luther was concerned about Scripture, theology, and creed. In 1534 his translation of the entire Bible was published. At the end of the decade, in a preface to the Wittenberg Edition of his German writings (1539), Luther gave three rules for the correct way of studying theology, that is, the Holy Scriptures: *oratio, meditatio,* and *tentatio*. The rules are derived from David the Psalmist. Thus, Scripture provides its own interpretation. These rules apply only to theology; thus theology is a unique discipline. One does not need prayer or the Holy Spirit to read *Aesop's Fables*. Using David's rules in the study of theology, says Luther in his preface, will lead to singing to the honor and glory of God.

Between 1535 and 1545 Luther was lecturing on Genesis. At the time of the Smalcald Articles he was treating chapter three. This undertaking was the exegetical context for the first article in the third part of the Smalcald Articles, the article dealing with sin. In his commentary on Genesis three Luther dwells on the immensity of original sin, how "hideous and awful" it is.

In 1536 there appears the *Disputation concerning Justification.* Here Luther reflects on the "mystery of God, who exalts His saints." Justification is "not only impossible to comprehend for the godless, but marvelous and hard to believe even for the pious themselves." To consider justification brings one to the mystery of who God is and what God does. It is "incomprehensible as far as our human nature is concerned." Justification is as *ex nihilo* as was creation. So also theology is *ex nihilo* as far as human possibilities are concerned. A true theologian is created by working frequently on this article.

Something else with which Luther was busy four hundred and fifty years ago was writing a short work published a year later, on the three oldest Christian confessions of faith. He wanted to elaborate on the first part of the Smalcald Articles, "on the lofty articles of the divine majesty." The three symbols or creeds of the Christian faith were the Apostles' Creed, the Athanasian Creed, and Luther's favorite "hymn in honor of the Holy Trinity," namely, the "hymn of St. Ambrose and St. Augustine" (*Te Deum Laudamus*). Luther reviews the heresies that threaten the three articles. All three must be truly believed. If any one is lacking, then all three are lacking. The Christian faith must be whole and complete. In this work he centers on the Trinitarian mystery and the person and work of Christ. The creed sung in the mass every Sunday is to be confessed and not interpreted. Luther is critical of modern, human interpretation. The teaching of Scripture concerning God is to remain uninterpreted and is simply to be confessed as the faith of the church in the form of a hymn.

In the year that Luther published the Smalcald Articles (1538), he also began to write *On the Councils and the Churches,* in which he reviews the councils of the early church. In his treatment of the early centuries, Luther does not employ nineteenth-century notions of the development of doctrine. The Christian faith does not develop by the interpretation of theologians or Christians in general. The Christian faith does not become more complete or better understood with the passage of time. The church is a confessing church—confessing, not interpreting, the creed. The creed is a mark of the church, along with the Word of God, baptism, the eucharist, the keys, the ministry, and the cross.

Thus, Luther's writings concurrent with the Smalcald Articles concerned Scripture, theology, and creed. The next matter which must be considered is Luther's foundational theological orientation. Throughout his life Luther identified with the understanding of theology as the discipline of the sacred page with a unique grammar, what here will be called the grammar of faith.

For generation after generation, from early times on up through the Reformation, theology was practiced as the discipline of the sacred page (*sacra pagina*). The monastery with its daily liturgy, connected to the sacred page, was the place and context of theology. The final goal of theology was to get home, home to God, home to the Trinity (in Augustine's words).

With the rise of universities in the twelfth century, theology shifted to sacred doctrine (*sacra doctrina*) as the place shifted to the schools. The schoolmen wrote Bible commentaries; they also wrote theology. Theology was based on the method of *quaestio* and dialectic. The final goal of theology was still the beatific vision. The shift from sacred page to sacred doctrine is the shift from locating the stuff of theology in Scripture to locating the stuff of theology in doctrine ("faith seeking understanding").

With the arrival of the printing press and the scholarship of the Christian humanists, however, theology was seen not as the monk's work of prayer and praise nor as the professor's academic questions and propositions but as the educative task of reviving the classics, both pagan and Christian. The study of the sacred letter of Scripture was to lead not so much to God as to a better society, church, education, and government. Theology as the study of the philosophy of Christ was to lead to piety, morality, and justice.

These approaches of sacred page, doctrine, and letter were mixed and matched during the early and late Reformation. Luther continued the discipline of the sacred page minus monastic discipline. The Council of Trent continued the discipline of sacred doctrine. The rise of the historical-critical methods of biblical introduction, biblical theology, and biblical hermeneutics during the sixteenth to nineteenth centuries continued humanistic methods. The goal of the historical-critical method is to understand the letter of the text. The goal of sacred doctrine is to understand the faith of the Roman Catholic Church. The goal of the sacred page is to prepare for the kingdom of God.

For some (few) today theology is still allied with the sacred page. For many (most) theology has become allied in the modern era with philosophy, psychology, sociology, politics; in other words, theology becomes interdisciplinary studies in the humanities. Theology is a science with such a plethora of allies; theology has many friends. But does theology today have any enemies? For Luther, if theology is true to its discipline of the sacred page, it will have a whole host of enemies; the demonic forces will be stirred up. Theology is engaged in a cosmic battle in Augustine's and Luther's world (not so for Erasmus). For Luther, theology does not engage in friendly interdisciplinary conversations. It speaks for God in the public arena. In his various commentaries on Galatians throughout his life Luther was conscious of the public character of his work and that the public included the demonic forces. Theology's enemies are God's enemies, the pseudo-apostles who come to the centers of faith. Theology is to speak for God against the false teachers in the public arena.

Luther's understanding of communication of theology was different from his contemporary and our contemporary humanist methods. For the humanist, sacred literature is in print for public edification. Luther was not so interested in printing the Gospel as in publishing the good news which is the Word of God. The church is not a pen house but a mouth house, said Luther. Luther was a leader in advocating schools for boys and girls so that they could learn to read. Education must be publicly supported; otherwise Germany might lose it as did Greece and Rome. But education is not communicating theology.

To communicate or speak for God entails a continual public battle. The cosmic battle between God and Satan does not take place in print. The form that the defense of God takes is the theology of Scripture. The form that the defense of Satan takes is blasphemy. Both are public in nature. To allow blasphemy to take place is to commit complicity. Blasphemy is a continual problem. To be silent in complicity is to support the opposition. There is no neutral zone. Either God is winning or the devil is. One way to understand Luther's opposition to the Jews, rather fierce at the time of the Smalcald Articles, is to understand his view of complicity. He believed that the Jews were perpetrating blasphemy publicly. Luther did not attack particular Jewish individuals. No, it was their Judaism and blasphemy. The Gospel must be publicly defended and the opposition attacked. Then one is true to the discipline of the sacred page.

Why did Luther publish another commentary on Galatians in the same year in which the Smalcald Articles were published? Had he not just published such a work three years earlier in 1535? Had not several editions of Galatians appeared earlier than that? Did Luther change his mind or come up with new interpretations during these years? Absolutely not; it was necessary to publish a commentary on Paul because of Luther's understanding of a *commentarius*.

One cannot assume that a commentary in one century is the same as a commentary in another. When Luther's *Commentary on Galatians* is edited and translated in modern editions, one cannot call it a commentary in the sense of modern exegesis. In fact, Luther himself says that, if one wants a commentary, he should see Erasmus. Luther says that his work is "less a commentary than a testimony to my faith in Christ." Both his so-called commentary and the so-called Smalcald Articles are singular testimonies to his singular faith in Christ. Luther's own word for his public defense of Galatians is *enarratio*. *Enarratio* connotes a public dimension. He is making public the one doctrine, truth, grace, and Christ. Luther is not primarily concerned about the text of Galatians. That would be *narratio*, narrating the text. *Enarratio* is to take out of the text the theology and to apply it in public. It is to publish the doctrine, the soteriology, and the Christology of Paul.

The modern introductions to Luther's various works on Galatians, which are perceived as commentaries in the modern sense, describe them as containing revisions, being shorter or longer, as making progress, or being abbreviated. Such descriptions are ridiculous. When one realizes what Luther's work is, namely, theology, such an idea would be equivalent to saying that Luther revised the doctrine of the Trinity, shortened or lengthened his soteriology, made progress in his Christology, or abbreviated his faith. The treatment of Scripture in the genre of *enarratio* is very old. It goes back to Augustine, the Psalter, and Isaiah. It is to praise the glory of God. A Scriptural *enarratio* is a *catena* (chain) of praises to the glory, the grace, and the justice of God. In the dedication to his commentary on Galatians Luther says that his purpose is to interest others in Pauline theology. Thus, his *enarratio* on Galatians seeks to promote the Gospel that Paul promotes. It is not a matter of interpreting Paul. It is a matter of publishing Paul's theology.

In his various publications of Galatians Luther is always conscious of Paul's linguistic style. Paul's peculiar language must be taken very precisely. Today we would say that Paul says what he means and means what he says. One of Luther's strongest statements on the interpreta-tion of Scripture is his assertion that Christ Himself gave Paul these special phrases. Luther indeed attempts to describe the various indi-vidual aspects of Paul's peculiar language: Paul's mode of argument, Paul's logic, Paul's use of metaphor, Paul's rhetoric, and Paul's gram-mar. "If you want to be studious in Christian theology, you must dili-gently observe this kind of Pauline language," says Luther in 1535. If you want to understand this kind of theology, you have to pay special attention to Paul's vocabulary and syntax, the logic and the idioms, the rhetoric and the grammar.

Paul uses a unique grammar as does all of Scripture. The grammar of the Psalter is different from the grammar of Aristotle. Each of these grammars has its place, but one must deal with each in terms of what it is. Paul's grammar is not that of nineteenth-century German idealism. The Bible was not written in Germany. The grammar of the Psalter is not that of nineteenth-century European notions of development, progress, and evolution. There is no progress in the Psalter. There is no development in God. Paul's theology does not evolve.

The challenge to modern historical-critical methods is that of consistency in method. To deal with Scripture on the basis of nine-teenth-century philosophical hermeneutics is not consistent. To use modern grammars to interpret Scripture's unique grammar is to cast Scripture into a world that is not its own. One must deal with Scripture in terms of what it is.

What is Scripture? Scripture was written from faith, to faith, about faith, for faith in God. Scripture has its own grammar, meaning, and vocabulary. The basic form of Scripture proceeds from faith to faith. It is the faith of the Christian creed. Scripture comes from God; the me-chanics bring us outside the realm of faith. God has a word to say. The promise is unconditional. The promise is given to faith. The promise is validated in the death and resurrection of Jesus Christ. The inher-itance is guaranteed by the Spirit who moved over the waters at cre-ation and who moves over the waters of our baptism. It is the Trinity, then, that provides the unity of the vocabulary, the morphology, the syntax, the grammar of faith.

What insights can be gained from the discipline of *sacra pagina* to deal with the grammar of faith? The distinct feature of *sacra pagina* is that it sees sacred matters as a page, not as doctrine and not as liter-ature. Sacred doctrine and literature have their place, but their status is derivative. They come from Scripture but they are not *pagina*. The sacred page is directly of God. It is *divina* and not *humana*. The grammar of assent has to do with doctrine and linguistics. The grammar of faith has to do with *divina* directly. The grammar of Athens has to do with the dialect of the city. The grammar of faith is a unique dialect. Luther often claimed in the face of the medieval four-fold sense of Scripture that Scripture has one single, simple grammatical sense. The grammatical sense most often refers to Christ. The grammar of faith is from God, about God, for God, and finally to God, Three in One.

Luther's foundational theological orientation should now be clear from the preceding aspects of it—the discipline of *sacra pagina*, the public character of theology, his commentary as the publication of Pauline theology, and the uniqueness of Paul's grammar. Luther's theology, then, is derived from the grammar of faith, which in turn comes from God the Father, Son, and Holy Spirit. Having considered Luther's other writings at the time of the Smalcald Articles and his theology as derived from the grammar of faith based on the Trinity, the *prima pars* of the Smalcald Articles takes on a new significance. It treats *divina* in Trinitarian and creedal form:

> I. The Father, Son, and Holy Spirit ... are one God, who created heaven and earth.
> II. The Father is begotten of no one; the Son is begotten of the Father; the Holy Spirit proceeds from Father and Son.
> III. The Son became man.
> IV. The Son became man in this manner ... as the Creed of the Apostles, as well as that of St. Athanasius, and the Catechism in common use for children teach.

The Smalcald Articles were to serve two purposes: to provide a distinctly Lutheran confessional identity and to serve as Luther's testament. Luther's testimony based on the grammar of faith is Trinitarian and creedal. Thus, Luther's preface concludes: "Do thou, then, help us, who are poor and needy, who sigh to Thee, and beseech Thee earnestly, according to the grace which has been given us, through Thy Holy Spirit, who lives and reigns with Thee and the Father, blessed forever. Amen."

THE HISTORY OF SCRIPTURE IN THE CHURCH

PART ONE: EARLY CHURCH TO THE REFORMATION

Modern biblical scholars have dealt with Scripture since the sixteenth century in terms of the various critical methods. It was not always that way. The concern for "method," whether in theology or medicine or logic, etc., became important in the sixteenth century and has continued to dominate the intellectual scene. The crisis today in scriptural study is due largely to the development of the "historical-critical method" after the sixteenth century. Since that method has so dominated Protestant approaches to Scripture for centuries and Catholic approaches more recently, Part Two will look at the rise of the historical-critical method.

To look at the history of Scripture before the modern church, the material in Part One will be divided into four sections: (I) The Early Church, (II) The High Middle Ages, (III) The Late Medieval Period, and (IV) The Early Reformation. In each case the subdivisions will treat the place of the Bible in theology, the interpretation of the Bible, and a key figure (Augustine, Aquinas, Erasmus, and Luther, respectively).

I. THE EARLY CHURCH

A. The Place of the Bible in Theology

For about the first thousand years theology was *sacra pagina* (sacred page). From the age of the Fathers up to the rise of the schools (Scholasticism), the source of theology was the sacred page of Scripture. Theology was all wrapped up in the study of God's sacred imprint in Holy Writ.

Think of monastic life.[1] It was the monastic community (more so in the West) that preserved learning up to the time of the schools or

---

1 "The monastic vocation was as much for women as for men; indeed, it is often women who may justly claim the priority as monastic pioneers" (Kallistos Ware, "Eastern Christendom" in *The Oxford History of Christianity*, ed. John McManners [Oxford: Oxford University Press, 1993], 140).

universities. They were the bearers of classical and Christian civilization. Think of the monk in the Scriptorium working with Scripture before the movable printing press and the photocopier. The disciplined life entailed copying Scripture, singing it in the holy office, praying it, carrying it in the heart the whole day. The monk and nun lived in the world of the Bible. Their whole life was connected with Scripture. It was sometime in the Renaissance (different times for different places) that people began to see a difference between their contemporary culture and the age of the Bible. The monastics could not disassociate themselves from Scripture. It is hard for us to imagine that because we have the Bible in a black book, we can take it off the shelf, read it, and then put the book back (out of sight, out of mind). The monastic could not put the Bible away. The Bible was not a book. The Bible was in the heart.

From the earliest times on, the place of the Bible in theology was that the Bible was theology and theology was the Bible. The Fathers refuted heresies, the monks preserved the Scriptures and Traditions, all on the basis of the Bible. Theology was not some separate discipline as it became in the high Middle Ages and as it is today. For the early period the Bible was the source of all that is—God's work in his creation and in his Church, and that work is encapsulated in the monastic community.

B. The Interpretation of the Bible

The Bible was seen to contain various senses or levels of meaning, sometimes many levels. The Bible was so rich, so full of meaning, that its depth of meaning could not be exhausted by a literal reading.[2] The early church on up to the discovery of Aristotle was influenced by Platonic philosophy. In Platonic philosophy the particular thing (in Scripture, the letter of the text) is a mirror of reality. The reality is the fuller meaning. As the monastics read Scripture they find shades of meaning far beyond what first meets the eye.

"The letter kills, but the Spirit gives life" (2 Cor. 3:6) was New Testament warrant for the Fathers and the monastics to distinguish between the literal and the spiritual meaning. The New Testament

---

2   The literal approach of the Antiochene school in the early period was an exception. In fact throughout the medieval church, more so in manuscripts than in what later was printed, a literal approach can be found, although very much the exception.

itself, in its interpretation of the Old, distinguishes between the literal and spiritual meaning. The pattern for interpreting Scripture is contained within Scripture. Interpreting Scripture meant explicating the spiritual depths of meaning expressed in the letter. For us, interpretation means bridging the gap between an ancient text and the modern world. When there is only one world, there is no separation. So interpretation meant commenting, annotating, explaining the various levels of meaning the Spirit leads one to see.

The most famous of the multilevel approach became the *quadriga*, the fourfold sense: the literal tells what happened (historical sense), the allegorical teaches what is to be believed, the tropological or moral what is to be done, and the anagogical where it is going or "tending." The usual example is Jerusalem, which refers literally to the city, allegorically to the Church, tropologically to the soul, and anagogically to heaven. The monks put this to rhyme. The point is that the letter of Scripture is a mirror of the almost limitless depth of meaning.

C. The Key Figure is St. Augustine

Augustine pulled together the various strands of biblical study in the early period and became the pillar on which medieval theology was built, thus the most important theologian for the entire (thousand year plus) medieval era and well into the sixteenth century. Now we consider how Augustine put Scripture together: three aspects of his understanding of Scripture.

First, Augustine, as was typical throughout this period, saw two eras of salvation represented by the two great books of Scripture. The Old and New Testaments represent the old and new era of salvation. God had a plan for his people; he gave revelation progressively as the people were prepared and able to accept what it was that God had in mind. A progressive revelation went on in Scripture. The ages of Scripture correspond to a person growing up; corporately it is the human race growing up. In the Old Testament the human race was in its infancy or in adolescence, and only as the human race (Israel) became more mature was it ready to receive Christ and the higher revelation. By implication then the fuller understanding of revelation continues in the Church.

Another concept that Augustine used was that God is the "doctor of medicine" and is healing his people. Salvation is health (well-being). The goal of creation, revelation, and finally salvation is final and complete healing. So God the doctor prescribed medicine to the extent that the people would respond and grow until the coming of Christ, who is both the medicine and the cure. Christ is the cure as well as the curer. The healing process continues in the life of the Church. As Augustine, then, looked at Scripture, he saw God's plan, God's providence. He saw two eras of this plan, and in these two eras God is the doctor healing his people.

Second, Augustine also worked with the Scriptures as books. As a theologian he had the Jewish and Christian manuscripts or books to integrate. A great deal of early hermeneutical effort was spent on the relationship between the two great Testaments. Very generally, the New was considered to be the fulfillment of the Old. Augustine emphasized that what was hidden or veiled in the Old Testament was revealed or uncovered in the New Testament. What was prefigured in the Old was made clear in the New. This is a "both ... and" relationship, thus the necessity of both Testaments: the New is concealed in the Old, and the Old is made clear in the New. Since the Holy Spirit is the author of both, there is unity and harmony between them. The unity of the Testaments and the progress of revelation is the basis of holding that the New Testament is superior to the Old Testament. The New is new in relation to the Old, and vice-versa. Both are needed. The New is more excellent.

So Augustine looked at the Bible in terms of salvation-medicine and healing. He looked at the Bible as a theologian and saw a unity geared towards the superiority of the New Testament as the fulfillment of the Jewish Scriptures. Third, when Augustine looked at Scripture, he did so in terms of salvation; he saw the two Testaments as two types of people, two ways of life. This is another level on which he looked at Scripture and saw that there is not only the chronological development of the whole race and the whole doctrine, but there is also the situation that some people of faith back in Old Testament times were actually living ahead of themselves (John 8:56, [Jesus] "Your father Abraham rejoiced to see my day: and he saw it, and was glad"). The ancestors of faith were actually living the New Testament because they believed Christian doctrine (They saw the promise, embraced it, and died in faith, Heb. 11:13). It was common in the early and medieval church to say that Moses was a Christian, along with all the faithful described in Hebrews 11. Augustine also said that in New Testament times there were people who had not believed the message and were still living the Old Testament because they were living according to the flesh and not according to the Spirit. This is again Augustine's famous letter/Spirit dichotomy, and it becomes an important hermeneutical tool throughout the medieval period into modern times. We live either according to the letter, or according to the Spirit. "The letter kills, the Spirit gives life." So if we live according to the letter, according to the desires of the flesh, we are Old Testament. It does not matter when we live, chronologically speaking, but soteriologically speaking we are old, Augustine said. Or, if we live according to the Spirit and you see the Spirit in the letter of Scripture and can see through the veil to the pure light of Christ and Christian doctrine, then we belong to the New Testament and are new, no matter whether we are Abraham or someone in the New Testament or someone today. So, on balance, what we have from Augustine is a fairly complicated view of Scripture, a multinuanced view of Scripture; and it is these various strands of putting Scripture together and interpreting Scripture that continued through the medieval period.

In between the early period and the high Middle Ages is something of a transitional period focused on the abbey of Saint Victor in Paris, namely, the twelfth-century Victorines. In going from Augustine to Thomas Aquinas via these Victorines, we see that something of a shift in the approach to Scripture was underway, a shift that is developed in Thomas. The important thing about the Victorines is that some of them were oriented towards the literal sense of Scripture, toward the historical sense, and used Jewish exegesis for the understanding of the Old Testament. What we have in the Victorines was not so much a theoretical change; that is, they were really not developing a new hermeneutic. They were simply preoccupied with the literal-historical sense apart from the allegorical or spiritualizing senses.

II. THE HIGH MIDDLE AGES

A. The Place of the Bible in Theology

From the eleventh century on it is important to think of the school, the university, for it is at the schools that theology takes on a new focus. This period became known as Scholasticism because theology increasingly became school-theology at the newly founded universities. Theology and the study of Scripture underwent quite a shift as they moved from the monastery to the university classroom. We have pictured the monastics living, praying, eating, and sleeping Scripture, living their lives, as they continue to do to this day, in the context of the life of Scripture. Whereas in the school, not unlike our contemporary colleges and universities, Scripture became a subject of academic study. In the school approach was a distinction or separation between theology and exegesis, a distinction or separation between the discipline of theology and the discipline of biblical interpretation. This is partly because of the influence of Aristotelian philosophy away from Platonic philosophy. With Aristotle, reality is seen contained in the thing itself. Hence in scriptural study, attention shifts to the sense of the letter. With the reality seen in the thing itself, rather than being mirrored into some other-worldly realm of the spiritual, Scripture itself becomes the object of study. What the Holy Spirit intended to say is there in Scripture, and all the levels of meaning are in the letter of the text, not in some other levels of meaning.

With a shift in scriptural study there is a shift in theology. While work on the Bible becomes more "literal" and "historical" (though, remember, we are still in the twelfth and thirteenth centuries), theology becomes speculative. An important influence on this shift in theology is the interest in dialectic (a part of logic). In the university situation, dialectic is the analysis of a question. Speculation is looking into something. It could and did have mystical overtones because theology first and foremost is looking into God. A question is posed, alternatives analyzed, often followed by a resolution. The shift in theology is a shift away from *sacra pagina* to *sacra doctrina* (sacred doctrine).[3] The first question in Thomas's *Summa theologiae* is: What is sacred doctrine? Work on the sacred page is contained in the *Commentaries on Scripture*. Theological questions are dealt with in the *Summaries of Theology* (there were summaries in other disciplines as well). Theology then took on a life of its own. Scripture and the Fathers are the authorities (footnotes). The method is philosophical, faith seeking understanding.

---

3 Simon of Tournai (d. 1201), the most important Parisian (early Scholastic) theologian at the end of the twelfth century, wrote *Institutiones in sacram paginam*. Scripture is not the subject. With the use of dialectic, the work consists of a series of questions related to Christian doctrine: the work begins "Incipiunt Sententiae magistri Simonis Tornacensis." See Richard Heinzmann's edition of *Die "Institutiones in sacram paginam" des Simon von Tournai*. Einleitung und Quästionenverzeichnis (Munich: Verlag Ferdinand Schöningh, 1967).

B. The Interpretation of the Bible

Accompanying the separation of Bible and theology is a different approach to the Bible (with Aristotle and reason in the background). For a Platonist, the soul (spirit) was seen hidden or imprisoned in the body (letter). The Aristotelian sees the spirit expressed by the text. All meaning is contained in the letter, authored by God. The focus shifts away from the mirror of universal truths to the intention of the author (letter). To understand the author is to discern the words and their significance. The Latin word to understand (*intelligere*) means to read within, to penetrate the rational meaning. The truth of the matter is there in the Bible expressed by the letters.

So far in Scholasticism we have the separation of biblical study from the study of theology, a different approach to theology (*sacra doctrina*), and a different approach to Scripture (intention of the letter). Also we have something of a new hermeneutic; at least a great deal is made of that in the literature. (One is always suspicious of new theories, because in the practice of biblical interpretation, the traditional results usually pertain.) This new theory is seen developed by the important fourteenth-century Franciscan biblical scholar, Nicholas of Lyra, who in turn was the most important biblical commentator for the later Middle Ages and early Reformation. Nicholas's commentaries were often printed in columns along side the biblical text and the glosses of the Fathers in the later fifteenth and sixteenth centuries. The new hermeneutic is called the "double-literal sense": two senses or meanings expressed by the one letter or word. There is the historical-literal sense and the spiritual- or prophetic-literal sense. The example given is that Solomon may refer to Solomon the man or be a figure of Christ or both. If both, both were intended by the author, the Holy Spirit. As will be seen with Thomas, grounding everything in the letter does not preclude the use of the traditional fourfold sense (literal, allegorical, tropological, and anagogical). The theory of the double-literal sense is widely accepted in the later Middle Ages (via Thomas and Nicholas). The result is an increasing attention to the text.

C. The Key Figure is Thomas Aquinas

In the modern period Thomas is famous for his *Summa theologiae* (Summary of Theology). In the century following his own, his commentaries on Scripture were more influential. Note that the Aristotelian Thomas wrote on Scripture, and in a separate literary genre he wrote on theology. As an Aristotelian thinks in terms of causality rather than reflection, Thomas thinks of God as the first author of Scripture and the human authors as instruments of divine revelation, choosing their own words. The letter contains the intention of the inspired writer. Thomas outlined his approach to biblical interpretation in the following statement:

> The author of Holy Scripture is God, in whose power it is to signify his meaning, not by words only (as man also can do) but by things themselves. So, whereas in every other science things are signified by words, this science has the property that the things signified by the words have themselves also a signification. Therefore that first signification whereby words signify things belongs to the first sense, the historical or literal. That signification whereby things signified by words have themselves also a signification is called the spiritual sense, which is based on the literal, and presupposes it. For as the apostle says (Heb. 10:1) the Old Law is a figure of the New Law, and (Pseudo-) Dionysius says: "The New Law itself is a figure of future glory." Again, in the New Law, whatever our Head had done is a type of what we ought to do. Therefore, so far as the things of the Old Law signify the things of the New Law, there is the allegorical sense; so far as the things done in Christ or so far as the things which signify Christ are types of what we ought to do, there is the moral sense. But so far as they signify what relates to eternal glory, there is the anagogical sense. Since the literal sense is that which the author intends, and since the author of Holy Scripture is God, it is not unfitting, as Augustine says, if even according to the literal sense one word in Holy Scripture should have several senses.[4]

Thomas presents a relationship between the Old and New Testaments along the lines of sign and fulfillment. The pattern is from Old to New to "future glory." Augustine is cited to show that in one literal sense there are several (spiritual) meanings. (It is always amazing how current Augustine is for the medievals on into the sixteenth century.) God is at work in the Old Testament through types and signs of the New. In seeing the signs one sees the relationship between Old and New, and in seeing the spiritual sense of the New one sees the relationship between the New Testament and the Church. In the allegorical, moral, and anagogical senses, God uses visible words to signify invisible truths. The pattern of relationship, fulfillment, development from Old

---

4   Aquinas, *Summa theologiae* I.1.10.

to New to Church is the pattern of Thomas's theology, and his interpretation of Scripture fits within that organic pattern.

For Thomas, there is an organic unity between Old and New.
Augustine's view of the progress of revelation is expanded by Thomas
to include everything from beginning to end, from creation to history, through the history of Israel, Old and New, to the end of time.
Thomas's view of revelation is that it is salvation history developing
organically. God is working salvation in history, and so the history of
God's people is salvation history. The history of salvation in Scripture
is the development from Old to New, old law to evangelical law. The
unity is based on God. The organic continuum goes on in the Church
to "eternal glory."

The main focus of Thomas on the Old and New Testament is on
their organic development, a part of the larger focus of salvation history. In terms of Augustine's approach and categories, Thomas's approach is a blend of the providential and hermeneutical foci. The blend
is seeing Testament as both era and book. Certain things concerning
Christ are prefigured in the Old Testament through figures like David
and Solomon. This is so because things of Christ are of such magnitude and power that they could not have been introduced "suddenly":
"The things of Christ are so great that they would not have been believed unless they had first been disseminated gradually through the
growth of time."[5] The development in time (era of salvation) is the
development from imperfect to perfect. Also the Old Testament is a
"figure" of the New Testament. The New Testament Church is a "figure" of the glory of heaven. With the development of "figure," Old to
New and New to glory, the Old Testament is a "figure of the figure."
The development is the development of clarity. Thomas also refers the
relationship of Old and New Law to the relationship of seed to tree,
implicit to explicit, fear to love. The growth is continual.

III. THE LATE MEDIEVAL PERIOD

A. The Place of the Bible in Theology

The fourteenth and fifteenth centuries were a mixture of what went
before and new currents of thought and practice. The schools continued to be the main focus of theological and biblical studies. The new

---

5   Cited in Kenneth Hagen, *A Theology of Testament in the Young Luther*
     (Leiden: E. J. Brill, 1974) 47.

currents of spirituality (for example, German mysticism and *Devotio moderna*) approached Scripture more along the monastic lines of *sacra pagina*. Among the Nominalists (a new philosophy-theology) and others, attention was paid to the relation of the Scriptures to the Traditions of the Church. Tension and even conflict between them were posited. The concentration on Scripture as an ancient book and the use of Scripture to criticize the Church was intensified in the (very) late medieval movement of Humanism.

The Humanists were not theologians in the usual sense of the profession at the end of the Middle Ages, that is, they were neither monastics nor scholastics. Often they were independent scholars, sometimes lay, interested in culture and learning and the effects of culture and learning on the reform of Church and society. Interest in Bible and theology was a part of a broader commitment to reap the wisdom of the pagan classics and the Christian Fathers. The discipline of biblical and theological study meant language study, classical Latin and Greek (and Hebrew for some).

The Humanists were involved in all kinds of humane studies. For our purposes we peg their efforts around the printing press and the production of sacred literature (*sacra littera*). So the approaches to Scripture in the medieval church differed as it was handled by the monks (*sacra pagina*), by the schoolmen (*sacra doctrina*), and by the printers (*sacra littera*). That is an enormous development, the effects of which we are still appropriating: the relation of the Holy Book to the traditions of the Church, to the study of theology, and to the life of faith.

B. The Interpretation of the Bible

The fourfold method continued. The double-literal sense was used. The imitation of Christ was another emphasis. The use of Jewish resources for a more historical understanding of the Old Testament increased. Study of Hebrew and Greek grew tremendously. All of these interests and approaches were filtered into the Reformation through the Humanists. The most important work on Scripture at the beginning of the sixteenth century was done by the Humanists. In the Catholic Reformation the Humanists led the way for critical editions of Scripture, vernacular translations, and the study of the Greek and Latin classics (as opposed to the Scholastics). In these matters they were defeated at the mid-sixteenth century Council of Trent. It has been in our century that Catholics have adopted Humanist and modern critical approaches to Scripture. The Protestants generally welcomed and used Humanist scholarship.

The effect of the Humanists on the place and interpretation of Scripture in the Church centered around their sense of history, study of the classics, expertise in the biblical (original) languages, preparation of critical printed editions of the Bible, and the use of Scripture for the reform of the Church. (Note that their effect on the place and interpretation of Scripture is on the Church in general, not just on theology, since their programs were broader than monastic and scholastic theology.)

A growing sense among the Renaissance thinkers (south of the Alps) and Humanists (north) was that the historical past is distant and different from present culture. This sense was not universally accepted, and it took until the nineteenth century for historical consciousness to be widely accepted and then largely only in Western culture. Their sense of history was that the time and place of classical culture was in the ancient world—not their own. In general for the medievals the age of the Bible was their own, a timelessness to it all. The Humanists perspective was the separation of past from present.

The Humanists were scholars, students of antiquity. The general Renaissance of the time was a revival of the arts, literature, and learning. The Humanists were interested in the learning contained in classical literature. The study of the classics was to go along with the study of Scripture, which also was from the classical world, for the purpose of moral and intellectual reform of the Church, theology, philosophy, education—the whole program. The critical study of the past had the edge to it of informing and often attacking the present. The study of the past included the editing, printing, and learning from the church fathers.

The Humanists were a part of the revival of Hebrew and Greek studies. Study of the ancient world meant the recovery of their languages. Study of the original languages of Scripture raised questions about the Latin Bible. The study of the Bible in the original often led to a criticism of the way the Bible had been translated into Latin and interpreted. Study of ancient languages was not what we would call strictly an academic exercise. Ancient literature—classical and Christian—was presumed to have value. The Humanists were often critical of Scholastics and others who concentrated only on the literal meaning of the text.

Humanist interest in original languages included an interest in original manuscripts and codices. With their historical perspective on the editing, translating, and transmission of texts, they were concerned to get as far back as possible to the original version of a writing. For scriptural study, this concern led to the discovery, collating, and printing of early Hebrew and Greek codices of the Bible. In 1516 Erasmus published the first Greek New Testament. The sixteenth century witnessed several critical editions of the Bible, printed by movable type. The new method in printing made possible the multiplication of both critical editions and vernacular translations.

The study of the classics, the Bible, and church fathers was critical and scholarly. The purpose of it was to reform the present. The Humanists were among those who were disturbed about corruption, lack of education, and the generally sorry state of society. The Church was often blamed for most of it, blamed for being too interested in money, politics, war, everything but the care of souls. The attacks were bitter and sarcastic. Theology (Scholasticism) was reproached for being interested only in syllogisms and not the simple piety of Scripture. The goal of their work was the reform of Church and society through education for the purpose of piety and knowledge.

C. The Key Figure is Erasmus of Rotterdam

Writing at the turn of the sixteenth century (died in 1536), Erasmus was very critical. He lambasted the superstitions of current monastic practice, the ritualism and legalism connected with the mass, Scholastic theology (especially its preoccupation with propositions, corollaries, definitions, and conclusions), the worldliness of the Pope (especially his preoccupation with war, money, excommunications, and interdicts), the begging of mendicant friars, clerical concubinage, and so on. The basis of his attacks was a call to return to the source of Scripture in its purity and original meaning for Christian living. The "pagan" classics and church fathers were to serve as an orientation to Scripture.

Erasmus edited and published a number of the works of the Fathers. Against criticism, he continued to advocate the study of the classics. "A sensible reading of the pagan poets and philosophers is a good preparation for the Christian life." He distinguished between the bad morals of the pagans, which are not to be followed, and their many examples of right living. "To break in on" Scripture without the preparation of the classics is "almost sacrilegious." "St. Cyprian has worked wonders in adorning the Scriptures with the literary beauty of the ancients."[6] So guided by the Fathers of the Church, classical studies were taken as a necessary introduction to understanding Christian revelation.

Schooled by the Brethren of the Common Life (a part of late medieval *Devotio moderna*), Erasmus's orientation to theology was away from speculation toward piety. His orientation to Scripture, the source of Christian piety, was toward the example of Jesus. The ethical life, preaching, and teaching of Jesus combine into the philosophy of Christ, the source of reform for everything from the papacy to peasantry.

Erasmus's main interest and work was on the New Testament. His Greek New Testament with critical annotations was a milestone in Reformation work on the Bible. It was used by Luther immediately. Erasmus could be very critical of the people of the Old Testament, for their superstitious and barbarous ways, in comparison with the "good letters" from Greece and Rome. In medieval terms his approach to the New Testament was largely tropological—as in Christ, so in me.

Erasmus's sarcasm against Scholastic theology included his charge of supercilious speculation, especially their use of dialectic. Theology was too intellectually preoccupied with doctrine, and not with its main task—persuading and bringing people to the way of Christ. Practical piety is the point of it all. When contemporary commentators dealt with the New Testament, Erasmus complained that they concentrated only on the literal sense:

> Let me mention another requirement for a better understanding of Holy Scripture [the first being reading Scripture with a clean heart]. I would suggest that you read those commentators who do not stick so closely to the literal sense. The ones I would recommend most highly after St. Paul himself are Origen, Ambrose, Jerome, and Augustine. Too many of our modern theologians are prone to a literal interpretation, which they subtly misconstrue. They do not delve into the mysteries, and they act as if St. Paul were not speaking the truth when he says that our law is spiritual. There are some of these theologians who are so completely taken up with

6 *Enchiridion* (1503) cited in *The Essential Erasmus*, ed. J. P. Dolan (New York: New American Library, 1964) 36.

these human commentators that they relegate what the Fathers had to say to the realm of dreams. They are so entranced with the writings of Duns Scotus that, without ever having read the Scriptures, they believe themselves to be competent theologians. I care not how subtle their distinctions are; they are certainly not the final word on what pertains to the Holy Spirit.[7]

In their theology the Scholastics were too speculative; in their commentaries on Scripture they were too literal. So a leading scholar of the Renaissance calls for a pious reading of the Bible as the source for Christian living.

IV. THE EARLY REFORMATION

A. The Place of the Bible in Theology

The early reformers, for example Luther, Zwingli, Calvin, were very concerned about the place of Bible in everything— Church, theology, and especially preaching. The main point of the Reformation was that the Gospel must be proclaimed. To continue our schematization (monastery—university—printing press), now think pulpit, think of the Evangelical cities (Wittenberg, Zurich, Geneva) where the medium for information was the pulpit (along with the important pamphlets). The Reformation was a movement of the Word: Christ, Scripture, preaching—in that order. They all are the Word of God. The reformers used the printed Word, studied the Word, prayed the Word. Their concern was to bring preaching back into the mass, preaching in the vernacular, and preaching on the text of Scripture. When Luther said that the Church is not a pen-house but a mouth-house, he meant that the good news cannot properly be put in (dead) letters but is to be proclaimed loudly in German.

What the Scholastics separated—theology and commentary on Scripture—the early reformers sought to bring together again, along the lines of *sacra pagina* (minus the monastery). Scripture alone is the sole authority for the Church, the discipline of theology, and the life of faith. The reformers continued the call for the reform of the Church on the basis of Scripture. Every office and activity in the Church falls under the judgment of Scripture. All of theology is contained in Scripture. God has revealed all that we need to know about him in Christ. Calvin is especially strong on the knowledge of God,

---

7　Ibid., 37.

the beginning point of the *Institutes of the Christian Religion*. God is revealed in Scripture, and to see the revelation of God in nature we need the spectacles of Scripture. Theology must be biblical theology; any other kind is human invention.

Scripture is its own authority because it is clear. No other authority is needed to see through its meaning. The early reformers were not concerned about some theory of inspiration. That came later. The Bible is the Word. The reformers were aware of the "critical" discussions among the Humanists about the text, authorship, language, etc. Luther engaged in some of this. The point of the Word is the presence of the Word in Scripture-Church-preaching. The Humanist sense of the distance of Scripture from the present was not accepted. The scholastic separation of theology from Scripture was attacked. The purpose of theology is to serve preaching, the main task of the Church. The vast amount of theological literature from the early Reformation was intended to clear the roadblocks to Scripture and to facilitate the proclamation of that Gospel.

B. The Interpretation of the Bible

The early reformers were premodern; they continued the general medieval understanding of interpretation as commentary, annotation, and exposition. The modern interpreter continues to develop the Humanist perspective of the historical past; thus interpretation in modern time is bridging the gulf between ancient literature and modern thinking. The early reformers continued the monastic approach of total immersion into the thinking and language of Scripture so that there is only one language, one biblical theology.

In their Catholic context, the reformers emphasized that Scripture was its own interpreter (a very old principle, grounded in Scripture itself). Luther argued that the papacy had built a wall of authoritative interpretation around itself so that Scripture could only be read as the papacy saw fit. One late medieval synthesis had it that Scripture is to Tradition as foundation is to interpretation (Occam). Strong in the sixteenth century was the question of an authoritative interpretation of Scripture. The Catholic Council of Trent decreed in midcentury:

> that no one, relying on his own skill, in matters of faith, and of morals pertaining to the edification of Christian doctrine, wresting the Sacred Scriptures to his own senses, presume to interpret the said Sacred Scripture contrary to that sense which holy mother church,

whose it is to judge of the true sense and interpretation of the Holy Scripture, has held and does hold.[8]

For Calvin at this time, the interpretation of Scripture by Scripture alone is aided by the internal testimony of the Holy Spirit. Scripture itself attests to its message and meaning. Christ and the Spirit are at work in the Word. The reformers insisted that postapostolic claims of authoritative interpretation were precisely the reason why the Word of God lost its/his central place in the life of the Church.

The Reformation interpretation of Scripture was caught up in theological polemics. The Humanists used Scripture to attack the Church, but they were not so much interested in the pure doctrines of Scripture as they were in exposing the corruption and folly of the present situation in the light of the piety of Scripture. The early reformers fought for pure doctrine on the basis of Scripture (and the Fathers). The doctrine of justification by faith alone, by grace alone (by Christ alone), was seen as the central doctrine of Scripture. The doctrine of justification by faith is the criterion by which all other doctrines, offices, and practices in the Church are judged. The criteriological priority of justification by faith is established in Scripture. The Church stands or falls, said Luther, on the scriptural teaching of justification. There were other issues, other polemics, but the procedure was the same. Doctrinal reform was forged and pleaded on the basis of Scripture.

C. The Key Figure is Martin Luther

Basic for Luther's understanding of Scripture is his distinction between law and Gospel. The Gospel of Jesus Christ is the fulfillment and end of the Mosaic law. Law and Gospel are in all books of the Bible. The Gospel is the good news that salvation is in Christ alone. Abraham and others saw that Gospel in the promises, believed, and were justified. Luther transposes Augustine's distinction between Old and New Testament as ways of salvation to law and Gospel as ways of salvation. The way of the law is do this ... and don't do that ... . The way of the Gospel is believe ... and it has already been done for you in Christ. The law is command, the Gospel is gift, the gift of forgiveness. When the law commands, failure results because one cannot fulfill the law on one's own power ("The good I would, I do not," said Paul). The law humbles; the Gospel picks up. One cannot be picked up unless

---

8   P. Schaff, *The Creeds of Christendom*, Vol. 2 (New York: Harper, 1919) 83.

one is put down to size. Being brought low (law) and being raised up (Gospel) are the daily struggles of the Christian life, the experience of sin (brought by the law), and the experience of forgiveness (brought by Christ). The distinction between law and Gospel, the doctrine of justification by faith apart from works, and the understanding of the core of Scripture are all the same for Luther.

The center of Scripture for Luther is Christ, present in both the Old and New Testament. Christ is the eternal Word of God, present in Old Testament times in the form of promise, present in New Testament times in the person of Jesus, and present in the Church through Word and sacrament. In all cases, Christ the Word is the effective means of grace (healing salvation for Augustine). The center or core of Scripture is "what drives Christ" (*was Christum treibet*), i.e., what preaches Christ, what promotes or points to Christ. Christ is at the core of God's plan of salvation. God promises through prophets; God delivers in person. All of Scripture leads to Christ, and Christ leads to salvation.

Luther's response to the various senses of meaning in the Middle Ages (fourfold, double-literal) was that Scripture has one simple sense (most often, Christ). The grammatical sense is the simplest sense and is the meaning of the text, the grammatical meaning and the theological meaning are the same. Luther availed himself of Humanist scholarship (and Humanists saw an early ally in Luther) and was a part of a late medieval trend to highlight (once again) the christological meaning of a text. Luther also used allegory, not to establish a doctrine, he said, but to embellish it. He also used the other spiritual senses. Luther on Scripture is often presented as a total break from the medieval world. That came later. (You can take the boy out of the monastery, but you cannot take the monastery out of the boy.) In the area of the senses of meaning, Luther is a part of the medieval trend to call for a return to the letter of the text, and then, in practice, to go on and find other senses of meaning. After all (and all the medievals knew this) the New Testament itself uses allegory.

Luther's distinction is his construction of Scripture as containing a single testament (will, promise) of Christ. God's last and only will and testament is that he would die for our salvation. The promise is the declaration of the will and testament. The death of the God-Man validates his testament. The inheritance is the forgiveness of sins and eternal life. The (new) testament of Christ is eternal. It is played out in time, but there is no development in the eternal. Augustine and the medievals generally saw a development and transformation within and between the Old and New Testament. Luther held that the New Testament is older than the Old because it is the oldest (eternal). The Old Testament begins and ends in time.

We have come a long way (to the sixteenth century). Or have we? What often is seen to be new is not so new after all. The monastery (*sacra pagina*), the university (*sacra doctrina*), the printing press (*sacra littera*), and the pulpit (Holy Gospel) all represent shifts and emphases. The whole enterprise, however, was still "sacred."

PART TWO: THE MODERN CHURCH

In the modern period the historical-critical method dominates most Protestant approaches to Scripture and, since 1943 (*Divino Afflante Spiritu*), also most Catholic approaches. By the middle of the eighteenth century the historical-critical method is in place. One way of picturing the shift that takes place between the medieval approach (including early Reformation) and the modern approach of the later seventeenth and eighteenth century is to consider their views of the relation between the letter and the real, the correlation between the text of Scripture and the events Scripture describes. In the medieval approach the letter of the Bible was read as historical and real; there was never any question that what was said actually took place. Scripture was read as religion, history, geography, liturgy, prayer, and so on. Scripture is God's Word on the subject. The approach of historical criticism is first to question the relation between the letter and the real, then to posit a separation between the two, and finally to see the text as a faith response to a stimulus, an interpretation of an event but not the event itself. What we have in the text are the responses of the communities of faith, not the stimuli. In the nineteenth century it was said that what we have in the New Testament is the Christ of faith and not the Jesus of history. In any case, it came to be perceived in historical criticism that the Bible is the interpretation of facts and not the facts themselves. It was written from faith to (our) faith.

The historical-critical method is concerned about the origin of individual books of the Bible. Moderns study individual books in their life-setting-in-history, using history to understand the Bible, not using the Bible to understand history. Concerned about the books as theological literature and not history, it uses the best critical (objective, analytic) tools available for the study of ancient literature. The modern approach develops some of the humanist interests detailed earlier here—interest in the historical past, the original text, and language.

There were and are various methods within the historical-critical method. These will be detailed by others in this volume. Here the concern will be to trace the rise of the historical-critical method, to detail the shift from medieval-early Reformation to (early) modern approaches (from the middle of the sixteenth century to late eighteenth century). The medievals treated Scripture as the Church's holy book, authored by God. The moderns treat Scripture as a product of human history with the secular tools of historical and literary criticism in order to understand it better in its ancient setting.

Among the elements that contributed to the rise of the historical-critical method, in addition to the separation between the letter and the real, include the following: (1) methodology, (2) Deism and rationalism, (3) the disciplines of biblical introduction and biblical theology, (4) textual criticism, and (5) historical consciousness.

1. Methodology. Theology became interested in the questions of "method" (way of interpretation) in the sixteenth century.[9] In 1555 Nils Hemmingsen, a student of Luther and Melanchthon (especially the latter), published a book *On Methods*, the first part for philosophy, the second for theological method. It was important because of its subject—*methodus*. Earlier in the sixteenth century method as a technical term came into medicine, and in the second half of the century lawyers discussed method. So theology joined the other branches of learning in their concern to tidy up their discipline. Also important is that Hemmingsen brought logic (particularly dialectic) into theology in the discussion of method. For biblical study this meant that discussion of "exegetical method" was carried on in the part on philosophical method, and then carried over and practiced in theology and "exegesis," the actual word being used.

"Exegesis" was widely used in the seventeenth and eighteenth century as the art for interpreting Scripture. Exegesis is an ancient and early modern word, not to be found in ecclesiastical Latin in the ancient or medieval period. Medieval work on Scripture was done in the genre

---

9   K. Hagen, "'De exegetica methodo,' Niels Hemmingsen's *De Methodis* (1555)," *The Bible in the Sixteenth Century*, ed. David Steinmetz ("Duke Monographs in Medieval and Renaissance Studies," Vol. 11; Durham, N.C.: Duke University Press, 1990) 181–96, 252–55.

of annotation and exposition. "Interpretation" meant the translation and explanation of obscure and enigmatic words or dreams. Modern "interpretation" presupposes a historical separation between the interpreter and the text; and in the case of the "methodists," there is the necessity of first discussing the method or way of interpreting before the actual interpretation or exegesis takes place. For Luther, Scripture was its own interpreter. The difference is that the (early) modern becomes conscious of the discipline, or problem, of interpretation.

What comes out of this work on method of interpretation is reflection on the need for an introduction to a biblical book. Already in the third quarter of the sixteenth century, this is found in Hemmingsen and Matthias Flacius Illyricus who is often credited with being the father of modern hermeneutics. In Hemmingsen's methodology four questions need to be asked in an introduction to a particular book of the Bible in order that it will be understood "more explicitly," "more skillfully and correctly," "more easily," or "more clearly." In the introduction the first question of *authorship* determines the authority of the writing. The second, the *occasion*, leads to an understanding of the literary structures. The third, the *status* or principal question of the writing, leads to a perception of the ultimate goal and scope of the whole writing. The fourth is the *method* or order of presentation. Flacius also reflected on the need for an introduction, covering the same four questions, before one begins with the biblical writing itself.

The shift away from the medieval-early Reformation to early modern approaches, somewhere in the middle of the sixteenth century, is seen in the modern focus on the proper order of methodology, introduction, exegesis, in other words, on the problem of interpretation (hermeneutics). For the medievals there was no problem of interpretation. There were rules for reading Scripture, summarized by Luther as prayer, meditation, and experience. For the modern, these become hindrances rather than helps. The modern needs a method to understand. Luther often said he needed more time.

2. **Deism and rationalism.** To discuss the next major advances in the rise of the historical-critical method would mean jumping to the late seventeenth and eighteenth century, with the developments in Deism and rationalism. To understand the attacks from these quarters, generically all rationalists, one needs to see what it was they were attacking, namely, what is known within (Western) Europe and Protestantism as Orthodoxy and Pietism.

In the later sixteenth and seventeenth century the question of method in theology was central in Lutheran and Reformed Orthodoxy. The concern was for pure doctrine in its proper place in the dogmatic system. Scripture is the source for systematic and doctrinal theology. In the give and take with Roman theologians, the Orthodox Protestants developed nuanced theories of the inspiration of Scripture, the only infallible authority. Revealed theology is drawn only from the revealed Word. Scripture is divine, supernatural revelation. It is the very Word of God in its letters, words, doctrines, and precepts. Scripture is the instrumental source of theology: God is the "principle of the being" of theology—the first cause of theology; and Scripture is the "principle of knowing" God—hence the instrument of theology. It is the Orthodox theory of revelation and inspiration that drew the ire of Deism and rationalism.

Their theory of inspiration is known as the dictation theory. The definition of inspiration was that act of God whereby he conveyed the content of what he wanted to be written and the very words expressing that content. It is also the doctrine of plenary inspiration—everything in Scripture was inspired and dictated. If the inspiration of one verse is denied, the inspiration, authority, and infallibility of the whole Bible falls. It is also the doctrine of verbal inspiration—every word. The Holy Spirit actually dictated the very words. The biblical authors were defined as "secretaries," hands of Christ or penmen of the Holy Spirit. It is also the doctrine of inerrancy—the secretaries were kept from error in the writing by the Holy Spirit. The method of inspiration was discussed in much detail. The effect was to secure a supernatural revelation (Scripture) that was inerrant, authoritative, sufficient, clear, and efficacious.

The responses to Orthodoxy in the late seventeenth and eighteenth century were as different as Pietism is from rationalism. And Orthodoxy did not die. Hence a three-ring circus, which is still being played today.

What is a Pietist? He's one who hears the Word.
And lives a holy life in terms of what he's heard.

There were Pietists in seventeenth-century England, Holland, and Germany. They were interested in nontheological study of the Bible for personal experience and holiness. They were more interested in the effect of Scripture than its origin. Scripture was the source of providential guidance for the pious. They encouraged direct access to the Bible without postbiblical interpretation. They were (and are) responsible for the massive distribution of inexpensive editions of the Bible. The developing historical-critical method was of little or no interest. The Pietists were in opposition to the rationalism of the age. A Bible in everyone's hand. For the Orthodox, the Bible was a source book of doctrine; for the Pietist, it was the mirror of holiness.

A rival to Orthodoxy and Pietism, but way over on the secular side of things where the historical-critical method was developing, was Enlightenment Christianity. Enlightenment Christianity included English Deists, Dutch skeptics, French naturalists, and German rationalists—all generically rationalists.

A central concern of the English Deists (rational belief in the deity), who were more influential in France and Germany than in England, was to attack supernatural views of revelation and to argue rather for natural religion—the natural, the rational, and the universal. The Anglican philosopher, John Locke, provoked much controversy with his book *The Reasonableness of Christianity* (1695). Other works, typical and influential, from the Deists were John Toland, *Christianity Not Mysterious* (1696); and Matthew Tindal, *Christianity as Old as Creation* (1730). Reason is the judge of revelation. Belief in the Creator God (Deity) is reasonable; but belief in God's subsequent intervention—prophecies, miracles, atonement—is not reasonable and therefore rejected. The truth of Christianity must be discoverable in all ages. Natural religion is the innate core of all religion. The universality of reason is the only criterion of truth. The authority of the biblical record is doubtful.

What comes then from the Deists, naturalists, and rationalists is that the enlightened are freed from the dogmatics of Orthodoxy and any supernatural theory of inspiration. Doctrines like the divinity of Christ, original sin, atonement, sacraments, and miracles are put aside. The New Testament never meant them to be taken seriously. Views of the supernatural were regarded as superstition. Scripture was interpreted historically and critically. The "unworthy," "impossible," and "unreasonable" parts of Scripture were explained away.

3. **The disciplines of biblical introduction and biblical theology.** By the middle of the eighteenth century (John D. Michaelis, *Introduction to the New Testament*, 1750), the discipline of biblical introduction was in place. We have seen writings about biblical introductions already

in the second half of the sixteenth century with Hemmingsen and Flacius. Their reflection on the need for an introduction in order to prepare the way for understanding the book more clearly is not recognized in secondary literature. Richard Simon, a French Catholic in the seventeenth century, is often credited with being the "forerunner" of the discipline of introduction (1678, *Critical History of the Old Testament*; three volumes on the New Testament, 1689–93).

In this discipline the Bible is treated as ancient literature with a historical setting. To understand a writing is to understand its situation in time and space, the book's setting-in-life. An introduction raises all the questions necessary to understand the book. In one introduction, Michaelis asks the following questions: What type of literature is it? Where is it cited elsewhere? To whom is it written? What was its place in the community? When was it written and in what language? What questions are there about the Greek translation? Who wrote it? What about the literary technique? Is it canonical? What is its content? In this line-up there are ten questions raised before the question of content, because the message is linked to its historical place.

The discipline of introduction presupposes the relativity of each book. Each book is unique unto itself and demands a thorough, objective (i.e., critical) study in order to understand it. Later in the eighteenth century, John Eichhorn developed further the humanist-rationalist introduction (three volumes on the Old Testament, 1780–83). The Old Testament must be studied like any other literature, free from all authorities, dogma, and tradition.

The discipline of biblical theology followed closely on the discipline of biblical introduction. The discipline of biblical theology, seen by some as the crown of biblical scholarship, comes out of the Enlightenment and the critical methodologies we have been detailing. More particularly, Gotthold Lessing's *Education of Mankind* (1780) constructed a view of the Bible which parochialized it as preparatory to the maturation of the human race. The Old Testament came at the stage of the childhood of the race, which was motivated by temporal rewards and punishments (law). The New Testament fits into the adolescence of the race, where one is willing to put up with temporary hardships with the promise of greater (spiritual) rewards later (resurrection). And finally the race matured into adulthood by the time of the Enlightenment, where one lives in the here and now guided by reason alone. In effect, then, the Bible is put in its time and place.

Later in the eighteenth century the concern was to separate biblical theology from dogmatic theology (1758, *The Advantage of Biblical Theology over Scholasticism*; 1787, *The Difference between Biblical Theology and Dogmatic Theology*). Dogmatic theology, perhaps connected to philosophy, could have permanence, while biblical theology is connected to its history. Late eighteenth-century romanticism, with its emphasis on empathy, aided the discipline of biblical theology. Something like today's nostalgia, one could emotionally immerse oneself into the spirit of a past generation. Biblical theology is the theology of a book. If a book has a human situation—authorship, time, audience, language, purpose, content, method—then it also has a particular theology. As there are various books with various historical situations, so there are various books with various theologies. As a result of this eighteenth-century development, there is no such thing as biblical theology in the singular, only biblical theologies in the plural.

Rationalism, connected with Deism, led to the rise of biblical introductions and theologies, as well as with advances in textual criticism, all a part of the developing historical-critical method.

4. **Textual criticism.** Textual criticism as applied to the Bible concerns the analysis of codices, variant readings, earliest manuscript evidence, with both theory and practice. Erasmus's text of the Greek New Testament, the first published in 1516, as mentioned earlier, remained the "critical" edition (*textus receptus*) until well into the nineteenth century. Although the Complutensian Polyglot relied on earlier manuscript evidence, and was actually printed earlier (*New Testament*, 1514) though made public in 1522, and is now regarded as better, it was Erasmus's text, through subsequent editions, that was "received by all" (*textus receptus*) and seemed to have an over three hundred year right to be. Robert Stephanus's text (Paris, 1550), which followed Erasmus (1535 edition), became the *textus receptus* for Britain.[10] The edition of the printing firm, Elzevir (Leiden, 1633), which followed Stephanus, became the *textus receptus* for the Continent. Richard Simon, later in the seventeenth century, engaged in a critical investigation into textual variants. In 1734 Johann Bengel (Tübingen) issued a critical text, not exactly the *textus receptus*, and is regarded as important for modern scientific textual criticism because of his principles (e.g., the more difficult reading is preferred) and theories of manuscript

---

10 Stephanus's 1551 New Testament introduced verse divisions still in use today.

families (groupings of manuscripts). Johann Wettstein's Greek New Testament (1751–52, Amsterdam) contained many important (new) variants. Johann Griesbach (text, 1774–75) agreed with Bengel on the grouping of manuscript families. His theories have lived on in textual criticism (e.g., a reading must have an ancient witness, the shorter as well as the more difficult is preferred).

And so on went the reception of the *textus receptus* until 1831, when Karl Lachmann set it aside and published a text based entirely on ancient manuscripts. In 1881, Westcott and Hort published *The New Testament in the Original Greek*, which has become in effect a new *textus receptus*.

Textual criticism, with the thousands and thousands of manuscripts and the tens of thousands of variant readings, was complicated not only by the discipline itself but also by the tradition (Church) that has received the biblical text. Critical interpretation of the text developed earlier under the aegis of rationalism. Critical rendering of the text itself was slower to develop not only because Erasmus's text was based on late evidence but also because it has seldom been regarded as purely a scientific task.

5. Historical consciousness. Historical consciousness is the dawning of perspective on the past and present, on distance and difference. What developed in Humanism, a sense of antiquity's distance from the present, including Scripture, continued to develop in the early modern period with all the critical methodologies.

Historical consciousness is part and parcel of what we have been discussing. The problem of hermeneutics as the problem of understanding and language is brought into the nineteenth century by Friedrich Schleiermacher and beyond our scope. Hermeneutics as the problem of expression, interpretation, and translation is brought into focus in the early modern period with the rise of the historical-critical method. Key in this development is the separation between text and reader, namely, the consciousness of the separation.

One way of describing this development is to use the distinction between internalization and externalization used in the sociology of knowledge. In the medieval-early Reformation period, as our argument has gone, the reader internalized Scripture, morning, noon, and night. With Humanism—printing, editing, translating, introducing—developed the externalization of the Bible as an ancient text. The concern of methodology is to find the way(s) of bridging the gap between text and interpreter. Once interpretation (with historical consciousness) becomes the focus of biblical study, then the Orthodox needed to set up a system, with logical coherence, to make the Lutheran interpretation the correct one vis-à-vis the Roman and the Reformed traditions. The emancipator from Orthodox dogmatism is always described as reason (and on to rationalism). But Orthodoxy used philosophy, and Pietism contributed another crucial element in the emancipation— the subjective experience of the individual. So this perspective suggests that orthodox philosophy plus pietist individualism helped create the atmosphere for rationalism, where the externalization process is advanced. The Bible is to be treated as any other ancient document, in need of historical introduction and linguistic-literary analysis. The distance and task is enormous.

Biblical theology belongs to the ancient world. Dogmatic theology, conscious of its methodology and distance from Scripture, is part of the Church's tradition, also past. If there is to be a bridge between biblical theology and contemporary thinking, it is the task of hermeneutics (translation, interpretation, understanding) to bridge the gulf— and on to the problems of the nineteenth century.

It is with historical consciousness that problems are perceived that were not before—method, exegesis, critical text, interpretation, and hermeneutics—all with the positive use of reason. The rise of the historical-critical method itself is a historical phenomenon. Its posture today is that it is purely objective and scientific. It did not begin that way nor develop untouched by human historical elements. Practitioners of the historical-critical method may want to use the method on itself and see it in its historical setting, which this essay has tried to set out with pure objectivity. The usual survey of the historical-critical method is described with "advance" language, not totally absent from the foregoing. As one author put it, going through the centuries, "It finally won out!" What did it win, outside of control of academic biblical studies? Did it win any new or better or clearer understanding of the text that was unavailable to St. Augustine, Thomas, Luther, or Calvin?

RECOMMENDED READINGS

Aldridge, John W. *The Hermeneutic of Erasmus*. Richmond: John Knox, 1966. Basic level; concentrates on the philosophy of Christ, erudition, and philology.

Cambridge History of the Bible, 3 volumes. Cambridge: University Press, 1963–70. Reference volumes by specialists that cover the early period (I), medieval (II), and modern (III).

Chau, Wai-Shing. *The Letter and the Spirit: a History of Interpretation from Origen to Luther*. New York: Peter Lang, 1995. A survey of historical approaches to Scripture, focusing on law and Gospel in the Pauline epistles.

Grant, Robert. *A Short History of the Interpretation of the Bible*. New York: Macmillan, 1963; 2nd edition with David Tracy, Philadelphia: Fortress, 1984. Basic introduction that starts with the Bible itself.

Hagen, Kenneth. *Luther's Approach to Scripture as seen in his "Commentaries" on Galatians*. Tübingen: J. C. B. Mohr (Paul Siebeck), 1993. Places Luther in the context of the whole history of biblical interpretation.

Hahn, Herbert F. *The Old Testament in Modern Research*. Philadelphia: Fortress Press, 1954/66. Extensive survey of Old Testament criticism; strong on the moderns.

Kooiman, Willen J. *Luther and the Bible*. Translated by John Schmidt. Philadelphia: Muhlenberg, 1961. Introductory level aimed at a broad coverage of many facets.

Kümmel, Werner G. *The New Testament: The History of the Investigation of its Problems*. Translated by S. M. Gilmour and H. C. Kee. Nashville: Abingdon, 1972. Extensive survey of New Testament criticism; several primary sources. Emphasis on the moderns.

de Lubac, Henri. *The Sources of Revelation*. Translated by L. O'Neill. New York: Herder and Herder, 1968. An abridgment of his monumental work in French on patristic and medieval exegesis; emphasis on the spiritual understanding of Scripture.

Smalley, Beryl. *The Study of the Bible in the Middle Ages*. Oxford: Blackwell, 1952. Scholarly and readable history from the Fathers of the Church to the friars of the thirteenth century.

Stuhlmacher, Peter. *Historical Criticism and Theological Interpretation of Scripture*. Translated by R. Harrisville. Philadelphia: Fortress, 1977. Short overview from the ancients to the twentieth century; reconstruction of the current dilemma.

WHAT DID THE TERM *COMMENTARIUS* MEAN
TO SIXTEENTH-CENTURY THEOLOGIANS?

INTRODUCTION

The *Problemstellung* for this study was the question of the meaning of *commentarius* in sixteenth-century *exegetica*. Initially this question was put to Luther's so-called "commentaries on Galatians" (1516-1538). While modern editors considered Luther's work to be a "commentary," it became clear to me that *commentarius* for Luther in these works had a special, particular, and different meaning, namely, *enarratio*.

So then the question was put to other so-called commentaries in the sixteenth century—What did their work on Scripture entail? What did *commentarius* mean in sixteenth-century theology?

I discovered that there was no uniform understanding of what a *commentarius* on Scripture meant or entailed in the sixteenth century, which only made the question for this study more interesting if not also more complicated and difficult.

Occasional references to the "commentaries" of others were made by Luther, Cajetan, Hemmingsen, Sasbout, the Rhemes NT, and Bèze.[1] These references to the works of others as "commentaries" are

---

1 In the 1519 Dedication to his "Commentary on Galatians," Luther says his work "is not so much a commentary as a testimony of my faith in Christ." He also distinguishes his work from the "commentaries" of Erasmus. — Cajetan refers to his own work in the Explicit as "Commentariorum Thome de Vio Cajetani Cardinalis sancti Xysti ... finis" (p. 361, dated 1. Iunij 1529). He refers to what Jerome says about Is. 6 as "Commenting on Is. 6." Cajetan views all those who offer an opinion on the Pauline authorship of the Epistle to the Hebrews as "commenting." — Nils Hemmingsen, in his discussion of exegetical method, includes a small section on the Use of Commentaries (*De methodis libri duo*, [Rostock, 1555], p. 140; cf. my Paper at Second International Colloquy on the History of Biblical Exegesis in the 16th Century, Duke University, September 1982, entitled "'De exegetica methodo': Nils Hemmingsen's *De Methodis* [1555]").— Adam Sasbout, "Epistolae D. Pauli ad Hebraeos expositio fratris Adami Sasbout," *Biblicus Apparatus*, ed. R. Walton (Zürich: Bodmer, 1673), pp. 533–534.

to works which were not always entitled Commentary (e.g. we know Chrysostom's work as Homilies, and Erasmus's as Annotations; the reference to Calvin by the Rhemes NT is to a work entitled Commentary). I found no explicit discussion of the meaning of the term *commentarius* anywhere. Perhaps I could conclude that I could not discover a uniform understanding of *commentarius*, since there was none.

In an effort to find perspective elsewhere in sixteenth-century exegetica, that is, to find out what a non-"commentary" entailed, other kinds of work on Scripture, e.g. *enarratio, annotatio, explicatio*, were consulted.[2] Again, I found variety and difference of form.

— *Rhemes New Testament* (Rheims: J. Fogny, 1582), p. 610.— Théodore de Bèze, "Epistola Pauli ad Hebraeos," *Novum D. N. Jesu Christi testamentum* (Geneva: R. Estienne, 1556–1557), f. 289r. Lefèvre d'Etaples refers to his own "commentariorum libri" (in Epistle 96, Eugene F. Rice *The prefatory Epistles* New York, [Columbia University], 1972, p. 298).— Bullinger entitles his work on Hebrews "commentarius" and in the "Prefatio" he refers to it as "my commentary" (Zürich, 1532, p. 490). He entitles his work on the Acts of the Apostles "commentariorum libri VI" (Zürich, 1535). Bullinger discusses "De commentariis" as guides to Bible study in his *Studiorum ratio— Studienanleitung*, edited by Peter Stotz (Zürich: Theologischer Verlag, 1987), I,108–111. — Various editions of Œcolampadius on the prophets contain the word Commentary—in the plural. *In Isaiam Prophetam Hypomnematon, hoc est, Commentariorum* ... (Basel, 1525). *In Heremiam Prophetam Commentariorum libri tres Ioannis Œcolampadii* (Argentinae, 1533). *Commentarii omnes in libros prophetarum* (Geneva, 1558). — Note that the word *Commentarius* is used in Zwingli's *Commentarius de vera et falsa religione* of 1525 (CR 90 (3) 590–912). In his ad lectorem, Megander praises Zwingli's "expositio brevis" on Hebrews. In so doing, he says, "It seems unnecessary to expand on these things since all things are learned from the commentaries of Bullinger, my beloved brother and fellow priest" (cf. my *Hebrews Commenting from Erasmus to Bèze, 1516–1598* ["Beiträge zur Geschichte der biblischen Exegese," vol. 23; Tübingen: J.C.B. Mohr [[Paul Siebeck]], 1981], p. 40).

2 The *Annotationes* of Bugenhagen (Nuremberg, 1524) are very selective and discursive. — The *Elucidatio* of Titelmans (Antwerp, 1528) consists of short paraphrases of the text printed in the margin (*elucido*, according to Lewis and Short, means to light, to enlighten).— Le Grand (Le P. Nicolas). *In divi Pauli Epistolam ad Hebraeos enarratio a fratre Nicolao Grandis* (Paris, 1537). The work is an anthology of the authorities. — Estienne's *Breves variarum tralationum annotationes* (Paris, 1541) are brief indeed. — Gasparo Contarini's *Scholia in epistolas divi Pauli* (Paris 1571) are so short and selective that they tend in the direction of a treatise on Christ, faith, justification and

What did *commentarius* mean in Latin originally? in the early church? in the Middle Ages? Was *commentarius* a classical form? What do modern authors say about "commentary"? A check of contemporary descriptions of the form "commentary" in the sixteenth century disclosed only abstractions and generalities.

Unable to find a concrete answer to the original *Problemstellung* in modern scholarship and in the sixteenth century, I turned to the Middle Ages.

Among the medievals, I found three different approaches to Scripture, and, once I gave up my effort to define *Commentarius* in the singular for the sixteenth century, I realized that these three differing medieval approaches continued into the sixteenth century. I had been searching for something quite elusive; in fact, at one stage I described my research as "In search of the elusive 'commentary'"; I wondered "When did it become the standard form?" My answer, after searching for patterns, frequency of usage, trends, forms, before, during, and after the sixteenth century, was that a variety of commentary forms existed from the beginning of Christianity to today.[3]

My conclusion and thesis for this study is to suggest that the three medieval forms of Scriptural interpretation I call sacred page, sacred doctrine, and sacred letter serve as a clue to the variety of forms of biblical interpretation in the sixteenth century. In other words, the variety and differences of form among sixteenth-century biblical interpreters can be traced, if not attributed, to the variety and differences among the medievals. The sixteenth century did not exist in isolation; neither, as we will see, was it a carbon copy of what went before.

---

their interrelation. — Johannes Gagnaeus's scholia (Paris, 1539) followed the style of the *Glossa ordinaria*. — Jean Benoît, *Novum testamentum ... scholiis* (Paris 1543). The scholia consist of very brief *marginalia*. — Claude Guilliaud's work was entitled *Collatio in omnes divi Pauli apoostoli epistolas* (Lyon, 1543). — In Veit Dietrich's *Summaria* (Frankfurt, 1545), whole chapters were summarized.

3   Gerhard Lohfink in the Berkeley Colloquy on «The Commentary Hermeneutically Considered» lists eight types of commentary («Kommentar als Gattung,» *Protocol of the colloquy of the Center for Hermeneutical Studies in Hellenistic and Modern Culture* [Berkeley, 1978], pp. 17–18). For a discussion of the forms of commentary in antiquity, cf. Karlfried Froehlich, "Bibelkommentare-Zur Krise einer Gattung," *Zeitschrift für Theologie und Kirche* 84 (1987), pp. 465–492.

In effect, I have not answered my initial question, the technical and explicit meaning of the word *commentarius* in the sixteenth century. I have rather broadened the question; namely, to the form(s) of biblical commentary in the sixteenth century.

To put my findings in other words, the search for the meaning of *commentarius* in the "commentaries" on Scripture revealed no uniformity of meaning but, rather, variety and differences. The uniformity I discovered was in terms of the revising and nuancing of medieval forms, i.e., the variety and differences were the continuation and revision of medieval forms.

To put the matter most simply, I could make sense out of the sixteenth-century commentaries only when I considered the sixteenth-century "commentary" in the context of medieval forms of biblical interpretation.

Commentarius in Latin

My first instinct when working on new material is to look up the terms, in this case *Commentarius [commentor]*, in Lewis and Short's Dictionary. (1) Originally, *Commentarius* (sc. volumen) was "a notebook, sketch-book, memorandum." (2) "As the title of a book on any subject, but esp. historical, which is only sketched down or written without care (mostly in plur.)," *commentarius* meant "a sketch, a paper, memoirs, a commentary." (3) Commentary meant exposition, brief explanation, annotation[4]; in law, a brief; the day book of an accounting officer; a collection of examples or citations; or a pupil's notes of a lecture. *Commentor* (atus sum) (classically) meant "to consider thoroughly, meditate, think over, study, deliberate, weigh, prepare one's self mentally."

Commentarius in the Vulgate

Also an early instinct of mine is to consult a Vulgate concordance.[5] *Commentarius* is found in 2 Reg 8.16, 2 Reg 20.24, 3 Reg 4.3, 1 Par 18.15. These are all references to Josaphat I. "Josaphat, filius Ahilud, erat a

---

4   *an-noto* meant "to put a note to" something, "to write down" or "to note" something, and finally, "to comment on" (post Augustine).

5   *Concordantiae bibliorum sacrorum vulgatae editionis* (Prati: ex officina Fratrum Giachetti, 1861).

commentariis," which the Douay translates "recorder" or "chancellor." The upshot of this is that Solomon retained David's recorder [=Jehoshaphat]: The Jerusalem Bible on 1 K 4, regarding Solomon's officials, notes the following: "The recorder (lit. 'remembrancer') is head of the diplomatic service and intermediary between king and people."[6]

THE "COMMENTARY" IN SECONDARY LITERATURE

Secondary literature tends to use the word commentary non-technically to describe all types of biblical exegesis. What follows in this section are explicit descriptions of "Commentary."

Was commentary a classical (possibly rhetorical) form? No. According to "The four position papers" at the Berkeley Colloquy on the commentary hermeneutically considered, it never existed in a single form, in any culture, at any time (Berkeley 1978).

"The Gnostics invented the form of Scriptural exegesis which we call the Commentary, even though Origen greatly expanded, developed and popularized it."[7] Regarding the important Origen, Quasten distinguishes between his sco,lia (= brief explanations of difficult passages), o`mili,ai (homilies), and to,moi [to,moj] (commentaries). Quasten describes the commentary in Origen, written to give a scientific exegesis, as a "strange mixture of philological, textual, historical, etymological notes and theological and philosophical observations."[8]

Jerome and others (followed by Erasmus) describe a commentary as involving two things, (1) discussion of the interpretation of others and (2) the clarification of difficult texts. In his *Commentary on John*, Theodore of Mopsuestia states, "I judge the exegete's task to be to explain words that most people find difficult; it is the preacher's task to

---

6   Joha I ("herald Joah" in the Jerusalem Bible) reads, "Joahe, filius Asaph, a commentariis" (Joha I is discussed throughout 4.Reg 18 and Isai 36; cf. also 2.Par 34.8). Also in the Vulgate are the following: 1 Esdr 4.15: et invenies scriptum in commentariis; 1 Esdr 6.2: talisque scriptum erat in eo commentaries; Esth 12.4: quod gestum erat scripsit in commentaries; 2.Mac 2.13: commentariis Nehemiae haec eadem.

7   R. P. C. Hanson, "Biblical Exegesis in the Early Church," *The Cambridge History of the Bible* (Cambridge: University Press, 1970), I.419.

8   J. Quasten, *Patrology* (Westminster, Maryland: The Newman Press, 1953), II.45–48.

reflect also on words that are perfectly clear and to speak about them."[9] Jerome on the purpose of a commentary: "To explain what has been said by others and make clear in plain language what has been written obscurely," and Scripture is full of obscurities.[10]

Thomas Reist discusses Bonaventure as biblical commentator with a "Reflection on the Bonaventurian Biblical Hermeneutic." He observes the following:

> From the very beginning, the Seraphic Doctor's approach to the Scriptures is eminently practical; the Scriptures are ordered to the salvation of mankind and to eternal happiness. They proceed from God with the purpose of dwelling in the heart of the listener or reader so as to bring about his return to God. Thus, all of scripture's modes (e.g. narration, exhortation, threat, etc.) are merely descriptions of the ways in which an individual might be moved from evil to do good.[11]

The importance of this reflection is that much of commenting on the Scriptures (note the plural) in the sixteenth century was itself reflecting on the reflections refracted within the sacred writings themselves.[12]

Beryl Smalley lists *commentarius* along with several other types of Scriptural exposition deriving from the schools and says that usage was not consistent:

> Here a word of warning is necessary to the student who embarks on the study of scholastic or pre-scholastic commentaries. He must not hope to find a precise terminology for the various types. He will meet *commentaria, commentariola, expositiones, glosae, glosulae, lectiones, lecturae* and *postillae. Lectiones* and *lecturae* ... denote

---

9   M. F. Wiles, "Theodore of Mopsuestia as Representative of the Antiochene School," *The Cambridge History of the Bible*, I.491.

10   R. P. C. Hanson, "Biblical Exegesis in the Early Church," *The Cambridge History of the Bible*, I.535.

11   Thomas Reist, *Saint Bonaventure as a Biblical Commentator* (New York: University Press, 1985), p. 45.

12   Also recently appeared the two volume work of G. R. Evans on *The Language and Logic of the Bible* (Cambridge: University Press, 1984, 1985). Never far from my reach when the matter of *lectio, disputatio, predicatio* comes up for review (as in the case of Evans) is the work of Beryl Smalley. When the matter of "Exegesis and the theory of signification" is discussed (Evans again), I turn to my own work (cf. my paper on Hemmingsen at the last meeting of this group in Durham).

lecture courses. "Gloss" came to have the increasingly specialized meaning of a short comment inserted into the margin or between the lines of the text or of a collection of glosses of this kind. *Postilla,* a word of uncertain derivation, appears in the thirteenth century and normally means a commentary which originated in the classroom, but can be used more widely. "Exposition" is a very general term. "Commentary" is not very usual. It can refer to patristic; but it was customary to refer to the Father quoted *in originali,* meaning his original commentary (understood) as distinct from an excerpt.[13]

"To avoid confusion," Smalley decided to distinguish between "lecture courses" and "commentaries" to cover all exposition deriving from the schools.

It was in 1511, writes Denis Janz, and thus before the beginning of the reformation controversies, that Cajetan completed his commentary on the *prima secundae.* Thus, unlike Konrad Kœllin's commentary, Cajetan's could in fact stand on its own as "an independent theological treatise."[14]

The introduction to Erasmus's *Paraphrases on Romans and Galatians* discusses the origin and character of the Paraphrase in itself and in relation to Commentary. Payne, Rabil, and Smith are precise about paraphrase but conjectural about commentary.

Their definition of a paraphrase is as follows: it is to clarify a text by rephrasing what the author says in the paraphraser's own words; it is a continuous narrative.[15] It differs from a commentary; a commentary is an interrupted narrative. Erasmus can blur this distinction between a paraphrase and commentary by referring to the paraphrase as a kind of commentary. Erasmus "probably" understood a commentary as more akin to a critical analysis of the text both philological and theological.

Two other differences between a paraphrase and a commentary are that "A paraphrase does not attempt to clarify all the difficulties of the text of the New Testament," "Nor does a paraphrase summarize

---

13   Beryl Smalley, "The Bible in the Medieval Schools," *The Cambridge History of the Bible* (Cambridge: University Press, 1969), II.203–204.

14   Denis Janz, *Luther and late medieval thomism: a study in theological anthropology* (Waterloo, Ontario: Wilfrid Laurier University Press, 1983), p. 126.

15   "The Paraphrases of Erasmus: Origin and Character" *Collected Works of Erasmus* 42 (Toronto: University of Toronto Press, 1984), p. xv.

(or even mention explicitly) the opinions of previous commentators"; "presumably" for Erasmus a commentary does these two tasks.[16]

Erasmus himself, I note in the original 1516 Preface, distinguishes between "short annotations" and "commentaries," which the editors of CWE say implies "a difference between philological notes and continuous theological exposition."[17]

A word about Calvin. The title of most if not all of Calvin's individual works on the New Testament are "commentarii." T. H. L. Parker is surprised that Calvin does not have Renaissance perspective on the distance between text and contemporary time.[18] Parker situates Calvin in the Renaissance and, as Calvin himself says, in the flow of Melanchthon, Bullinger, and Bucer.

In his work on Calvin's OT commentaries, Parker distinguishes between commentary, lecture, and sermon. Parker says that except for the works on the *Mosaic Books, Psalms,* and *Joshua,* Calvin's so-called commentaries on the OT are not in fact genuine commentaries but are expository lectures or sermons: "by 'commentary' we mean a work written or dictated by an author."[19] In the section on "Characteristics of the three forms," the forms of commentary, lecture, and sermon all give "exegesis" and "exposition." When considering of the form of commentary, Parker (blandly) gives: translation, theme, linguistic exegesis, possibly "an elucidation of historical, geographical, or cultural fact, or it may simply be the explanation of some point in a narrative." References to previous commentators are often made anonymously, the intention being "to keep the reader's mind on the matter in hand instead of letting it stray to a particular person." "Finally, he will usually apply the message of the verse to his readers."[20]

---

16   *Ibid.,* p. xvi.

17   *Ibid.*

18   *Calvin's New Testament Commentaries* (Grand Rapids: Eerdmans, 1971), p. 91. Parker follows a typical pattern in Renaissance studies, namely, that of treating ones favorite figure, Calvin in this case, as the best thinker of the age; thus Parker considers Melanchthon as one-sided, Bucer as different, but Calvin as the best of all worlds (pp. 52–55).

19   *Calvin's Old Testament Commentaries* (Edinburgh: T. & T. Clark, 1986), p. 9.

20   *Ibid.,* pp. 34–37.

Conclusion to secondary literature
Summary of the various descriptions of commentary
with reference to particular figures:
While the commentary is not a classical (rhetorical) form, for Origen it is a mixture of philological, textual, historical, etymological notes, and theological and philosophical observations.

For Jerome, it is a discussion of the interpretation of others and the clarification of difficult texts.

Scripture's modes (e.g. narration, exhortation, threat, etc.), for Bonaventure, are merely descriptions of the ways in which an individual might be moved from evil to do good .

Commentarius, for the Schoolmen, is the original exposition of a Father.

It is an independent theological treatise (Cajetan).

In Erasmus, a commentary is an interrupted narrative, a critical analysis of the text both philological and theological to clarify all the difficulties of the text and to summarize the opinions of previous commentators; it is continuous theological exposition.

For Calvin, commentary is a work written or dictated by an author; it provides thematic and linguistic exegesis. Historical, geographical, or cultural details may be considered. References to previous commentators are often made anonymously in order to keep the reader's mind on the text. He usually applies the message of the verse to the reader.

Evaluation:
Such descriptions of the "Commentary" in the tradition, while generally true in their particular applications and generalities, did not provide sufficient help for understanding the variety of commentaries in the sixteenth century—in most instances, they did not intend to do so. With the exception of Quasten's description of Origin's commentaries as notes and observations, I find that none of these descriptions apply uniformly to every instance of *commentarius* in the sixteenth century, or to put it the other way around, each commentary is an exception to one or more of these generalities.

Every attempt at generalization, including my own, did not prove fruitful in my attempt to define or understand the commentary in the sixteenth century. There is no guide to The Commentary in the Sixteenth Century (that I know of).

My own conclusion is that one cannot posit trends or developments or make any generality about the commentary as the dominant or typical form of Scriptural interpretation. Furthermore, it would be difficult to show that there was one form of commentary, just on the basis of *commentary* in the title,[21] to say nothing about the other titles. My instinct, namely that each work on Scripture was unique, turned out to be true.

In titles the use of the term *commentary* in the plural (*commentarii, commentaria, commentariola*) as well as in the singular I find positively fascinating. We are accustomed to referring to *a* commentary on *a* book. Among the medievals and continuing into the sixteenth century, the sacred writings were a collection of the manifold mysteries of God (just as *traditio* can means traditions in the plural). We tend to refer to a work as *a* commentary, whereas in the sixteenth century, when in the plural, it is less *a* commentary and more a series of notes. Thus what we think of as a commentary turns out to be a series of comments on the many ways that God has spoken and acted. I think the difference is that when referring to a commentary we presume that there is a need to make sense out of the biblical text, to provide some kind of unity or coherence that is not immediately apparent; that is, it is shrouded in some kind of enigma that requires the exegetes' expertise to unravel. In the sixteenth century, many of the biblical texts were taken as clear and full of sense(s); the unity and coherence of Scripture was seen as grounded in God, not the exegete. Perhaps the difference is not so great, but there is a difference in my mind between *a commentary* and *comments*.[22]

Among works on Scripture, then, can we find some similarity or uniformity between or among them? This must be answered in the negative on the basis of secondary literature and the sixteenth-century material alone, and can only be answered in the positive in the light of medieval approaches to Scripture.

---

21   My own check of titles on Hebrews in the sixteenth century compared with the first half of the seventeenth century indicates that the use of *commentary* in the title does not increase or decrease (perhaps half of the titles in a given time frame are given as *commentary*).

22   Consider the title of my book *Hebrews Commenting from Erasmus to Bèze*. It was the title suggested originally by an English publisher. While it is not a good idea to use a noun as an adjective, it seems acceptable in sloppy American, particularly if sanctioned by a Brit! Twice in my paragraph on Cajetan I use "commenting" regarding Jerome and all the others. Perhaps rather than *a commentary*, *comments* or *commenting* is closer to what several of these biblical scholars were doing.

MEDIEVAL PERSPECTIVE[23]

From early times through the Reformation, theology was practised as the discipline of the sacred page (*sacra pagina*). The monastery became the place and the monks' daily liturgy was the context, for the practice of theology. Holy Writ is the sacred page; the canon of Scripture was the rule of faith. The goal of life for the medieval pilgrim (*viator*) as well as the final goal of theology was to get home, home to God, home to the Trinity (in Augustine's words).

The sacred page was seen as directly from God, about God, and for the pilgrim's journey to God. The sacred page bore the imprint of God just as the tablets of stone were carved by the fingernails of God. Theology as commentary served the purposes of the sacred page. Theology, whether expressed in doctrine, liturgy, or catechesis, was the discipline of the sacred page. Page etymologically meant *pago, pango, pax, pagina*. The covenant, peace, and the page came from the direct initiative of the Lord God of history. The sacred page was the record of God's creation and redemption. All theological matters were matters of the page, and matters of the page were matters of God. Theology, Scripture, Commentary, and God were bound up in one world and were focused on the sacred page.

From the perspective of Augustine, the understanding of theology as the discipline of the sacred page goes back to David and Isaiah, continued by Paul and John. The discipline is rigorous (disciplined); its identity and purpose is clear.

The rise of Scholastic theology in the twelfth century was linked to the discipline of dialectic and its use of the question. The discipline of Scholastic theology practised in the schools (universities) was the discipline of faith seeking understanding, the understanding of the faith. The seeking was done by posing problems in the form of question, distinction, and conclusion. The problems concerned the content of the *doctrina* of the church. Thus the goal was understanding the *doctrina*, and the means was the question. Theology was concerned with sacred doctrine.

With the Universities in the twelfth century, theology shifted to sacred doctrine (*sacra doctrina*). The Schoolmen wrote Bible commentaries, and they also wrote sacred theology. St. Thomas Aquinas, for example, wrote commentaries that were along traditional lines of

---

23   K. Hagen, "The History of Scripture in the Church," *The Bible in the Churches* (New York: Paulist Press, 1985), pp. 3–18.

providing comments on the sacred page. His theology took the form of a *Summa*, a form different and separate from biblical commentary. The form of *summa* was common in other disciplines as well at the time, providing a summary of the discipline (of Christian doctrine in the case of theology). Theology used Scripture but it was not exegetical theology. The first question in St. Thomas' *Summa* concerned the nature of Christian doctrine.

Scholastic theology was based on the method of *quaestio* (question) and dialectic. To be sure, the final goal of theology was still the beatific vision. The shift from sacred page to sacred doctrine is the shift from locating the substance of theology in Scripture to locating the substance in doctrine.

With the printing press and the scholarship of the Christian humanists, theology shifted to the sacred letter as literature. Theology was seen not as the monk's work of prayer and praise nor as the professor's academic questions and propositions but as the educative task of reviving the classics, both pagan and Christian. The study of the sacred letter of Scripture was to lead not so much to God as to a better society, church, education, and government. Theology as the study of the philosophy of Christ (Erasmus) was to lead to piety, morality, and justice.

The rise of historical-critical methods, during the sixteenth to nineteenth centuries, continued Humanistic methods. These methods included the discipline of biblical introduction, biblical theology, and, finally, biblical hermeneutics.

It seems to me that a key, if not *the* key, to the rise and triumph of the various historical-critical methodologies was the growing consciousness of the distance between the biblical world and the contemporary world. Such a consciousness arose among the Humanists and became a major presupposition in the nineteenth-century discipline of hermeneutics. That such a gap or distance was perceived in Humanist literature and art is generally accepted in the scholarly literature.

The goal of the historical-critical method is to understand the letter of the original text. The goal of sacred doctrine is to understand the faith of the church. The goal of the sacred page is God (the Trinity).

These approaches to the sacred page, sacred doctrine, and sacred letter continued in the early and late Reformation. Luther continued the discipline of the sacred page minus monastic discipline. The Council of Trent and Lutheran Orthodoxy continued the discipline of sacred doctrine. Melanchthon approached Scripture as sacred letter (literature).

THE FORM(S) OF BIBLICAL COMMENTARY IN THE SIXTEENTH CENTURY

The following seeks to provide some perspective on the various types of "Commentaries" (forms of biblical comments and commenting) in the sixteenth century on the basis of the medieval approaches of sacred page, sacred doctrine, and sacred letter. It seeks to line up differences in the sixteenth century among those who continued the tradition of commenting on the *sacra pagina* (Luther, Calvin, Arboreus), those who approached Scripture for its sacred doctrine (Hemmingsen, Flacius), and those who advanced humanistic methods.

Erasmus worked on Scripture as sacred literature (the paraphrase was aimed at discovering the *philosophia Christi*). Work on Scripture as sacred literature can be seen among those who wrote notes, annotations, and the like (Zanchius, Camerarius, Sasbout, Rhemes NT). The focus on Scripture as sacred letter, following Erasmus's lead, is a concentration on the words, their etymology, their equivalents in Greek, Hebrew, Latin. Beza's *Annotations* are a good example of this approach.

MELANCHTHON

Melanchthon followed Erasmus's use (*usus*) of Scripture for its "sacred letters."

The Preface in the 1519 edition of Luther's *Commentary on Galatians*[24] was written by Melanchthon under the pseudonym of Otho Germanus.

Melanchthon praises Luther's *commentary* on Galatians because it treats the *locus* on Justification so diligently.[25] The problem with this evaluation is that it is not completely accurate. At least Luther, it seems, did not think of the work as a "commentary."

---

24   *In epistolam Pauli ad Galatas, F. Martini Lutheri Augustiniani commentarius* (Leipzig: Melchior Lotther, 1519). Both the Preface by Otho Germanus and the Nachwort by Paulus Commodus Brettanus were identified as being authored by Melanchthon in the *Supplementa Melanchthoniana* VI.1.59, edited by Otto Clemen (Leipzig, 1926), and *Melanchthons Briefwechsel*, I:Regesten 1–1109 (1514–1530), edited by Heinz Scheible (Stuttgart, 1977) number 54, p. 60. The WA accepts the Preface by Otho Germanus (1519).

25   *In epistolam Pauli ad Galatas Martini Lutheri commentarius* (Wittenberg: Joh. Grünenberg, 1523).

In his Dedication Luther says that his work is "not so much a commentary as a testimony of my faith in Christ."[26] The question of whether Luther's *commentary* is a commentary, and in what sense, is a question that I deal with in another manuscript. Melanchthon thought it was a commentary. The publishers of the editions of 1519, 1523, and following gave Luther's work the title of *Commentarius*. This has been followed in the modern critical editions and translations. One simply cannot assume that a commentary means the same thing in every age. Luther's commentary is not the same as a Humanist's commentary nor the same as a modern commentary. So, to cast Luther's work into Melanchthon's Humanist world by calling it a commentary and describing its content in Humanistic Latin[27] is perhaps not accurate.

To praise Luther's commentary because it treats a certain *locus* is a way of casting Luther into a mold other than his own. *Locus* for Melanchthon means place, a place in a system comprised of topics that all have their proper place. *Locus* in Melanchthon's mind is connected with reason (*ratio*), order, method (*methodus*), system, and use (*usus*): "Unless you seek the *ratio* for the *locus* in the Scriptures, I do not see in what *usus* you read the sacred letters," says Melanchthon using language from Erasmus's treatise of 1516, *On Method*.[28] For Melanchthon, then, Scripture contains an ordered system of topics, and in the following work of Luther on Galatians, says Melanchthon in his Preface, Luther treats one of these topics so diligently.

The difficulty with Melanchthon's description is that *locus* is an abstraction which superimposes Melanchthon's ordered system on Scripture. For Luther *locus* means *textus*, a particular text or passage in Galatians. For Luther any use of Scripture was "to be with Christ." Melanchthon's use of Scripture was involved with order or method or system, all of which in the Medieval world were connected to Dialectic and Logic. Rolf Schäfer describes Melanchthon's *Commentary on Romans* as rhetorical and dialectical.[29]

---

26   1519, folio A iiiii verso.

27   The Humanistic Latin of Erasmus follows a different grammar. It is the grammar of classical Latin. The point here is that by using Erasmus' grammar, Melanchthon takes Luther out of his grammar and introduces Luther's work in a light different from what it is.

28   Melanchthon, Preface, 1523.

29   "Melanchthons Hermeneutik im Römerbriefkommmentar von 1532," *Zeitschrift für Theologie und Kirche* 60 (1963), pp. 216–35.

Melanchthon was cited above as saying that one should find the reason and order in the "sacred letters." To see Scripture as a letter is vastly different from Luther's view of Scripture as a pagina (page). For Melanchthon and Erasmus, Scripture was seen as classical, sacred literature along with classical, pagan literature. The pagan classics were seen as preparation for the sacred letters, both regarded as important for philosophy and morality.

The Preface of Otho Germanus is an effort in 1519 to introduce Luther. It is conceivable that Melanchthon is trying to package Luther in a way that will present him favourably to the Humanists.

LUTHER

Luther was concerned to revive the earlier, patristic and early-medieval approach to theology as the discipline of the sacred page. This can be seen in the rules he suggested (in 1539) to be followed in the practice of theology: prayer, meditation, and temptation (experience). The discipline of theology was the reading of Scripture. The rules themselves are found in the Psalter.

If Luther does not consider his work "so much a commentary," what does Luther consider his work on Galatians to be? On Gal. 1.9-10, Luther gives an answer; it has to do with the particular vocabulary of theology as "*Enarratio.*"

Editors of the *American Edition of Luther's Works* and the *Weimarer Ausgabe* have a different and necessarily modern understanding of what a commentary is. Accordingly they view Luther's work on Galatians from 1519 to 1538 as five different editions of Pauline exegesis. They compare the different editions, supposing them to be literary interpretations. As literature, such expressions as the following are appropriate: expanded, shorter, longer, revised, abbreviated; or, there is progress between 1519 and 1523. These descriptions put Luther into a world other than his own. In their editorial practice, Luther is pictured as an exegete who is interpreting an ancient text. Therefore, where he is wrong, he should be corrected. Such practice reflects a modern presupposition about what interpretation is; namely, a kind of procedure that can be corrected by supplying a supposedly more accurate Scriptural reference.

If Luther's work is not a nineteenth-century commentary, what is it? Does Luther himself provide an answer to what his work is? Yes.

It is possible to get at Luther from his own perspective rather than from the perspective of the nineteenth-century editors.

Read him in the original!

In the 1519 Dedication, when Luther says his work "is not so much a commentary as a testimony of my faith in Christ," he distinguishes his work from the "commentaries" of Erasmus.

The word that Luther uses instead of "commentary" is the verb "*enarrare*" or the noun "*enarratio*."[30] "*Enarrare*" for which there is no simple English equivalent means to speak, tell, or set forth in detail. A public context is connoted. It means, thus, to speak in public in detail. "*Enarratio*" includes "*narratio*," which means to narrate, but involves both "detail" and "public." "*Enarrare*" means to take out (to narrate) and to apply; in other words, to take the theology out of the text and to apply it in public.

What is it that Luther says he is talking about and applying? The one doctrine, truth, grace, Christ. It is the very substance of theology contained in the sacred page.

To see Luther's work as a modern commentary in terms of its length, revisions, and progress would be equivalent to saying that Luther revised the doctrine of the Trinity, shortened the truth, lengthened his soteriology, made progress in his Christology, or abbreviated his faith.

The term "*enarratio*" is very old. It goes back to Augustine, the Psalter (c. 18), and to Isaiah (c. 53)—in the medieval Latin translation of the Bible. It is to set forth in the public arena praise to the glory of God.[31] A Scriptural "*enarratio*" is a *catena* (chain) of praise to the glory, the grace, the justice of God. In the case of an "*enarratio*" of Galatians, for Luther, it is to publish the doctrine, the soteriology, and the Christology of Paul.

CALVIN

Calvin also, I would argue, approached and practised theology as the discipline of the sacred page. This is especially clear with Calvin's sense of the immediacy of the message of the sacred page. Scripture is addressed to "us."

---

30   1519 (1520), 1535, and 1538.

31   1535 Galatians, ff. 52 r°–54 r°.

He glorifies Christ in these praises so as to bring us to reverence Him, for since the Father has made all things subject to Him, we too belong to his kingdom.[32]

The Commentary (commenting) entails carrying the theology of the page to the audience with the Pauline urgency not to backslide but to grow up in the faith and to persevere. The comments on Hebrews are not notes to an ancient text; it is applied theology—throughout Calvin draws "us" into the message of the text. Calvin continues the tradition of treating Scripture as the sacred page.

He does discuss the interpretation of others without giving names (e.g. on Heb. 6.6), though Chrysostom[33] and Erasmus[34] are mentioned. Rather than describing the work as an interrupted narrative, I think it better to describe the *Commentary* as a thematic approach to, or selective analysis of, the whole (e.g. Law and Gospel in his commentary on Hebrews Chapter 1, Christ is worthy of greater honor than Moses in Chapter 3, the power and efficacy of the living word of God in Chapter 4, Christ's sitting at the right hand of the Father in Chapter 10). He does recognize and explain difficult texts (such as Heb. 6.4-6,[35] and 9.19-21).[36] He does criticize the interpretation of others (the "hallucinating interpreters" of Heb. 11.3).[37]

Calvin himself considers his work as providing important observations on the material: "many things are most worthy to be noted" (on Chapter 8 of Hebrews).[38]

In his Dedication (1551) before his comments on 1. and 2. Peter, Calvin says,

> To return to you, most illustrious king, you have here a small pledge, my Commentaries on the Catholic Epistles, in which many things which have been thought obscure and recondite, I have tried so to

---

32 *The Epistle of Paul The Apostle to the Hebrews and the First and Second Epistles of St. Peter*, translated by William B. Johnston ("Calvin's Commentaries"; Edinburgh: Oliver and Boyd, 1963), p. 6.

33 *Ioannis Calvini Commentarii in Epistolam ad Hebraeos* (Geneva: Ioannes Gerardus, 1549), p. 14.

34 *Ibid.*, pp. 164, 181, 199.

35 *Ioannis Calvini Commentarii in Epistolam ad Hebraeos* (Geneva: Ioannes Gerardus, 1549), pp. 72–75.

36 *Ibid.*, pp. 123–124.

37 *Ibid.*, p. 156.

38 *Ibid.*, p. 108.

explain that easy access to the true meaning may be open to a reader who is not wholly lazy.[39]

ARBOREUS

For Arboreus (doctor Sorbonicus), also in the tradition of *sacra pagina*, I would use only slightly different words to describe his commentary; namely, he summarizes and amplifies the text.[40] He is more interested in restating the message of the material than engaging in conflicting interpretations (e.g. the conflict between Erasmus and Faber over Heb. 2.3);[41] he prefers the common judgment of the Church on the matter.

HEMMINGSEN

For Hemmingsen, the focus is more on sacred doctrine, the teaching of Scripture as article of faith. Scripture as doctrinal teacher is seen in words like reason, proof, proposition, argument, conclusion ("Haec propositio continet praecipuum caput doctrinae Ecclesiae Dei ...,[42] "Haec propositio, confirmat articulum fidei nostrae de Sessione Christi"[43]). With Hemmingsen there is a unique blend of seeing Scripture as sacred page and seeing Scripture as the basis of sacred doctrine. The blend is termed by him as Exegesis of [every] Chapter with the observation of doctrines ("exegesis ... capitis cum observatione doctrinarum").

He does not discuss the position of others, nor seem to recognize certain texts as difficult (e.g. Heb. 2.3, 2.7, 6.6, 9.19). He rather culls out the doctrines and sets them forth. The whole is in no way interrupted; neither is it thematic; it is systematic-doctrinal, even "evangelical-philosophical."

While Hemmingsen repeats the first person plural of the text, the text of Scripture is in need of explanation in order for the

39   "Calvin's Commentaries," p. 226.

40   The approach and dates of Ambrosius Catharinus Politus are close (*Commentaria ... in omnes divi Pauli, et alias septem canonicas epistolas* (Venice: Vincenzo Valgrisi, 1551; Paris: Bernardus Turrisanus, 1566).

41   *Doctissimi et lepidissimi Commentarii Ioannis Arborei Laudonensis ... in omnes divi Pauli epistolas* (Paris: Jean Roigny, 1553), f. 250r°.

42   *Commentaria in omnes epistolas Apostolorum, Pauli, Petri, Iudae, Iohannis, Iacobi, et in eam quae ad Hebraeos* (Frankfurt a. M.: Georg Corvinus, 1579), p. 833.

43   *Ibid.*, p. 834.

argumentation to be clear. The reader is not drawn into the text in the manner of Luther or Calvin, the reader is not drawn towards God; rather the text is the teacher whose proofs seek to persuade.

FLACIUS

Flacius does not discuss the position of others either, nor does he seem to recognize texts as difficult (Heb. 2.3, 2.7, 6.6, 9.19). His title describes the work as a "shortened gloss." Flacius calls Chapter 1 of the Epistle to the Hebrews an *expositio* of the many doctrines,[44] which could also describe his "Gloss." The Pauline authorship of Hebrews is necessary because of the importance of the "doctrines" treated in the Epistle.[45] He uses the same words as Hemmingsen—reason, proof, proposition, argument, conclusion. Flacius differs from Hemmingsen's systematic organisation of the material. The gloss of Flacius is a unique work, an *expositio* of the necessary doctrines concerning Christ.

For both Hemmingsen and Flacius, with their more critical introductions, the text of scripture seems one step removed. Flacius discusses the Epistle in the third person; namely, Paul, he, and the Hebrews.[46]

Work on Scripture as sacred doctrine can be seen in Hemmingsen's distinction between exegesis and observation of doctrine. There is no medieval tradition that I have established that sees a scriptural commentary yielding *sacra doctrina*; rather *sacra doctrina* in the Middle Ages is a scholastic way of doing theology. The approach to Scripture as the resource of sacred doctrine by Hemmingsen and Flacius in the form of commentary and gloss may be a new element in the sixteenth century.

CONCLUSION

"What did the term *Commentarius* mean to sixteenth-century theologians?" has turned out to be a difficult question. The term was not used in any uniform or technical sense in the sixteenth century, as far as could be determined. Given its frequent use in the plural when referring to a single work, its meaning is close to its traditional Latin meaning of comment or note. A commentary in the sixteenth century

---

44   *Novum Testamentum* (Basel: Perna and Dietrich, 1570), p. 1109.

45   *Ibid.*, p. 1103.

46   E.g. Flacius, p. 1120.

referred generically to a work on Scripture. I could not find any other common denominator, nor could I (as Erasmus did not) differentiate between a commentary and, say, an annotation.

The search for an answer to the question, "What did the term *Commentarius* mean to sixteenth-century theologians?" led to the Middle Ages. In previous writing I have characterized the approaches to Scripture (from Augustine to Erasmus) as threefold (sacred page, sacred doctrine, sacred letter). Such distinctions help explain the variety of commentaries, so entitled, and the variety of other work on Scripture in the sixteenth century. I have found the pluriformity of commentary in the sixteenth century to be in continuity with the Middle Ages.

The term *commentarius* to sixteenth-century theologians meant something basically no different from anyone else in the tradition, namely, comment or note; but the form the commentary took in the case of Hemmingsen and others was different from what existed in the Middle Ages. Thus something old continued, the approach to Scripture as sacred page by Luther and Calvin; and something new took shape. Perhaps a definition of the term *commentarius* could be comment on *sacra* as page, doctrine, or letter.[47]

No attempt has been made to provide a typology of exegesis, neither have hermeneutical questions been pursued (typology and hermeneutics are recent in origin).[48]

The attempt has been to deal with the variety of approaches to Scripture in terms of the world of the sixteenth century. Thus Luther's so-called commentary was really an *enarratio*, and Erasmus's annotations a kind of commentary (a real commentary in Luther's mind). Other commentaries took more the form of the Scholastic summaries of doctrine.

"Commentaries," whatever the form, did exist as did references to the "commentaries" of others, both of the Fathers and of contemporaries. Their approach to Scripture continued the medieval practice of seeing Scripture as something *sacra*.

---

47 Commentary comes close to *interpretatio* in the medieval sense of explanation using the clear parts to explicate the whole chapter, book, Testament.

48 The terms *sacra pagina*, *sacra doctrina*, and *sacra littera* are medieval in origin, whereas typology seeks to organize material around modern categories.

OMNIS HOMO MENDAX:

LUTHER ON PSALM 116

Trained in the classical medieval tradition as a *doctor in Biblia*, Martin Luther[1] also stood at the watershed between the medieval and emerging modern approaches to the Christian Scriptures, where he participated in the increasing attention to the "literal" sense of Scripture characteristic of his age. Nevertheless, as a biblical interpreter Luther remained firmly rooted in the medieval approach to the text, the so-called "spiritual reading" (*lectio divina*). As professor in Scripture at the University of Wittenberg from 1513 to his death in 1546, Luther spent his entire career wrestling with the whole Bible, but returning again and again to those texts that he loved best:. the Psalms, the letters of Paul, and the Gospel of John.[2]

1   This tribute, dedicated to an old friend and colleague in the field of exegetica, is an attempt to say something (truthful) about Luther's ALL-or-nothing theology. New research and writing took place at Hill Monastic and Manuscript Library, Collegeville, Minnesota, where I was plunged into the marvelous world of medieval manuscripts. The good folks in Collegeville, at HMML, Alcuin Library, the Watrys at St. John's University Special Collections, the Benedictines (Cyril, David, Gregory, Kilian, Peregrin), and, above all, our sponsors at the Institute for Ecumenical and Cultural Research deserve thanks for their splendid cooperation.

2   Among the many Luther biographies that one might cite, the most comprehensive and up-to-date is probably Martin Brecht's three volume *Martin Luther*, trans. James L. Schaaf (Minneapolis: Fortress Press, 1985-1993). Still helpful, however, is Julius Köstlin's classic study, revised by Gustav Kawerau, *Martin Luther, sein Leben und seine Schriften*, 5th rev. ed. (Berlin, 1903). For an in-depth study of Luther's development after 1521, see Heinrich Bornkamm, *Luther in Mid-Career 1521-1530*, trans. Theodore E. Bachmann, ed. Karin Bornkamm (Philadelphia: Fortress Press, 1969). The best English-language introduction to Luther studies remains Mark U. Edwards, Jr., "Martin Luther," in *Reformation Europe: A Guide to Research*, ed. Steven Ozment (St. Louis: Center for Reformation Research, 1982), pp. 59-83. Essential for advanced research is Kurt Aland's aptly titled *Hilfsbuch zum Lutherstudium*, 3d rev. ed. (Witten: Luther-Verlag, 1970). Current Luther studies may be tracked through the annual

Led by Gerhard Ebeling's pioneering studies of Luther's herme-neutics, the tendency in Luther studies generally has been to distance Luther from his medieval context. Indeed, Ebeling's claim that Luther departed from medieval allegory (1519) has dominated the modern picture of Luther as a biblical interpreter.[3] My own research, how-ever, has called into question any connection between Luther and Enlightenment approaches to the biblical text. On the contrary, we now know that Luther was deeply rooted in the traditional monastic approach to Scripture as *sacra pagina*. Like his patristic and medie-val predecessors, for example, Luther saw Christ as the heart of the Psalter.[4]

Lutherjahrbuch, which contains over a thousand bibliographic entries. In addition, *Luther Digest* annually condenses about thirty-five Luther studies (about half originally written in German).

3   See his *Evangelische Evangelienauslegung. Eine Untersuchung zu Luthers Hermeneutik* (Munich: Chr. Kaiser, 1942; 3d ed. [erweitert um ein Nachwort], Tübingen: J. C. B. Mohr [Paul Siebeck], 1991; idem, "Die Anfänge von Luthers Hermeneutik," *Zeitschrift für Theologie und Kirche* 48 (1951): 172-230; idem, "Luther und die Bibel," in idem, *Lutherstudien* (Tübingen: J.C.B. Mohr [Paul Siebeck], 1971), 1:286-301. The standard introduction to Luther as a biblical interpreter is Jaroslav Pelikan's *Luther the Expositor: Introduction to the Reformer's Exegetical Writings* (St. Louis: Concordia, 1959). Among the many specialized studies of Luther's bibli-cal interpretation, one might also mention Heinrich Bornkamm, *Luther and the Old Testament*, trans. Eric W. and Ruth C. Gritsch, ed. Victor I. Gruhn (Philadelphia: Fortress, 1969); Scott H. Hendrix, *Ecclesia in Via: Ecclesiological Development in the Medieval Psalms Exegesis and the Dictata Super Psalerium of Martin Luther* (Leiden: E. J. Brill, 1974); James Samuel Preus, *From Shadow to Promise: Old Testament Interpretation from Augustine to the Young Luther* (Cambridge, Mass: Harvard, 1968); and David C. Steinmetz, *Luther and Staupitz: An Essay in the Intellectual Origins of the Protestant Reformation* (Durham, N.C.: Duke University Press, 1980).

4   See Kenneth Hagen, "What did the term *Commentarius* mean to six-teenth-century theologians?" in *Théorie et pratique de l'exégèse biblique*, ed. Irena Backus and Francis Higman (Geneva: Droz, 1990); idem, *Luther's Approach to Scripture as Seen in His "Commentaries" on Galatians, 1519-1538* (Tübingen: J.C.B. Mohr [Paul Siebeck], 1993).

I. *OMNIS HOMO MENDAX*—"EVERYONE IS A LIAR:"[5]

PSALM 116:11 IN THE EXEGETICAL TRADITION

Study of patristic and medieval commentators helps one to appreciate better what Luther was doing when he came to comment on Ps. 116:11. The numbering of Psalms varies, especially Psalm 116, which in some Vulgates is entitled "a continuation of the previous Psalm." In the Latin Vulgate and for the tradition in which Luther worked, it is known as Psalm 115, without any formal verse numbering.

Psalm 116 was a favorite psalm of Luther's because it expresses a central theological truth about the Truth.[6] Moreover, because of the way Paul repeated the Psalm in Rom, 3:4, "Every person is a liar," and filled out its meaning with the phrase, "God alone is true," Luther frequently pondered the theological truths about *homo* and God contained in just three Latin words: *omnis homo mendax*. Given the repetition of the Psalter in Paul, the echo of Scripture within and throughout Scripture, and Luther's own hermeneutical assumption that Scripture is its own interpreter, he believed that Psalm 116 is made clear in Romans 3. Together with Luther's paradoxical theology and the unity of Scripture, one could say, therefore, that Rom. 3:4 is actually on the *sacra pagina* of Ps. 116:11.[7]

Did Luther change his mind about any theological or technical aspects of the Psalm verse? No. His rendering of the German text is

5   In deference to contemporary sensitivities about gender and language, wherever possible I will render *homo* as "everyone." Where I need to contrast "man" with God, I use man since in the Psalter and in Luther man/homo (*mendax*) is such a derogatory term and contrasts with the *verax* (true) so well. Also, where the contrast comes in between "man" as the former self under the wrath of God and the "god" we become in faith, "man" as the individual person needs to be used in order to convey that I am no longer such a man, but a child of the Most High.

6   Cf. Luther, *Römerbriefvorlesung*, on Rom. 3:4 (WA 56:212.12): "confessio veritatis Dei."

7   At HMML, *Omnis homo mendax* was always my starting point as a way of focusing on the Psalter as a whole; the number of known manuscripts seems to be endless. Time and eternity seem to blend together in the Psalter. The monks copied the Psalters and sang them. Prayer and work blended together in their devotion to God. Working with manuscripts, especially Psalms manuscripts, brings one closer to the church at work in the Middle Ages.

the same in 1524, 1528, 1531, and 1545.[8] The variations in the Latin Psalters on this verse for over a thousand years are inconsequential. His comments on the text are consistently the same from 1513 onward; what he calls the various senses in the *Dictata*, for example, *literaliter*[9] and *moraliter*,[10] turn up with exactly the same emphases and content later.

Examination of patristic and medieval authors places Luther's exegesis of Psalm 115 (116) in its proper historical context: Luther knew and used the work of such authors as Jerome, Augustine, Arnobius the Younger, Gerhoh of Reichersberg, Peter Lombard, Rusch's Strassburg Bible, and Faber Stapulensis. Furthermore, much of what was written in medieval work on the Psalter, including Luther's comments, is a continuation of what Jerome and Augustine said. Since Augustine used the Gallican Psalter of Jerome, we will consider Jerome first.[11]

Jerome's first examination of our text occurs in his *Brief Commentary on Psalms*.[12] We now switch to the Vulgate numbering (Psalm 115). To paraphrase Jerome: Pope Symmachus and the Septuagint render the Psalm, "I said in the excess of my mind: Everyone is a liar" (*Ego dixi in excessu mentis meae: omnis homo mendax*). The liar (*mendax*) in Hebrew is KIVZHB which Symmachus renders falsehood (*mendacium*)[13] and elsewhere failure (*defectio*). Isn't this saying that not only are we *mendax* but also *mendacium* and *defectio*, and that our life is quickly

---

8   The marginal note to *lügener* is the same for 1531 and 1545 (WADB 10/1:489): "Das ist, es ist auff keinen menschen zu bawen, Er kan doch zu letzt nicht helffen, und mus feilen."

9   Luther, *Dictata super Psalterium* (1513-16), on Ps. 116:11 (WA 4:268.29).

10   Luther, *Dictata* on Ps. 116.11 (WA 4:269.3).

11   In addition to the Roman and Gallican Psalters associated with Jerome, his third Psalter (late fourth century) was translated from the original, hence known as "Hebrew Psalter." *Psalterium iuxta hebraeos Hieronymi*, ed. J. M. Harden (London: SPCK, 1922) p. v. For a discussion of the scholarship on *Hebraica Veritas* and Luther on Jerome, see Christoph Markschies, "Hieronymus und die 'Hebraica Veritas'—Ein Beitrag zur Archäologie des protestantischen Scriftverständnis." *Die Septuaginta zwischen Judentum und Christentum*, ed. Martin Hengel and Anna Maria Schwemer (Tübingen: J. C. B. Mohr [Paul Siebeck], 1994), esp. pp. 176-81.

12   Text of Jerome's *Commentarioli in psalmos* is found in CCSL 72:177-245.

13   *Mendacium* is derived from *mendax: mendacium* is the lie or falsehood produced by *mendax*, the liar. KIVZHB is Jerome's attempt to transliterate KŌZĒB: see CCSL 72:234.

over since the next verse reads, "I will receive the cup of salvation"?[14] Yes, since he goes on to say that the God who made me out of nothing (*de nihilo*) and sustains me deserves to be offered in return what he, my creator, has given me. Jerome lines up the *mendax* with the *ex nihilo* of creation, which is behind us as then our life moves on—to become as gods, as Jerome proposes in his later *Treatise on the Book of Psalms*.[15]

What is important for the medieval tradition on the Psalter in Jerome's Preface to the Hebrew Psalter (*Praefatio in libro Psalmorum iuxta Hebraeos*) is his assertion that this Book of Hymns is one book and is to be read in the church of Christ as one book, whereas with Jews (he says) it consists of single words with disastrous consequences.[16]

Jerome's *Treatise on the Book of Psalms*[17] begins with a question, "What is earth and the ruin of destruction? I said in my excess: Everyone is a liar."[18] That truth (*veritas*) is not in our substance, but shadow (*umbra*) is, is a prominent theme throughout this section. *Mendacium* is in corporeal substance, not in the soul. Considering all the diverse errors in the human condition, I will not find truth in this world but rather falsehood, shadow, and phantom.[19] The long and short of it is that all we have on this earth is puff and poof.

---

14   The verses to follow "our" Psalm 115 verse (Vulg.) are sometimes in different order: sometimes the *Calicem* verse, sometimes the *retribuam* verse follows. Sometimes the numbering of the whole Psalm can vary in manuscripts; I have seen 115 as 114.

15   See CCSL 72:234.1-12 of Ps. 115 for this paragraph.

16   Donatien De Bruyne, *Préfaces de la Bible Latine*, ed. Auguste Godenne (Namur: Auguste Godenne. 1920), pp. 46-47. For bibliography, see Samuel Berger, *Les préfaces jointes aux livres de la Bible dans les manuscrits de la Vulgate* (Paris: Imprimerie Nationale, 1804).

17   Text of Jerome's *Tractatus in Librum Psalmorum* is found in CCSL 78:3-352.

18   Psalm 115: "Quid autem est terra et cinis? *Ego autem dixi in excessu meo: omnis homo mendax.*" The Hebrew Psalter reads, "Ego dixi in excessu meo: Omnis homo mendacium"; Jerome, *Tractatus* on Ps. 115 (CCSL 78:240.15-18).

19   "Mendacium hic dixit, quasi umbram, quasi imaginem … ." Now we can say, Omnis homo mendacium: hoc est, omnis homo umbra. We have the Hebrew and the Septuagint; I follow the church [on the matter of *mendax*]: *Ego dixi in excessu meo: omnis homo mendax*; see Jerome, *Tractatus* on Ps.115 (CCSL 78:240.27-241.35).

Then (which can also serve as a summary of Jerome's exposition) he asks if David, as shadow, is telling the truth when he says "Everyone is a liar"; or is that Psalm verse itself a lie, that is, not true? Whatever way Jerome looks at this question, the end result is contradiction. How do we know that a phantom is not lying when it says, "Everyone is a liar"? Let's turn to Aristotle. After turning syllogisms around some more à la Aristotle, Jerome remembers Col. 2:4 and the deception of philosophy and so declares: David is telling the truth because he is no longer a shadow. As long as we are "men," we lie; when we become gods, we cease to be liars (see Ps. 81:6). When you are made god, you cease to be man and do not lie.[20]

St. Augustine treats *Omnis homo mendax* throughout his immense *Enarrationes in Psalmos*[21] as well as at Psalm 115 itself.[22] Thus, Ps. 36:19, "They will not be confounded in the evil time." What does this mean? In the day of tribulation, when hope was lacking, they did not hope in God but in "man" (*in homine*). Cursed is he who puts his hope *in homine*, hence in falsehood and deception.[23] If you put your hope in your God, you will not be confounded because he in whom you hope cannot deceive.[24]

Similar is the comment on Ps. 52:1, "The fool said: There is no God. You are 'man,' the liar; he is God and God is true. Separate your heart and life from those who are abominable in their lies."[25] Or again, Ps. 91:5 and John 8:44: He who speaks *mendacium* speaks of himself.

---

20   Jerome, *Tractatus* on Ps.115 (CCSL 78:241.36-242.63).

21   Augustine's *Enarrationes in Psalmos* comprise vols. 38, 39, and 40 in the CCSL.

22   Augustine uses v. 11 ("Everyone is a liar") for the First Sunday after Easter; see William L. Holladay, *The Psalms through Three Thousand Years* (Minneapolis: Fortress Press, 1993), p. 167. I would say that if one were to come to the Psalter in Romans (3:4) from within the Greek and Latin traditions, from the early centuries (CE) on, one could hardly say, as Holladay does (p. 122), that Paul "alludes" to Ps. 116:11; he is citing it: ἄνθρωπος ψεύστης. See the excellent chapter on the utilization of the Psalms in the first Christian centuries by Pierre Salmon, *Les "Tituli Psalmorum" des Manuscrits Latins* (Paris: Les Éditions du Cerf, 1959), 10-15; for Rom. 3:4, p. 11.

23   "Confunderis, quia fefellit te spes, fefellit spes posita in mendacio; omnis enim homo mendax"; Augustine, *Enarratio* on Ps. 36 (CCSL 38:352.9.7-8).

24   Augustine, *Enarratio* on Ps. 36 (CCSL 38:352.9.1-10).

25   Augustine, *Enarratio* on Ps. 52 (CCSL 39:640.4.22-28).

Every sin is a *mendacium* against the law and against truth. Therefore it says in Rom. 3:4, "God alone is true *(verax)*; everyone else, however, is a liar." Be careful not to lie since you are a man. In order to be *verax*, drink truth; tasting of God, and you will be true.[26] These texts provide some background for Augustine's reading of Ps. 115:11, *Ego autem dixi in ecstasi mea: omnis homo mendax.* The *ecstasi* is the voice of a martyr. What pertains to everyone is *mendax*; it is the grace of God that effects *verax*, lest one falls just as Peter fell and speaks not what one believes, but negates.[27] Concerning humankind, nothing should be taken for granted. Well, therefore, are they who see in *pavore suo* (their holy awe, awesome fear) that everyone is a liar. By the gifts of God we do not fall. Thus it is most truly said: *Omnis homo mendax*, but God is true who says, "You are gods, sons of the Most High" (Ps. 81:6).[28] If all are liars, the only way they can cease being liars is to become gods and sons of the Most High.[29]

Much of medieval commenting on this Psalm verse focuses on the various renderings and meanings of liar. Next to the amount of time spent on the word for liar, medieval commenting pays attention to the word for the condition of the speaker; that is, the one who says *Omnis homo mendax* does so in a state of ecstacy *(ecstasi)*; or …? Augustine

---

26 Augustine, *Enarratio* on Ps. 91 (CCSL 39:1283.6.10-18).

27 "Hoc itaque considerans deuotissimus populus fidelium testium, quomodo infirmitatem humanam Dei misericordia non relinquat, in cuius infirmitatis pauore dictum est: *omnis homo mendax*, quomodo consoletur humiles, et impleat spiritu fiduciae trepidantes, ut pene mortuo corde reuiuiscant, nec in semetipsis fidentes sint, sed in eo qui suscitat mortuos, et linguas infantium facit disertas, qui ait: *Cum autem tradent uos, nolite cogitare quomodo aut quid loquamini: dabitur enim uobis in illa hora quid loquamini; non enim uos estis qui loquimini, sed spiritus patris uestri qui loquitur in uobis:* haec ergo omnia considerans ille qui dixerat: *ego dixi in pauore meo: omnis homo mendax*, et uidens gratia domini se factum ueracem, *quid retribuam*, inquit, *domino, pro omnibus quae retribuit mihi?*" Augustine, *Enarratio* on Ps. 115 (CCSL 40:1654.1-1655.4.15).

28 "Proinde uerissime dictum est: *omnis homo mendax*; sed Deus uerax, qui ait: *Ego dixi: Dii estis, et filii Altissimi omnes; uos autem sicut homines moriemini, et sicut unus ex principibus cadetis.*" Augustine, *Enarratio* on Ps. 115 (CCSL 40:1654.3.19-22).

29 "Si enim omnis homo mendax, in tantum non erunt mendaces, in quantum non erunt homines; quoniam dii erunt, et filii Altissimi." Augustine, *Enarratio* on Ps. 115 (CCSL 40:1654.3.25-27).

says that *ecstasi* is *pavor* because the Psalm verse is the voice of a martyr facing impending suffering and death. The verse is said by someone "whose fearful awe of infirmity God's mercy does not abandon." Thus it reads *ego dixi in pauore meo: omnis homo mendax*, which seems quite different from the usual *Ego autem dixi in ecstasi mea*; in fact, isn't it the opposite? On the face of it, *pavor* is fear, anxiety, panting for fear. Pursuing the matter further, *pavor* can mean religious fear, that is, awe; and, earlier in classical Latin, *pavor* can mean joyful trembling. *Pavor* is on the fearful side of amazement; whereas e;kstasij *(ekstasis)* in Greek, the origin for *ecstasis* in Latin, is on the wondrous side of amazement; *ekstasis* basically means both astonishment and terror. For example, *ekstasis* was the amazed reaction at Jesus' healing the twelve-year-old girl (Mark 5:42); it is used in Gen. 27:33 (LXX)—Isaac trembled.

Again Augustine opens an aspect of the text that had not been clear to me before. Augustine's reading has the opening phrase saying: If indeed everyone is a liar, dead because of sin and, as men and women all, everyone is never anything as *homo* but a liar without hope of anything except eternal death, then we are in a deadly serious situation as *humana*. Such a situation calls forth from the depth of *humana infirmitas*[30] a loud exclamation that expresses both a sickness unto death (the fearful tone) and an almost joyful yelp of amazement that this *mendax* by the grace of God is no longer a *homo*. This is precisely Luther's point about the liar-man. In Christ I am no longer a man. In Augustine's citation of Ps. 81:6, I am a god among the children of the Most High.

The *mendax* verse comes in *Enarrationes*, finally, in connection with Ps. 115:13: "I will receive the cup of salvation and call upon the name of the Lord." O *homo*, in your sin you are *mendax*; by the gift of God, *verax*; thereby, thereby, no longer *homo*. Who gives to you the cup of salvation? It is none other than the one who said: "You will be able to drink the cup I will drink."[31]

Arnobius, who died after 451, is hard to locate in time, place, and position; he did write his *Comments on the Psalms* sometime in the fifth century.[32] On Ps. 115:11, he writes, "Albeit (or however much) he says that man is to be subject to the interchange of his benefits,

---

30   Augustine, *Enarratio* on Ps. 115 (CCSL 40:1654.3.4).
31   Augustine, *Enarratio* on Ps. 115 (CCSL 40:1655.5.1-8).
32   Arnobius, *Commentarii in Psalmos* (CCSL 25:1-258).

everyone is a liar."[33] To paraphrase Arnobius: Before he says what he is to say, he [the Psalmist] expresses his faith; "I have believed," he said. What did you believe? Birth and death; and because I have believed, therefore I am humbled. Because I have believed, this I have said: If the Lord again humbled himself and for me took on the form of a servant, how wretched I make (myself). How do I repay to the Lord for all he has repaid me? As much as he says that man is to be subject to the interchange of his benefits, every man is a liar. What is the worth of man's repayment to the Lord, except perhaps by compensating passion with passion.

Some question exists about Arnobius the Younger and his position on the spectrum between Augustine and some kind of semi-Pelagianism. Arnobius's comments on Psalm 115 indicate a fair amount of exchange that is to take place between the wretch and his redeemer, an emphasis not seen so far on this verse.

The *Anonymous Gloss on Psalms* (Seventh Century) contains what seems to be a standard biblical text and comment;[34] it turns out, however, to have a different combination of comments. The Gloss speaks in the voice of the church: I am greatly humiliated, as if the church says, because I both believe and preach thus, I will endure tribulation. EGO DIXI IN EXCESSU MENTIS MEAE: OMNIS HOMO MENDAX. Others read, "in extasi mentis," but *ekstasis* in Greek is what in Latin means *alienatio mentis*. The alienation of the mind means to transcend the physical senses as did Peter and Paul (*mentis excessus*, Acts 10:10-11), and Paul in 2 Cor. 12:2-3 (*raptum ... ad tertium caelum*). The church seeks to despise (to be alienated from in the sense of *alienatio sensus corporis*) the five exterior senses and to contemplate God with interior gifts. *Omnis homo mendax* means that whatever is of us is *mendacium*, and whatever is of God is of *veracio* (truth). When we cleave to God we are then *veraces*, as 1 Cor. 6:17 puts it: "Whoever adheres to God is one spirit."[35] Simply put, to be true is to be in Truth, who is God.

---

33 "Quantumuis dicat se homo seruire ad uicissitudinem beneficiorum eius, omnis homo mendax est"; Arnobius, *Commentarii* on Ps. 115 (CCSL 25:183).

34 *Anonymi Glosa Psalmorum ex Traditione Seniorum*, Teil II: Psalmen 101-150, ed. Helmut Boese, Vetus Latina, Die Reste der altlateinischen Bibel, vol. 25 (Freiburg: Verlag Herder Freiburg, 1994).

35 *Anonymi Glosa* on Ps. 115, p. 82.1-19.

Gerhoh of Reichersberg's (1093-1169) *Commentarius in Psalmos*[36] should probably be placed before Peter Lombard's work on the Psalter.[37] Gerhoh's commentary offers us the following: Psalmus CXV, *De confessione Martyrum*. [Vers. 11] *Ego dixi in excessu mentis meae: Omnis homo mendax.* The excess of mind is taken in two ways, either *pavore* or *inspiratione*. The *pavor* means human infirmity and death; in confessing Christ, we remember his death. *Omnis homo mendax* is said in fear; since I am a man, I am not able to be fulfilled in the truth. In Hebrew *Omnis homo mendacium*, that is, in this life everyone is shadow, an imitation (*imago*), not true and not the truth. Everyone in sin is a liar; true by a gift of God.[38]

Peter Lombard's *Commentary on the Davidic Psalms* (115)[39] indicates that the *proprium* (property) of man is that he is *mendax*, which is not easily known except in *excessu mentis*—a comment I have not seen before. The *exstasi mea* is mental rapture unto the eternal. The essence of human stuff is liar (*Omnis homo mendax est ex se*). The ecstasy is both *pavore* and *inspiratione*. Nothing of good is our *proprium*. Thank goodness for the power of God who makes us true.[40]

Rusch's Strassburg Bible (1480-81)[41] provides a significant exemplar of the glossed test of Psalm 115. Here, the interlinear gloss has *ex se*, meaning in and of ourselves we are all liars, whereas in and of God we are true (*ex Deo verax*). A more extended interlinear gloss of *omnis* is given: "I have suffered many tribulations on account of the word of God which I will hold firmly, whence the truth shines more brightly."[42]

---

36   Paris: Beauchesne, 1986. Also, HMML project no. 2770. Gerhoh of Reichersberg's *Opera* (vol. 1): *Commentarius in Psalmos* 1-20 contains the typical dedicatory to the Trinity.

37   See *Dictionnaire de Spiritualité*, s.v. "Psaumes."

38   "*Omnis homo* peccando est *mendax*, dono Dei verax," Gerhoh of Reichersberg, *Commentarius in Psalmos* on Ps. 115 (PL 194:717-20).

39   Peter Lombard, *Commentarius In Psalmos Davidicos* (PL 191:55-1296).

40   Peter Lombard, *Commentarius* on Ps. 115 (PL 191:1029-30).

41   *Biblia Latina cum Glossa Ordinaria*, Facsimile Reprint of the Editio Princeps Adolph Rusch of Strassburg 1480/81 (Brepols: Turnhout, 1992). At CXV (2:604, hand numbered), *Ego dixi in excessu meo: omnis homo mendax*.

42   *Biblia Latina cum Glossa Ordinaria*, 2:604.

The *Glossa ordinaria* records the comment of Augustine and provides other standard readings found in medieval expositions.[43] At "What shall I render to the Lord?" Augustine is cited: "The power and grace of God shall conquer weakness and he shall not be consummed."[44] The *Glossa ordinaria* provided Luther with a wealth of resources, as did Faber Stapulensis.

The origin of Faber Stapulensis' *Qvincvplex Psalterium*[45] (Five Psalters) stemmed from Faber's philological interest in establishing a clear and intelligible Psalter, needed in and of itself, and needed in the French Church since the Breviary of the day contained psalms that were obscure and unintelligible. The *Vetus* (Old), a very literal translation of the LXX, is pre-Vulgate, established from Old Latin versions, beginning probably around A.D. 150; it existed in a plurality of versions. The *Vetus* was used, for example, by Augustine, who said the *Vetus Itala* was the best version,[46] and by Cyprian.[47] The *Psalterium Romanum* is still used today in the Holy Office at St. Peter's in Rome. The Gallican version was widely used, contra the *Hebraica*. The *Textus conciliatus* is a "new text, established by a comparison of the readings supplied by all the witnesses," by all the evidence or readings supplied from before Jerome.[48] So the *Conciliatum* is a reconciliation of many Latin versions with the Hebrew text of Jerome, available in Latin translation at St. Germain since the ninth century, that Faber prepared for his *Quincvplex Psalterium*. In his *Ad Reverendissimum* (preface to his patron), Faber says that he added or changed a few things *ad gallicum*, by which effort this Psalter (*Conciliatum*) accords more accurately and beautifully with the Hebrew original.[49]

---

43 *Biblia Latina cum Glossa Ordinaria*, 2:604.

44 *Biblia Latina cum Glossa Ordinaria*, 2:604.

45 *Qvincvplex Psalterium. Gallicum. Romanus. Hebraicum. Vetus. Conciliatum* (Paris: Henricus Stephan, 1509).

46 Augustine, *De doctrina Christiana*, 2.15.22 (CCSL 32:47-48).

47 It is probable that Tertullian used the Old Latin, but "certain" that Cyprian did; see Ernst Würthwein, *The Text of the Old Testament. An Introduction to the Biblia Hebraica*, trans. Erroll F. Rhodes, 2d ed. (Grand Rapids: Eerdmans, 1995), p. 91.

48 E. Amann, "Lefèvre d'Etaples," *DTC*, 9/1:136-37.

49 Faber, *Quincvplex Psalterium*, p. 3 of preface.

A literal translation of the *Argumentum*[50] would read, "A Psalm, which Christ always resolved to be heard by God, concerning his ecstasy in which he renews [i.e., refreshes his mind about] the *errata* of every person, and concerning his great humiliation and cup of passion that he took up for our redeeming, which pure host of his body he offered for the whole people of Israel in the middle of the people at Jerusalem to God the Father and the highest divine Trinity."

The Hebrew version has *mendacium*; the others have *mendax*. The *Conciliatum*, Gallican, and Roman Psalters have *excessu*; the *Vetus* has *exstasi*, and the Hebrew, *stupore*.[51] Faber's Epilogue to the Psalms says that Psalm 115 speaks of the ecstasy of Christ and his chalice. Does *exstasi* mean joy here? Yes, *exstasis* by 1500 can easily be ecstasy in the American sense as well as fear, fright, and agony.[52]

II. LUTHER'S INTERPRETATION OF PSALM 116:11

Luther's exegesis on Psalm 116 (115) will be treated chronologically. From the beginning, Luther knew the two sides of *excessus* ("In my excess I said" conveys both fear and joy), the contrast between the liars and the gods (and how one moves from being a liar to being true), and

---

50   "ARGVMENTVM. Psalmus, quod semper Christus certus esset exaudiri a deo, de eius extasi in quo omnium hominem errata novit, de nimia humiliatione eius & passionis calice quem pro nobis redimendis suscepit, quod hanc puram sui corporis hostiam vidente vniuerso Israelis populo in medio populi Ierusalem deo patri & superdiuinae trinitati obtulerit." See *Quincvplex Psalterius.*

51   "Psalmus CXV

VET.: Ego autem dixi in exstasi mea: omnis homo mendax.
CONCIL.: Ego dixi in excessu meo: omnis homo mendax.
GALL.: HALELVIA.CXV. Ego dixi in excessu meo: omnis homo mendax.
ROM.: HALELVIA.CXV. Ego dixi in excessu mentis mee: omnis homo mendax.
HEB.: Ego dixi in stupore meo: omnis homo mendacium."

52   *peur, effroi, angoisse.* See Albert Blaise, *Dictionnaire Latin-Français des Auteurs Chrétiens,* ed. Henri Chirat. Gerhoh says *excessu* can be *pavore* or *inspiratione* (PL 194:718). In a variety of Latin dictionaries consulted, the meaning of *exstasis* ranges from great rejoicing, through terror and amazement, to stupor.

the tradition of the martyrs.[53] In his *Annotations* (1513-) on Faber's *Quincvplex Psaltrium*, Psalmus CXV, Luther identifies "my excess" as being in an elevated state, illumined to see how one is nothing; and Luther identifies how we through faith and the martyrs are gods, no longer liars but the truthful ones.[54]

In his *First Lectures on Psalms* (1513-1515), the *Dictata super Psalterium* reflecting what the literature calls the double-literal sense of Scripture, Luther says the Psalm is spoken in the person of the Psalmist and in the person of the Lord Christ (*in persona sua et domini Christi*).[55] The note in the Gloss adds the reference to 2 Cor. 4[:13] which shows that, although Augustine says that the Psalm is the voice of martyrs, the early church of Corinth understood that the Psalm referred to Christ.[56] After liar, Luther comments that everyone is such because God alone is true along with those born of God;[57] only those who believe are the truthful ones because faith is truth.[58]

In the Gloss on *in excessu meo*, Luther identifies *excessu* as ecstasy. He speaks of it, first, as the meaning of faith (*sensus fidei*), which exceeds the literal sense, the domain of unbelievers (remember: only those of the Spirit understand the words of the Spirit). Second is the rapture of the mind unto a clear knowledge of faith, which is ecstasy proper. Third is the mind's awesome fear in persecution. Fourth is *excessus*, in which reference is made to Luke 9[:31], speaking of the *Die Verklärung Jesu* and of Jesus' *Ausgang* to Jerusalem (in Luther's German Bible) that martyrs make.

---

53 Luther, *Annotationes Quincvplici Fabri Stapulensis Psalterio manu adscriptae* (1513ff.) (WA 4:466-526).

54 Luther, *Annotationes*, on Ps. 116:10-18 (WA 4:519.26-30): "*Ego dixi in excessu meo*. Iste est excessus, quando homo elevatur super se secundum Ieremiam et illuminatus videt quam sit nihil, et quasi de supra respicit in seipsum in suas nebulas et tenebras, tanquam in monte positus infra respiciens, supra ps. 30 in fine. *Omnes homo mendax*: nos autem sumus dii, ideo veraces, sicut martyres."

55 In the *Dictata*, it is "Glossa: Psalmus CXV [CXVI v 10-19.]" (WA 4:265.15-17).

56 Luther, *Dictata* on Ps. 116:11 (WA 4:265.22): " *in excessu meo* raptu mentis seu pavore passionis."

57 Luther, *Dictata* on Ps. 116:11-12 (WA 4:266.1-2).

58 Luther, *Dictata* on Ps. 116:11 (WA 4:266.25-28).

The Scholia contain an amazing section on "I have been humbled exceedingly" (*Ego humiliatus sum NIMIS*). "When I speak on account of the word of faith, they persecute me. Why are you not then silent so as to avoid affliction? Because I believe; because of what I believe, I speak. Faith compels me to speak against every lie in the world." Luther was and is famous for his rhetoric. Even though more often than not he attacks dialectic, Luther engages in fierce analysis of what I call elsewhere "the logic of faith," because to do otherwise would aid the opposition. The opposition will rise up; faith is a battle with the evil ones. Luther must speak out. A silent faith is a theological oxymoron. "The zeal and fervor of faith and truth does this to me and makes this happen, just as the apostles opposed Jews, as doctors opposed heretics (*Apostoli contra Iudeos, doctores contra hereticos*), as up to today every Christian opposes false Christians, so Psalm 39 'I have not concealed your truth from a great council.'"[59]

"If I speak and if my zeal consumes and compels me, what happens?" This is Luther's lead into the Psalm verse: "I said in my excess: Everyone is a liar." Liar means without faith; the status as true comes about through the confession of faith. As long as I was a man I did not see that everyone is a liar. Liars by definition are blind. Now that I believe and am *in excessu* and made spiritual through faith, I see that they who are not *in excessu* are the liars. Some very strong synonyms for "liars" come roaring off the page: *stulti, vani, mali;* then the all-powerful "etc." The *veraces* are righteous and wise.[60]

Luther employs the two-kingdom distinction to say that many of the most truthful people on earth (*coram hominibus*) are liars *coram deo* since they do not say, "I have believed." And it also goes the other way: Those who are the truthful ones through the truth of faith are persecuted and humiliated in this world (*coram hominibus*).[61]

In commenting on the remaining verses, Luther continues to emphasize the strong contrast between truth and lie.[62] If there is the realm of God, the "sons of men" are not there. Luther's strongest Latin,

---

59   Luther, *Dictata* on Ps. 116:10 (WA 4:267.6-13).

60   Luther, *Dictata* on Ps. 116:11 (WA 4:267.16-22). The same analysis of *Ego dixi* is given again in a paragraph entitled Literaliter (WA 4:268.29-269.2). Under "Moraliter" Luther writes: "Quod intelligitur de mendacio, non quo coram hominibus est mendax, sed coram deo" (WA 4:269.10-12).

61   Luther, *Dictata* on Ps. 116:11 (WA 4:269.12-15).

62   Luther, *Dictata* on Ps. 116:14-15 (WA 4:270.16-271.8).

albeit avoiding scatological overtones, goes in opposite directions; one way to the "gifts of God," the reverse to the idiot, the fool, *homo* the liar, the libeler.[63] On verse 16, "O Lord, for I am your servant," three exclamations (*Trinitas*) are expressed in this confession: *pater, o domine fili,* and *o domine spiritus sancte.*[64] The Psalter was a major source of trinitarian theology in the early and medieval church.[65] Either God is three in one or he is not; three in one from day one to all eternity is the claim of faith.

In his *Vorwort zu Bugenhagens In Librum Psalmorum Interpretatio* (1524)[66] Luther offers the broadly applicable hermeneutical comment that the bishop of the Church of Wittenberg offers the Psalter in the spirit of Christ who is the key (*clavis*) to David.[67]

In his *Summaries* (*Summarien über die Psalmen und Ursachen des Dolmetschens* (1531-1533), Luther writes on the psalms and the matter of translation. Psalm 116 is a *Danckpsalm,* as are 114 and 115. He is so thankful that God has heard his prayer. This Psalm engages in extremely deep *anfechtung.* He confesses his faith and the Truth of God (*die warheit Gottes).*[68] All men are false (line 22). The pious must

---

63 Luther enters into the medieval discussion using the various senses: in addition also *spiritualiter* [*sacramentaliter*], set in brackets but the Latin requires it, and *exemplariter.* The last refers to the martyrs: Luther, *Dictata* on Ps. 116:15 (WA 4:271.12-15).

64 Luther, *Dictata* on Ps. 116:16 (WA 4:271.18-21).

65 An ancient discipline was "prosopologique": to discern the Psalms that apply to God the Father, to Christ, and by extension to the church. Working with *prosōpon* and persona comes Augustine's dictum: "una persona (una quaedam persona) et nos transfiguravit in se (Christus)"; see *Dictionnaire de Spiritualité,* 12:2567.

66 Luther, "Vorwort zu Bugenhagens In Librum Psalmorum Interpretatio" (WA 15:8).

67 Luther, "Vorwort zu Bugenhagens (WA 15:8.9-13). Luther holds David, Isaiah, Paul, and John on the same level (WA 15:8.30). See Luther's preface to Roth's German translation of his *Operationes in Psalmos* ("Vorrede zu 'Das erste Theil der lateinischen Auslegung des Psalters D. M. Luthers [*Operationes in Psalmos*] verdeutischt durch Stephan Roth," 1527. Prefatory Title:"Allen meinen lieben herrn und brudern ynn Christo Ihesu" (WA 23:389.1-31).

68 Luther, *Summarien* on Ps. 116 (WA 38:56.21).

suffer in the world. Again, Luther starkly contrasts between truth and those who would be holy but are false.[69]

The only sermon on Psalm 116:10 I could find from Luther's *Predigt am Montag nach Trinitatis* 1534.[70] The thrust of the sermon is that to utter "I said in my excess" is the work of the devil; whereas the purpose of the Psalm verse is to utter praise to God. The devil seeks to bring us only to *anfechtung*, not to truth.[71] The devil would have us see how sour Christ is. In such a situation comes the judgment that the whole world is full of liars *(totus mundus sit lügner)*. And there is nothing worse than being a liar. The world is not able to hear that God gives grace. These people are not in faith; they bear lies, are dumb, and live in false faith. Luther will preach the word of the cross *(verbum crucis)*.

III. LUTHER'S ORIGINALITY IN THE LIGHT OF HIS PREDECESSORS' EXEGESIS

By Luther's time, Scripture as its own interpreter had taken on various configurations of meaning—including various combinations of the sufficiency, clarity, efficacy, and authority of Scripture alone. Among others earlier, whether in the Gospel of John, Augustine, or Aquinas, the same principle of Scripture-interprets-Scripture obtained, but the configuration of issues congealed differently. For Luther the authority of Scripture alone focused on "what drives Christ" *(was Christum treibt)*, seeing that the unity of Scripture is grounded in the unity of the Trinity.

For a proper interpretation of Luther, it is important to note that Rom. 3:4 used and explained Ps. 116:11 (RSV) and that Ps. 116:11 actually says what Paul said. Therefore, it is necessary to have some understanding of Scripture as a whole in order to understand any of its parts. That everyone is a *mendax* (liar) is not an assertion about human nature, nor is it a pessimistic anthropology; rather, it is an optimistic assertion about God in the form of doxology. Paul (Rom.

---

69   Luther, *Summarien* on Ps. 116 (WA 38:56.20-24).

70   Luther, "Predigt am Montag nach Trinitatis" (edited in WA 37:419.15-424.30). The title also includes "1. Juni 1534. Lunae post Trinitatis." It is found in the WA section entitled "Predigten des Jahres 1534." Under *Credidi, ideo locutus sum* is a chatty style with a mixture of German and Latin.

71   Luther, "Predigt am Montag nach Trinitatis," on Ps. 116:11 (WA 37:423.18).

3:4) makes it clear that there is more to the Psalm than first meets the eye. The "more" is its opposite, namely, God alone is true (*verax*). Opposites express theological truth in Paul and, therefore, in Luther. When the text says liar, Luther sees Truth.

The Psalter repeats over and over the basic truth that everyone is a liar and God alone is true. Sometimes, as in the case of Psalm 116, only "Everyone is a liar" appears. No more need be said. Both parts of the contrast are the message even though only one appears at this point on the page. As Luther saw it, the message of Scripture is consistent and not everything has to be said over and over. Praise of the truthfulness of God is the central message of the Psalter, which is why Psalm 116 was such a favorite of Luther's throughout his life.

Luther resonated with Psalm 116 not only because the *mendax/verax* contrast expressed a truth about the Truth, but also because the contrast was so reflective of the biblical, and later patristic and monastic, view of the two ways (wickedness/righteousness), presented in the form of contrasts. While Luther shares with his predecessors all the exegetical particulars about the verse, perhaps unique to Luther on this Psalm is that he uses the form of contrast to drive the wedge deep between the opposites of lie and truth. The contrast is the basis for his paradoxical way of practicing theology as the discipline of the sacred page. I do not see the overall theological constructs of Augustine, Jerome, Lyra, and Faber built on constructs of sharp antithesis; if Luther is paradoxical or antithetical (supply your favorite term) through and through, the others mentioned here are not so in their whole theological program. For Luther the sacred page is full of paradox; focus on the lie casts the truth into the clearest of light. In the truth of Christ, my lie ceases to be.

In sum, Luther worked on the Psalter with Moses and David in one breath and then with Jerome and Faber in another in order to sing the praises of *verax* by way of contrast with *mendax*.

IV. CONCLUDING REFLECTIONS

(1) The lie and the liar are theological terms with reference to the *coram Deo* in Luther's famous distinction between "before God" and "before human beings." In the exegetical tradition there is some speculation about whether the Psalm verse (*Omnis homo mendax*) is itself a lie. For Luther, the answer is "No." Clearly not. Liar, just as sinner, is apparent only to the person of faith. It is the law that brings the lie

to light. In Paul's mind, as Augustine and Luther knew well, there is the cosmic battle between the forces of Satan and the call of the Holy Spirit. No neutrality. For Luther, keeping silent about the lies amounts to complicity with Satan.

(2) The Psalm verse in Latin uses the generic word for humankind (*homo*), neither the Latin word for a male person (*vir*) nor the Latin word for a female person (*mulier*). The Hebrew text says that each person (*hā'ādām*)[72] is a liar; that is, we humans are untrustworthy and ultimately unable to create or redeem Israel to be a Light to the Nations. In other words, this Psalm verse does not engage in constructive or philosophical anthropology. Luther constantly emphasizes that what Aristotle does in logic is fine for philosophy, but Aristotle is not a theologian since the test of one's standing as a theologian is whether or not one gives honor and glory to the Almighty Creator and Redeemer. Since Aristotle does not give God the glory, he is no theologian. Luther recognizes the other disciplines of philosophy, medicine, and law; and he emphasizes that, while all are needed, medicine is not theology. Paul is clearly the theologian since he gives God the glory in his doxological Rom. 3:4, "God alone is true, everyone is a liar."

Homo, therefore, is a theological term equivalent to pagan or sinner. When a person actually says something that is true, the operative linguistic category is adjective. Given Luther's attachment to the Gospel of John, however, Truth is God, a person—"I am the Way, the Truth, and the Life"—and not an adjective. Those who live in the Truth are truthful in their speaking. The reverse does not work, for that would be Aristotle; that is, by speaking truthful words, a good habit to maintain to be sure, one does not become truth. As good as good habits may be, habits do not save; only God saves.

(3) *Omnis* is a key word in this verse that is often overlooked—*omnis* excludes no one. Outside of Christ, all fall short of the glory of

---

72 In Gen. 1:27, the "*hā-'ādām* is not one single creature who is both male and female but rather two creatures, one male and one female." Since a shift occurs from singular to plural pronouns, humankind "from the beginning" consisted of two creatures, both equal and free (to lie). Genesis 1:26 RSV: "Let us make humankind (*ādām*) in our image, after our likeness; and let them have dominion … ." For a discussion of Genesis, see Phyllis Trible, *God and the Rhetoric of Sexuality* (Philadelphia: Fortress Press, 1978), esp. p. 18. For an analysis of *'adham* in the Psalter and Ps. 116:11, see G. Johannes Botterweck and Helmer Ringgren (eds.), *Theological Dictionary of the Old Testament* (Grand Rapids: Eerdmans, 1974), 1:82.

God. Luther spoke in outrage against all, be they Turk or Schwärmer, against all false brethren who besmirch the holy name of Jesus. Luther did not and could not, given his Augustinian presuppositions, entertain the possibility of salvation outside of Christ; and as *doctor ecclesiae* he felt compelled to take a stand on the side of Truth. To be silent, in his worldview, meant complicity with the other side, which is every bit as evil as the lie. Without Truth, serious sickness is close at hand. This coincides with Luther's ALL-or-nothing theology.

(4) Everyone is interested in truth, in knowing, being, and seeing it. The question is, How does one arrive at Truth? This is a theological, spiritual, and epistemological question. The theological move that Luther most often makes is to move to the goal by way of the opposite. Contemporary parlance usually dubs it a dialectical or dualistic thought-structure. For Luther it would be better to term this move paradoxical; theology "through (*per*) antitheses" is antithetical theology. Luther uses the strongest German and Latin idioms possible to make a point. At one point, in 1531, Luther even says that *Lugner ist zu schwach*.[73]

(5) Truth involves both reality and the perception of reality. When 1 Kings (RSV) 10:6 says, "And the Queen of Sheba said to Solomon, 'The report was true which I heard in my own land of your affairs and of your wisdom …,'" was the report true, that is, historically accurate (by anybody's understanding of history)? No, only half true, or only the half of it, as v. 7 goes on to say. What is the "it"? Truth and reality are often thought of as a philosophical problem. The central claim of the Bible (Rom. 3:4: God alone is true) is that God's words are true; only God can be trusted to never tell a lie. The words of those in the status of "men" are always lies, not completely and consistently trustworthy, because "men" are not God, only God is God, "men" are against God. If Luther were asked, "Are you a man?" his answer, consonant with Paul, would be, "I was a man; now, in Christ, I am no longer a man of my former ways." Luther is talking about our relationship with God (*coram Deo, von oben*). When that relationship is out of kilter, then everything else is also off. To make such a statement offends us all

---

73 That is, that "'Liar' is too weak a term"; see Luther, "Revisions-Protokoll zum Psalter 1531" (WADB 3:145.30). Although the note says that Luther stayed with *Lügner*, it occurs already (without umlaut) in, e.g., *Psalterium … in linguam germanicam translata* (1456; Codex Vindobonensis Palatinus 2671; HMML, no. 15,924), fol. 246ʳ.

because it is making a religious judgment that goes to the core of our being. If we are at heart a liar, we are awful, putrid, sick unto death—some of the milder of Luther's idioms. But is that not exactly what is ailing our world—deep, serious, sickness, sickness of the soul? People cease to be liars when they are claimed by God.

(6) The effort to situate Luther as the first modern historical-critical exegete does not work; neither does it work to make Luther the first Lutheran.[74] After working on Luther and hermeneutics, sometimes together, more often separately, for over twenty-five years, I have come to see Luther as a part of his medieval, Roman Catholic, Augustinian-Benedictine, Bernardian traditions. Like any good late-medieval theologian, Luther had to pick and choose his way through the issues he confronted. Given his near genius talents of language, in which I would include logic as well as Greek, his conclusions are there for all who wish to ground their contemporary theology in Scripture.

---

74   See my *Luther's Approach to Scripture*, n. 4, above.

DID PETER ERR? THE TEXT IS THE BEST JUDGE

LUTHER ON GALATIANS (1519-1538)

Gal. 2.11 caused a controversy between Jerome and Augustine. Erasmus followed Jerome and Luther Augustine. Gal. 2.11 reports that when Peter came to Antioch, Paul opposed him to his face, since Peter was manifestly in the wrong. Jerome attributed deception to Paul, whereas Augustine attributed error to Peter.

Luther takes up the battle between Jerome and Augustine.[1] Jerome thought that Paul acted similarly to Peter in Galatians as he did to Timothy in Acts 16 (when he circumcised him because of Jews in the area). In Acts 18 and 21, reports Jerome, Paul had an offering for the temple. Jerome further cites Acts 18, 21, and 1 Cor. 12 (where Paul says that he is a Jew when he is among Jews). The net effect of the Jerome collection of texts is that Paul continued to be very Jewish; and Peter is protected from any wrongdoing. Furthermore, Peter was an apostle to the Jews and Paul to the Gentiles. So Jerome asks, by what authority would Paul dare to reprehend this in Peter when Peter was the apostle of circumcision and Paul of the Gentiles? Jerome's conclusion is that Paul faked a rebuke or reprehension, which, unbelievable to Luther, Jerome calls a "new art of fighting."

Next, Luther turns to Erasmus and the Greek text of Galatians, which, temporarily, Luther thinks supports Jerome and Erasmus. The Greek has "on the face of it" in place of "to his face." The effect of the argument from Jerome and the Greek is that Paul simulated a rebuke.

From the Greek, Erasmus points out that the text does not say that Peter was reprehensible or worthy of rebuke; but that he was rebuked or reprehended. Erasmus concludes that Peter, who was not reprehensible, was rebuked for the sake of the weak and ignorant.

The net effect of Jerome's interpretation is to go all over Scripture to protect Peter.

---

1   Luther, *In epistolam Pauli ad Galatas, F. Martini Lutheri Augustiniani commentarius*, Leipzig, 1519, [WA 2.438."A"], 1519, f. 15 v. (The Luther citations are from the original prints and cited by year and page/folio reference).

The Greek and Erasmus seem to support Jerome: Paul could not and did not rebuke Peter.

Luther turns to Augustine.

Augustine, reports Luther, keys on "PAUL." Paul said, "I write before God ... I do not lie." Augustine's argument is that if Jerome is correct Paul is not telling the truth; he is lying. Thus (Luther adds to Augustine) the authority of the whole of Scripture vacillates if in one place it says one thing but means another (cf. 2 Pet. 3.16). Luther consistently maintained that the text says what it means and means what it says, as he did in the lectures on Hebrews (1.5) when dealing with the so-called double-literal sense. Luther might come across as a literalist in the modern sense; no, he attacked the "Buchstabilisten" who actually did violence to the text.[2] Luther operated with a single or simple grammatical sense (the simplest sense). When the text says that Paul reprehended someone, it means that the someone was reprehensible.

Augustine's line of argument is that it is necessary that Peter was reprehensible and was truly corrected, otherwise Paul is a liar. Strongly opposed to Jerome's argument, Augustine holds that Paul acted out of humility and corrected Peter appropriately, openly, and directly. He did so with the same concern that the Lord had about Peter's steadfastness when the Lord said three times, Do you love me? Feed my sheep.

One way to reconstruct the difference between Jerome-Erasmus and Augustine-Luther is to say that theologians Augustine and Luther have their eyes on the whole "page," (the whole context of what has come before and what is soon to come), whereas grammarians Jerome and Erasmus have their eyes fixed on one word (kata,). The problem is not with the kata, but with the next word and whether in Latin it should be in the accusative or ablative. And to anyone or for anyone who knows Latin the difference is enormous. Luther is unconvinced by the word-argument because of the whole, that is, all the words, the style, and the theology of Paul.

The next paragraph in Luther begins, "The text in this case is the best judge."[3] The text says what it means and means what it says. The "text" in this case is both the preposition and the whole "page."

---

2   Bernhard Lohse, "Die Aktualisierung der christlichen Botschaft in Luthers Bibelübersetzung," *Luther*, Zeitschrift der Luthergesellschaft, 51 (1980), 9–25.

3   1519, f. 16 r.

Throughout the whole argument one cannot forget what happened to Peter; he denied the Lord. And one cannot forget the potential for church polemic of "saint" Peter as the first Pope. There might be such a polemic in Luther's phrase: "the holy man made an error." What is on Luther's mind concerning this text are the questions: What is a saint? Can saints err?[4]

Luther's point thus far is that Paul is fighting for freedom.[5]

Next, Luther entertains a medieval question, did Peter sin mortally? Initially Luther is not interested in the question because it contains a scholastic distinction about mortal and venial sin, which would be an abstraction superimposed on the "text" of Scripture. The more Luther thinks about the distinction the more angry his argument becomes. Luther does not care about the distinction between mortal and venial sin. In Luther's mind, sin is sin. It was a very serious situation. Paul does not act lightly (or venially). Peter offered an occasion for a scandal of faith.

As Luther thinks through the various positions, one can almost feel his blood pressure go up and up as the argument becomes clear. Jerome and others have missed the very point of the text. Any attempt to protect Peter is misguided and contrary to the text.

Luther's conclusion is that Augustine is right; Jerome and Erasmus are wrong; the final judge is the gospel; and the text is the best judge.

Interesting that Erasmus gives the title "BEATI" to Peter in the title of his first Epistle, never to Paul, and only to the "Apocalysis Beati Ioannis Theologi." Is some editing of the original going on? Of course.

---

4   In the paragraph, Luther states his textual argument against Jerome and Erasmus; the WA breaks the paragraph in the wrong place. In the 1519 print, PAUL is capitalized throughout this section and Peter is not. Only rarely does the WA follow the original in capitalizing words. The capitalization of PAUL supports the very point of the text, namely, that Paul was right and Peter committed an error.

5   Peter erred out of fear and not out of ignorance, and what is necessary, contra Jerome, is the "faith of Christ" (1519, f. 16 v). In response to Jerome, Luther says, on the basis of the Greek, that "reprehended" refers to those who accused Peter for withdrawing reprehensibly which then moved Paul to reprehend Peter who was reprehensible. There is no warrant to offer excuses for the saints, and especially if they deviate from the power of Scripture to offer them praise. It would be better, as the text says, if Peter AND PAUL were damned than "one iota of the gospel perish" (1519, f. 16 v).

Erasmus refers to a dispute between Jerome and Augustine concerning "mendacio." Jerome has the peace of the faithful and the faith of the church in mind. At stake for him is the blasphemy of the Neo-Platonic Bishop of Gaza.[6]

A review of some of the medieval discussion of the passage would be helpful to clarify Luther's context and position.

The *Glossa ordinaria* refers to Jerome's commentary on Galatians. The Gloss comes out on Jerome's side.[7]

Lyra thinks that the whole issue is about the force of the law, that is, whether and when the law was in force—or not.[8] Augustine, cited approvingly by Lyra, distinguishes three times. One is before the passion when the law had its course. Another time is after the publication of the gospel when the law is dead and deadly. The third time is between the passion and the publication when the law is dead but not deadly. During this third time, in the in-between situation, there were varieties of practice depending on the Jew and Gentile situation. This explains why Paul circumcised Timothy (Acts 16).[9] The effect of Lyra's argument is that Augustine is upheld and Jerome opposed. The text of Scripture is kept as is and thus no lying has taken place. And Peter is saved by the distinction between venial and mortal sin.

Augustine's differentiation of "time" clarifies Luther's distinction between the Word (the person of Christ), the words (the oral preaching about Christ), and the written, published text.

---

6   Jerome, *Opera*, edited by Erasmus and Amerbach, Basel, 1516, 83 H.

7   "Paul is not able to reprehend in Peter what he himself did nor accuse him of hypocrisy of which he himself was guilty" ([Biblia Lat.] *Cum postiliis Nicolai de Lyra*, Basel, 1508, p. 80 F).

8   Jerome, reports Lyra, distinguishes between the time before the passion when the law was in force, and the time after the passion of Christ when the law was not in force, and thus to serve it would be deadly (mortal). Furthermore Jerome's position is that Peter, the "principal apostle," never served the law as though it were the truth, but only with a certain kind of pious hypocrisy so as not to scandalize those converted (1508, p. 81 B).

9   Lyra asserts that on the basis of "catholic Scripture" Paul could not lie, and on the basis of the canonical I John 1 Peter could sin. Lyra's conclusion is that Peter sinned venially because, according to Augustine's differentiation of "times," observance of the law by a Jew was not deadly (thus it was venial) (1508, p. 81 C).

Erasmus offers a different and Humanist reason why the text should read, "on the face of it," rather than "to his face."[10]

From Luther's point of view, Augustine and Lyra are right to hold on to the text that Peter was reprehensible. On the way to folio 15 verso on Gal. 2.11 in his 1519 "Commentary" on Galatians, the marginal has "Divinatio Lutherii," which calls attention to Luther's statement, "if my divining [of divina] is worth anything, what we have here is ...." Luther is concerned about "correctly understanding Scripture" in contrast to the "the schools."[11] The importance of the text (Gal. 2.11) and the question of Paul's reprimand of "Peter's error" (Luther) is the "definition of the gospel."[12]

Luther distances himself from Lyra and the distinction between venial and mortal sin. Sin is sin, period, not sort of. Peter sinned, period. The whole point of Galatians for Luther is to glorify God, not Peter or Paul. Since "Peter offered an occasion for a scandal of faith," it should be remembered what Luther remembered from the "rule of faith": sin and forgiveness. The "rule" (regula in Latin, kanon in Greek) of faith is expressed in the Creed. The Creed is structured around the Trinity. As

---

10   It is his first of two reasons. It would have been "ugly" for Paul to confront him to the face. The second reason is the Greek text (Erasmus *Novum Instrumentum omne diligenter ab Erasmo Roterodamo*, Basel, 1516, Vol. II, p. 512). Manners before grammar??!!

11   Whether Luther correctly reports on "Personam" as subjection (u`potagh,) or not is difficult to tell; he contrasts the way "Personam" was understood long ago and the way it is now used in the schools: in the schools, rationalem individuamque substantiam. For Luther and longe aliter accipi: externam qualitatem vitae .... Et quicquid non fuerit in spiritu iuxta illud, i. e. Rho (1519, f. 14 r).

12   *In epistolam S. Pauli ad Galatas commentarius ex praelectione D. Mart. Luth. collectus. Iam denuo diligenter recognitus, castigatus etc.*, Vittebergae, 1538 [WA 2.40.1.14."C"], f. 45 v. The evangelium is the revelatio, doctrina de Christo. In the many places in the Old and New Testament de operibus, the theologicam grammaticam [1519, *Operationes*, grammatica] equals nova vocabularis. While the humanist editors and printers were concerned with the study of 3 languages, Christian philosophy, and Christian piety, Luther offers a "testimonium" of the healthy faith in solum Iesum Christum (1519, f. 1 r; *In epistolam Pauli ad Galatas, D. Martini Lutheri Augustiniani commentarius*, Basel, 1523 [WA 2.439."G"], f. 1 r). Luther knew three languages, testimonium, marturian, Zeugnis (Rev. 1.2), but the difference is the translation of the Hebraica (cf. PAULUS COMMODUS, BRETTANUS, LECTORI S., CR col. 125).

is often the case with Luther, what seems to be an insignificant discussion of a little preposition turns out to be most significant because the whole sacred page and, thus, God himself is involved.

The seriousness of the situation with Peter was that he was in danger of losing the freedom of the Gospel and slipping into slavery under the law, says Luther. Forgiveness, freedom, giving glory to God is the way of faith, trust in God the Father, Son, and Holy Spirit.[13]

In 1535, already in his treatment ("*enarratio*") of chapter one, Luther is very concerned about this passage in chapter two: Peter erred. In response to the debates about the passage, the conclusion Luther draws is as earlier, namely, that he will listen only to those who assert and teach "the pure Word of God" (Christ). Neither the church, the fathers, nor the Apostles will Luther hear except and insofar as they affirm Christ.[14]

Also in 1535 the rhetoric is sharp. Everything is at stake, namely, the point of Galatians and the point of the chief article of the Christian faith. At stake is the defense of the truth of the gospel. If the dignity of Peter is what is to be magnified, then both the text and the praise of God is lost.

Luther's "*enarratio*" on Galatians is clearly not exegesis of an ancient text. As Augustine stipulated in his well-used book *On Christian Doctrine*, with which Luther is familiar, the final goal of studying Scripture is not correct interpretation. Luther is engaged in a life and death battle. Ditto Augustine, who reminiscent of Rom. 3.4, had commented on Romans before Galatians. Both Augustine and Luther key on PAULUS, and the Psalter, Paul, and Luther are praising God. The reason Luther keeps publishing Pauline theology over and over in the form of a printed *enarratio*, it seems to me, is that the truth of the

---

13   In the 1523 edition the same points are emphasized. Jerome is dismissed. The text is the judge. The situation is serious. The "force" of Scripture is at stake. Luther has no time for excusing Peter. "Better Peter and Paul having lapsed into infidelity indeed be anathematized, than one iota of the gospel perish" (*In Epistolam Pauli ad Galatas Martini Lutheri commentarius*, Wittembergae, 1523 [WA 2.439."H"], f. Eiii r). The urgency is in the "force of sacred Scripture" (1523, f. Eiiii v). There is "power" in the words of Scripture because they come from the Creating-Redeeming-Sanctifying Lord God Almighty, Creator of heaven and earth.

14   *In Epistolam S. Pauli ad Galatas Commentarius, ex praelectione D. Martini Lutheri collectus*, Vitebergae, 1535 [WA 40.1.13."A"], f. 59 v.

gospel must continually be defended; otherwise, the opposition gains ground.

An interesting question is how good Jerome's Hebrew was. It may be that, according to Luther, Hieronymus has distorted Hieremias and the problem is with inaquosa (Vulg. Ps. 62 [.3]), because Luther's translation has "da Kein Wasser ist" (Luther 63 [2]), and Hieronymus ends up with Kein Sünde. Knowing that there is a slight difference between water and sin in anybody's vocabulary, after checking out a half dozen texts in about as many languages, my answer to the question of Jerome's Hebrew is that the LXX is wrong and he follows it. Or, in the language of Augustine and the Psalter:

> We saw him in the temple. Perfect love is his name. Strange. He had no form. The form he had was "unworthy" of the King of kings and Lord of lords. So we sing on and see that we do not see with our (meta)physics but with our faith.

The argument is that Moses is to be preferred to Aristotle. You can go to school and learn a lot of Aristotle. Or, "as it is written,"[15] you can hear the Angels. And, never to any angel did he say, "Today I have begotten thee." The God of gods and King of kings says "I am who I am," and Hermes, who has to explain Method, is in jail. And so I ask, who speaks the liberating word? Paul, Habakkuk, and David.

---

15   The "as it is written" is Scripture's way of nailing down an assertion. The New Testament's citation of an Old Testament passage is equivalent to the modern footnote. In contrast to the modern footnote, however, it need not be complete. It is often elliptical. Paul's style of citing the Old Testament elliptically is imitated by Luther. Luther is so intent on promoting Pauline theology that he adopts the style of Paul. The basic assumption of "as it is written" is the unity of Scripture. The Epistle to the Hebrews shows the Christological core to both Testaments for Luther. The unity of Scripture is grounded in the unity of God, or another way of saying the same thing is that Scripture is a whole piece (a sacred page), that Scripture sees itself as a whole piece—of faith in and for God. The idea that Scripture interprets itself is not unique to Luther, it seems to me. In trying to be the faithful student of Scripture he was, Luther acquired the idea from the Bible itself by simply seeing the echo of Scripture in Scripture. Consider, for example, how the Psalms echo throughout Scripture. Scripture comments on Scripture. According to Luke (4.16-21), Jesus cited and commented on Isa. 61.1-2 when he began to teach in the synagogues. For Paul, the Hebrew Scriptures were written to provide "us" example, lesson, and teaching (Rom. 15.4; 1 Cor. 10.11).

With texts from Isaiah, Habakkuk, Romans, Galatians, Hebrews, and the Psalter, and from the perspective of Augustine and Luther, the difference between some philosophy of history and theology is the difference between eros and dsh (hiesed).[16]

What infuriates Luther is that those who think they know Aristotelian theology do not know the difference between Moses and Aristotle. Moses spoke Hebrew; the disgruntled student of Plato spoke a different dialect. The noises, the squiggles, and the wiggles are all different. Put in Greek, the assertion of Paul is simply that Christ is God and not Eros.[17]

What Luther says he is after is the *res* (the reality of the Word of God) that Paul is after. That reality is that the prophets erred and Peter sinned gravely. Luther goes on to list the sins of the saints. If the church is made up of saints, then the church is "simultaneously holy and sinful. Christ is our complete holiness."[18]

Luther takes up the text that Jerome had to twist here and turn there, namely, 1 Cor. 9 (to the Jews I am as a Jew). Luther attacks and corrects Jerome on the basis of freedom from the law. Paul is free to eat this or that. And he is free not to eat this or that. Jerome has not understood the text of Galatians.

Peter's problem was hypocrisy. Peter's problem, which Jerome cannot see, is the difference between eating and the meaning of eating. Peter needed to be recalled to the freedom in Christ.

Everything is at stake and it is contained in the "etc."! What is in danger of being lost is the "Gospel and Christ etc." Contained in the "etc." is the "blood of the cross, the Holy Spirit, God, and all *divina*."[19] The Trinity, or the "HOLY TRINITY" as Luther says,[20] is implicit and explicit in all of Luther's theology. One has to keep track of the material contained in the etc.'s.

Luther was a passionate theologian and a passionate Saxon. Seldom is the connection so clearly seen as in Luther's assertion about the

---

16　Heiko A. Oberman, "Der reformatorische Durchbruch," *Luther. Mensch zwischen Gott und Teufel*, Berlin, 1982, p. 172.

17　1519, f. 20 r; *In epistolam Pauli ad Galatas, F. Martini Lutheri Augustiniani commentarius*, Basel, 1520 [WA 2.439."F"], p. 63; 1523 p. 88.

18　1535, f. 95 r-96 r.

19　1535, f. 97 v.

20　In chapter 4 of Galatians, the SANCTAM TRINITATAM (one God) is highlighted (1519, f. 39 v).

relation of God to "friend and brother man." If the greater danger is to lose "friend and brother man" rather than God, the opposite will happen. If Father God is lost, brother man will not remain for long.[21] Luther's passionate plea to the Mayors to support education becomes a little clearer in the light of this theology. The Greeks lost it; the Romans lost it; and now the Saxons are in danger of losing the Word of God. To lose God is to lose everything. The source of faith and life is God the Creator, Redeemer, and Sustainer.

Interesting would be to suggest that continuity exists in Luther's head from 1516 to 1535 *even* to 1543. The continuity is the devil, that is, the devil's hatred of the gospel.[22] God, Christ, Evangelium do not have a beginning or an ending vis-à-vis the devil until "that day."[23] The battle is continuous "until that day which will be the end of his tyranny."[24]

The text of Scripture must not be distorted. Peter erred. There is a power in the words that mediate the Word. Not one iota of the gospel of freedom should perish. God is to be praised and not brother Peter. Brother Peter is dependent on God for life, forgiveness, and freedom. If "friend and brother man" is placed above God, everything is lost.

In the middle of his comments on Gal. 2.16, Luther says, "now let us return to the text." What is the "text"? The text of Scripture is the sacred page.

On the force of the Latin Vulgate, Luther can equate covenant (*pactum*) and testament (*testamentum*)—because of both the theology and the Latin. The Latin Vulgate translates b'rith (*pactum*) as testament. In both cases—the theology and the Latin—the key, it seems to me, is the giftedness of the sacred page.

Luther's theology is that salvation is *ex nihilo*; so was Creation; God created from null and void. Everything came from God at the beginning and in the Incarnation. Christ is a gift. Christ is the Word; the

---

21   1535, f. 97 v.

22   Heiko A. Oberman, "Die Juden als Wegweiser zur Reformation," *Wurzeln des Antisemitismus. Christenangst und Judenplage im Zeitalter von Humanismus und Reformation*, Berlin, 1981, pp. 135-143.

23   1543, qui finis erit tyrannidis eius. The devil works through the plurality and variety of sects; he attacks the Ecclesiam et religionem of the one Christ from the beginning of the church to now (f. iiii r).

24   1543, f. iii v.

Word is the promise of the testament of Christ which includes the promise, death, and inheritance. The testament is all from God.

The linguistics on *pactum* connect it to page.[25] The sacred page has the smudge and finger prints of God on it.

Both covenant and testament are from God. They are both human and legal. What God does leaves a permanent imprint. The covenant bore the imprint on stone of God's fingers. Covenant is both a legal contract and a human agreement. The handling of inheritance in a testament and will in Hebrew culture was a family matter. The testament of Christ was validated and sealed by the human blood of Christ.

For Luther there is no dichotomy between human and legal in God's way of doing something. The only dichotomy is what is from God and what is not from God.

Luther sought to revive the earlier, patristic, early medieval, and monastic way of understanding theology as the discipline of the sacred page (*sacra pagina*). Among the Scholastics, theology concerned sacred doctrine. Among the Humanists, at the end of the Middle Ages theology concerned classical, sacred literature. The distinctive feature of *sacra pagina* is that it sees sacred matters (*divina*) as a *pagina*, a page, not as doctrine and not as literature. Sacred doctrine and literature have their place, but their status or place is derivative and secondary. Sacred doctrine is derived from Scripture but it is not *sacra pagina*. Sacred literature is a view of Scripture that is far from the primary purpose of the sacred page. Sacred doctrine and sacred literature do not bear the imprint of God. Sacred page is directly and immediately of God. It is *divina* and not *humana*.

To cast Luther's view of Scripture in terms of *sacra pagina* and not in terms of the later problems of Scripture and tradition, inspiration, and hermeneutics is historically more accurate and helpful. One is thus able to see why Luther was so concerned about faith and faith alone, not doctrine or literature. The primary form of the grammar of faith is from faith, to faith, about faith, for faith in God.

---

25   Derivatives from page in Latin are as follows: *pago, pango, pax, pagina.* *Pax* (peace) as well as *pagina* (page) all come from God. The page is directly from God and of God. The page is the pango bango of God on stone— hence pactum, covenant/testament, are all from God.

I love Michael Beyer's sentence, "Whoever talks foolishly in the pulpit (wer auf der Kanzel wesschet), should not have entered it in the first place."[26]

Scripture as sacred page is Luther's view of the "text" as a gift. The works of God—Creation, Incarnation, and Sanctification—are all gifts of God. Luther's work on the sacred page is theologically aimed at promoting Pauline theology. Luther is concerned about what he sees to be the demise of Paul among the Scholastics. The "fall" of Paul was due to the fact that the Scholastics did not see any difference between the grammars of Aristotle and Paul or Christ. The grammar of Aristotle is different from the grammar of Paul.

"It is no wonder that Pauline theology fell so quickly when people, who knew neither Aristotle nor Paul and Christ, taught (lied) that the moralia of Aristotle agrees with the teaching of Christ and Paul. Thus PAUL stands firmly."[27]

The "moralia" (Ethics) of Aristotle teach about good habits in the area of morals and ethics. If one does just deeds habitually one becomes just, one acquires the virtue, according to Aristotle. Paul teaches otherwise. Justice comes from God; it is a gift and not a human habit. Paul teaches *divina* and Aristotle *humana*. What a difference!

Those who hold that Paul and Aristotle are arguing from the same grammar make Luther absolutely furious. Paul is to be promoted in his area of theology and Aristotle passed off as a theologian is to be attacked. It is Paul who gives God all the glory for justice, goodness, righteousness, wisdom, holiness.

Different grammars require different disciplines. Theology as the discipline of the sacred page has a unique discipline. Luther learned his theology from Paul and, along with all other medieval theologians, from Augustine. Thanks to the rotting dijk (Erasmus of) Augustine was edited and PAUL stands firm.

In his comments on this section in Gal. 2, Luther makes reference to the famous work of Augustine *On the City of God against the Pagans.* The full title as well as the content of Augustine's work indicates that it is a work of theology and not a book about the writing of history as is commonly thought.

---

26 Michael Beyer, "Luthers Ekklesiolgie," *Leben und Werk Martin Luthers von 1526 bis 1546. Festgabe zu seinem 500. Geburtstag,* ed. by H. Junghans, Göttingen, 1983, pp. 93-117.

27 1519, f. 20 r.

On the City of God against the Pagans is an "*enarratio*" on Ps. 87, Isa. 53, Hab. 2, Rom. 1, Heb. 10, and so on. It is theology in praise of the most glorious city of God. Those who see Augustine's work as Christian philosophy take it out of its own tradition of *sacra pagina* and place it in the nineteenth century, where theology, as in Scholasticism, was heavily influenced by philosophy.

I see Augustine's work as a "commentary" on Romans and Romans as a commentary on Isa. 53. The message of both is the same—in praise of the city, and the city is feminine.[28]

To state the argument succinctly: Paul is not Aristotle; Scripture is not philosophy; Augustine is not philosophy. Luther seeks to follow Isaiah, Paul, and Augustine.

For Luther theology has to do with God. Its text is the sacred page. The sacred page is a gift from the Creator, Redeemer, and Sanctifier. It is the sacred page against the pagans and their pagan gods.

Gal. 4.12-13 uses language about the weakness of the flesh. For Luther, the "infirmity of the flesh" is a peculiar Pauline trope, figure of speech.[29] Jerome had said, reports Luther, that Paul adapted his language about weakness to accommodate himself to the weak Galatians. Luther argues vehemently against Jerome and Erasmus throughout chapter 4. To Luther's way of understanding the "art of translating," Jerome, followed by Erasmus, is wrong to accuse Paul of HYBERBOLEN (hyperbole), that is, excessive speaking. Luther says that Paul's examples are "most beautiful examples" for teaching the truth.[30]

A typical pattern in Luther's dealing with a problematical ("obscure") text in Galatians emerges again with regard to 4.12.[31] The pattern is that Luther finds Jerome's reporting of multiple opinions itself problematical; Augustine in the process is slighted (by Jerome); Luther says 'no' to Jerome; Luther avoids variety of opinions if they lead to "obscurity" and confusion; Luther pays close attention to Paul's vocabulary in the "obscure" text and elsewhere; and the end of the pattern is that Luther concludes that the text (4.12) in the context of other Pauline writings and the whole sacred page makes an important

---

28   As Luther Augustine went from Romans to Galatians; CSEL (ad Gal. 4.1): gloriosissimam civitatem Dei.

29   1523, f. M.

30   1519, f. 43 v, 44 r; 1520, p. 145.

31   1516, WA 57,II.91.7-92.14; 1519, f. 42 r; 1520, pp. 135-138.

and basic theological point about the Christian faith so that what might seem like a technical, grammatical matter in Greek for Luther is very important precisely because all technical, grammatical matters in Greek and Latin are the very essence of Pauline theology. The basic theological point in 4.12 (as also found in 1 Cor. 2.3, 2 Cor. 11 and 12, and Ps. 67.10) is that we are weak and God is strong. Paul and Luther glory in the weakness of their flesh so that the power of Christ may dwell within them. Furthermore, the flesh for Paul is in relation to the Holy Spirit; thus it is theological and Trinitarian and not anthropological. Luther cites Rom. 1 where Jesus Christ is born of the flesh and declared Son in the power of the Spirit of sanctity "etc." By triggering the memory of Rom. 1, the work of God the creator, redeemer, and sanctifier readily comes to focus. For Luther 1 Pet. 3 also shows the character of flesh in relation to Spirit (put to death physically, made alive in the Spirit).[32]

Luther has arrived at his resolution of the problematical text with the use of stark contrast (Luther's familiar contrast of "Every Man is a Liar, God Alone is True" readily comes to mind).[33] As Luther sees Paul, the more "Man" is put down (lowered) the higher Christ is elevated. A consistent point that Luther makes is that Paul is never singled out for praise—just the opposite is the case in order to praise the only one worthy of praise.

The kind of faith that Luther sees Paul evangelizing (4.12) is not an inarticulate or irrational faith. It is solid, reasonable, and healthy.[34] Luther has been charged with fideism—an old Roman Catholic problem with Protestantism. But for Luther the faith principle—the "main article" of justification by faith and not by works—is not itself salvific. Only Christ saves; articles and doctrines do not. Plus, for Luther, Paul not only has a consistent vocabulary and grammar, but he also has a logic that he adheres to strictly. For example, on the meaning of Arabia (Gal. 4.25), Luther says that in Scripture it "always" means desert.[35]

---

32   1523, f. M.

33   On Gal. 4.27 (regarding the sterilis ... multi filii) Luther says haec scripta sunt [Isa. 54], miraque antithesi et antilogia (1520, p. 155; 1523, f. Nii v).

34   1535 (with marginal Fructus sanae doctrinae), f. 50 v; 1538, f. 247 r.

35   1519, f. 47 v.

Why? Because law is always law; in this case it signifies the rigid and frigid Synagogue.[36]

To understand both Paul and Luther a modern interpreter needs as much language and logic as can be attained. Heiko A. Oberman taught a generation of us how to read a text in the original language, print, and context. He also emphasized in the 1960's that the history of Christian thought is not church history, a discipline perhaps more appropriately taught in a history department. The history of Christian thought is divinity.

For Paul and Luther only a healthy faith can say, 'I am weak,' because it is a strong faith statement to say that 'whatever strength I possess' is Christ's. It would be interesting to compare the relation between "'Reagan's revolution' and Bush's evolution"[37] with the relation between Luther and Melanchthon. A common suggestion today is that Lutherans and Catholics could live together with Melanchthon's moderation but not with the excesses of Luther. The comparison might also work with Jerome and Augustine, but that would be a tougher play to call [pun intended]. My preference will always be with the excesses, or as Paul says, the σκάνδαλον of the εὐαγγέλιον.

The logic of this kind of faith proceeds along the following lines: if God saves, God *alone* saves; to praise Paul does not give glory to God; the law is not the gospel; God works in ways contrary to ours; and so on.

Conclusions

Gal. 2.11 caused a controversy between Jerome and Augustine: Did Peter err? Jerome's conclusion is that Paul faked a rebuke or reprehension. The Greek and Erasmus seem to support Jerome: Paul could not and did not rebuke Peter. Augustine's argument is that if Jerome is correct Paul is not telling the truth; he is lying. For Luther the authority of the whole of Scripture vacillates if in one place it says one thing but means another. Luther operated with a single or simple grammatical sense (the simplest sense).

"The text in this case is the best judge" (Luther) means the text says what it means and means what it says. The "text" in this case is both the preposition and the whole "page." Luther's conclusion is that

---

36 Arabia means desert (law) ut significet sterilem et desertam Synagogam (1519, f. 47 v; 1520, p. 153).

37 THE MILWAUKEE JOURNAL, Sunday, 7-23-89.

Augustine is right; Jerome and Erasmus are wrong; the final judge is the gospel; and the text is the best judge.

From Luther's point of view, Augustine and Lyra are right to hold on to the text that Peter was reprehensible. Peter sinned, period. The whole point of Galatians for Luther is to glorify God, not Peter or Paul. As is often the case with Luther, what seems to be an insignificant discussion of a little preposition turns out to be most significant because the whole sacred page and, thus, God himself is involved. In 1535, the conclusion Luther draws is as earlier, namely, that he will listen only to those who assert and teach "the pure Word of God" (Christ).

The reason Luther keeps publishing Pauline theology over and over in the form of a printed *enarratio* is that the truth of the gospel must continually be defended; otherwise, the opposition gains ground.

Luther attacks and corrects Jerome on the basis of freedom from the law. What is in danger of being lost is the "Gospel and Christ etc." Contained in the "etc." is the "blood of the cross, the Holy Spirit, God, and all *divina*."[38]

The Trinity is implicit and explicit in all of Luther's theology.

One has to keep track of the use of the etc.

God is to be praised and not brother Peter. If "friend and brother man [Peter]" is placed above God, everything is lost.

Scripture as sacred page is Luther's view of the "text" as a gift from God.

Luther is concerned about what he sees to be the demise of Paul among the Scholastics. The "fall" of Paul was due to the fact that the Scholastics did not see any difference between the grammars of Aristotle and Paul or Christ.

On the City of God against the Pagans is theology ("*enarratio*"), not philosophy, in praise of the most glorious city of God.

A typical pattern in Luther's dealing with an "obscure" text is as follows:

> Jerome's reporting of multiple opinions is problematical;
> Augustine in the process is slighted (by Jerome);
> Luther says 'no' to Jerome;
> Luther avoids variety of opinions if they lead to "obscurity" and confusion;
> Paul's vocabulary is to be attended to carefully; the text makes a basic theological point.

---

38   1535, f. 97 v.

What might seem like a technical, grammatical matter in Greek for Luther is very important precisely because all technical, grammatical matters in Greek and Latin are the very essence of Pauline theology. Paul and Luther glory in the weakness of their flesh so that the power of Christ may dwell within them.

The kind of faith that Luther sees Paul evangelizing is solid, reasonable, and healthy. The faith principle is not itself salvific; only Christ saves. For Luther, Paul not only has a consistent vocabulary and grammar, but he also has a logic that he adheres to strictly.

The logic of this kind of faith proceeds along the following lines:

> if God saves, God and God *alone* saves;
> to praise Paul does not give glory to God;
> babies are not adults;
> the heir will receive an inheritance because God is faithful to his promise;
> the law is not the gospel;
> God works in ways contrary to ours;
> and so on.

For Paul and Luther only a healthy faith can say, 'I am weak,' because it is a strong faith statement to say that 'whatever strength I possess' is Christ's.

Zusammenfassung

DID PETER ERR? THE TEXT IS THE BEST JUDGE
Luther on Galatians 2.11
KENNETH HAGEN
übersetzt von Michael Zamzow

Der Streit zwischen Hieronymus und Augustin um Galater 2,11 und die Frage nach dem Fehltritt des Petrus wurden durch Erasmus und Luther fortgeführt. Nach Luther "ist in diesem Fall der Text der beste Richter", d.h. daß Augustin recht hatte, indem er die Wahrheit der Schrift und die Zurechtweisung des Petrus durch Paulus verfochten hatte. Petrus hat gesündigt. Nach Luther ist die ganze Absicht des Galaterbriefes, Gott die Ehre zu geben, nicht dem Petrus oder dem Paulus. Wenn "Freund und Brudermensch [Petrus]" über Gott gestellt wird, ist eben alles verloren. Der Text ist die ganze "Schriftseite". Die Schrift als heilige Schriftseite ist Luther's Auffassung des "Textes" als

Geschenk Gottes. Die Dreieinigkeit ist zugleich unausgesprochen und ausdrücklich im ganzen der Theologie Luthers. Der "Sündenfall" des Paulus ist darauf zurückzuführen, daß die Scholastiker die Grammatik des Aristoteles von der Grammatik Paulus und Christus nicht zu unterscheiden vermochten. Eine scheinbar bloß formale und grammatische Sache im griechischen Text (*kata*) ist von großer Bedeutung für Luther. Eben sind alle formalen und grammatischen Sachen im griechischen und lateinischen Text das Wesentliche der paulinischen Theologie. Paulus und Luther rühmen sich der Schwachheit ihres Fleisches, damit sie Christus die Ehre geben möchten, der alleine heil machen kann.

IT IS ALL IN THE ET CETERA

LUTHER AND THE ELLIPTICAL REFERENCE

1. Introduction

"It is all in the et cetera." One needs to know the full page of Scripture in order to follow Luther's argument. The medieval practice of Luther's day was to reference Scripture elliptically or in an abbreviated manner.[1] Only a few words had to be supplied in print in order to trigger the memory of the whole text, chapter, and letter. For Luther, the whole sacred page is a part of his argument. Since the modern scholar tends not to carry in his head and heart the amount of Scripture Luther did, all the Scripture contained in the "etc." needs to be supplied in order for the Weimarer Ausgabe (henceforth WA) to edit Luther correctly.[2] My thesis (and experience) is that sometimes the most important part of Luther's argument is contained in the et cetera and not in the passage cited—hence the whole (all) is in the "etc." The modern use of etc. in English—appropriate mostly for informal writing—is to convey more of the same; where appropriate in scholarship, it is preferably confined to parenthetical references. For Luther, however, following high academic usage of the day, key words actually referenced often appear not *before* the et cetera but *after*.

These and other conclusions pertinent to the elliptical style of referencing have been reached by working with the original prints of Luther's "Commentaries" on Galatians (1519, 1521, 1523, 1525 [German], 1534, 1535, and 1538). Luther's lectures on Galatians of 1516-1517 have also been compared.[3]

---

1   The incunabula and early-sixteenth century Bibles available to Luther that contained Lyra's *Postilla* cited the Scripture headings for Lyra's commentary elliptically with various abbreviated Latin forms of "etc."

2   The reproduction of the "etc." in the American Edition of Luther's Works is only occasional. When it is supplied, I require my students to read the whole passage of Scripture in order to see what Luther saw; such a procedure is necessary, as one of my students put it, "to find Luther's argument."

3   For a fuller treatment of the points made in this article, see my *Luther's Approach to Scripture as seen in his "Commentaries" on Galatians, 1519-1538*, Tübingen, 1993 (J.C.B. Mohr [Paul Siebeck]).

Luther was not interested in a correct proof text. He did not think of Scripture in terms of verses and thus did not refer to Scripture by chapter and verse. He had whole sections, chapters, and books committed to memory. The text for him in the tradition of *enarratio* was a sacred page, not a series of chopped-up verses. (*Enarratio* meant to narrate, to exit the text, and to apply the message in public.) As will be shown, Luther's references were often elliptical — a portion of some text cited was shorthand for a whole piece. So the entire effort by the WA to add chapter-and-verse references in the margins changes both the format and the argument of the original. The references are distracting, not always accurate, and miss the point of Luther's usage of Scripture. The original marginalia are far more helpful and consistent with Luther's genre of biblical commentary.

Furthermore, the practice of the WA and modern editions to add quotation marks around Scripture changes Luther's publication. Quotation marks were not used by Luther nor given in his original prints. The use of quotation marks sets Scripture off as a reference, separate from Luther's own words and work. The medieval practice was to weave Scripture into the flow of the commentary.[4] As far as Luther was concerned, he did not add anything to Scripture, certainly not interpretation. Interpretation was to be avoided. The flow of scripture and comment is interrupted in the WA by the use of quotation marks around the scriptural words. It gives the effect of putting Scripture in the category of ancient references, proof texts, or footnotes. It separates Luther's text from the text of Scripture. The modern scholar is trained to skip over the citations and look for the interpretation. Through the use of quotation marks, Scripture is set apart; whereas for Luther, his *enarratio* of Scripture is a whole piece in praise of God. Luther's language is the language of the Psalter and the Prophets, the Gospels and the Epistles. The use of Scripture in such a manner *is* the "interpretation," the setting forth in detail the praise to the glory, the grace, and the justice of God. What gives better expression to the praise of God than the Psalter itself? The Psalter is not a footnote to some argument. It is daily liturgy in Wittenberg.

Obviously Luther knew the difference between Paul's Greek and his own Latin and German. Luther never claimed his text to be the Word

---

4   The language of pre-Scholastic theology was the language of the Latin Vulgate. Thus it is very difficult to distinguish the Latin of the author from the Latin of the Bible.

of God. But my point is that Luther knew the performative power of words, and what he was seeking to drive (*was Christum treibt*) was not his own point of view but the same that Paul was seeking to promote, namely, Jesus Christ.

The blending of Scripture and comment assumes the unity of Scripture. Here, I think, is the difficulty and difference with modern methods, the modern methods of biblical interpretation, and the modern method of the critical edition. The modern assumption is that every biblical writer has his/her point of view, thus as many biblical theologies exist as there are biblical authors. For Luther Scripture has only one author and a singularly consistent point of view. Luther is able to weave a set of texts from all over Scripture because Scripture is of God—and there is only one Trinity.

Luther's assertion that there was nothing new in Galatians challenges the assumption of the critical edition, since, by definition, there can be nothing new in Luther's *enarratio*. The assumption of the critical edition is that the edited author has his/her own point of view and in order to set that view in clear perspective, footnotes of identification, clarification, and especially comparison need to be given as copiously as the publisher will allow in order to show the distinctiveness of the edited author's interpretation. However, for Luther novelty comes from the pseudo-apostles. Luther sought to imitate and promote Paul, and he should not be expected to have a new interpretation. "Scripture interprets itself" is true for Luther because it is the form that Scripture itself takes—"as it is written." Scripture interprets (cites) itself. Scripture itself is a *catena*, a chain of scriptural citations and allusions. Scripture is full of echo. As theologian, Luther was conscious of his task to publish an *enarratio*, to go public with the voice of the Gospel, the words of Christ, the Word of God.[5]

Scripture for Luther was a whole piece, a sacred page, not verses, not a proof text, not an ancient reference, not something to be interpreted; Scripture was to be published. In the tradition of *enarratio*, his "commentary" was to remove (take out) the message and set it forth in

---

5   Theology presents that Word, that "doctrine concerning the Son of God," that "good Word," that "announcement of peace" in ways different from philosophy and law (1519, f. 8 r): *In epistolam Pauli ad Galatas, F. Martini Lutheri Augustiniani, commentaries*, Leipzig 1519 [Melchior Lotther]; the print designated as 'A' in WA 2,438.

detail in the public arena. There was no need in both the theological and printing praxis of Luther's day to supply the full biblical reference.

2. Et Cetera

After working with the material contained in the etceteras, it became clear to me that much more of Scripture appears on Luther's page than first meets the modern eye and that the Latin is more abbreviated than the modern editions indicate. Remember, medieval Latin was shaped by the Vulgate.

On Galatians 1:9-10 contrasts are EMPHASIZED: Scripture/ Philosophy, Paul/Aristotle. They who learn from the tree of Aristotle "love man," whereas they who understand Scripture "love truth." Luther's words sparkle with scriptural overtones and the WA has no references.[6] In the original print of 1519 (designated print "A" by WA), it says, "Ita" (thus) MAN IS LIAR meaning "and so on" with the whole of it implied; the whole of it is a reference to Romans 3:4 where Paul fills out the Psalm MAN IS LIAR with GOD ALONE IS TRUE.[7] More is actually being conveyed by the text with the frequent use of "et cetera" than the modern editor or reader realizes.

In medieval practice, a word of Scripture called up a whole set of associations. One has to trace the cross-references to see what Luther sees. The word that drives Luther's understanding of Galatians 1:9-10 is not in Galatians 1:9-10. The key word is "testimonium" in Revelation 1:2 (*marturian* in Greek and *Zeugnis* in German). My guess is that the

---

6   The WA could have referenced Matthew 24:32, Galatians 1:12 regarding the tree-disco; remember how much Luther used the tree-fruit expression. Paul did not "learn" the Gospel from homo; he "received" it. I really think Luther was as concerned as Aristotle to "please man," but he was concerned that the Aristotelians end up with the opposite, namely, to displease, when measured by Christ (the CANONICUM). Theology's teaching concerns the *doctrina de filio dei, sicut scriptum est.*

7   Strong contrasts are pointed to in the 1535 margins (on Gal. 1:9-10): Paul. divina docet (f. 53), or soli Dei placere (f. 54 r). Preaching (enarrant) is to be done to the grace and glory of God (caeli gloriam Dei [= Ps. 18:1] damnatis universis hominibus [f. 52 r]); omnes homines esse impios (f. 51 v). We (Paul and Luther) condemn everything in the world: Liberum arbitrium; vires humanas; sapientiam; iustitiam; omnen religionum voluntariam (f. 52 r): *In Epistolam S. Pauli ad Galatas Commentarius, ex praelectione D. Martini Lutheri collectus,* Vitebergae, 1535 (per Ioannem Luft); WA 40,1.13, 'A.'

"witness" is by those willing (hoping) to die in faith and for faith, i.e., die to self so as to live in the source of life here and in the hereafter. What then becomes clear, if that is true, is that the witness-martyr is not some model or example of faith because that would put him/her in the range of virtue rather than faith. The VAPOKALUYIS (apoka-lupsis, revelation) of Jesus Christ gave John, Paul, and Luther courage to live in faith.

The medieval practice of Luther's day was to reference Scripture elliptically or in an abbreviated manner. Other disciplines also cited their authorities elliptically with the use of the "et cetera." Just a few words were needed to be supplied in print in order to reference and recall the whole authority. For Luther, the text in the context of all the Holy Writ was the content of his argument. Just as the abbreviated Latin of Luther's day conveyed the whole word, so the abbreviated references to Scripture conveyed the whole page. The task of an *enarratio* was to get the whole message out.

Medieval commentators have accurately been described as "walking concordances." They had so much of Scripture committed to memory that, for example, if the word "justice" were in mind from a particular Pauline text, the other biblical usages of justice would also readily come to mind.

The modern (editor, reader) does not carry Scripture in the heart but in the hand. For the WA to edit Luther correctly, all the Scripture contained in the "etc." should be filled in. Otherwise, those of us not trained to memorize massive amounts of Scripture in Latin and Greek miss too much valuable information. For the modern to see what Luther saw in a text, he or she should have an open Bible plus Latin and Greek concordances that reference the words of the text. This advice comes from experience. At one point, serious consideration was given to entitling my recent book on Luther "It is all in the et cetera." I found that to follow Luther I had to read massive amounts of contexts and cross-references, in Luther's Greek, Latin, and German in order to understand his word associations and follow his argument.

For example, the WA consistently identifies MAN IS LIAR with the marginal reference Psalm 116:11. From a modern point of view, that is correct. That is all the modern eye sees. From Luther's point of view, the full reference is also Romans 3:4. Luther cannot think of his favorite Psalm without hearing the rhythmic echo in Romans.

On Galatians. 1:11-12, Luther continued the contrast between man (law) and Christ (Gospel).[8] He did so with a very elliptical citation of Romans 3 and 4. For one not having Galatians 1 and Romans 3 and 4 in Greek and Latin committed to memory, it is necessary to read these chapters in their entirety several times to obtain the linguistic parallels with which Luther was working. Often Luther had a special Pauline word in mind and would cite a verse from somewhere else in the passage so that what he was saying is not actually on the printed page as we know it. One has to know what is in the "et cetera" to know what Luther was saying.

The linguistic parallels that Luther worked with are a pattern basic to Paul.[9] The contrast is between man and Christ, *humana* and *divina*. Paul taught *divina* (things of God) not *humana* (things of man). Paul did not receive the Gospel from men but from Christ. In Romans 3:4 Paul highlighted the truth (*verax*) in contrast to lie (*mendax*), as it is written (Psalm 116:11).

On Galatians 2:11. Everything is at stake, and in Luther's text the "everything" is contained in the "etc."(!) What is in danger of being lost are the "Gospel and Christ, etc." Contained in the "etc." is the "blood of the cross, the Holy Spirit, God, and all *divina*."[10] In other words, the "etc." refers to the Creed and the Trinity, or the "HOLY TRINITY" as Luther said.[11] The Trinity was implicit and explicit in all of Luther's theology. One has to keep track of the material contained in the etceteras to see the Trinitarian fundament to Luther's *enarratio*. Only after working with the original texts of Luther on Galatians did it become clear to me that the form and continuum of the faith of the people of God is shaped by the Trinity, and that the Trinity is the hermeneutical unity of Scripture (*kanon, regula*) and the unity of the Church's Creed. Likewise it became clear to me that just as Luther is accustomed to reference the Scripture elliptically with an "etc.," so Luther gives reference to the Creed elliptically with only a word or two from it.

On Galatians 3:13. When Scripture says that Christ was cursed, the general evidence is that the curse is by God. Sometimes Scripture speaks in an abbreviated manner. Scripture does not have to say

8   1519, f. 7 r.

9   Non ... sed, sicut scriptum est (not ... but, as it is written, 1519, f. 7 r).

10   1535, f. 97 v.

11   In Chapter 4 of Galatians, the SANCTAM TRINITATAM (one God) is highlighted (1519, f. 39 v).

everything (as in "by God") everytime (the divine passive). Some of the truest thoughts need not to be spoken. Augustine already discussed the problem of valuing a certain word or passage in Scripture according to the number of times it appeared in a text, thus interpreting the Bible by statistics:

> What in the holy Gospel is spoken briefly ought not briefly to be expounded, so that what is read may be understood. The words of the Lord are few, but great; to be valued not by number, but by weight: not to be despised because they are few, but to be sought because they are great.[12]

3. Apokope

Luther noted in 1516 that the abbreviated or short verse, Galatians 3:15, is an abrupt or elliptical expression (*apokope*): "To give a human example, brethren: no one annuls even a man's will, or adds to it, once it has been ratified." Paul was verbose in Chapter 3 in regard to other matters, but he quickly slid over the example of a ratified testament. He did, however, pick it up a few verses later with "inheritance" and "heir" terminology.

In contrast to Jerome, who saw the little verse as a crude example for the crude Galatians, in 1519 Luther saw the abrupt or elliptical expression of testament as shorthand for an extremely necessary example. Without the example of testament, Galatians would be more difficult to understand and more difficult than Romans 4, where inheritance and promise are discussed. The example of testament says so much so clearly.

On Galatians 4:4. An example of *apokope* comes in Luther's treatment of Galatians 4:4: "When the fullness of the time was come, God sent his Son, made of a woman ...." The Gospel of John, noted Luther, does not even "mention" woman or virgin. "In the beginning was the Word, etc." It is important to put the "etc." inside the quotation because it covers about thirteen verses. The whole passage is on the page, and it is all in the et cetera. Then Luther quoted "and was made flesh"

---

12 I am indebted to Dr. John M. Norris for this reference: Augustine, Tractates on the Gospel of John, 37,1, in : *Nicene and Post-Nicene Fathers of the Christian Church*, Vol. 7, Grand Rapids (Eerdmans) 1956, 213.

(1:14). In John's Gospel, thus, "there is not even one word mentioning mother."[13]

4. Sicut Scriptum Est

Galatians 3:15 for Luther was an apocope. The argument here is that Scripture cites itself elliptically or in an abbreviated manner. The "as it is written" (*sicut scriptum est*) is another form of biblical self-referencing. It is Scripture's way of nailing down an assertion. The New Testament's citation of an Old Testament passage is equivalent to the modern footnote. In contrast to the modern footnote, however, it doesn't need to be complete. It is often elliptical. Paul's style of citing the Old Testament elliptically was imitated by Luther; Paul himself was imitating the Hebraic use of ellipsis (ECLIPSIS).[14] Luther was so intent on promoting Pauline theology that he (unconsciously ?) adopted the style of Paul.

Galatians 4:12, 21, 24, 27. The reference from Isaiah "Rejoice, oh barren one" in Galatians 4:27 begins with "as it is written" (*sicut scriptum est*). On Galatians 4:24 the central biblical tradition of praising God as Father—for he is your maker—was continued by Luther. Therefore, ringing throughout the sacred page is this refrain in praise of our maker: "Rejoice, oh barren Sarah, Hannah, Mary, [? Eve ?]." The Bible provided the precedent for medieval usage. It would certainly follow, then, that the medieval pattern of allegory followed the biblical precedent and usage of allegory and, likewise, that the use of the "etc." by Luther and others in his day as a form of cryptic biblical referencing had itself biblical warrant or precedent. In the case of Jesus' reference to the burning bush (Lk. 20:37), the whole passage was being referred to by an allusion to Exodus 3:2. In Luther's mind, Christ's lament on the cross (Ps. 22) was a reference to the whole Psalm which ends in victory and includes "I am a worm and no man." The rich medieval tradition coming from Origen about the whale, the hook, and the worm was

---

13   1538, f. 220 r.: *In epistolam S. Pauli ad Galatas commentarius ex praelectione D. Mart. Luth. collectus. Iam denuo diligenter recognitus, castigatus etc.*, Vittebergae, 1538 (in officiana Iohannis Lufft); WA 2,40,1,14, 'C'.

14   1519, f. 12 v-13 v; the *ecliptica oratio* of Paul's grammar emphasized by Luther in dealing with Gal. 2:7-10 was accented in the margin as *tropus Paulinus* (1519, f. 15 v).

one of Luther's favorites.[15] If Luther was following the biblical pattern of elliptical referencing, then Paul was citing the whole of Isaiah 54, triggered for the audience's mind by citing just the first verse.[16]

The manner of biblical citation employed by medieval commentators that led to their description as "walking concordances" was also for Luther the biblical form of referencing.[17] This means that just as

15 In his German translation, Luther calls this Psalm the passion song of Christ. I like to think that Luther often hummed this tune as did Christ himself. In early Christian theology, Christ's descent into hell was pictured as a worm on a hook cast into the great sea: the little worm (*vermiculus*, Luther) in cosmic battle with the devil. In First Clement, Ps. 22:6 was used to describe the humiliation of Christ. In Origen, the worm as Christ's humanity is used as bait to catch the devil and his angels. In Cyril of Jerusalem, new life comes from worms as evidenced by the birds and the bees. The transformation of the Phoenix from a worm is proof of Christ's resurrection. In Gregory of Nyssa, the gluttonous fish is lured by the flesh of Christ as bait. The divinity of Christ is the hook. Luther referred to Gregory, probably Gregory the Great. God took a sharp fishhook, put an angleworm on it, and threw it into the sea. The worm is the humanity of Christ, the hook the divinity. On the hook, the worm is bound, namely, the humanity. The devil says "should I not swallow the little worm?" He did not see the hook. For Luther, the testator on the cross is pure man, a worm. The testator is also the one who made the promise of the eternal inheritance, "the humanity did not conquer sin and death, but the hook that was hidden under the worm at which the devil struck conquered and devoured the devil who was trying to devour the little worm" (1535, f. 236 r; Hagen, "En Metemarks Testament," *Norsk teologisk tidsskrift* 80, 1979, 239251.)

16 So C. H. Dodd, *According to the Scriptures. The Sub-Structure of New Testament Theology*, London, 1953 (Nisbet & Co. Ltd.), 126. In the quotation of passages from the Old Testament by the "early Christian biblical Scholars" of the New Testament, a "certain *method* of biblical study was established… The method included, first, the *selection* of certain large sections of the Old Testament scriptures, especially from Isaiah, Jeremiah and certain minor prophets, and from the Psalms. These sections were understood as *wholes*, and particular verses or sentences were quoted from them rather as pointers to the whole context than as constituting testimonies in and for themselves. At the same time, detached sentences from other parts of the Old Testament could be adduced to illustrate or elucidate the meaning of the main section under consideration. But in the fundamental passages it is the *total context* that is in view, and is the basis of the argument."

17 According to Robert H. Gundry, citing earlier authorities as well, Luther was right, as least regarding "the whole semitic culture" (*The Use of the Old*

Luther had much if not all of Scripture committed to memory so, he argued, did Paul and Isaiah in the case of Galatians 4:27 and Isaiah 54:1. Luther's point was that the Apostle cited Isaiah (whole chapter) and Isaiah was citing "1 Kings 1" (1 Sam. 1) regarding Hannah (the barren one) and Peninnah, "especially," he added, "with the addition of the song of Hannah," which is actually Chapter 2 of 1 Samuel. So Luther cited Scripture elliptically, and he thought Paul and Isaiah did the same. The audiences of these people would know the Song of Hannah; some would know it by heart—in uninflected Hebrew, at that! How can Luther hold such a position? He said that it was the same Spirit illuminating Isaiah as inspired Samuel.[18] Scripture cites itself for Luther because of the illumination of the one and same Holy Spirit. For Luther, it was absolutely necessary that God's Word be consistent in its grammar, rhetoric, and theology. Luther invariably grounded the unity of Scripture in the HOLY TRINITY.

When Luther's work is seen not as a nineteenth-century commentary but as a medieval *enarratio*,[19] then his use of Scripture is not to provide evidence or proof for an interpretation. Rather, Scripture is used to promote what Scripture promotes throughout: GOD. The WA tests and corrects Luther's "Commentary" with the criterion of the modern footnote. Contrary to the function of the modern footnote, Luther often carried on his argument after the citation of the text with the use of "etc." The words of Scripture for the tradition of

---

Testament in St. Matthew's Gospel, Supplements to Novum Testamentum, Vol. 18, Leiden, [Brill] 1967, 2).

18   1519, f. 49 r.

19   We are accustomed to referring to *a* commentary on *a* book. Among the medievals and continuing into the sixteenth century, the sacred writings were a collection of the manifold mysteries of God. We tend to refer to a work as *a* commentary, whereas in the sixteenth century when commentary appears mostly in the plural it is less *a* commentary and more a series of notes. Thus what we think of as a commentary turns out to be a series of comments on the many ways that God has spoken and acted. I think the difference is that when referring to a commentary we presume that there is a need to make sense out of the biblical text, to provide some kind of unity or coherence that is not immediately apparent; that is, it is shrouded in some kind of enigma that requires the exegetes' expertise to unravel. In the sixteenth century, many of the biblical texts were taken as clear and full of sense(s); the unity and coherence of Scripture was seen as grounded in God, not the exegete.

a biblical *enarratio*, cited explicitly and implicitly, served to advance God's cosmic battle against the demonic forces.

5. Outline of the Main Points

Luther was not interested in a correct proof text. The practice of the WA and modern editions to add quotation marks around Scripture changes Luther's work. Scripture for Luther was a whole piece, a sacred page, not verses, not an ancient reference, not something to be interpreted; Scripture was to be published. There was no need in both the theological and printing praxis of Luther's day to supply the full biblical reference.

The WA consistently identifies MAN IS LIAR with only the marginal reference Psalm 116:11. From a modern point of view, that is all the eye sees. From Luther's point of view, the full reference is also Romans 3:4.

Just as Luther is accustomed to reference Scripture elliptically with an "etc.," so Luther gives reference to the Creed elliptically with only a word or two from it.

Luther sees the abbreviated or short verse, Galatians 3:15, as an abrupt or elliptical expression (*apokope*). Paul's style of citing the Old Testament elliptically was imitated by Luther. The use of the biblical phrase "as it is written," along with elliptical citations and the et cetera, assumes the unity of Scripture.

One has to keep track of the etceteras. "It is all in the et cetera." One needs to know the full page of Scripture in order to follow Luther's argument. The medieval practice of Luther's day was to reference Scripture elliptically or in an abbreviated manner. Only a few words had to be supplied in print so as to trigger the memory of the whole text, chapter, and letter. For Luther, the whole (sacred) page is a part of his argument. Since the modern scholar does not carry Scripture in the head and heart, all the Scripture contained in the "etc." needs to be supplied in order for the WA to edit Luther correctly.

The manner of biblical citation among medieval commentators that led to their description as "walking concordances" was also for Luther the biblical form of referencing. Luther cited Scripture elliptically, and he thought Paul and Isaiah did the same. It is the same Spirit illuminating Isaiah that inspired Samuel. Scripture cites itself for Luther because of the illumination of the one and same Holy Spirit.

A RIDE ON THE QUADRIGA WITH LUTHER[1]

INTRODUCTION

The most common assertion about Biblical Interpretation in the Middle Ages and the Reformation is that medieval theologians employed the fourfold method of interpreting Scripture known as the *quadriga* and the reformers rejected it[2]: the Quad, the four senses were history, allegory, tropology, and anagogy.

"The medieval *quadriga*" is the common coinage.[3] But if you look in your classical Latin dictionary you will find that *quadriga* means "A chariot with its team of four horses running abreast," or "a team of four chariot horses," "four abreast," "a four-horse team," "four-horse chariot," or just "chariot." We might say a four-horse rig. Medieval and ecclesiastical Latin dictionaries continue defining *quadriga* as "chariot" or "wagon."

How do we go then from a four-horse rig to the four senses of Scripture? Histories of hermeneutics will tell you that it's medieval and comes from John Cassian (360-430). All medievals used a threefold or fourfold scheme to designate the multiple senses of Scripture. The fourfold scheme is the *quadriga*, right? Well, it not only is not so easy; it may not be true. And then there is Luther; he rejected allegory and the whole *quadriga*, right? Well, here again it is not so easy and may not be true.

---

1   An earlier version of this was given as a paper at The 33rd Annual Reformation Lectures, Bethany Lutheran College and Seminary, Mankato, Minnesota, October 2000, entitled "Biblical Interpretation in the Middle Ages and Reformation" and subsequently published in: *Lutheran Synod Quarterly* 41 (March 2001) 6–43.

2   *Quadriga(e)* is a contraction from *quadrijugae*. *Quadrijugus* is formed from *quattuor* (4) and *jugum*. *Jugum* is a yoke for oxen and a collar for horses. Hence, four-yoked horses making a four-horse team.

3   See "*Quadriga*: the fourfold pattern of medieval exegesis" in *Dictionary of Latin and Greek Theological Terms,* Drawn Principally from Protestant Scholastic Theology, Richard A. Muller, Grand Rapids 1998, 254.

I. DATA ON QUADRIGA

If you want to know the meaning and use of a word in medieval theology, you must know its usage in the Vulgate because the Latin of medieval theology is the Latin of the Bible. The Latin Vulgate permeated the style and vocabulary of most medieval literature and certainly all of medieval theology. Medieval theologians have been described as "walking concordances" because they carried the whole of Scripture in their heads and hearts. Melanchthon said that Luther had memorized the whole Bible.

I.I. MEANING OF *QUADRIGA* IN THE LATIN BIBLE

The six instances of *"quadriga"* in the nominative singular in the Vulgate all translate "chariot."

Zech. 6:1–5 is cited throughout the Middle Ages:

NRSV Zech. 6:1–5. And again I looked up and saw four chariots coming out from between two mountains—mountains of bronze. The first chariot had red horses, the second chariot black horses, the third chariot white horses, and the fourth chariot dappled gray horses. Then I said to the angel who talked with me, "What are these, my lord?" The angel answered me, "These are the four winds of heaven going out, after presenting themselves before the Lord of all the earth."[4]

There are eight instances of *quadrigae* in the plural, all mean chariots. Example:

NRSV Isa. 66:15. For the LORD will come in fire, and his chariots like the whirlwind, to pay back his anger in fury, and his rebuke in flames of fire.[5]

The four instances of *quadrigam* (in accusative singular) all mean chariot:

---

4 VUL Zech. 6:1. Et converses sum et levavi oculos meos et vidi et ecce quattuor quadrigae egredientes de medio duorum montium et montes montes aerei [2] in *quadriga* prima equi rufi et in *quadriga* secunda equi nigri [3] et in *quadriga* tertia equi albi et in *quadriga* quarta equi varii fortes [4] et respondi et dixi ad angelum qui loquebatur in me quid sunt haec domine mi [5] et respondit angelus et ait ad me isti sunt quattuor venti caeli qui egrediuntur ut stent coram Dominatore omnis terrae.

5 VUL Isa. 66:15. Quia ecce Dominus in igne veniet et quasi turbo *quadrigae* eius reddere in indignatione furorem suum et increpationem suam in flamma ignis.

NRSV Isa. 43:17. ... who brings out chariot and horse, army and warrior; they lie down, they cannot rise, they are extinguished, quenched like a wick.[6]

The eleven instances of *quadrigarum* (genitive plural) all translate chariots:

NRSV 1 Sam. 8:11. He said, "These will be the ways of the king who will reign over you: he will take your sons and appoint them to his chariots and to be his horsemen, and to run before his chariots."[7]

The four instances of *quadrigas* (accusative plural) mean chariots:

NRSV 1 Chron. 18:4. David took from him one thousand chariots, seven thousand cavalry, and twenty thousand foot soldiers. David hamstrung all the chariot horses, but left one hundred of them.[8]

Five instances of *quadrigis* (ablative plural), all chariots:

NRSV 2 Chron. 16:8. Were not the Ethiopians and the Libyans a huge army with exceedingly many chariots and cavalry? Yet because you relied on the LORD, he gave them into your hand.[9]

Conclusion regarding *quadriga* in the Vulgate: The thirty-eight instances of *quadriga* (in various case endings) in the Latin Vulgata all translate and mean chariot(s). Plain old rigs, all connoting horses, charioteers, battles, blood and guts—there is no connection to senses or meaning of anything, let alone Scripture. As I imagine sitting behind a "stink-en" old four-horse team, what flies in my face is anything but the sweetness of Scripture.

1.2. WHAT HAPPENS TO THE WORD QUADRIGA IN THE MIDDLE AGES?

In the electronic *Patrologia Latina Database* (PLD) are 311 instances of *quadriga* in the nominative singular. There is some variation on *quadriga* in the Middle Ages. Beyond the biblical references to chariots

6   VUL Isa. 43:17. Qui eduxit *quadrigam* et equum agmen et robustum simul obdormierunt nec resurgent contriti sunt quasi linum et extincti sunt.

7   VUL 1 Sam. 8:11. Et ait hoc erit ius regis qui imperaturus est vobis filios vestros tollet et ponet in curribus suis facietque sibi equites et praecursores *quadrigarum* suarum.

8   VUL 1 Chron. 18:4. Cepit ergo David mille *quadrigas* eius et septem milia equites ac viginti milia virorum peditum subnervavitque omnes equos curruum exceptis centum *quadrigis* quas reservavit sibi.

9   VUL 2 Chron. 16:8. Nonne Aethiopes et Lybies multo plures erant *quadrigis* et equitibus et multitudine nimia quos cum Domino credidisses tradidit in manu tua.

on earth engaged in battles, using horses and soldiers, the word *quadriga* takes on a figure of speech beyond the temporal world. To use patristic language, it becomes an image, a symbol, a metaphor[10]:

* Martyrs are carried away in chariots to glory (PLD, vol. 17).
* The New Testament—Matthew, Mark, Luke, and John—is the chariot of the Lord (vol. 22 and elsewhere).
* The Lord sits in the heavens in his chariot and the angels praise him (26).
   Lie (falsehood) is the chariot of the demons (39).
* Spousal obedience, you are the perfect ladder to heaven, you are the chariot by which Elijah was carried to heaven, you are the gateway to paradise (40).
* Prudence, justice, temperance, fortitude—these are enclosed in the regions of heaven; you chariot as charioteer of Christ carries to the goal (30).
* Virtues, four cardinal virtues: chariot of the virtues of heaven (46).
* Chariot of friends, full of love (100).
* Ancient customs are brought together into one chariot— Richard, Hugo, Willelmus, Hamo (163).
* The chariot of Christ (*Quadriga Christi*) is the Gospel; the four wheels are the four evangelists. The chariot of Aminadab are the four Gospels (172).

In Scripture and throughout the Middle Ages, *quadriga* means chariot (singular or plural), a four-horse chariot. Most often in the Middle Ages, *quadriga* means one of the chariots of battle cited in Scripture. Less often but sometimes in the Middle Ages, *quadriga* takes on metaphoric usage, the four horses become four virtues, four vices, four Gospels. One could say that it would be a short step from *quadriga* as four Gospels to *quadriga* as the four senses of Scripture. The question is "Who first took that step and when?"

---

10 Joseph W. Trigg (ed.), *Biblical Interpretation*, Wilmington 1988, 65, 115—Origen.

The fourfold sense or meaning (*quadrifariam*) of Scripture, i.e. Jerusalem, goes back to the early period (Jerome, Cassian).[11] A three-fold division goes back to Origen's anthropology of body, soul, and spirit, hence historical, moral, and mystical senses of Scripture. Images of three and four abound. One threefold, classic image, having to do with building a house, came from Gregory the Great and was used by Hugh of St. Victor: the historical sense is the foundation, the structure built thereon is the allegorical sense, the decoration is the tropological sense.[12] Configurations of four abound: four Gospels, four corners of the world, four winds, four rivers of paradise, four legs of the table in the temple. The fourfold division emerged as the dominant practice by the end of the Middle Ages.

The fourfold meaning was put to rhyme, nobody knows exactly when for the first time, and called a "verse" by Lyra; Lyra refers to these four senses (*istorum quatuor sensuum*). The most comprehensive and respected survey of medieval exegesis by Henri De Lubac finds the earliest usage of the rhyme (distich) to come from a Dane, Augustine (Aage) of Denmark, in a document published around 1260.[13] Lyra's dates are 1270–1349.

The verse (distich, a verse couplet[14]) is as follows:
Littera gesta docet, quid credas allegoria,
Moralis quid agas, quo tendas anagogia.

The letter teaches what happened, the allegorical what you are to believe,

the moral what you are to do, the anagogical where you are going.

Jerusalem (literally) is the city; Jerusalem (allegorically) is the church;

11	*Quadrifariam* in Ezek. 45:2 is translated in Douay as "foursquare":

	VUL Ezek. 45:2. Et erit ex omni parte sanctificatum quingentos per quingentos *quadrifariam* per circuitum et quinquaginta cubitis in suburbana eius per gyrum.

12	Rebecca Moore, *Jews and Christians in the Life and Thought of Hugh of St. Victor*, Atlanta 1998, 68.

13	*Exégèse Médiévale: Les quatre sens de l'Écriture*, Paris 1959–64, I,1:23.

14	In my (next) section on medieval manuscripts, I will argue that "distich" has some medieval warrant; *quadriga* does not.

Jerusalem (morally) is the human soul; Jerusalem (anagogically) is heaven.

I see three stages:
1. the fourfold meaning of Jerusalem goes back to Cassian,
2. the Verse comes with Aage and Lyra,
3. *Quadriga with verse has yet to appear.*

Nobody up to Lyra applies the word *quadriga* to the well-known verse (from my research); neither does Lyra. Lyra says, "Sacred Scripture has *quadruplicem sensum* [fourfold meaning]" and later cites "the verse."[15] I think it is safe to say that if anyone were to assign the verse (distich) to *quadriga* the greatest biblical scholar of the age, Nicholas of Lyra, would have done so. Lyra, like Luther's amanuensis Rörer, was a vacuum cleaner that sucked up the wealth of medieval biblical learning.

Now mind you that Lyra is not just some fourteenth-century manuscript, though many copies were made of his commentaries (*Postillae*). LYRA WAS IN THE BIBLE, LUTHER'S BIBLE (literally!). That is, when the Great Froben Bibles were printed in Basil, starting in 1498 and continuing to 1508, Lyra's commentaries occupied the whole right side of the page of the Bible. The Froben Bible (1506–1508) was the edition available to Luther in Wittenberg. So when Luther opened his Bible to his favorite Epistle, Galatians, there he saw Lyra say, "Sacred Scripture has quadruplicem sensum [fourfold meaning]"; *quadruplex* not *quadriga*.

I.3. DOES *QUADRIGA* AS THE SENSES OF SCRIPTURE EXIST IN MEDIEVAL MANUSCRIPTS?

So far printed material has been considered. This section looks at manuscripts. What follows is a summary of findings from searches for the word *quadriga* in medieval manuscripts, as either a verification or falsification of the findings so far.

The conclusion from my searches was/is that the word *quadriga* as the fourfold meaning of Scripture does NOT appear in any of the some forty manuscripts I consulted at the Hill Monastic Manuscript Library (HMML is located in Collegeville, Minnesota), neither in the texts themselves nor in the marginal notations. I was especially hoping that if *quadriga* as the senses of Scripture were so pervasive in the Middle Ages I would find it written in the margins. I tried to find those places where the manuscript used *quadruplicem* or *quadrifariam*

---

15   Lyra on Galatians 4[:24] in *Biblica sacra* (Lugduni, 1545) VI:85v.

or *quattuor sensum* (what I will call the "quads" and "quats"), the medieval variations on the word "fourfold" senses of Scripture. Here I
hoped/supposed that if *quadriga* was a sort of shorthand oral tradition for the senses of Scripture I would find it in the margins. Since I
had not found the word as the senses of Scripture in printed material,
I thought it could be an oral tradition, a gnomic device that everyone
knew by heart.

Karlfried Froehlich wrote a chapter on Trithemius and the fourfold
interpretation of Scripture, and said, "Trithemius himself speaks of
the *modi intelligendi*, and affirms the indispensability of the *quadriga* as
well as its versatility." [16] Since a microfilm copy of the only manuscript
(at Trier) of Trithemius's work is at HMML, I thought it would be
an excellent place to start. [17] *Quadriga* as the sense of Scripture is not
Trithemius's actual word. I see many *quatuor*'s but not *quadriga*. In the
very section where Froehlich says Trithemius "affirms the indispensability of the *quadriga*," Trithemius's text reads "ita quatuor isti modi
intelligendi totius sacra scriptura." I see the "quats," the four rivers, the
four doctors, as Froehlich reports, the modes for interpreting (*intelli-
gentias*) Scripture, but no *quadriga* (f. 196r-v). [18]

The texts from the PLD reported above that used the "quads" and
"quats" were often commentaries on Scripture. I checked what I
thought to be all the likely places where the manuscripts would discuss the multiple senses of Scripture (and did in print). The one place
in the Vulgate where "allegory" is used is Gal. 4:24, "quae sunt per *allegoriam* dicta haec enim sunt duo testamenta unum quidem a monte
Sina in servitutem generans quae est Agar." I consulted nine films that
were single commentaries on Galatians.

---

16   Karlfried Froehlich, "Johannes Trithemius on the Fourfold Sense of
      Scripture: The *Tractatus de Inuestigatione Sacrae Scripturae* (1486)," in:
      Richard A. Muller and John L. Thompson (ed.), *Biblical Interpretation
      in the Era of the Reformation*, Essays Presented to David C. Steinmetz in
      Honor of his Sixtieth Birthday, Grand Rapids 1996, 38.

17   Item 21. Tractatus de investigatione sacre scripture Joannis abbatis
      spanheimensis is on HMML (H) film # 40536; Trier. Bibliothek des
      Priesterseminars Hs 84.

18   Where Froehlich says Trithemius begins the fourth chapter with the
      four rivers of paradise (p. 45) and that the "rubricator refers to them as the
      quadruplex via sacrae scripturae" (p. 38), the text reads "De quadruplici viA
      sacre scripture Sequitur" (f. 196r).

In Thomas Ebendorfer de Haselbach is a version of the tradition-al distich.[19] Is it fair (linguistically clean) to say "traditional distich"? What would be the difference from saying the "traditional *quadriga*"? *Quadriga* comes close to the medieval words, the "quads and quats," and gives the impression that it is the medieval word. Whereas dis-tich is obviously a (modern) poetic term. Lyra does refer to "the verse" (*unde versus*), so there is medieval warrant for "distich," not *quadriga*. In Lewis and Short, versus is used in poetry for verse. In this manuscript someone wrote in the margin: "hystoricus, misticus, allegoricus, ana-gogicus." No *quadriga's*.[20]

I tried a dozen commentaries on all of Paul, with an eye on the Galatians text. No *quadriga*.

In the PLD material the "quadrifariam sacrae Scripturae intelligen-tiam" came up in Honorius Augustodunensis, *Expositio in Cantica*. So I tried some commentaries on the *Cantica Canticorum* with an eye for Sol. 6:11 and "*quadriga(s)* Aminadab." Song of Solomon 6:10 "de-scendi ad hortum nucum ut viderem poma convallis ut inspicerem si floruisset vinea et germinassent mala punica [11] nescivi anima mea conturbavit me propter quadrigas Aminadab." (I went down to the nut orchard, to look at the blossoms of the valley, to see whether the vines had budded, whether the pomegranates were in bloom. I knew not: my soul troubled me for the chariots of Aminadab.)

In some of these manuscripts I found the "*quadrigas* Aminadab" to refer to four virtues. In three manuscripts, I found "quadrigas Aminidab: prima rota sanctitatis vitas secunda fixa humilitas. ter-tia singularis castuas, quarta perfectissima caritas" (the first wheel is

---

19 H 17,435. Oesterreichische Nationalbibliothek, Vienna. Codex Vindobonensis Palatinus 4233. 15.c. (1454 et 1455), Thomas Ebendorfer de Haselbach. Lectura super epistolam Pauli ad Galatas. F 1a–41a. F.23r. gives a version of the traditional distich at the bottom.

20 In H 17,555 Nicolaus de Dinkelsbühl NB Ad Galatas [4:24] "de que sunt per allegoriam dicta. Habet omnis sacra scriptura quadruplicem sen-sum, scilicet hystoricum quae per voces significata …." And then a little later the distich is given. The marginal notes do not treat the senses of Scripture. F. 77r. Oesterreichische Nationalbibliothek, Vienna. Codex Vindobonensis Palatinus 4355. Nicolaus de Dinkelsbhhl. 66a–84a: Lectura in Epistolam ad Galatas.

holiness of life, second firm humility, third moral purity, fourth is most perfect love).[21]
Hugh of St. Victor and Thomas Aquinas relate the "*quadrigas Aminadab*" to the four evangelists.[22] In the same vein is the manuscript of Honorius Augustodunensis, *Super Cantica Canticorum.* The "*Quadriga*" paragraph is set out as new paragraph with a large Q. In the Patrologia Latina (172:454D) it all runs together; only the (numbered) verses are set out in new paragraphs. The point here is that the eye is drawn to the "*Quadriga*" in the manuscript: "Quadriga est christi evangelium. Quatuor rote sunt quatuor evangeliste qui circa finem seculi per totum mundum current." (The "*Quadriga*" is the gospel, and the four evangelists.)[23] In another Honorius manuscript on the Canticle are marginal notes, "hystoria, allegoria, tropologia." The text of Honorius is full to *ad literteram, allegorice, tropologice, anagogice.* No marginals at the "Quadriga est christi evangelium."[24]

Another likely text I tried was 1 Cor. 14:6 ("Nunc autem fratres si venero ad vos linguis loquens quid vobis prodero nisi si vobis loquar aut in revelatione aut scientia aut prophetia aut in doctrina") which prompted Rabanus Maurus (PLD) to elaborate on "quadrifariam sacrae Scripturae intelligentiam." I called up several films, classified in

---

21   H 6704. Stift Zwettl, Austria. Codex Zwettlensis 112. 14.c. F 2a–81b. Expositio in Cantica Canticorum. H 6879. Stift Zwettl, Austria. Codex Zwettlensis 289. 14.c. F 34a–78a Nicolaus de Lyra (?), Postila super Cantica Canticorum. H 4797. Stift Heiligenkreuz, Austria. Codex Sancrucensis 259. 14.c. F.1a–85a. Expositio in Cantica Canticorum.

22   H 36,958. Bischöfliche Priesterseminarbibliothek Mainz. Stadtarchiv K`ln. Hs W kl. f. 132. Expositio Hugonis de sancto Victore super Cantica canticorum. 162 f. 15.c [1452]. f. 66v *quadrigas* Aminidab. "Quadriga est evangelium christi quatuor rote quatuor evangeliste."

H 4797. Stift Heiligenkreuz, Austria. Codex Sancrucensis 259. 14.c. Thomas Aquinas. F 85a–117b. Expositio in Cantica Canticorum. F.108v. "quadrigas appellat quia evangelii predictio quatuor evangelistarum."

23   H 6678. Stift Zwettl, Austria. Codex Zwettlensis 88. 14.c. f.31a–68b Honorius Augustodunensis. Super Cantica Canticorum. F 58r.

24   H 14,434. Oesterreichische Nationalbibliothek, Vienna. Codex Vindobonensis Palatinus 3894. 15.c. (1425). F. 1a–70a. Honorius Augustodunensis. Super Canticum canticorum.

Kapsner as Epistles of Paul,[25] with an eye to both Galatians 4 and 1 Corinthians 14. No *quadriga*.

The final place I thought to look were manuscripts that contained Lyra's first prologue to his "Postilla," where after citing the distich he says, "Et istorum quatuor sensuum potest poni exemplum in hac dictione Jerusalem ...." I checked both the "Postilla in Sacra Scripturam" and the "Postilla mistica."

In one "Expositio moralis" someone wrote in at top "Prologus generalis." The "versus" is given followed by a discussion of the *litera, allegoria, moralis, anagogia*. No *quadriga*.[26]

In another "Postila mistica seu moralis" we find (f.1r–v): "Prologus generalis." It is well said that Scripture is written *intus et foris*. "Foris quantum ad sensum literalem, intus vero quantum ad sensum mysticum sub literam latentem." The exterior meaning is the literal sense. The interior meaning lying hidden under the letter is the mystical sense. This so designed by God the author. After further discussion of this, "unde versus Littera gesta docet ..." followed by the example of Jerusalem, he continues to discuss the "senses" (*sensus/m*). He brings in Galatians 4—through allegory the two testaments are signified. No *quadriga* or *quattuor*, the emphasis is on literal and mystical senses.

Enough of this. What I have written about printed materials is born out by the manuscripts I have worked on. If, as Froehlich says about "unoriginal" Trithemius, the medievals confirm "the indispensability of the *quadriga*," you would think they would use the word accordingly. Trithemius "allows us to catch a glimpse of late medieval hermeneutics in its most normal, most traditional, and most trivial form."[27] No *quadriga* in Trithemius.

My research into Triethemius and other manuscripts shows a consistent pattern of referring to the senses (*sensus*) of Scripture as fourfold (*quadrifariam, quattuor sensus*), without ever using the word *quadriga* as the senses of Scripture. The medievals knew the biblical usage and meaning of the four-horse chariot, and in the manuscripts as well

25   Oliver L. Kapsner, O.S.B. *A Catalog of Bible Texts and Bible Commentaries in Hill Monastic Manuscript Library*, Collegeville, Minn. 1984.

26   H 4219. Schottenstift, Vienna, Austria. Codex Scotensis-Vindobonensis 373 (373). Nicolaus de Lira. Expositio moralis seu mystica super omnes libros Bibliae.

27   Froehlich, 24.

as printed material on occasion amplified a spiritual meaning of the *quadriga* to imply/signify virtues, Gospels.

I tried in vain to find at least one marginal comment with the word *quadriga*. If the method of *quadriga* so dominates medieval biblical interpreting, as so many moderns say, where is it?

Someone, and it may be Luther who started this, has played a trick on medieval biblical interpreters by attributing the word *quadriga* to their method of exegesis (to use another anachronistic term). It is the same with those who refer to "Luther's hermeneutics" when he was opposed to the whole idea of "interpretation," and worse yet, to the problem of interpretation. Luther (and Trithemius) had no hermeneutics, neither did the medievals. Nor could they have the *quadriga* as senses of Scripture given the biblical meaning of the word.

I may be wrong, and certainly my choice of manuscripts (and printed material as well) is far from complete. No one can cover all medieval theology in either print or in manuscript form. But one would think that if *quadriga* were so extensive and dominant that the word as the fourfold meaning of Scripture would show up at least once in the materials I examined.

When you think about it, modern scholarship is full of anachronisms. We devise categories to help classify vast amounts of materials. We all do it. One thing about the *quadriga* that has been of concern is that modern scholars are not aware of the biblical meaning of *quadriga*. Another thing is the *quadriga*, certainly starting with Luther and following, has had a pejorative connotation. Any fourfold scheme does not dominate or even pre-dominate medieval biblical scholarship. Biblical scholarship then had far too many variables to be influenced by any overarching twofold, threefold, or fourfold scheme. These schemes do not account for the splendor and variety of medieval theology. And in the case of the *quadriga*, the vocabulary is simply wrong.

If one needs a category that is not medieval per se but close, distich (ala Lyra's "verse") would be a good replacement for *quadriga*.

I looked at every place in my manuscripts on Scripture where the multiple senses are commented on to satisfy my conscience that I was only relying on printed material. A critic of my manuscript/conference paper said that the *quadriga* must be there in common usage pre-Luther, and that we haven't yet just found it. I would say it is far more likely that Luther started a linguistic tradition and that the history of the word *quadriga* (as fourfold meaning of Scripture) begins with Luther.

2. *QUADRIGA* IN LUTHER

At the end of the Middle Ages the famous "verse" is given by the best-known and most influential biblical scholar, Lyra. The word used by everyone to describe this verse, *quadriga*, cannot be located and connected to the verse in printed or manuscript form. I believe the first person to use the verse and the word *quadriga* is Luther (between 1517 and 1521). You might think that this is an acceptable solution, Luther put *quadriga* on the map; Luther is better known and more influential than Lyra. The problem with this is that when Luther does refer to *quadriga* he does so in a manner that seems to indicate it is a well-known word descriptive of the four senses. Furthermore, Luther's use and comments about *quadriga* are not unequivocal (he vacillates somewhat): at first he is critical of *quadriga*, calling it a game and saying it does not lead to true understanding of Scripture. About two years later he is mildly supportive of *quadriga*. Then about two years later still he attacks *quadriga*. Then after 1521, he reverts to the medieval usage of *quadriga* as "chariot" in the biblical sense of the word and not the four senses of Scripture (see below).

In 1516, as in 1513, Luther uses the traditional four senses, and then in 1516 (on Galatians) he recites the verse (distich) as well. However, no word *quadriga* is attached. In his 1516 comments on Gal. 4:24, Luther introduces the distich with these words: *Quadruplex sensus scripturae habetur in usu* (there is a fourfold meaning of Scripture in use today).[28] Note that Luther says "quadruplex," not *quadriga; quadruplex* was the customary word (Lyra's word).[29] In 1516 he sees prob-

---

28   Clemens/Vogelsang ed. 5:339.31.

29   Joannes Cassianus, Collatio 14, Caput VIII, "De spiritali scientia" in: *Joannis Cassiani Abbatis Massiliensis Collationum XXIV Collectio in tres partes Divisa* PLD 49:0962B–0965B. Cassian Caput VIII: Jerusalem quadrifariam possit intelligi. Quadrifariam adverb comes from quattuor.

Rabanus Maurus (c. 780-856) has quatuor species ad quadrifariam sacrae Scriptureae intelligentiam, history, tropology, allegory, anagogy (PLD 112).

Lyra has the versus, "Littera gesta docet ... quo tendas anagogia" in his first Prologue to the Bible (de commendatione sacrae scripturae), which he describes as quattuor sensuum (*Biblia sacra* [Basel: Froben, 1501] I:3v; PLD Lira).

lems with the usual delimitation of the four senses as too narrow and too inconsistent.

The first usage of *quadriga* comes in a Sermon on the Ten Commandments early in 1517. Here, he is negative, saying that the most impious deal with "*that quadriga*."[30] "The most impious" are called Scholastic doctors. Their most accurate name, however, is "stage actors," "humorists," and "mockers" because they make inept games out of the literal, allegorical, moral, and anagogical senses.[31]

The word "that" (*Illam*) denotes *that* famous *quadriga*, as though everyone knew what Luther was talking about. The demonstrative pronoun (that) puzzles me since I cannot (nor can anyone else) find *quadriga* as the "famous fourfold meaning" in print or in manuscript form. In 1519, when he gives mild approval, he refers again to "*that quadriga*" with a different demonstrative pronoun (*ista*) as though it is well known (in this case he seems to use *ista* with a negative connotation).

In 1519 (on Gal. 4:24), Luther again knows and uses the word *quadriga* applied to the four senses of Scripture.[32] He does so in a way that indicates that he is not making any of this up. He speaks of the usual interpretation of the four senses and even calls it a "game" played by some, which is okay if it is not used to the extreme and if it adds ornamentation to the legitimate sense. Often for Luther allegory means an example for the not well instructed, or a "milky teaching." Then Luther's next point is "That QUADRIGA, though I do not disapprove of it, is not sufficiently supported by the authority of Scripture, by the custom of the Fathers, or by grammatical principles" (LW 27:311). The American Edition translates "*quadriga*" as "four-horse team" which makes no sense as translation but is correct as to its classical usage.

Quattuor sunt regulae sacrae scripturae (Bede; see Froelich, "Johannes Trithemius on the Fourfold Sense of Scripture," 41).

Gerson: quadruplicem (Feld, p. 138 n. 50).

Wycliff: sensum quadruplicem and quattuor species (*De veritate sacrae scripturae*, ed. R. Buddensieg [London: 1905] vol. 1, ch. 6, pp. 119–121).

Jacobus Faber Stapulensis: quatuor sensus (*S. Pauli epistolae XIV*. Faksimilie-Neudruck der Ausgabe Paris 1512. Paul on Gal. 4:24, p. 159a).

30   Decem praecepta Wittenbergensi praedicata populo. 1518 (zwischen 29. Juni 1516 und 24. Februar 1517). WA 1,508,3.

31   WA 1,507,35–39.

32   In epistolam Pauli ad Galatas commentaries, 1519. WA 2,550,34.

Soon after 1519, in his second commentary on the Psalms from 1519-21, Luther has another thought about the *quadriga*, this time completely unfavorable. His concern here is with those who slice up Scripture into various pieces, going back to Origen and Jerome and continuing up to Scholasticism and the Antichrist. Actually Luther's term is very strong; he attacks those corrupters who "lacerate," mangle, Scripture into four parts and "divide the robe of Christ." To paraphrase, toward the end of the *Operationes in Psalmos*:

> Scripture began to be lacerated with the falling apart (down) of the Fathers and to deteriorate in succeeding generations. Then with the Universities and the reigning of the Antichrist, confirmed in the hand of the Roman Pontiff, came not the mystery of iniquity but iniquity itself in control and its abomination standing in the holy place openly, as Christ and his Apostles became extinct. Soon Saint Thomas with Lyra and his kind began to publish to the world *quadrigam illam sensuum scripturae, literalem, tropologicum, allegoricum et anagogicum*, and thus divide the robe of Christ into four parts; and all the authors, doctors, inquisitors were audacious corrupters of Scripture.[33]

Luther sees the *quadriga* to be so named (made known to the world) by Thomas, then Lyra and others. He goes on to repeat that the Scholastics in their lacerations of Scripture know nothing of the legitimate meaning of Scripture. What we may have here I have seen elsewhere in medieval theology, namely, that some position is attributed to someone and that attribution continues to be repeated without any basis in fact. I cannot see where *quadriga* in Thomas is used in any way other than chariots and horses, and as noted above in one place he relates "*quadrigas* Aminadab" to the four evangelists.[34]

These three references, 1517, 1519, 1521, are the only three references in all of Luther's works where he connects *quadriga* with the four senses of Scripture; otherwise, in thirteen other uses *quadriga* refers

---

33 Operationes in Psalmos. 1519–1521. WA 5,644,19–28. Also in 1521, in a German work Against Emser, Luther attacks those who out of "ignorance" attribute "four senses" (*vier synn*) to Scripture. "There is no basis for it" (WA 7,652).

34 See *quadriga* in *Index Thomisticus* # 67561.

to chariot(s), [35] except in one place where it means "fourfold meaning of sins." [36]

I must conclude that Luther in 1517 is the first to use *quadriga* in print as applied to the fourfold meaning of Scripture. You could even say the four-horse chariot has become the fourfold meaning of Scripture, a logical extension of medieval metaphor. Now mind you that Luther is not terribly excited about the fourfold meaning (now called *quadriga* by him), and says that it cannot be used to establish a doctrine of faith (which is Aquinas's position as well). In addition, he says that the distinctions among the four senses are not clearly and consistently made among the Fathers. Nevertheless, Luther uses the three spiritual senses off and on throughout his life, not for doctrine but for example and ornamentation.

I see three possible explanations of how this all hangs together, namely, that Luther was the first to use *quadriga* as the fourfold meaning of Scripture and yet uses demonstrative pronouns that seem to indicate that everyone was familiar with this meaning of *quadriga*. One is that he found and adopted the word *quadriga* from an, as yet, unknown source. Two, he heard it used in the lecture hall as an oral shorthand reference to the fourfold meaning, sort of as a figure of speech, much the same way the word *quadriga* apparently has been used from the sixteenth century on. You say *quadriga* and everyone knew and knows that you mean the traditional medieval fourfold meaning of Scripture. He even ascribes its origin to Thomas and Lyra who were most likely sources, believable and repeatable by everyone. I say "from the sixteenth century on," since *quadriga* is so defined in Muller's *Dictionary of Latin and Greek Theological Terms, Drawn Principally from Protestant Scholastic Theology* (see note 3). The way Luther and this Latin Dictionary for the sixteenth century read, *quadriga* as the fourfold meaning was a kind of oral tradition never put in print.

For my third possibility, Lyra (again) unlocks the door I have been trying to open. Once it dawned on me that in Luther's Bible *quadruplex* and not *quadriga* was used, Luther had to be the first to use the term *quadriga* as the medieval fourfold meaning of Scripture. Or put it another way, if anyone was going to use *quadriga* before Luther it would have been Lyra (and wasn't). Luther is famous for making up

35 See *quadriga* in the Index of Latin Words in Luther's Works WA 67,603.
36 WA 8,82,26.

German words; why not Latin? And the demonstrative pronouns were good Luther rhetoric.[37]

Perhaps Luther was not aware of the importance of his use of *quadriga* for Scripture at that instance in 1517. Nevertheless, his use of the word is consistent with his new understanding of Scripture. For the medievals, and this is Luther's consistent complaint, the four senses of Scripture could and did become a biblical game, a spiritual game without the Spirit. Scripture could be manipulated by the clever allegorist. How many allegories can you find? For Luther, Scripture is not to be interpreted; it is not up to the interpreter to show off the many meanings of Scripture. Scripture is a performative force that drives, propels, promotes, transports Christ. The interpreter is to get out of the way and let the moving force of God's Word do God's work (law and Gospel). The other consistent criticism of Luther is that the *quadriga* slices up the wholeness of Scripture into bits and pieces. He goes on in the *Operationes* to say that Scripture has one, most simple sense; Scripture remains the most simple doctrine of faith, hope, and charity. The word "most simple" (*simplicissima*) means most plain, open, straightforward, frank, and honest. No hidden mysteries that require the scholastic doctors to cull and carve out the meanings of Scripture.

3. SCRIPTURE AS CARRIER

Let's back up our wagon and take another run at this topic. I would suggest that in our next ride through the Middle Ages and Luther we extend the medieval metaphor a bit and consider the *quadriga*, chariot, in the sense of journey. Specifically Scripture becomes a means of transportation to God, both in the Middle Ages and in a different way in Luther.

Biblical Interpretation in the Middle Ages and Reformation begins and ends on a journey. The image of a journey and carriage is not just a metaphor or symbolic language. It is the actual language of understanding and interpreting the Bible in the early church and Middle Ages, continuing into the Reformation.

The language of journey is actually the first term used to describe those who also became known as "Christian." Those who followed

---

37   Dr. Franz Posset, who read this manuscript, asked: "Could it be that Luther as the Dr. Exaggerator made up a straw man with this *quadriga*: in order then to knock it down?"

Jesus were known as followers of the "Way" or those who belonged to the Way (see six references in Acts).[38]

Augustine set the stage for understanding the Christian life as a journey, a journey home to God. The medieval believer was described as a *viator* (pilgrim), on the way, on a journey, the goal of the journey is home, and home is the Trinity (in Augustine's terms). What I am suggesting is that the medievals viewed the understanding and interpretation of Scripture as a journey into the depth of the riches and wisdom and knowledge of God. As the journey home to God is a life-long effort, so the understanding of God's Word is a lifelong quest. As one never gets to the bottom of God, so one never gets to the bottom of Scripture.

The medieval four senses was/is often maligned as an escape from the letter of Scripture into fairy tale and allegory. This criticism is actually as old as the Middle Ages; that is, the criticism of excesses in allegory is a constant in the Middle Ages and Reformation. The twelfth-century Victorines were critical of the allegorists of their day.

Two points in defense of allegory: One, allegory is used in Scripture. Two, it is an attempt to penetrate the spiritual depths of meaning in Scripture; for Luther, allegory is an example, a good story. Plus, for Aquinas and Luther no doctrine could be based on allegory or any of the spiritual senses, but only on the literal sense of Scripture.

---

38 Acts 9:2: ... and asked him for letters to the synagogues at Damascus, so that if he found any belonging to *the Way*, men or women, he might bring them bound to Jerusalem.

Acts 19:9: ... but when some were stubborn and disbelieved, speaking evil of *the Way* before the congregation, he withdrew from them, taking the disciples with him, and argued daily in the hall of Tyrannus.

Acts 19:23: About that time there arose no little stir concerning *the Way*.

Acts 22:4: I persecuted this *Way* to the death, binding and delivering to prison both men and women.

Acts 24:14: But this I admit to you, that according to *the Way*, which they call a sect, I worship the God of our fathers, believing everything laid down by the law or written in the prophets.

Acts 24:22: But Felix, having a rather accurate knowledge of *the Way*, put them off, saying, "When Lysias the tribune comes down, I will decide your case."

The point of the four senses is not the horse but the number. The number four, as stated earlier, was very suggestive and symbolic. As far as I can tell, the first use of the quadruple word was in Cassian, where he uses *quadrifariam*, an adverb descriptive of the action in penetrating the depths of Scripture.

By the end of the Middle Ages the number four was firmly in place; Luther used the word *quadriga*. In the earlier Middle Ages, the senses and rules for understanding Scripture could very often be three or even seven. At the end of the Middle Ages two senses of Scripture were offered by Aquinas and Lyra. The importance of these numbers is that they are more than one. The reason was the oft-cited verse "The letter kills, but the Spirit gives life." That verse was understood to mean that the letter of Scripture, while inspired by God, was not the end of Scripture. The end of Scripture is the spirit of God, life in God. Second Cor. 3:6: "[God] has made us competent to be ministers of a new covenant, not of letter but of spirit; for the letter kills, but the Spirit gives life." The combination of this verse and Augustine's famous letter/Spirit dichotomy led to a sharp distinction between letter/spirit, exterior/interior, flesh/spirit, OT/NT.

In the background of the early medieval view of the multiple senses of Scripture was neo-Platonic philosophy, that reality lies above and beyond the historical particular. As Aristotle came into medieval theology, the value of the historical entity, the letter of Scripture, increased to the point that all spiritual meaning was seen contained in the letter (double-literal sense: literal historical, literal prophetic). The spiritual senses allowed the medieval pilgrim to penetrate the heights and depths of the mysteries of God. The quest for meaning was the search for God. The monastic quest was a human quest aided by the graces of God. Scripture and the sacraments of the Church were the means for living the Christian life of piety and service. Augustine said that the proper end of Scripture was charity. If you had correct interpretation but not charity, you had not understood the Bible. On the other hand, if your interpretation was not accurate (not the intention of the author) but your reading led to charity, you are not deceived and will reach the proper end of the Bible.[39] I have tried here to suggest that the medieval perception of Scripture as a means of transportation home to God, as a means to another end, was cast in terms of reaching beyond

---

39   Augustine, *On Christian Doctrine* I: 35–36. In the D.W. Robertson edition in the Library of Liberal Arts, it is pages 30–31, New York 1988.

the letter of Scripture and searching for God in spiritual realms. The search for God in spiritual realms was to lead to a life of virtue. Within the monastery the Bible was also a *regula vivendi*. It was God's supreme directive guiding the monk along the *via regia* to his heavenly homeland. This principle is clearly enunciated in St. Benedict's Rule (chap. 73): "For what page or what saying of the divinely inspired books of the Old and New Testament is not a most correct rule of human life?" The Bible was, therefore, in monastic circles not only a source of truth but also a source book of morality which proposed to the monk the virtues to be acquired in his religious life. The fourth chapter of St. Benedict's Rule presents a list of monastic virtues, derived from the Bible, which the monk is to acquire and exercise.[40]

With Luther, Scripture as carrier ends with a different focus. One of his rules for reading Scripture was *was Christum treibet*. Scripture is what carries Christ. And what carries or promotes Christ is at the heart of Scripture. *Treiben* is an old Germanic word connoting transportation. The journey image with Luther ends up right at the heart and letter of Scripture. For Luther the move is not away from the letter but directly to the letter as the conveyer of Christ.

3.1. CONCLUSION TO SCRIPTURE AS CARRIER

The situation is this. We have allegory in Scripture, typology, moral application, and heaven as the end of it all. Scripture resonates with Scripture; Scripture is full of echo, repetition, explanation, commentary. As Luther says, Scripture interprets itself. This inner scriptural action of comment and application continues in the history of the Church. Add the ingredient of 2 Cor. 3:6, "The letter kills, but the Spirit gives life," and you have the extension of multiple senses of Scripture. The lifelong search for God is the search for the spiritual meaning of Scripture in medieval theology. For Luther, however, the Second Corinthian passage is not license for allegory, nor is it a diminution of the letter, but rather teaches the distinction between law and Gospel, the law which kills and the Gospel that gives life.

Luther's response to the various senses of meaning in the Middle Ages (threefold, fourfold, double-literal sense) was that Scripture has one simple sense (most often, Christ). The grammatical sense is the simplest sense and is the meaning of the text, the grammatical-historical

---

40   Robert E. McNally, S.J. *The Bible in the Early Middle Ages*, Westminster 1959, 9.

meaning and the theological meaning are the same. The literal meaning is the spiritual meaning because the letter is of the Spirit. "The Holy Spirit is the simplest writer and adviser in heaven and on earth."[41] Luther's objection to the fourfold meaning is that it is based on a faulty reading of 2 Cor. 3:6, "The letter kills, but the Spirit gives life." The letter does not kill, Christ himself used the letter of Scripture. Luther concluded: "From this it is now clear that the words of the apostle, 'The letter kills, but the Spirit gives life,' could be said in other words: 'The law kills, but the grace of God gives life.'"[42]

Another of Luther's objection is that the multiple senses of Scripture would mean that Scripture could have more than one meaning. It is unthinkable that Scripture could say one thing and mean something else. Luther's further contention is that the *quadriga* arbitrarily superimposes a fourfold scheme onto Scripture, which does not come from Scripture itself. For Luther the only rules for interpreting Scripture must come from Scripture itself.

4. CONCLUSION

In this research I have tried to solve the mystery of where the word "*Quadriga*, the fourfold pattern of medieval exegesis" actually came from. Since *quadriga* in all the Latin Dictionaries I know means a four-horse team, a "stink-en" old wagon pulled by four horses under four collars, how do we get the four senses of Scripture out of this word?

The earliest source I have found is Luther, and that in a fairly brief time frame in his life, between 1517 and 1521. I have suggested that he may have heard it and certainly used it as a figure of speech. The final history of the word *quadriga* may never be written.

I must confess that in my writing (heretofore) I too have repeated what everyone else has repeated, namely, that the medieval approach to Scripture was dominated by the *quadriga* as the fourfold meaning of Scripture. I have tried to explain the results of this fresh research.

As said, Luther vacillated a bit on his use of *quadriga*, briefly "not disapproving" though mostly disapproving strenuously. This is not the first instance of Luther shifting his opinion on a Latin or Greek word. The impression I have is that when Luther realized what the

---

41 Auff das ubirchristlich, ubirgeystlich und ubirkunstlich Buch Bocks Emszers zu Leypczick Antwortt D. M. L. WA 7,650, 21–24. LW 39,178.
42 Ibid., WA 7, 655, 3–7. LW 39,183.

quadriga really entailed, that is, finding several meanings for one word and one passage, all his hermeneutical rules came into play. One such prominent rule is that Scripture says what it means and means what it says, and does so in a straightforward manner. Scripture interprets itself and is clear. No need to search for meanings other than what is said. After Luther realized this, he went back to using *quadriga* in the biblical sense of a four-horse chariot.

Bear in mind that Luther, very much a theologian of his day, continued to use allegory and the other spiritual senses throughout his life. So, it is not fair to say that Luther dumped the *quadriga* in the sense of dismissing all spiritual senses. His use of the spiritual senses, however, was under tightly controlled rules.

What I think is important about Luther as a theologian of his day on the issue of Scripture is that medievals used Scripture as a means of spiritual formation, the formation of virtuous habits. Remember that for Augustine the proper end of Scripture is charity. For Luther there is more to Scripture than virtue, charity, and good habits, however desirable they all are. The purpose of Scripture is to promote Christ and Christ alone. Scripture is an end in itself in that there in the heart of the sacred page is Christ himself.

LUTHER'S PREACHING TO THE HOMETOWN FOLKS

The sermon is "perhaps the most significant genre of literature stemming from the Lutheran Reformation." It served to transfer the new ideas and reforms to audiences far and wide. The reason for this is twofold: in the largely oral culture, the spoken word was the vehicle through which the majority of the population received information; and second, the sermon was dominant in print culture, so much so that Luther's sermons appeared in mass quantities in the first decade of the reform movement. Between 1518 and 1525, over eighteen hundred vernacular works of Luther, including numerous reprints, were published; two of every five were sermons.[1]

Luther's preaching ministry began officially in May 1512, commissioned by the Vicar-General of the Augustinian Order, Johann von Staupitz. At the request of the city council, he took on preaching responsibilities from the ailing pastor (Simon Heinz) for the city/parish church; thus from 1514 until Bugenhagen's appointment in1522, and in Bugenhagen's frequent absence, Luther continued to preach at St. Mary's.

It is virtually impossible to get a handle on all of Luther's approximately 2,300 sermons (in print). Two recent full-length studies have focused on just the year 1522.[2] Articles tend to focus on one pericope, one sermon, or one category of sermon (Luther on daily bread, for example).

Scholars have tried to characterize all of Luther's sermons. Harold Grimm says Luther's sermons can be classified as kerygmatic, didactic, paracletic (consolation), and polemical.[3] John Doberstein

1   Beth Kreitzer, "The Lutheran Sermon," *Preachers and People in the Reformations and Early Modern Period*, ed. Larissa Taylor (Leiden: Brill, 2001) 35, 40.

2   Susanne bei der Wieden, *Luthers Predigten des Jahres 1522, Untersuchungen zu ihrer Überlieferung*. Archiv zur Weimarer Ausgabe der Werke Martin Luthers 7 (Cologne: Böhlau Verlag, 1999). Neil R. Leroux, *Luther's Rhetoric, Strategies and Style from the Invocavit Sermons* (St. Louis: Concordia, 2002).

3   Harold J. Grimm, "The Human Element in Luther's Sermons," Archive for Reformation History 49 (1958): 50.

says Luther uses direct address, dialogue, and the dramatic form.[4] Robert Schaibley says Luther's method was coherence, interface, and correlation.[5] Irving Sandberg and Tim Wengert say Luther's use of "direct address, paraphrase and exaggeration, as well his identification of the characters with his own situation, served to crucify and raise his hearers ..."[6] David Yeago says, "Although the sermons are typically leisurely, rambling and discursive, Luther's *argument* nonetheless has a clearly defined logical structure.[7]

The real problem with trying to characterize Luther's preaching is that the sermons were of such a varied form, largely due to their historical situations: sermons on the pericope, sermon series on the catechism, sermon series on a succession of biblical chapters, sermons on theological topics, sermons for various occasions—baptisms, funerals, inauguration, sermon series on different days of the week.

It is impossible to say that Luther followed one style throughout. Secondary literature comes down on opposite sides of the following: he had concern for form or he did not;[8] his was a homily or not a homily;[9] thematic or not thematic; rhetorical or not; Luther was dependent on Quintilian or not (and interest in rhetoric came later in the sixteenth century);[10] he used Greek and Hebrew in his sermons or he did not; he abandoned allegory or continued to use allegory.[11]

---

4   John Doberstein, "Introduction," AE 51:xx.

5   Robert Schaibley, "Lutheran Preaching: Proclamation, Not Communication," Concordia Journal 18 (1992): 14.

6   "Introduction," in *The 1529 Holy Week and Easter Sermons of Dr. Martin Luther*, trans. Irving L. Sandberg, annotated with an introduction by Timothy J. Wengert (St. Louis: Concordia, 1999), 26 (hereafter referred to as *1529 Holy Week and Easter Sermons*).

7   David Yeago, "The Bread of Life: Patristic Christology and Evangelical Soteriology in Martin Luther's Sermons on John 6," *St Vladimir's Theological Quarterly* 39/3 (1995): 258.

8   The "no form" is Yngve Brilioth, *A Brief History of Preaching*, trans. Karl Mattson (Philadelphia: Fortress, 1965), 112.

9   "Not homily" is Fred W. Meuser, *Luther the Preacher* (Minneapolis: Augsburg, 1983) 47.

10   Concern for rhetoric came later in the sixteenth century according to Grimm, "Human Element," 53.

11   The variations in secondary literature regarding what Luther did or did not do in his sermons could be accounted for in terms of what slice of

Because of the complexity and variety of Luther's sermons, I decided to study three different sets of sermons from the 1520s, when the Reformation really took off. The three I worked on were in different historical situations and of different genre, my purpose being to cut across different types and forms to see what conclusions I could make. I concluded that certain themes and issues came to the fore in all the sermons I read. These issues are Luther's "form of address," his doctrine of vocation, his teaching on ethics, the current issue of rhetoric, and the last is a question: "What must sermons do?"

The three sets of sermons I studied are 1) the famous Invocavit Sermons (1522), that is, the eight sermons at St. Mary's which were given immediately upon Luther's return from the Wartburg. He left the safe confines of the castle to exercise his pastoral calling under the protection of God alone in order to quell radical departures at the parish church. I include these because of the unique historical situation (*Notsituation*[12]) and because of the new critical edition.[13] 2) The second set is the Catechism Sermons (1528), the third series, because of their proximity to the Small and Large Catechisms and also because they are instruction for children (*Kinderlehre*).[14] 3) The third set is the 1529 Holy Week Sermons because the editors say that they show "Luther at the height of his expository power and demonstrate the depth of his pastoral concern."[15]

My paper is organized around the issues and themes, citing primary material as I go along from the three sets of sermons in roughly chronological order.

---

sermons the scholar takes. You might say that what everyone says is true, is true for the selection of sermons they make.

12   Hanfried Fontius, "Martin Luthers Predigt in Aktueller Notsituation der Kirche, die Invokavit-Predigten von 1522," *Luther als Prediger*. Veröffentlichungen der Luther-Akademie e.V. Ratzeburg, 9 (Erlangen: Martin-Luther-Verlag, 1986), 77-88.

13   "Eight Sermons at Wittenberg, 1522," AE 51:60-100. "Dominica Invocavit. Sermon DML," Studienausgabe (StA) 2:530-58.

14   "Ten Sermons on the Catechism, 1528," AE 51:137-93; "Katechismuspredigten, Dritte Predigtreihe," WA 31/I:57-122.

15   *1529 Holy Week and Easter Sermons*. Trans. from "Predigten D. Martin Luthers auf Grund von Nachschriften Georg Rörers und Anton Lauerbachs," ed. Georg Buchwald (Gütersloh: Bertelsmann, 1925), hereafter referred to as *Predigten*, vol. I or II.

The question of the reliability of the sources need not detain us long. As in the case of Luther's *Lectures on Genesis*, some have raised the critical suggestion that Luther's sermons reflect more the words of the transcriber(s) than Luther himself.[16] Ulrich Asendorf and others have set aside such suggestions.[17] My own view is that chief scribe Rörer (especially) was a virtual vacuum cleaner, sucking up every word of Luther. Besides, Luther was *tardiloquus*, a slow, deliberate preacher, and the secretaries were accustomed to writing in abbreviated Latin— in other words, they were good at shorthand![18]

I am using "sermon" as distinct from the "postil" (sermon guide) and as distinct from works entitled *Sermo* but never preached. Furthermore, it is often said that Luther's lectures were sermonic and that it is hard to distinguish the lectures from the sermons. I'm not so sure about this anymore. The lectures included technical, linguistic analyses, and philosophical arguments, which his sermons tended not to include. Luther criticized Zwingli for bringing Greek and Hebrew into his sermons at Marburg.[19]

LUTHER'S FORM OF ADDRESS

The issue of Luther's form of address—first person, second person, or third person, or some combination thereof—is to assess the relation of preacher to people and to see how the Gospel is presented. Another reason for looking at Luther's "form of address" (as I am calling it) is that Rev. Maxfield and I agreed at the outset of this assignment that we wanted to see what Luther actually wanted his people to hear. Out of this came the title "Luther's Preaching to the Hometown Folks."

In addition to being a professor, Luther was "father" (Rev. Father), pastor, doctor of the church, and friar (not monk!)—all

---

16　Emanuel Hirsch, „Vorrede," *Luthers Werke in Auswahl* (Berlin: Walter de Gruyter, 1950), 7:vii.

17　Ulrich Asendorf, *Die Theologie Martin Luthers nach seinen Predigten* (Göttingen: Vandenhoeck & Ruprecht, 1988), 18-19.

18　Luther's transcribed sermons were often in macaronic, a mixture of Latin words and the vernacular. The copyists had only Latin abbreviations in their repertoire, so it was easier and quicker to transcribe, e.g., "faith" with "f" (*fides*) than with *der Glaube*. Rörer was the most accomplished and had developed his own system of abbreviations and signs.

19　Walter von Loewenich, *Martin Luther, The Man and His Work*, trans. Lawrence W. Denef (Minneapolis: Augsburg, 1986), 356.

religious-pastoral titles in Luther's late medieval setting. Luther was a Wittenberg pastor. In the Second Invocavit Sermon, Luther speaks of Wittenberg beer in the famous paragraph about the Word doing everything while he slept or drank Wittenberg beer with friends. In the First Invocavit Sermon Luther is concerned that Wittenberg not become a Capernaum and end in worse fate than Sodom. Likewise in this sermon Luther is concerned not to "overwhelm" his people, literally cover them (überschütten) with many texts,[20] and even says that he "loves" them (poetic meaning of meinen).[21]

You could say that Luther's so-called "ten commandments" for good preaching (Conditiones boni praedicatoris) reflect a concern for effective communication with his people:

> (1) teach well (to be understood), (2) have a good head, (3) be a good speaker, (4) have a good voice, (5) have a good memory, (6) know when to stop, (7) be convincing (and diligent), (8) put body and life on the line [my version of "sol leib und leben dran setzen"; or maybe risk life and limb], (9) be prepared to be ridiculed by everyone, (10) endure patiently, and know that the world sees nothing more quickly in preachers than their mistakes.[22]

In the Introduction to the American Edition of Luther's Sermons, John Doberstein says concerning the form of address:

> Luther has the persons of the text speaking to one another or goes into an imaginary dialogue between the preacher and his listeners or the preacher and his opponents. And every sermon is part and parcel of his own struggle, not only the dialogue he is carrying on with his opponents, the papists and the enthusiasts [Schwärmer], but also of that existential encounter which is constantly being enacted on the cosmic, eschatological level.[23]

In other words, the sermon is in nuce a retelling of the saving event and is the saving event, where the ultimate battle between God and Satan is fought out every day in the ears and hearts of the hearers. The sermon is proclamation of the proclamation, the Word of Christ addressing the folks directly in the second person.

---

20   AE 51:70; StA 2:530.14. Also 51:165 (Catechism Sermons of 1528).
21   AE 51:73; StA 2:532.32.
22   WATr 2:2580. Somewhere I saw: "Stand up, speak up, shut up."
23   "Introduction to Volume 51," Sermons, AE 51:xix-xx.

I find that Luther's form of address is often that of the Scripture cited: Come unto me, all who labor ... and I will give you rest (an often-cited text). The third person is merged with the first and second person, singular and plural: Christ has ... , me, us, we, I, and you—all blend together in total identification of preacher and people (Easter Monday Afternoon, 1529).[24] The Gospel is the personal form of address: *your* sins are forgiven. Even the demons know on a historical level that Christ died for the sins of the world, called "the faith of the demons," which is not saving faith. Saving faith ends the cosmic conflict; Christ is risen, the ultimate apocalyptic victory over Satan. The thesis here is that the sermon is this form of address that announces Christ's apocalyptic victory "for us," "for me." People understood evil, sin, the grace of the sacraments, "a troubled conscience"; they understood the difference between the pangs of a guilty conscience and the assurance of forgiveness (St. Matthias' Day, 1525).[25]

Though I am light on generalizations, one conclusion I have reached is that Luther's sermons reflect his personal engagement. The sermons are for the people present. His style was *extempore* (to speak without written text). This style allowed him to speak directly to his audience, rather than read a sermon prepared in his study (I have not seen anybody make this point). *Extempore* is different than *impromptu* and offhand because he did prepare. His preparation consisted in writing out a *Konzept*—which can be translated as concept, but more accurately as rough copy or outline. When I first read references to Luther's *Konzepte*, I thought it was akin to what I have done in the past, i.e., right down a few words on the back of a communion card before giving a lecture. Some fourteen of these have been found and printed in the WA. These *Konzepte* are really brief outlines, for example, one is 24 lines for a 94-line sermon.[26]

The personal engagement was also with the subject matter. I am convinced that one of the motives of Luther's "reformatory program" (as Germans would put it) was his conviction that his beloved German people deserved to hear the Gospel. Luther the pastor saw the need

---

24   Christ uses "I" with Mary ("Do not hold on to me because I have not yet ascended") so that we may allow the third and first person singular to be a unity; when Christ says "I" we should see that it concerns us (*1529 Holy Week and Easter Sermons*, 145; *Predigten*, I:377).

25   "Sermon on St. Matthias Day, 1525," AE 51:129, 131.

26   Number 5 of "Vierzehn Predigtkonzepte Luthers," WA 48:339-40.

to lift the burden of medieval laws off the shoulders of his people. Frequently Luther says in his sermons, "previously, we were taught" to do this, to avoid that—restrictions upon restrictions. For Luther the Middle Ages meant law, lowercase "l," uppercase "L": Germanic and Roman laws, canon laws of the church as well as a doctrine of salvation by Law. His people deserved not another "pen house," writing more laws, but a "mouth house," where their Christian freedom was proclaimed.

The scholastic sermons of the day were on the academic side for the university audience.[27] The sermons of the mendicant friars, often given at the center of the cities and towns, were edifying and entertaining. Homiletic sermons continued in limited circles.[28] None came with Luther's conviction of the performative power of the Word—the medium of the words perform the message that for Christ's sake your sins are forgiven. "My word does not return void but accomplishes that which I purpose" (Is 55:11). The various sermonic forms—academic, sensational, homiletic—all had their place (say I). I am convinced that Luther saw the need for a new form, toning down the entertaining and literary forms, and lifting up the text of Scripture as written from faith to faith for the faith of his people. The "grammar of faith," Scripture, was the discipline in which Luther was trained and to which he committed all his energies. John O'Malley's conclusion is that Luther fits into the tradition of the "Christian grammarian" in his exposition of the text.[29] The living voice of God (*viva vox Dei*) emanating from the

---

27 The Scholastic method of preaching: *modus ... praedicandi per divisiones et per thema* (Brilioth, *Brief History of Preaching*, 82).

28 John O'Malley, "Introduction: Medieval Preaching," in *De Ore Domini, Preachers and Word in the Middle Ages*, ed. Thomas Amos, Eugene Green, Beverly Kienzle (Kalamazoo: Western Michigan University, 1989), 10.

29 O'Malley distinguishes between rhetoric and grammar as two components within the complex movement of humanism. Relating Luther to humanism is a "difficult task because of its complexity." O'Malley distinguishes between primary and secondary rhetoric, and in grammar between philological and poetic levels of interpretation, and posits a fundamental distinction between the grammarian and the rhetorician. Grammar was text-related, rhetoric was action-related. For example on one end of the spectrum is the scribe poring over his text, at the other end is the statesman arguing before the senate for the declaration of war. Origen's heritage to the Fathers was *explication de texte*, homiletical exposition verse by verse of the text using techniques of classical grammar. How does Luther fit in: he fits

grammar of faith is what his dear Saxon flock needed and deserved to hear.

VOCATION AND ETHICS

I came into this project with an eye to see if and how Luther's doctrine of vocation played out in the pulpit. In the First Invocavit Sermon Luther says that faith is directed to God's Son and love to the neighbor.[30] In the Second Sermon, Luther begins with the same point. On the matter of what is of necessity (must) and what is of choice (may), Luther says one "must" love the neighbor in the same manner as God dealt with us.[31] On the face of it, it may seem rather simplistic to say that faith is directed to God and love to the neighbor, but just as we know in the case of "justification by faith" that faith is hardly simplistic and Luther took a hundred volumes to explain it, so also Luther's ethic of love is hardly simplistic.

The key to Luther's ethic of love, not well understood in general and not at all in classics such as Paul Althaus and George Forell, is that Luther preaches and writes on love as an ethic *in the classic sense of ethics*.[32] In my recently published article on vocation, I argue that Luther had an ethic, other than doing good and avoiding evil, other than

---

first and foremost into the tradition of "the Christian grammarian" and the *explication de texte*. As to *doctrina* and *exhortatio*, Luther related teaching with the practice of dialectics. So, with Luther we have homiletical form conditioned in part by the classical *contio* ("Luther the Preacher," in *The Martin Luther Quincentennial*, ed. Gerhard Dünnhaupt [Detroit: Wayne State University Press, 1985], 6-10, 13). *Contio* is oration before a public assembly.

30 AE 51:72.

31 AE 51:75.

32 Ethos (which Paul Althaus uses interchangeably with ethics) in classical Greek and the New Testament denotes the habits of people, their manner of living (which is the way we use ethos today). In Luther's Vulgate, the Latin for ἔθος was derivatives of *consuetudo* (custom, habit, usage), and *mos* (conduct, behavior). For his German Bible, Luther rendered ἔθος as *Gewohnheit* (custom), *pflegen* (be in the habit of), and *Weise* (manner, way). In my own manuscript, I conclude: Luther does have a Christian ethic, a theory, a doctrine, beyond the description of behavior; Luther sees "ethics" as a *ratio*, a doctrine, a principle of nature.

encouraging the basics of Christian living.[33] My thesis on ethics is that Luther's ethic was a principle, the principle that the love of the neighbor is an end in itself, a radical principle in the late medieval scene, whether scholastic, humanist, or monastic. Across the board among the late medievals, love of the neighbor was an act for the benefit of the *doer*, not the recipient, the neighbor. The motive was ulterior: my works of love toward the neighbor for the glory of God accrue back to me in my formation of virtue. For Luther there is no ulterior motive, namely, the enhancement of my standing before God. The motive, the goal, is the neighbor, the improvement of the neighbor's life. This has been called the "radical horizontalization of social ethics."[34]

Luther's Invocavit Sermons that seem to be in the genre of exhortation—and exhortations do abound—are at base an exercise in Luther's ethic. The point is that while Luther preached and wrote so extensively on faith, the end or purpose is love of the neighbor. I think Luther's "reformatory plan" was motivated by his desire, along with the intentions and desires of all the humanists and "pre-reformers," to effect a reformation of church and society. But Luther took a different approach. Rather than attacking abuses from the pulpit and in the pamphlets as the others did, Luther deemed that bad fruit was the result of a bad tree, and hence proposed the basics of his theology.

The bad fruit in Wittenberg, while Luther was at the Wartburg, wanted to change everything overnight and institute radical changes in liturgy and custom. Upon return and in the First Invocavit Sermon Luther got down to basics, the *Hauptstück* (principles, the main points) that are Christian: we are children of wrath, that is, nothing; God's Son makes us *ein kind gottes* (children of God); we must love one another and have patience, thus not abolish the mass in an unorderly manner. Faith without love is no *warhafftigs* (real, true) faith, only *scheyn* (pretense); love is necessary for the neighbor. We must

---

33 Kenneth Hagen, "A Critique of Wingren on Luther on Vocation," *Lutheran Quarterly* 16 (Autumn 2002): 249-73.

34 Heiko A. Oberman, cited in Robert J. Bast, "Je geistlicher ... je blinder: Anticlericalism, the Law, and Social Ethics in Luther's Sermons on Matthew 22:34-41," *Anticlericalism in Late Medieval and Early Modern Europe*. Studies in Medieval and Reformation Thought, 51 (Leiden: E. J. Brill, 1993), 376.

care for our neighbor as a mother for her child—milk, eggs and soft food. No hard reforms that offend.[35]

What we have here is analysis and action, analysis of what the emergency situation demanded and admonition to patience for the weak in faith. How often in Luther is the concern for the weak in faith, which is about all our faith ever is. We live in fear of the devil and act in humility towards what is best for our weak brother and sister. The Word pours forth from Luther's lips, words that place us at the mercy of God to be His children, and children we are through faith in Christ. *Wir müssen* have a *warhafftigs* faith. We daily fight and face death. Change of heart will come and service must follow, as we love one another as God has done to us.

Luther's teaching on vocation is also the foundation for my second set of sermons I examined: *Ten Sermons on the Catechism* of 1528, the third and last series of sermons on catechism before the publication of the Catechisms (1529);[36] they are instruction for children (*Kinderlehre*). Parents are appointed by God to instruct the young, thereby carrying on the ministry of the church (*Predigtamt*).[37] Parents as bishop and bishopess (*Episcopus, Episcopa*) are to teach the Ten Commandments, Creed, Our Father, etc. (the important "etc." usually omitted in translations). The verbs *predigt, ediscat, educat, mandat, docet, intelligit* (third series) all indicate the action of presenting the *Christliche lehre* (second series).[38] Parents perform their office (*officium, Amt*) when they discipline.[39] Father and mother, master and mistress, prince, burgomaster, and preacher occupy appointed offices,[40] which stand in God's stead (*Gottes Statt*).[41] Marriage is an estate (*Stand*) established by God.[42] God even established the marketplace.[43] God

---

35 StA 2:530-34.

36 Preachers in Wittenberg had weekday sermons on the catechism four times a year: March, May, September, and December.

37 AE 51:137; *Predigten* I:73.

38 WA 30/I:27.34.

39 AE 51:146; WA 30/I:73.5; *Predigten* I:83.

40 AE 51:150-51, 178.

41 AE 51:152; *Predigten* I:89.

42 AE 51:154; *Predigten* I:91.

43 AE 51:156; *Predigten* I:99.

ordained the office of government.[44] Luther is conscious of his office
(*Amt*) of preacher.[45] The Holy Spirit, Christ, and the church all have
their *officium*, to fill out the vocabulary of vocation in these sermons.[46]
What we are talking about here is often called "the orders of creation" (Luther: "order of creation"); this is probably better called the
callings or vocations established by God for the sustaining of creation.
So when Luther enunciates what seem to be exhortations to his flock,
it is not simply that Luther is calling for a better morality, better discipline, or more education (a la humanist style). He is calling his flock
to remember their God-given, God-created vocations. As parents and
princes they are engaged in a high calling to carry out God's work,
what Luther elsewhere calls co-creators.[47]

I have the impression that these injunctions are sometimes seen
as Luther instructing his people in the do's and don'ts of Christian
living, emboldening what today is called "a Christian lifestyle." There
is more here than what the humanists were calling for in the reform
of Christian morals and manners. In Luther's structure of thinking,
the behavior of Christians (and of all people for that matter, believers
and unbelievers) is a matter of civil order, under the control of the left
hand of God. The kingdom of this world with its orders and offices
is created by God and ruled by law, reason, and the holy angels. The
"more here" is that the faithfulness of parent and prince to their calling
is a part of a theological construct, grounded and sustained in and by
God. The two kingdoms all have their place in the rule of God.

I am concerned that Luther's sermons not be seen as an exercise
in "the third use of the Law" (the function of Law in the life of the

---

44   AE 51:159.

45   AE 51:160; *Predigten* I:103.

46   Francis Pieper gives a two-page quotation from Luther's Sermon "Von
     unserer seligen Hoffnung" (Titus 2:13), 1531, on the high calling of clean-
     ing the stable and feeding the horses compared to the seemingly more
     glamorous though not God-commanded works of the monks. Pieper gives
     several more references in the footnote to Luther's praise of the seemingly
     lowly works of the patriarchs in their performance of their calling. Francis
     Pieper, *Christian Dogmatics* (St. Louis: Concordia, 1950), III:40-42.

47   For a good example of how this relates to Luther's concept of time, see
     David Speers, "Vocation and the Concept of 'Time' in Martin Luther's
     Lectures on Ecclesiastes," *Sanctification: New Life in Christ*. The Pieper
     Lectures 7 (St. Louis: Concordia Historical Institute & The Luther
     Academy, 2003), 1-18, esp. 13.

Christian). The issue seldom comes up in the literature, though when it does and the "third use" is supported, the support comes from the Confessions and not Luther. If ever Luther employed a "third use of the Law," you would expect it in the sermons, for here Luther's instruction on everyday Christian living comes to the fore. I must admit that the question of Luther and the "third use" of the Law never entered my mind while working on the sermons this time.

Luther's use of the imperative, "you must," "you should," following the commands of the Commandments, is an exercise in a Christian ethic for the left hand of God. Robert Bast says that in the sermons he selected, Luther's use of the Law cannot be forced into the "simple schema" of the two uses (and there are only two), found for example in the Large Galatians, namely, theological use to drive the sinner to grace, civil use to restrain sin and punish sinners. Luther's appeal to the Ten Commandments to teach good works and to define the godly social orders goes "far beyond the traditional understanding of the civil use of the Law." Bast finds in the sermons that after 1528 Luther insists "with ever greater intensity that obedience to the Law must be a normative part of the Christian life for the believer who has been justified by Christ."[48] I might suggest sometime that Luther's understanding of the first use of the Law embraces what later is included under the third use. Or, if that does not prove satisfactory, perhaps the way to put this point is that the positive aspects of Luther's understanding of the "civil use" have not been satisfactorily explored.[49] The talk about Luther not having a third use of the Law sometimes glosses over his emphasis on the tasks and admonitions that the new man avoid sin

---

48   Bast, "Je geistlicher ... je blinder," 374-75.

49   The third use in Melanchthon and the Solid Declaration it seems to me follows the line of Luther that the flesh is to be bridled, first and second use, that the Christian is to grow in faith and holiness beginning each day, as Luther counsels, on the knees for the forgiveness of sins. The *simul* is *totus* and *semper* for Luther. Remember the knees before you get carried away with sanctification. The Summer Postil, cited in the Solid Declaration on the Third Use of the Law, is not law-oriented. Luther speaks of the new man who has clear knowledge of Christ, whose heart is illumined, whereby he follows the Word through faith in Christ, not relying on external works but on inward faith in Christ, and is disposed to lead a godly life in harmony with the commandments ("Am XIX. Sontag nach Trinitatis, Epistel," WA 22:311-22). The Postil speaks of the new man and the Christian life; this seems to me to be all Gospel talk, no Law talk.

and seek righteousness and holiness. Faith, after all, is the most difficult work, said Luther.

In the Catechism sermons on Baptism and the Lord's Supper, Luther
makes it clear that faith is needed to receive the benefit and fruit of
the sacrament "for you." Unbelief does not alter God's Word, however.
Baptism is dependent on God's Word, not my faith. It is God's Word
and God's Word alone with the water that makes Baptism "genuine."
Heiko Oberman always taught that the sacraments are valid and effective for Luther because the Word is effective *ex opere operato*. "My
Word does not return void" was a favorite and oft-cited text of Luther.
I remember Oberman asking me in an oral exam, "Why for Luther do
you need the Lord's Supper when you have everything in the Word?"
He was reading these Catechism sermons of Luther since Luther asks
this question. Luther's answer: "I go because it is a body and blood
which is given and shed for me; that's why I go."[50] Elsewhere Luther
says we go because of the command.

For Luther there is power in the Word, the Word of God, the Word
of Christ, written and preached because the Word of God is Christ,
the Logos of God. God said, "Let there be ... and there was." God has
set everything from day one in place. The whole creation out of nothing ordered everything to exist in its proper place. God's calling is His
willing what is to be. God executes His will through the *voco/vocatio*,
even on non-Christians. Our calling is God's calling. Everything is set
by God and works best when so followed; to do otherwise is idolatry.
Hence Luther emphasizes the need to remain in the work or vocation
to which you have been called. Everything works best when everyone
does what he was made to do. "A woman can handle a child better
with her little finger than a man can with both fists."[51] Let everyone
remain in that work (*opus*) to which he has been called and constituted by God. Christian doctrine is to be carried out through vocation,
learning, knowing, teaching the content of the Catechism and doing
the work of one's calling. Pieper also says that angels serve believers in
their work and calling.[52] Luther often speaks of the rule, protection,

50 AE 51:189-90.

51 "Notes on Ecclesiastes," 1526, AE 15:131. For an elaboration of Luther
    and women, see John A. Maxfield, "Martin Luther on the Vocation(s) of
    Women," in *Feminism and the Church*, ed. John A. Maxfield (St. Louis: The
    Luther Academy, 2003), 1-20.

52 Pieper, *Christian Dogmatics*, I:506-7.

and influence of the angels in the governments (*Regimente*) of God that rule life.

THE CURRENT ISSUE OF RHETORIC

Two general studies are often cited in secondary literature. This will lead us into the current interest in rhetorical studies.

One is by Fred W. Meuser, *Luther the Preacher*.[53] It is set up as pastor to pastor, Meuser to his audience. He says Luther preached some 4,000 sermons, 2,300 preserved.[54] Meuser points to Luther's self-styled habit of going to the heart of the text (*Sinnmitte*) in an expository style, giving *Lehre* (doctrine) and *Ermahnung* (admonition).[55]

The other introductory study is by Harold J. Grimm, *Martin Luther as a Preacher*.[56] Grimm records a Table Talk: "A preacher must be both a dialectician and rhetorician" (*dialecticus et rhetor*). Dialectic supplies the body of the sermon, rhetoric the ornamentation.[57]

The older literature took a dim view of Luther having any positive appreciation for or use of rhetoric. The more recent literature has re-examined the matter and has argued that Luther had high regard for Quintilian (first-century Roman rhetorician who wrote the book on the subject), was taught rhetoric in Erfurt, and advocated the study of Quintilian in the University curricular reforms of 1518.

By virtue of training and age I must admit I come from the old school. The reaction of Bernhard Lohse, a granddaddy of Luther studies, to the book by Ulrich Nembach, who argued Luther's dependence on Quintilian, was also my reaction (even before I read it in Lohse).[58] Lohse says that it is one thing to say that Luther was familiar with Quintilian and another to say that Luther was dependent

---

53   Meuser, *Luther the Preacher*.

54   Ibid., 18. The weekly schedule: Sun. at 5:00 AM sermon on the Epistle; 10 AM sermon the Gospel; afternoon on one of the lessons, OT, or the Catechism; Mon. and Tues. on the Catechism; Wed. on Matthew; Thur. and Fri. the Apostolic Letters; Sat afternoon usually on John (ibid., 37-38).

55   Ibid., 25, 46-47.

56   Harold J. Grimm, *Martin Luther as a Preacher* (Columbus: Lutheran Book Concern, 1929).

57   Ibid., 88-89. Grimm's Table Talk reference comes from A. Nebe, *Zur Geschichte der Predigt* (Wiesbaden: Julius Niedner, 1879), II:24-25.

58   Ulrich Nembach, *Predigt des Evangeliums, Luther als Prediger, Pädagoge und Rhetor* (Neukirchen-Vluyn: Neukirchener Verlag, 1972). Bernhard

on him. Lohse says to do so is as simplistic as it is to recite Luther's criticisms of Quintilian as the final word on the subject. O'Malley says that Nembach overstates his case regarding Luther and Quintilian.[59] In the early stage of my research I found the line of Nembach extremely odious. I don't know how many times I tried to reread—and quit in frustration—the book of Neil Leroux, who follows the Nembach line.[60] My problem with this line is that it takes rhetoric out of context and blows it way out of proportion. I found other scholars, most notably the Swedish Stolt, the German Masser, and the American O'Malley, to be more moderate. These "moderate" scholars, with a more "balanced" approach, place rhetoric in the context of dialectic and grammar.[61]

My argument is that Luther's sermons are not all rhetoric. If you take the premise of humanistic curricular reform involving Quintilian in Wittenberg, the whole tradition of the seven liberal arts needs to be recognized, especially the trivium: grammar, rhetoric, and dialectic.[62]

The exclusive use of rhetorical criticism has been a trend now for a few decades in biblical studies. More recently it has come into popularity in Reformation studies, a step beyond the prevalent social history—but one more nail in the coffin of the history of ideas. The tendency is to take the categories of classical rhetoric and modern rhetoric and apply them to the sixteenth century, a tendency I find

---

Lohse, *Martin Luther: An Introduction to His Life and Work* (Philadelphia: Fortress, 1986; German original 1980), 102.

59   O'Malley, "Luther the Preacher," 9.

60   Neil R. Leroux, *Luther's Rhetoric*.

61   A seminal article by Birgt Stolt argued that Luther's language was not just folksy and simple for the unlearned, but well-structured, learned, and folksy based on rules of dialectic and rhetoric in order to move and delight ("*Docere, delectare* und *movere* bei Luther: Analysiert anhand der 'Predigt, dass man Kinder zur Schulen halten sole,'" *Deutsche Vierteljahrsschrift für Literaturwissenschaft und Geistesgeschichte* 44/3 [1970]: 474).

62   The difficulty for me with using rhetoric to analyze Luther is that Luther was a medieval man, perhaps also a part or start of modernity—but that only in hindsight. In the Middle Ages rhetoric was also a part, a third part of logic, which was a subdiscipline of philosophy. Logic consisted of grammar, dialectic, and rhetoric. Having had to work in medieval logic, I came to the conclusion, reinforced and confirmed by a modern expert, that medieval logic (to put it bluntly) was a mess. Or, more simply put, medieval logic did not exist—only a plethora of medieval logicians plied their trade.

both anachronistic and reductionistic. I am always suspicious when people come to Luther with methods extraneous to the (medieval) discipline of theology. Leroux describes Luther as a choreographer of thought.[63] Luther's complaint about medieval allegory was that allegorists made a game of language out of Scripture.

One more thing that bothers me is that I find something that smacks of an agenda among some historians, namely, that Luther and humanism were not so far apart as previously thought. The argument goes that Luther studied Quintilian, at Erfurt biblical humanism was prevalent, he promoted humanistic studies in liberal arts at the University during the reform of the curriculum in 1518, and praised and followed classical rhetoric in his writings. Therefore, Luther not only followed the humanist program of classical studies—study of Hebrew, Greek, and Latin, back to the sources, aversion to scholastic theology; he also employed classical and humanist methods of rhetoric. So, the implication is that humanism and Luther were not such strange bedfellows.

A more appropriate approach to Luther, it seems to me, would be to use terms and methods germane to the discipline of theology, such as eschatology (as noted above), *enarratio*, and grammar of faith (the latter two to be explained shortly).[64] For eschatology: Luther lived in a world dominated by an Augustinian worldview, that there is a cosmic conflict between the devil and God. No neutral ground. One is either for God or against God. Hence the sermon, life itself, is a matter of life or death. Images of God and the devil were personal. Discussions of faith and forgiveness were hardly academic. Luther's sermons are as graphic as the flames of hell; likewise the reality of the body and blood as the answer to life's natural direction is cast as God's victory over sin, death, and the power of the devil. This is not just rhetoric, this is the truth.

---

63   Peter Matheson, *The Rhetoric of the Reformation* (Edinburgh: T & T Clark, 1998), 20, referring to Leroux's dissertation. Nor do I find it helpful when Leroux says that Luther's concept of faith was deeply indebted to rhetoric, faith an affective phenomenon derived from the Holy Spirit as rhetor (*Luther's Rhetoric*, 12).

64   It is one thing to say that Luther knew and appreciated Quintilian (and Cicero), and another to say that he used their methods in his extempore preaching. Scripture provides the logic of Christ, which is the grammar of faith—the method and message Luther sought all his life to imitate and serve.

Through a word search for rhetoric in AE on CD-ROM, I saw Luther's positive regard for the trivium—grammar, dialectic, rhetoric. Luther highly valued the study of classical poetry and rhetoric, cited and used such.

I took another look at Nembach[65] and Leroux and reconsidered rhetorical analysis. I have wondered if rhetoric may be helpful for those not in the theological discipline (linguist Stolt, historian O'Malley, speech communication specialist Leroux). Visiting Prof. Zwanepol responded quickly to my query about rhetorical analysis: "That belongs to the post-modern-type thinking, which does not deal with truth," he said.

If one needs to go outside theology to philosophy and logic, wouldn't dialectic be more appropriate since, as cited, Luther says that a preacher must be a *dialecticus* and a *rhetor*: *dialecticus* gives the body of the sermon and *rhetor* the ornamentation. Dialectic penetrates to the argument and proof of the matter at hand and rhetoric gives the embellishment.[66] For example, Luther says:

> And now there comes the preacher, the holy patriarch [Melchizedek, Gn 14:19], who did not end this address in so bald a manner as Moses relates but without a doubt added dialectical arguments and all sorts of rhetorical embellishments.[67]

> Therefore it is one thing to teach and another thing to exhort. Rhetoric, which is useful for exhorting, often plays games and often hands you a piece of wood, which you suppose is a sword. But dialectic carries on war and busies itself with matters that are serious. Therefore it does not show the opponent pieces of wood; it shows iron.[68]

---

65   So much of Nembach's argument is circumstantial; he points out similarities between Luther and Quintilian without demonstrating dependence. This is Lohse's point: similarity does not mean dependence. Both Nembach and Leroux speculate what Luther must have done: it's understandable that Luther followed Quintilian (Nembach, 140). It's also understandable that he did not.

66   Also cited in Birgit Stolt, *Martin Luthers Rhetorik des Herzens* (Tübingen: Mohr Siebeck, 2000), 68-69, from WATr 2:2216.

67   On Gn 14:19; AE 2:389.

68   On Gn 18:4; AE 3:191.

The trivium and logic, with grammar, dialectic, and rhetoric, are all great disciplines in their own sphere, but at one point Luther called for a new language:

> 38. Thus, in particular liberal arts, or rather crafts, if you look them over, you will never discover that the same thing is true in all of them. 39. How much less is it possible for the same thing to be true in philosophy and theology, for the difference between them is infinitely greater than that between liberal arts and crafts. 40. We would act more correctly if we left dialectic and philosophy in their own area and learned to speak in a new language in the realm of faith apart from every sphere.[69]

The work by Wolfgang Maaser put an end to my misery over this issue by clarifying for me the subject of Luther and rhetoric. Maaser makes clear that Luther emphasized the interrelatedness of dialectic and rhetoric; you can't just have rhetoric, or you have nothing to say. Luther says that just as faith and hope cannot be separated, so

> *Dialectica* and *Rhetorica* are distinct arts and yet are connected and not able to be separated one from the other, *Quia Rhetor sine Dialectica nihil firmi docere posset*, and likewise *Dialectica* without *Rhetorica* does not affect the hearers; both are joined, to teach and persuade.[70]

---

69 "The Disputation Concerning the Passage: 'The Word was Made Flesh,'" AE 38.242. Ulrich Moustakas studies the famous disputation theses of 1539 on philosophy and theology and argues that while Luther seems to abandon all philosophy for the new language, he (Luther) used philosophy for his arguments on the sacrament. See *Luther Digest* 11 (2003): 123-30.

70 WA 40/II:28.15-18: "Sicut autem Dialectica et Rhetorica distinctae artes sunt et tamen adeo inter se cognatae sunt, ut altera ab altera separari non possit, Quia Rhetor sine Dialectica nihil firmi docere potest, Et econtra Dialecticus sine Rhetorica non afficit auditores, Qui vero utramque coniungit, is docet et persuadet." Cited in Maaser, „Rhetorik und Dialektik, Überlegungen zur systematischen Relevanz der Rhetoriktradition bei Luther, *Luther* 69/1 (1998): 33, citing WA 40/II:28.15-18. The same is mentioned in his book which is more concerned with Jüngel and Bayer's philosophical interests, metaphysics, and *Naturwissenschaften*. *Die schöpferische Kraft des Wortes: Die Bedeutung der Rhetorik für Luthers Schöpfungs- und Ethik Verständnis* (Neukirchen-Vluyn: Neukirchener, 1999).

Likewise, says Luther: *Grammatica* is necessary and true but is not to rule the *res* (the facts) but must serve them.[71]

While reading a footnote in Pieper regarding Luther and preaching, it hit me that for Luther rhetoric is embellishment and allegory is embellishment. So just as doctrine must be based on the literal sense of Scripture, so rhetoric must be based on dialectic. Neither rhetoric nor allegory stands alone. Pieper's Luther quote concerns Gal 4:22 (Sarah and Hagar): the doctrine of faith is based on the historical sense, allegory makes faith very clear and embellishes it.[72]

The often-cited (classical) phrase from Luther, "Dialectica docet, rhetorica movet" (WATr 2:359), makes clear the interconnection of doctrine and exhortation. This also strengthens my contention that Luther used all three of the trivium—grammar, dialectic, and rhetoric.

With the help of Stolt's book on Luther's "Rhetoric of the Heart," the way I resolve this matter of dialectic and rhetoric in my own mind is to say that for Luther the Word of God (Scripture, preaching) is effective and affective. The teaching is effective—the Word creates faith. "My Word does not return void." Stolt points out that Cicero was the main authority for the scholastics, with his emphasis on *ratio* (understanding of the mind), while the Wittenberg reform (1518) favored Quintilian, with his emphasis on *affectus* (understanding of the heart).[73] The effect of God's Word is that God says, and it is accomplished. The affect is that God's Word brings about a change, it moves the heart and mind and soul and body into action. God's work *ad extra* is *ex nihilo*, in creation, redemption, and sanctification for Luther. The *Exhortatio* moves the hearer to love of the neighbor for the neighbor's own sake. The dialectic of the sermon is the definition, argument, and analysis of the text, themes, and issues. The rhetoric is affective communication. The good tree does bear fruit. The Law must be fulfilled. The Holy Spirit is a most effective and affective rhetor.

Luther liked to point out that Christ did not write anything, God's Word is His work. The power of preaching thus is the power of God's Word to effect and affect. That's as far as I am able to go with Luther and rhetoric. I am not able to go as far as to say that what we once

---

71   WA 42:599.6-8: "Grammatica quidem necessaria est et vera, sed ea non debet regere res, sed servire rebus." Cited in Maaser, "Rhetorik und Dialektik," 38.

72   Pieper, *Christian Dogmatics*, I:290, n. 97.

73   Stolt, *Martin Luthers Rhetorik des Herzens*, 42.

thought of as the sermon we must now call a "speech act." Can you imagine the Sunday bulletin that reads, instead of the Sermon Hymn, the speech-act song!

Now back to Luther.

WHAT MUST SERMONS DO?

Primary Luther material will now come mainly from the third set of sermons from the 1520s: *The 1529 Holy Week and Easter Sermons of Dr. Martin Luther.*[74]

MAKE CHRISTIANS OUT OF CHRISTIANS

Luther is concerned throughout his sermons that his parishioners believe and do, believe the Gospel and do their calling. The fruit of faith is the Christian song of praise that no one sings except Christians. This is what Christians do, praise Christ and give to the poor (this on Palm Sunday Morning).[75]

Luther's personal engagement is seen in his direct form of address: Dear friends, you. You have the greatest treasure in the spoken Word and absolution.[76] Then he says "We admonish you to become a Christian" (affective communication):

> If because of pride you go to the sacrament without confession, you despise what no Christian despises. When we admonish (*ermahnen*) you to go to confession, we admonish you to become a Christian (*ermahnen wir dich, ein Christ zu werden*).[77]

To "become a Christian" is to do what Christians do. Are you a Christian, that is, do you yearn for what Christ has commanded? A

---

74   The editor(s) often add subtitles to the sermon headings, which prove useful, except in the case of "Easter Sunday Morning (28. March) 1529. The Resurrection of Christ" to which is added "and Its Meaning." The contemporary meaning of meaning and its common usage in English translations of the Second Article, "What does this mean?" is discussed and dismissed as a correct translation of "Was ist das?" by Gottfried Krodel in *Ad fontes Lutheri: Toward the Recovery of the Real Luther: Essays in Honor of Kenneth Hagen's Sixty-Fifth Birthday*, ed. Timothy Maschke, Franz Posset, and Joan Skocir (Milwaukee: Marquette University Press, 2001), 134-36.

75   *1529 Holy Week and Easter Sermons*, 30-31.

76   Ibid., 31-32.

77   Ibid., 33; *Predigten* I:276.

Christian is a disciple of Christ.[78] I point this out because this admonition "to become a Christian" seems rather strange since Luther is preaching to his Saxon fold who have all been baptized.

A sermon at Weimar helps clarify what it means "to become a Christian" when you are already a Christian. In the sermon (at Weimar, October 19, 1522), Luther speaks of being a Christian—"if you want to be a Christian," take up the cross of Christ:"When I help my neighbor, I prove my name as a Christian."[79] This is not a matter of being or becoming saved: "If I have faith, I am already saved, without any works or merit." Christ lives in us for the "betterment" of the neighbor, which is performing our office in love."God does not want our work"; the neighbor not only wants but also needs our work. "My Christian name would not be sufficient, despite my baptism and my faith, if I did not help my neighbor."[80] Key here, it seems to me, is bearing the *name* Christian. The name Christian denotes those who call upon Christ.[81] "We are all Christians through faith and baptism." Christ lives in us through faith "in such a way that I do these works" for the benefit of my neighbor.[82] So becoming, being, bearing, proving my name as a Christian is fulfilling my calling as a servant to my neighbor.[83]

TEACH AND ADMONISH

In the 1529 Holy Week Sermons, Luther "urges through teaching and admonition" (*mit Lehren und Ermahnen*).[84] These two are often cited in the literature as the sum and substance of all of Luther's sermons. But Luther also uses alarm and illustration, offers consolation, and

---

78   1529 Holy Week and Easter Sermons, 73, 75.

79   AE 51:117 (Second Sermon at Weimar, the Afternoon).

80   Ibid., 116.

81   Ibid., 111; see also the 1528 Catechism Sermons at Wittenberg, AE 51:165.

82   Ibid., 113, 116.

83   See how *freundlich* the Lord attracts us to the *Christenstand*, "dass wir gern sollen Christen sein!" (*Predigten* I:325). To be(come) a Christian is to fulfill one's *Stand*. Love alone will teach you what to do; love is the final command. Before I teach a mother what to do with her child she has already done it. Her heart knows. Love and serve. *1529 Holy Week and Easter Sermons*, 84.

84   1529 Holy Week and Easter Sermons, 37; Predigten, I:279.

gives chastisement. In one 1529 case: This is a sermon of comfort.[85] Or in another: Every preacher should teach, comfort, and admonish.[86] The teaching and admonition is not always a fifty-fifty, half-and-half proposition. How about ten to one, *Lehre* to *ermahnen*: We must always admonish (*ermahnen*) people to do good, but the *Lehre* (*Hauptstück* of the Christian faith) is ten times more necessary to uphold.[87]

Listen to the teaching and admonition in summary form, along with proclamation and vocation in the following. You must learn, you must know ... [88] Injunction upon exhortation. Defend yourselves with the clear and plain words of Scripture.[89] The battle is on, against the fanatics and the devil: the jackasses should be crowned with donkey farts (a thistle).[90] Satan fears the cutting edge of the Word.[91] This is no time for uncertainty—believe with certainty; it's a yes or no situation.[92]

The content is constant. Luther was very careful with his language, knowing that the words he spoke were not his; the words carry a message beyond normal discourse. He used grammar, dialectic, and rhetoric in various combinations. All linguistics, argument, and technique served to proclaim the Word, the *Hauptstück* of the Christian faith: that Christ died not only for the sins of the world but also for my sins.[93] For it was my sin that put Him on the cross, sins so enormous that they led to Christ being forsaken by God. Our sins drowned Christ. There is no more Christ (*kein Christus mehr da ist*).[94]

---

85   *1529 Holy Week and Easter Sermons*, 142; *Predigten*, I:374.

86   *1529 Holy Week and Easter Sermons*, 153; not in *Predigten*.

87   *Predigten* I:340.

88   *1529 Holy Week and Easter Sermons*, 39.

89   Ibid., 46.

90   Ibid., 40.

91   Ibid., 49.

92   Ibid., 65.

93   Also for Easter there is a great difference between "Christ is *a* Savior" and "Christ is *my* Savior." *1529 Holy Week and Easter Sermons*, 123.

94   *1529 Holy Week and Easter Sermons*, 116; *Predigten*, I:350.

The sermon is the Word. The Word is command and promise.[95] The Word is power—to make bread into body.[96] Sacrament is an exercise of Christ's mediatorial office.[97]

PROCLAIM THE GOSPEL

The Word proclaims (*verkündigt*) the forgiveness of sins, speaks the work of the cross.

> Words of Christ at the Last Supper, and now in Sacrament are as much Gospel as when I preach: I proclaim to you [*Ich verkündige euch*] that Christ died for your sins.[98]

Along with teaching and exhorting, Luther engages in proclamation. He not only discusses the power of the sacrament, power of Christ's words, he also announces in direct address the forgiveness of sins, the great treasure for you.

Proclamation is of the essence of the Gospel, without proclamation the tomb is empty (Easter Sunday Afternoon). The work of the resurrection was so secret that no one would have found out about it had not the angels come and proclaimed it (*es verkündigten*). Although the work was right in front of their eyes, if the Word was not added, the tomb remained empty. Christ did not want to appear to anyone at His resurrection; the oral Word had to be first, and lest it happened without the Word, the angels came from heaven. The treasure of Christ's resurrection will never come to us if it is not proclaimed. This is the preaching of the Gospel, that Christ is heard through hearing, through the sermon (*Predigt*).[99]

The difference between Luther and the Middle Ages is that preaching for him is a means of grace.[100] The sermon is salvific. The sermon is the medium of the message of God's Word to man.

---

95 *1529 Holy Week and Easter Sermons*, passim, 50.

96 Ibid., 63.

97 Ibid., 58; *Predigten* I:299 : *Mittleramts*.

98 *1529 Holy Week and Easter Sermons*, 67-68; *Predigten* I:307.

99 *1529 Holy Week and Easter Sermons*, 131-32; *Predigten*, I:363-65. The work of the resurrection is accomplished through preaching (*1529 Holy Week and Easter Sermons*, 137; *Predigten*, I:369).

100 Smalcald 8:10, and for example "Sermons on the Gospel of John." AE 26:151.

Luther begins the Good Friday morning sermon with an exhortation. The exhortation is the teaching. The *Vermahnung* is our *Lehre*[101] or, in the words of Hermann Werdermann, religion and ethics are inseparable in Luther.[102]

Our works remain on earth. Suffering serves to improve things on earth. Do not mix your suffering with Christ's suffering; separate them like heaven from earth. Christ's suffering is His *Amt*.[103]

"Der grösste Artikel zu glauben" (the greatest article to believe) is that Christ alone takes away our sins.[104] The thief on the cross is the first saint of the New Testament: in repentance he says, "I am a sinner," then turns and calls on Christ, "Lord, remember me," words of faith.[105] The thief belongs to the Kingdom through the Word, "Today you will be with me."[106]

These Holy Week sermons emphasize proclamation, teaching, comfort, admonition, doing one's vocation, and the great treasure of the forgiveness of sins.

These Holy Week Sermons of 1529 are a part of the two-volume work of Luther sermons prepared by Georg Buchwald, in which he edited the manuscripts of Rörer and Lauterbach from 1528-32. The work is unexcelled.[107] Also in my mind not replaced is the work

---

101 *Predigten*, I:327, 330.

102 This a Karl Holl-sounding phrase. Hermann Werdermann, *Luthers Wittenberger Gemeinde, wiederhergestellt aus seinen Predigten* (Gütersloh: Bertelsmann, 1929), 154.

103 *1529 Holy Week and Easter Sermons*, 90, 92-93; *Predigten* I:343.

104 *1529 Holy Week and Easter Sermons*, 93; *Predigten*, I:330.

105 *1529 Holy Week and Easter Sermons*, 110-111; *Predigten*, I:345.

106 *1529 Holy Week and Easter Sermons*, 141; *Predigten*, I:373. The office of forgiving sins belongs to the Holy Spirit. Contra Anabaptists and Donatists the ungodly can preach the Gospel. The preaching office and Holy Spirit remained among the papists (*1529 Holy Week and Easter Sermons*, 152). The office remains though people abuse it. Parents have their office. The office of preacher is to preach the Gospel (153). The preaching office exists to forgive sins (157). Preachers carry in their mouth the Word of God that brings death and life (159). Death to sin and life to righteousness. May the Word bite you (164). The sermon is to stick in our hearts (171-73). Paul warns and threatens at the same time—*vermahnet und drohet zugleich* (*Predigten* I: 394)—in the sermon.

107 Buchwald standardized the German, turning the macaronic notes back into all German.

by Hermann Werdermann in which he combed through these sermons (ed. Buchwald) on a variety of topics reflecting the life of the
Wittenberg community, parents, usury, government, and the like.
Throughout Werdermann's summary, Luther's teaching on vocation
is prominent. In addition to teaching, exhortation, and alarm, woven
throughout is the admonition to fulfill one's office (ampt, Stand). The
ämpter and Stände are not a part of the Gospel or revelation but are
governed by reason, applicable to Christian and non-Christian territories.[108] Luther emphasizes the force and honor of being told that you
are a mother with a God-given calling; every office is an important
part of the fabric of God's good creation.

Werdermann cites Luther. A sermon must do two things: first,
preach the rich treasure of faith in Christ; second, preach "Remember
your Stand which is pleasing to God." Therefore: "Du Knecht, tue, was
deines Amptes ist!" (You servant, do what your calling is!).[109]
Elsewhere Luther says what all sermons must do:

> For all sermons and the entire heavenly doctrine must be directed
> to the end that faith may increase, that the promise concerning the
> grace of God may be praised and take root in the hearts of men, and
> that patience and other fruits of faith may be increased.[110]

It is often said that Luther's preaching after 1521 turned to biblical
preaching, "expository, not thematic or topical," along the lines of a
free-moving homily.[111] It is forgotten, and Werdermann reminds us,
that Luther often preached without a biblical text, for example on
the catechism and Baptism. When he did preach on the text it was
the style of Auslegung, says Werdermann. Luther also preached on
themes—justification, Law and Gospel.[112]

Werdermann goes on to describe Luther's Predigtkunst (art, method,
and style). No fancy artistic introductions for Luther. His first sentence
went directly to the text, or previous sermons, or the church year. He
ended his sermons with a summa summarum, with the exhortation to
prayer. The sermons were often in the form of a dialogue—questions

---

108 Werdermann, 92.
109 Werdermann, 154-55; Predigten II:467, 260.
110 Lectures on Genesis, AE 5:79.
111 Doberstein, xviii. This line of interpretation goes back to Emanuel
       Hirsch, "Luther's Predigtweise," Luther 25/1 (1954): 2.
112 Werdermann, Luthers Wittenberger Gemeinde, 173, 175.

and answer; also in the form of an argumentative dialogue with the devil, Pope, and Schwärmer. Sometime the dialogue took on an apologetic form, with "du." He also used "ich" and "wir."[113] The Gospel speaks directly to present-day Germans and Wittenbergers; for example, "Luke has written this against our Schwärmer."[114]

The world of the Bible and the world of Wittenberg merge. The text is contemporary—no Lessing's ditch.[115] "This goes even today (*noch heute*)."[116] Judas is a *Mönch*.[117] "The Carthusians and Franciscans are Herod's farm hands (*Gesinde*)."[118]

Werdermann confirms exactly the same that I found in my work on Luther's so-called "commentaries." The works of Luther described as "commentary" I found to be in the form of an *Enarratio*. *Enarrare* means to speak, tell, or set forth in detail. A public context is connoted. It means to speak in public in detail. *Enarratio* includes *narratio*, which means to narrate, but involves both detail and public. *Enarrare* means to take out (to narrate) and to apply. In other words this process takes the theology out of the text and applies it in public to the audience.[119] *Enarratio* is a biblical and historical form of treating Scripture.

CONCLUSION

What has the preceding yielded that we could consider relevant for Lutheran preaching? As a hearer in the pew, what have I learned in this research? What is needed?

1. The personal, second-person form of address: *your* sins are forgiven. Not just the sins that Staupitz said to Luther were uninteresting, but the big sins, the sins of judgment, priorities, anger, selfishness, and on.

---

113   Ibid., 177-87.

114   Ibid., 189.

115   What became the unbridgeable gulf between religion and reason, between Scripture and history: "the accidental truths of history [religion] can never become the proof of necessary truths of reason" (Lessing's ditch).

116   *Predigten*, I:335.

117   *Predigten*, I:337.

118   *1529 Holy Week and Easter Sermons*, 101; *Predigten* I:338.

119   Kenneth Hagen, *Luther's Approach to Scripture as seen in his "Commentaries" on Galatians, 15191538* (Tübingen: J. C. B. Mohr [Paul Siebeck], 1993), 50.

2. My daughter needs to hear that changing diapers in the whole scheme of things is as important as the lectures her father gives, that the least is the greatest in God's eyes.
3. Respect for the next-door neighbor is necessary for the ongoing of created vocations, mine and his. Civility is an ethic for social order.
4. Every Sunday is the last. The ultimate battle between God and Satan is not a thousand years away in the cosmos, it is now, in our little town, this day, this hour, in my head and heart.
5. Every sermon is an apocalyptic event. Yogi Berra was wrong—the game of life is "not over til it's over"—because life has been lived, suffered, crucified, risen, and ascended. The game has been played: the victory is mine.
6. Preaching is where the rubber hits the road. Not basic Bible, moral instruction, interesting stories, word studies, clever quotes from the Internet. Without the oral Word, the tomb was empty. The work of the resurrection is accomplished through preaching. Preach it, teach it, admonish Christians to be Christians!
7. The sermon is a public event. The Word, while written out of necessity because of distortion, is a mouth house. Narrate and explicate the message from the grammar of faith, grammar that leads to analysis and action.

Let me leave you with what Luther in 1530 says he has been doing in the pulpit:

> I have spoken so far about the works and miracles which your son [Luther] does for individual souls, helping them against sin, death, and the devil. Beyond that, however, he does great and mighty works for the world. He informs and instructs the various estates on how they are to conduct themselves outwardly in their several offices and estates, so that they may do what is right in the sight of God. Every day he can comfort and advise those who are troubled, compose difficulties, relieve troubled consciences, help maintain peace and settle and remove differences, and countless other works of this kind. For a preacher confirms, strengthens, and helps to sustain authority of every kind, and temporal peace generally. He checks the rebellious; teaches obedience, morals, discipline, and honor; instructs fathers, mothers, children, and servants in their duties; in a

word, he gives direction to all the temporal estates and offices. Of all the good things a pastor does these are, to be sure, the least. Yet they are so high and noble that the wisest of all the heathen have never known or understood them, much less been able to do them. Indeed, even to the present day no jurist, university, foundation, or monastery knows these works, and they are not taught either in canon law or secular law. For there is no one who regards these offices as God's great gifts, his gracious ordinances. It is only the word of God and the preachers that praise and honor them so highly.[120]

120 "A Sermon on Keeping Children in School," AE 46:226.

A CRITIQUE OF WINGREN ON LUTHER ON VOCATION

Gustaf Wingren's 1942 dissertation, *The Christian's Calling: Luther on Vocation* has dominated our understanding of Luther's doctrine of vocation. This is unfortunate because, as I intend to show, Wingren's book presents a one-sided, and thus misleading, reading of Luther on the key topic of our calling before God and for the neighbor.

German mystics were the first to advance the idea of a worldly call.[1] First Corinthians 7:20 is the key text ("Every one should remain in the *Beruf* [klh/sij] in which he was called"). Laity are called by God to do their worldly work in whatever station/occupation they find themselves. Everyone has a calling from God. Luther was the first to provide a theological basis for understanding calling in the sense of secular work. Luther also was the first to challenge the notion that monasticism and clerical ministry were higher callings than secular work.

---

1   It seems that no one has successfully challenged Holl's history (1924) of the word "Beruf." See F. Lau, "Beruf III," *Religion in Geschichte und Gegenwart*, ed. Kurt Galling, 3rd edition (Tübingen: Mohr Siebeck, 1957-62), 1078. See Karl Holl, "Die Geschichte des Worts Beruf," *Gesammelte Aufsätze zur Kirchengeschichte*, vol. 3 (Darmstadt: Wissenschaftliche Buchgesellschaft, 1965), 189-219. Nikolaus Paulus found Holl's history unacceptable and attempted (1925) to offer proof that in the 11th and 12th centuries theologians were applying "Beruf" (*vocatio*) to the status of marriage as in 1 Cor. 7:20. Nikolaus Paulus, "Zur Geschichte des Wort Beruf" in *Historische Jahrbuch* 45 (1925): 308-16. My perspective on this is that Paulus's theologians were saying such in their commentaries on 1 Cor. 7:20, where of course they would repeat the text of 1 Cor. 7, as medievals must. Luther did the same thing. For Holl's thesis to be revised, medieval scholarship would have to go outside biblical exegesis on the text of 1 Cor. 7 and in the usual theological treatises find what was said by Tauler and others on worldly callings. Alfons Auer also tried to counter Holl's history, which I find unconvincing since he focuses on the value of work (man as *Mitarbeiter Gottes* in Aquinas) which is a different slant on *Beruf* as such: "Zum christlichen Verständnis der Berufsarbeit (Nach Thomas von Aquin und Martin Luther)" in *Beiträge zur Begegnungn von Kirche und Welt*, 8 (Rottenburg, 1953), 2-16.

One of Luther's early points in his 1520 *Address to Christian Nobility* was that all Christians share the "spiritual estate" (*geystlichs stands*) formerly reserved for popes, bishops, priests, and monks.[2] Near the end of his life, Luther repeated that "there is the universal calling" (*generalis vocatio*) to believe in Christ and to be baptized in his name.[3] All Christians are equal in that baptism, gospel, and faith alone make us spiritual. The spiritual estate is common to all Christians, while "office" (*ampt*) and "work" (*werck*) refer to one's particular situation.[4] All are one body, yet everyone has his or her own work by which he serves others.

The main thrust of Luther's doctrine of vocation is that (1) all Christians are to serve God in their occupation, that (2) every occupation is equal in the sight of God, and that (3) the purpose of vocation is to serve the neighbor.

The three estates are: first, the priestly *Amt* (pastors, those who supervise the common chest, sextons, servants and messengers of these); second, the married estate (husband/wife, parents, children, servants, widows, single people); third, the worldly authorities (civil government) including princes, lords, judges, civil officers, state officials, notaries, and servants for these persons.

In his 1528 *Confession concerning Christ's Supper*, Luther discusses the three "orders and true religious institutions": *Ecclesia, oeconomia, politia* (church, household, government). After a paragraph on each of the three, he says, "Above these three institutions and orders is the common order of Christian love, in which one serves not only the three orders, but also serves every needy person in general with all kinds of benevolent deeds, such as feeding the hungry, giving drink to the thirsty, forgiving enemies, praying for all men on earth, suffering all kinds of evil on earth, etc."[5] All Christians are members of the church, a household, and society, and beyond all that is the common order of Christian love. All these stations and orders and the "common

---

2 *Luthers Werke*, Kritische Gesamtausgabe, 57 vols., ed. J.F.K. Knaake, et al. (Weimar: Böhlau, 1883ff.), 6:407,14 [hereafter cited as WA; *Luther's Works*, American Edition, 55 vols. ed. J. Pelikan and H. Lehmann (St. Louis and Philadelphia: Concordia and Fortress, 1955ff.) 44:127 [hereafter cited as LW].

3 WA 42:641.38-39; LW 3:131.

4 WA 6:407.16; LW 44:127.

5 WA 26:505,11-15; LW 37:364-65.

order" are created by God. The created order of God's civil kingdom is structured with a myriad of occupations and obligations, all geared to make the kingdom of God's world work, and the working of it all is pleasing to God.

RESPONSE TO WINGREN

By everyone's admission, the classic expression of Luther's doctrine of vocation was given in Gustaf Wingren's *The Christian's Calling: Luther on Vocation*.[6] The Swedish original was published in 1942 as his doctoral dissertation and underwent at least three subsequent and, as far I can tell, unchanged editions or printings in Sweden; the third appeared in 1960. It is amazing that Wingren remains the prevailing word on the subject of Luther on vocation. How many dissertations are even read after fifty years, let alone defining and dominating the field? Kolden speaks of this as "Wingren's masterful work."[7] Lohse cites it as the only work on the subject.[8] Nowhere in secondary literature on vocation have I read any criticism of Wingren.[9] I have seen work by Finnish, German, British, and American scholars build on Wingren and pursue related lines of thought, but never challenge any

---

6   Gustav Wingren, *The Christian's Calling: Luther on Vocation*, trans. Carl C. Rasmussen (Edinburgh: Oliver and Boyd, 1958) from the second printing, *Luther lära om kallelsen* (Lund: C.W.K. Gleerups Förlag, 1948). Hereafter cited as Wingren. The first printing was in 1942.

7   Marc Kolden, "Luther on Vocation," *Word & World* 3 (1983): 389.

8   Bernhard Lohse, *Luthers Theologie in ihrer historischen Entwicklung und in ihrem systematischen Zusammenhang* (Göttingen: Vandenhoeck & Ruprecht, 1995), 264. Translated by Roy A. Harrisville under the title *Martin Luther's Theology: Its Historical and Systematic Development* (Minneapolis: Fortress Press, 1999), 247.

9   In his "critical study" of *Luther's Two Kingdoms Doctrine* Per Frostin criticizes Wingren as an example of what is wrong in most Luther studies, namely a circularizing, harmonizing, paraphrasing method that ignores the contradictions and paradoxes in Luther and that renders, when following the proposed historical-critical method, any attempt at a complete picture of Luther on the Two Kingdoms (or any non-contradictory system in Luther) as impossible. See *Studia Theologica Lundensia*, vol. 48 (Lund: Lund University Press, 1994), 45-47.

of his points. Recently, Froehlich called this "the standard book on Luther's thought in this matter."[10]

The historical and philosophical context of Wingren's thought was the Danish philosophy of Knut Løgstrup,[11] who argued that the "universal element" is creation. As a result, throughout his education and writing, Wingren had a hard time accepting Christology and gospel theology as a basic frame of reference. Instead he opted for creation and law.

Wingren interpreted Luther's doctrine of vocation along these lines. Vocation belongs to our situation before the resurrection, where there are two kingdoms, two contending powers, and two antagonistic components within the Christian; Christians are involved in constant struggle. Vocation is our calling in our situation in life, through which we serve God's creative work by being under the law. The old man must bear vocation's cross as long as life on earth lasts and the battle against the devil continues. As long as he continues in his earthly vocation, there can be no end to the struggle. After death comes a new kingdom free from the cross; heaven has taken the place of earth, and God has conquered the devil.

LAW, VOCATION, CROSS

A prominent, though questionable, feature of Wingren's presentation is his emphasis that law and vocation belong together: "Vocation falls within the kingdom of the law."[12] In vocation is one's cross. "The cross of vocation" is an operative phrase throughout the book—"and on this cross the old human nature is to be crucified."[13] Here we hear of the toils of a broken world in which we bear our cross in service of the neighbor.[14]

Luther does use "cross" as in "world of toil and cross" (*in terra operis et crucis*)[15] in one of Wingren's early and favorite references (he cites

10   Karlfried Froehlich, "Luther on Vocation," *Lutheran Quarterly* 13 (1999): 195.

11   Henry Vander Goot, *Creation and Gospel, The New Situation in European Theology: Gustaf Wingren* (New York: The Edwin Mellen Press, 1979), xxxviii ff.

12   Wingren 26.

13   Ibid., 29.

14   Ibid.

15   WA 40/I:469,27; LW 26:301, "the flesh of works and torment on earth."

it twice in one paragraph from the 1535 Galatians commentary). In this text, Luther does speak of "the cross on earth" but not of vocation. Nor is it only a "world of toil" for in the very next sentence not cited by Wingren it reads: "And then the troubles that the flesh is forced to bear will not be difficult, for the promise is sweet and delights the heart in a wonderful way."[16]

When Wingren cites Luther's 1519 *Treatise on the Sacrament of Baptism*, he links dying to the old man with the cross of one's vocation, "and on this cross the old human nature is to be crucified."[17] Wingren confuses Luther's two kingdoms when he identifies exclusively the dying to sin with learning to die in one's vocation. Luther does speak here of belonging to an estate (in this example, the estate of marriage), with its toils and sufferings, "in order that he may grow used to pleasure and sorrow, avoid sin, and prepare himself for death better than he could do outside of that estate."[18] It is the Christian who knows "in what estate he may best slay sin and put a check upon his nature."[19] I get the strong impression from Wingren, with his identification of law and vocation and both with cross, that it is the vocation (with our attachment to it) that must die, and that the Christian is crucified by the law only in his vocation. Wingren: "The Christian is crucified by the law in his vocation, under the earthly government; and he arises through the gospel, in the church under the spiritual government."[20] From Wingren it seems that when the Christian is freed from the law, he is free from his vocation.

Wingren's mistake is to link vocation with law, without clearly distinguishing civil law from spiritual use of the law. Both Wingren and American Evangelicalism confuse the first and second uses of the law. For them, the law, civil and spiritual, is to bridle the flesh, to restrain sin, to punish transgressions. But for Luther, the vocations are a part of the civil orders of creation (which Wingren knows), and the Christian does not die to the civil law. Yes, the Christian, who lives in God's creation and who occupies more than one vocation, must daily die to sin through the exercise of the spiritual law. The dying to sin

---

16   WA 40/1:469,27-28; LW 26:301-2.
17   Wingren, 29.
18   WA 2:736,10-12; LW 35:41.
19   WA 2:735,38; LW 35:41.
20   Wingren, 30.

may well include slaying sin as a parent, spouse, and in one's occupation; but, just as service to God is not limited to serving God only in one's vocation(s)—remember the "common order" of Christian love in addition to one's vocation—so dying to sin is not dying to sin only in one's vocation.[21]

Luther, in Wingren's sources, always distinguished between the inner person and outward works and between the person and office. To be sure, the outward works are full of pain and suffering, but also joy. Luther does speak of our bearing our cross in and out of our vocations, but it is not the vocation that dies. From Wingren, one gets the impression that vocation is only suffering, trouble, and death (his words). What happened to the joy of serving Christ also in one's vocations?

In his chapter in *This is the Church*[22] and in his famous book, Wingren's key text by Luther is from the *Treatise on the Sacrament of Baptism*, where Luther says that "God instituted many estates in life in which men are to learn to exercise themselves and to suffer."[23] In our station in life we learn to fulfill the work and purpose of baptism "namely, to slay sin and to die in order that Christ's burden may thus grow light and easy and not be carried with worry and care."[24] There is nothing about law here. Along with striving, tasks, and sufferings that are the work of God,[25] baptism also brings comfort, mercy, and forgiveness.[26] All one hears from Wingren is suffering and dying, not that "God receives us sinners, spares us, and makes us pure from day to day, then our heart must be joyful, and love and praise God."[27]

---

21 Ibid., 32. The identification of cross and vocation renders such statements very misleading as, "the crucifixion of the old nature in vocation," and "Christ's cross and man's cross, for these two are the same." It is one thing to say, as Luther does, that we share in the crucifixion and resurrection of Christ. It is another to say that it is the vocation that suffers and dies.

22 Gustaf Wingren, "The Church and Christian Vocation," *This is the Church*, ed. Anders Nygren, tr. Carl C. Rasmussen (Philadelphia: Muhlenberg Press, 1952), 281-93 (esp. 282-86).

23 WA 2:734,24-25; LW 35:39.

24 WA 2:735,21-23; LW 35:40.

25 WA 2:733,1-6; LW 35:37.

26 WA 2:731,3-734,13; LW 35:34-38.

27 WA 2:737,6-9; LW 35:42.

WINGREN CONTRA BILLING

Wingren has lumped together law, vocation, suffering, and death in a one-sided manner. Wingren's lopsided approach may stem from an effort to correct Einar Billing. Billing had sought to correct only a negative view of vocation in Luther with "brighter colors."[28] Wingren went out of his way to paint the dark colors, which he sees are Luther's. Wingren was concerned that Billing's picture with the "brighter colors" had won the day. Wingren also criticizes another Swede, Arvid Runestam, for "an altogether too optimistic view of vocation."[29] Later in his book, Wingren does bring in something a bit more positive about vocation in Luther. "It is the old man who endures the cross of vocation, it is the new man who rejoices in vocation, and from within gives it new character."[30] In the same sentence, however, this is cast in terms of living in prison, between the night of despair and the peaceful day of labor. Wingren keeps coming back to Billing and hence emphasizes against Billing, "To Luther world-affirming joy in culture is utterly strange."[31]

Wingren's book on Einar Billing contains a section on Luther.[32] Important for Wingren is Billing's discussion of Two Kingdoms ("realms") and law in Luther. For Billing, the Two Kingdoms become one in the forgiveness of sins. This may have lead Wingren to emphasize the future Kingdom of God yet to come. Moreover, Billing defines law as Old Testament legalism. This may have lead Wingren to emphasize law and cross and vocation. There is a confusion of two uses of law and the two realms here, although it is not exactly clear where this confusion lies, whether in Billing or in Wingren (or in both). Where Wingren describes the influence of Luther on Billing, he says that Luther constructed a theology in such a way that the formal elements became a doctrine of two different realms: church-gospel

---

28 Wingren, 74-75. In his (untranslated) footnotes, Wingren amplifies his critique of Swedish scholarship. See *Luthers lära*, 84-88.

29 Wingren, 75.

30 Ibid., 119.

31 Ibid., 141.

32 Gustav Wingren, *Einar Billing—En studie i svensk teologi före 1920* (Lund: C. W. K. Gleerup, 1968). Translated by Eric Wahlstrom under the title *An Exodus Theology. Einar Billing and the Development of Modern Swedish Theology* (Philadelphia: Fortress Press, 1969).

and state-law. In the church the "forgiveness of sins" dominates and became the *leitmotif* in Billing. "A certain tendency to isolate the gospel from the law was therefore present in Billing's thought from the beginning."[33] The "law" in this paragraph means the law of the state, whereas the law/gospel construct in Luther is within the realm of the church. This is the confusion throughout Wingren, namely, that the civil (use of the) law (in the realm of the "state") becomes confused with the spiritual (use of the) law.

The confusion of the two uses of the law in Luther becomes apparent again in the "Doctrine of the Two Realms."[34] Even though Billing and Wingren see (and at least on some level correctly report) the two uses of the law in Luther,[35] in the process of analyzing Billing, Wingren confuses matters. Billing sees (and rejects) the second accusatory use of the law as a decadent, medieval, ascetic hangover in Luther. This "law" has "a disciplinary, mortifying and crucifying, function to perform in the hearts of men."[36] Wingren states that Billing "rejected Luther's 'medieval asceticism'"[37] and thus "the two realms tended to become *one realm.*" The one realm for Billing is centered on the forgiveness of sins. The problem and confusion here is that for Luther both the second use of the law (Billing's "medieval asceticism") and the forgiveness of sins already belong to the one realm of the church (the kingdom of God), whereas in Wingren's mind law is associated with cross and earthly calling. Hence we slip from the spiritual realm of the cross (crucifying the heart) to the earthly realm of law. In fact, Billing cannot and did not reject the "state" (the civil realm; see the importance of the national church in Billing). By rejecting Luther's second use of the law, Billing did not reject the two realms; he rejected the second use of the law within the realm of the church.

Thus, Wingren's dissertation was a club, a polemical weapon, aimed minimally at Billing. This is no surprise, since most often dissertations have a polemical edge to them. It is also understandable that Wingren delimited his dissertation topic to the aspect of vocation within the limits of law in Luther (though this is confusing and worth

---

33   *An Exodus Theology,* 66.
34   Ibid., 73ff.
35   Ibid., 74-75.
36   Ibid., 75.
37   Ibid., 76.

challenging). But, as this dissertation became the standard work on the topic through at least three editions in Swedish and numerous translations, severe distortions have emerged in our general understanding of Luther on this subject for over a half-century.

LAW AND GOSPEL?

Wingren cannot see any joy in culture in Luther. What is strange about Wingren on this point is how contrary it is to Luther, who was highly appreciative of music and the arts, and the whole civil realm. "Martin Luther has taught us to recognize in music a gift of God."[38] Other scholars have recognized the positive function of law and reason for the affairs of this world. In the earthly kingdom "reason is an excellent gift of God."[39] "Luther praises the law in its first use as 'the most excellent of all things in the world.'"[40] Luther praises humanity in his 1536 *Disputation Concerning Man*; he gives "tribute to the reason of man and the majestic position he occupies on earth."[41]

The kingdom of the world is not identical with the kingdom of the devil; the secular realm includes state or government, nature, the family, the arts, and all the sciences.[42] These are the orders of God's creation wherein the Christian serves the neighbor in vocation. The problem with Wingren is that he limits vocation to law and understands the orders of creation as ruled by the devil. He says that "the new man" has no law, but surely the "new man" has a vocation. After all, the "new man" is a whole person (*totus homo*).

38   Theodore Hoelty-Nickel, "Luther and Music," *Luther and Culture*, Martin Luther Lectures 4 (Decorah, Iowa: Luther College Press, 1960), 161.

39   Brian A. Gerrish, *Grace and Reason* (Oxford: At the Clarendon Press, 1962), 26.

40   Kolden, 384.

41   LW 34:135, editor's preface. For Luther on the good life that God has made for the use of man, see his comments on Ecclesiastes: "Gold is good, and riches are conferred by God. A woman is a good thing, made to be a helper for man (cf. Gen. 2:18). For God has made all things to be good and to be useful for some human purpose." See WA 20:10,35-11,11; LW 15:8.

42   Bernhard Lohse, *Martin Luther, An Introduction to His Life and Work*, trans. Robert C. Schultz (Philadelphia: Fortress, 1986), 188. "Luther had a high regard for the sciences, including astronomy." See also Donald H. Kobe, "Copernicus and Martin Luther: An encounter between science and religion," *American Journal of Physics* 66, (1998): 193.

It seems that Wingren at times recognizes the difference between the two uses of the law and the difference between the kingdom of the devil and the kingdom of this world, but more often than not these crucial distinctions are blurred, as, for example, in the following: "On earth vocation implies the cross as a consequence of the ceaseless enmity of evil against every work of God,"[43] or earlier referring to Luther's "belief in a real devil who holds sway here in the darkness"; only "Eschatology is the first field to restore harmony and meaning to what happens in earthly life. For that reason faith yearns for death and heaven."[44] This is simply an incorrect view of Luther's theology of the cross. For Luther, God is revealed in suffering; God is not just hiddened on the cross. Moreover, Wingren ignores the Resurrection.

Crucified by the law through the cross of one's vocation, one is made alive, says Wingren,[45] but then faith stretches to life after death, "away from the present." The strong (and welcomed) eschatological character of faith and justification in Wingren seems to leave an enormous gap between the present under the law and heaven. No vocation under the gospel, only drudgery under the law. The gospel of forgiveness is only a future eschatological referent; "Thus the forgiveness of sins is the same as eternal life"![46] This is qualified a bit later by emphasizing love of the neighbor in this world;[47] heaven is on earth;[48] the "new man" has no law.[49] More typical is "The gospel speaks about the eternal kingdom in the resurrection, where Christ rules without law."[50] No gospel on this earth!

The connection of vocation with law in Wingren has more to do with the theological situation in Sweden at the beginning of the twentieth century than with Luther. According to a historical analysis of Wingren's theological development by Henry Vander Goot, Wingren was moved to emphasize law and creation because of his opposition to the theology of Agape of his antagonist, Anders Nygren, and out of

---

43   Wingren, 142-43.
44   Ibid., 142.
45   Ibid., 37.
46   Ibid., 38.
47   Ibid., 44.
48   Ibid., 47.
49   Ibid., 50.
50   Ibid., 212.

his opposition to Lundensian methodology of motif research which surrounded him. In Agape theology, a Christian ethic is derived from the New Testament concept of love, that is, the gospel. Wingren responded to this by stating that, "An ethic derived from the gospel was theologically impossible for us."[51] In his student years leading up to his dissertation on vocation, Wingren claimed to see that Luther developed his doctrine of vocation out of the Genesis story of creation and the doctrine of law as the means by which God coerces humanity under sin to serve the neighbor in the earthly kingdom, thus fulfilling the purpose of creation.[52]

The debate, conflict, and tension with Nygren's Agape theology finally led to a personal and theological parting of the ways between the two in the mid-1950s. Feeding this animosity was that Wingren's appointment to succeed Nygren in the chair of theological ethics at the University of Lund.

Wingren's dissertation on vocation was a polemical work, cast in opposition to Billing of the rival faculty in Uppsala, and developed in opposition to Lundensian methodology, specifically against the gospel theology of Nygren. Wingren was obsessed and upset with Nygren and Nygren's motif research; against Nygren's Agape motif, Wingren propounded creation and law as the context for vocation.

Wingren's book on vocation, reprinted and translated time and time again, was no objective treatment of the subject. Our understanding of Luther's teaching on vocation has suffered in this century from Swedish theological battles far removed from sixteenth-century Wittenberg. Why and how Wingren's dissertation has survived for over fifty years as the last word on the subject of vocation remains a mystery, especially considering the fact that Wingren was neither a church historian nor a Luther scholar. Despite the praise Wingren has received for his work on Luther's doctrine of vocation, he himself seldom ever mentioned the subject in his subsequent publications. In fact, after 1951 the professor of systematic theology seldom mentioned Luther. The work of this graduate student should be read as a part of the history of Swedish theology in the early part of the twentieth century and not as a full treatment of Luther on the topic.

Wingren was correct to speak of the cross of vocation. In addition, for Luther vocation defines one's place in God's good creation, in the

51   Vander Goot, xix.
52   Ibid., xx.

estates of creation, in the civil realm ruled by reason, order, love, and service. Vocation is the work of believers as Christs under the gospel. Vocation is the calling of priests in the service of Word and sacrament, and even of professors.

Luther says that we grasp our *Beruf* or *Stand*, in God's Word so that we can say to the devil, today I have done thus and so and know God's work.[53] Many texts in the Weimar Ausgabe on *vocatio*, do not speak so much of law and suffering as of grace and help of God. Remain firm in faith and in your particular calling, and God will bless you richly. The *Beruf* is the connecting point in this world with God's left hand.

A WORD STUDY OF VOCATIO/BERUF
IN THE WEIMARER AUSGABE

This critique of Wingren demonstrates that the topic of vocation needs to be completely redone. The topic needs at least a balanced treatment of law and gospel, the two uses of the law, and the distinction between the kingdom of the devil and the civil kingdom. The following analysis of several key texts represents a step in that direction.[54]

HOLY LIFE

The first reference to *vocatio* in the Latin Subject Index is to a sermon on 1 October 1531.[55] The text is Ephesians. 4:1-4: walk worthily in "your calling" (*vocatio, Beruf*) in which you have been called. "We have

---

53   WA 52:395.12-20.

54   *Luthers Werke, Lateinisches Sachregister zur Abteilung Schriften Band 1-60, S — Zythum*, vol. 68 (Weimar: Verlag Hermann B`hlaus Nachfolger, 1999). While this volume was being published and before the German Index appeared, the Institut fhr Sp@tmittelater und Reformation, Thbingen, kindly supplied me a list of references to *vocatio* and *Beruf*. Because the references I am using are from the WA Index, I will use the WA edition. I am conscious of being the blind man who touches only the tail of the elephant (and thinks everything is tail). It would be easy to see all of Luther speaking of *vocatio*. My Teaching Assistant, Silviu Bunta of Romania, kindly photocopied over 1100 pages from the WA on this subject. We must keep in mind that the Sachregister is not a *Wortindex*, it is (*als*) an *Auswahl*. See "Einleitung," WA 64:XII.

55   WA 34/II:298-308: "Predigt am 17. Sonntag nach Trinitatis, nachmittags."

a twofold vocation: spiritual and external."[56] The spiritual vocation is that we are called (*vocati*) through the gospel to baptism and Christian faith; through word and baptism we are incorporated into Christ and called *bruder, geselschafft Jesu Christi*.[57] The *vocatio* is common to all.[58] Caesar does not have a better baptism than the beggar. We are called into Christ to live a holy life as he did.[59] But the office of all members is not the same. Diverse, thus, is the order of external works.

The external *vocatio* distinguishes persons, man is other than woman, teacher than disciple, father than son. This is a "bodily or external Beruf" (*leiplicher* or *eusserlich beruff*).[60] In this regard we are all unequal or different (not the same), just as in the former we are all equal. In the external situation/station (*Stand*) we are called to do our office (the *Materfamilias* has her own things to do).[61] Luther concludes that Paul admonishes each "to his spiritual and bodily station."[62]

This sermon is very clear about the two callings: baptism and office. Wingren does not have this distinction so clear. The places where Wingren discusses baptism are different from Luther. In Wingren,[63] baptism is the daily putting the old creature to death. Citing the 1519 *Treatise on the Sacrament of Baptism*, Wingren quotes Luther as saying that the best way to fulfil the work of baptism is "to slay sin and to die." The 1531 sermon is quite different from Wingren's interpretation of Luther. Both the dying and also living the holy life are in Luther, but Wingren concentrates only on death. In the sermon, Luther states that Christ is the head to which we have been called, just as he is justice, salvation, life, and so forth. So also we ought to live; I consider myself baptized so that I have received a holy *standt*, called into a holy, heavenly life (*caelestem statum*),[64] therefore also I live.[65]

---

56 "Duplicem habemus vocacionem, spiritualem et externam" WA 34/II:300.23-24).

57 WA 34/II:300.25.

58 Ibid., 300,11.

59 "Communis est vocacio omnium" WA 34/II:301,21-22.

60 WA 34/II:306,27.

61 Ibid., 307.

62 "ad suum statum geistlich und leiplich" WA 34/II:308,12-13.

63 Wingren, 28.

64 WA 34/II:302.13.

65 WA 34/II:301,26-302,19. See also, "Sermon on 17th Sunday after Trinity" (1544), on Ephesians 4:1ff. The text speaks of your call,

CALLED THROUGH THE GOSPEL

In his work "'This is by body' Against the Enthusiasts," Luther uses Irenaeus to combat Oecolampadius' inclination to make earthly and heavenly bread a single thing. With Irenaeus, the point for Luther is that the *Vocatio dei* is God's naming ("This is my body") ordinary bread to become *Eucharistia odder sacrament.*[66]

Luther's point is that the *Vocatio dei* makes the thing what it is or what it becomes as in creation (let there be light, and light it is) and sacrament (this is my body, and body it is). He cites Romans 4:17: "God names or calls into existence the things that do not exist." Key here is the power of God's word to name, call, speak, declare, and thus it so happens. The implication thus is that the call to being a father, student, maid is done by the power of God's word, and so it happens. Can it not be said, thus, that the earthly vocations are set in place by God so naming and calling?[67]

The stations/vocations are set into the fabric of the universe by God. In his Christmas postil of 1522, Luther asks "How is it possible

---

nostra/vestra vocation, WA 49:615-20. This is to a special *Stand*, which the world does not know, which after this life is with Christ in eternity, WA 49:615,26-28. Paul praises our call because it is *herrlich* (WA616.12-13). It is a *geistlichem stand*, WA 49:618,21.

66   "Daß diese Wort Christ'Das ist mein leib' etc noch fest stehen wider die Schwarmgeister" (1527 [Drucke]), WA 23:233,10-15; LW 37:117: "Also redet hie Ireneus auch vom Gotts nennen oder ruffen, wie auch Moses Gene.1 zeuget, Das Gott durch nennen oder ruffen (das ist durchs wort) alles schaffet. Odder sey du meister und sage mir, was Vocatio dei sonst heyssen müge, quando deus vocat, dicit, appellat, nominat. Das ist sein wort, da er spricht:'Das ist mein leib', gleich wie er ynn Genesi spricht:'Es sey liecht', so ists liecht. Lieber, es ist Gott, der da nennet odder rufft und was er nennet, das stehet so balde da, wie Psal. xxxiii. sagt 'Es spricht, so stehets da.'"

67   On Zechariah 4:10, Luther brings in Romans 4:17 that God gives life to the dead, calls into existence the things that are not. The "call" of God in Romans 4:17 (see John 5:21) is the Word that brings life. This call into existence and naming things (vocations) what they are connects to the immediate power of God's speech in creation. Luther draws on the *ex nihilo* power of the creating, redeeming word of God of Genesis 1 and John 1 to emphasize that God's word produces immediate results, WA 13:592,14, "Praelectiones in prophetas minores, Zacharias" (1524-26; end 1525 to beginning 1526).

that you are not called? You have always been in some station (*stand*), you have always been a husband or wife, boy or girl, servant or maid."[68] Each and every *Stand* entails much to be done, the vocations are a given, the tasks all time consuming. "He will have so much to do that the time will be too short." Luther's point here is that we have no choice but to do what our calling requires: a man-servant who plows and drives a team travels straight to heaven, while another who goes to St. Jacob or to church and lets his *ampt und werck* lie goes straight to hell.[69]

All Christians are called.[70] The reference is to Matthew 22:9: "*Ladet, wen ir findet*" (invite everyone you find). He (king, Jesus) makes no distinction, he invites, calls man, woman, young, old. *Sic omnes sumus vocati*, meaning thus we are all called, without distinction. "That is, come, believe in Christ, be baptized, hear the gospel, love one another, that is the invitation." Come to the banquet. "What you will find to eat is the forgiveness of sins, eternal life, victory over death, hell, etc. Thus all are invited, no one should say that he is not called (*vocatus*)."[71] The noun (*vocatio*) and verb (*vocare*) are closely associated theologically and linguistically, because the noun derives from the verb. Further references from Sermons from 1533 and the *Dictata* of 1513-15 make clear that throughout Luther's writings all are called (*vocati*) to the gospel and eternal life. Prophets, biblical figures, all are equally called through baptism. The common call is to eternal life.

If Wingren did not have such a negative view of vocation (earthly work under the law), he could see the positive linkage between call to the gospel and eternal life as well as the call to everyday office. At the beginning of his book, Wingen says, "We do not deny that included as well in earthly vocation is the call to be the child of God through the gospel."[72] Better than "not to deny" would be to affirm the positive aspect of all God's callings.

---

68   WA 10/I,1:308,6-9, "Weinachspostille" (1522) on John 21:19-24. No one is without a *befelh, beruff, niemand on werck* WA 10/I,1:309,14-15. Cf. *The Sermons of Martin Luther*, ed. and trans. John Lenker, 8 vols. (Grand Rapids, Mich.: Baker Book House, 1988).

69   WA 10/I,1:309,18; 310,10-13).

70   "[Christiani]: omnes sumus vocati." "Predigten des Jahres 1533 (26 Oct. 1533) on Matt. 22:2ff., WA 37:181,16.

71   WA 37:181,15-21.

72   Wingren, 2.

Wingren made a serious mistake when he separated the call through the gospel from the call to earthly vocation. Of course, a dissertation needs to reduce the scope of the project. Perhaps the problem lies with the title of his dissertation: *Luthers l@ra om kallensen.* The title is global sounding, Luther's teaching on the call, on vocation. A more accurate title would be "Luther on Vocation from the Perspective of Law." At base, the distortion his work produced is to separate the law from the gospel to such an extent that the whole purpose and context of the law are lost. The purpose of the law is not just to die in vocation.

The *vocatio* is a seamless continuum of "call." The call embraces the Christian's life from beginning to end. We are called out of darkness to the gospel through baptism. We are to call upon the name of the Lord in prayer and praise. We live our callings both on earth as children of the heavenly father and as fathers and mothers, teachers and pastors. And in the last day we will be called out of the grave. In each of these cases, the operative word is *vocare/vocatio.*

God creates/calls out of nothing the things that are not and gives them life. The *vocatio* is the connection with and to God. God contacts, reaches out to his creatures through the call. The breath of God breathes (new) life into his creatures by direct contact. The call is likewise direct contact from God to his creatures. God communicates through call. The Holy Spirit calls and gives faith. As Luther states in his explanation of the third article of the Apostles' Creed, the Holy Spirit calls me through the gospel.

Vocation is the connection between the right and left hands of God. The continuum of the call (*vocare/vocatio*) provides the contact and connection between the two kingdoms. It is always said that the two kingdoms cannot be separated in Luther, but how they are connected has never been clearer than in seeing the connection and movement from the right hand to the left as the continuum of "call." From Genesis 1 to the eschaton God calls.[73]

THORNS AND GLORY

Contrary to Wingren, who has long sections on "Cross and Desperation" (despair, anxiety), for Luther vocation entails both thorns and glory.[74]

---

73   There are extensive references in Scripture to *vocare/vocatio* and derivatives in the Vulgate Bible concordance.

74   "Lectura in Genesis," WA 44:439-448; LW 7:189-202, on Genesis 41:45, Pharaoh appointing Joseph to rule.

In the context of carrying out the duties of magistrate, bishop, husband (and the like), Luther says, "Consider that you are born and called to this, to serve the neighbor."[75] Note both "born" and "called" to serve the neighbor. Then Luther goes on to speak of holding civil office as a bitter punishment for original sin, both because it is onerous and also because it is designed to curb malice. Finally Luther notes that Joseph does well. Luther says, "I know I am serving God's will when I do my duty to the best of my ability."[76] "Whatever success I have redounds to the glory of God." Luther cites Joseph as an example for all to press on when we have been called to our office (*officium nostrum*).[77] Young people should resolve to serve God *meo loco*.[78] I shall have "thistles and thorns"; nevertheless, I shall be "content with this glory, that I am certain of divine grace and benevolence in this office and obedience."[79]

In this section Luther uses as synonyms *officium*, *locus*, and *munus* in the context of Joseph's and our being called to serve God in our place. *Munus* is connected to duty; Luther links it to obedience. Stelten's dictionary gives "office" as one meaning of *munus*.[80] Of course, *munus* also means gift. In Lewis and Short,[81] *munus* means service, office, post, employment, function, duty—all these with the connotation of public service. For Luther, the office carries both thorns and glory.[82]

---

75 "Cogita igitur te ad hoc natum et vocatum esse a Deo, ut servias proximo," WA 44:443,23-24; LW 7:194.

76 WA 44:444,25-26; LW 7:196.

77 WA 44:445,5; LW 7:196.

78 WA 44:445,7; LW 7:196: translated in LW "in my station"; literally "in my spot."

79 "quod de gratia et benevolentia divina in hoc munere et obedientia certus sum," WA 44:445,8-11; LW 7:197.

80 Leo F. Stelten, *Dictionary of Ecclesiastical Latin* (Peabody, Mass.: Hendrickson, 1955).

81 Charlton T. Lewis and Charles Short (based on E. A. Andres), *A Latin Dictionary Founded on Andrew's Edition of Freund's Latin Dictionary* (New York: Oxford Press, 1969).

82 WA 44:445,9-10; LW 7:197.

CALLED TO SERVE

The purpose of vocation is to bear fruit.[83] In the context of the ordinary (often earthy) activities of the patriarchs in comparison to (often exemplary) deeds of the heathen (praised by Erasmus), Luther says it is faith and the Word that make the works of Christians important and of great worth. For God himself is in the Christian. We have been given the promise, baptism, and absolution; we are to be vigilant and bear fruit in our faith and calling.[84] Interesting in this section vis-B-vis Wingren is that when God imposes a cross—to be a *Christianus* is to be a *Crucianus*[85]—it is for the dual purpose of being purged and bringing forth greater fruit.[86] The *vocatio/Beruf* (of Moses) brings great action.[87] In the context of a true (God) and false call (anyone), Luther says, when God calls, he *dringt* and *zwingt* (presses and compels; pushes and shoves we might say) and then there is great action, as happens here. God acts and liberates his people through the calling of Moses.

The purpose of our calling (*vocati* and *vocatio*) is to serve; Luther emphasizes over and over that "we have been ... called into such a ministry through baptism."[88] Building on Matthew 18:19-20 ("wherever two or three are gathered in my name"), Luther says that we gather in his name, pray, choose bishops and ministers of the word from among us. Even before such choosing we have been born and called into such

---

83   "Memento te vocatum esse ad vigilandum," WA 43:617,26; LW 5:274, "Lectura in Genesis" (on Gen. 29:1-3). Promises (to Jacob) are given "ad laborandum, ad vigilandum et ad fructificandum."

84   "quae et fidei sunt, et vocationis" WA 43:617,23-27; LW 5:274.

85   WA 43:617,34; LW 5:274.

86   In one reference Luther says our vocation is to fight against the devil. "Predigten des Jahres" 1535, WA 41:10,6. Every Christian knows that he is called into the army of Christ (*vocatus in militiam Christi*) in order to fight against the devil. It is a holy slaughter of the devil. The body and soul are not killed, rather the opposite. "Das ist unser vocatio," WA 41:10,13. The vocation is to fight through sin to victory.

87   "Ubi Deus vocat, dringt et zwingt et tum fit opus magnum," WA 16:32,5, "Predigten hber das 2. Buch Mose" (1524/27). Chapter 3 of Exodus describes the *vocatio/Beruf* of Moses. On pages 31-33 the word *vocatio* and *officium*, which appear in the top text, are translated *Beruf* and *Ampt* in the bottom text, respectively. See esp. top text, 33.

88   "per baptismum ... vocati sumus ad eiusmodi ministerium," WA 12:191,37; LW 40:37,"De instituendis ministeria Ecclesiae" (1523).

a ministry through baptism. Further, every Christian should feel obligated to fill any need without a call from the community.[89] Apollos came to Ephesus without call or ordination and taught fervently. By what right? The right common to all Christians.[90] The eunuch accomplished much through no other right than that inherent in baptism and faith, especially in places lacking other ministers.[91]

For Luther, everything from day one has been set in place by God. The whole creation out of nothing implies that God ordered everything to exist in its proper place. God's calling is his willing what is to be. God executes his will, even on non-Christians, through the *vocare/vocatio*.[92] Our calling is God's calling. Everything is set by God and works best when so followed; to do otherwise is idolatry.[93] Hence Luther emphasizes the need to remain in the work to which one has been called.[94] Everything works best when all do what they were made to do. "A woman can handle a child better with her little finger than a man can with both fists."[95] Let everyone remain in that work (*opus*) to which he has been called and constituted by God.[96]

Therefore let us presume nothing without the word of God. He who knows that he is driven (propelled) by vocation works securely in his

---

89 WA 12:192,6; LW 40:38.

90 WA 12:191,40; LW 40:37-38.

91 WA 12:192,22; LW 40:38.

92 He calls the Vandals to destroy Rome: "Vandali ... iactabant se vocatos ad perdendam Romam," WA 25:141,31, "Vorlesung hber Jesaia 1527-29" (Scholia 1532/34). God appropriates (arrogates) to himself all the power of kings and rulers (Rom. 13; Jer. 28). He commands the kings of Babylon. He calls the Medes his sanctified ones. The Vandals throw themselves called into destroying Rome.

93 "officium: in quod vocatus est," WA 5:135,16, "Operationes in Psalmos" (1519-21). Speaking of idolatry and disobedience, Luther says it is more atrocious today with those called to office ("officio, in quod vocatus est") who desert the office and seek to adorn themselves with splendid property, WA 5:135,15-21.

94 "maneat unusquisque in eo opere, ad quod vocatus est a Deo," WA 20:149,22, "Ecclesiastes Salomonis cum annotationibus D.M. Lutheri" (1532, 30 July – 7 Nov. 1526).

95 WA 20:149,20-21; LW 15:131.

96 See also "Der 147. Psalm Lauda Jerusalem ausgelegt," (1532), WA 31:1.437,7-8; LW 14:115.. This is the context of the callings, work and performance, as the "Masks of God."

office undaunted; whatever happens he is certain that he is pleasing to God.[97] We are certain in and of our vocation. To be sure, it is a call under the cross. However, it is to be said concerning cross and love toward enemies that we suffer all evil and pray for persecutors, by which practice we acquire hope and certainty of our faith and vocation.[98] Note here (contra Wingren) that cross in the context of vocation leads to hope and certainty of our faith (not toil and death).

In fact our life is lived for the glory of Christ.[99] The Christian is one with Christ, member of member, flesh of flesh, as the woman shares the substance of the man in marriage. The Christian in his or her entire being participates in God. We are totally Christ's, by the calling of Christ, and all our works are not ours but Christ's. We are said to have been created for the glory of Christ.[100] The Christian's vocation is a high calling to carry out God's work in God's creation. The Christian is under law and gospel. The offices (callings) are God's means to slay sin and to serve the neighbor.

REMAINING IN ONE'S VOCATION

The largest number of references is "Let everyone remain in his vocation" (*Maneat quisque in sua vocatione*).[101] Interestingly, Luther says, "It is evil to stand (*stare*) in a *standt* which is not commanded by God." *Stare* (according to dictionaries of ecclesiastical Latin) means to stand or remain, stand firm in the faith, stand firm, persist, persevere. God is changeless, his commandments persevere, his command is that we live (stand tall) and remain in our *standt*, vocation.

---

97   WA 16:594,15, "Predigten hber das 2. Buch Mose" (1524-1527) on Exodus 24-30 (1526).

98   WA 10/II:482,19, "Ein Betbhchlein der 10 Gebote" (1522), "Certitudo nostrae fidei et vocationis."

99   "totum sumus Christi vocacione Christi" WA 31,II:332,26; LW 17:90, "Vorlesung hber Jesaias (1527-1530). Isaiah 43:7, "everyone who is called by my name, whom I created for my glory, whom I formed and made."

100 WA 31/II:332,21-28; LW 17:90.

101 WA 12:644,29, "Predigten des Jahres (1523). In the context of the need to do the will of the father, namely bear good fruits outwardly to the neighbor. It is not the will of the father to become a monk. It is evil to stand in a *standt* which is not commanded by God. Everyone should remain in his vocation.

Already at an early date Luther admonishes the following. Be obedient to the vocation in which you were called. God has set (established) his ways and put them into laws. These are called vocations (*vocatio*) and stations (*officio* and *status*). To seek another or better station is an abomination *coram deo* and to go against the ways (laws) of God. I see here no development in Luther's terminology or theology on vocation. [102]

In a very large number of references Luther notes God (via St. Paul) prefers works that are proper to one's vocation to works (however more glorious) of other callings. [103] "And whoever does not provide for relatives, and especially for family members, has denied the faith and is worse than an unbeliever." Paul prefers the works proper to one's vocation (all of them) to other works, however great they be. The context here for Luther is criticism of those who abandon family to become nuns and monks, seemingly to achieve higher status. Paul imposes on widows domestic tasks even though they are not as spectacular as those spiritual tasks. We are to obey even (especially) disgraceful tasks.

Suffering in vocation is based for Luther on 1 Peter 2:21, "For to this you have been called, because Christ also suffered for you, leaving you an example, so that you should follow in his steps." [104] I am to live in a holy calling which brings nothing other than suffering. [105] If you are Christian, you are called to live under the holy cross. [106] Our holy calling, which gives eternal life, brings torment and trouble. Wingren ignores the scriptural base for Luther's linking cross with vocation.

---

102   See WA 4:484,10, "Annotationes Quincuplici Fabri Stapulensis Psalterio manu adscriptae" (1513ff.) Also in the *Dictata* at this time Luther equates *vocationes* with *officia* and *ministeria*, WA 4:313,33-34, In "Predigten des Jahres" (1520). First Corinthians 7:20 is cited: "in qua vocatione vocatus es" means "there remain and exercise your work," WA 4:710,23-24. The same equation of vocation and office is in WA 1:451,24, "Decem Praecepta Wittenbergensi praedicta populo" (1518; between 29 June 1516 and 24 February 1517).

103   "praefert opera propriae vocationis omnibus aliis operibus" WA 26:87,16; LW 28:217-384, "Vorlesung hber den 1. Timotheusbrief" (1528) on 1 Tim. 5:8.

104   "oportet pati ... martern, plagen" WA 45:74,6, "Predigten des Jahres 1537" (Apr. 15).

105   WA 45:73,22.

106   Ibid., 73,28.

One would think that in Wingren's section on Imitation,[107] 1 Peter 2:21 and Luther's sermon on the text would come up. Luther is following Scripture here, and 1 Peter 2:21 is not the only scriptural text mandating suffering/cross bearing. In Matthew 16:24 (and parallels) Jesus told his disciples, "If any would come after me, let them deny themselves and take up their cross and follow me." The First Peter text links calling with suffering.[108]

> Summary: the cross is given us in baptism and marked on our forehead, which means we have come into the true order of the cross order [*rechten krewczorden*; R`rer's word, *cruciger* means cross-bearer]. Therefore suffer. Summary: your vocation, O Christian, is to suffer just as the magistrate's calling is to rule and the calling of the mother is to bear children. Therefore no one is ashamed of his vocation but glories in it. Christ has left us the example.[109]

Christ is our example: he suffered, we suffer. This is what Luther has to preach given the sermon on First Peter 2. Why did Christ suffer? Suffering is salvific.[110] Echoing Romans 5:3, Luther argues that we are to glory in our vocation (*glorietur in illa*). There are only nine references to this theme In the Subject Index, compared to hundreds that lead beyond Wingren's limited perspective. It is true that the Index (WA 68) is a selection and not an Index *verborum*. Nevertheless, if Wingren's interpretation were correct then all the references should be to cross-suffering-vocation, which is far from the case.

---

107 Wingren, 171-84.

108 The 1 Peter 2 text is the basis of "Predigt am Sonntag Jubilate, nachmittags" from "Predigten des Jahres 1531" (April 30), WA 34/I:354-360.

109 WA 34,I:355,19-26.

110 Another reference to cross in vocation is addressed to papists and *Schw@rmer*, those who pretend to perform (new) works of humility and suffering, thereby representing themselves as Christ and Christ's way of suffering. Luther's response is that Christians in their vocation bear the suffering (cross) of Christ. Everyday living of father and mother, *burgermeister* and *paterfamilias*, involves pain and suffering. Perhaps one could say that for papists and *Schw@rmer* suffering was salvific, a means to humility and to righteousness. Whereas for Luther, suffering is part and parcel of living in the world (left hand). All matters salvific are in Christ's hands, WA 27:467,15, "Predigten des Jahres" (1528) on John 1:19ff.

CONCLUSION: PUBLIC SERVICE TO THE NEIGHBOR

As noted, Luther uses as synonyms *officium, locus,* and *munus. Munus* means service, office, post, employment, function, duty, all these with the connotation of public service.[111] In the papacy it is completely different.[112] The text "Behold my servant" (*Ecce servus meus* from Isa. 42:1) is cited in Matthew 12:18. It is to be diligently noted that servant (*servus*) here is a public name. This is said contrary to the familiar error in the papacy where to serve God signifies fleeing the world, deserting the public office of teaching, guiding, and performing it, which every vocation requires. In abdicating their public office they become monks, anchorites, and private men, who by their own chosen work presume to serve God, because they cannot bear public dangers and troubles.

The public sphere is the left hand of God. Vocation is an ethic for the left hand, an ethic for living in the civil kingdom. The ethic for the left hand is "love of the neighbor is an end in itself." Love of the neighbor is serving the neighbor in one's vocation. Luther has an ethic, a norm for living in this world of God's sustaining power. The connection between God and his world are the offices God has ordained to be the means of carrying out his will in his world. This analysis of Luther's ethic shows that one key ethical norm is that the Christian loves the neighbor for the neighbor's own sake, not as a means for some further good or reward, but as an end in itself. The direction of Christian love is this-worldly, and that is where it stops because one's neighbor is that important and deserves that much.

Luther's essay on First Corinthians 7 of 1523 shows this ethic for the left hand. Commenting on 1 Corinthians 7:24, "So, brethren, in whatever state each was called, there let him remain with God." Luther says that this *Ruff* is not the *stand* wherein you are *beruffen*, but the text speaks of *dem Evangelischen ruff*; remain in your office as you were when called by the gospel. These comments make the crucial distinction between the two kingdoms, "relation to God" and "relation to your neighbor."

---

111 WA 44:445,9-10; LW 7:197.

112 "in *Papatu* ... servire Deo significabat ... deserere ... ea, quae uniuscuiusque vocatio requirebat," WA 38:535,29, "Annotationes in aliquot capita Matthaei" (1538).

Therefore notice this and differentiate between the freedom existing in your relation to God and the freedom existing in your relation to your neighbor. In the former this freedom is present, in the latter it is not, and for this reason: God gives you this freedom only in the things that are yours, not in what is your neighbor's. There differentiate between what is yours and what is your neighbor's. That is why no man can leave his wife, for his body is not his own but his wife's, and vice versa. Likewise the servant and his body do not belong to him himself but to his master. It would be of no importance to God if the husband were to leave his wife, for the body is not bound to God but made free by Him for all outward things and is only God's by virtue of inward faith. But among men these promises are to be kept. In sum: We owe nobody anything but to love (Rom. 13:8) and to serve our neighbor through love. Where love is present, there it is accomplished that no eating, drinking, clothing, or living in a particular way endangers the conscience or is a sin before God, except when it is detrimental to one's neighbor. In such things one cannot sin against God but only against one's neighbor.[113]

"God does not need my good works but my neighbor does" is the usual phrase. Luther makes it even stronger here. "It would be of no importance to God if the husband were to leave his wife." But, it would make all the difference in the world of the wife. In matters of outward things "one cannot sin against God but only against one's neighbor." Or again, "All things are free to you with God through faith; but with men you are the servant of every man through love." The love of the neighbor is directed (only) to the neighbor. The direction is unilateral, "his body is not his own." The *vocatio/Beruf* is the link between the right and left hand of God. The *Beruf* of the gospel is that "you were bought with a price (1 Cor. 7:23). The only thing required is "to believe and confess" God (which is the whole work of the church). Otherwise you are free vis-B-vis God—not free vis-B-vis the neighbor. The vocation of love, serving the neighbor, is not optional. The whole structure of God's world is ordered so that the neighbor is served in and by vocation.

Wingren has voided the very goal and direction of vocation in Luther. In Luther the direction of vocation is the neighbor. In Wingren the direction is the self—all the works of the law aimed at killing the self. By making the gospel an eschatological referent, Wingren missed Luther's vocation by gospel (good tree) serving the neighbor (good fruits) in the present.

113   WA 12:132,6-22; LW 28:46.

Alms-giving and other penitential acts in the medieval world were geared toward serving the giver. Poverty was praised as pleasing to God. For Luther, giving is to benefit the recipient. The principle of loving the neighbor for personal ends is selfish and self-serving. The Christian, rather, is to give not out of ulterior motives, but simply for the sake of serving. Luther's ethical motivation for reformation was to free the Christian from medieval burdens of all kinds of laws that weighed the pilgrim down. Freed from such baggage, the theory or principle is that the love of Christ in the Christian is a more effective agent for works than the threats and anxious obligations of Moses, the Pharisees, the pope, and canon law. Just as Luther placed all his trust in Christ to save, and Christ alone, so Luther placed all his trust in the gospel to free from the law and make good trees that would bear good fruit.

LUTHER'S DOCTRINE OF THE TWO KINGDOMS

INTRODUCTION

The understanding of "Luther's doctrine of the two kingdoms" is complicated for several reasons: the doctrine is not Luther's[1]; Luther had more than two kingdoms; Luther had more than one doctrine, or so it seems; the terms kingdom and government are not technical terms; and the doctrine is often criticized, misunderstood, and misused. Since the problems of misunderstanding and misuse lie in modern philosophical assumptions (such as Liberalism) and political agendas (such as Nazism), I see no need to force Luther into modern problems.

Let us try to set our focus on Luther, on his time and corpus, setting aside modern agendas. To do so, I offer seven assertions.

Let us first set aside the assumption that the two kingdoms equal church and state. The kingdom of God for Luther includes more than the church militant and the kingdom of this world includes more than the single, divinely instituted secular government.

Second, the two cities of Augustine's *City of God Against the Pagans* do not equal Luther's two kingdoms. The two cities for Augustine are two loves—one of the flesh and one of the spirit; the two cities represent the cosmic conflict between the divine and the demonic. The two loves and the cosmic conflict are also in Luther but do not equate with the two kingdoms of God and this world. Both kingdoms of God and the world in Luther are in conflict with the devil.

Third, the famous charge of "quietism" leveled and led by Reinhold Niebuhr, that particularly German Lutherans were passive with regards to the kingdom of this world, has been adequately rebuffed by Brent Sockness.[2] Furthermore, I always remind my students that

---

1   It began to take shape in the nineteenth century. Bernhard Lohse finds the first usage of the term in 1922; see his *Martin Luther, An Introduction to His Life and Work*, trans. Robert C. Schultz (Philadelphia: Fortress, 1986) p. 188.

2   Brent Sockness, "Luther's Two Kingdoms Revisited, A Response to Reinhold Niebuhr's Criticism of Luther," *The Journal of Religious Ethics* 20 (1992): 93-110.

when you think of the man Martin Luther who lived in and taught the two kingdoms, "defeatism" and "quietism" are the last words that come to mind. Erasmus wished that Niebuhr would have been right.

Fourth, to focus on Luther in his context, remember that everything in the Middle Ages, above the earth, on the earth, and beneath the earth, was under the rule of God. No independent, neutral, secular realm, no secular state existed apart from God. The *saeculum* is God's creation.

Fifth, remember for Luther that the "kingdom of the devil," the third kingdom, was active but not in control of the kingdom of the world. The *regnum diaboli* stands as a threat to both the kingdoms of God and the world.

Sixth, still trying to focus on Luther in his historical context, Luther's distinction between the two kingdoms developed vis-à-vis the polemical contexts of Rome on the right and the Radicals on the left. The papal middle ages had confused the two kingdoms such that they were often indistinguishable. Erasmus preceded Luther in reminding the Pope to tend the flock and not to engage in political warfare. The Radicals wandered between wanting to establish the kingdom of God on earth by divine law or force, thereby collapsing the two kingdoms, and wanting to separate totally from all political and social involvements.[3]

Seventh, Luther had two different configurations of two kingdoms, most often called "two kingdoms" and "two governments." Since the terms are interchangeable and not technical, I find it helpful to picture two schemes or two sets of kingdoms in Luther. The two are separate but overlap and intersect. The two governments are the right and left hands of God. Some of the subsequent confusion over Luther's teaching results from not seeing and distinguishing the two configurations and how they relate. I do think that Luther had one general doctrine, which I will come back to at the end.

---

3   Luther condemns both the Anabaptists and the Pope for confusing the rod of the Word and the rod of wood: "they all reach for the sword, the Anabaptists, Münzer, the pope, and all the bishops." *Sermons on the Gospel of John* (1537-38), AE 22:225.

MODERN SCHOLARSHIP

What is needed here is not a discussion of R. Niebuhr, Liberation Theology,[4] Political Theology,[5] T. Rendtorff,[6] or K. Barth,[7] à la recent secondary literature, but a more systematic-historical view of Luther's whole doctrine of the kingdoms. It is typical of secondary literature to state the complexity of Luther's doctrine, but then in my view to contribute further to the complexity. I have found no full treatment in the secondary literature. All too often the doctrine is discussed in reference to some issue extraneous to Luther.

My own contribution is intended to sort out the complexity and thereby clear up any ambiguity. Luther was not confused over the issue; Luther was clear about heaven and earth, the hangman and the preacher, Christ and the devil. It is true that Luther did not use a technical vocabulary for the two kingdoms-regiments, such as he did with law, gospel, church, and so on. But his mind was consistent and clear about keeping the two separate, and he employed a wealth of terms to do so.

I have not seen anyone do what I intend to do: distinguish two different schemes of the kingdoms, isolate a third kingdom of the devil, identify a third government-regiment of the angels, and suggest that it all hangs together in one theological framework.

A word about the doctrinal character of the doctrine, apart from the fact that Luther did not use the phrase "the doctrine of the two kingdoms." Some wish to argue that the doctrine of the two kingdoms in Luther is not a doctrine in the sense of that to which faith is attached. That is true; faith is attached to the Word. The doctrine is not an article of faith, such as those in one of the Creeds. But it is a doctrine in the sense of important teaching; to confuse the two kingdoms by

---

4   Craig Nessan, "Liberation Theology's Critique of Luther's Two Kingdoms Doctrine," *Currents in Theology and Mission* 16 (1989): 257-66.

5   Andreas Pawlas, "Evangelische politische Theologie, Zwei-Reiche-Lehre von der Königsherrschaft Christi als ihre Kriterien und Interpretamente," *Kerygma und Dogma* 36 (1990): 313-32.

6   Ernst-Wilhelm Wendebourg, "Die Reformulierung der lutherischen Zweireiche-Lehre in Trutz Rendtorffs Ethik—der Versuch einer theologischen Bewertung," *Kerygma und Dogma* 38 (1992): 199-229.

7   Gérard Siegwalt, «Les Deux Règnes (Concernant la relation entre Eglise et Etat),» *Revue D'Histoire et de Philosophie Religieuses* 70 (1990/2): 165-72.

collapsing or totally separating them is the work of the devil, according to Luther.[8] Luther did have a doctrine of the earthly realm and a doctrine of the kingdom of God, as seen, for example, in his *Commentary on the Sermon on the Mount* (AE 21.50); you might say that he had a doctrine of each of the kingdoms separately but not a doctrine of the two, that is, a doctrine of their relationship.

The doctrine of the kingdom of Christ is the "chief doctrine."[9] In his comments on Isaiah 60:19 (1527-30), Luther speaks of distinguishing "Christ's kingdom from the kingdom of the world"; the "visible sun, which rules the world, the elements, and government," and the other sun who is Christ who instructs us in divine righteousness; the Gospel tribulation, the light of Christ. At the end he says, "These are articles of faith which are spoken in the school of the cross."[10]

While one could criticize the older scholarship—Wingren, Cranz—for the heaven/earth dichotomy at the expense of the kingdom of the right and left hand, they were accurate to see heaven in Luther.[11] Today

---

8   *Commentary on Psalm 101* (1534); AE 13:194-95: "Constantly I must pound in and squeeze in and drive in and wedge in this difference between the two kingdoms, even though it is written and said so often that it becomes tedious. The devil never stops cooking and brewing these two kingdoms into each other. In the devil's name the secular leaders always want to be Christ's masters and teach Him how He should run His church and spiritual government. Similarly, the false clerics and schismatic spirits always want to be the masters, though not in God's name, and to teach people how to organize the secular government. Thus the devil is indeed very busy on both sides, and he has much to do. May God hinder him, amen, if we deserve it!"

9   *Sermons on the Gospel of John*, AE 23:178.

10   AE 17:324-25.

11   A problem with Luther's doctrine of the two kingdoms arises when men like Cranz and Wingren reduce all of Luther's distinctions between the two kingdoms to a two-level, horizontal scheme of heaven and earth. See F. Edward Cranz, *An Essay on the Development of Luther's Thought on Justice, Law, and Society*, Harvard Theological Studies (Cambridge, 1959); Gustaf Wingren, *Luther On Vocation*, trans. Carl Rasmussen (Philadelphia, 1957). Luther, indeed, partially fits into this scheme. But there are also parts of Luther's distinction of the two kingdoms which cut across the two-level scheme of heaven and earth. These may be represented as emphasizing two vertical realms extending from heaven and earth. These two schemes or ways of distinguishing Luther's discussion of the two kingdoms are not self-contradictory. In fact, both must be kept together in mind always.

with a dualistic (existential) orientation, heaven seems to have slipped away in treatments of Luther; the same with the angels. Ebeling it seems is symptomatic of a dualistic treatment when he links the two kingdoms with law and gospel. At the outset it appears that the two kingdoms do parallel law and gospel in that law is the instrument of God's left hand, and the gospel the instrument of the right hand. But Ebeling and others miss Luther when they identify law with devil, death, sin, and flesh (*diabolus, mors, peccatum, caro*).[12] Has Ebeling missed the point in Luther that the civil use of the law is different from the spiritual use? The identification of the two kingdoms with the kingdom of God and the kingdom of the devil goes back to Johannes Heckel.[13] The kingdom of the world is not identical with the kingdom of the devil; the secular realm includes state or government, nature, the family, the arts, and all the sciences.[14]

WHOLE PICTURE

Allow me to state the whole picture in three paragraphs.

(1) A systematic or coherent and historical view of Luther's whole doctrine of the two and three kingdoms focuses on the distinction between the kingdom of God and the kingdom of the world against the medieval inclination to unite the two under the papacy. Here the horizontal distinction between heaven and earth pertains. The kingdom of the devil, the kingdom of the underworld, is at work attacking both God's eternal kingdom of redemption and God's created world. The Christian belongs to both the earthly and heavenly kingdoms. Since there are so few true Christians, the civil use of the law is needed to maintain order and justice in the earthly realm.

(2) Intersecting this scheme, that is, the horizontally oriented kingdoms of heaven and earth, a wholistic treatment of Luther notes another aspect to Luther's doctrine of the kingdoms, namely, the two governments as the kingdom of the right hand and the kingdom of the left hand of God. This scheme is vertically oriented in that it represents God's outreach, his rule over all on earth. Luther's doctrine is that God rules indirectly with his left hand in the created order through the

---

12   Gerhard Ebeling, *Word and Faith*, trans. James W. Leitch (Philadelphia: Fortress Press, 1963) p. 391.

13   Lohse, p. 189.

14   Lohse, p. 188.

God-ordained institutions of government, family, schools, etc.; and God rules directly with his right hand in the church through Word and sacrament. This vertical scheme of two governments-regiments includes a third government; it is the rule of the angelic realm or government through reason and the understanding.

(3) These two, what I am calling schemes or configurations of how the world here and beyond is governed, are complementary and always in force together.[15] To put it simply, think of Luther who lived in both of the horizontal kingdoms: in the visible earthly kingdom as a citizen of Wittenberg and in the invisible heavenly kingdom as a Christian in the company of all the saints and angels. Furthermore, Luther was an instrument of God's left hand as professor, father, and civil judge, and an instrument of God's right hand as priest and preacher. Furthermore, Luther's doctrine of *Anfechtung* meant he was in daily struggle with Satan and his kingdom, and his morning prayer called for charge of the holy angel.

RELATION TO OTHER DOCTRINES

Many seek to connect "Luther's doctrine of the two kingdoms" with some other of his well-known distinctions such as law and gospel, creation and redemption.[16] James Atkinson relates the two kingdoms to the two aeons:

> For the biblical foundation of his social ethic, Luther rooted his doctrine of the "two kingdoms" of creation and redemption in the Pauline eschatology of the "two ages" (aeons), in Adam and in Christ (Romans 5). In the kingdom of God, the Redeemer rules all regenerate believers through Christ and the gospel in personal faith and love. In the kingdom of men, the Creator rules all sinful but rational creatures through Caesar and the law in civil justice and order. As both Redeemer and Creator, God is at once the Lord

---

15   Below is a discussion of the two schemes present in Luther's distinction of the two kingdoms. I am perhaps in danger of misrepresenting Luther by separating them, but I do so because interpreters of Luther tend to emphasize one or the other, and even one to the exclusion of the other. Furthermore, I present two schemes separately because more often than not Luther uses one or the other in a given work. Occasionally, both are present.

16   The one who does the most interrelating of doctrines is Franz Lau, "The Lutheran Doctrine of the Two Kingdoms," *Lutheran World* 12 (1965): 355-72.

of both kingdoms; as both righteous and sinful, the Christian is at once a subject of both kingdoms. Hence for an evangelical theology of society, the two kingdoms must always be properly distinguished, but never separated in secularism or equated in clericalism.[17]

To be sure, all of Luther's theology forms a coherent whole; but to use one distinction as a key to unlock some other theme, I do not find helpful. I recommend seeing each of Luther's ideas as a whole piece using the vocabulary from within that article of faith.

Let us try and see how the doctrine of the two kingdoms interconnects with Luther's other main ideas.

Law and Gospel: civil use of the law is for the left hand, spiritual use for the right hand; both uses of the Gospel, alien and proper, are used by the right hand.

Christian Freedom: the Christian is free only in the kingdom of God through the power of Christ to redeem from bondage to sin.

Christian Vocation: all are called to be children of God; in the kingdom of this earth, we have different callings.

Faith and Good Works: faith is vertically directed to God; works are horizontally directed to the neighbor; God does not need my good works but my neighbor does.

Christian Society: God rules the world; rulers will be held accountable; human reason and will are to reign to create peace and justice.

The Two-Kingdoms Doctrine relates best to Luther's **doctrine of God:** God is the creator of all that exists, seen and unseen.

Except for the doctrines of God and vocation, the two-kingdom theology does not gain a great deal set in relation with other key ideas. It is really a theological construct, a *Weltanschauung*, to set up the whole picture. Most of Luther's distinctive ideas relate to the kingdom of God and do not achieve any greater clarity in relation to the other kingdom(s): such is the case where we have to deal with biblical interpretation, Trinity, Christology, pneumatology, ecclesiology, sacramentology, soteriology, and eschatology.

HEAVEN AND EARTH

Next I wish to present two key documents of Luther's that highlight the scheme of the two kingdoms as heaven and earth, namely, *The Large Commentary on Galatians* and *The Bondage of the Will*.

---

17   Introduction to *The Christian in Society*, AE 44:xiii-xiv.

Gustav Wingren points out the importance of the distinction between the two kingdoms in *Galatians* and *Bondage* by saying "that this demarcation between earth and heaven is the main point in two of Luther's central writings: *Large Commentary on Galatians* and *The Bondage of the Will*."[18]

In *Bondage* Luther makes the distinction between the two kingdoms very clear by the terminology of things which are "above" us and things which are "below" us. For Luther, man and woman, in their special place within the pyramid of creation, were created to have free dominion over all things, even though they have lost their freedom before God.[19] Luther says that if we do not wish to drop the term "free will" altogether "let us at least teach men to use it honestly, so that free choice is allowed to man only with respect to what is beneath him and not what is above him."[20] Thus human will is free in earthly matters, but not before God. Later, in *Bondage* Luther reaches the same conclusion in a discussion of Sirach 15:14-17 by dividing mankind into two kingdoms:

> We thus learn from Ecclesiasticus that man is divided between two kingdoms, in one of which he is directed by his own choice and counsel, apart from any precepts and commandments of God, namely, in his dealings with the lower creatures... In the other kingdom, however, man is not left in the hand of his own counsel, but is directed and led by the choice and counsel of God, so that just as in his own kingdom he is directed by his own counsel, without regard to the precepts of another, so in the Kingdom of God he is directed by the precepts of another, without regard to his own choice.[21]

The distinction of the two kingdoms is between the kingdom of man and the kingdom of God. Near the end of his work, Luther again makes use of the distinction between the kingdom of earth and the kingdom of heaven: "We are not disputing about nature but about grace, and we are not asking what we are on earth, but what we are in heaven before God."[22] And so Luther again continues to solve

---

18　Wingren, p. 14.

19　Gordon Rupp, *The Righteousness of God* (New York: Philosophical Library, 1953) p. 275.

20　Martin Luther, *On the Bondage of the Will*, AE 33:70.

21　AE 33:118-19.

22　AE 33:284-85.

the problem of free will by making the distinction between the two kingdoms. Hence in *Bondage* Luther used the distinction of the two kingdoms as the conceptual framework and as the eyeglass by which he constructs his reply to Erasmus. And on this account I would disagree with Gustav Wingren's point that the demarcation of the two kingdoms is "the main point" of *Bondage*. Luther does not seek to establish the point or to prove it, but he rather assumes the distinction of the two kingdoms as his basic frame of reference. The main point of the treatise is to show that our salvation is utterly beyond our powers, will, and works and is absolutely dependent on the free will of God.

Luther gives a very clear picture of the two kingdoms in his *Large Commentary on Galatians*. At times he uses the distinction of the two kingdoms to indicate the two realms of existence. This can best be seen in Luther's fundamental contrast between the two justices (*Gerechtigkeit*).[23] He says, "We set forth two worlds, as it were, one of them heavenly and the other earthly. Into these we place these two kinds of righteousness, which are distinct and separated from each other."[24] The two realms of justice are the contrast between passive and active justices. Christian justice, that is justice before God, is passive justice: "For here we work nothing, render nothing unto God; we only receive and permit someone else to work in us, namely, God. Therefore it is appropriate to call the righteousness of faith or Christian righteousness, 'passive.'"[25] This worldly justice, that is justice among humans, is active justice—it is "all other kinds of righteousness" than righteousness before God: "There is a political righteousness, which the emperor, the princes of the world, philosophers and lawyers consider. There is also a ceremonial righteousness, which human traditions teach ... There is, in addition to these, yet another righteousness, the righteousness of the Law or of the Decalog."[26] Luther equates the distinction between the two justices with the basic biblical distinction between law and the gospel and argues that just as God carefully separated heaven and earth, so we should carefully separate these two justices:

---

23   AE 26:4f.
24   AE 26:8.
25   AE 26:5.
26   AE 26:4.

Therefore whoever knows well how to distinguish the Gospel from the Law should give thanks to God and know that he is a real theologian... The way to distinguish the one from the other is to locate the Gospel in heaven and the Law on earth, to call the righteousness of the Gospel heavenly and divine and the righteousness of the Law earthly and human, and to distinguish as sharply between the righteousness of the Gospel and that of the Law as God distinguishes between heaven and earth.[27]

Luther distinguishes the two justices because the Christian lives in both the realm of God's kingdom and the realm of the human kingdom, and as long as Christians are in the human kingdom they may never "mix" them.

Luther uses a number of other contrasts to indicate the two realms of existence. For example he urges the distinction between morals and faith, works and grace, and polity and religion.[28] He urges that the political and economic realm of reason be distinguished from the spiritual realm: "For the kingdom of man's reason and the spiritual kingdom must be separate far asunder."[29]

Distinguishing between the life of religion and life of secular polity, Luther says, "Where religion and the Word of God are the issue, there must be no partiality. But apart from religion, apart from God, there must be partiality."[30] He corrects his "adversaries" by distinguishing the realm of natural or moral works from the realm of theological works and matters of divinity: "Therefore 'doing' is always understood in theology as doing with faith, so that 'doing' with faith is another sphere and a new kingdom, so to speak, separate from moral doing."[31] "The boundaries and the kingdoms of the Law or works and of faith should be correctly distinguished from one another."[32]

At other times Luther uses the distinction of the two kingdoms to indicate the two realms of discourse. Certain propositions and

---

27 AE 26.115.

28 WA 40 I, 51, 10f.: "Audistis heri subiectum huius Epistolae, quod Paulus docet illam iusticiam Christianam, et, sicut dixi, diligenter est observanda ista distinctio, ne confundantur mores at fides, opera et gratia, politia et religio, et valde multum conducit istas 2 iusticias disiungere."

29 AE 26:174.

30 AE 26:97.

31 AE 26:262-63.

32 AE 26:273.

concepts apply only to the kingdom of heaven, other times only to
the realm of human reason. And sometimes statements have different
meanings as they are applied in one or the other realm. For example,
Luther says at one point, "For we must note here that Paul is dealing
(*quia Paulus versatur*) not with a political topic (*non in loco politico*)
but with a theological and spiritual one, with something in the sight
of God (*sed theologico et spirituali coram deo*)."[33] Commenting on Paul's
statement that God is no respecter of persons, Luther says this is true
in the realm (*in loco*) of justification: "We must pay careful attention to
this distinction, that about theological issues we must speak in a way
that is vastly different from the way we speak about social issues."[34]
Considering some of the statements of the "sophists," Luther illustrates the two realms of discourse by saying, "We do not then deny
that these sentences are true in the corporeal realm; but if you drag
them into the spiritual kingdom before the presence of God, I utterly
deny them."[35]

To sum up this scheme of the two kingdoms, from another source in
Luther: "Christ did not come to establish a worldly kingdom; He came
to establish a kingdom of heaven."[36]

LEFT AND RIGHT HAND

Now I wish to present two other documents of Luther's that highlight
the other scheme of the two kingdoms as the left and right hand of
God, namely, *Secular Authority: To What Extent It Should Be Obeyed*
and *Whether Soldiers, Too, Can Be Saved.*

Luther also thinks of the two kingdoms in terms of two governments (*Regimente*) established by God in order to rule the human race.
The scheme is two vertical governments and kingdoms, representing
the extension of the left and right hand of God: the secular kingdom,
being the kingdom of the left hand, which God rules through secular authority; and the spiritual kingdom, being the kingdom of the
right hand, which God rules through the church. "*Weltliches Regiment*
is spoken of as *Gottes Reich* for God wills it to remain and wishes us to
be obedient within it. It is the kingdom of God's left hand where God

---

33   AE 26:249.
34   AE 26:96.
35   AE 26:174.
36   *Sermons on the Gospel of St. John* (1537), AE 24:155.

rules through father, mother, Kaiser, king, judge, and even hangman; but His proper Kingdom, the Kingdom of His right hand, is where God rules Himself, where He is immediately present and His Gospel is preached."[37] This aspect of Luther's teaching of the two regiments must be seen within the context of his doctrine of providence and creation, that is, as Gordon Rupp says, "*coram Deo*."[38] The two kinds of rule are ways by which God himself runs his world. Hence, as Anders Nygren says, it is with God whom we deal in matters spiritual and temporal—God himself rules both realms.[39]

Luther divides all of mankind into two groups: the Christians who belong to the kingdom of God and the non-Christians who belong to the kingdom of the world. Each group and kingdom has its own government, with its special means for government, and with its particular goals and purposes for governing: "We must divide all the children of Adam into two classes; the first belong to the kingdom of God, the second to the kingdom of the world. Those belonging to the kingdom of God are all true believers in Christ and are subject to Christ... He [Christ] also calls the Gospel a Gospel of the kingdom of God, because it teaches, governs, and upholds God's Kingdom."[40] "All who are not Christians belong to the kingdom of the world and are under the law. There are few true believers, and still fewer who live a Christian life, who do not resist evil and indeed themselves do no evil. For this reason God has provided for them a different government outside the Christian estate and God's kingdom. He has subjected them to the sword so that, even though they would like to, they cannot practice their wickedness, and if they do practice it they cannot do so without fear or with success and impunity."[41] "For this reason these two governments must be sharply distinguished, and both be permitted to remain; the one to produce piety, the other to bring about external

---

37 Martin Luther, "Sermon for the Third Sunday of Advent," WA 52.26.22-27 (1544), translated by T. F. Torrance, *Kingdom and Church* (London: Oliver and Boyd, 1956), p. 24; cf. also WA 36.385.6-11 (1532) for a slightly different version of the same.

38 Rupp, p. 289.

39 Anders Nygren, "Luther's Doctrine of the Two Kingdoms," *Ecumenical Review* 1 (1949): 304.

40 *Temporal Authority: To What Extent It Should Be Obeyed* (1523), AE 45:88.

41 AE 45:90.

peace and prevent evil deeds. Neither one is sufficient in the world without the other."[42]

Gordon Rupp summarizes Luther well: "God's spiritual government is that of the 'Kingdom of God,' the 'Kingdom of Christ,' and is exercised through the Gospel, as a 'Kingdom of Hearing' (through faith)."[43] Luther says, "Christians can be ruled by nothing except God's Word."[44] This means that if all were Christians there would be no need of secular law and sword:

> If all the world were composed of real Christians, that is, true believers, no prince, king, lord, sword or law would be needed. They would serve no purpose, since Christians have in their hearts the Holy Spirit, who instructs them and causes them to wrong no one, to love everyone, willingly and cheerfully to suffer injustice and even death from every one... Therefore, it is not possible for the secular sword and law to find any work to do among Christians, since they do of their own accord much more than all laws and doctrines can demand.[45]

Since, however, "the whole world is evil and that among thousands there is scarcely one true Christian ... it is out of the question that there should be a common Christian government over the whole world, or indeed over one land or company of people, since the wicked always outnumber the good."[46] For this reason God rules the two different groups of people in the world by two different instruments. In *Whether Soldiers, Too, Can Be Saved* Luther states the "sum and substance of it":

> God has established two kinds of government among men. The one is spiritual; it has no sword, but it has the Word, by means of which men are to become good and righteous, so that with this righteousness they may attain everlasting life. He administers this righteousness through the Word, which He has committed to the preachers. The other kind is worldly government, which works through the sword so that those who do not want to be good and righteous to eternal life may be forced to become good and righteous in the eyes of the world. He administers this righteousness through the sword.

---

42   AE 45:92.
43   Rupp, p. 290.
44   AE 45:117.
45   AE 45:89.
46   AE 45:91.

And although God will not reward this kind of righteousness with eternal life, nonetheless, He still wishes peace to be maintained among men and rewards them with temporal blessing.[47]

Thus according to Luther, God has established and rules two *Regimente* and *Reiche*: the temporal for *iustitia civilis* through the law by the sword, and the spiritual for *iustitia christiana* through the Word. "Thus God Himself is the founder, lord, master, protector, and rewarder of both kinds of righteousness."[48]

KINGDOM OF THE DEVIL (*REGNUM DIABOLI*)

Luther also speaks of a *regnum diaboli* which must now be understood. I think his discussion of the *regnum diaboli* can best be understood as presupposing his emphasis on the two horizontally oriented kingdoms of heaven and earth.

A further difficulty in trying to specify what Luther means by the two kingdoms arises when Luther speaks of a *regnum diaboli* distinguished from a *regnum dei*: for example, "Whatever is flesh is ungodly, under God's wrath, and a stranger to his Kingdom. And if it is a stranger to God's Kingdom and Spirit, it follows of necessity that it is under the kingdom and spirit of Satan. For there is no middle kingdom between the Kingdom of God and the kingdom of Satan, which are mutually and perpetually at war with each other."[49] Gordon Rupp says that the conflict and dynamism in history, the ferment of evil, to which Luther's doctrine of the devil bears witness, "blurs all theorizing and prevents a smooth and rounded doctrine in this matter."[50] When confronted with Luther's thought on the *regnum diaboli*, it must be kept in mind that both the spiritual and temporal *Regimente* and *Reiche* are under the rule of God. It is only because the kingdoms are governed by God that they continue; whereas if the kingdoms should be left to themselves for a moment, they would be overthrown by the devil. Thus, as E. M. Carlson points out, the *regnum diaboli* is not to be identified with either regime, but can affect both: "Both regimes are ideally and properly a defense against evil, but both of them may

---

47   AE 46:99-100.
48   AE 46:100.
49   AE 33:227.
50   Rupp, p. 290.

be corrupted."[51] The devil's dominion seeks to prevent submission to God which is demanded in both regimes.

Luther on Psalm 101:5:

> Such divine direction is especially necessary in that secular government in which David and God-fearing Christian princes rule; for they are supposed to do both—serve God and rule the people. The devil is much more hostile to these than he is to the heathen, who are his subjects. . . As the Bible teaches us, therefore, God Himself has always had to protect and preserve His people's kingdom through His own power and miraculous deeds, through all the extraordinary leaders whom He chose and awakened for this purpose. While the devil is also hostile and opposed to the secular government of the heathen, still he hates the government of the saints of God on earth much more fanatically. Against this he has always used the kingdoms and the powers of the heathen, as is shown by all the heathen who have been round about Jerusalem; and he will never quit until the Last Day, when he will finally have to stop.[52]

GOVERNMENT OF THE ANGELS
(ENGELISCHES REGIMENT)

Just as the doctrine of the two kingdoms as heaven and earth has a third kingdom, that of the devil, so the doctrine of the two kingdoms-governments as the right and left hand of God has a third government, that of the angels. In Luther's works, I have only seen the view of the angels as a third government spelled out in his *Commentary on Zechariah* of 1527.[53] Certainly Luther speaks of the rule, protection, and influence of the angels often. I have not seen anyone in secondary literature point out the existence of both the—third—kingdom of the devil and the—third—government of the angels.

---

51   E. M. Carlson, "Luther's Conception of Government," *Church History* 15 (1946): 270.

52   AE 13:201.

53   My conclusion is also that of Franz Lau (p. 357), whom I read at the end of my study.

Commentary on Zechariah (WA 23.513.36—514.31):

> He has, then, three outward governments and in addition three outward ways or means for His own divine rule. In the secular government it is the sword and the fist, in the spiritual government it is the Word and the mouth, in the angelic government it is reason and the understanding. These are the three means: sword, Word, reason. By the sword, however, I understand all that pertains to the secular rule, such as secular justice and laws, customs and habits, manners, estates, various offices, persons, clothes, etc. By the Word I understand all that pertains to the spiritual government, such as spiritual gifts, 1 Cor. 12:5, Eph. 4:11, Rom. 12:6f., and the sacraments and the like. By reason I understand everything that the dear angels use to move us, to keep us from evil or to nudge us toward the good. For they do not rule by the sword or the Word, though they might. The spiritual rulers, on the other hand, cannot rule by reason, like the angels, nor do they rule with the sword, though they could do that too, but by the Word. The secular rulers cannot rule by reason, like the angels, nor by the Word, like the spiritual rulers, but govern by the sword. Thus each has its designated work and limit: the lowest cannot perform the office of the highest, but the highest can indeed perform that of the lowest. The secular government, however, is the lowest and least of the governments of God; for it makes no one pious but only punishes the evil and resists the rebellious. But more of that elsewhere.[54]

---

54 This passage in *Commentary on Zechariah* AE 20:172 and first paragraph in Karl H. Hertz, ed. *Two Kingdoms and One World* (Minneapolis: Augsburg, 1976), entry 61, pp. 63-64; translation my own. The text continues: "And none of these governments is against the other, and none crushes or destroys the other; but the one serves the other. The lowest, the rule of the sword, serves the Gospel by maintaining peace among the people; and without that one could not preach. The Gospel, in turn, serves the sword by teaching, holding people to the obedience of the sword and bearing witness to the fact that the sword is the ordinance and rule of God (Rom. 13:1ff.) and is therefore to be feared and respected. Without this fear and respect, however, the sword would have a very wretched rule. And the angels serve both the Gospel and the sword by helping to promote them and moving the people toward them through reason. The sword and the Word, in turn, serve the angels; for they create opportunities and through peace and prosperity prepare the people so that the angels may all the better approach them and promote their rule. For in the midst of strife and error the angels find it difficult to rule through their reason."

Going beyond the Luther texts covered, one could cite Luther forever on the topic of the two kingdoms. Let me provide a further sample of a document where the horizontal scheme dominates, a sample where the vertical dominates, and a text where both are present.

First, the distinction between heaven and earth. In his comments on Psalm 8 (1537/1572), Luther, following John 18:36 ("My kingship is not of this world"), distinguishes "sharply" between Christ's kingdom, an eternal, heavenly, imperishable kingdom and the kingdom of the world, an earthly, perishable, mortal kingdom.[55]

Next, the vertical scheme. In his comments on Psalm 101 (1534), Luther distinguishes "two areas of authority," the secular kingdom and God's kingdom. The secular government of the godless is God's ordinance and creation: "both kingdoms were in Rome at the same time— Emperor Nero ruled the one against Christ, Christ ruled the other through His apostles Peter and Paul against the devil."[56]

Last, a good example of both schemes present:

> The spiritual government or authority should direct the people vertically toward God that they may do right and be saved; just so the secular government should direct the people horizontally toward one another, seeing to it that body, property, honor, wife, child, house, home, and all manner of goods remain in peace and security and are blessed on earth. God wants the government of the world to be a symbol of true salvation and of His kingdom of heaven, like a pantomime or a mask.[57]

CONCLUSION

I have tried to present the whole picture of the various ingredients that go into "Luther's doctrine of the two kingdoms." Without repeating what I have set forth, let me indicate how I diagram the matter for my students: I see two horizontal planes, that is, the two horizontal kingdoms of heaven and earth overlapping two vertical lines. I see the two vertical lines reaching out from the left and right hands of God extending from the heavens above to the earth below, both the secular and spiritual governments ruling and intersecting the kingdom of this earth.

---

55   AE 12:103.
56   AE 13:193-94.
57   AE 13:197.

For Luther it is doctrinally necessary to separate the two kingdoms. For our purposes, I have separated the two schemes of the two kingdoms, calling the one a horizontal configuration of the heavens above and the earth beneath and calling the other a vertical picture of God's two governments as his two hands. For Luther the kingdom of heaven is not the earth, and yet on this earth God is present and at work through sword and word. Also, the earth is not heaven; our temporary abode here is sustainable because we participate in the heavenly realm and worship Christ in the company of all the saints. Both schemes are further nuanced by the kingdom of the devil and the government of the angels.

The reason I have separated the two schemes is that in Luther's writings usually only one is present. The two are very different. Refusing to believe that Luther contradicts himself, and refusing to isolate the one as the mature and real Luther by ignoring the other, as is sometimes done, the only way I could avoid the confusion so prevalent from the literature on the subject is to see that Luther has two complementary views of the two kingdoms.

As is typical for all of Luther, he has the whole theological picture in his head. I see Luther in general as operating with a complete theological arsenal from which he draws particular weapons depending on the situation. I see Luther as having a complete and coherent picture of the complexities of heaven, earth, word, hangman, devil, angels, and all their interrelationships in his huge storehouse of a mind; however, since most of his writing was occasional in some polemical context, he drew out and developed what was needed for the moment.

The two conceptions of the kingdoms provided him with a theological structure to organize his thoughts in a particular context. Just as all of Luther's nuances complement each other, so the two sets do not conflict but complete each other.

And not only are the two complementary, they are both necessary. The horizontal scheme alone could lean in the direction of other-worldliness, as it did in the case of the Spiritualists, or secularism, as it did in the medieval papacy. The vertical configuration alone could lead to immanentism; and it has, as in Enlightenment Christianity.

It may be that the difficulties associated with Luther's two-kingdom doctrine in the history of Lutheranism are attributable to the isolation of one scheme at the expense of the other. The two views, then, are not only both complementary and necessary but also serve as correctives to each other.

Finally, we may ask, does Luther have a doctrine of the two kingdoms? I am willing to say yes not only because it is such a commonplace in the literature but also because I think Luther had one doctrine with several nuances and complementary configurations depending on the historical (and polemical) situation. I see no problem with the term "two" kingdoms while there were actually four or six. Predominantly there were two kingdoms and two governments, namely, two different schemes, two configurations in one overall framework. The point here is that for Luther it all hung together. As the heavens are higher than the earth, so the kingdom of God is to be separated from the kingdom of the world. So too as the word is mightier than the sword, the right hand of God is to be differentiated from the left hand. Luther frames his understanding of the kingdoms with basically two horizontal and two vertical kingdoms. The frame is under siege by the devil and guided by the angels.

THE DOCTRINES OF VOCATION AND ETHICS
AND MARTIN LUTHER

INTRODUCTION

Those responsible for this project ("Confessional Lutheran Ethics") are to be congratulated for taking on the topic of Lutheran ethics, since in some circles Lutheran ethics is considered an oxymoron (hear the old and still current critique of quietism). Or, to put another face on it, ethics means works, Lutheranism means faith, and everyone knows how that all goes; so why a publication on the obvious?

Furthermore, Luther on vocation is an old topic, covered by Gustaf Wingren's classic volume, so what is new there? Luther on ethics means either Luther on Christian living, and faith-active-in-love takes care of that; or the topic means Luther on Aristotle, and Luther takes care of him in short order. While these caricatures abound, actually the topic of Luther on vocation and ethics involves much that needs rethinking.

The question of ethics in Luther, namely whether he had a doctrine of ethics, occupied much of my research time, since the secondary literature treats ethics in Luther as Christian living and not as a separate theological discipline. Hence my focus will be on principles, norms, and structures relative to ethics and not on particulars, for example, sexuality, usury, or the state. The question of vocation in Luther became for me a problem with the work of Wingren, which resulted in the need to critique what I will call his lopsided reading of Luther.

Next some basic theological distinctions will orient our discussion.

BASIC THEOLOGICAL DISTINCTIONS: FREEDOM/SERVANT HOOD

Luther's treatise on *The Freedom of a Christian* "established the connection between his doctrine of justification and the Reformation ethic":[1] freed under the gospel from all law, the Christian is a slave to the neighbor.

---

1   Bernhard Lohse, *Martin Luther, An Introduction to His Life and Work*, trans. Robert C. Schultz (Philadelphia: Fortress, 1986), 130.

LAW (TWO USES) AND GOSPEL

The civil use of the law (*usus politicus legis*) is to maintain peace and order in the kingdom of this world. The spiritual use (*usus theologicus legis*) of the law is to convict of sin and lead to the gospel. The two uses of the law are as distinct as heaven is from earth, though an individual in this world is subject to both. The gospel is the proclamation of the forgiveness of sins. The distinction between the second use of the law and the proper use of the gospel is what makes a true theologian.

TWO KINGDOMS

The spiritual and temporal *Regimente* and *Reiche* (governances and kingdoms) are under the rule of God. As E. M. Carlson points out, the *regnum diaboli* (kingdom of the devil) is not to be identified with either regime, but can affect both: "Both regimes are ideally and properly a defense against evil, but both of them may be corrupted."[2] Ethics and vocation have to do with the kingdom of this world. The temporal governance "pertains to the secular rule, all secular rights and laws, customs and habits, actions, stations, various offices, persons, clothes, etc. By the Word I understand all that pertains to the spiritual rule, such as spiritual gifts, 1 Cor 12:5, Eph 4:11, Rom 12:6f., and the sacraments and the like" (*Commentary on Zechariah*, AE 20:172).

VOCATION TO WORK VS. VOCATION TO RELIGIOUS LIFE

The German mystics were the first to advance the idea of a worldly call, according to Karl Holl's history of the word Beruf. First Corinthians 7:20 is the key text ("Every one should remain in the Beruf [klh/sij] in which he was called") in Holl's discussion. Laity are called by God to do their worldly work wherein they find themselves. Everyone has his call from God.[3] According to Bernhard Lohse, Luther was the first to provide a theological basis for understanding calling in the sense of secular work. Luther also was the first to challenge the notion that monasticism and clerical ministry were higher callings. In Roman Catholic territories "calling" (*vocatio*) continued to mean the vocation to enter a religious order, where ethics, as in the Middle Ages,

---

2   E. M. Carlson, "Luther's Conception of Government," *Church History* 15 (1946), 270.

3   Karl Holl, "Die Geschichte Des Worts Beruf," *Gesammelte Aufsätze zur Kirchengeschichte* (Darmstadt: Wissenschaftliche Buchgesellschaft, 1965), 3:205–8.

continued to be two-tiered, one for the laity and a higher one for the clergy.[4]

"ETHICS"

Luther knew the New Testament word for calling (κλῆσις). Is there a New Testament word for ethics? No. In the Septuagint? No. Is the word "ethics" in Luther's vocabulary? Yes. Where does it come from? Aristotle. Is that all Luther meant by ethics, namely, Aristotle's *Ethics*? No. My point here is that the doctrine of vocation has a clear biblical and historical background. The same is not true for ethics. Ethics is a post-Luther, modern theological discipline; and it is a classical genre of philosophical literature (nothing in between). Is Luther the first to discuss "Christian ethics" as a theological discipline? I think so.

Now to some linguistics on "ethics" as to what Luther knew (from the classics and the New Testament) and what he meant by "ethics."

"ETHICS" IN GREEK AND LATIN

τὰ ἠθικά (τὰ ἠθικα) in classical Greek is a treatise on morals, as in Aristotle's *Nicomachean Ethics*, a work on which Luther lectured (1508–9).[5]

In classical Latin *ethice* means moral philosophy, ethics; *ethicus, a, um* (post-classical, pagan) = moral, ethic, with *res* = ethics, with *dictio* = character; *ethicos* = morally. *Moralis* (Lewis and Short), meaning morals or moral, is a word formed by Cicero (cf. *moratus* [character of a person]), which the Greeks call ἦθος because it pertains to mores. Cicero, Seneca, and Quintilian speak of three parts of philosophy: moral, natural, and rational. ἠθικά (ἠθικά) is that part of philosophy called *moralis*.

Ethics, then, as Luther knew it was a classical genre of moral treatise: showing, expressing, and discussing moral character. The term is not in the New Testament.

ἤθη (ἦθος) is in the New Testament six times, and signifies custom, habit, or manner. ἦθος appears in the New Testament (1 Cor 15:33);

---

4   Lohse, *Martin Luther*, 120.

5   For some help on Luther and Aristotle see Richard Klann, "Luther on Teaching Christian Ethics," *A Lively Legacy: Essays in Honor of Robert Preus*, ed. K. E. Marquart, J. R. Stephenson, and B. W. Teigen (Fort Wayne, IN.: Concordia Theological Seminary, 1985), 96–104.

ἦθος as [good] manners or morals. These mean customs of the fathers, or customs of the Jews.

Ethos, which Paul Althaus uses interchangeably with ethics, in classical Greek and the New Testament refers to the habits of people or their manner of living, which is the way we use the word today. In Luther's Vulgate, the Latin for ἦθος (éthos) was a derivative of *consuetudo* (custom, habit, usage), and *mos* (conduct, behavior). For his German Bible Luther rendered ἦθος (éthos) as *Gewohnheit* (custom), *pflegen* (be in the habit of), and *Weise* (manner, way).

For Luther, then, linguistically there was no "Christian ethics" in Scripture nor any discipline or doctrine of such in the history of the church. There were descriptions of Christian behavior, manner of living, the Christian ethos. There was moral philosophy from classical times, but no moral theology; that came later, in Roman Catholic circles.

LUTHER'S USE OF "ETHICS"

Luther knew and used the word "ethics" ("Christian ethics"). When discussing the Genesis account of Abraham turning Sarah over to Pharaoh (Gn 2:11–13), Luther sees an example of faith in the promise: both Abraham and Sarah "commend themselves to the mercy of God" (AE 2:296). Luther considers and rejects the views of Aristotle and Cicero about suspicion and concludes that Scripture commands us to consider not the conduct of another but the Word and fear of God (AE 2:299). Luther's last sentence is: "Thus the holy Scriptures teach ethics, or the theory of duties, far better than any Ciceros or Aristotles" (*Ethicam, seu Officiorum rationem*, WA 42:478.24).

In a similar fashion Luther refers to Abraham's buying a field to bury Sarah (Gn 23:10–20) as a better source for the "whole doctrine of ethics" than Aristotle, the jurists, and canonists. (*Tota ethicorum doctrina hinc colligi posset melius, quam Aristoteles et Iuristae et canonistae tradiderunt*, WA 43:292.8–9).

Luther does have a Christian ethic, a theory, a doctrine, beyond the description of behavior. On Rom 12:1 Luther says that Paul is about to teach "Christian ethics" (*Christianam ethicam*, WA 56:440.20). Luther discusses Aristotle's description of the five stages of nature (nonbeing, becoming, being, action, being acted upon) as an example of how the life from sin to righteousness proceeds:

> Thus it is most correct to say that man is always in privation, always in becoming or in potentiality, in matter, and always in action. Aristotle philosophizes about such matters, and he does it well, but people do not understand him well. Man is always in nonbeing, in becoming, in being, always in privation, in potentiality, in action, always in sin, in justification, in righteousness, that is, he is always a sinner, always a penitent, always righteous. [AE 25:434]

Luther does not seem to use this particular structure from Aristotle, mentioned in his early *Lectures on Romans*, later in his work. What is significant from the references I have cited, from the early *Lectures on Romans* to the late *Lectures on Genesis*, is that Luther sees "ethics" as a *ratio*, a doctrine, a principle of nature.

MORAL PHILOSOPHY AND CHRISTIAN ETHICS

Luther criticizes the moral philosophy of Aristotle when adopted by the scholastics:

> Therefore they snatch the words "do," "work," and the like, from moral philosophy and from the Law [*ex philosophia moralis et legali*, WA 40/I:410.1–2.], and transfer them to theology, where they act in a way that is not only evil but ungodly. Philosophy and theology must be carefully distinguished. [AE 26:261; 1535 on Gal 3:10]

Luther complains here about the transference of moral philosophy to theology. "Philosophy also speaks of a good will and of right reason"; in and of itself, this is its proper domain, not to be brought into theology. In the next paragraph, Luther speaks about "where the philosophers come to a halt." Moral philosophy means a good will and right reason to do well, and does not have God as its object and final cause. A philosopher and a lawyer seek civil good: welfare of the state and tranquility and honesty. They do not ascend any higher; they do not suppose to attain forgiveness of sins and eternal life, as the sophist or monk does. "Therefore a heathen philosopher [*Gentilis Philosophus*, WA 40/I:411.17] is much better than such a self-righteous person, because he remains within his limits, having in mind only honesty and tranquillity, and not mixing divine things with human" (AE 26:262).

Ethics usually means a principle of right conduct, a system of moral principles (from my *American Heritage Dictionary*). If faced with such a definition Luther immediately thinks of the classical teachers of morals, Cato or Aesop (whom he prefers), Cicero or Aristotle. "So far as moral precepts are concerned, one cannot find fault with the industry and earnestness of the heathen" (1535 on Genesis; AE 2:160), although they are inferior to Moses. "Concerning morals the philosophers of the heathen, too, are capable of giving instruction, although they are completely without a knowledge of faith" (AE 2:152).

Luther knows how the principles of doing and acting in moral philosophy differ from the principles of doing and acting in Christian theology. He does have a clear picture of the distinctively Christian life, which is governed by ethical principles. These principles include the following: the Christian in all matters of the law—ceremonial, judicial, and moral—is free: freed in Christ. The good tree will bear good fruit; faith is active in love. The Christian as a little Christ is a slave to the neighbor. Service to the neighbor is an end in itself; God does not need my good works, my neighbor does.

It is in this picture that I think we see Luther's Christian ethics. The key to this picture is that these genuine Luther items are principles of Christian behavior; they do not specify the content or course of one's action in any particular circumstance. They are norms that are valid in all circumstances.

Throughout his book Wingren is very insistent that those who criticize Luther for separating faith and love and for giving no content to the love ethic end up wanting to turn Luther's position into a new legalism, that is, they want to specify the do's and don'ts of the Christian life. One cannot stipulate what should be done for the neighbor at any given moment because works are spontaneous acts in service of the neighbor, and the needs of the neighbor are always changing.[6]

To be sure Luther discusses at length the specific content and course of Christian living; the moral injunctions abound in his sermons and letters of spiritual counsel. But I have also been trying to establish here that Luther does have Christian ethics as a system of Christian principles for daily living.

---

6   Gustaf Wingren, *The Christian's Calling. Luther on Vocation*, trans. Carl C. Rasmussen (London: Oliver and Boyd, 1958) 40–41, 48–50. Wingren accuses Karl Eger and Paul Heinz Schifferdecker of wanting to make a law for the new man, but, says Wingren, "the new man has no law" (50). See footnotes through this section (not translated) in Wingren's original dissertation: *Luthers* lära om kallelsen (Lund: C. W. K. Gleerups Förlag, 1942), 49–60.

All modern categories relative to Luther's ethics, such as indicative ethic, Reformation ethic, political ethic, personal ethic, social ethic, intentional ethic—and they are all there in the literature—are indeed modern constructs. I prefer to use Luther's constructs. The one that stands out in my mind that would meet the criterion for an ethical principle by classical and modern standards is the one that stipulates "service to the neighbor is an end in itself."

LUTHER'S ETHICAL STRATEGIES

Luther had formal ethical principles; he also gave moral directives. His primary work, however, was that of a theologian.

It seems to me that one aspect of his theological efforts had an ethical motivation to it. I like to think that one of Luther's guiding principles on behalf of reformation was a plan to wipe out the bad fruit in Christendom. Other reformers attacked immorality in high and low places — to no avail in Luther's mind, because they attacked only the bad fruit. Corruption could not be effectively reformed by preaching good conduct, because corruption stemmed from corrupt people who were hell-bent on evil. Luther's strategy was to replace bad trees with good trees rooted in the gospel; then the good conduct would flow.

In other words, Luther's strategy was to move away from the moral admonition of contemporary humanists, from ethics in the classical sense, where they advocated the practice of good manners, civil behavior, imitation of the moral life of Jesus, and the like. Luther focused instead on theological doctrine, on the distinction between law and gospel, between the civil and spiritual realms, on a theology of vocation. In Luther's mind, as I see it, he was convinced that moral discourse was not what the church or society needed. Moral discourse was good in and of itself, and good behavior is highly desirable. But love and justice do not save. There is more to the good life than the good; the "more" is God. Furthermore the good life cannot best be achieved by the imitation of virtue. The gospel produces powers within the Christian to love the neighbor in ways far more effective, because it is the way of Christ.

Luther's concern was always that of a theologian and pastor. His beloved (German) people deserved more than more of medieval law; they deserved and needed the gospel. Luther's training as a doctor of Scripture meant he was committed to the biblical perspective. While Moses was an improvement over classical moralists because he also gave instruction in the worship of God (WA 2:160), the law and ceremonial worship of God do not save. We have two testaments, and the New is older than the Old because the testament of Christ is the oldest testament; and it is the only testament that ever saved. Salvation in Christ releases the individual from the burden of law to the freedom of the gospel.

To say that Luther had an ethical motivation for reformation of church and society does not mean that Luther was a moral theologian; that would be Erasmus. Luther was a pure theologian, a doctrinal theologian. In the area of doctrine, Luther was convinced that ethical behavior in society would happen automatically with the proper distinction between law and gospel and the consequent spread of good trees.

There was an ethical aspect to Luther's distinction between law and gospel, as well as to the distinction between the civil and spiritual realm. When the civil realm was properly conceived, the civil realm would function properly, justice would prevail, the civil and moral law would be followed. This means that the civil realm is not the ladder that leads to heaven. The civil realm leads to civility when the civil realm performs its God-given tasks. The civil realm is ordered by God.

Luther's strategy for reform is his view that the civil realm, ordained by God, works best when ruled by law and reason, that the civil realm when so ordained and ruled would take care of all issues of morality. Public issues of morality today, such as homosexuality, abortion, and euthanasia, were unthinkable and unquestionable in Luther's day. All the sexual sins were inconceivable in the sense of being issues for public discussion. Immorality is immorality, enforced by centuries-old laws and customs of society—period. Luther had a high view of the civil realm because of its basis in law and reason, ordained by God.

Where it is hard, I think, to bring Luther's perspective into our society today is that civil morality and the laws to enforce it were very different in Luther's day. Civil morality is next to nonexistent in our society. That needs no proof or comment. Where our situation today as Lutherans is different than Luther's is that the church cannot rely on society for the enforcement of the morality ordained by the left hand of God. Luther certainly did admonish princes, mayors, soldiers, parents, and the like to do their jobs; and he provided a doctrine of vocation to support secular responsibility. Beyond them Luther could rely on the hangman to be the guardian of the civil realm, as the pastor was the guardian of the spiritual realm. All of society was seen to be under the rule and wrath of God.

So the ethical strategies of reformation were to put the individual, society, and God in proper perspective, seeking to insure that solid doctrine would drive ethical behavior, both Christian ethical behavior and civil morality.

LUTHER ON VOCATION VIS-À-VIS WINGREN

Within Luther's doctrine of the two kingdoms comes his special consideration of the call (*Beruf*), a theology of the call. And the doctrine of the two kingdoms also contains an ethic of vocation, where the performance of one's vocation does not lead to heaven but to civility in this world and a life pleasing to God.

Modern Germans like to point out that Luther's description of *Beruf* has continued to influence modern German language and culture, such that everyone has one; *Beruf* is used on all civil documents (name your *Beruf*). The secularization of Luther's vocabulary can also be seen: words that once were central to Luther's theology are now used with reference to the telephone (which connection I have not seen any German recognize): *anrufen* which meant "to call upon the name of the Lord," now means "to ring up" (in telephone commercials: "ruf mich an"); *wählen*, which meant "the Lord's choosing," now means "to dial"; *Vermittlung*, which meant "mediator," now means "the operator"; and the word which was a synonym for *Beruf*, namely, *Amt*, now means "a line out or extension."

One of Luther's early points (*Address to Christian Nobility*) was that all Christians share the "spiritual estate"; it is common to all Christians, while "office" and "work" refer to one's particular situation (AE 44:129–30). The spiritual estate that all Christians have and are means that all are popes, bishops, priests, and monks, which were considered the spiritual estate in contrast to the temporal estate of princes, lords, artisans, and farmers in the Middle Ages (AE 44:127).

After 1522 Luther uses Beruf as synonymous with *Stand, Amt,* and *Befehl,* based on 1 Cor 7:20[7] (*Ständen, Orden, Stiften, Ämtern, Hierarchien*).[8] The main thrust of the doctrine of vocation is that

---

7   Holl, "Die Geschichte Des Worts Beruf," 217.

8   Bernhard Lohse, *Luthers Theologie in ihrer historischen Entwicklung und in ihrem systematischen Zusammenhang* (Göttingen: Vandenhoeck & Ruprecht, 1995), 262.

every Christian is to serve God in his occupation, every occupation is equal in the sight of God, and the purpose of vocation is to serve the neighbor.

The three *Stände* or *Hierachien* are, first, the priestly *Amt* (pastors, those who supervise the common chest, sextans, servants and messengers of these); second, the married estate (parents, children, servants, widows, maidens); third, the worldly authorities (civil government), including princes, lords, judges, civil officers, state officials, notaries, servants for these persons.[9]

In his *Confession Concerning Christ's Supper* (1528) Luther discusses the three orders, *ecclesia, oeconomia, politia*. After a paragraph on each of the three, he says, "Above these three institutions and orders is the common order of Christian love, in which one serves not only the three orders, but also serves every needy person in general with all kinds of benevolent deeds, such as feeding the hungry, giving drink to the thirsty, forgiving enemies, praying for all men on earth, suffering all kinds of evil on earth, etc." (AE 37:364–65). All Christians are members of the church, a family, and society, and beyond all that is the common order of Christian love. All these stations and orders and the "common order" are created by God. The created order of God's civil kingdom is structured with a myriad of occupations and obligations, all geared to make the kingdom of God's world work, and the working of it all is pleasing to God.

By everyone's admission, the classic expression to Luther's doctrine of vocation was given in Gustaf Wingren's *The Christian's Calling: Luther on Vocation* (London: Oliver and Boyd, 1958; hereinafter abbreviated W). The Swedish original (abbreviated W Sw) was published in 1942.[10]

A prominent though questionable feature of Wingren's presentation is his emphasis that law and vocation belong together: "Vocation falls within the kingdom of the law" (W 26). In vocation is one's cross. "The cross of vocation" is an operative phrase throughout the book: "and on this cross the old human nature is to be crucified" (W 29).

---

9   In *Confession Concerning Christ's Supper* (1528), AE 37:364–65.

10   Wingren seems to be the final word on the subject of Luther on vocation. Marc Kolden speaks of this volume as "Wingren's masterful work" ("Luther on Vocation," *Word & World* 3, no. 4 [Fall 1983], 389), Lohse cites it as the only work on the subject (*Luthers Theologie*, 264). No one I have read in the secondary literature criticizes Wingren at all.

Here we hear of the toils of a broken world in which we bear our cross in service of the neighbor (W 29).

Luther does use "cross" as in "world of toil and cross" (*in terra operis et cruces*, WA 40/I:469.27) in one of Wingren's early and favorite references (he cites it twice in one paragraph from the 1535 Galatians). Luther does speak of "the cross on earth" but not of vocation in this text cited. Nor is it only a "world of toil," for in the very next sentence, not cited by Wingren, it reads: "And then the troubles that the flesh is forced to bear will not be difficult, for the promise is sweet and delights the heart in a wonderful way" (WA 26:301–2).

When Wingren cites Luther's *Treatise on the Sacrament of Baptism* (1519), he links dying to the old man with the cross of one's vocation: "and on this cross the old human nature is to be crucified" (W 29). Wingren confuses Luther's two kingdoms when he identifies exclusively the dying to sin with learning to die in one's vocation. Luther does speak in the *Treatise* of belonging to an estate, in this example the estate of marriage, with its toils and sufferings, "in order that he may grow used to pleasure and sorrow, avoid sin, and prepare himself for death better than he could do outside of that estate" (AE 35:41). It is the Christian who knows "in what estate he may best slay sin and put a check upon his nature" (AE 35:41). With his identification of law and vocation, and both of these with the cross, Wingren gives the strong impression that it is the vocation (with our attachment to it) that must die, and that the Christian is crucified by the law only in his vocation: "The Christian is crucified by the law in his vocation, under the earthly government; and he arises through the gospel, in the church under the spiritual government" (W 30). From Wingren it seems that when the Christian is freed from the law, he is free from his vocation. Hardly!

Wingren's mistake is to link vocation with law, without clearly distinguishing civil law from spiritual use of the law. The vocations are a part of the civil orders of creation, which Wingren knows—but the Christian does not die to the civil law. Yes, the Christian, who lives in God's creation and who occupies more than one vocation, must daily die to sin through the exercise of the spiritual law. The dying to sin may well include slaying sin as a father, husband, and one's occupation; but just as service to God is not limited to serving God only in one's vocation(s), so dying to sin is not dying to sin just in one's vocation.[11]

11 The identification of cross and vocation renders such statements very misleading: "the crucifixion of the old nature in vocation," and "Christ's

Luther, in Wingren's sources, always distinguished between the inner person and outward works and between the person and office. To be sure, the outward works are full of pain and suffering, but also joy. Luther does speak of our bearing our cross in and out of our vocations, but it is not the vocation that dies. From Wingren, one gets the impression that vocation is only suffering, trouble, and death (his words). What happened to the joy of serving Christ also in one's vocations?

In his chapter in *This is the Church*[12] and in his famous book, Wingren's key text of Luther is Luther's 1519 *Treatise on Baptism*, where Luther does say that "God has instituted many estates in life in which men are to learn to exercise themselves and to suffer" (AE 35:39). In our station in life we learn to fulfil the work and purpose of baptism "namely, to slay sin and to die in order that Christ's burden may thus grow light and easy and not be carried with worry and care" (AE 35:40). There is nothing about law here. Besides, along with striving, tasks, and sufferings that are the work of God (AE 35:37), baptism also brings comfort, mercy, and forgiveness (AE 35:34–38). Wingren speaks only of suffering and dying, not that "God receives us sinners, spares us, and makes us pure from day to day, then our heart must be joyful, and love and praise God" (AE 35:42).

Wingren has stitched together law, vocation, suffering, and death in a one-sided manner; I call it "lopsided stitching." I think he became lopsided in his effort to correct Einar Billing, who had sought to correct only a negative view of vocation in Luther with "brighter colors" (W 74–75).[13] Wingren, concerned that this picture with the "brighter colors" had won the day, went out of his way to paint the dark colors that he sees are Luther's. He also criticizes another Swede, Arvid Runestam, for "an altogether too optimistic view of vocation" (W 75). Later in his book Wingren does allow a bit more positive view about vocation in Luther; for example, "It is the old man who endures the cross of vocation, it is the new man who rejoices in vocation, and from

---

cross and man's cross, for these two are the same" (W 32). It is one thing to say, as Luther does, that we share in the crucifixion and resurrection of Christ. It is another to say that it is the vocation that suffers and dies.

12   Gustaf Wingren, "The Church and Christian Vocation," *This Is the Church*, ed. Anders Nygren, trans. Carl C. Rasmussen (Philadelphia: Muhlenberg Press, 1952), 281–93 (esp. 282–86).

13   In his (untranslated) footnotes, Wingren amplifies his critique of Swedish scholarship (W Sw 84–88).

within gives it new character" (W 119). In the same sentence, however, this is cast in terms of living in prison, between the night of despair and the peaceful day of labor. Wingren keeps coming back to Billing, emphasizing: "To Luther world-affirming joy in culture is utterly strange" (W 141).

Speaking of "strange," what is strange about Wingren on this point about culture is how contrary it is to Luther, who was highly appreciative of music and the arts and the whole civil realm. "Martin Luther has taught us to recognize in music a gift of God."[14] Other scholars have recognized the positive function of law and reason for the affairs of this world. In the earthly kingdom "reason is an excellent gift of God."[15] "Luther praises the law in its first use as 'the most excellent of all things in the world.'"[16] Luther praises man in his *Disputation Concerning Man*; he gives a "tribute to the reason of man and the majestic position he occupies on earth" (1536; AE 34:135; from Lewis W. Spitz).[17]

The kingdom of the world is not identical with the kingdom of the devil; the secular realm includes state or government, nature, the family, the arts, and all the sciences.[18] It seems that Wingren at times recognizes the difference between the two uses of the law and the difference between the kingdom of the devil and the kingdom of this world, but more often than not these crucial distinctions are blurred, as for example in the following: "On earth vocation implies the cross as a consequence of the ceaseless enmity of evil against every work of God" (W 142–43), or earlier, referring to Luther's "belief in a real devil who holds sway here in the darkness." Only "Eschatology is the first field to restore harmony and meaning to what happens in earthly life. For that reason faith yearns for death and heaven" (W 142). This is simply a wrong view of Luther's theology of the cross. For Luther,

---

14   Theodore Hoelty-Nickel, "Luther and Music," *Luther and Culture*, Martin Luther Lectures 4 (Decorah, IA: Luther College Press, 1960), 161.

15   B. A. Gerrish, *Grace and Reason* (Oxford: Clarendon Press, 1962), 26.

16   Kolden, "Luther on Vocation," 384.

17   For Luther on the good life that God has made for the use of man, see his comments on Ecclesiastes: "Gold is good, and riches are conferred by God. A woman is a good thing, made to be a helper for man (cf. Gen. 2:18). For God has made all things to be good and to be useful for some human purpose" (AE 15:8).

18   Lohse, *Martin Luther*, 188.

God is revealed in suffering; God is not just hidden on the cross. Plus, something happened after Good Friday, which you would never know reading Wingren.

Crucified by the law through the cross of one's vocation, one is made alive, says Wingren (W 37), but then faith stretches to life after death, "away from the present." The strong (and welcomed) eschatological character of faith and justification in Wingren seems to leave an enormous gap between the present under the law and heaven: no vocation under the gospel, only drudgery under the law. The gospel of forgiveness is only a future eschatological referent: "Thus the forgiveness of sins is the same as eternal life" (W 38)! This is qualified a bit later by emphasizing love of the neighbor in this world (W 44); heaven is on earth (W 47); the new man has no law (W 50). More typical is: "The gospel speaks about the eternal kingdom in the resurrection, where Christ rules without law" (W 212). No gospel on this earth!

Wingren's misunderstanding of Luther's theology of the cross is a real problem (W 53–55). Cross, Wingren says, has to do with earth and neighbor and is "excluded from heaven" (W 54). Wrong. Luther's theology of cross precisely has to do with God and not the neighbor. Wingren complains that newer German literature sees Luther's theology of the cross as the bankruptcy of reason (which is a correct reading of Luther) rather than the concrete and tangible hardships which arise in vocation and purely earthly matters (which is not correct) (W 55).

The problem with Wingren is that he limits vocation to law and misunderstands the orders of creation as ruled by the devil. He says that the new man has no law, but surely the new man has a vocation. I have considered the work of Wingren in some detail not because as a Norwegian American I want to criticize a Swede, but because the topic of vocation needs to be reexamined. The topic needs a balanced treatment of law and gospel, the two uses of the law, and the distinction between the kingdom of the devil and the civil kingdom.

LUTHER'S CIVIL ETHIC

In his widely cited study of Luther's ethics Paul Althaus equates Luther's ethics with the Christian life.[19] Althaus focuses mainly on

---

19   Paul Althaus, *The Ethics of Martin Luther*, trans. Robert C. Schultz (Philadelphia: Fortress Press, 1972), 101.

Christian behavior.[20] Those who treat Luther's "ethics" per se do so not in terms of theory but of practice. It seems to me the subject of Luther's ethics, properly speaking, has received scant attention[21] because scholars have looked in the wrong place in Luther. Generally scholars have looked into Luther's theology and ended up discussing Luther and Christian living, law and gospel, works, vocation, love of the neighbor, faith active in love, two kingdoms, family, work, politics, commandments, education, and so on. Nothing is wrong with these topics and they do impinge on what we mean by ethics, but they do not get at the heart of what ethics means in the classical sense, namely, moral discourse.

Luther's ethics, properly speaking, is located in his discussion of the civil use of the law, the first use of the law. Hence I suggest the phrase Luther's "civil ethic." The reason, I suppose, that this location of ethics has not been recognized is that Luther is seen, as he should be, as a theologian. But in the structure of his thought and in his activity as civil adjudicator the civil use of the law is as important for the kingdom of this world as the spiritual use is for the kingdom of God. The structure of society is governed, or should be, by reason and law. When Luther talks about the high morality of the Turks and that they put the Germans to shame, he is not talking about Christian living.

Remember that loving the neighbor for his own sake is an ethic of significance for the Christian. Here I am interested in the more classic meaning and discipline of "ethics."

Luther has a clear vision of civil law and the civil order. On Gn 9:6 ("Whosoever sheds the blood of man, by man shall his blood be shed"), Luther says no one should shed the blood of a human being. "For if God will require the blood from an animal that kills a human being, with how much greater severity he will require it from the hand of a human being!" (AE 2:139). Here, he says, we have the source of

---

20 Lohse, whose *Luthers Theologie* was geared to replace Althaus's similar work, entitles his short section on Luther's ethics as "Der Ansatz der Ethik." In his footnote Lohse praises Althaus's work as a quick and good overview.

21 Oswald Bayer agrees; see his "`~Ich bin der Herr, dein Gott …`': Das erste Gebot in seiner Bedeutung für die Grundlegung der Ethik." In "`Ich bin der Herr, dein Gott…`": Das erste Gebot in säkularisierter Zeit, Veröffentlichungen der Luther-Akademie e. V. Ratzeburg, vol. 24 (Erlangen: Martin-Luther-Verlag, 1995), 109–20 (esp. 116).

all civil law and law of nations. For this reason courts have been established and procedures prescribed (AE 2:140). The governments should punish all sins forbidden in the second table of the law (disobedience of children, theft, adultery, and perjury; AE 2:141).

Genesis 24:1–4 (Abraham making his servant promise that Isaac would not take a wife from among Canaanites) leads Luther to say that children entering into betrothal need parental consent, otherwise the marriage is neither lawful nor valid (AE 4:218). In the course of his arguments against "the canonists of the pope" Luther appeals to natural right, laws and civil rights, examples of Scripture, written laws, examples of the fathers, civil law (AE 4:219), reason and common sense (AE 4:220).

Luther says of Gn 18:20–21 (God saying that He will come down to Sodom and Gomorrah to see if what is reported is true) that this passage offers moral teaching for the benefit of officers of the state and judges "that verdicts would not be reached in haste; nor would only one side be heard, but there should be a full investigation of a case" (AE 3:230).

On Gn 20:2, Luther in harmony with the testimony of Scripture praises civil works; "for God wanted us to bear the common hardships and misfortunes of human nature, and he tells us not to despair in them but to be confident that he will be with us. Indeed, he has provided us with natural reason, by means of which we are to exercise control over those civil works ..." (AE 3:322). Luther then wonders how Sarah at age 75 could still be beautiful and seizable, and he concludes that people at that time were more moderate and aided by a mild climate: "Today we not only injure and weaken our bodies by gluttony, but we also contaminate the climate by our sins; that is, we provoke God, with the result that the inclemency of the weather is greater than it was in those times" (AE 3:323). Some kind of nature ethic going on here.

The civil order is to be civil. Luther praises civility (AE 6:169).

I would not say that Luther had a civil ethic all worked out, but several ingredients are there in his mind. Luther's ethic is often considered an individual ethic: faith active in love is the Christian automatically doing the works of faith. This is true. I think there are also the seeds of a societal or civil ethic grounded in his first use of the law;[22] I hate to use the term social ethics because of modern connotations.

---

22 Bayer, "*Ich bin der Herr, dein Gott ...*"

It may well be that the content of the civil ethic is traditional, the laws of the land, or what they should be. However, if Luther's doctrine of the two kingdoms is unique to Luther then the civil realm is uniquely conceived as being under the left hand of God. If this is true, we may then speak of both Luther's Christian ethics and Luther's ethics in the ordinary sense of the word.

LUTHER'S ETHIC OF SERVANTHOOD IN VOCATION

Christian ethics is a modern discipline. Moral theology in Roman Catholic circles emerged later in the sixteenth and seventeenth centuries. In medieval times there were penitential books with guides for handling of moral cases by priests; there were books for confessors.[23] Moral issues were dealt with in terms of the virtues. It was a system of legalistic casuistry based on the penitentials.

Luther's dictum of Christian freedom was freedom from all laws in relation to the gospel. The Christian is not free, nor is anyone else free, from the structures of society ordained by God. The freedom of the gospel allowed Luther to "horizontalize" the Christian's love of the neighbor. One of Luther's ethical principles mentioned above is love of the neighbor for the neighbor's sake, as an end in itself. The principle concerns the end in itself; it does not stipulate the particulars of individual conduct. It is a principle within the construct of the two kingdoms, law and gospel.

The principle of "the end in itself" means that God's love flows through the Christian to the neighbor. The neighbor needs and deserves the love that the little Christ gives. The fruit is really good for the neighbor. The Christian life is a life of servanthood, serving God by serving the neighbor.[24] The neighbor, in the church, the economy, and the government, as well as all those in need, is the goal of Christian ethics.

Luther put a great deal of ethical charge in his optimistic principle that love of the neighbor for the neighbor's own sake would be more genuine and effective than the Roman Catholic view that love of the neighbor was oriented to earning merit before God for the one giving

---

23   Bernard Häring, *The Law of Christ*, trans. Edwin G. Kaiser (Westminster, MD: The Newman Press, 1963), 1:10–20.

24   So also Hans Schwarz, "Martin Luther's Understanding of Vocation in the Light of Today's Problems," *Lutheran Theological Journal* 30 (May 1996), 11.

the love. In the Roman Catholic version, the neighbor is used for personal gain. In Luther's view, the neighbor receives all the gain of ethical activity. God does not need my good works; my neighbor does.

Alms-giving and other penitential acts in the medieval world were geared toward serving the giver. Poverty was praised as pleasing to God. For Luther, giving is to benefit the recipient. No one is to have more than he needs, and all excess is to be given away. The principle of loving the neighbor for personal merit before God is selfish and self-serving. The Christian rather is to give not out of ulterior motives, but simply for the sake of serving. Luther's ethical motivation for reformation was to free the Christian from medieval burdens of all kinds of laws that weighed the pilgrim down. Freed from such baggage, the theory or principle is that the love of Christ in the Christian is a more effective agent for works than the threats and taxing obligations of Moses, the Pharisees, the pope, and canon law. Just as Luther placed all his trust in Christ and Christ alone to save, so Luther placed all his trust in the Gospel to free from the law and make good trees that would bare good fruit.

Luther's civil ethic is with reference to the left hand of God or the kingdom of this world. Just as Luther was optimistic about the power of Christ to work in the Christian, so he was confident that the orders of creation were ordained by God. The doctrine of the two kingdoms contains the ethical principle that all vocations are the means for carrying out God's will for His world. Just as the spiritual kingdom is to preach the gospel, so the civil kingdom is to promote civility, honesty, reason, and common sense.

"LUTHERS KORSTEOLOGI"

The occasion for this piece initially was an invitation by Prof. Bøckman to lecture in Trondheim to his students in the institute for religious studies.[1] This allowed me to expand my interest in Luther's early theology. The actual lecture in 1980 was only the beginning of an expanded relationship with the Bøckman family that has enriched the Hagen family as well on both sides of the puddle known as the Atlantic ocean. This author has reached only 50. Sixty must be terrific.

SECTION I. CROSS IN THE CONTEXT OF TESTAMENT

Testament for Luther was the means for theologizing about the Christian faith. He says the promise was given to Abraham "per modum testamenti," through the medium of testament. Testament is also the message as well as the means, "and so that little word testament is a short summary of all God's wonders and grace fulfilled in Christ." The "whole Gospel" is summarized in the testament of Christ. Hermeneutically for Luther, the New Testament book illumines the Old Testament. "The books of Moses and the prophets are also the Gospel," for the New Testament is the light of the Old Testament. The Old Testament is the fountain of the New; the New is the light of the Old.

The first element in testament is the promise initiated by God from the beginning. "It must happen in this manner ... that God alone without any entreaty or desire of man must first come and give him a promise." The promise is "the beginning, the rock, the foundation"; "God is the testator, for it is he himself who promises and bequeaths." The testament is the promise and the promise is in both books: "all the fathers in the Old Testament together with all the holy prophets have the same faith and gospel as we have," because "it is all the one truth of the promise." For Luther there is no book in the Bible which does not contain both law and promise. The testament is eternal. Some would say that the prophets and the New Testament add something to the books of Moses. "No," said Luther regarding all books of the Bible,

---

1 Torsdag 14. februar, Aud. VIII, Dragvoll.

"throughout them all there is one and the same teaching and thought." In every promise, there is a word and a sign just as notaries affix their seal or mark to make a will binding and authentic. The signs were rainbow, circumcision, and rain on the ground; in baptism—water, and in the Lord's Supper—bread and wine. "The words are the divine vow, promise, and testament. The sacred signs are the sacraments, i.e., sacred signs. Now as the testament is more important than the sacrament so the words are much more important than the signs."

The second element in testament is Luther's theology of Word. The word is the living eternal promise of the testament of Christ. The Gospel of Christ is not a writing but a word of mouth, "this report and encouraging tidings, or evangelical and divine news, is also called the New Testament. For it is a testament when a dying man bequeaths his property after his death to his legally defined heirs. And Christ, before his death, commanded and ordained that his Gospel be preached after his death in all the world." Luther preferred the Gospel of John over the synoptics because John is much more about the preaching of Christ. "If I had to do without one or the other, either the works or the preaching of Christ, I would rather do without the works than without the preaching. For the works do not help me but his words give life." Christ did not publish anything. The New Testament is a living word. Consequently for Luther, the church is a "mouth house" not a "pen house." Luther often bemoaned the fact that we have the New Testament in written form because it is primarily proclamation to be sung loudly in German.

The testament is the word of Christ, "'this is my body ....' In like manner he says over the cup 'take it and all of you drink of it: this is the new and everlasting testament in my blood.' In proof and evidence of this, he left his own body and blood under bread and wine, instead of letter and seal." Everything depends on the words of Christ's testament, says Luther: "you would have to spend a long time polishing your shoes, preening and primping to obtain an inheritance, if you had no letter and seal with which you could prove your right to it. But if you have a letter and seal, and believe, desire, and seek it, it must be given to you even though you were scaly, scabby, stinking and most filthy. So if you would receive this sacrament and testament worthily, see to it that you give emphasis to these living words of Christ." The word is the promise. The word is the testament. The word is Christ. Christ's testament is the Lord's Supper. "Let this stand, therefore, as our first and infallible proposition, the mass or sacrament of the altar is Christ's testament."

Now, says Luther, "you have the testator, the testament, the substance of the testament, and those for whom it was made. Now it remains that it be ratified, that is, made valid through the death of Christ." Hebrews 9:16 was often cited by Luther "'for where there is a testament, the death of the testator must of necessity occur.' Now God made a testament, therefore, it was necessary that he should die, but God could not die unless he became man, thus, the incarnation and the death of Christ are both comprehend most concisely in this one word, 'testament'". Testament is not a vow to be altered or recalled by the living. It is an irrevocable will of one about to die. The cross, then, is in the context of the promise of the testament "that God would became man, and die, and rise again in order that this word in which he promises such a testament might be fulfilled and confirmed."

SECTION 2: THEOLOGIA CRUCIS

One early instance and component of Luther's theology of the cross is contained in his 1517 lectures on Hebrews. The component is that Christ's death is a sacrament and an example. It comes up in the context of Luther's comments on Hebrews 10:19, "therefore, brethren, since we have confidence to enter the sanctuary by the blood of Jesus" and the verse goes on to say "let us draw near with a true heart" (verse 22). "Since we have confidence to enter the sanctuary by the blood of Jesus," draws Luther to deal with the work of Christ in terms of sacrament and example. Luther began his interpretation by saying that "the apostle wants us to imitate Christ who suffered and by dying passed over to the glory of the Father." The passion and resurrection of Christ is "the sacrament for imitating Christ," a sacrament "for the mortification of concupiscence" and "for our new life." Luther then says, "almost all of Paul's epistles are full of this mystical and exemplary suffering of Christ."

The passion of Christ, for Luther, is "exemplary" in a twofold way. Referring to St. Augustine, Luther says "we pass over in flesh and spirit, but Christ in flesh alone, therefore, the passing over of Christ's flesh is at the same time an example of the passing over of our flesh (for we will be like him) and a sacrament for the passing over of our spirit." The reference to Augustine made in the lectures on the Hebrews and the earlier lectures on Romans and Galatians show that the sacrament of Christ's passion and resurrection is the work of Christ for our salvation. We are called to imitate Christ's sacrament by dying to sin and walking a new way with Christ. Christ's death and resurrection is also an example for man to die physically in order to be reunited with Christ in heaven.

In the light of earlier medieval exegesis of this verse the conclusion which Luther draws from his discussion of sacrament and example is striking. For Luther, because of the sacrament and example of Christ, "we have confidence to enter the sanctuary by the blood of Jesus." Medieval interpretations ranged from one text that argued that we have confidence because the realities of the New Testament are greater than the types of the Old Testament. Another interpretation emphasizes that our certainty comes from the fact that Christ was first to enter. For another, Christ is an infallible leader. For another, Christ prepared and demonstrated, opened and initiated the way for us to enter.

For Luther, the example of Christ is that he "passed over before everyone else and leveled the rough road in order to elicit our confidence." However, Christ does more than show us the way, "he also holds out his hand for those who are following." Our confidence rests in the fact that "Christ alone is not only our companion on the way but also our leader, and not only our leader but also our helper, in fact, he carries us over." Christ as example, therefore, shows us how to die confidently. Christ as sacrament made it possible for us to die confidently, and he continues to do so.

In the light of medieval exegesis, the significance of Luther's interpretation of Hebrews 10:19 is that "we have confidence to enter the sanctuary" not because Christ's testament is greater than the old but because of Christ alone, his sacrament and example. Furthermore, our confidence arises from the fact that Christ not only opened the way, but he also carries us over.

For Luther, then, the only way to God is by way of faith in the lowly humanity of Christ seen totally humiliated on the cross. This humanity is the holy ladder of ascent to God. Christ became the most abject of men in his passion and death. Luther concentrates on Christ on the cross by way of emphasizing that our righteousness is effected by Christ's righteousness and our penance by Christ's purgation. It is Christ who accomplishes salvation in us rather than our commitment to him. The cross is both sacrament and example.

The next and key document where Luther develops his theology of the cross is the Heidelberg Disputation of 1518. The Heidelberg Disputation is key for two reasons. One, it is Luther's explanation to his fellow Augustinian brothers of his key ideas with regard to sin, free will, and grace, topics which had been debated in this Disputation against Scholastic Theology (1517). The other important thing about the Heidelberg Disputation is that it is the key text in all of Luther's writings for his theology of the cross. The immediate historical context for the Heidelberg Disputation was the posting or the submission of Luther's 95 theses. There has been considerable debate as to whether Luther actually nailed the 95 theses to the door of the Castle Church in Wittenberg. Some ecumenically motivated Catholic scholars have felt that there is really no evidence for the posting and that Luther rather followed the channelsystem and submitted his theses to the proper church officials. The matter really has not been resolved to the specific question of the posting. Perhaps you could say that Luther studies have come too far when this has become such a matter of debate. In any case, the 95 theses created quite a stir.

Pope Leo the 10th was very concerned to prosecute Luther. He hoped to silence Luther through the regular channels by asking the general of the Augustinian hermits in Rome to do that. The Augustinian general, Gabriel della Volta, in turn transmitted this request to the head of the German congregation of the Augustinian hermits, Luther's spiritual fathercounselor, Johann von Staupitz. Staupitz decided to use the regularly scheduled meeting of the German Augustinians on Jubilate Sunday, that is the third Sunday after Easter, in 1518, to discuss Luther's theology. The brothers met at Heidelberg. Luther had been asked by Staupitz to avoid arousing animosity and to avoid controversial subjects, in short, to deal with some of the central items that had been brought up in the Disputation against Scholastic Theology. Historically, that was an important meeting because here is Luther explaining to his Augustinian brothers some of the basics of his theology; some of the younger men (Martin Butzer, Johann Brenz and Theobald Dillichanus), influenced by Luther, turned to the evangelical reformation and were later leaders of the reformation in other cities. They spearheaded the reformation in Strassburg, Wurtenberg, and Nordlingen, respectively.

Then let us move to the key texts in the Heidelberg Disputation relative to the theology of the cross. They are Theses 19, 20, 21, and

22. The Heidelberg Thesis 19 reads, "that person does not deserve to be called a theologian who looks upon the invisible things of God as though they were clearly perceptible in those things which have actually happened." Luther's explanation of this, with reference to Romans 1:20, ("His invisible being can be seen so that it is perceived in his works"), is, "This is apparent in the example of those who were theologians and still were called fools by the apostle in Romans 1." So, those theologians who seek to know God by speculating through the work of their reason into the invisible things of God clearly perceived in those things which have happened are fools. That is what Luther has said so far, but then, typical Luther, if you really want to know what these invisible things are of God, Luther says "the invisible things of God are virtue, godliness, wisdom, justice, goodness and so on. The recognition of all these things does not make one worthy or wise." So a theologian of glory speculates into the invisible things of God as though they were perceptible in the things which have actually happened.

Now a theologian of the cross, which is the subject of Thesis 20, is different. Heidelberg 20: "he deserves to be called a theologian, however, who comprehends the visible and backside of God seen through suffering and the cross." A theologian of the cross looks at what is visible. What is visible is suffering and cross, and suffering and cross are the back parts, the backside of God. There is a problem here with the way this Heidelberg 20 has been translated. It has been mistranslated in the American edition and other places. The word in question is *posteriora dei*. Heidelberg 20's reference to the *posteriora dei* is a reference to Exodus 33:18 where a view of God's face was denied to Moses. Moses was put up in the rock and only could see God from the backside as God walked by. He could not see God face to face, so the revelation of God is from the rear, therefore, indirect. This foreshadows Luther's distinction developed later between the hidden and the revealed God. The visible things (which is now theologyofthecross talk) turn out to be the backside of God. So God is both hidden and revealed, or revealed in his hiddenness. God is revealed on the cross, but what we see on the cross is the backside, the *posteriora dei*. We do not see, as Moses could not see, God face to face. So a theologian of the cross is the only legitimate type of theologian; the theologian of glory is a theologian in name only, and is actually a fool. The theologian of the cross comprehends the visible and the backside of God seen through suffering and cross.

The theologian of glory, discussed in Thesis 19, seeks a knowledge of God and his attributes, or the invisible things of God, by perceiving and understanding the things which have actually happened. In other words, the theologian of glory comes to a knowledge of God through God's works. He does this by his own works, that is, by his intellectual activity. Luther believes that the powers of reason are contaminated. Just as in morality where the human being misuses the law and appropriates goodness to his works, so in the intellectual sphere he assumes the knowledge of God to be his work.

In contrast to the theologian of glory, the theologian of the cross seeks knowledge of God in suffering. The suffering here has a twofold meaning—the suffering of God in Christ and the suffering of the Christian united with Christ. But the main point of the contrast is that knowledge comes in and through suffering rather than in and through works; and this is the key to the theology of the cross in Heidelberg 19 and following. Theology of glory equals works of reason, whereas theology of the cross equals suffering, the suffering of Christ and the Christian with Christ.

Knowledge comes then for the theologian of the cross in and through suffering rather than in and through works. Furthermore, visible things are perceived rather than invisible things understood. What is perceived is the backside of God rather than understanding through those things which actually happened. The theologian of the cross comprehends the visible backside that is perceived, whereas the supposed theologian of glory claims to perceive the invisible things that are comprehended.

Thus, God is hidden in the revelation, or God reveals himself through concealment. He is concealed because his face is not turned towards us. His brilliance and glory are hidden in their opposites, that is, in suffering, weakness, foolishness, and the cross. Such knowledge cannot be misused by humans as the knowledge from works can be misused.

Luther's explanation of Thesis 20 continues the distinction between glory and cross:

> The manifest backside and the visible things of God are placed in opposition to the invisible, namely, his human nature, weakness, and foolishness. The Apostle in 1 Corinthians 1 calls them the weakness and folly of God. Because men misused the knowledge of God through works, God wished again to be recognized in

suffering, and to condemn wisdom concerning invisible things by means of wisdom concerning visible things, so that those who did not honor God as manifest in his works should honor him as he is hidden in his suffering. As the apostle says in 1 Corinthians 1, "for since, in the wisdom of God, the world did not know God through wisdom, it pleased God through the folly of what we preach to save those who believe." Now it is not sufficient for anyone, and it does him no good to recognize God in his glory and majesty, unless he recognizes him in the humility and shame of the cross. Thus God destroys the wisdom of the wise as Isaiah says, "truly thou art a God who hidest thyself." So also in John 10 where Philip spoke according to the theology of glory, "show us, Father." Christ forthwith set aside his flighty thought about seeing God elsewhere and led him to himself saying, "Philip, he who has seen me has seen the Father." For this reason, true theology and recognition of God are in the crucified Christ, as it is also stated in John 19, "no one comes to the Father but by me." "I am the door," and so forth.

Throughout this passage Luther uses the word "knowledge" or "to know." This means that in the theology of the cross he has worked out a principle of knowledge that stands over against the principle of knowledge from works that the theology of glory offers. This is especially clear in the sentence "for this reason, true theology and recognition of God are in the crucified Christ." Luther rejects the works of creation as firmly as he rejects moral works as a way to God. He fights rationalism as strongly as moralism. He sees religious speculation as a human desire for direct communion with God and as building a staircase to heaven through knowledge. This desire constitutes the theology of glory. In actuality for Luther, indirect knowledge of God is possible so long as we know the situation for what it is. The theologian of the cross knows that this knowledge is found only through suffering and the cross. To find the cross and Christ is to find God hidden in suffering.

The theologian of glory gets things reversed and in his confusion fails to find reality. As Luther says in Thesis 21, "A theology of glory calls evil good and good evil. The theology of the cross calls the thing what it actually is." I find Luther to be a very "isy" theologian, a theologian of the cross tells it like it is. The isness of the situation is the isness of the human situation and the isness of the divine situation. Through his own experience and through his own theology, Luther is absolutely convinced that human nature is rotten to the core, that God is God, that God is quite capable of being God, and that God has bridged the gap in Christ. Philip Watson some years ago wrote a book entitled *Let God Be God.* This was the brunt of Luther's early theological work: to get human mediators, ecclesiastical mediators, any kind of mediators out of the way so that God is free to be God. A theologian of the cross calls the thing what it actually is. In his explanation to this thesis, Luther says "this is clear, he who does not know Christ does not know God hidden in suffering." The way to know the only God there is to know, is to know the God in Christ who is visibly showing the backside of himself seen through suffering and cross. To continue the quotation:

> Therefore, he prefers works to suffering, glory to cross, strength to weakness, wisdom to folly and, in general, good to evil. These are the people whom the apostle calls "enemies of the cross of Christ," for they hate the cross and suffering and love works and the glory of works. Thus, they call the good of the cross evil and the evil of a deed good. God can be found only in suffering and the cross, as has already been said. Therefore, the friends of the cross say that the cross is good and the works are evil, but through the cross, works are dethroned and the old Adam, who was especially edified by works, is crucified. It is impossible for a person not to be puffed up by his good works unless he first be deflated and destroyed by suffering and evil until he knows that he is worthless and that his works are not his but God's.

Luther's istheology begins with the assumption that human nature prefers works, human nature prefers the Tower of Babel, human nature prefers to be God rather than man, and the way up to God through the theology of glory is through the knowledge of reason. Luther's presumption is that human nature will only end up deadended and that this puffed up works oriented human nature, works of will, works of reason, need to be dethroned and destroyed. Works of the law need to be totally destroyed and that's what happened in the Gospel. The Gospel completely dethroned the works of law. So the isness of the situation is that we are puffed up by good works and that the only way we are to find God is to know God in Christ, God hidden in suffering on the cross. That is the only beginning point of knowledge and the only beginning point of contact with God.

In the Heidelberg Thesis 22 Luther goes on to say, "That wisdom which sees the invisible things of God in works as perceived by man is completely puffed up, blinded, and hardened." Then one other Heidelberg thesis that shows the isness orientation of Luther is

Heidelberg number 26. Heidelberg 26 shows the character of Luther's ethic as indicative rather than imperative. An imperative ethic deals with thou shalt do this or thou shalt not do that. An indicative ethic tells it like it is, is rather than what it ought to be. Heidelberg 26 reads, "The law says 'do this' and it is never done; Grace says 'believe in this,' and it is already done." In his explanation to 26, Luther says "through faith, Christ is in us, indeed, one with us. Christ is just and has fulfilled all the commands of God." The Christian is just in Christ. This for Luther then is the greatest source of ethical activity, namely, that Christ is in us. There is no need or place for the law to tell us what we ought to do because Christ in us will do whatever the law commanded us and more than what the law commanded. So Luther's confidence in the isness of the situation is that human nature can get nowhere and God can get everywhere. This makes clear then that the knowledge of God for Luther is not theoretical because this rotten reason can get nowhere. The theologian of the cross comes to know God not by thinking but through suffering. Only when one is crucified and dies with Christ does one know God. This knowledge is the wisdom of the cross that is folly to humans. This knowledge comes to us through an encounter with God in Christ crucified rather than by human reasoning. The knowledge of this hidden God encountered in Christ is a faith knowledge. "Our life is hidden in God, that is, in the simple confidence of his mercy."

A rereading of Theses 19-21 will now be clearer: "That person does not deserve to be called a theologian who looks upon the invisible things of God as though they were clearly perceptible in those things which have actually happened. He deserves to be called a theologian, however, who comprehends the visible backside of God seen through suffering and cross. The theology of glory calls evil good and good evil. The theology of the cross calls the thing what it actually is.

The cross meant suffering a humiliation for Luther, the wounds of Christ, the blood of Christ, and Christ as worm on the cross. Christ as worm meant total humiliation. "I am worm and no man" (Psalm 22:6), said Christ on the cross according to Luther. We find him dying a "shameful death."

SECTION 3: CHRIST AS WORM ON THE CROSS

Let me conclude with a section on Christ as "worm" on the cross based on texts from Luther that range from 1517 well into the later Luther.

The first text is from his Hebrews lectures in reference to Hebrews 2:7 where it says, "thou didst make him a little lower than the angels." There was considerable debate in the tradition as to who the "him" is in, "thou didst make him a little lower than the angels," and as to what the author of Hebrews means by "a little lower." Luther first discounts those who understood "him" to be human nature, thus a "little lower than the angels" in dignity. Next Luther opposes those who understood "him" to be Christ in so far as they had an inadequate Christology. He says, "others understand this verse to refer to Christ as being lower than the angels, not according to his soul but according to his body which is capable of suffering, but even this interpretation is not precise enough since he not only made lower than the angels but as he himself says, 'I am worm and not a man' (Psalm 22:6)." Being made "lower than the angels" meant for Luther the time of total humiliation on the cross, and the time between the cross and the resurrection, namely, the three days, when forsaken and deserted by God, "thou didst hand him over into the hands of sinners."

The meaning of Christ as worm on the cross carries the connotation of Christ being abject, the object of contempt, forsaken, nauseating, abominable, rotten stench, scandal, or, simply, rotting worm (these are all depictions from Luther at various times and places). "The prophets have a special way of speaking but they mean exactly what the apostles preach for both have said much about the suffering and glory of God and of those who believe in him. Thus, David says of Christ in Psalm 22:6, 'I am a worm and no man.' With these words he shows the depth of his abject humiliation in his suffering" [from 1522]. Christ as worm refers to "the mode of his passion as pure man." The state of pure man is that he is a bag of worms. The first enemy that tempts the Christian away from the word of God and faith is "our own flesh," a rotten old bag of worms hanging heavy around our neck. "We are nothing other than filth, corruption, and worms." In death, the flesh turns to dust, and the worms consume it. Faith looks beyond death and the consumption by worms and believes that the body will rise. "For thus it has pleased God to raise up from worms, from corruption, from the earth which is totally putrid and full of stench a body more beautiful than any flower, than balsam, than the sun itself and the stars" [from 1535].

The inheritance for the worm of faith is eternal life. Christ destroyed the devil's tyranny over death. God chose not to use heavenly muscle, such as Gabriel, Michael, and the others, but he "degrades himself so profoundly and becomes a man, yes, even degrades himself below all men, as it is written in Psalm 22, 'I am a worm and no man, scorned by men and despised by the people.' In such physical weakness and poverty, he attacks the enemy, lets himself be put on the cross and killed, and by his cross and death, he destroys the enemy and the avenger" [1537].

How is it that a worm on a cross destroys the enemy's tyranny over death? The force of the image of worm is illumined by an examination of some early Christian literature. In First Clement 16:15, Psalm 22:6 is used to describe the humiliation of Christ and later (25:3), the worm is used with reference to the resurrection, the worm comes forth from the decaying flesh of the Phoenix bird. The resurrection of the mythical Phoenix is used as an illustration of the Christian doctrine of resurrection, "now from the corruption of its flesh there springs a worm which is nourished by the juices of the dead bird and puts forth wing." In Origen, the worm as Christ's humanity is used as bait to catch the devil and his angels. In Cyril of Jerusalem, new life comes from worms as evidenced by the bees and the birds. The transformation of the Phoenix from a worm is proof of Christ's resurrection. In Gregory of Nyssa, the gluttonous fish is lured by the flesh of Christ as bait. The divinity of Christ is the hook. Luther refers to Gregory, probably Gregory the Great (cf. Gregory the Great's Moralium in Job, Book 33).

Now Luther [1530]: God took a sharp fish hook, put an angle worm on it and threw it into the sea. The worm is the humanity of Christ, the hook is the divinity. On the hook, the worm, namely the humanity, is *gebundene*. The devil says "should I not swallow the little worm?" He did not see the hook.

For Luther, the testator on the cross is a pure man, a worm. The testator is also the one who made the promise of the eternal inheritance, "the humanity did not conquer sin and death, but the hook that was concealed under the worm at which the devil struck conquered and devoured the devil who was attempting to devour the worm."

FINALLY for Luther as theologian of the cross (thinking of Luther and Heidelberg 21), the theologian of the cross tells it like it actually is. For Luther, God is there in Christ and Christ is there on the cross. In the Lord's Supper we receive the inheritance which is the forgiveness of sins. Inheritance is received by the worm of faith. In cross, in suffering, in worm, is Christ.

DR. ROBERT D. PREUS

CONFESSIONAL SYSTEMATICIAN & TEACHER OF THE CONFESSIONS

INTRODUCTION

Robert Preus "was a witness for the truth .... He did not waver; he did not compromise the Lutheran Confessions. He followed his mentor, Luther; and taught the theology of the cross. And he lived the theology of the cross, which is never easy" (David Scaer in his Commemoration Sermon).[1]

One of the last manuscripts Preus wrote was entitled "The Theology of the Cross" (dated 18 February 1994). He sent me this for inclusion in *The Luther Digest*.[2] It was a typical Preus work: 55 pages in manuscript form, 82 pages in print, given as a lecture before an International Lutheran Confessional Congress in Kenya, published in Helsinki (1994), and edited by well-known Finnish scholars.

Our assigned topic is "Dr. Robert D. Preus: Confessional Systematician and Teacher of the Confessions." Could the theology of

---

1   In the commemorative volume of *Logia: A Journal of Lutheran Theology* 5/3 (Holy Trinity 1996): 10. Dr. Scaer speaks of Dr. Preus as a *doctor ecclesiae*.

2   His manuscript was published in *The Theology of the Cross*, ed. Reijo Arkkila and Richard O. Olak, Second International Lutheran Confessional Congress, 14-18 March 1994, Matongo, Kenya (Helsinki: Helsingin Painotuote, 1994), 40-122. Preus supplied me this publication data (personal correspondence will be filed at Concordia Historical Institute) when he submitted the manuscript for inclusion in *Luther Digest*, a publication inspired and sponsored by Preus. I have not seen the book. As far as my searches reach (and they are far), this book is not available in the United States; hence my references are to page numbers in the manuscript (hereafter abbreviated TC). The first published record that I know of in the United States is the digested version in *Luther Digest* 1997, 121-31. In March 1999, late in this writing, I received the two-volume edition of articles on Luther in *Reformation and Revival* 7 (Fall 1998) and 8 (Winter 1999) wherein, in two parts, is contained Preus's "The Theology of the Cross"; since the footnotes of Preus's article in this journal rendition are not as complete as in the manuscript (and key information for me is missing), I will refer to the manuscript.

the cross provide an entrée into "The Theology and Life" of our honoree? To answer this question, we will seek to determine if Preus discussed the theology of the cross *as* a confessional systematician, that is, did he use the Confessions as a point of reference for understanding and explaining Luther's theology of the cross? If so, is this reading history backwards? Was the theology of the cross central to Preus as a confessional theologian?

In a section that blends Luther, Smalcald, and the Apology, Preus wrote,

> Why must the theology of the Cross reign supreme? Why must this one article or principle, which we might call the *solus Christus,* have total prominence? The theology of the Cross must judge all doctrine in the church and guide the teaching of the church for two reasons. First, this doctrine opens up the entire Scripture to us and teaches us to know Christ aright and give Him proper honor and brings to our troubled consciences the most abundant consolation.[3]

Or again, "We note once again that the Lutheran Confessions represent as central this theology of the Cross."[4]

To provide some further focus for my daunting assignment, I will pay particular attention to what occupied Preus's mind and pen towards what we now know as the end of his life. I do so because he sent me his manuscript on the theology of cross; plus he invited me to become a member of The Luther Academy in June of 1991 (also sending me his monograph on the call with that letter). My personal and professional contacts with him thus were in this last period of his life.

In addition to the theology of the cross and the doctrine of the call, his last written works were on "The Unity of Scripture" and on "Luther: Word, Doctrine, and Confession" (given at Bethany Lutheran Theological Seminary in 1992).[5] As stated in the response at Bethany, this article on Luther, Word, doctrine, and confession is patterned on

---

3   TC 6.

4   TC 11, speaking of Luther.

5   The latter being another 80-page production given at Bethany Lutheran Theological Seminary in Mankato for their twenty-fifth annual Reformation Lectures (28-29 October 1992) and published in *Lutheran Synod Quarterly* 32 (December 1992), 1-80. Preus also sent me this manuscript/publication for inclusion in *Luther Digest* (1995): 68-77.

the familiar "We believe, teach and confess."[6] He was a confessional systematician to the end.

In all his publications up to the end (including his last written work),[7] Preus considered whether the confessional Lutheran theologian might legitimately use the historical-critical method for the study of the Bible. The necessity for this topic (historical-critical method) was dictated by one of Preus's "guiding theological principles," namely, subscription to the Confessions involves agreement with their hermeneutics for reading Scripture.[8]

I find that in treating these two issues, the theology of the cross (vis-à-vis Luther scholarship) and the historical-critical method (vis-à-vis modern biblical scholarship), Preus was confessional to the core, historically erudite, and critically creative in his systematic work (which is the highest praise a university professor can give).[9]

Actually my competence suffers from the fact that whereas Preus was born in Saint Paul[10] I am from sinful Minneapolis, thus not worthy to speak as sinner about the saint. (Think about the twin *simul* here.) He went to Luther Seminary in St. Paul and Bethany Lutheran Theological Seminary in Mankato, both committed to godliness, whereas I went to godless Harvard. He was ordained to the holy

---

6   Harstad in *Lutheran Synod Quarterly* 32 (December 1992): 100.

7   "The last written work our father produced before his unexpected death on November 4, 1995" (Daniel and Rolf Preus), *Justification and Rome* (St. Louis: Concordia Publishing House, 1997), 11; for treatment of "The Historical-Critical Method and *Sola Scriptura*" see 109-11.

8   "Guiding Theological Principles. A Lutheran Confessional Approach to the Doctrine of Creation," in *Rock Strata and the Bible Record.*, ed. Paul A. Zimmerman (St. Louis: Concordia Publishing House, 1970), 12-13.

9   For corroboration of my competence on these two issues, I can report that I have been in and around the historical-critical method for over 40 years, going back to Harvard (in fact, some of those whom Preus criticized I had as teachers); and I have published on the history of the historical-critical methods. Also, I gave a lecture in Norway on Luther's theology of the cross in 1987 and have kept up on the literature ("Luthers Korsteologi," in *Teologi på tidens torg: Festskrift til Peter Wilhelm Bøckman.* "Publikasjoner utgitt av Religionsvitenskapelig institutt Universitetet i Trondheim," vol. 23 [Trondheim: Tapir, 1987], 71-81).

10   Kurt E. Marquart, "Robert D. Preus," in *Handbook of Evangelical Theologians*, ed. Walter A. Elwell (Grand Rapids, MI: Baker Books, 1993), 353.

ministry, while I am just a layman. For those who know the Oslo situation, he was connected to (conservative) *Menighetsfakultet* whereas I, unbeknownst to me, was professor at the (liberal) university faculty.

In spite of these deprivations in my life, I will do what I as a doctor and a university professor am able to do to add to the Preus commemoration, namely, read books, use the languages, and provide analysis and perspective on my theme.

THEOLOGY OF THE CROSS: SOLUS CHRISTUS

In his work on "Luther: Word, Doctrine, and Confession," Preus said, "The most important principle of Luther's theology, the dominating theme of all his prodigious theological work as preacher and teacher of the church and confessor in the church, is *solus Christus*."[11] Preus cites Part II of the Smalcald Articles, a favorite of his, cited in many of his writings:[12] "The first and chief article is this, that Jesus Christ, our God and Lord, was 'put to death for our trespasses and raised again for our justification.'"[13]

Solus Christus means the theology of the cross. As he says later in the manuscript, the terms are interchangeable.[14] *Solus Christus* has "total prominence":

---

11   Robert D. Preus, "Luther: Word, Doctrine, and Confession," *Concordia Theological Quarterly* 60 (July 1996): 187.

12   In the manuscript on "The Theology of the Cross" Preus says that "the most important statement in the Smalcald Articles is found exactly in the middle of this great confession (II.i.1-5): 'the first and chief article...'" (TC 5). In "The Influence of the Formula of Concord on the Later Lutheran Orthodoxy," Preus spoke in a loving tone of "our Book of Concord" (91); of the Formula's "masterful discussion on the nature of justification"; and of Melanchthon's treatment of justification in the Apology as "one of the finest ever written on the subject" (91). Both Formula and Apology offer explicit treatment of the work of Christ in the discussion of justification; in this context the "first and chief article" (Smalcald) comes up on the saving work of Christ (92). Preus lists cross along with repentance, confession, good works, and prayer in treatment of later orthodoxy on the Christian life (93). Robert D. Preus, "The Influence of the Formula of Concord on the Later Lutheran Orthodoxy," in *Discord, Dialogue, and Concord. Studies in the Lutheran Reformation's Formula of Concord*, ed. Lewis Spitz and Wenzel Lohff (Philadelphia: Fortress Press, 1977), 86-101.

13   Preus, "Luther: Word, Doctrine, and Confession," 190.

14   TC 11.

It is clear from Melanchthon's words that he is making the theology of the Cross, or the article of justification, a hermeneutical principle for the interpreting of all Scripture, a principle which was not understood by the Papists and was never followed by the Reformed.... The articles of faith, although agreeing with each other in truth, do not agree at all with each other according to human reason .... The agreement is in Christ and in theology and event of the Cross.[15]

The linkage here is *solus Christus*, cross, the Apology of the Augsburg Confession (IV:2), and the "first and chief article" of Luther's Smalcald Articles. "The entire Smalcald Articles, which were written to be a confessional for an ecumenical council, are structured around the *solus Christus*."[16] "All of Luther's works are, in a sense, nothing but his confession of faith."[17] "In fact, the entire public ministry of preaching the Word and administering the sacraments is nothing but a confession of faith according to Luther."[18] The confession of faith is that Jesus Christ, our God and Lord, was put to death for our trespasses and raised again for our justification.

AFFLICTIONS OF THE FAITHFUL

To preach the gospel and to confess Christ inevitably brings "crosses, affliction, and persecution upon the Christian and the church."[19] God has attached suffering to the teaching of the gospel, and He does so for our own benefit.

Already we have come full circle around Preus as confessional systematician and writer on the Confessions: Luther and the Confessions teach *solus Christus*, the theology of the cross; to confess such, said Preus, brings crosses. "C" is a prominent letter in our commemoration: C for Christ, C for Confession, C for cross, and C for carry (the Confessions commend the Christian to carry the cross of Christ).

The cross of Christ is our salvation (the *Hauptartikel*); and the cross of Christ is also what we suffer—for our own good. Strange business here. No wonder this is called the "foolishness of the cross."

---

15   TC 6.

16   Preus, "Luther: Word, Doctrine, and Confession," 202.

17   Ibid., 207-8.

18   Ibid., 207.

19   Ibid., 213-16. Section 4 is "Confession and the Cross."

What is the relationship between these two crosses, Christ's and ours? I need to ask this because some claim that the cross of Christ is fulfilled in our suffering. Roman Catholic doctrine teaches that the cross of Christ is filled out and completed in the church. Experience-based soteriology needs more than the cross. No, for Luther, the cross of Christ fulfills the law and completes salvation. Whether or not we suffer (whether or not the cross fills the church or the individual), Christ has died for our sins; and that's that. The victory is won. We do not carry wood on our backs or have nails pierced in our hands. Only One did that. As I like to instruct my students about Luther's difficulty with Mary as co-mediator or any notion of the saints sharing in the mediation of Christ: How many were on the cross? One. How many suffered there? One. How many died for sins? One.

DEFINITION OF TERMS

Preus makes clear the relation between what we might call the cross of Calvary and the cross of faith. Luther's phrase for what Christians carry is "the afflictions of the faithful."[20] The "cross of faith" is a phrase that suggests itself after reading Preus's 55-page manuscript "The Theology of the Cross." What Preus makes clear is that there are two crosses: Christ's and ours.

Preus is very careful in his work to define terms, and this is typical of his writing. He is constantly wanting to know the origin of a phrase or etymology of a word. Here again we have the confessional systematician at work. Usually systematicians invent words and phrases and redefine meanings to go along with new concepts. Not so our doctor of the Confessions: the Confessions are precise in their usage of words and phrases because it was often controversy over words and phrases that gave rise to the Confessions in the first place. Hence our confessional systematician, called to teach the Confessions, must be faithful to the precise meaning of words and phrases explicated therein.

Careful explication of words and phrases is how we are to interpret the Confessions because the Confessions explicate Scripture

---

20   For the meaning of the "cross of Christ" in Gal 6:14, see Luther on Galatians in 1531/1535: the cross of Christ does not signify the wood Christ bore and to which He was nailed, "but it signifies all the afflictions of the faithful, whose suffering are Christ's suffering. As it is written: 'The sufferings of Christ abound in us' (2 Cor 1:5).... The cross, therefore, signifies all the afflictions of the Church, which is Christ's Body" (AE 27:134).

correctly.[21] If you want to know Luther's method for explicating Scripture in a nutshell, it is this: Scripture says what it means and means what it says; Luther constantly harped on this.

The theology of the cross concerns the work of Christ on the cross. It is the doctrine of *solus Christus* and the *Hauptartikel*. Preus is very clear that the phrase "theology of the cross" came into our vocabulary from Luther's Heidelberg Disputation. While the phrase has stuck in theological jargon, the phrase disappeared in Luther's writings after 1518. What is meant by "the theology of the Cross is epitomized in the article of justification by grace through faith taught all over Lutheranism to be the *articulus stantis et cadentis ecclesiae*."[22] As Preus explains.

> the article of redemption, or justification as Luther so often termed it, or, what is the same thing, the theology of the Cross, really sums up all of our theology, sums up the meaning and implications of the *sola scriptura*, the *sola fide*, and *sola gratia*. The theology of the Cross, the article of justification, is not divided or separated from the other articles of faith, creation, sin, grace, baptism, church, Lord's Supper, Christ's return and eternal life. Rather all these articles take their meaning from the article of redemption and the theology of the Cross, and one understands and applies all other articles only in the light of the Cross, which points to Christ's atoning and saving work of redemption.[23]

Or again,

> The reader will no doubt have observed that I have used the term "theology of the Cross" interchangeably with the doctrine of justification by grace, or the teaching of redemption and the vicarious atonement through Christ's suffering and death. This is altogether

---

21 Robert D. Preus, "Can the Lutheran Confessions Have Any Meaning 450 Years Later?" *Concordia Theological Quarterly* 44 (April-July 1980) 104-7. Preus gives five reasons that the Lutheran Confessions have meaning today: (1) the Confessions convey knowledge about God, man, sin, grace, and salvation; (2) the meaning of the Confessions has remained the same; (3) the meaning of the Confessions, drawn from Scripture, cannot be falsified; (4) the Confessions are a correct exposition of Scripture; (5) the center of Christian theology is the article of Christ and His work, including reference to SA II.ii.1.

22 TC 3.

23 TC 1-2.

warranted. Actually Luther seldom uses the term "theology of the Cross" as such. But he is constantly referring to the theme as the real meaning and center of the Christian Gospel.[24]

When Luther did use the phrase *theologia crucis* in the Heidelberg Disputation of 1518, early in his career:

> There he shows the theology of the Cross is simply the way God reveals Himself graciously to man, namely, as a poor suffering human dying for the sins of the world. There Luther tells us that the theology of the Cross is *the* revelation of God, the very opposite of God's glory which no man can see or conceive. This basic theme runs through all of Luther's works. God can only be known through the revelation of His Son who came to us and for us in the flesh, and then only by His suffering. Thus Luther can say, "Therefore in the crucified Christ is true theology and the knowledge [*cognitio*] of God." Again Luther says, "God can only be found in sufferings and the Cross."[25]

The Lutheran Confessions represent as central this theology of the cross. Cited are the Augsburg Confession, the Apology, and the "chief article" in Luther's Smalcald Articles.[26]

At this point in the Preus manuscript is a long footnote on the history of writing on "Luther's *Theologia crucis*."[27] Preus refers to Hermann Sasse, Walther von Loewenich, Regin Prenter, Alister McGrath, and to one I have not seen anyone else refer to in recent times, namely, Otto Ritschl. I thought I had read everything on the theology of the cross in Luther (and had graduate students over the years do research papers on the subject); none of us knew about the old Ritschl thesis. (I must say as an aside that in my efforts to track down the Ritschl thesis I ended up using the very volume our honoree used at Luther Seminary; his signature and the date 29 November 1951 are on the library card.) While Preus was a confessional systematician, this long footnote on historiography tells me that he was also a first-rate historian. In the most recent edition of *Archive for Reformation History* is an article on "The Medieval Origins of Luther's Theology of the Cross";

---

24   TC 11.
25   Ibid.
26   TC 11-12.
27   TC 12.

no mention of Otto Ritschl, yet the author criticizes others for not treating the subject of Luther and the Middle Ages. Preus did.[28] At this point we are only on page 12 of Preus's 55-page manuscript. We need to change our pace. Faith receives the theology of the cross;[29] faith involves suffering. What happens through preaching of the Word? God saves. He who witnesses to the cross will experience rejection. And he will have to bear his own cross.[30] Afflictions are thrust upon us to bless us and make us theologians of the cross.

Preus reflects in a personal way on the different kinds of crosses, namely, that he had not lost his head like St. Cyprian, lain in a Nazi prison camp like Bonhöffer, or been forbidden to worship like the Christians in the Soviet Union for more than 70 years. "But God does send crosses to those who believe, teach, and confess the theology of the Cross. It happens without fail. It must happen. And it is God who sends them.... God sends them in order to bless us and make us theologians of the Cross."[31]

There is no soteriological connection between the two crosses. Ours is a result of His. "And so the Christian, especially the Christian pastor, suffers crosses for the sake of the theology of the Cross."[32]

LUTHER AND THE CONFESSIONS

Turning to the *Book of Concord* (Tappert), we find several entries under Cross, Afflictions, Mortification (all inter-referenced). Let me offer a thesis, what for me is an insight gained from doing my homework in Preus and the Confessions: Preus's theology of the cross is confessional and based on the whole of Luther, that is, it is not strictly based on Luther's Heidelberg Disputation, where cross is a way of knowing God (theological epistemology). While including the cross as our way of knowing God hidden in suffering and death, the cross in the later Luther (*On the Councils and the Churches*) and in the Confessions is a mark of the church and the Christian. In the Apology the cross

---

28   Graham S. Tomlin, "The Medieval Origins of Luther's Theology of the Cross," *Archive for Reformation History* 89 (1998): 22-40.

29   TC 33, 51.

30   TC 52.

31   TC 53.

32   TC 55.

"belongs to the confession of faith" (Ap. XXIV.38), and "Christ's kingdom is concealed under the cross" (Ap. VII/VIII.18).

In Luther literature (especially the more recent),[33] "theology of the cross" usually means suffering with the disenfranchised of the world, solidarity with the poor. In a minority of Luther interpreters (reflecting the older approach),[34] "theology of the cross" means theological epistemology (God is known only in hiddenness). In another case, "theology of the cross" is presented as the way of conversion (how we are saved).[35] Seldom is the broader picture in Luther presented. The focus is always on the Heidelberg Disputation, where the neat theses are an attractive base for drawing out either a theology of suffering with the poor, or of knowing God, or of being saved. The broader picture in Luther must connect the Heidelberg Disputation with *On the Councils and the Churches*.

When Preus speaks of the cross, he means "cross" in the use of the total (whole) Luther and the Confessions: Christ, Our God and Lord, was "put to death for our trespasses and raised again for our justification." "Cross" is also knowledge of God hidden in suffering; the mark of the church; the afflictions Christians bear; and the burden of one's vocation.

It is Preus as confessional theologian who brings the whole theology of the cross together. Other theologians appeal only to parts of this rich theological construct, mostly by focusing on the young Luther. Nowhere else have I seen "cross" embrace affliction and mortification, the work of Christ as death for sins (per Smalcald), and theological epistemology, along with the mark of the church.

At the outset I asked if Preus discussed the theology of the cross as a confessional systematician, that is, did he use the Confessions as a point of reference for understanding and explaining Luther's theology of the cross? Was the theology of the cross central to Preus as a confessional theologian? By now I hope it is abundantly clear that Preus's

---

33   See for example Franceen (Vann) Neufeld, "The Cross of the Living Lord, the Theology of the Cross and Mysticism," *Scottish Journal of Theology* 49 (Spring 1996): 131-46.

34   Walther v. Loewenich, *Luthers Theologia crucis* (Munich: Chr. Kaiser Verlag, 1929), "Theologischen Erkenntnisprinzip," 9-10, 13ff.

35   Gerhard O. Forde, *On Being a Theologian of the Cross. Reflections on Luther's Heidelberg Disputation, 1518* (Grand Rapids, MI: William B. Eerdmans, 1997).

treatment of the theology of cross was as a confessional theologian; certainly this is true in comparison with others who treat Luther. I would even claim that Preus's approach to Luther as a confessional systematician is unique among his peers; and it is this approach that allowed him to see and present a holistic theology of the cross. This is reading history forwards and backwards, from Luther to the Confessions and back.

Furthermore, the Confessions are faithful to the whole of Luther on the cross. See Luther's "Sermon at Coburg on Cross and Suffering" (1530): Christ's suffering saved us from the devil, death, and sin; His suffering is also an example for our suffering that we may be conformed to him. "Each one must bear a part of the holy cross."[36]

The more I read on cross in Preus, the Confessions, and Luther, the more I am convinced that what passes for the theology of the cross is very limited and skewed to the Heidelberg Disputation. Many have puzzled over the fact that Luther never again used the distinction given in the Disputation (theology of cross vs. theology of glory) after 1518 in his literary output of over one hundred volumes.[37] The Confessions do not pick up the cross-vs.-glory phraseology. Preus knows the whole of Luther and covers the Heidelberg Disputation, but the Disputation does not govern Preus's theology of the cross, as in fact it did not govern Luther's either. In other words, the Confessions follow Luther, and Preus followed both.

Is that true, that Luther himself was not governed in his theology of the cross by what he wrote for his confreres to be discussed at the Heidelberg conference? This had never occurred to me before I read Preus on the subject.

Let's check this out with Luther. See the "Preface to the Wittenberg Edition of Luther's German Writings" (1539), where the third rule for the study of theology is *tentatio*. Here, drawing his three rules from David (prayer, meditation, and temptation), Luther describes how

---

36   AE 51:198.

37   While everyone knows the famous distinction between theology of the cross and theology of glory in the Heidelberg Disputation, what seems largely to be overlooked is that in the same year, in his *Explanations of the Ninety-five Theses* (1518), Luther uses the same distinction and again gives the clear definition: a theologian of the cross speaks of the crucified and hidden God (AE 31:225-27).

David complains about all kinds of enemies, arrogant tyrants, false spirits, and factions.

> For as soon as God's Word takes root and grows in you, the devil will harry you, and will make a real doctor of you, and by his assaults [*Anfechtungen*] will teach you to seek and love God's Word. I myself (if you will permit me, mere mouse-dirt, to be mingled with pepper) am deeply indebted to my papists that through the devil's raging they have beaten, oppressed, and distressed me so much. That is to say, they have made a fairly good theologian of me, which I would not have become otherwise.[38]

Following prayer and meditation by repeating and rereading, *tentatio*, *Anfechtung*, is the touchstone, which teaches not only to know but also to experience God's Word.[39] The experience of how sweet, lovely, and mighty God's Word is comes via the opposite of sweet and lovely, namely, via distress, attack, and affliction. Luther's own experience, recounted in 1539 in his preface to the first complete edition of his German writings, is corroborated, also in 1539, in his description of the seven marks of the church in his treatise *On the Councils and the Churches* (cited in the Solid Declaration of the Formula of Concord, III: 21). Hear the seventh mark:

> Seventh, the holy Christian people are externally recognized by the holy possession of the sacred cross. They must endure every misfortune and persecution, all kinds of trials and evil from the devil, the world, and the flesh (as the Lord's Prayer indicates) by inward sadness, timidity, fear, outward poverty, contempt, illness, and weakness, in order to become like their head, Christ. And the only reason they must suffer is that they steadfastly adhere to Christ and God's word, enduring this for the sake of Christ, Matthew 5 [:11], "Blessed are you when men persecute you on my account." They must be pious, quiet, obedient, and prepared to serve the government and everybody with life and goods, doing no one any harm. No people on earth have to endure such bitter hate; they must be accounted worse than Jews, heathen, and Turks. In summary, they must be called heretics, knaves, and devils, the most pernicious people on earth, to the point where those who hang, drown, murder, torture, banish, and plague them to death are rendering God a service. No one has compassion on them; they are given myrrh and

38   AE 34:287.
39   AE 34:286-87.

gall to drink when they thirst. And all of this is done not because they are adulterers, murderers, thieves, or rogues, but because they want to have none but Christ, and no other God. Wherever you see or hear this, you may know that the holy Christian church is there, as Christ says in Matthew 5 [:11-12], "Blessed are you when men revile you and utter all kinds of evil against you on my account. Rejoice and be glad, for your reward is great in heaven." This too is a holy possession whereby the Holy Spirit not only sanctifies his people, but also blesses them.[40]

Yes, this squares with Luther, namely, the whole of Luther is more than the Heidelberg Disputation. So, once again, we have come full circle, Luther, the Confessions, and Preus, on a theological topic: cross, experience, and affliction.

Preus also said that this theology of the cross is "taught all over Lutheranism." Is that true? Yes, this squares with what Preus lovingly called "the old Lutheran Dogmaticians."[41] "The Cross and Affliction" come as the Tenth Rule for the study of theology in David Chytraeus. Referring to Luther's *tentatio* as a requirement for making a theologian: "All other skills will never make one a theologian unless God adds the *crux* (the cross) by which He works in us appreciation and understanding of Christ and His promises and by which He works in us hope, patience, humility, and other virtues." It is not enough for the mind to be instructed with excellent learning, unless there are present in the will and heart the activities of piety, penitence, faith, comfort .... Nor can we ever understand the nature of such activities without serious afflictions, difficulties, and temptations. "Crosses are as necessary for the life of the theologian as food and air for his bodily sustenance."[42]

In Abraham Calov and the "Silver Ages" of Lutheran Orthodoxy, *tentatio* (affliction) is the third requisite for becoming a theologian, along with prayer and study.

---

40   AE 41:164-65.

41   Robert D. Preus, *The Inspiration of Scripture: A Study of the Theology of the Seventeenth-century Lutheran Dogmaticians* (Edinburgh: Oliver and Boyd, 1955, 1957).

42   Robert D. Preus, *The Theology of Post-Reformation Lutheranism*, vol. 1, *A Study of Theological Prolegomena* (St. Louis: Concordia Publishing House, 1970) 106-7.

We are tested by the weakness of our own flesh, by crosses of God's sending, and by the siftings of Satan. But really God is the one who tests us, and hence affliction is the practical experience of the one who listens to God's speaking. In the school of the cross and of persecution one learns to lift his eyes to God's Word of light and comfort; cf. 2 Cor. 4:17.[43]

It is Preus who makes the broad connections between the early and later Luther and shows the continuity between Luther and the Confessions into the age of orthodoxy. As it has turned out, the theology of the cross has provided an entrée into "The Theology and Life" of our honoree. The theology of the cross has served as a focus that shows the interrelation of Luther, the Confessions, and Preus—our confessional systematician and teacher of the Confessions at work.

HISTORICAL-CRITICAL METHOD

I could rest my case here: I have read his books, used the languages, and tried to provide analysis and perspective on my theme. But one further aspect of Preus's prodigious publications remains, one that puts him at the cutting edge of biblical scholarship today, namely, how can a confessional theologian relate to the historical-critical method. This method is modern, post-Lutheran Orthodoxy. Should we hide our heads and "just say no" to the most important development in the study of Scripture to hit the modern church? Preus didn't. He didn't "just say no." He offered a significant perspective on how to use method (critical and any other kind) in the study of the Bible.

SUBSCRIPTION TO CONFESSIONAL HERMENEUTICS

Preus confronted the historical-critical method for at least two reasons: (1) It is today's great heresy, he said;[44] (2) it is not appropriate to its subject.[45] More importantly, Preus *had* to confront the

---

43 Ibid., 221-22.

44 Robert D. Preus, "Den historisk-kritisk metode" in *På Ordets Grunn. Festskrift til professor dr. theol. Carl Fr. Wisløff,* ed. S. Hunnestad, J. Kvalbein, G. Prestegård (Oslo: Luther Forlag, 1978), 71-78. The historical-critical method is "en dårlig metode" (73) and is today's great heresy (77).

45 Robert D. Preus, "Biblical Authority in the Lutheran Confessions," *Concordia Journal* 4 (1978): 16-24. The purpose of the Confessions is to confess (= *quia* subscription, 18). Preus attacks Robert Smith, Kent Knutson, Gerhard Forde (19). This is like reading Luther: Scripture is the

historical-critical method because of his claim that subscription to the Confessions involves agreement with their hermeneutics for reading Scripture. In other words, the hermeneutics of the Confessions are to be defended as much as the content of said Confessions—method and content cannot be separated. These claims about consistency of method and content affect a confessional theologian.

A confessional theologian subscribes to the method and content of the Confessions. Scripture and the Confessions are of a piece, and subscription is based on the principle of *quia* subscription. Confessions are the *Begriff, Form, Fürbild, summa* of biblical doctrine and derive their authority by virtue of their agreement with Scripture. Subscription to the Confessions should conform what the Confessions themselves thought subscription should be. *In quatenus* subscription is a relativistic stance whereby one could improve on the scriptural character of the Confessions with new confessions. *Quia* subscription conforms to the Confessions themselves and their authority.[46]

Hermeneutics of the Confessions was the subject of several of Preus's publications. The approach to Scripture in the Confessions precludes and excludes the historical-critical method for Preus because this method does not consider what Scripture is, the sacred Word of God. In this regard Preus is absolutely correct. The decline of the confessional approach to Scripture and the coordinate rise of the historical-critical method have meant the desacralization of Scripture.

Historical-critical practitioners generally relativize the Confessions along with Scripture as relics of the past. Even given that pagan presupposition, Preus still offers a significant perspective on method, as critical and historical as you want to make it. That perspective I have called the method of consistency.[47]

---

divine authority, norm, source, and judge of all doctrine and teaching (20). No canon within the canon (20). Biblical hermeneutics must be appropriate to its subject (22). Amen.

46 Robert D. Preus, "Are There New and Current Issues Calling for Confessional Statements?" in *The Confession-Making Process*. (Chicago: The Division of Theological Studies of the Lutheran Council in the USA, 1975), 31-35.

47 Kenneth Hagen, *Luther's Approach to Scripture as seen in his "Commentaries" on Galatians, 1519-1538* (Tübingen: J. C. B. Mohr [Paul Siebeck], 1993), 39, 41, 47, 62.

METHOD OF CONSISTENCY

Beginning with his dissertation, Preus was concerned about the divine nature and content of Scripture. One of the rules he applied to the method of interpreting Scripture was that biblical hermeneutics must be appropriate to its subject. "A basic principle in any methodology" is that the subject with which the method deals determines the method. "And now the method of dealing with Scripture is a hermeneutical one.... This means first of all that we who interpret the Scriptures must first understand what we are dealing with, what the Scriptures claim to be and *are* in terms of their form and content ...."[48]

This I can tell you, ladies and gentlemen, is what the historical-critical methodists do *not* do. Their fundamental fallacy is that Scripture is seen to be a historical book, the product of Near Eastern religious history. I don't know how many times I was taught that Scripture must be read like any other product of Near Eastern culture. To be understood it must be seen in its full historicity. The only problem with this is that history is not one kind. Scripture is divine history; to approach Scripture we must take off our shoes and bend the knee, for we are not dealing with any old book.

Whether in Norwegian or English, Preus's plea was for consistency in method. It is on this note that I think he offers a challenge to the historical and critical presuppositions of modern methodology, in effect remembering the difference between apples and oranges. The historical-critical method approaches Scripture as a human book, and does not consider what Scripture is; it cannot, given its philosophical assumptions derived from the seventeenth and eighteenth centuries; the historical-critical method does not recognize the historical setting of the Bible, namely, God's Word in history.[49] Philosophical methods do not jell well with theological subjects. Preus ends the article to which

---

48   Preus, "Biblical Authority in the Lutheran Confessions," 21-22.

49   Robert D. Preus, "The Hermeneutics of the Lutheran Confessions and the Historical-Critical Method," in *The Function of Doctrine and Theology in Light of the Unity of the Church* (Chicago: Lutheran Council in the USA, 1978), 72-75. A Swedish version of this (trans. Natanael Granath of Stockholm) appeared in 1971 (word for word): "Bibeln och de Lutherska Bekännelseskrifterna," *Ditt Ord Är Sanning. En handbok om Bibeln tillägnad David Hedegård* (Uppsala: Stiftelsen Biblicum, 1971), 214-33. This version lacks the section on the historical-critical method's incompatibility with the approach to Scripture found in Confessions.

I am referring with the observation that the incompatibility of the historical-critical method with the hermeneutics of the Confessions means that to try and mix the two does an injustice to both methods.

DIFFERENCE BETWEEN HISTORICAL-CRITICIAL METHOD AND CONFESSIONAL METHOD

My experience is that practitioners of the modern critical methods want nothing to do with church, prayer, meditation, temptation; these are all seen as hindrances to their objectivity. The secular academicians enjoy their independence from the norms of faith and confession; they have spent centuries attacking and distancing themselves from such. My point is that they recognize that the two methods Preus refers to are incompatible. In other words, the standoff is mutual.

The confessional hermeneutics of Preus do meet the standards of modern methodology (which is the point I am trying to make here); in fact, I would argue that a confessional hermeneutic is more historical and more accurate in the treatment of Scripture than its secular counterpart, and thus need not "just say no" to the modern questions of method.

Let's put this very bluntly. The Bible was not written in Germany, or in the nineteenth century, home of the historical-critical method. To write the history of the Bible from the canons of nineteenth-century German scholarship is anachronistic. Who would explain Aristotle from the perspective of Kant or Hegel and expect to be credible? The Bible was written from the perspective of the open tomb, the wilderness, and the Red Sea; it was written from faith to faith; it is the church's book. To step out of faith (and worse, to trample the faith), to take the Bible out of its historical context, is to commit the methodological fallacy of inconsistency, that is, to make the Bible something it isn't. It is inconsistent to treat Aristotle as a German Idealist. Let the Bible be the Bible it claims to be. Let German critical philosophy be what it claims to be.

I am suggesting that Preus's biblical hermeneutic is consistent with the Bible. All he asked is that the nature of the subject determine its interpretation.[50] It seems to me that, rather than being a throwback to dead orthodoxy, the call for consistency is avant-guard. *Hermeneutica*

---

50 Robert D. Preus, "May the Lutheran Theologian Legitimately Use the Historical-Critical Method?" *Affirm*, Occasional Papers (Spring 1973): 31.

sacra must come from Scripture itself.[51] Further, what comes to my mind is how the traditional Roman Catholic approach and modern historical-critical method are alike in that Scripture as such is unclear and requires the church or the biblical scholar to bring meaning to the text. Following Luther and the Confessions, Preus lets the Bible supply its own meaning. What an innovation: let the text interpret the text, let the text govern the interpretation.

The modern historical-critical practitioner is blinded by modern philosophical presuppositions. This has been proved many times over; Preus said it over and over. He who has ears to hear, let him hear. Only those in tune with the sacred understand the sacred mysteries. Seculars complain when theologians impinge on their (secular) disciplines—sociology or history or the like; theologians are attacked for not knowing what they are talking about. Why should it be any different when the tables are turned? Should anybody be surprised when theologians attack the seculars for not knowing what they are talking about in matters of biblical studies?[52]

When it comes to understanding the blood of Calvary, the profane historian is at a loss. He looks for themes of blood sacrifice in Gnostic religions. The sacrifice of bulls, roasting over the grate, blood dripping down, cleansing the receptacles, "explains" Calvary. This Gnostic explanation will be etched forever in my memory as my Harvard professor explained the meaning of blood sacrifice. (This was over 40 years ago and I still don't get it.)

Luther's problem with profane philosophy was that Aristotle was not the Bible: these are two different worlds. Profane history is a world

---

51   Robert D. Preus, "A Response to 'The Unity of the Bible,'" in *Hermeneutics, Inerrancy, and the Bible*, ed. Earl D. Radmacher and Robert D. Preus (Grand Rapids, MI: Zondervan Publishing House, 1984), 681. This chapter also appeared in "The Unity of Scripture," *Concordia Theological Quarterly* 54/1 (January 1990): 12.

52   Let's be very clear that from both sides, the (secular or) pagan and the (Christian or) confessional, we are talking about two different methodologies. Christian or confessional scholars employ the method I like to call the logic of faith. The pagan uses the logic of secular science. Pagan is not a pejorative term, but is used by such proponents to distinguish their method from the Christian: pagans choose to differ from Christians. Likewise the confessional scholar chooses not to be pagan. The divide is never clearer than in the mind of the pagan practitioner of the historical-critical method.

unto its own. For Luther, profane philosophy was fine as long as it did what it was good at, which did *not* include the study of Scripture.

The reason Preus spoke out against the historical-critical method is the same reason Luther spoke out against the use of Aristotle in the explanation of Scripture. They had to: silence meant complicity. The pagan point of view clashes with the Christian perspective when it uses its pagan presuppositions to explain Christian claims— always has, always will.

The history of the rise of the historical-critical method is the history of distancing modern hermeneutics from Christian presuppositions about revelation and the infallibility of Scripture. Preus was very clear that a confessional hermeneutic could not employ the pagan historical-critical method, and what I am saying here is (1) that there are different methods at work, intentionally so, by both sides, and (2) that the historical-critical methodists do not have the corner on method (just a different method).

When explaining Scripture, Luther liked to say, God does not lie. A good refrain to remember is something a student of mine said, "Die Bibel ist die Bibel."

Before concluding, let me indicate what other subjects occupied Preus's mind and pen toward the end of his life. He published a booklet on *The Doctrine of the Call*.[53] In this and in another article at the time he considered four issues in church and ministry: church fellowship, open communion, ministry and "lay ministry," women pastors.[54] His last manuscript was on "Justification and Rome," a study on the "historic *status controversiae* between Rome and the Church of the Augsburg Confession on every substantive aspect of the doctrine of justification." Driving Preus's study were the dialogues between Lutherans and Roman Catholics during the previous thirty years in the USA and Europe (beginning with the Lutheran World

---

53   Robert D. Preus, *The Doctrine of the Call in the Confessions and Lutheran Orthodoxy*. Luther Academy Monograph # 1 (Houston, Texas: Our Savior Lutheran Church and School, 1991). [Revised edition: Robert D. Preus, "The Doctrine of the Call in the Confessions and Lutheran Orthodoxy," in *Church and Ministry Today: Three Confessional Lutheran Essays*, ed. John A. Maxfield (St. Louis: The Luther Academy, 2001).]

54   Robert D. Preus, "Confessional Lutheranism in Today's World," *Concordia Theological Quarterly* 54 (1990): 99-116.

Federation assembly at Helsinki).[55] This work was of special interest to me personally since I served on the national commission that produced *Justification by Faith*, a document that came under Preus's critical scrutiny. It is not my place to commend or condemn the document. After teaching Roman Catholics for over thiry years I can say this, however: Preus is right on target when he describes the Roman Catholic position on justification as a process. I like to tell my students that the Roman Catholic position was well described by that famous theologian Yogi Berra, when he said, "It ain't over 'til it's over." Another aspect of the Roman Catholic position that has become clear to me is just how foreign the *solas* (or *solae*) are to the Roman Catholic position. Scripture does not exist alone: its fullness (and interpretation) is realized in the tradition of the church. Christ's atoning work does exist alone: the church is the extension of the incarnation, which means that Christ and the saints complete the atonement in the sacramental fullness of the church. Faith does not exist alone, nor grace, nor cross. The "alones" of the Lutheran position cannot be accommodated in Roman Catholicism.

The voice of Preus cries out through his published works, to call the church to faithfulness to God's holy Word, to bear the afflictions that necessarily come, and not to compromise on the doctrine of justification as expressed in historic Lutheranism.

CONCLUSION

Listen to Luther from *The Magnificat*, connecting cross with affliction: God has "laid the cross of Christ together with countless sufferings and afflictions upon his beloved children and Christians."[56]

Preus taught and lived the theology of the cross. In the foregoing coverage of Preus's writings, we have seen a blend and interweaving of Luther, Confessions, and doctrine; all interconnected, defending the truth against false doctrine. When heresy encroaches on the truth, the confessional theologian must speak. God does not lie. The doctor of the church, Robert David Preus, has spoken.

False prophets have always arisen and claimed to know God's Word; they arise at the very centers of faith. They shall be known by their fruits; their fruits are discord, denial, and destruction of God's holy

---

55 Preus, *Justification and Rome*, 14, 22-26.
56 AE 21:301.

Word. Is the historical-critical method one more cross the church must bear? Listen to Luther and substitute the modern popes of historical criticism in place of Luther's popes:

> Pay no heed to the papists' holy possessions from dead saints, from the wood of the holy cross. For these are just as often bones taken from a carrion pit as bones of saints, and just as often wood taken from gallows as wood from the holy cross. There is nothing but fraud in this. The pope thus tricks people out of their money and alienates them from Christ. Even if it were a genuine holy possession, it would nonetheless not sanctify anyone. But when you are condemned, cursed, reviled, slandered, and plagued because of Christ, you are sanctified. It mortifies the old Adam and teaches him patience, humility, gentleness, praise and thanks, and good cheer in suffering. That is what it means to be sanctified by the Holy Spirit and to be renewed to a new life in Christ; in that way we learn to believe in God, to trust him, to love him, and to place our hope in him, as Romans 5 [:15] says, "Suffering produces hope," etc.[57]

Preus placed his hope in nothing less than Jesus' blood and righteousness. He ended his manuscript on "The Theology of the Cross" as follows:

> And so the Christian, especially the Christian pastor, suffers crosses for the sake of the theology of the Cross. His zeal is interpreted as anger, his courage as stubbornness, his orthodoxy as heterodoxy, his suffering as self-inflicted. And throughout it all he sings in his heart, happy in forgiveness of sins, confident in the sure hope of a gracious God who has saved him forever through the blood of Christ.[58]

---

57   AE 41:165.
58   TC 55.

LUTHER ON ATONEMENT — RECONFIGURED

Dedicated to the Memory of Dr. Robert Preus

L uther writes in his 1535 commentary on Galatians:

"I believe in Jesus Christ, the Son of God, who suffered, was crucified, and died for us." This is the most joyous of all doctrines and the one that contains the most comfort. It teaches that we have the indescribable and inestimable mercy and love of God. When the merciful Father saw that we were being oppressed through the Law, that we were being held under a curse, and that we could not be liberated from it by anything, He sent His Son into the world, heaped all the sins of all men upon Him, and said to Him: "Be Peter the denier; Paul the persecutor, blasphemer, and assaulter; David the adulterer; the sinner who ate the apple in Paradise; the thief on the cross. In short, be the person of all men, the one who has committed the sins of all men. And see to it that You pay and make satisfaction for them." Now the Law comes and says: "I find Him a sinner, who takes upon Himself the sins of all men. I do not see any other sins than those in Him. Therefore let Him die on the cross!" And so it attacks Him and kills Him. By this deed the whole world is purged and expiated from all sins, and thus it is set free from death and from every evil.[1]

Luther on atonement presents a puzzle. As we use the term atonement, we normally think of some kind of payment in blood for sins. Ever since Gustaf Aulén's published *Christus Victor* we have tended to think in terms of theories: objective, subjective, classical.[2] The English word atonement suggests "At-One-Ment" with God. None of this helps with regard to Luther. I will argue in this paper that atonement

---

1   *Lectures on Galatians* (1535), Chapters 1-4, in *Luther's Works*, edited by Jaroslav Pelikan and Walter A. Hansen, 55 volumes (St. Louis and Philadelphia: Concordia and Fortress, 1958-1986), 26:280. Volumes in this series are hereafter abbreviated *LW*.

2   Gustaf Aulén, *Christus Victor. An Historical Study of the Three Main Types of the Idea of the Atonement*, translated by A. G. Hebert (London: SPCK, 1953).

for Luther is more than the expiation won in Christ's blood, more than being "At-One" with God.[3]

The real puzzle with Luther on atonement is that the words that Luther used to describe the earthly work of Christ do not precisely include atonement. For Luther reconciliation is the prominent word for the work of Christ (*versöhnen* or *Versöhnung*), and the key text is 2 Corinthians 5:19: "God was in Christ reconciling the world unto himself." *Versöhnung* is often translated atonement. But *versöhnen* is used in Matthew 5:24 where we are to be reconciled with our neighbor before going to the altar. "Be atoned" with your neighbor does not work.

In addition to *Versöhnung*, other words in Luther's German that are translated atonement in the American Edition and elsewhere include *Bezahlung* (payment), *Opfer* (sacrifice), and *gnug thun* (be sufficient). Latin words that are translated atonement include *placare* (appease), *propiciatio* (propitiation), *satisfactio* (satisfaction), and *reconciliatio* (reconciliation). If one looks up "atonement" in the Index to the American Edition of Luther's Works, several words appear.[4] However, the references do not point the reader to "atonement" in the texts. Words that are indexed to atonement are sacrifice, mediate forgiveness, satisfaction, reconciliation, ransom, forgiveness, merit of His blood, reconciled. In the subject index in the *Concordia Triglotta*, atonement does not appear; reconciliation does.[5] The same is true for Tappert's edition of *The Book of Concord*.[6]

The use of terminology in discussing Luther on atonement is difficult since atonement (*Versöhnung*) is a term that Aulén put on the map of Luther studies. Aulén's vocabulary in translation, however, is not Luther's vocabulary in the original. Should atonement therefore be banished from our vocabulary for Luther? No. My solution to the terminology problem has been to see that "Luther's theology of atonement" is similar to other phrases we use to encompass several parts of

---

3 Years ago when lecturing on Luther, I was asked what Luther's theory of atonement was. My immediate reply was that Luther had no theory of atonement. Research for this paper confirms the same assessment.

4 LW 55:17.

5 *Concordia Triglotta: die symbolischen Bücher der evangelisch-lutherischen Kirche, deutsch-lateinisch-englisch* (St. Louis: Concordia Publishing House, 1921).

6 *The Book of Concord. The Confessions of the Evangelical Lutheran Church*, translated by Theodore G. Tappert (Philadelphia: Fortress Press, 1959).

Luther's thought, such as his sacramental theology, forensic [and sanative] justification, his doctrine of the two kingdoms, and his hermeneutics. Atonement for Luther serves as an important interpretative tool for packaging many genuine Luther articles such as reconciliation, expiation, cross, *fröhlicher Wechsel*, redemption, sacrament and example, justification, and yes, salvation. To have a more exact understanding of Luther on atonement one needs to be grounded in Luther's actual usage of the "genuine articles." This essay seeks to understand some of those "genuine articles" as a way of reconfiguring Luther on atonement, articles that come from my reading of Luther in the light of medieval theology.

Hence, the several items that atonement embraces in Luther include the method of *enarratio*, joyous exchange, theology of testament, theology of the cross, theology of the worm and the devil, sacrament and example. These are the many pieces to the picture of Luther on atonement.

Aulén seems to have difficulty specifying the meaning of atonement by claiming that for Luther atonement equals salvation and salvation equals atonement—that atonement and justification are the same thing.[7] In Aulén's chapter on the New Testament, atonement is not used in translating Scripture; words that do appear are propitiation, payment, ransom, redemption, reconciliation.

Aulén has done us the service of providing a panoramic view of atonement in the Christian tradition, using the Ludensian method of motif-research. The disservice of this method is that it is abstract typology. Aulén speaks of atonement theories: idea, type, and motif. Luther did not have time for theories; he worked as a theologian on the death-resurrection of Christ to give God glory and preserve the mysteries of the faith. Luther trusted only biblical truths.

Enarratio

Enarratio means to explain and expound in detail. Luther preoccupied himself with the Epistle to the Galatians and published throughout his life what are called in Latin and English "commentaries" on that book. Luther himself did not consider his work to be a commentary. He said that his work "is not so much a commentary as a testimony of my faith in Christ." Rather, Luther identified the genre of Erasmus's

---

7 Aulén, *Christus Victor*, 135, 167.

Greek and Latin New Testament, the *Novum instrumentum* of 1516, as a commentary (and he did so in a sarcastic way).

The term that Luther used to describe his publications on Galatians was "enarrare" or "enarratio." Committed to kindling interest in Pauline theology, Luther set out to "enarrate" Pauline theology—to set forth in detail Paul's theology in the public arena. "Narrate" (*narratio*) means to tell the story. "Enarrate" (*enarratio*), which is not an English word, means to take the message out and to apply it, that is, to tell the story in public. The story concerns the "one true faith in Christ alone." In the Preface of 1535, to "enarrate the Epistle" means to go public against the devil.

To tell Paul's story in public is not to do something new, but rather to do something very old: to fight the devil with the doctrine of "solid faith." From his lectures of 1516 to the printing of 1535, Luther's purpose with Galatians was to go public with the "faith of Christ." Hardly an academic exercise, Luther views this as the battle of life against death. It means to defend the faith against the pseudo-prophets and pseudo-apostles, the false teachers, who both Paul and Luther were convinced return all too quickly to the very centers of faith. To make public the faith—the Gospel of Christ—will inevitably stir up demonic forces and cause eschatological conflict.

In the Large Galatians, after describing the complete death and victory over sin, Luther says that the doctrine of Christian righteousness is too great to describe or understand.[8] This leads to my claim that any theory of the atonement explains away one of the mysteries of the faith. How Christ took the place of the murderer and adulterer, and all the sins of mankind, and made satisfaction by his blood is not open to theorizing but to praise. "Thanks be to God, who gives us the victory through our Lord Jesus Christ" (1 Corinthians 15:57).[9] Any theorizing takes away the mystery.

Working on the atonement has led me to conclude that, in spite of theories prevalent in Luther's day, the reconciling work of atonement is one of those precious mysteries that escapes theory. Atonement is a mystery rather than a theory developed by reason. It is not clear to the eye of reason how the blood of a Nazarene shed on a cursed tree between two criminals one Friday afternoon in Jerusalem could redeem the sins of humankind the world over. The eye of faith sees

8   LW 26:280.
9   LW 26:277, 280.

my sins dying in the work of the one who has taken my place in the incarnation.

Much of the Luther on atonement research and writing has been spent on Luther and Anselm. My own angle on Anselm and Luther is to remember the rule for doctrinal development in the Middle Ages, namely, *potuit, decuit, fecit.* Concerning a doctrinal matter, the medieval theologian asks (1) is it possible (*potuit*); if yes, then (2) is it becoming of God (*decuit*); if yes, the conclusion is (3) it happened (*fecit*). Anselm worked out his view of atonement on the level of *deceo*, what is fitting or becoming of God, all in the framework of faith seeking understanding. Luther, however, worked on the level of *fecit*: what happened. Without analyzing the reasons (fittingness) for God's actions, Luther wants to get the message out (*enarratio*).

If there has been anything of a theological breakthrough for this author in this project on atonement, it is seeing the difference between the dynamic of doctrinal development in the Middle Ages (and continuing in the modern Roman Catholic Church) and Luther's approach to theology. The method of faith seeking understanding in the Middle Ages employed reasons in speculating about what is possible and fitting for God to have done. For Luther, the method of *enarratio* meant getting the message out into the public sphere, the message of what God has in fact done in Christ. What God could have done, however beautiful and fitting, was theology of glory for Luther, based on reason. The medieval approach kept theology and doctrine an in-house affair. For Luther theology meant confession of faith, proclamation, profession in public, "the testimony of my faith in Christ."

Der fröhlicher Wechsel

For some, Luther's "doctrine of atonement" is summarized in the phrase "the joyous exchange." Burnell Eckardt, in his insightful book on Anselm and Luther, says: "*fröhlicher Wechsel* occurs only by imputation; it may in fact be termed Luther's version of the vicarious satisfaction." [10]

According to Ulrich Asendorf, the incarnation is the joyous exchange (*fröhlicher Wechsel*) of our flesh and Christ's. [11] We are born

---

10   Burnell Eckardt, *Anselm and Luther on the Atonement*: Was It "Necessary"? (Lewiston, New York: The Edwin Mellen Press, 1992).

11   Ulrich Asendorf, *Die Theologie Martin Luthers nach seinen Predigten* (Göttingen: Vandenhoeck & Ruprecht, 1988).

of Mary; Christ's birth is our birth; Mary is our mother, Christ our brother, God our father.[12] In the Lord's Supper in faith we are in a joyous exchange with Christ in that we become one with him.[13] Ultimately, Asendorf argues that the joyous exchange leads in the direction of theosis.[14]

The joyous exchange that is seen as a prominent feature of Luther's theology has its precedent in Staupitz, from Augustine. Augustine says in his sermons that the property of man is sin, untruth, and death, but the property of God is goodness, truth, and life. "The sinner with his property possesses God and is possessed by him.... What is properly God's (namely, life) becomes man's; and what is proper to human nature (namely, death) becomes God's."[15] Staupitz and Luther use this *commercium admirabile* in Augustine's sermons and add to it both a marriage metaphor and the exchange of sin and righteousness.

Luther used the bridal imagery to convey the idea of common property: the bridegroom turns over to the bride all of his property just as God does to man. Luther said that it would be a fragile love if the groom had not turned over to his bride his keys and the power over wine, bread, and everything else in the house. Luther extended the idea of common property to the idea of the holy exchange (*fröhlicher Wechsel, admirabile/sacrum commercium*).

In his *Lectures on 1 John* (1:3) regarding 2 Peter 1:4, Luther remarks that we are partakers of the divine nature because we have all the good things God has. The Father and Son have life, truth, and eternal salvation. "On our side there are nothing but sins. We share His good things; he shares our wretchedness. I believe in Christ. Therefore my sin is in Christ."[16]

In his work *On Two Kinds of Righteousness*, where he treats 2 Peter 1:4 and several other texts, Luther says God has granted us very great and precious gifts in Christ. Bride and bridegroom have all things in common. Christ and the Church are one spirit. Through faith in

---

12   Asendorf, *Theologie Martin Luthers,* 80, 88.

13   Asendorf, *Theologie Martin Luthers,* 296.

14   Asendorf, *Theologie Martin Luthers,* 423.

15   David C. Steinmetz, *Luther and Staupitz: An Essay in the Intellectual Origins of the Protestant Reformation,* Duke Monographs in Medieval and Renaissance Studies, volume four (Durham: Duke University Press, 1980), 29.

16   LW 30:225.

Christ, his righteousness becomes our righteousness and all that he has becomes ours; rather, he himself becomes ours. He swallows up all our sins in a moment for it is impossible that sin should exist in Christ.[17]

The secret of the divine grace for the sinner is that through a wonderful exchange our sins are no longer ours but Christ's, and the righteousness of Christ is not his but ours.[18]

Theology of Testament

Luther's theology of testament, the testament of Christ, embraces five parts. Testament was the means for theologizing about the Christian faith for Luther. He says the promise was given to Abraham "through the medium of testament" (*per modum testamenti*).[19] Testament is the message as well as the means, "and so that little word testament is a short summary of all God's wonders and grace fulfilled in Christ."[20] The "whole Gospel" is summarized in the testament of Christ.[21]

The first element in testament is the promise initiated by God from the beginning. "It must happen in this manner . . . that God alone without any entreaty or desire of man must first come and give him

---

17 LW 31:297-98.

18 On Psalm 22:1-2, *Operationes in Psalmos* (W² 4:1241.41). Other texts on *admirabile commercium*: Christ has *admirabile commercium* with creatures (WA 5:253,10-11). Christ has *admirabili commertio* with us sinners. Our sins are exchanged for Christ's righteousness. Bride/bridegroom become one flesh (WA 5:608.5-22). LW 26:284 "fortunate exchange" equals *feliciter commutans* (WA 40,I:443,23); *commutans* means total exchange, to alter wholly, change entirely, replace, substitute.

19 *Divi Pauli apostoli ad Galathas epistola* (1516), WA 57,II:24.9-10.

20 *Ein Sermon von dem neuen Testament* (1520), WA 6:357.25-27; LW 35:84.

21 *Ein Sermon*, WA 6:374.3-9. Hermeneutically for Luther, the New Testament illumines the Old Testament (*Evangelium in der Christmesse, Luk. 2,1-14* [1522], WA 10,I,1:79-84; one may compare *Ein klein Unterricht was man in den Evangeliis suchen und gewarten soll* [1522], WA 10,I,1:14.16-15.9). "The books of Moses and the prophets are also the Gospel," (*Epistel S. Petri gepredigt* [1523], WA 12:275.5) for the New Testament is the light of Old Testament. The Old Testament is the fountain of the new, the new is the light of the old (WA Tr 5:378.25-26, #5841).

a promise." The promise is "the beginning, the foundation, the rock."[22] "God is the testator for it is he himself who promises and bequeaths."[23] The testament is the promise and the promise is in both books; "all the fathers in the Old Testament together with all the holy prophets have the same faith and gospel as we have," because "it is all the one truth of the promise."[24] For Luther there is no book in the Bible which does not contain both law and promise.[25] The testament is eternal. Some would say that the prophets and the New Testament add something to the books of Moses. "No," said Luther regarding all books of the Bible, "throughout them all there is one and the same teaching and thought."[26] In every promise, there is a word and a sign just as notaries affix their seal or mark to make a will binding and authentic.[27] The signs were rainbow, circumcision, rain on the ground; in baptism—water, and in the Lord's Supper—bread and wine. "The words are the divine vow, promise, and testament. The sacred signs are the sacraments. Now as the testament is more important than the sacrament so the words are much more important than the signs."[28]

The second element in testament is Luther's theology of Word. The Word is the living eternal promise of the testament of Christ. The Gospel of Christ is not a writing but a word of mouth.[29]

> This report and encouraging tidings, or evangelical and divine news, is also called the New Testament. For it is a testament when a dying man bequeaths his property after his death to his legally defined heirs. And Christ, before his death, commanded and ordained that his Gospel be preached after his death in all the world.[30]

The New Testament is a living Word. Consequently for Luther, the Church is a "mouth house" not a "pen house."[31] Luther often bemoaned

---

22 *Ein Sermon*, WA 6:356.3-8; LW 35:82.
23 *Ad Galatas* (1519), WA 2:519.5; LW 27:264.
24 *Das Magnificat* (1521), WA 7:600.1-9; LW 7:354.
25 *Adventspostille* (1522) WA 10,I,2:159.7-8; one may compare *Ein Sermon von dem neuen Testament*, WA 6:356-57.
26 *Von Menschenlehre zu meiden* (1522), WA 10,II:73.7-18; LW 35:132.
27 *Ein Sermon*, WA 6:358.35-359.3.
28 *Ein Sermon*, WA 6:363.4-7; LW 35:91.
29 *Ein klein Unterricht*, WA 10,I,1:17.4-11.
30 *Vorrede auf das Neue Testament* (1522), WA DB 6:4.12-17; LW 35:358.
31 *Adventspostille* (1522), WA 10,I,2:35.1-2; 48.5.

the fact that we have the New Testament in written form because it is primarily proclamation to be sung loudly in German.

The testament is the Word of Christ, "this is my body. In like manner he says over the cup 'take it and all of you drink of it; this is the new, everlasting testament in my blood.' In proof and evidence of this, he left his own body and blood under bread and wine, instead of letter and seal."[32] Everything depends on the words of Christ's testament, says Luther.

> You would have to spend a long time polishing your shoes, preening and primping to obtain an inheritance, if you had no letter and seal with which you could prove your right to it. But if you have a letter and seal, and believe, desire, and seek it, it must be given to you even though you were scaly, scabby, stinking and most filthy. So if you would receive this sacrament and testament worthily, see to it that you give emphasis to these living words of Christ.[33]

The Word is the promise, the Word is the testament, the Word is Christ. Christ's testament is the Lord's Supper. "Let this stand therefore, as our first and infallible proposition, the mass or sacrament of the altar is Christ's testament."[34]

Now, says Luther, "you have the testator, the testament, the substance of the testament, and those for whom it was made. Now it remains that it be ratified . . . that is, made valid through the death of Christ."[35] Luther often cited Hebrews 9:16: "'for where there is a testament, the death of the testator must of necessity occur.' Now God made a testament; therefore, it was necessary that he should die, but God could not die unless he became man, thus, the incarnation and the death of Christ are both comprehended most concisely in this one word, 'testament.'"[36] Testament is not about to be altered or recalled by the living. It is an irrevocable will of one about to die. The cross, then, is in the context of the promise of the testament "that God would

---

32 *Von den guten Werken* (1520), WA 6:230.10-25; LW 44:55-56.

33 *Ein Sermon*, WA 6:360.29-361.9; LW 35:88.

34 *De captivitate Babylonica ecclesiae praeludium* (1520), WA 6:513.14-15; LW 36:37.

35 *Ad Galatas* (1519), WA 2:519.38-520.6; LW 27:265.

36 *De captivitate Babylonica*, WA 6:514.6-10; LW 36:38.

become man, and die and rise again in order that his Word in which he promises such a testament might be fulfilled and confirmed."[37]

The third part of Luther's theology of testament is the cross. Because for many Luther's entire theology is a theology of the cross, we will return to that in Part Four.

The fourth aspect of Luther's theology of testament is grace. Grace for Luther is unilateral gift. One of the primary functions of testament is that it is unilateral, the testator makes out his will without the recipient having to do anything to deserve the inheritance. Testament, at least God's way, is totally gratuitous. The heir in no way merits the inheritance. Testament for Luther stands in contrast with covenant. Often Luther uses covenant as a synonym for testament and understand it as unilateral gift. The covenant, in late medieval covenant theology and elsewhere, is a bilateral, two-way pact, bond or agreement. The various covenant theologies in the later Middle Ages were at least semi- if not fully pelagian, because they called for some human action as necessary part of the pact. This model of covenant does not call for a death. The grace of the unilateral testament is the cross and resurrection. The unilateral act of grace proves that God's promise is true. The cross is final proof that God's testament is valid. The resurrection completes God's action. For Luther, then, grace is God's self-authenticating Word that accomplishes its purpose without requiring any act on our part.

The fifth aspect of testament is faith or trust in the inheritance. One receives faith through the Word accomplishing its purpose. Faith is a gift of grace. Trust is confidence that Christ not only died for the sins of mankind but that he died for me. Trust is intimately bound up with Luther's notion of the certitude of salvation. The Christian has an absolute ground of the certainty of his salvation because his salvation is in Christ—Christ for us and for me. If salvation were dependent on something that I were to do—free will, free reason, free whatever—then Luther in no way can have any confidence. Confidence rests in Christ alone.

Luther's theology of testament is soteriological, having to do with salvation. Luther sometimes, like other medieval theologians, discusses testament in terms of the books of the Old and New Testament and the great eras of divine providence covered by the books. Luther's principle interest in the category of testament, however, is not in terms

37 *Ein Sermon*, WA 6:357.22-24; LW 35:84.

of books or eras but in terms of soteriology. Luther was quite similar to Saint Augustine in this regard in his understanding of testament as way of salvation, though Luther's doctrine of salvation is different from Augustine's. Luther and Augustine see Old and New Testament as old and new ways of salvation, both ways being present in both books and eras. When Luther and Augustine discussed old and new, they often meant old man/new man, letter/spirit, flesh/spirit. The man of faith is a New Testament man; that is, for Luther, he has received the testament of Christ in faith and trust because the testament of God is eternal and his Word eternally effective. Those who lived during the era of Old Testament but believed and trusted in the promise in faith belong to the New Testament. Luther does not conceive of salvation in terms of progressive transformation as did Augustine, but in terms of the ever present Word of God, faith, inheritance, all grounded in the death of Christ. The full force of God's testament is present at every point in time. Those who respond in trust belong to the New Testament of Christ.

The New Testament person is at the same time both totally just in Christ and totally sinful in himself, simultaneously and totally sinner and saint. That is, the human situation never changes, and the divine situation never changes. We cannot build a staircase to heaven, we are totally dependent on the effectiveness of the divine testament for our salvation. Another way of saying this is that as there are both Old and New Testaments, both old and new men, so also the man of faith himself is both old and new at the same time—old in himself, new in Christ, totally, simultaneously, and continuously (Augustine could not say any of this). The Christian, at whatever point in time and space, is sinful and saved. Luther says that just as Christ on the cross is suspended between heaven and earth so the Christian lives between the Old and New Testament, totally old, totally new, waiting for final glory when he will be totally and finally new. A Christian is simultaneously sinful and saved or, put another way, a Christian is simultaneously Old Testament and New Testament.

Theology of the Cross
The theology of the cross has an anti-speculative force to it which is directed against a theology of glory. The theology of the cross is contextual, working within the framework of what God, in fact, did in Christ on the cross. It is not speculative, looking into the infinite

number of possibilities available to divine power. Remember Luther's difference with his predecessors in his interest to concentrate on what God has done in order to get the message out (*enarratio*), whereas they speculated about the fittingness of what God could do. Rather than using philosophical terms, Luther talks about the wounds of Christ on the cross and about Christ as a worm on the cross, emphasizing the total humiliation of the God-man. The humiliation of the cross is God's total identification with the human situation in order to redeem that situation so that we can live by faith. The meaning and effect of the cross is a continual reality for all of God's faithful people in all times and places; the faithful of all ages live at the foot of the cross. The cross is the Word historicized making credible God's eternal promises.

Luther speaks of the death of Christ as the alien work of God through the devil, the lord of death. Death is used to destroy the lord of death. Life wrought through death is closed to reason and open only to faith. The alien deed is indirect revelation. God is *not* known through the works of creation or his invisible attributes (for example, immutability). He is known through suffering and the cross. Speculation as a way to God is eliminated. God revealed himself in the hiddenness of this One who is crucified. Life is the proper work of God. God uses the devil's proper work to destroy the devil through his own work of the death of Christ.

> He destroyed the devil, not by a work of God but by a work of the devil himself. For this is the most glorious kind of victory, namely, to pierce the adversary with his own weapon and to slay him with his own sword, as we sing: "He fell prostrate on his own darts." For in this way God promotes and completes His work by means of an alien deed, and by His wonderful wisdom He compels the devil to work through death nothing else than life, so that in this way, while he acts most of all against the work of God, he acts for the work of God and against his own work with his own deed. For thus he worked death in Christ, but Christ completely swallowed up death in Himself through the immortality of His divinity and rose again in glory.[38]

Christ became the death of death.

The key document where Luther develops his theology of the cross is the *Heidelberg Disputation* of 1518.[39] The *Heidelberg Disputation*

---

38   *Lectures on Hebrews*, LW 29:135.

39   LW 31:40.

is key for two reasons: (1) It is Luther's explanation to his fellow Augustinian brothers of his key ideas with regard to sin, free will, and grace—topics which had been debated in his *Disputation against Scholastic Theology* the previous year. (2) It is the key text in all of Luther's writings for his theology of the cross.

> That person does not deserve to be called a theologian who looks upon the invisible things of God as though they were clearly perceptible in those things which have actually happened. He deserves to be called a theologian, however, who comprehends the visible back sides of God seen through suffering and cross. A theology of glory calls evil good and good evil. A theology of the cross calls the thing what it actually is.[40]

Luther's explanation of Thesis 19, with reference to Romans 1:20 ("His invisible being can be seen so that it is perceived in his works") is: "This is apparent in the example of those who were 'theologians' and still were called fools by the apostle in Romans 1."[41] So, those theologians who seek to know God by speculating through the work of their reason into the invisible things of God clearly perceived in those things that have happened are fools. That is what Luther has said so far, but then typical Luther, if one really wants to know what these invisible things are of God, "the invisible things of God are virtue, godliness, wisdom, justice, goodness, and so forth. The recognition of all these things does not make one worthy or wise."[42] So a theologian of glory speculates into the invisible things of God as though they were perceptible in the things which have actually happened.

Now a theologian of the cross—the subject of Thesis 20—is different. A theologian of the cross looks at what is visible. What is visible is suffering and cross, and suffering and cross are the back parts of God (*posteriora dei*). The visible things turn out to be the back side of God. God is revealed on the cross, and what we see on the cross is the back side. We do not see, as Moses could not see, God face to face. A theologian of the cross is the only legitimate type of theologian; the theologian of glory is only a theologian in name and actually a fool. The theologian of the cross comprehends the visible and back sides of God seen through suffering and cross.

---

40 LW 31:40.
41 LW 31:52.
42 LW 31:52.

The theologian of glory discussed in Thesis 19 seeks a knowledge of God and his attributes, or invisible things of God, by perceiving and understanding the things which have actually happened. In other words, the theologian of glory comes to a knowledge of God through God's works. He does this by his own works, that is, by his intellectual activity. Luther believes that the powers of reason are contaminated. Just as in morality man misuses the law and appropriates goodness to his works, so in the intellectual sphere he assumes the knowledge of God to be his work. In contrast to the theologian of glory, the theologian of the cross seeks knowledge of God in suffering. Suffering here has a twofold meaning: the suffering of God in Christ and the suffering of the Christian united with Christ. The main point is that knowledge comes in and through suffering rather than in and through works, and this is the key to the theology of the cross in Heidelberg 19 and following. Theology of glory equals works of reason, theology of the cross equals suffering. Furthermore, visible things are perceived rather than invisible things understood. What is perceived is the back side of God.

Thus, God is hidden in the revelation, or God reveals himself through concealment. He is concealed because his face is not turned towards us. His brilliance and glory are hidden in their opposites, that is, in suffering, weakness, foolishness, and the cross. Such knowledge cannot be misused by humans as knowledge from works is.

Heidelberg Thesis 21 shows Luther to be an "is-theologian." The "is-theologian" must get the message out as to what the situation is. The theologian of the cross knows that knowledge of God is found only through suffering and the cross. To find the cross and Christ is to find God hidden in suffering. The theologian of glory gets things reversed and in his confusion fails to find reality. As Luther says in Thesis 21, "A theology of glory calls evil good and good evil. The theology of the cross calls the thing what it actually is." The "isness" of the situation is the "isness" of the human situation and the "isness" of the divine situation. Through his own experience and through his own theology, Luther is absolutely convinced that human nature is rotten to the core, that God is God, that God is quite capable of being God, and that God has bridged the gap between mankind and himself in Christ. A theologian of the cross calls the thing what it actually is. In his explanation to this thesis, Luther says, "This is clear, he who does not know Christ does not know God hidden in suffering." The way to know God is to know the God in Christ who is visibly showing the back sides through suffering and cross.

The cross meant suffering and humiliation for Luther, the wounds of Christ, the blood of Christ, Christ as worm on the cross. Christ as worm meant total humiliation. "I am worm and no man" (Psalm 22:6), said Christ on the cross according to Luther. We find him dying a shameful death, says Luther, which is his theology of the worm and the devil.

Christ as Worm on the Cross

The texts from Luther for this part range from 1517 well into the later Luther. The first is from his Hebrews lectures (1517-18). Hebrews 2:7 says "thou didst make him a little lower than the angels." The medievals debated as to who the "him" is in this text and what the author means by "a little lower." Luther first discounts those who understood "him" to be human nature, a little lower than the angels in dignity. Next Luther opposes those who understand "him" to be Christ, which is on the right track, but lack an adequate Christology. He says,

> Others understand this verse to refer to Christ as being lower than the angels, not according to his soul but according to his body which is capable of suffering. But even this interpretation is not precise enough since he was not only made lower than the angels but as he himself says: "I am worm and not a man" (Ps. 22:6).[43]

Being made "lower than the angels" meant for Luther the time of total humiliation on the cross and between the cross and resurrection. For three days when forsaken and deserted by God "Thou didst hand him over into the hands of sinners."[44] The meaning of Christ as worm on the cross carries the connotations of Christ being abject, the object of contempt, forsaken, nauseating, abominable, rotten stench, scandal, offensive or, simply, rotting worm.[45]

The prophets have a special way of speaking but they mean exactly what the apostles preach for both have said much about the suffering and glory of God and of those who believe in him. Thus, David says of

---

43   WA 57,III:117.4-10; LW 29:126.

44   WA 57,III:119.1-5; LW 29:127.

45   *Operationes in Psalmos*, WA 5:614.4-24.

Christ in Psalm 22:6, "I am a worm and no man." With these words he shows the depth of his abject humiliation in his suffering.[46]

Christ as worm refers to "the mode of his passion as pure man."[47] The state of pure man (*purus homo*) is that we are a bag of worms. The first enemy that tempts the Christian away from the Word of God and faith is "our own flesh," a rotten old bag of worms hanging heavy around our neck.[48] "We are nothing other than filth, corruption and worms." In death, the flesh turns to dust, and the worms consume it. Faith looks beyond death and the consumption by worms and believes that the body will rise.[49] "For thus it has pleased God to raise up from worms, from corruption, from the earth which is totally putrid and full of stench a body more beautiful than any flower, than balsam, than the sun itself and the stars."[50] The inheritance for the worm of faith is eternal life.[51]

Christ destroyed the devil's tyranny over death. God chose not to use heavenly muscle, such as Gabriel, Michael and the others, but

> He degrades himself so profoundly and becomes a man, yes, even degrades himself below all men, as it is written in Psalm 22, "I am a worm and no man, scorned by men and despised by the people." In such physical weakness and poverty, he attacks the enemy, lets himself be put on the cross and killed, and by his cross in death, he destroys the enemy and the avenger.[52]

How is it that a worm on a cross destroys the enemy's tyranny over death? The force of the image of worm is illumined by an examination of some early Christian literature. First Clement (16:15) uses Psalm 22:6 is used to describe the humiliation of Christ and later (25:3) the worm is used as a resurrection symbol. The worm comes forth from the decaying flesh of the Phoenix bird. The resurrection of the

---

46   *Epistel S. Petri gepredigt und ausgelegt* (1522), WA 12:279.23-27; LW 30:24.

47   *Operationes in Psalmos*, WA 5:614.8-9.

48   *Das fünfte, sechste und siebente Kapitel Matthaei gepredigt und ausgelegt* (1532), WA 32:308.13-14; 489:34-38; LW 12:105, 230; LW 24:44.

49   *Lectures on Genesis* (1535-45), WA 43:318.22-23; 303.36-304.6.

50   *Lectures on Genesis* (1535-45), WA 43:272.37-39; LW 4:190.

51   *Das 16. Kapitel S. Johannes gepredigt und ausgelegt* (1537), WA 46:54.36-55.8.

52   *Der 8. Psalm Davids, gepredigt und ausgelegt* (1537), WA 45:220.14-22; LW 12:110.

mythical Phoenix is used as an illustration of the Christian doctrine of resurrection, "now from the corruption of its flesh there springs a worm which is nourished by the juices of the dead bird and puts forth wing." In Origen, the worm as Christ's humanity is used as bait to catch the devil and his angels.[53] In Cyril of Jerusalem, new life comes from worms as evidenced by the bees and the birds. The transformation of the Phoenix from a worm is proof of Christ's resurrection.[54] In Gregory of Nyssa, the gluttonous fish is lured by the flesh of Christ as bait. The divinity of Christ is the hook.[55] Luther refers to Gregory's notion of how God took a sharp fishhook, put an angle worm on it and threw it into the sea.[56] The worm is the humanity of Christ, the hook the divinity. On the hook, the worm is *gebunden*, namely, the humanity. The devil says, "Should I not swallow the little worm?" He did not see the hook.[57]

For Luther, the testator on the cross is pure man, a worm. The testator is also the one who made the promise of the eternal inheritance. "The humanity did not conquer sin and death, but the hook that was concealed under the worm at which the devil struck conquered and devoured the devil who was attempting to devour the worm."[58]

The time frame for the worm action, described by Aulén as gross imagery, is primarily the descent into hell. It can also, however, refer to the whole incarnation.[59] God in the incarnation acts like a fisherman, with hook and worm. The devil finds him like "a worm and no man" and swallows him up. But this is to him as food which he cannot digest. For Christ sticks in his gills, and he must spew him out again, as the whale the prophet Jonah, and even as he chews him the devil chokes himself and is slain, and is taken captive by Christ.

For Luther, thinking of Heidelberg Thesis 21, the theologian of the cross tells it like it actually is. God is there in Christ, Christ is there on the cross. In the Lord's Supper, Christ is there: we receive the inheritance, the forgiveness of sins. Inheritance is received by the worm

53 *Selecta in Ps.* 21.7, Migne, *Patrologia Graeco-Latina* 12:1254C.

54 *Catechesis* 18.8, Migne, *Patrologia Graeco-Latina* 33:1026-27.

55 *Oratio Catechetica* 24, Migne, *Patrologia Graeco-Latina* 45:66A.

56 Luther likely means Gregory the Great; one may see *Moralium in Job*, lib. 33, Migne, *Patrologia Latina* 76:682C,D.

57 Luther, *Predigt am Ostersonntag* (1530), WA 32:41.12-26.

58 *Ad Galatas* (1531/35), LW 26:267; WA 40,I:417.31-33.

59 Aulén, *Christus Victor*, "grossest" symbol, 119.

of faith. The beauty of the "is" is that that is the way it is—in the life of faith there is no ought, must, do, wait and see. A man of faith can only have faith because Christ has totally redeemed our human situation in all its worminess. Christ as worm, less than man, decimates the deadly forces and we are totally victorious—from worm to glory; and with Luther's theology of revelation in hiddenness, the glory is in the worminess. The contradictions exist in tension. The tensions are not resolved. In cross, in suffering, in worm is Christ.

Sacrament and Example

Christ's death is a sacrament for dying to sin and walking a new life every day of our lives. Christ's death and resurrection is also an example for us to die confidently since he is not only our companion and leader, he carries us over to the other side.

In his 1517 *Lectures on Hebrews*, Luther speaks of Christ's death as a sacrament and an example (*sacramentum et exemplum*). It comes up in the context of Luther's comments on Hebrews 10:19, 22: "therefore, brethren since we have confidence to enter the sanctuary by the blood of Jesus ... let us draw near with a true heart." These words move Luther to deal with the work of Christ in terms of sacrament and example. Luther began his interpretation by saying that "the apostle wants us to imitate Christ who suffered and by dying passed over to the glory of the Father."[60] The passion and resurrection of Christ is "the sacrament for imitating Christ," a sacrament "for the mortification of concupiscence" and "for our new life." Luther then says, "Almost all of Paul's epistles are full of this mystical and exemplary suffering of Christ."[61]

The passion of Christ, for Luther, is "exemplary" in a twofold way. Referring to St. Augustine, Luther says, "We pass over in flesh and spirit, but Christ in flesh alone. Therefore, the passing over of Christ's flesh is at the same time an example of the passing over of our flesh (for we will be like him) and a sacrament for the passing over of our spirit." [62] The reference to Augustine made in the lectures on the Hebrews and the earlier lectures on Romans and Galatians shows that the sacrament of Christ's passion and resurrection is the work of Christ for

---

60   WA 57,III:222.12-14; LW 29:225.

61   WA 57,III:222.23-223.5; LW 29:225.

62   WA 57,III:223.11-14; LW 29:225 citing *De Trinitate* IV.3.5-6.

our salvation.[63] We are called to imitate Christ's sacrament by dying to sin and walking a new way with Christ [first example]. Christ's death and resurrection is also an example for man to die physically in order to be reunited with Christ in heaven.

In the light of earlier medieval exegesis of this verse, the conclusion which Luther draws from his discussion of sacrament and example is striking. For Luther, because of the sacrament and example of Christ, "we have confidence to enter the sanctuary by the blood of Jesus" (Hebrews 10:19). Medieval interpretations ranged from one text that argued that we have confidence because the realities of the New Testament are greater than the types of the Old Testament. Another interpretation emphasizes that our certainty comes from the fact that Christ was first to enter. For another, Christ is an infallible leader. For another, Christ prepared and demonstrated, opened, and initiated the way for us to enter.[64]

For Luther, the example of Christ is that he "passed over before everyone else and leveled the rough road in order to elicit our confidence." However, Christ does more than show us the way, "he also holds out his hand for those who are following." Our confidence rests in the fact that "Christ alone is not only our companion on the way but also our leader, and not only our leader but also our helper, in fact, he carries us over."[65] Christ as example, therefore, shows us how to die confidently and as sacrament makes it possible for us to do so.

In the light of medieval exegesis, the significance of Luther's interpretation of Hebrews 10:19 is that "we have confidence to enter the sanctuary" not because Christ's testament is greater than the old but because of Christ alone, his sacrament and example. Furthermore, our confidence arises from the fact that Christ not only opened the way, but he also carries us over.

For Luther, then, the only way to God is by way of faith in the lowly humanity of Christ seen totally humiliated on the cross. Christ became the most abject of men in his passion and death. This humanity is the holy ladder of ascent to God. Luther concentrates on Christ on the cross by way of emphasizing that our righteousness is effected

---

63   WA 56:320.11-16; LW 25:308; WA 57,II:54.4-9.

64   Kenneth Hagen, *A Theology of Testament in the Young Luther: The Lectures on Hebrews*, Studies in Medieval and Reformation Thought, volume 12 (Leiden: E. J. Brill, 1974), 115.

65   WA 57,III:223.24-224.10; LW 29:226.

by Christ's righteousness and our penance by Christ's purgation. It is Christ who accomplishes salvation in us.

Conclusion

This paper chooses not to focus on themes that are in Anselm and Luther, themes commonly associated with atonement, such as payment for sin, substitution, satisfaction, redemption by blood. Rather it has attempted to reconfigure Luther on atonement. Being convinced that atonement is a broad category that encompasses many genuine Luther items, it suggested several aspects to God's work of atonement, for example, the alien work of God through the devil, the back side of God, Christ as worm, the curse of Christ as sin, in addition to the main themes of the method of *enarratio*, joyous exchange, theology of testament, theology of the cross, theology of the worm and the devil, sacrament and example. The contextual, nonspeculative character of Luther's theology runs through much of the foregoing, namely, the *fecit*, the cross, and Luther's "is-theology." The certitude of salvation rests on the conviction that the testament of Christ is for me.

In all fairness to medieval theology, scholastic speculation was done from the posture of faith seeking understanding; reason was used in the genre of approbation, convincing only to those already convinced. And yet for many critics of scholastic theology—Luther among them—the speculative questions did not help explain basic biblical truths. The use of dialectic, question, reason, and doubt had a life of its own; theology was for theologians. Theology had become divorced from the study of Scripture.

For Luther, theology is in service of the Church; its purpose is to get the message of the truth of Christ out into the public sphere. Theology must protect the mysteries of the faith and speak out against the false prophets. Question, reason, debate were appropriate for the training of young theologians in the university; the weekly Friday afternoon disputations were reintroduced into the curriculum at Wittenberg. The main curriculum, however, as well as the whole purpose of theology under Luther's leadership was to teach, serve, and guide the faithful, especially the weak in Christ.

A NOTE ON THE 450TH ANNIVERSARY OF THE DEATH OF
MARTIN LUTHER (FEBRUARY 18, 1996).

The importance of Luther for our time, as I see it, is his clear perception and practice of theology—in the tradition of *enarratio* and the discipline of the sacred page. Often Luther is brought into the contemporary situation to bolster a current agenda (which the history of Luther research bears out). The usefulness of Luther for me is his insight into the task of theology, a discipline with a tradition and an agenda sufficient unto itself. In recent times, studies of theology *and*, or theology *as*, or *adjectival* theology have become popular. In other words, in some circles theology has become copulative, adverbial, and adjectival: theology *and* (society), theology *as* (history), and (*feminist*) theology.[66] Luther practiced theology *as* theology.

In the tradition that Luther worked, theology had (and has) more than enough to do to keep track of the demands of the sacred page, the public, and the demonic. The thesis here is that theology has a discipline, an identity, and a long history that stretches back into Scripture itself. Its starting and ending point is God. It is important to me that other disciplines do not worry about the reality of the Logos present in the flesh, the reality of Christ Jesus present at the table, the forgiveness of sins, and the meaning of redemption, among others. It is important that theology be a disciplined study of God and that Scripture, in the name of consistency, be approached for what it was and is.

Above all else, I have come to see that the discipline of theology is characteristized by uniqueness, sufficiency, and finality. Its uniqueness consists in its focus on God and his sacred page. Its sufficiency lies in its tasks to protect the mysteries of God and to ward off the pseudo-apostles; it is best equipped to accomplish these tasks by reliance on the resources deep within the discipline and not by liaisons with other disciplines. Its finality consists in its eschatological dimension. In the grammar of Scripture, there is a finality to *eschaton* which the Latin Vulgate translates "in the newest days." The eschatological referent of theology differentiates it perhaps most clearly from philosophy, history, and psychology.

---

66   A Harvard Professor said in the early 1960s that when theology has to be qualified with an *and*, *as*, or *adjective*, it has lost its discipline.

The eschatological referent was the guiding light behind the work of two doctors of the Church, Dr. Martin Luther and Dr. Robert Preus. In his Preface to the Burial Hymns, Luther writes:

> We Christians, who have been redeemed . . . by the dear blood of the Son of God should by faith train and accustom ourselves to despise death and to regard it as a deep, strong, and sweet sleep, to regard the coffin as nothing but paradise and the bosom of our Lord Christ, and the grave as nothing but a soft couch or sofa, which it really is in the sight of God; for He says, John 11, "Our friend Lazarus has fallen asleep."[67]

---

67   "Preface to the Burial Hymns," LW 53:326.

DOES METHOD DRIVE BIBLICAL STUDY?

How to study the Bible often means in contemporary circles, "What is your method?" *How* means *method*, the necessary prerequisite to interpretation. Every interpretation is based on a method, or so goes the current consensus; therefore it is best to make one's method clear before interpretation can effectively take place. The question here is whether it is true that method precedes interpretation, that every interpretation is based on a method, and, therefore, that method drives biblical interpretation.[1]

Methodenlehre has been a preoccupation of biblical interpreters for a few centuries, especially in historical-critical circles. It has not always been that way. In fact the church existed quite happily for a good sixteen hundred years or more before the M-word came into prominence.

Methodenlehre is important, to be sure, along with other associated disciplines reaching prominence in the nineteenth century, such as hermeneutics and exegesis. My concern is not to challenge the importance of the discussion of method in and of itself. My only concern here is to test the widespread assumption (1) that method is prior to interpretation, (2) that method is clean and clear of philosophical presuppositions, and (3) that method then is the necessary prior discipline, that is, the prolegomenon upon which are built systems of particular points of view.

IS METHOD PRIOR TO INTERPRETATION?

The assumption of contemporary "method-ists" is that method drives practice. They assume that every interpretation of Scripture is governed by a method. And so, in the twentieth century, the discussion of method is carried on up-front, with the assumption that one needs to be clear about one's method in order to make one's interpretation clear. The scholars of the Bultmann generation were very proud of announcing that they were open and up-front about methodological

---

1 Author's meaning of terms: "interpretation" means to understand and explain; "method" means the manner of proceeding; "study" means immersion into the text or reading; *Methodenlehre* means the question, problem, or topic of method.

presuppositions.[2] The claim was that all scholars should come out of their closet and declare their method.

Is it possible to engage in biblical study without a method? Of course. Biblical scholars for centuries did so—and continue to do so. Not only did Luther not have a hermeneutic, but he also spoke against the idea of interpreting the Bible. "Interpretation" suggested to him that it was the interpreter who was providing the understanding—that is, the clarity, the importance, and the message. For Luther, Scripture was quite capable of interpreting itself.

Much is to be gained in the contemporary discussion of hermeneutics and method for those so interested and so inclined.[3] My concern here is the relation of method to interpretation. My objection to the claim that every interpretation employs a method and therefore that method of necessity drives interpretation is that such a claim is reductionistic and deterministic. It is similar to the claim that all language presupposes a philosophy. Whenever it is claimed that "all" something is determined by something else, disciplines become blurred. What is worse, it assumes some neutral beginning point in the human endeavor of understanding that is itself uncaused and is the unmoved mover. Human understanding is complex and every discipline has something to offer; but to make one discipline, for example, *Methodenlehre*, the basis of another exceeds the discipline's capabilities. At best, method drives method, which means it needs to be tested and revised by interpretation, to examine its philosophical and historical presuppositions, and to sustain its own discipline of inquiry without trying to run the world of understanding.

Does method drive the practice of biblical interpretation even among the modern practitioners of the historical-critical method? I think not. The rise of the historical- critical method has a history, a fairly long history; and it is not over yet, since the method continues to change. I would argue that the history and changes in the historical-critical method are the result of the fact that method does not always produce

---

2 Rudolf Bultmann and his immediate students were explicit about theology's necessary relation to philosophy, which carried over into the post-Bultmannians' discussion of method as well.

3 The Ebeling school has done much for promoting the understanding of the Word of God in Luther's theology via a discussion of the hermeneutics of the young Luther. Hermeneuticians have built on the idea of the power of the text of Scripture for the transmission of understanding.

perfect or satisfying practice, hence the method needs to be adjusted and revised to accommodate the new results. The new results are not the product of the previous method but of the new method forged in practice. The history of the historical-critical methods—and you need more than two hands to count them—means that method evolves with interpretation, which suggests to me that interpretation drives method at least as much as method drives interpretation.

New methods arise when old methods do not work. This only confirms what I have observed for years in the practice of interpretation, namely, that method comes as a result of work. I have observed this especially in my own field of historical theology. Method is *a posteriori* not *a priori*. In research one tries as many angles and approaches as possible to get to the bottom of the problem, question, or text. Method is forged in the heat of research. What works one time may not work well the next time, hence new results. My experience is that people write their introductions after all the results are in and not before. It is in these introductions where methodological claims of superiority are often made.

What bears this out, and it is too embarrassing to mention names, is when a scholar announces in a second book that he rejects the method employed in the previous publication. This is most likely not at all what happened and is off the mark. Two different books entail two different sets of sources, circumstances, problems, and issues, which result in different methods that solved the new venture. The second successful book is the result of new research, not a new method. The new research followed a new course and came up with new results. This is then abstracted for the purpose of an introduction into claims of a new and superior method. Contrary to these claims, the rule seems to be that method follows practice.

IS METHOD CLEAR OF PHILOSOPHICAL PRESUPPOSITIONS?

One of the attractive claims of those who insist on the priority of method over interpretation is that, while interpretation can be colored by one's biases, method is free of bias. This claim is based on the notion that method is an "objective"[4] science more closely related to the pure science of history, to philosophy and logic, than to the muddied waters of biblical commitments. Method does not dictate results, so it would

---

4 Author's meaning of term: "objective" means a static starting point.

seem, since results come from interpretation, while method is neutral, historical, and prior to what is actually to be found in Scripture. It is a simple fact that method—as some kind of a neutral starting point—has never driven interpretation. Method is too closely tied in with results, with interpretation that works, to be considered separate and prior to interpretation. The venture of method and interpretation involves a whole complex of research tools, no one of which is necessarily prior to another. In the practice of interpretation, one tries time-honored methods and never-heard-of methods to see what works, what is true to the text. Method and practice go hand in glove. The text, not method, drives the interpretation.

The idea of a value-free method means to me that it is free of value, that is, valueless or worthless. Method is a part of historical inquiry. Human history does not yield objective pure truth. Only God produces objective pure truth, and history is not God. The pursuit of historical truth, especially the truth of Scripture, involves passion and plenty of it. The idea of scientific neutrality is a myth. Ask any scientist how objective his work is. What convinced me was when our mathematics chairman told me that numbers are relative.

There is no clean and clear neutral point of beginning. Nineteen hundred years of biblical interpretation show that the study of the Bible, with or without a method, is inextricably coupled with all kinds of theological commitments. What else would you expect when we are dealing here with God and his word? How can one be objective and scientific about God? The Bible is certainly not a neutral document.

Just as the rise of the historical-critical method has a history, so the discussion of method, namely, *Methodenlehre*, has a history.[5] My research indicates that *Methodenlehre* came into theology in the sixteenth century from philosophy—more specifically, in the case of Niels Hemmingsen, from logic, and within logic from dialectic. It was a part of the general trend of the time to organize and order one's discipline, an admirable venture, to be sure. As the quip goes: What is the opposite of organized religion? Disorganized religion.

Method came into several disciplines in the sixteenth century as a way of tidying up the mass of information. This was parallel to the

5   See my study "De Exegetica Methodo. Niels Hemmingsen's De Methodis (1555)," in *The Bible in the Sixteenth Century*, ed. David Steinmetz, Duke Monographs in Medieval and Renaissance Studies 11 (Durham, N.C.: Duke University Press, 1990), 181-96, 252-55.

discipline of *summa* in Aquinas's generation. Providing order in the discipline did not mean that method must be prior to interpretation. Method seeks to be clear about the *via docendi* (the way or manner of teaching)—the ancient, classical and philosophical definition of method—where the logic of interpretation must be laid out. But logic is not a presuppositionless discipline. It has a very long history; just try to sort out the history of medieval logic. I did and was relieved when an expert told me that there was no logic to medieval logic.

The point here is that what arises in history is not clean and clear of presuppositions. Method has a history. It is the history of *Methodenlehre*. My concern here is not to debunk the discipline of method, but only to dethrone it as the necessary prolegomena to the study of the Bible. Order, definition, presupposition, *via docendi*, and principles of interpretation are all important areas of study, and they are all interrelated.

After being accepted in other disciplines, *Methodenlehre* became a theological question. Likewise in the seventeenth and eighteenth centuries, the disciplines of biblical introduction, biblical theology, and dogmatic theology became separate subjects of theological work and publication. These fields, along with exegesis, hermeneutics, historical theology, and systematic theology all became a part of the plethora of theological inquiry by the end of the nineteenth century.[6] Each subject had—and continues to have—a history and a place in theological discussion. Each of the disciplines mentioned in this paragraph has a place in the effort to understand Scripture.

The claims of "method-ists" are simply unrealistic. They cannot possibly deliver on the claims of objective neutrality. The fact that there are a plethora of method-ists should tell you something about objectivity.

By saying that a discipline has a history, I mean that it arises in particular historical circumstances with the usual influences of time and space. Method is not presuppositionless. These influences shape its historical development. I dare say that all theological disciplines, including theology itself, arise in human-historical circumstances. Only Scripture is God-given and divinely inspired. The point is that until very recently no one theological discipline enjoyed lordship or dominance over all the others. Even so today, many segments of the

---

6   See my chapter "The History of Scripture in the Church," in *The Bible in the Churches*, ed. Kenneth Hagen, 3rd ed. (Milwaukee: Marquette University Press, 1998), 1-28.

theological world outside of Western Europe and the U.S. are not dominated by *Methodenlehre.*

A peculiar thing about method—and perhaps one could add herme-neutics and exegesis—is that it is something of an intrusion into the-ology from the outside. Method in its classical definition of *via docendi* does not come from Scripture, councils, creeds, or confessions. It is not a part of any of the ordinary and traditional theological subjects from creation to eschatology. It is a philosophical abstraction from the practice of biblical study.

Another aspect to method that makes it problematical is that it is anachronistic to the study of Scripture. It is extraneous to Scripture and superimposes agenda and presuppositions that do not arise from Scripture itself. Hence it violates one of its own presuppositions, namely, consistency. Method is not consistent with the document it seeks to clarify. Method is an abstraction. Is God driven by method? Scripture is a faith document. Eschatology in Aristotle is very differ-ent from eschatology in Paul. A document should be approached for what it is and to whom it is addressed. The task of interpretation is to lay out the message of Scripture. Otherwise it is ripped out of histor-ical context and made to float on the horizons of Western philosophi-cal inquiry. *Methodenlehre* is a modern discipline. Scripture should not be expected to have a *Methodenlehre.*

The argument here is based on historical, theoretical, and practical considerations. Historically, *Methodenlehre* is itself a historical disci-pline. Theoretically, the history and variety of methods—to say noth-ing about the variety of interpretations—show that method is not neutral or objective, that is, never a static starting point. Practically, the actual exercise of interpretation, which produces variances on meth-ods, shows that method proceeds from interpretation, not the other way around.

IS METHOD THE NECESSARY PRIOR DISCIPLINE?

To make such a claim, that method dominates or drives interpretation, limits the interpretation to what is consistent with the method. For over thirty years of teaching and researching historical theology and for forty years of observing changes in biblical methods of interpre-tation, I have come to see what a shackle a method can be. When a professor is an adherent to one method, then the student must pur-sue research within the confines of that method. In the old days of

German theological scholarship, it took a generation of students to go beyond their professor and forge a new corrective to the method. Now these students change methods at will, which only goes to prove that a new method comes as a result of new research, not a new method.

When it comes to understanding Scripture, interpretation is in the driver's seat, not method. To make rules of interpretation the necessary prolegomena to the actual interpretation prejudices the result at the start. Rules are restrictive and delimiting.

If you want to talk about method, be realistic. We begin with the text, the Book. We begin with eyes, hands, minds, questions, issues, goals, and, yes, deadlines. The task is study and interpretation. How to read the Book? The best way is to start by reading—slowly.[7]

---

7 I offer seven rules on how to read the Bible to my university students; here abbreviated:

(1) *Read it.* This rule is important especially for those who think they know a lot of Scripture. The trained theologian is most apt to skip step one, since he has read it all before.

(2) *Read it SLOWLY.* Since the goal of reading Scripture is not the quantity of consumption, it is best read carefully and slowly. If good food takes time, certainly food for the soul takes an abundance of time.

(3 *Read it slowly, OVER AND OVER.* We often come to Scripture with many other things on our mind. We are not ordinarily tuned in to the extraordinary. It is better to grasp a little well than to try for too much and miss it all.

(4) *Read it slowly, over and over, FORWARDS.* Take it as it comes, verse by verse.

(5) *Read it slowly, over and over, forwards, and BACKWARDS.* To read backwards means to take the chapter and start with the last verse and take it verse by verse backwards. If you are very familiar with Scripture and are accustomed to reading only forwards, you are likely to skip and jump precisely because you are so familiar with the material. If you also read backwards, it forces you to concentrate more.

(6) *Read it slowly, over and over, forwards, backwards, and SIDEWAYS.* The procedure of reading sideways is important because that is how Scripture interprets itself. To read sideways means to read across the terrain of Scripture. It means to check out parallel verses in both Testaments.

(7) *Read it slowly, over and over, forwards, backwards, sideways, and, above all, ENJOY it.* St. Augustine says that we are to enjoy God and not to use him. Things are to be used. God is to be enjoyed. Since Scripture is all about God, its proper use is that he should be enjoyed.

The point is that the scholar begins with a task. Method is far down on the list of priorities. Reading the text is the most ancient of disciplines. It still works. Study drives interpretation. Study brings understanding. *Methodus?* She might show up during coffee to see how we are doing. Reading and more reading are the only way to read and see.

I see nothing wrong with scholars coming along with new results on the basis of new procedures, and then in their introductions or conclusions claiming insight, victory, and nirvana, as far as their method was concerned. What I do find objectionable is the claim that all subsequent research must follow the same procedures or method.

My own concern about method and *Methodenlehre* is not just that it has come to dominate modern historical studies—I am thinking specifically of the use the historical-critical method for the study of the Bible or "social history" for the study of the Reformation—but that it distorts the study of the history of the church prior to the rise of *Methodenlehre*. To put it bluntly, for three-fourths of the church's life, method did not exist. And for a few hundred years after that, it was only one of many new kids on the block. To force everyone prior to the discovery of method to have a method is anachronistic.

To ask about Augustine's method is horrible. It turns history upside down. Luther said that the Holy Spirit was a master rhetorician, but not a method-ist. To ask about Augustine's rules for the study of Scripture is consistent with his document *On Christian Doctrine*. To ask about Luther's method—likewise his hermeneutics and exegesis— would make as much sense as to ask about Luther's inclusive language, racial toleration, multiculturalism, or ethic of cloning. Questions do have their time and place. Method is not a timeless question.

When *Methodenlehre* dominates the history of biblical study prior to the Renaissance, all sorts of distortions occur. Again these distortions are too embarrassing to mention by authors' names. What I have in mind here is the study of historical figures on the basis of *Methodenlehre*, where these figures are studied for their "methods" of biblical interpretation. This is usually based on their prefaces or introductory sections to their commentaries (the *Argumentum*), or methodological-sounding statements made elsewhere. The resulting study claims to portray the history of biblical methodologies. The main flaw is not just that method did not exist, but that the authors' actual interpretation of Scripture does not seem to follow their stated methods in the *Argumenta*, and elsewhere. A biblical commentator's actual interpretation—not its methodological justification—is the most important source for the history of biblical study.

To put this a little more imaginatively and daringly: to study the *Argumenta* of historical figures—let us say, Augustine, Aquinas, Luther, and Calvin—and take their methodological sounding statements at face value, and then write a history of hermeneutics is utter nonsense. Such authors in the history of biblical interpretation did not assume that "method" was a necessary step prior to interpretation. What they wrote in their prefaces were time-honored claims about literal and spiritual interpretation, without ever thinking that they should follow their "method" in their practice of interpretation. I do not know how else to explain the fact that these historical authors did not practice what they preached in their introductions. In other words, it never occurred to them that method drives interpretation, especially since method didn't exist. For historical authors, biblical study drove biblical study.

Not only is method *not* the necessary prior discipline, namely, the prolegomenon, upon which interpretation is built; it never has been so, and it never should be. To make method dominate interpretation exceeds what method is good for. Systems of particular points of view are built not on method but on particular points of view. About the only thing that is built on method is method. Hemmingsen's work *On Methods* included a discussion of a method for method. It is easy to imagine where the logic of a method for method leads: more method.

Luther's well-known rules for biblical interpretation—prayer, meditation, and experience—are consistent with the text under investigation and are the kind of prior preparation that yields results.[8] Method is abstract, removed from the sacred page. The method-ist seeks a neutral point of entry so as not to prejudice the results. Scripture's response to neutrality is hardly a point of entry, since God says, "I will spew them out of my mouth." Scripture rather speaks the language of prayer, song, and meditation. Approached in such a vein, the results are very rewarding.

---

8 Luther's "rules" are sometimes called the principles of biblical interpretation, which are to be considered before interpretation can fruitfully begin. "Principles of biblical interpretation" are necessary and important to have clear in mind. Whether they *must* be discussed first before interpretation can take place effectively is another matter.

LUTHER'S SO-CALLED JUDENSCHRIFTEN:

A Genre Approach*

Martin Luther has been accused of being anti-Semitic, of being a predecessor for the actions of some German professors during the Third Reich, and of being an apologist for the ideology of Hitler. These charges are based on his so-called *Judenschriften*.

In modern editions of Luther's writings, the term 'Judenschriften' is used to classify those of his writings which supposedly were directed "against the Jews." Where is the origin of this classification and what is its history? Did Luther actually publish anything "against the Jews"— as this phrase has come to be understood—if one judges his writings by the standards of his day and not by those of the post-Holocaust era? These are the questions which I will pursue in the following materials. My objective is not to amplify the century-old debate on Luther and the Jews, and I have no intention of rewriting the history of Jewish-Christian relations. My objective is to ascertain when the classification 'Judenschriften' came to be applied to some of Luther's writings (I, II) and identify the literary genre of these writings by reading them in their literary context (III, IV). I approach the topic 'Luther and the Jews' from a literary point of view, setting aside all post-Holocaust agendas vis-à-vis Luther and all pro- or anti-Semitic sentiments. I am interested in the intended audience of a treatise; I am also interested in the genre of a treatise if it is judged by historical precedent; and, finally, I am interested in the problem how modern classifications create a literary product other than the original. This genre approach allows Luther's writings to be examined in their historical, that is, their medieval context; therefore I have read Luther's so-called *Judenschriften* in their original printings rather than in modern editions.[1] "Context" and

---

1 *Abbreviations: Aland: Kurt Aland: *Hilfsbuch zum Lutherstudium* (3d ed., rev. and enl. Witten, 1970; 4th ed., rev. and enl. Bielefeld, 1996). —HAB: Herzog August Bibliothek, Wolfenbüttel. —WA: *Dr. Martin Luthers Werke.* Kritische Gesamtausgabe (Weimar, 1883ff.). —From 1979 to 1991, I have worked on the original printings of Luther's works on Scripture, which in modern editions are classified as 'Exegetical Writings'. In that process I also examined the so-called *Judenschriften*. In the following I present the results of

"audience" need to be safeguarded against false expectations. I will deal with the literary contexts of these writings, and not their socio-political contexts. And I exclude the reception of a treatise by the audience and all the problems connected with such a reception. Enough has been written about the possible, actual, or assumed reception of these writings.

This approach is based on the assumption that words make all the difference: To call a writing something, gives it a frame of meaning; to call it what it is gives it an accurate frame; to call it something other than what it was historically to be casts it into a foreign frame of reference. There may be nothing wrong with modern terms which are foreign to Luther's days, but they are "other." By using the term 'Judenschrift', which, as will be demonstrated below, is of rather recent origin, a framework is created for the writings thus classified. This framework suggests that the *Judenschriften* were directed to Jews and were written as an attack on Jews. Logically, then, by extension all other writings not so classified would not deal with Jews.[2] Yet Luther discussed many of the subjects raised in those Judenschriften also in many other writings not so classified. Saying that words make all the difference affirms the fact that meaning is conveyed by words; therefore it is important to know the meaning of words in their historical context. For example, the word 'man' (*homo*), gender neutral, in medieval Latin designated something quite different from what the word 'man', gender specific, conveys today. For Luther the word 'Jew', no gender, designated 'nonbeliever'. To us this sounds strange since Jews are in many cases fervent, practicing believers. But for Luther any belief other than that founded on the Gospel was not another belief but false belief; for him nonbelief and false belief were synonyms. The idea of

---

this examination. I am grateful to Marquette University for a Faculty Research Grant in 1993, and to the Institute for Ecumenical and Cultural Research at Collegeville, Minnesota, for its Resident Scholar Program (1994–95).

    For the difficulties and dangers of reading Luther in modern editions, especially WA, see Kenneth Hagen: *Luther's Approach to Scripture as seen in his "Commentaries" on Galatians, 1519–1538* (Tübingen, 1993).

2   To illustrate further: The classification 'Exegetical Writings' suggests that all writings so grouped are exegesis of Scripture and all others not included in this classification are not exegetical; in the case of Luther's writings this would be absurd since there are very few of his writings which do not include exegesis.

a tolerable plurality of belief-systems is modern and was unthinkable in Luther's day.

I. THE HISTORY OF THE CATEGORY 'JUDENSCHRIFT' IN COLLECTED WORKS OF LUTHER

I have attempted to check all editions of collected works of Luther from the sixteenth century to WA for the category 'Judenschrift[en]' as a classification of certain writings. Unless noted, the title pages of individual volumes contributed nothing to the problem at hand; therefore they may be ignored. I concentrated on sections of text which can be found in some—not all—volumes of the early collections of Luther's Latin and German works. These sections are titled "catalogue" (*Catalogus*), or "register" (*Register*), or "list" (*Verzeichnis*), and in some cases they have no title at all. The titles of these sections vary and certainly would present problems to the present-day book designer or bibliographer. Yet the materials presented in these sections are simply lists of the individual writings printed in the volume (a table of contents) in which such a catalogue, register, or list can be found.

I used three bibliographic aids to organize my work: The shelf list, *Luther's Works. Comprehensive Collections*, prepared by, and available in, Special Collections, Luther Seminary Library, in St. Paul, Minnesota; the entry, "Luther: Gesammelte Schriften," in the card catalogue of the Herzog August Bibliothek (in which the editions of Luther's works are grouped by site of publication); and the entry, "Luther: Spätere Ausgaben," in the same catalogue.

A. Special Collections, Luther Seminary Library, St. Paul, Minnesota: Luther's Works. Comprehensive Collections

1. LATIN WORKS: WITTENBERG, 1545–1561. 6 Volumes.
In vol. 1 Luther's salutation is followed by that of Melanchthon and by "Catalogvs Scriptorvm Qvae in hoc I. Tome Continentvr." In vols. 2, 3, 4, and 5 are lists of writings contained in each volume. And in vol. 6, after the preface to the *Lecture on Genesis* (which fills the whole volume), is inserted an "Index rerum memorabilium in enarratione Libri Primi Moisi Reverendi Viri D. Doctoris Martini Lutheri" of about 22 folios in length;[3] within this index is listed (on Biiijʳ): "Contra Iudaeorum gloriam

---

3   This is a name and subject index to Luther's lectures on Genesis. Pertinent to our problem is the entry "Iudaei," where we find subsections such as *Iudaei*

de carnali nativitate ...." (361).[4] In the lists of the writings contained in vols. 1–4 no classification of writings is given; there is no list in vol. 5.

2. GERMAN WORKS: JENA, 1555–1558. 8 Volumes.

Each volume contains a list of the books printed in that volume. The list at the end of vol. 1 records the "Bücher und Schrifften" by year of origin. The same kind of list at the beginning of vol. 2 includes *Das Jesus Christus ein geborner Jüde sey* (1523). The list at the end of vol. 3 covers the years 1525–27; for 1525 is listed the classification "Etliche Stuck von der Bawren Auffrhur." In the list at the end of vol. 4 (covering the years 1528–30) appear a few classifications ("Two Prefaces to Sermons on Genesis," "Three Writings," "Two Prefaces for the Large and Small Catechisms"). The list at the beginning of vol. 5 records the writings for 1530 to 1533, and in this list, too, a few classifications appear ("Three Beautiful Writings to Duke John, Elector of Saxony," "Some German Writings to the Theologians at Augsburg"). Such lists and classifications are also given in the beginning of vol. 6 (1533–38),[5] vol. 7 (1538–42),[6] and vol. 8 (1542–47). *Without any classification or category*, vol. 8 contains *Von den Jüden und jren Lügen D. M. L., Vom Schem Hamphoras und vom Geschlecht Christi D. M. L.,* and *Von den letzten Worten Davids D. M. L.*

---

proditores Germaniae, Iudaei hodie opprobrium omnium hominum, Iudaei omnia amiserunt quae Abrahae promissa sunt, Iudaei terrae Chanaan haeredes usque ad Regem suum Christum, Iudaei extenuant incestum Ruben, and so on. The index also includes *Iudaeorum glossa* and ends with *Iudaei destituti Christi, non intelligunt promissiones.*

4 This reference is to Luther's comments on Gen. 25:21. Luther's point is that both Jews and Turks have "glory of flesh"; the Jews also glory in their blood, that they are born of the fathers and prophets (361).

5 In the *Verzeichnis* is listed for 1537: "Schrift D. M. L. an einen Jüden / Warumb er im Fürschrifft versage." A longer and more descriptive title is given at the beginning (533ʳ) of the "Schrift" (*Dem fürsichtigen Jesel Jüden zu Rosheim meinem guten Freunde*) which reads: "Schrifft D. M. L. an einen Jüden / Warumb er im schrifftliche Fürbitte an Churfürstliche Durchleuchtigkeit zu Sachssen / versage, Anno 1537" (2 folio pages). This "Schrift" is not listed in Aland for 1537 or for "Juden," nor is it listed by name, place, or chronology in the indexes in WA 61–63.

6 In the *Verzeichnis* is listed for 1538: "Brieff D. M. L. wider die Sabbather an einen guten Freund." See n. 8.

3. LATIN WORKS: JENA, 1556–1570. 4 Volumes.
The edition is chronologically organized. Each volume gives a list of the titles of the books printed in the specific volume; in vol. 1 the list is at the end, but in vols. 2, 3, and 4 it is at the beginning. Only in the list of vol. 1 are there some minor classifications—for example, "Duae Conciones Lutheri," "Quatuor Epistolae ... Luth.," "Sex Conciones viri Dei, D. M. L." Otherwise the titles are listed as they appear in their respective volumes.

4. GERMAN WORKS: JENA, 1558–1562. 8 Volumes.
This chronologically organized edition is of special importance for our discussion. Each volume has a list of Luther's books printed in that volume; the list is organized by title and date of the original publication of the books. The lists for vols. 1, 2, 3, 5, 6, and 8 (all at the beginning of each volume) are the same as in the earlier Jena German edition. The list for vol. 4 is the same as in the earlier Jena edition (see above, A.2), except for the minor difference that the classification "Three Writings" is not given. (Vol. 7 is missing at Luther Seminary.) As in the first Jena edition, the titles of Luther's German writings (including those now called *Judenschriften*) are listed in vol. 8 according to the title Luther gave them, but without any category or label.

In addition to these lists, the edition has what appears to be the first book-length subject index (in the modern sense of the term). It was prepared by Timothy Kirchner and was printed in 1564 as a separate volume by the publisher of vol. 8: "Index oder Register über die Acht deudsche Tomos ... Gestellet Durch M. Timotheum Kirchnerum." This index was also published in connection with later Jena editions (beginning in 1573; see below, B.2). In 1592 it was reissued as a separate volume with the title: "Index oder Register uber die acht deudsche Tomos / Ersten und andern Drucks / alle Bücher und Schrifften des thewren und seligen Mann Gottes / Doctor Martini Lutheri. Gestellet durch D. Timotheum Kirchnerum," printed at Jena "durch Thobiam Steinman 1592." The Kirchner index is arranged by subjects (two-thirds of the volume) and names (one-third); at the end is a short list of Hebrew, Greek, and Latin words, and a brief index of Scripture passages. In the index of names, under "Abraham" are listed the subjects of promise, faith, circumcision, blessed seed, and Gospel, all vis-à-vis Abraham. Under "Doctor Martinus Luther" some titles of his writings are listed along with some topical sentences. Some of the writings are listed under certain categories; for example: "Erzelung etlicher Artikel darin es D. M. L. zu erst mit dem Bapst gehalten, aber hernach widerruffen etc."; "D. Mart. Luth. verdampt"; "Handlung mit Caietano." Nothing is listed for the Jews. In the index of subjects, references to Jews cannot be found in the entries "Enemies of Christ" or *Lügen*. They can be found scattered in the entries "Circumcision," "Christ's Priesthood," "Ten Commandments," "Law of Nature," "Messiah," "Sabbath," and *Heiden*. *However, in the 220 leaves of the 1564 and 1592 printings of this index there is no entry "Jude ...," and no entry "Judenschrift[en]."*

5. GERMAN WORKS: LEIPZIG, 1729–1740. 22 Volumes.
The edition is organized in twelve "Main Divisions." The first two cover almost all of the first 21 volumes. The third begins in vol. 21 on page 531 and ends on page 687. The remaining nine main divisions can be found in vol. 22 and the supplement section of the *Register* volume.

The third main division is titled "D. Martin Luthers Schrifften wider die Jüdischen und Türckischen Irrthümer." It contains the following writings against "Jewish errors": *Send-Schreiben an einen guten Freund wider die Sabbather A. 1538* (21:531); *Von den Jüden und ihren Lügen. Anno 1543* (544); *Vom Schem Hamphoras und vom Geschlecht Christi* (614); *Das Jesus Christus ein geborner Jude* (646). Then follow two writings against "Turkish errors," beginning with Luther's Preface to *Bruder Richards Verlegung des Alcorans* (657).

For this edition M. Johann Jacob Greiff prepared an index volume (in the modern sense of the term) which was published separately and by another publisher: *Vollständige Register über die XXII Leipziger Teile der gesammten Schriften Des seligen D. Martin Luthers* (Leipzig: Bernhard Christoph Breitkopf, 1740). In the list of Luther's writings we find the category "Writings Against Jewish and Turkish Errors." In the index of subjects ("Real-Register") we find the entry "Jews" (565–570). Here are listed references to Jews in the Old Testament, Jews in the New Testament, Jewish errors, their blasphemy and blindness, conversion of Jews, etc.

This "Register" volume of 1740 is the first index of a Gesammelte Schriften edition that I have seen, in which Luther's writings are classified with reference to Jews: "Writings Against Jewish and Turkish Errors." The term 'Judenschrift' is not used, however. In the index of subjects there are entries pertaining to Jews, but there is no entry "Judenschrift[en]." That term has yet to appear!

B. Herzog August Bibliothek, Wolfenbüttel: Luther: Gesammelte Schriften
The second collection I consulted was *Luther: Gesammelte Schriften* in
the HAB. The card catalogue groups the editions according to site of
publication.

1. WITTENBERG EDITIONS:

Luft Editions: 1539–1551, 4 volumes; 1552–1559, 12 volumes; 1556–
1559, 12 volumes; 1568–1581, 12 volumes.

For the present discussion only vols. 1 and 2 of these four editions are
important. At the end of vol. 1 are indexes to three exegetical writings
(*On Galatians*, 1531/35, *On 1 Corinthians 7*, 1523, *On 1 Corinthians 15*,
1534), in which are various entries of subjects related to Jews, but no entry "Judenschrift[en]." Vol. 2 of all four editions has the subtitle "Darin
alle Streitschriften ..." The "Schriften wider den Türcken" are listed as a
separate group, but there is no separate group of *Streitschriften* for Jews;
hence the term 'Judenschrift[en]' is not used. None of the writings now
called *Judenschriften* are in the 1539–51 edition. They are printed in vol.
5 of the subsequent editions as Luther had titled them and without any
classification.

2. JENA EDITIONS:

1555–558, 8 volumes; see above, A.2.
1558–562, 8 volumes; see above, A.4.
1563–573, 8 volumes; see above, A.2: "Zum 3. mal gedruckt." As in
above, A.4, we find Timothy Kirchner's *Index oder Register*, Jena 1573
(which is the earlier Kirchner index of 1564).
1572–581, 8 volumes; see above, A.2: "Zum 4. mal gedruckt." The index
volume contains the 1573 printing of Kirchner's *Index*.
1585–1606, 8 volumes; see above, A.2: "Zum 5. mal gedruckt." The index volume contains the 1573 printing of Kirchner's *Index*.

3. ALTENBURG EDITION, 1661–1664. 10 Volumes.

In vol. 10 we find the "Haupt Register." Its eleventh and last "Capitul" is
an index of theological subjects arranged "nach den Locis Theologicis"
of Johann Gerhard. "Juden" is listed in locus XXVII: *Von der weltlichen
Obrigkeit*, in subsection *Von den Weltlichen Gesetzen* (esp. 1174–16).

4. LEIPZIG EDITION, 1729–1740. 22 Volumes.
See above, *A*.5.

5. HALLE EDITION, 1740–1753. 24 Volumes (Walch, 1st ed.).
Vol. 20: *Die Schriften wider die Sacramentirer, Fanaticos, Jüden ūnd Turken.* In the third section of this volume we find "Schriften Luthers wider die Juden und Türcken." Vol. 23: *Hauptregister:* Entry: "Jude, Juden." There are references to many topics (for example, "Von der Juden Blindheit, Irrthumen und Unglauben," "Judengenossen," "Jüdisch Reich,""Jüdisch Kirche"), but there is no entry of, or reference to, "Judenschrift[en]."

6. ERLANGEN-FRANKFURT EDITION, 1826–1857. 68 Volumes.

Vols. 66–67: *Alphabetisches Sach-Register über Dr. M. Luther's sämmtliche Schriften in 65 Bänden,* ed. by Johann Konrad Irmischer (Frankfurt/Main: Heyder and Zimmer, 1857). Important are the index of subjects and the index of words. In the "Sachregister" we find many entries pertaining to Jewish matters; for example, "Juden," "Judenthum,""Jüdisches Land." In the "Fünftes Register ... über die ... hebräischen und griechischen Wörter" are listed Hebrew words and their meaning. Among the wealth of materials presented in these index volumes there is *no entry* "Judenschrift[en]."

C. Herzog August Bibliothek, Wolfenbüttel: Luther: Spätere Ausgaben.
The card catalogue of the HAB designates a second category of Luther's collected works as "Spätere Ausgaben." In this group we find the following editions:

1. LEIPZIG, 1844–1846. 22 Volumes.
See above, *A*.5, *B*.4.
2. ST. LOUIS, 1880–1910. 23 Volumes (Walch, 2d ed.).
Vol. 20: *Reformations-Schriften. Zweite Abtheilung. Dogmatisch-Polemische Schriften. B. Wider die Sacramentirer und andere Schwärmer, sowie auch wider die Juden und Türken.* In the two Walch editions (see above, *B*.5), Luther's writings are classified as "against" (*wider*) the Jews, which is the connotation of the label 'Judenschriften'. That label is yet to appear.

Vol. 23 (1910): *Haupt-Sachregister, Spruchregister, Berichtigungen und Nachträge.* The bulk of the 30 columns of references are to "Jews after Christ"; within these are about 18 topics such as "The messiah of Jew and heathen is joy and comfort," "Jews are vexed by the humble form of Christ," "Jews expect a worldly kingdom," "Turks and Jews accuse Christians of praying to three gods," "The general conversion of Jews is not to be hoped for."

3. In this group is also listed WA; it will be discussed below in II.

In sum: "Judenschrift[en]" as a category for classifying some of Luther's writings did not appear in any of the examined collections of Luther's works, or their lists of Luther's writings, or their indexes. The only category that comes close is "Schriften wider." It can be found in vol. 21 of A.5, the Leipzig, 1729–1740 edition and its index volume, prepared by M. Johann Jacob Greiff. It also can be found in vol. 20 of B.5 and C.2, the first and second editions of the Walch edition.

II. 'JUDENSCHRIFT[EN]' IN THE WEIMARER AUSGABE

The first use of the term 'Judenschrift' (singular and plural) can be found in WA 53, published in 1920. The term is used in the introduction to *Von den Juden und jren Lugen* (WA 53:413). On page 413, the editors, Ferdinand Cohrs and Oskar Brenner, refer to *Das Jesus Christus ein geborner Jude sey* as Luther's "erste Judenschrift," and on page 414 they refer to Luther's later "Judenschriften," those published by Luther after *Von den Juden.* Yet in the WA text of *Das Jesus Christus ein geborner Jude sey*, published in 1900 (WA 11:314–336), and of *Wider die Sabbater*, published in 1914 (WA 50:312–337), the term 'Judenschrift' is not used!

In *Von den Juden und jren Lugen* Luther announced another writing (WA 53:513.14–19). In the WA introduction to *Vom Schem Hamphoras* this writing is identified as a "Judenschrift" (WA 53:573). The editors, Cohrs and Brenner, refer to *Von den letzten Worten Davids* (which soon followed *Vom Schem Hamphoras*) as Luther's "letzte Judenschrift" (WA 53:574).

In the WA introduction to *Von den letzten Worten Davids*, "Judenschrift" is used to refer to *Von den Juden und jren Lugen* (WA 54:16) and to *Von den letzten Worten Davids* as Luther's last "Judenschrift." And in WA 54:22, published in 1928, the editor,

Cohrs, lists as the "eigentlichen Judenschriften": *Das Jesus Christus ein geborner Jude sey, Wider die Sabbather, Von den Juden und jren Lugen, Vom Schem Hamphoras,* and *Von den letzten Worten Davids.* It is this list (minus *Wider die Sabbather*), established in 1928, that has become the canon of Luther's *Judenschriften. Von den letzten Worten Davids* belongs "gewissermaßen anhangsweise" to the "Judenschriften" and contains the same harsh judgment as the other "Judenschriften" (WA 54:20). In reference to Luther's *Judenschriften,* Cohrs speaks of Luther's judgment about Reuchlin's "Streit über die Juden" (22), of Luther's sharpest writing "gegen die Juden"—that is, *Von den Juden und jren Lugen* (23)—and of Luther's "Judenstreit" (24).

According to these materials, the designation 'Judenschrift' connotes controversy ("Streit") and writings *against* the Jews ("gegen die Juden"). It is then only natural that Heiko Oberman affirms that Luther's "harsh writings against the Jews" were used in the 1930s to furnish "the historical and religious legitimation for hatred of the Jews."[7]

The category 'Judenschrift[en]' had not been used prior to the WA volumes published in the 1920s. The history of the editing of Luther's writings—to say nothing about the history of Luther interpretation—says more about the editor and interpreter than it does about Luther himself. According to the WA classification, a *Judenschrift* is a *writing against the Jews.* But "writings against Jewish errors"—to say nothing about Jewish *and* Turkish errors—as these writings were called in vol. 21 of the Leipzig edition (1729–1740) and its index volume by Greiff, are not directed against a group of people but against certain theological positions deemed heretical; whoever affirms such heretical positions is totally unimportant.

Kurt Aland in his *Hilfsbuch* (3d ed., 1970; 4th ed., 1996), in the *Schlüssel* to the 22-volume Leipzig edition (see above, A.5) uses "Juden- und Türkenschriften" as a category for Luther's writings printed in vol. 21. Yet the original classification in that volume was "Luthers

---

7 Heiko A. Oberman: "The Nationalist Conscription of Martin Luther," in: *Piety, Politics, and Ethics. Reformation Studies in Honor of George Wolfgang Forell,* ed. by Carter Lindberg (Kirksville, Mo., 1984), 69. Marianne Awerbuch, speaking of Luther as a "Judenfeind," calls the writings "Judenhetzschriften"; see her "Humanismus—Reformation und Judentum," *Jahrbuch für Berlin-Brandenburgische Kirchengeschichte* 55 (1985): 34. And Kurt Meier refers to the writings as "Luthers späten Kampfschriften gegen die Juden"; see his *Kirche und Judentum. Die Haltung der evangelischen Kirche zur Judenpolitik des Dritten Reiches* (Göttingen, 1968), 138.

Schrifften wider die Jüdischen und Türckischen *Irrthümer*." By the time of the third edition of the *Hilfsbuch*, the classification 'Juden- und Türkenschriften' is common coinage. Yet this shift in the classification of a text changes the original into what the classifier or editor supposes or wants the text to be. In the case of Luther's writings we are able to establish their true nature, however, by reading them in the light of their historical and literary setting. Therefore the question is whether the classification 'Judenschrift' is accurate, if the text is judged in light of its literary *Sitz-im-Leben*.

III. LUTHER'S WRITINGS CLASSIFIED AS 'JUDENSCHRIFTEN' READ IN THEIR HISTORICAL CONTEXTS

An examination of Luther's so-called *Judenschriften* in their historical and literary contexts reveals a picture of these writings that is different from that which one perceives on the basis of WA and Aland, and from what is forthcoming in most post-Holocaust agendas vis-à-vis Luther. Of special interest to us is the issue of Luther's intended audience, specifically the questions: Are these so-called *Judenschriften* addressed to Jews? Are these so-called *Judenschriften* writings against Jews?

Among the sixteen categories of Luther's writings, established in WA 61 (1983), we find "Disputationen." In "Disputationen" appears the category "Judenschriften" (WA 61:52) with a numbered list of four writings: *Das Jesus Christus ein geborner Jude sey* (1523); *Von den Juden und jren Lugen D. M. Luth.* (1543); *Von den letzten Worten Davids* (1543); *Vom Schem Hamphoras und vom Geschlecht Christi* (1543). In the following these four books will be examined in the order in which they are listed here, and I will use the original printings.[8]

---

8 A work printed together with Luther's *Von den Juden* and *Vom Schem Hamphoras* (designated as "Judenschriften" in WA 61) in a 1577 edition of Luther's works (*Von den Jüden und iren Lügen. Vom Schem-Hemphoras der Jüden / und von Geschlecht Christi. Wider die Sabbather / und der Jüden Lügen und betrug. Durch D. Martinum Lutherum*) published by Nikolaus Selnecker (Leipzig: Heirs of Jacob Berwald, 1577. HAB Alv.: Ba 109 [1]) is a letter which has the subtitle: *Wider die Sabbather*. I examined the original printing at HAB: *Ein Brief D. Mart. Luther. Wider die Sabbather. An einen guten Freund* (Wittenberg: Nickel Schirlentz, 1538), 31 Bl 8° = WA 50:309: A = HAB Li 5530 SLG HARDT (63,1287). This examination confirmed the decision not to list it among the "Judenschriften" in WA 61 (1983); it is a letter to a friend. Therefore this text will be excluded from the following investigation.

DAS JESUS CHRISTUS EIN GEBORNER JUDE SEY, 1523. In this book[9] Luther answers the charges, leveled against him by the papacy, that he taught the following heresies: Jesus was the son of Joseph and Mary; Mary was not a virgin before and after the birth of Jesus; Mary and Joseph had more children; Christ was of the seed of Abraham.

It is Luther's intention to demonstrate his faith that Christ was born a Jew by a virgin. In this process, directed against the pope, bishops, sophists, and monks, Luther hopes to teach a pure(r) faith to the Jews as well. In effect, Luther is reversing the charges—his accusers are the false teachers; he argues that the Jews have not turned to the Gospel because they have not heard it. Then he demonstrates from Scripture that Jesus must be of human nature but not of the seed of a man under Satan's power; Jesus must be of the seed of a woman under the special work of God. Jesus was born of real flesh and blood by a virgin—not from the evil lust of a man.

In this book traditional Marian piety is reflected. Perhaps instead of a *Judenschrift* this book should be classified as a *Marienschrift* since it contains a beautiful treatment of Mary's virginity (Bi[r-v]). I always thought that Luther avoided the approach to the Incarnation which is reflected in Anselm's *Cur Deus homo* (because it offers reasons for God's actions and because Luther seems quite content to let God do what God does without raising questions). Yet it is striking how vigorously and extensively Luther argues in this book for the *necessity* (according to God's plan) of the virgin birth (Bii[r]). The Anselmian approach of offering reasons for God's actions reflects a very traditional and important purpose for theology in the Middle Ages. The function of theology in this tradition is to offer 'proofs' to those already convinced—proofs in the genre of approbations. Theology operates on the level of the 'fittingness' of something and attempts to demonstrate how it was appropriate for God to do something (*decuit*).[10] And for

---

The "good friend" is Graf Wolf Schlink zu Falkenau. At the beginning (Aii[r]) Luther states that he will give his counsel in the form of a brief letter. He argues that because of their sin the Jews have been for 1500 years exiled from Jerusalem and without temple, worship, priesthood, and political leadership. On the last page (Dii[r]) he states that he has "bestettigt" our faith.

9   Wittenberg, 1523 [Cranach & Döring]. WA 11:308: A = HAB Li 5530. SLG HARDT (40,716).

10   A rule for doctrinal development in the Middle Ages is *potuit, decuit, fecit*. Concerning a doctrinal matter, the medieval theologian asks: (1) Is it possible

Luther the birth of Jesus by a virgin fits into this scheme. He deals
with Scripture passages about the Virgin and affirms the perpetual
virginity of Mary (speaking in terms of traditional Marian piety),
though he points out that Scripture does not speak of her virginity
postpartum (Bii^r). This affirmation of *semper virgo* is a perfect example of theology operating on the level of 'fittingness' (*decuit*). Virginal
conception is typical of the work of God *ex nihilo*, that is, conception
without a man (Cii^r): "Certainly no one can doubt that it is not impossible that God made a maid pregnant without a man *syntemal er auch
alle ding aus nicht gemacht hat.*" (Cii^r). Since we know that God created
out of nothing, it is consistent for God to work the miracle of the birth
of Jesus Christ by a virgin without the cooperation of a man.[11]

In sum: In what amounts to a first part of this book Luther focuses
on Mary, and in what amounts to a second part he focuses on Jesus
Christ as the fulfillment of Old Testament prophecies. *The treatise is
hardly a work against the Jews. It is a Marian work in the theological
genre of decuit— what is appropriate, consistent, typical about God.* The
literary context for the work is Luther's 1521 German rendering of
the *Magnificat*.[12]

(*potuit*)? If yes, then (2) is it becoming of God (*decuit*)? If yes, then the conclusion is (3) it happened (*fecit*). Anselm worked out his view of Atonement
on the level of *decuit*, what is fitting or becoming of God in the framework of
faith seeking understanding. See Burnell Eckardt: *Anselm and Luther on the
Atonement: Was It "Necessary"?* (Lewiston, N.Y., 1992).

11   For Luther justification by faith alone is on the level of 'fittingness'
      (consistency); in essence, Luther is saying that God creates and redeems
      ex nihilo.

12   *Das Magnificat vorteutschet und auszgelegt durch D. Martinum luther Aug.*
      (Wittenberg, 1521 [Melchior Lotther]). 44 B 8° = WA 7:540: A = HAB Li
      5530 SLG HARDT (4,41). Traditional Marian piety appears immediately
      in the preface, to which Luther adds his "aus nichts" theology: God lifts up
      the lowly and the nothings (Mary) of this world and puts down the high and
      haughty. He cites Scripture passages from Daniel and Isaiah similar to those
      cited in *Das Jesus Christus ein geborner Jude sey.* He speaks against the works
      of monastic sects (Biii^r). He emphasizes the mighty works of God with the
      Virgin. The book is, as the title suggests, a rendering in German of the praises
      ("magnification") of God's mighty deeds by the lowly Virgin.

VON DEN JUDEN UND JREN LUGEN D. M. LUTH., 1543. It is significant that Luther on purpose titled this book[13] "Von den Juden und jren Lugen" and not "Wider die Juden und jren Lugen."[14] "Luther wanted, first of all, to strengthen the faith of Christians and refute the blasphemies of the Jews for them."[15] In what amounts to a first part (Aii-Jiii), Luther deals with the privileges about which the Jews brag. In a detailed discussion of rabbinical exegesis of biblical passages, Luther deals in what amounts to a second part (Jiiii-biii) with the messiahship of Jesus Christ. In these two parts, Luther focuses on five major topics, declaring in light of biblical evidence the Jewish positions on these topics to be lies: The Jews in the history of mankind and salvation,[16] circumcision,[17] the law of Moses,[18] the land of Canaan with Jerusalem and the Temple,[19] and the messiah and the piety of Jews who are expecting the messiah yet to come.[20] In what amounts to a third and final part, Luther makes suggestions about what to do with the Jews in light of these lies. Here he makes those statements which eventually placed him at the root of the Holocaust. Brecht pointed out that the first two parts are "kaum mehr bekannt," and whoever knows the secondary literature will affirm this statement. But if one ignores the first two parts and their close connection with this third part, then it is understandable that Luther supposedly wrote a

---

13   Wittenberg: Hans Lufft, 1543. 144 Bl 4° = WA 53:415: A = HAB Li 5530 SLG HARDT (47,852).

14   So according to the opening statements of *Schem Hamphoras* (Aiiʳ).

15   Martin Brecht: *Martin Luther. The Preservation of the Church, 1532–1546*, trans. by James Schaaf (Minneapolis, 1993), 3:341.

16   The Jews are special children of Abraham (Aiiiiʳ); Jews and Gentiles have the same grandparents (up to Ciii); all people share the same familial lineage.

17   Luther emphasizes the circumcision of the heart, repeats the prophetic threat against uncircumcised hearts, and draws a parallel between circumcision and the sacrificial acts of the papists as an *opus legis* or *opus operatum* (Fii, iii).

18   Gii. "Learn, dear Christian," that we cannot keep the law; we are guilty before God; only by pure grace are we forgiven through Christ (through Hiiii).

19   Ji. "Jews, Turks, papists, radicals" all claim to be God's people, boasting of their works (through Jiii).

20   Jiiii. Luther does not want to debate with Jews; he seeks to strengthen the Christian's faith concerning the Messiah (to Kii).

"Hetzschrift."[21] One also violates the principle of interpretation that a text is a unit and has to be interpreted as a whole; one has missed the flow of Luther's argumentation and the issues which are at stake for him. On the basis of Jewish literature[22] and folklore among Jews and Christians, and his own interpretation of biblical texts, Luther deals in parts one and two with theological subjects; he demonstrates that, in light of biblical evidence, Jewish positions are lies which slander the Christian faith and offend the believer. In the third part Luther answers the question: What now? In a Christian community it may not be tolerated that all that is sacred to the believers be slandered; therefore action has to be taken against those who publicly blaspheme the faith. This line of argumentation may be questioned in theological terms. Does there exist something like a Christian community? Does the faith of the Christian need to be defended by means outside of the faith? May such a defense take place and yet the integrity of the faith be preserved? Therefore this third part raises theological questions and also questions about Luther's judgment.[23]

At the beginning of the book, Luther underscores that he wishes neither to speak with the Jews (later he calls it "disputiren"; Ki[r]) nor try to convert them. He understands his book to be an answer to questions Christians might have about Jewish matters and as a strengthening of the Christian's faith (Aiii[v]). The book deals with matters pertaining to Jews, yet according to the author's stated purpose, it is *not addressed to Jews—it is addressed to Christians*; if one wishes to press the point one could suggest that it is directed to the questions Christians might

---

21   See Awerbuch in n. 7.

22   In addition to Lyra (see n. 26), Luther derived his knowledge about the Jews from Antonius Margaritha's book, *Der ganz Jüdisch Glaub* (Augsburg, 1530), and Porchetus Salvaticus's book (see also n. 61), *Victoria adversus impios Hebraeos* (Paris, 1520).

23   Brecht's summary (3:346f.) is worth considering: "It is obvious how Luther was ultimately contending in this book for his faith in Christ. At the same time there is a deep contradiction in his argumentation that is apparent: He wanted to defend his non-violent Christ with the power of the Christian state. His bias in favor of the existing political and social system of evangelical Christianity of that time induced him to suggest completely inappropriate, even dangerous measures. Because of his fear and hate, there was little room for confidence and love. The weaknesses and false consequences of Luther's piety, which drew sharp distinctions, are nowhere more clearly visible than here."

have as a result of certain Jewish positions. Thus the classification of this book among the "Schriften wider"— found, for example, in the first and second edition of the Walch edition of Luther's works—is contrary to Luther's stated purpose. In the light of medieval precedent, Luther could not write against the Jews since they were heretics, and one does not reason with heretics. As David Bagchi reminds us in his book on the Roman Catholic controversialists against Luther,[24] authority does not argue with a heretic.

In attempting to discover the genre of this book in its historical setting, certain words are important, and so is the way in which Luther works with one of his sources. Throughout the book, Luther uses the following words and phrases: prove ("*beweisen*"), strengthen ("*stercken*") the Christian faith; honor and strengthen ("*ehren und stercken*"); strengthened and made (or be) certain ("*gesterckt und gewis*"); strongest proof ("*sterckest beweist*") for the Christian faith.[25] These key words suggest that Luther is concerned with proving the correctness of the Christian faith and strengthening the faith of the individual believer. Luther addresses Christians on matters which in his opinion are important to them. That these matters are raised because there are Jews around is of secondary importance. But the book as a whole is not written for or against Jews but for Christians. It is an *apologia* for the Christian faith addressed to Christians for the purpose of strengthening, building up, and defending the faith, a faith which is sorely

---

24   David V. N. Bagchi: *Luther's Earliest Opponents, Catholic Controversialists, 1518–1525* (Minneapolis, 1991). The controversialists feared that their writings might be construed as an attempt to debate with a heretic. They "were fully aware of the tradition that heretics were not to be reasoned with but simply confronted with the choice of either submitting to the church's authority or rejecting it and therefore, as it were, condemning themselves. But in supplying *auctoritas* with *rationes*, the controversialists could be seen as bringing these matters into dispute. The resulting tension was expressed by Eck when, in 1523, he urged the pope to issue a new bull of condemnation to take account of Protestant heretics other than Luther." Eck affirmed the convention that legal judgments never contained reasoned opinions so that they would not invite arguments and so lessen the authority of the court. "But was there not a greater risk to the Curia's authority, he wondered, if such reasons were again to be omitted from such a bull, as they had been from *Exsurge Domine?*" See Bagchi, 250f.

25   See, e.g., Aiii^v, Ki^r, Miiii^v, Oiii^v, Piii^r, Piiii^r, Tiii^v.

offended by certain Jewish positions. This quality becomes even clearer when we consider the way Luther works with one of his sources. Luther uses and cites *Contra perfidiam Judaeorum* by Nicholas of Lyra, a book written in the medieval genre of a *defensio fidei*.[26] He argues that Lyra's description of the apostasy of the Jews is a "right, good, and strong argument" (Tiiiiᵛ). Jeremy Cohn states that Lyra began *De Iudeorum perfidia*—Cohen prefers to call it *Quodlibetum de adventu Christi* since this title does not highlight the polemical tone—as a scholastic discourse in 1309 and revised it in the 1330s.[27]

According to Lyra, the first question derived from "the Scriptures of the Jews" was: can it be proved effectively that our Savior was God and man ("possit efficaciter probari salvatorem nostrorum fuisse deum et hominem"); the second was: can it be proved that the incarnation of the divine person, thus that the messiah promised in the law and prophets, is true God and true man ("verus deus et verus homo"); and the third was: whether the time of the incarnation is past (or whether the Messiah is yet to come).[28] In *De Iudeorum perfidia*, Lyra deals with these questions at great length (and also with others) by developing proofs and lengthy arguments for his answers. A key word in his presentation is *probatio* (proof). In medieval theology, the offering of *probationes* had the purpose of strengthening those who believed; they were not offered as means to prove the faith to nonbelievers.[29] Cohen affirms the contention of Bernhard Blumenkranz and Herman

---

26 Nicolaus de Lyra: "Contra perfidiam Judaeorum," in: *Biblia Latina cum postillis Nicolai de Lyra* (Venice: Johann von Köln & Nicolas Jenson, 1481): "Incipit libellus editus per magister Nicolaum de lyra ordinis minorum theologie professorem in quo sunt pulcherrime questiones iudaicam perfideam in catholica fide improbantes" (4:1566ʳ–1570ʳ). For this text, see also below, n. 28. —Peter of Blois, known as a twelfth-century English humanist and political thinker, also wrote a treatise *Contra perfidiam Judaeorum* (Migne: *Patrologia Latina*, 207:825). Lyra's "second anti-Jewish polemical treatise" was titled *Responsio ad quemdam Iudeum ex verbis Evangelii secundum Matheum contra Christum nequiter arguentem* of 1334; see Jeremy Cohen: *The Friars and the Jews. The Evolution of Medieval Anti-Judaism* (Ithaca, 1982), 185.

27 See Cohen, *The Friars and the Jews*, 180–91.

28 *Biblia Latina* (Venice, 1481), 4:1566ʳ, 1567ᵛ, 1569ʳ. The treatise is also located in the back of the Basel Bibles (see below, IV); there the three questions are found on fols. 275ᵛ, 276ᵛ, and 277ᵛ of vol. 6.

29 *Probatio* in medieval Latin means approbation; see Lewis and Short, *A Latin Dictionary*, s.v. Quintilian argues that in rhetoric, *probatio* is also called

Hailperin that Lyra's *Quodlibetum*, that is, his *Contra perfidiam Judaeorum*, should not be classified as anti-Jewish since there were no Jews in France at the time that Lyra authored this text; the book was written for the internal use of Christians rather than for a missionary program (and we might add, an anti-Jewish program).[30]

Throughout Luther's text we find repeatedly the word "beweisen." One may suggest, then, that Luther's book is an *apologia* in the medieval genre of *probatio*, directed toward believers for the purpose of giving them reasons and proofs for their faith which is challenged from the outside,[31] that is, by what Luther has tried to prove, namely, the lies of the Jews. If one compares Lyra's text with that of Luther, it becomes clear that many of Luther's questions and points are also treated by Lyra. And Luther does not hesitate to use Lyra's materials and give him credit.[32] In terms of genre, *Von den Juden und jren Lugen* is an *apologia*, or more precisely, a *probatio*-based *defensio fidei* in the vein of Lyra's *Contra perfidiam Judaeorum*. It is an argument concerning certain articles of the Christian faith that arises when that faith is confronted with certain Jewish positions or arguments. The book is Christian apologetic in the medieval sense of giving proofs (confirmation) to those already convinced for the purpose of bolstering their faith — however strong or, more likely, weak that faith may be.[33]

The only connection between *Von den Juden und jren Lugen* and *Das Jesus Christus ein geborner Jude sey* is the genre of proof. (In *Das Jesus Christus ein geborner Jude sey* the proof concerns the virginity of Mary.)

---

confirmatio or *fides orationis*, in which the orator enumerates his arguments (ibid.).

30   Cohen, *The Friars and the Jews*, 187, 190.

31   See James J. Murphy: *Rhetoric in the Middle Ages. A History of Rhetorical Theory from Saint Augustine to the Renaissance* (Berkeley, 1981), 13: Cicero: "*Confirmatio* or proof is the part of the oration which by marshaling arguments lends credit, authority, and support to our case."

32   E.g., Aii, Tiiii^v, hiii^v, dii^v.

33   See Heinrich Lausberg: *Handbuch der literarischen Rhetorik. Eine Grundlegung der Literaturwissenschaft* (Munich, 1960), 190: "Die πίστις ... *argumentatio* ... *quaestiones* ... *probatio* ... *confirmatio* ... *confirmation* ... dient der Herstellung der Glaubwürdigkeit ... des vertretenen Parteistandpunktes: ... *confirmatio est, per quam argumentando nostrae causae fidem et auctoritatem et firmamentum adiungit oratio.*" (The material in the ellipses are references to classical authors.)

Both books are "theological treatises"[34] in which Luther treated topics—virgin birth, circumcision, law, Messiah—which he treated also in many of his other writings without mentioning Jews at all. Hence the classification of *Von den Juden und jren Lugen* as a 'Judenschrift' gives the wrong impression. For this book to be a *Judenschrift* it should be addressed to Jews and be a writing against them. Neither is the case unless one separates the last part from the first two parts and reads it separately. I seek neither to exonerate nor condemn Luther for this third part. My point is that, while as a result of this third part, the book as a whole is painted in negative terms, in terms of genre the book may not be understood as a *Hetzschrift*.[35] It has to be understood as a Christian apologetic in the medieval genre of *probatio*; that is where the document fits historically. The book should not be understood as background to Jewish-Christian relations of twentieth-century Germany.

VON DEN LETZTEN WORTEN DAVIDS, 1543. The issue in this book[36] is the rabbinical exegesis of 2 Sam. 23:1–7 and the impact of that exegesis on the Christian faith. In contrast to that exegesis, Luther develops his own exegesis. His goal is to demonstrate that the rabbinical exegesis distorts the Word of God and to prove that Christians have the truth from God's Word.

In the opening sections, Luther discusses problems connected with translations of the Bible and the Jewish argument that Christians do not have the proper biblical texts. Then he develops an *expositio* on the Trinity (Giii, iiii) by means of a trinitarian reading of biblical passages along the line of expounding, explaining, giving theological comments, and meditating. He begins with 2 Sam. 23:1–3 and discusses the Holy Spirit as an article of faith (Ci). He argues that the Last Words of David confess the highest article, the three indistinguishable

---

34   So Wilhelm Maurer; see his "Die Zeit der Reformation," in: *Kirche und Synagogue: Handbuch zur Geschichte von Christen und Juden. Darstellung mit Quellen*, ed. by Karl Rengstorf and Siegfried von Kortzfleisch (Stuttgart, 1968), 1:363–452, esp. 388f., 407. For a discussion of Maurer's presentation, see Mark U. Edwards: "Against the Jews," in: *Essential Papers on Judaism and Christianity in Conflict*, ed. by Jeremy Cohen (New York, 1991), 366.

35   See n. 7.

36   Wittenberg: Nickel Schirlentz, 1543. 84 Bl 8° = WA 54:26: A II = HAB Li 5530 SLG HARDT (8,126).

persons in God (Ciii^v, Di). Then he comments on 2 Sam. 7:11–16 and 1 Chron. 17:11–14 (Di^v-ii^r), and the three persons in God (Dii) are at the center of his comments. The Trinity is the key to the *expositio*: Father; Son, the builder of the eternal house (1 Chron. 17:12), the church;[37] Scripture (words of the prophets) spoken by the Holy Spirit. Combining Isaiah, chap. 9, with 1 Chron. 17:11–14, Luther argues that Isaiah and David agree with the New Testament affirmation that Christ is the eternal king (Fii^r). He says he will bring in other texts (which he has been doing all along the way) to support the Christology of David's Last Words in order to strengthen ("stercken") our faith (Hiii^v-iiii^r). Luther's overriding goal is to strengthen and confess ("zu stercken und zu bekennen") the trinitarian faith of the believer (Ki^r, Lii^r). He is very careful and extensive in his comments on the nature and work of the individual persons of the Trinity, but the distinctions of the persons always lead to the unity of the Trinity.[38] When Luther comes to summarize this little book at the end (Tiiii), he repeats his main theme: there are three speakers, the Spirit of the Lord, the God of Israel, and the Rock of Israel, and yet there is only one speaker.

In his preface Luther complains about the old and new Hebraists (those who follow the rabbis too closely, the *Buchstabilisten*). In the last folio he warns about rabbis and the false interpretation of Scripture, and about the enemies of Christ, Jews, Mohammed, pope, and false spirits. If only this material of *Von den letzten Worten Davids* were read, then the point of the whole would be missed; this book could hardly be understood as an attack on Jews. In terms of genre, the book as a whole is a thoroughgoing *expositio* of a theological topic, the Trinity, which is based on a detailed exegesis of the Last Words of David and a collage of biblical passages.

VOM SCHEM HAMPHORAS UND VOM GESCHLECHT CHRISTI, 1543. The book[39] is divided into two parts. They are held together by three

---

37 The fact that the Temple in Jerusalem lies in ashes for fifteen hundred years proves (Luther uses "beweisen") that "house" does not designate that temple (Eiii).

38 Luther cites Augustine approvingly (Pi, Qiiii, Si): "Opera trinitatis ad extra sunt indivisa."

39 Wittenberg: Georg Rhaw, 1543. WA 53:575: A II = HAB Li 5530 SLG HARDT (2,21).

facts: Jesus Christ is the subject matter of both parts; the connection of the book with *Von den Juden und jren Lugen* (where Luther announced that he would deal with the *Schem Hamphoras*);[40] Luther's sources. This last point is important. In preparation for *Von den Juden und jren Lugen* Luther had studied Margaritha's book on the Jewish faith, and also another book, *Victoria adversus impios Hebraeos*, by a Carthusian monk named Porchetus Salvaticus (d. ca. 1315).[41] In both books Luther found the Jewish legend that Jesus cunningly got hold of the Schem Hamphoras (the ineffable, powerful name of God as encoded in a Cabbalistic speculation on letters derived from Exod. 14:19–21); therefore he was able to commit all sorts of miracles and other actions until the Jewish authorities caught and executed him as a sorcerer. In the first part of *Schem Hamphoras* Luther dealt with this legend. The second part of the book was the result of a no longer extant response to Luther's *Wider die Sabbather*;[42] in this response apparently the differing genealogies of Jesus found in Matthew, chap. 1, and Luke, chap. 3, were used in an effort to nullify the biblical basis for the affirmation that Jesus was the messianic offspring of the House of David. In the second part of *Schem Hamphoras* Luther dealt with this situation. In both parts Jesus Christ, his messiahship, and his birth by the Virgin were the central subject matters.

On the first page (Aii^r) Luther sets the same stage as in *Von den Juden und jren Lugen*: He does not intend to write against the Jews as if he hoped to convert them; there is no reason ever to hope that all the Jews could be converted. Rather, he wishes to instruct and warn Christians about certain Jewish subjects, and he wants to strengthen and honor ("stercken," "ehren") the faith of Christians. On Aiii begins a translated quotation from the book by Porchetus, *Victoria adversus impios Hebraeos*, in which the legend about Jesus and the *Schem Hamphoras* is recorded. Then Luther exposes these materials and their basis in Cabbalistic speculation to a loosely structured critique (Ciiii–Dii). He seeks to demonstrate the origin of the Cabbalistic speculations about the name of God and to point out that the Cabbala is sorcery which any proper interpretation of Scripture can unmask (Fii). Toward the end of this first part, Luther develops a theological

---

40   *Von den Juden*, biiii^v.

41   See also n. 22. Luther's notes in the margins of the book by Porchetus (Paris, 1520) are available; see WA 60:236–39.

42   See n. 8.

discourse about the name of God and closes with a rather extensive trinitarian theme (Fiii^v-Giii).

This first part may be considered to be a *quodlibetum*, a discussion of a specific topic (the legend of Jesus and the Schem Hamphoras) which crossed the author's desk; it is written for the purpose of setting the record straight, of instructing and warning the reader. Luther feels that Christians need to know about this legend and need to be warned of this "Teufelsmist."

Das ander Teil, Vom Geschlecht Christi is also *quodlibetum*. Built around *expositio, probatio,* and *assertio,* this part is more tightly structured than the first one. If one takes both parts together, it becomes clear that Luther, for the purpose of instructing and warning his fellow Christians and strengthening their faith (Piii^v), writes a theological treatise about Jesus Christ because in Jewish literature a picture of Christ had been developed which slanders the faith of the believer and is therefore unacceptable to Christians.

The issue in this second part is the geneology of Jesus and thus his messiahship. There are differences between the geneology reported in Matthew and in Luke; further, Mary was not listed as being a member of the House of David. Therefore, presumably, Jesus' lineage was not purely Davidic. Luther makes short shrift of rabbinical exegesis; on the basis of the Old Testament prophecies, Matt. 1:1, and other passages, for Luther Jesus' birth by the Virgin, his David-sonship, the Davidic lineage of Mary, and thus Jesus' messiahship, are givens—case closed.

In the closing paragraph of this book, Luther says he wants no further dealings with the Jews nor write any more about or against them ("noch weiter von jnen oder wider sie schreiben, Sie habens gnug"); may God give his grace that a few might turn so that we all may praise God the Father, together with our Lord Jesus Christ and the Holy Spirit (Qiiii^r). Yet in the preceding paragraph Luther announces that he "soon" will deal with the rabbinical exegesis of the Last Words of David, a passage so important for Christ's messiahship (Qiii). Thus at the end Luther makes clear that for him the overarching issue in this book is the understanding of biblical texts in general, rabbinical exegesis in particular. He feels so strongly about this that he has to write another book, his *Von den letzten Worten Davids.*

At the beginning of this second part of *Schem Hamphoras* (Giiii^r), Luther states that his purpose is to answer the Jews and to write about the Jews ("von den Juden"). His goal is to show that Mary is of the stem of Juda and the house of David (even though Matthew develops the Joseph lineage), since Jesus is the Messiah who must be of the House of David. In the style of a *quodlibetum*, Luther deals with several topics, but he concentrates on the affirmation that Mary must be of the house of David because Jesus is the Messiah. In order to prove his point, he develops a detailed *expositio* of Moses and the Messiah.[43] And then he returns to the *assertio* that Mary is of the house of David (Kiii^{r,v}). He uses the method of question, answer, and proof to state his main point—that Mary and Joseph are of one house, namely, the house of David (Kiii^{r,v}, Kiiii, Li^r, Li^v, Lii^v). Luther's materials lead to two articles of faith (*assertio*): Jesus is Messiah, Mary is a virgin (Liiii, Miii^r). In connection with these articles of faith, Luther assures his reader that he will do as he had stated earlier: leave the Jews alone, but strengthen and adorn ("stercken und schmücken") the Christian's faith (Nii^v, Piii^v).

Part One of *Vom Schem Hamphoras* is a *quodlibetum* on the Trinity. Part Two is a *quodlibetum* on Mary's familial lineage and Jesus as Messiah. The overarching issue in both parts is the interpretation of biblical texts by Jews and by Luther, and the consequences which arise from the Jewish interpretation for the faith of the individual Christian. I find myself not being as adamant about this work not being a Judenschrift. Luther himself in the closing paragraph speaks of writing about and against the Jews. Luther has Jews, that is, Jewish exegesis and all its claims, in mind when he writes this book. But foremost he has in mind the faith of the Christian. Luther seeks both to confront Jewish claims, claims which in his eyes are false, and strengthen the faith of Christians. But then confronting false theological claims and strengthening the Christians' faith are not restricted to the so-called *Judenschriften*!

I have read the original printings of Luther's four writings, listed as "Judenschriften" in WA 61: *Inhaltsverzeichnis*, in the order listed there. If one places these writings into their medieval context, then their genre is determined by the terms *decuit, expositio, probatio, assertio*, and *quodlibetum*. The modern classification 'Judenschriften' does not do justice to the genre of these writings if they are read in their

---

43   In the margin of page Ii^v of the HAB copy a reader noted: "Expositio verborum Mose ...." That note is accurate; the following pages (Ii^v to Ki) are indeed an *expositio* on the Messiah.

medieval context, free from any modern baggage. These so-called *Judenschriften* are not directed against, or addressed to, Jews. These writings are Christian apologetic for Christians.

How did Luther himself view these writings? How did he speak about them, specifically regarding their content as being "about" Jews, or "against" Jews, or "addressed to" Jews? In the opening sentence of *Von den Juden* Luther says he had decided "nichts mehr von den Juden noch wider die Juden zu schreiben." Such writing before *Von den Juden*, in the usual *Judenschrift* classification, would be *Das Jesus Christus ein geborner Jude sey*, which we have shown above to be a *Marienschrift*, if it must be classified.[44] In the beginning of *Vom Schem Hamphoras*, Luther states that he wrote *von* and not *wider den Juden* earlier and that likewise in the present treatise (*Vom Schem Hamphoras*) he wishes not to write *wider* the Jews. However, at the end of *Vom Schem Hamphoras* he states: "noch weiter von jnen [Jews] oder wider sie schreiben, Sie habens gnug." I take Luther at his word, namely, that he did not write *wider* the Jews in either of the 1543 treatises, and that this phrase "noch weiter von ... oder wider" at the end of *Vom Schem Hamphoras* is a sign-off sentence, meaning that he does not want to write any more on the subject addressed in the treatise; by this sign-off phrase he has not changed the genre of two treatises.

There is one more place (that I know of) where Luther stated—supposedly—that he had written a book against the Jews. In a table talk recorded by Heydenreich (1542/43) Luther stated: "O, die Hebraei— ich sag auch von den unsern—judentzen sehr; drumb habe ich sie auch in eo libello, scripsi contra Judaeos, auch gemeint." The text is entry No. 588 in Ernst Kroker, ed.: *Luthers Tischreden in der Mathesischen Sammlung. Aus einer Handschrift der Leipziger Stadtbibliothek* (Leipzig, 1903). In the introduction (64), Kroker identifies the "little book" with *Von den Juden und jren Lugen*. He argues that the booklet cannot be *Vom Schem Hamphoras* since that work appeared at the very beginning of 1543. This certainly is a peculiar argument. Why could *eo libello* not be identical with *Vom Schem Hamphoras* since the collection deals with materials from 1542/43? Besides, *Von den Juden* is hardly a "little book"! In any case, Kroker makes Luther contradict himself. In the opening of *Schem Hamphoras* Luther clearly stated that his last book (*Von den Juden*) was not against the Jews but about the Jews (and this

---

44 WA 54:22f. lists *Wider die Sabbather* among the "eigentlichen Judenschriften." See n. 8.

applies also to *Schem Hamphoras*). In his introduction (64) Kroker also states that the Mathesius collection contains "Nachschriften Heydenreiches, Besolds und Wellers" and that they "probably" do not "wesentlich" differ. These qualifiers (probably and essentially) do not specify anything, neither does the phrase "little book" prove anything. Such historical difficulties always accompany statements made in Luther's *Table Talk*. The standard rule in Luther scholarship is that a table talk can be used to supplement something known for a fact in the known works of Luther. That fact in this case is lacking. So nothing from Luther himself has changed the thesis here, namely, that Luther wrote to Christians "about" Jewish matters; he did not write *Judenschriften* against Jews or addressed to Jews.

Cast in modern terms, these treatises are a scholarly *Auseinandersetzung* in a pastoral frame. It is beside the point that we reject the rhetoric of one of the participants in this *Auseinandersetzung*— though we probably are not very familiar with the rhetoric of the other participant. Who still reads the book by Margaritha or Porchetus, or the Toldoth Jeschu writings, and tries to imagine how a sixteenth-century Christian must have felt when he read these materials? In his writings, Luther addresses Jewish claims and practices, but he does the same in other treatises not classified as 'Judenschriften'. The category 'Judenschrift[en]' is a device to systematize Luther's writings for the convenience of the modern edition, a device which turns these writings into something which they are not if one reads them with medieval genre in mind.

IV. LUTHER AND THE BIBLES PUBLISHED BY FROBEN IN 1501–1502 AND 1506–1508

At the beginning of vol. 1[45] of the Bibles published by John Froben in Basel in 1501–1502 and 1506–1508, we find texts in the genre

---

45 The front matter of vol. 1 of the 1501 Froben Bible contains the following: 1ᵛ: Froben's letter of dedication, where he announces the content of the following: interlinear and marginal glosses, the *postilla* of Lyra, the *additiones* of Burgos, *cum replicis* of Doering; 2ʳ: *De libris biblie canonicis et non canonicis*; 2ᵛ: *Translatores Biblie*; 3ʳ: In nomine sancte trinitatis: incipit *prologus primus venerabilis fratris Nicolai de Lyra ordinis seraphici Francisci: de commendatione sacre scripture in generali*; 3ᵛ: Incipit *prologus secundus de intentione auctoris et modo procendendi*; 4ʳ: *Venerabilis fratris Nicoli de lyra in moralitates biblie prologus*; 4ᵛ: Additiones ad postilam magistri Nicolai de lyra super biblia; 8ᵛ: Incipit *prologus in replicas defensivas postilile venerabilia ac [=in Replicas]*; 9ᵛ: Expositio

of questions on the nature and content of Scripture and in the genre of praise of Scripture. The first text is Froben's letter in praise of the biblical text, the whole page of divine history, which is called the Bible. The second is a treatise which deals with the problem of the canonical and non-canonical books. The third is a treatise which deals with translations of the Bible (Septuagint, Vulgata, and other texts involving Hebrew, Greek, and Latin). The fourth is Lyra's *De commendatione sacrae scripturae*. The fifth is Lyra's *De intentione auctoris et modo procedendi*.[46] Then follow prologues to Scripture by Lyra, Burgos, and Doering.

In vol. 6 of the two Basel Bibles, after the Explicit to the Apocalypse, we find Lyra's *Contra perfidiam Iudaeorum*.[47] In vol. 6 of the 1508 Basel Bible appears Lyra's "second anti-Jewish polemical treatise."[48] In terms of the position of both texts in the whole of the Bible and in terms of genre, both texts are a *defensio fidei* in the sense of a *probatio* of the truth recorded on the many preceding pages, especially the Old Testament.

---

epistolae sancti Hieronymi (itself glossed); 19ᵛ: Incipit *prologus sancti Hieronymi presbyteri in pentateuchum moyse*; 21ᵛ: *Prothemata glose ordinarie*; 23ʳ: Incipit *postilla Nicolai de Lyra super librum Genesis.*—The front matter is the same in vol. 1 of the 1506 Froben Bible.

46 Lyra deals here with the problem of how to read the intention of Scripture, that is, its literal and mystical senses. He develops the rule that what is written in Scripture is written about Christ and his mystical body, the church, because of the connection of the head (Christ) to the body of sacred Scripture.

47 The title printed in the Basel Bibles is *Libellus eiusdem venerabilis patris Nicolai de Lyra continens pulcherrimas questiones iudaicam perfidiam in catholica fide improbantes* (fols. 275ᵛ to 279ᵛ). Lyra's treatise was widely printed in Bibles "with Commentary." (See Hans Rost: *Die Bibel im Mittelalter* [Augsburg, 1939], 371f.) The library of the University of Würzburg has nine Bibles with Lyra's postils printed before 1500, and each contains Lyra's treatise; see Ilona Huray: *Incunabula der Universitätsbibliothek Würzburg* (Wiesbaden, 1966), 86–89.

48 See n. 26 for the title of the treatise (6:280ʳ–285ʳ). Although Cohen describes Lyra's two treatises as "Anti-Jewish" (*The Friars and the Jews*, 180–91), he notes that Lyra "sets out to prove three fundamental doctrines of Christianity" (188) regarding the incarnation, Trinity, and Christology. Lyra does this for a Christian audience. In this process he makes "frequent reference ... to the absurd beliefs of the rabbis" (189). Note that in the first paragraph of the second treatise, Lyra seeks to exhort "fideles in sana doctrina" and to argue against "infidels" (f. 280ʳ).

Working through the Froben Bible, I saw a remarkable similarity between the front and back matter of these Bibles and some of the materials Luther wrote on Scripture and in the books classified by modern editors as 'Judenschriften'. To put it imaginatively: As Luther studied this Bible,[49] he read in vol. 1 treatises in the genre of questions (*quodlibetum*) people might have about the nature of Scripture, and also in the genre of praise of Scripture. And in vol. 6 he read Lyra's *Contra perfidiam Iudaeorum*. He saw that the Bible did not begin with Genesis—Genesis begins on folio 23^v—but with a series of texts authored by the giants of biblical studies, Nicholas of Lyra, Paul of Burgos, and Matthias Doering, and before them Jerome. He found that the biblical text needs glosses and comments (*Glossa ordinaria et interlinearis*, Lyra's postil, Burgos's additions, and Doering's replies). And finally he was confronted with the fact that the Bible did not end with Revelation but with a treatise in which Lyra proves (*probatio*) the truth of the biblical message over against the Jews.—Soon Luther himself would join these illustrious authors!

In terms of genre, Luther's *A Brief Instruction on What to Look for and Expect in the Gospels*[50] (published in connection with the *Wartburg Postil*), his prefaces to the Old and the New Testament and to individual biblical books, including the Apocrypha, in *Das Neue Testament*

49 Gottfried Edel lists the 1498 Basel Bible (Froben and Petri) which contains Lyra's *Contra perfidiam Judaeorum* as a Bible used by Luther; see his *Das gemeinkatholische mittelalterliche Erbe beim jungen Luther. Beiträge zu einer methodischen Grundlegung* (Marburg, 1962), 25. The Froben Bibles of 1501–02 and 1506–08 were a continuation of what Edel calls the "Glossenbibel" of 1498, known and used by Luther (Edel, 26). The 1498 Basel Bible is a 6-volume edition, with the *Glossa ordinaria*, Jerome's prologues, Lyra's *Postilla*, Burgos's *Additiones*, and Doering's *Replices*, the texts which we find then again in the 1501–02 and 1506–08 Bibles. Peter Bietenholz (under Nicolaus of Lyra, *Opus totius Biblie cum glosa ordinaria et expositione Lyre*, Basel: Petri & Froben, 1498) lists the Basel Bibles of 1501–02 and 1506–08 as "reprints" of the 1498 edition; see his *Basle and France in the Sixteenth Century, The Basle Humanists and Printers in Their Contacts with Francophone Culture* (Geneva, 1971), 315. Furthermore, Sachiko Kusukawa (*A Wittenberg University Library Catalogue of 1536* [Binghamton, 1995], 17) lists the 1508 Froben and Petri Bible as present in Luther's Wittenberg University library along with Lyra's *Postillae Nicolai de Lyra ... cum libello contra judaica perfidia*, printed in Venice 1489.

50 *Ein Kleiner Unterricht, was man in den Evangelien suchen und erwarten soll*, 1522; WA 10.I.1:8–18.

Deudsch and in *Biblia Deudsch*, were parallels to what Luther had read in vol. 1 of the Froben Bible. Though their format differs, the marginal notes which we find in *Das Neue Testament Deudsch* and throughout *Biblia Deudsch* were parallels to the glosses he had read in the *Biblia Latina*. And his postils have to be considered parallels to Lyra's *Postilla*. For his extensive literary output in connection with the German version of the Bible, Luther used the genres of medieval biblical scholarship. Therefore it should not surprise us that Luther also created parallels to Lyra's *defensio fidei* vis-à-vis the Jews, which he had read in vol. 6 of the Froben Bible.

An old tradition links Lyra with Luther: "Nisi Lyra lyrasset, Lutherus non saltasset." Unfortunately the origin of this pun on Lyra's name is not known.[51] Luther refers to Lyra frequently throughout his writings. In his *First Lecture on the Psalms* (1513 to 1515) he refers to Lyra several dozen times, and by an overwhelming margin favorably. On the other hand, in his *Lecture on Romans* (1515–1516) his attitude toward Lyra is generally negative. By the last decade of his life, Luther's attitude has changed again. In his *Lecture on Genesis* Luther refers to Lyra over one hundred times, generally favorably. The passage most often cited by those who wish to show Luther's attitude toward Lyra comes from these lectures: "I prefer him to almost all other interpreters of Scripture."[52]

Luther used the medieval genre of *defensio fidei* when he was confronted with particular issues raised by Jews, which had an impact on the Christian's faith. In terms of genre, his so-called *Judenschriften* were, then, nothing new. He also used some of the materials which he had found in Lyra's *defensio fidei* and gave credit to his source.[53] With his own writings he placed himself in line with the medieval tradition

---

51   For this paragraph, see "Lyra's Influence on Luther" in the forthcoming volume entitled *The Postilla of Nicholas of Lyra on the Song of Songs*, ed. by James G. Kiecker, published by Marquette University Press in the series "Reformation Texts With Translation (1350–1650)." Edel suggests (85) that the Luther-Lyra verse is probably an adaptation (by someone after Luther's time) from Cornelius à Lapide (1567–1637) who supposely said: "Si Lyra non lyrasset, nemo doctorum in Bibliam saltasset."

52   *Luther's Works.* American Edition, 55 vols. (St. Louis, 1955–1986), 2:164 (WA 42:377.17f.).

53   See n. 26.

of biblical scholarship and in his own way met his professional responsibility as a doctor of the church and as a *Seelsorger*.

V. CONCLUSION

Work for this project has been done independently of modern secondary literature on Luther and the Jews, though an extensive bibliography has been consulted.[54] Secondary literature ranges in claims from conclusions that nothing new is to be found in Luther on the Jews, that everything he said and proposed about Jews was a medieval repeat,[55] to conclusions that Luther was the arch anti-Semite paving the way for Hitler.[56] The difficulty with secondary literature is that most of it assumes that Luther produced a specific body of writings against the Jews that has been so-classified in modern editions. If, as the above attempts to show, no such body of writings exists, and Luther did not produce a body of 'Judenschriften' as classified by modern interpreters and editors, then nothing is to be gained by an extensive discussion of such literature.

Heiko Oberman[57] and John Kleiner[58] worked on the topic 'Luther and the Jews' in Luther's own historical milieu rather than the contemporary context. While Oberman downplays the economic factors to explain the plight of Jews in early modern Europe, and Kleiner seeks to play up such factors, both seek to describe the situation in late medieval terms, without having to apologize for or denounce Luther.

---

54 An unpublished bibliography (deposited at the Department of Theology, Marquette University, Milwaukee, WI) of over 500 primary and secondary sources on Luther and the Jews has been prepared by Olaf Roynesdal for private circulation.

55 See Marc Saperstein: *Moments of Crisis in Jewish-Christian Relations* (London, 1989), 41.

56 See Simon Markish: *Erasmus and the Jews*, trans. by Anthony Olcott (Chicago, 1986), 152.

57 Heiko A. Oberman: "Three Sixteenth-Century Attitudes to Judaism: Reuchlin, Erasmus and Luther," in: *Jewish Thought in the Sixteenth Century*, ed. by Bernard Dov Cooperman (Cambridge, 1983), 326–64. Oberman recognized the plight of post-Holocaust historiography and argued (328): "At this point it is high time to abandon our concern with the historian and turn to history."

58 John W. Kleiner: "Martin Luther and the Jews," *Consensus* 19.1 (1993): 109–26.

Their contributions gave me courage to go public with the results of my examination of the sources.

Through my work on Luther's commentaries on Galatians, I became aware of the questionable handling of Luther's commentaries on Scripture.[59] This result raised the question about other classifications of Luther's writings at the hands of modern editors, namely, that of the *Judenschriften*. The goals of the preceding materials were to exclude modern classifications and research agendas and clarify whether Luther was the author of *Judenschriften* in the sense that this term has to be understood in the context of WA and modern historiography, how this modern classification does not do justice to these writings but distorts their medieval context, and how those of Luther's writings which are classified as 'Judenschriften' are to be understood in their historical and literary contexts.

The one author to whose work the results of my project come close is Walter Bienert. He stated concerning *Von den Juden und jren Lugen*: "Luther gave an apology of Christian doctrine against Jewish denials. He did this as a medieval-prereformational scholastic, who sought to prove the correctness of Christian dogmas in opposition to its detractors."[60] Bienert developed a bibliographic account of the four authors used by Luther (Lyra, Burgos, Porchetus, and Margaritha). He also emphasized the quote from Luther that influenced me, namely, Luther's statement that he understood his book as a "strengthening of our faith."[61] Brecht's treatment has been helpful to me, especially at the final stages of reviewing secondary literature; he presents a good

---

59 See Hagen in n. 1.

60 Walther Bienert: *Martin Luther und die Juden. Ein Quellenbuch mit zeitgenössischen Illustrationen, mit Einführungen und Erläuterungen* (Frankfurt/Main, 1982), 134.

61 Bienert, 138f. (*Von den Juden*, Aiii^v). Reinhard Schwarz also listed Lyra's *Libellus contra Judaeos* (*Contra perfidiam Iudaeorum*) and Burgos's *Scrutinium Scripturarum* as Luther's sources for *Das Jesus Christus ein geborner Jude sei*; see Reinhard Schwarz: "Luther," in: *Die Kirche in ihrer Geschichte*, ed. by Bernd Moeller, 3.I (Göttingen, 1986), 214–19. Schwarz pointed out that in *Von den Juden und jhren Lugen*, Luther, in addition to Lyra and Burgos, was influenced by Porchetus and by Antonius Margaritha's *Der ganz Jüdisch Glaub*. (Luther used either the first edition, Augsburg, 1530, or the better second edition, Leipzig, 1531, of Margaritha's book; Schwarz, 217, n. 20.) Some authors (seven out of over 300 consulted for this project) listed the four authors Luther cited in *Von den Juden und jren Lugen* (Lyra, Burgos, Porchetus, and

balance of the theological-pastoral side of Luther's writings along with the offense Jews were giving to Christians.[62] In some ways my work could be seen as providing literary proof for Steven Katz's claim that Luther is "wholly imitative—however fervidly held and however much fueled by a powerful apocalyptic sensibility—and is morphologically distinct from modern racial antisemitism."[63] The materials presented above confirm that Luther was unoriginal but adopted medieval genres of theological writing. These medieval genres do not permit us to classify his writings as anti-Semitic, as this term is understood in the present.

The term and classification 'Judenschriften' did not exist in any of those of Luther's *Gesammelte Schriften* or *Opera omnia* and their indexes prior to WA, which I examined. The only classification that comes close is "Schriften wider"—*Jewish errors, not Jews as such*. It can be found in the Leipzig edition (1733) and its index volume prepared by Greiff (1740),[64] and in the two Walch editions.[65] It is in WA (1920, 1928) that *Judenschrift* takes on the meaning of writing *against* the Jews.[66] The classification 'Judenschrift[en]' in WA is a modern invention which distorts the medieval genres in which Luther wrote. It turns Luther's books into writings *against* the Jews. If one disregards the factor that this classification was convenient for editors and bibliographers, then we are confronted with a new question: Why did this classification and its consequences for the understanding of Luther's writings emerge?

Margaritha), but they did not engage in genre analysis either of these titles or of Luther's book.

62   Brecht, 3:334–51.

63   Steven T. Katz: *The Holocaust and Mass Death before the Modern Age* (New York, 1994), 1:387–90.

64   See above, A.5.

65   See above, B.5.

66   See above, II, and n. 7.

DE EXEGETICA METHODO

NIELS HEMMINGSEN'S DE METHODIS (1555)

Exegesis is generally understood to be a modern discipline, and the current literature on the direction of its future is enormous. The history or "prehistory" of exegesis, regarding the sixteenth century at least, is neither clear and nor very accurate. Historical surveys of the historicalcritical method, hermeneutics, and the discipline of Einleitung (Introduction) credit various figures and works as the "real beginning" of this and the "father" of that.[1] I would suggest, visàvis the sixteenth century, that these terms (historicalcritical, hermeneutics, Einleitung) are not very helpful because they were not the terms used at the time. For example, the phrase "medieval hermeneutics" or "Luther's hermeneutics" suggests that the medievals and Luther actually had hermeneutics; whereas they only had "rules" for exposition. As Flacius held and is still accepted today, to use a philosophy (such as is entailed in hermeneutics) is to bring with it a whole host of presuppositions.[2] My point is simply that it would be more helpful to use sixteenth-century terms when discussing the sixteenth-century backgrounds to an eighteenth-century discipline (historical hermeneutics).

"De exegetica methodo" is the phrase Niels Hemmingsen used in 1555 in his first work, De methodis libri duo (the first book was for philosophy and the second for theological method).[3] My thesis is that

---

1 John Benson, "The History of the Historical-Critical Method in the Church: A Survey," Dialog 12 (1973): 98.

2 Günter Moldaenke, Schriftverständnis und Schriftdeutung im Zeitalter der Reformation. Teil I: Matthias Flacius Illyricus (Stuttgart: Kohlhammer, 1936), 558.

3 De methodis libri duo, quorum prior quidem omnium methodorum universalium et particularium, quarum usus est in Philosophia, brevem ac dilucidam declarationem: posterior vero ecclesiasten sive methodum theologicam interpretandi, concionandique continet. Authore Nicolao Hemmingio (Rostock, 1555; Wittenberg, 1559, 1562; Leipzig, 1565, 1570, 1578; Geneva, 1586). The Dansk bibliographi 1551–1600, ed. Lauritz Nielsen (Copenhagen, 1931–33), does not list the editions of Wittenberg, 1559, or Geneva, 1586.

Hemmingsen belongs in the historical surveys of socalled historical criticism, hermeneutics, and Einleitung—or, to use his term, the development of exegetical method. This thesis will be based on a word study of exegesis, Hemmingsen's work of 1555 and his subsequent commentaries on the New Testament Epistles, and on secondary literature, that is, accounts of who does qualify for these surveys and why.

People who write about historical exegetica do not seem to know about Hemmingsen, and, on the other hand, those who write on Hemmingsen do not seem to know about his work on exegetical method.[4] Carl von Kaltenborn's book *Forerunners of Hugo Grotius on Ius naturae et gentium* praises Hemmingsen as "epoch making" for considering the scientific form of law according to mathematical sciences. After all, it is Grotius's scientific method that is important, rather than the content of his work. It is the science of the principles of law for which he is important but completely unknown.[5] I would like to make the same claim for Hemmingsen regarding the rise of exegetical method. I will not use "forerunner" or "father" language, but I will contend that he is important for the methodical framework in which he places "exegesis," and that he is unknown.

Hemmingsen (1513–1600) was not unknown in sixteenth-century Europe. He was at the center of university and church life in Denmark. The *praeceptor universalis Daniae* was also the leader in the Philipist period of power. The "brilliant young Dane" was with Melanchthon in Wittenberg, 1537–42; then in Copenhagen (1542) as professor of Greek (1543), dialectic (1545), and theology (1553), until his dismissal in 1579 on grounds of Crypto-Calvinism regarding

4 Kjell Barnekow, *Niels Hemmingsens teologiska åskådning* (Lund, 1940); reviewed by B. Kornerup,"En svensk disputats om Niels Hemmingsen,"*Dansk teologisk tidsskrift* 4 (1941): 57–66 (hereinafter *DTT*); and J. O. Anderson, "Om Niels Hemmingsens teologi," *Kyrkohistorisk årsskrift* 41 (1942): 108–31; E. M. Madsen,"Om Forholdet mellem Niels Hemmingsens Enchiridion theologicum og Melanchthons Loci Communes," *DTT* 5 (1942): 137–51, 215–32; Madsen, "Er Calvin Niels Hemmingsens eksegetiske Forbillede?" *DTT* 9 (1946): 1–10. For various studies on Niels Hemmingsen, cf. the overview of nineteenth-century and twentieth-century literature by Jens Glebe-Møller, "Socialetiske aspekter af Niels Hemmingsens forfatterskab," *Kirkehistoriske samlinger* (1979): 7–11.

5 Carl von Kaltenborn, *Die Vorläufer des Hugo Grotius auf dem Gebiete des Ius naturae et gentiium, sowie der Politik im Reformationszeitalter* (Leipzig: Mayer, 1848), 237–38, VII.

the Lord's Supper. Trygve Skarsten says that "his fame and reputation throughout the learned circles of Europe brought renown and glory to the University of Copenhagen. His Latin and Danish works were to be found in the leading libraries in multiple editions and often in Dutch, English, and German translation. As he advanced in age, scholars and dignitaries made their pilgrimage to his door, and kings like James VI of Scotland counted it an honor to have talked with the famous Danish theologian."[6]

He published in the areas of exegetics, dogmatics, ethics, and pastoral theology. He published commentaries on individual epistles beginning with Romans in 1562 and continuing to write one or more every year until 1569. The bulk were published between 1564 and 1566. Then his *Commentaria in omnes epistolas apostolorum* appeared in 1572 (Leipzig), 1579 (Frankfurt), and 1586 (Strasbourg).

The reasons for this study on exegetical method for the Second International Colloquy on the History of Biblical Exegesis in the Sixteenth Century were twofold. First, in my study *Hebrews Commenting from Erasmus to Beze, 1516–1598*, it seemed to me that "Introductions" to Pauline Epistles in the second half of the century were quite different from those earlier in the century; particularly after Calvin's commentary 1549 commentary on Hebrews. M. E. Schild also sees a change "near the middle of the century." This change involved the removal of the traditional Vulgate prologues from their places in the Latin Bible of the Roman Catholic church, possibly because of "the new critical literary attitudes."[7] He says no more. My second reason was Hemmingsen's use of the words *method* and *exegesis*.[8] I learned that discussion of "Method" (Methodenlehre) was already under way earlier in the century. So Hemmingsen could be seen as a part of that transition to what Reinhard Kirste calls "methodological thinking in

---

6   Trygve Skarsten, "The Reception of the Augsburg Confession in Scandinavia," *Sixteenth Century Journal* 11 (1980): 96.

7   M. E. Schild, "Leading Motifs in some Western Bible Prologues," *Journal of Religious History* 7 (1972): 107.

8   "As the method of teaching is the *opus* in other disciplines, the *ratio docendi* is to be established especially in the Queen of the Disciplines, Theology," *Enchiridion theologicum* (1559) in *Opuscula theologica* (1586), 324. "*Exegesis*" is also used in his three works on the Psalter (1567, 1569, 1592) and throughout his commentaries on the Epistles, gathered together in *Commentaria in omnes epistolas apostolorum* (1586).

Orthodoxy."[9] What is significant is Hemmingsen's use of *exegesis*, particularly within a philosophical and theological framework.

EXEGESIS: MEANING AND HISTORY OF THE WORD

Hemmingsen's use of the word, *exegesis*, prompted an investigation into the meaning and history of the word itself. Independent lexographical work confirmed the overview given in the *Allgemeines RealWörterbuch* of 1784. The word *exegesis* is both an ancient and relatively modern word. As far as I can tell, it was not used in ecclesiastical Latin in the ancient or medieval period, but it was used in the seventeenth century, and certainly in the eighteenth century and afterward. In the modern period it is connected with the "art of interpreting Scripture" (*Auslegungskust der heiligen Schrift*). Regarding the ancient period it is related to grammar and interpretation of poetry. In classical Greek, exegetes were interpreters or expounders of sacred lore. With the Romans they were the augurs and *interpretes*, often meaning "translator" or "mediator" of some kind. In Christian theology well into the sixteenth century, work on the Bible was done in the genre of commentary, explanation, exposition, and annotation, but not in the more modern sense of interpretation. *Intepretatio* at that time referred more to translation and explanation of obscure and enigmatic words or dreams.[10] For Luther, Scripture was its own interpreter.[11]

A comparison of two types of lexicons—the sixteenth-century edition with the later seventeenth- and eighteenth-century versions— confirms the above overview. The types are the *Thesaurus linguae Latinae* and the *Vocabularium*, as classified in the subject catalogue of

9   Reinhard Kirste, "Massstäbe und Methoden biblischer Hermeneutik in der altprotestantischen Orthodoxie," *Bijdragen: Tijdschrift voor philosophie en theologie* 36 (1975): 290.

10 Johannes Altenstaig, *Vocabularius theologie* (Hagenau, 1517), "Interpretatio."

11 I consulted the *Vocabularia* by Reuchlin (1478), Calepino ([1510], 1542, 1598, 1647), Altenstaig (1517), *Dictionaire en Theologie* (1560), Arguerio (1567), Chaulmer (1672), Magri (1677), Du Cange (1688), and the *Thesaurus linguae Latinae* by Estienne (1543, 1740), Burer (1576), Pareus (1645), Morel (1657). *Exegesis* does exist in Zwingli's title, *Amica Exegesis, id. est. expositio Eucharistiae* (1527). *Exegematicum* is in Budé (*De Asse, Opera Omnia*. 1557, 2:8; *Exegetes*, p. 149), as is e`xhgh,sewj (*Commentarii linguae graeize, Opera Omnia*, 4:1062.34). *Exegetei, exegematicus,* and *exegeticon* appear in some sixteenth-century lexicons.

the HerzogAugustBibliothek in Wolfenbüttel. Within each type one can compare the various editions of the *Thesaurus* of Robert Estienne (Stephanus) (the 1740 edition verses the 1573 edition) and the various editions of Ambrosio Calepino's *Dictionarium latinarum* (1647 edition verses the 1598, 1542 and [1510] editions). In the later editions (seventeenth and eighteenth century) *exegesis* appears; while in the sixteenth-century ones it does not.

Minimally, it seems to me that Hemmingsen certainly played a role in development in the area of exegesis as well as in the area of *Methodenlehre*. Can one get at the beginnings of the discipline of exegesis? If so, I suggest that Hemmingsen was at least a part of it.

DE METHODIS LIBRI DUO (1555)

The Context of Hemmingsen's Book

Lutz Geldsetzer's introduction to Jacobus Acontius's work on method (*De methodo*, 1558) sets that work in the context of Erasmus's *Ratio seu methodus* (1520), Erasmus Sarcerius's ... *ad certam methodum* (1547), and Hemmingsen's *De methodis libri duo* (1555). These works, however, are not all in the same genre. Hemmingsen's is *De methodis*; but Sarcerius's is a *loci communes*, beginning with *De trinitate* and ending with *de sepultura* and is *ad certam methodum* and not *de methodo*. Erasmus's "pedagogical methodology"[12] is concerned, as he says, with "true theology" (*incipit, explicit*).

One might say, as Hemmingsen himself intended and as the Danish scholar E. Munch Madsen believes, that Hemmingsen's exegetical method comes from Melanchthon. Hemmingsen regarded his *Enchiridion theologicum* of 1557 as an introduction to Melanchthon, as a resource for a deeper understanding of Melanchthon's *opus sacrosanctum*.[13] And in *De methodis* he defers to Melanchthon's *Loci*. The only one who discusses *De methodis* in the secondary literature is Madsen, who accepts Hemmingsen's word about faithfulness to Melanchthon.[14] Madsen's thesis is that on method and dogmatics Melanchthon was Hemmingsen's teacher, but on exegetical particulars he turns to others (e.g., Calvin). Madsen's contention that Hemmingsen's method is "hardly original" is offered without proof, except to say that that is

12 N. W. Gilbert, *Renaissance Concepts of Method* (New York: Columbia University Press, 1960), 108.

13 Hemmingsen, *Opuscula theologica*: 332.

14 Madsen, "Er Calvin Niels Hemmingsens eksegetiske Forbillede?"

what one would expect.[15] I disagree. As to Hemmingsen's dependence in dogmatics on Melanchthon, in the Five Hundredth Jubilee of the University of Copenhagen Nils Andersen describes Hemmingsen's claim that his *Enchiridion* is an introduction to Melanchthon as "grossly exaggerated."[16] It is true that in the beginning of the second period of the *Loci* (1533) Melanchthon discusses method. But he does so in terms of the *ordo locorum* (*Corpus Reformatorum* 21:253); so he is not talking *about* method as such. Further, I would point to the beginning of the third period of the *Loci* (1543) where Melanchthon says that method has no place in theology. Method belongs to philosophy, which proceeds from experience, principles, and proofs. The doctrine of the church, however, proceeds from what God has said, from revelation (CR 21:603–4). It may well be that Hemmingsen thought he was carrying out Melanchthon's wishes, for it "seems" to N. W. Gilbert, who thinks Melanchthon's reputation as *artifex methodi* is illfounded, that Melanchthon emphasized the importance of method more in "oral teaching" than in his books.[17]

Taking my cue from Wilhelm Risse, a contemporary historian of logic covering the period from 1500 to 1640,[18] and Jodocus Willich, an earlier dialectician in the sixteenth century and principal independent of Melanchthon, it is clear that method was being discussed earlier in terms of dialectic. The context for Hemmingsen's *De methodis* is his own work, including teaching, in dialectics. This then concurs with the standard biography and treatment of Hemmingsen's theology (Kjell Barnekow's *Niels Hemmingsens teologiska åskådning*) as far as book 1 is concerned. Barnekow relegates it to a footnote and classifies it as a philosophy textbook,[19] as does the *Danish Biographical Lexicon* (vols. 1 and 2).[20] The problem with this is that book 2 is overlooked. Book 2, which parallels book 1, contains exegetical method for theology and method for spiritual rhetoric (hermeneutics and homiletics, in our terms). Hemmingsen's connection of dialectics (book 1) with

---

15   Ibid., 2, 4–5.

16   Nils K. Andersen, "De teologiske Fakultet, 1479–1597," *Københavns universitet 1479–1979* (Copenhagen, 1980), vol. 48.

17   Gilbert, *Renaissance Concepts*, 127.

18   Wilhelm Risse, *Die Logik der Neuzeit*, vol.1, *1500–1640* (Stuttgart, 1964).

19   Barnekow, *Teolgiska åskådning*, 34, n. 3.

20   *Dansk Biografisk Leksikon* (1895): 326 (hereinafter *DBL*); *DBL* 2 (1936): 55; *DBL* 3 (1980) does not mention it.

theological method (book 2) could well have come from Melanchthon. But, according to Risse, given Melanchthon's direction toward *Lehrunterricht*, his followers in logic tended to go their own way or to simplify Melanchthon for school purposes.[21] Also according to Risse, using some terms also found in Willich, Hemmingsen was his own person.[22] *Methodus* as a technical term came into medicine before the middle of the sixteenth century, and by the second half of the century lawyers were discussing *Methodus* as well.[23] Hemmingsen, then, is a part of the contemporary discussion of method. From Melanchthon he turned to Galen and Aristotle and the dialectical and rhetorical traditions. With this context in mind, we turn to the book.

BOOK I, DEFINITION OF METHOD AND THE METHODOLOGICAL FRAMEWORK FOR *DE EXEGETICA METHODO*

Before defining method, Hemmingsen gives high praise of *ordo* and *methodus* for teaching and learning. Since the "little book" is on method, it seems "commodius" to Hemmingsen that one should indicate what particular method will be followed in the discussion "of methods" (method for method). His is diai,resin—the method of definition and division (pp. 2–3, 1570 ed.). Method is defined, following the ancient Greek methodists, as *via docendi certa cum ratione*. It is the *via* or *ratio docendi* (p. 3). Synonyms include *via, ratio, forma, methodus*, and *ordo*.

The overall division of methods is between universal, which is the *via integrarum* (p. 4), and particular (pp. 21–23), which is divided into *simplex* and *composita* (plus rhetoric) with further definitions and divisions. At the end of Hemmingsen's discussion of universal methods, he asks whether one is preferable. The answer, contra Ramus, is no; each has its strengths and place (p. 19).

As with the universal, the subdivisions of *simplex particularis* are synthetic, analytic, and "definitive." This comes from Galen and is also the format of Flacius's well-known "*tabula* of theological methods."[24]

---

21 Risse, *Die Lotic*, 1:120.

22 Ibid., 1:111-12.

23 Gilbert, *Renaisance Concepts*, 92–100. Gilbert knows only of the 1570 edition of Hemmingsen's *De methodis*, and "unfortunately" has not consulted it. Also unfortunately, he places it after works on theological method by Zanchi (post-1568), Strigel (1581), Flacius (1567), and Melanchthon (Gilbert, 107–12).

24 Flacius. *Clavis Scripturae Sacrae* (Basel, 1567), pt. 2, pp. 41–45.

The section on exegetical method is in the second cluster of three methods in the *composita particularis.* "This second part especially helps the zeal for discovery, confirms the memory, and shows the way to read the best authors" (p. 40). It consists of *disputatio, collatio,* and *examen. Examen* is the exegetical method: "examination of those things written by others" (p. 22). The exegetical method is then divided into four aspects (pp. 89–108).

The first aspect, which is all inclusive, is *forma* or *ratio interpretandi authores.* Just as there are many ends of interpretation, so there are many forms. The grammatical pays attention to words and phrases, the dialectical to things, rhetorical to the *accidentia* of words and things, and the *interpretationis genus* to all these things *simul.* All these genera are to be found in the great disciplines of theology, mathematics, law, physics, and ethics. So far, then, exegesis is the examination or interpretation of other authors and includes the grammatical, dialectical, and rhetorical methods; it is the examination of the words, the thing itself, and the accidental.

The second aspect of exegesis prescribes the way of reducing to dialectical brevity the dialectical forms of interpretation. Included in this section, which is anything but brief, are the different forms of speech (*expositio, argumentation,* or both), rules for dialectics, oratorical forms, examples, and more rules. At the end of this second member is a summary of the dialectical *via* that discusses of the question of whether it comes from some firm principle, is a hypothesis, is absurd, or whatever, and whether the proposition follows dialectical precepts.

The third aspect examines *quae tradita sunt,* and they are (again) grammar, dialectic, and rhetoric.

The fourth is the method for learning to remember: know the thing well, count the parts, note the order of the parts and the "adornment."

Perhaps Kaltenborn could be repeated at this point, to the effect that *what* Hemmingsen is saying is not as important, visàvis Melanchthon or Willich, Hyperius or Flacius, as the fact that he discusses "exegetical method" as such, and then carries it over from philosophy into theological method in book 2. That is significant and at least deserves notice. Or, to put my thesis in other words, Hemmingsen puts together methodexegesistheology in such a way that neither Luther nor Melanchthon would be happy—i.e., independently. Luther, Melanchthon (at least in the preface to the third edition), Hyperius, and Flacius would not (in Luther's case) or did not (in the other cases) want to talk about method, and certainly not from the dialectical tradition. They would rather talk about Scripture (Luther and Flacius), revelation (Melanchthon), or a particular locus (Hyperius). Hemmingsen is also independent of the dialecticians both in the area of *Methodenfrage* and theology.

BOOK 2 AND THEOLOGICAL METHOD

Whenever we look at what God has made we see the most beautiful order; so too in sacred theology. The *ratio* for observing this order is, with a very apt metaphor, called *methodus*. Those who have a method become *periti* more quickly than those who become fatigued from reading the Bible without order or method (pp. 119–120). Visàvis book 1, "methodum Theologicam" comprises spiritual dialectic (*ratio interpretandi scripturam*) and spiritual rhetoric (*ratio formandi sacras conciones*). Theological method, then, is the *ratio* "et interpretandi scripturam et formadi sacras conciones" (p. 120). Theological method is the procedure or principle for interpreting Scripture and forming sacred speeches (i.e., sermons). The purpose of the former is that we might more easily understand other interpreters and grasp the interpretive forms. The latter's purpose is that we might be able to discuss (i.e., preach) the thing proposed (in Scripture) in ecclesiastical contexts.[25] The second part, then, is Hemmingsen's method for preaching (which we will not treat).[26]

The section on method for interpreting Scripture is divided into two parts: "division of Scripture" and "forms of interpretation" (pp. 122–40). Hemmingsen acknowledges the common division: Old Testament/New Testament, Law/Prophets/Gospels/Epistles, and so on. Moderns define the historicalcritical method as concerning first and foremost the origin of individual books, but also the canon. In the light of such concerns, it should be noted that in dividing the New

25 "Quapropter constitui Methodum Theologicam conscribere, in qua rationem et interpretandi scripturam, et formandi sacras conciones complectar, quorum prius faciet, ut facilius alios interpretes intelligamus, et ipsi interpretandi formas teneamus, quas sequi utile erit. Posterius vero, ut citra garrulitatem, dextre et copiose de re proposita disserere incoetu Ecclesiastico valeamus" (Hemmingsen, pp. 120–21).

26 J. H. Paulli, *Dr. Niels Hemmingsens Pastoraltheologie* (Copenhagen, 1851); P. G. Lindhardt, "Til belysning af Niels Hemmingsens indflydelse på dansk praediken omkring 1600," in *Festskrift til Jens Nørregaard* (Copenhagen: Gads, 1947).

Testament into Gospels, Acts, twentyone Epistles, and the Apocalypse, Hemmingsen comments on the canon: "All these books of the New Testament are in the canon except Second Peter, Second and Third John, the Epistles of James and Jude along with the Apocalypse. Some also place the Epistle to the Hebrews outside the canon" (p. 124). Such lists of inclusion/exclusion were not uncommon at the time.

Hemmingsen dismisses immediately the scholastic division of lawhistorywisdomprophecy. He offers the "most suitable" division: history and doctrine (p. 126). History is old and new, dividing at Christ. The *doctrina rerum* is law and gospel; the *doctrina signorum* is ceremonies and sacraments. A further distinction is important lest law and gospel be confused, as the Papists do by defining the gospel as a new law. The prophets and apostles teach nothing that Moses did not teach; but in the *modus tradendi* there is a great difference. Moses received the doctrine from God, and the Fathers passed it down from hand to hand, but it is more obscure than the prophets. The prophets are interpreters of Moses. What is an aphorism in Moses, the prophets explain fully. But what the prophets predict, the apostles see clearly. The apostles are clearer interpreters of Moses and the prophets. Note the medieval distinction of *clarior* just after his criticism of the Papists for calling the gospel a new law. With this distinction of *clarior*, Scripture can be read with greater fruit. At the outset Hemmingsen claims that the purpose of knowing the parts of Scripture is twofold: The parts may be recognized more easily, and the use of the individual parts may be seen more clearly (p. 121). What is important for theological method is that these distinctions are necessary for clarity. In other words, there is some historical perception here of a process of interpretation.

Concerning the *forms* of interpretation (*De formis enarrationum*)— the other part of his method for interpreting Scripture—there are four (pp. 129–40): (1) aids for the interpreter, (2) causes of interpretation, (3) the kinds of interpretations, and (4) the use of commentators.

1. *Aids for the interpreter*. The interpreter of Scripture is treating sacred mysteries, or, as Hemmingsen also says, "the mind of the interpreter ought always to be attentive to the first axioms of our religion" (p. 132). Such being the case, care is incumbent on one wishing to be free from error, one wishing not to deviate from *pietas*. He must, first, seek God and his will; second, have the word of God *pro regula*; third, compare Scripture so that the consensus of MosesprophetsChristapostles

appears, diligently observing the circumstances of the places (texts) lest they be taken out of context; and, fourth, refer every true interpretation "ad analogian fidei." Even if one is in error regarding the scope and mind of the author, so long as one is in agreement with the faith, one's salvation is not endangered. The analogy of faith means in respect to the first axioms of religion, which are law and gospel (pp. 130–33). Since the eighteenth century these four would be considered not aids but hindrances to biblical criticism. For Hemmingsen, every interpretation hangs on the constant word of God (p. 133), hence the consensus. In this section on aids I find Hemmingsen close to Augustine (book 3 of *De doctrina*).

2. *Causes of interpretation.* Hemmingsen refers here to the preface of Melanchthon's *Loci*. Again, the subdivision is four. (He is surely following his announced method for method.) The first is to understand the kind of language so as to retain its sense. The second is an examination of the order. Third is to bear witness to the true interpretation. The fourth is to refute false opinions (pp. 133–34). A comparison between Melanchthon (*Loci*, preface to third period, 1543) and Hemmingsen on this point shows a further differentiation between the two. On language and interpretation Melanchthon says, "Because the untrained do not everywhere know the *genus sermoni* nor immediately see the order of things, they are to be admonished by the voice of the interpreters concerning the genus of words and the order of things," and, because there are corrupters around, pious pastors and theologians are witnesses of the truth and refuters of false interpretations. On account of these "causes" God has restored the ministry of the gospel with studies in schools and temples so that we are keepers (*custodes*) of sacred books (CR 21:606). Hemmingsen's analysis, I submit, is very aware of the problem of translation and interpretation. For Hemmingsen, we are to understand the *genus sermonis* "for hearers or readers do not always understand the phrases of another language, even the most learned of men sometimes are lacking very much in this *palaestra*." He goes on to say that it often happens that where a speech is translated with words of another language, while corresponding in *significatio* they often do not retain the same sense in both languages, on account of dialect or the variety of phrases; thus, lest we be deceived, the work is to be done by an "expert interpreter" (pp. 133–34). Whereas Melanchthon's "pious pastors and theologians" are

custodians of Scripture, Hemmingsen's "expert interpreters" must pay attention to meaning, sense, and translation.

3. *Kinds of interpretation (interpretandi genera)*. Hemmingsen wants to be as clear as possible here because these genera are quite distinct. Reading the commentaries of others, he finds four kinds of interpretation: grammatical, dialectical, oratorical, and mixed. We will look particularly at the dialectical with its various subdivisions. The first is grammatical "exegesis" (p. 135), for which one needs to know Hebrew, Greek, and Latin (pp. 135–36). The second is dialectical, for which there are four Canons. First Canon: In the beginning of a commentary it is fitting to discuss the kind of doctrine in general and its authority, certainty, necessity, and utility. Second canon: Following the dialectical genus of interpretation there are four questions with regard to a particular writing. These four questions will structure the *argumenta* to Hemmingsen's commentaries, beginning with Romans in 1562. Here the former professor of dialectic lays out the methodology for interpretation that he will follow in his later commentaries. The first question, authorship, determines the authority of the writing. The second, the occasion, leads to an understanding of the literary structures ("*tractationis ordinem*"). The third, the status or principal question, leads to a perception of the ultimate goal and scope of the whole writing. Without the fourth, method or *ordo tractationis*, the effort will be to little or no advantage (pp. 137–38).

The third canon, what is being taught, follows on the question of method and is a part of it. The doctrine is often "dispersed" in admonition, praise, threat, consolation, etc., by which the author accommodates the doctrine to the hearer (p. 138). The fourth canon is on the explication of particular commentaries. There is a necessary order among as well as within these canons. The first is a summary of the whole commentary; next is how the commentary fits into the preceding and following commentaries; then is "*exegesis textus*" (pp. 138–39). In his commentaries on all the Epistles, beginning with *ad Romanos*, Hemmingsen follows the format detailed in the final canon of the dialectical genus: first a summary of the whole commentary, then its *ordo*, then "*exegesis*" —again the actual word.

4. The final form is on the use of commentaries (p. 140), which completes Hemmingsen's theological method for interpreting Scripture, divided into the division of Scripture and forms of interpretation.

The point I want to emphasize regarding *De methodis libri duo* is that "exegesis of the text" is grounded in dialectic, a part of philosophy. There is a definite method for exegesis or interpretation; in fact, there is a method for the method, which Hemmingsen consistently follows, with its definitions, divisions, and subdivisions. The purpose of method is clarity in exegesis. The interpretation of Scripture is grounded in *de exegetica methodo*.

COMMENTARIES ON NEW TESTAMENT EPISTLES

In his *argumenta*, or introductions, to New Testament Epistles, Hemmingsen announces that in order to understand them better, four items have to be discussed: authorship, occasion, principle question, and method. "In order that the *Argumentum* or general *Periocha* of this noble epistle written to the Romans be understood more explicitly by readers, four things need to be explicated by us in order."[27] On James (1563), these four "*introducunt*" skillfully and correctly the innermost reaches of Scripture as a light held before the reader.[28] On Galatians (1564), "In order that entrance (*aditus*) to this epistle be had more easily."[29]

The year that Flacius prefaced and published the *Clavis*, 1567, is the same year Hemmingsen prefaced his *Commentarius* on Hebrews (published in Wittenberg, 1568). What stands out in Hemmingsen's introduction, or *Argumentum in Epistolam ad Hebraeos*, is his explicit statement about what an introduction is supposed to accomplish and what questions should be asked in order to prepare the way for understanding the epistle: "But omitting these [questions of authorship] let us talk about the things which the argument of this epistle opens up to us: let us see what the occasion was for writing, what the principal point or question was, and what was the order of proceeding or method. For knowing these things well, we will have the way prepared for understanding this epistle more clearly" (p. 830).

For Hemmingsen, Beza (1556), and others at this time, questions of authorship—and not only of Hebrews—were regarded as "useless disputations" (Hemmingsen). They continue to discuss authorship, but one has the strong impression that the reason why the longstanding

---

27   *Commentaria in omnes epistolas apostolorum* (Leipzig, 1572), 7.

28   Ibid., 921.

29   Ibid., 315.

authorship question was regarded as useless is that no consensus regarding Hebrews had emerged from Erasmus on through Calvin, where the question was vigorously discussed. Hemmingsen does raise the authorship question in other introductions. The growing tendency regarding Hebrews is to emphasize that the Holy Spirit is the real author anyway. Besides, for Hemmingsen, other questions—the occasion, point, and method—were more important. After all, the purpose of an introduction is to prepare the way for understanding.

My point here is that because Hemmingsen reflects on the function of an introduction, even using the verb "to introduce" at one point, in his *argumenta* to the Epistles, he deserves notice in the history of exegetical method.

SECONDARY LITERATURE

Who, then, does receive notice in histories of historical criticism, hermeneutics, and so on, and on what basis? We began with the question of how Hemmingsen compares with his contemporaries. In the literature, the sixteenth century and the first half of the seventeenth are treated as background to the eighteenth century, when historical criticism "won out."[30] The picture presented is that the sixteenth and seventeenth centuries were a time of transition between the Dark Ages and dawn of historical consciousness in the eighteenth century.

In order to compare Hemmingsen with contemporary material, the Complutensian, Erasmus, Calvin, Karlstadt, Santes Pagnino, and Flacius were checked because of the claims made on their behalf and because, except for Flacius, they are earlier than Hemmingsen.

In his commentary on "Biblical Scholarship" in the *The Cambridge History of the Bible*, Basil Hall praises "the great Complutensian Polyglot of Alcalá, 1514–17." In discussing its content, he notes that it contains two statements about the method of studying Scripture.[31] After Brevard Childs evaluates Pagnino's *Isagogae* (1536) and Sixtus Senensis's *Bibliotheca sancta* (1566) as traditional, he says, "However the major contribution to the discipline of Introduction was the publication of the Complutensian Polyglot Bible (1514–17) which dramatized the new philological interest and set the stage for critical biblical

30 Benson, "History," 98.
31 Basil Hall, *The Cambridge History of the Bible*, 3 vols. (Cambridge: University Press, 1963), 3:50–51.

scholarship in the field of Old Testament."[32] Early in the Complutensian (vol. I) there appears a short section on "Modi intelligendi sacram scripturam," which turns out to be a discussion of the famous medieval *quadriga*. At the end is a section on "Introductiones artis grammatice hebraice." It is strictly grammatical—consonants, vowels, Hebrew sounds, vowel points, word order, nouns, and pronouns. A comparison of the Complutensian introduction to Hebrews with medieval introductions reveals that the Complutensian is a reprint of the medieval *Glossa ordinaria*. Certainly this is a "contribution," but it is not "the major contribution to the discipline of Introduction."

H. J. Kraus assesses Calvin and his discussion of the intention of the biblical author as an *Ansatz zur Kritik*. Calvin insists on investigating "the history, geography, and institutional *circumstances* which are determinative for the author's situation."[33] Then Kraus states, "He is clearly following the lead of Erasmus" (Greek and Latin New Testament, 1516). Erasmus also insists on study of the history and geographical setting, the customs, and institutions. "Then a marvelous light and, I might say, life, is given to what is being read" (Erasmus).[34] A check of Erasmus's introduction and the context of Kraus's quote reveals that Erasmus is actually citing Augustine's De doctrina christiana (2:16, also 2:28). This suggests that one should be very careful about such words as *historical* and *critical*. We have the words *historical, geographical, and institutional circumstances*. Do you think they mean the same for Augustine, Erasmus, Calvin, and Kraus?

Another kind of misjudgment, e.g., by Kraus and Otto Kaiser, is made about the importance of Karlstadt's De canonicis scripturis (1520). Kaiser evaluates the work as "at least the beginnings of a modern science of Old Testament introduction,"[35] and Kraus considers Karlstadt the first precursor of literary historical research on the Old Testament within Protestant theology.[36] I do not see it. What

---

32   Brevard Childs, *Introduction to the Old Testament as Scripture* (Philadelphia: Fortress, 1979), 32.

33   H. J. Kraus, "Calvin's Exegetical Principles," *Interpretation* 31 (1977): 14.

34   "Ratio sev compendium verae theologiae," in *Novum Testamentum* (Basel: Froben, 1519), 17.

35   Otto Kaiser, *Introduction to the Old Testamen*, trans. John Sturdy (Minneapolis: Augsburg, 1977), 7.

36   Kraus, *Geschichte der historisch-kritischen Erforschung des Alten Testaments*, 2d ed. (Neukirchen: Neukirchener Verlag, 1969), 28–29.

I see is a series of quotations, principally from Augustine and Jerome. Occasionally Karlstadt will argue with the Fathers (with Jerome on the Apocrypha, for example), but he gets permission to do so from Augustine.[37] An early section on the majesty of Scripture is reminiscent of Lyra's prologues. One way I can account for the misjudgment about Karlstadt is that these authors were misled by the title, which sounded scientific.

Some have listed Pagnino's *Isagogae* (1536) as a part of the history of the discipline of *Einleitung*.[38] Even as the full title indicates, it is very traditional and mystical. The first brief book discusses topical questions, for example, the four modes of expounding the law (from Augustine). The second, much longer, section is concerned with the mystical meaning of various words, listed alphabetically from *abyssus* to *uxor*.[39]

Almost everyone includes Flacius's *Clavis Scripturae Sacrae*[40] key to the development of the modern discipline of historical criticism. It has been described as the "real beginning of scholarly hermeneutics" (Werner Kümmel);[41] the first of a scientific biblical discipline;[42] for Hans Frei, it is the "first writing on hermeneutics."[43] The *Clavis* is a general and special (hermeneutical) guide to Scripture. Flacius lists fifty-plus causes for difficulty with regard to Scripture (which Olivier Fatio argues were plagiarized from Hyperius).[44] There are fifty-plus rules from Scripture for understanding Scripture (treatise 1); for

---

37   In: Karl Credner, *Zur Geschichte des Kanons* (Halle, 1847), 327.

38   Theodor Zahn, "Einleitung in das Neue Testament," *Realencyklopädie für protestantische Theologie und Kirche* (1898), 5:263.

39   Pagnino, *Isagogae ad sacras literas, liber unicus. Eiusdem Isagogae ad mysticos sacrae scripturae sensus* (Lyon: Hugo à Porta, 1536), 51–818.

40   Flacius, *Clavis scripturae sacrae, seu de sermone sacrarum literarum, plurimas generales regulas continens altera pars_*(Basel: Eusebius Episcopius 1581 [prefaced 1567]).

41   Werner Kümmel, *The New Testament: The History of the Investigation of Its Problems*, trans. S. McLean Gilmour and Howard Kee (New York: Abingdon Press, 1972), 27.

42   Kraus. *Edition*, 28–29.

43   Hans Frei, *The Eclipse of Biblical Narrative: A Study in Eighteenth and Nineteenth Century Hermeneutics* (London: Yale University Press, 1974), 37.

44   Olivier Fatio, "Hyperius plagié par Flacius. La destinée d'une méthode exégétique," *Histoire de l'exégese au XVIe siecle* (Geneva: Librairie Droz, 1978), 375–79.

example, the distinction between law and gospel is the "clavis" to "true religion." In addition treatise 1 considers the *ratio* for understanding Scripture (largely from Scripture, with a long section on multiple senses of Scripture). Treatise 2 contains rules from the Fathers for understanding Scripture; 3 and 4 are grammatical, 5 is literary (*de Stylo*), 6 is both grammatical and literary, and 7 is mostly on the tradition. The *Clavis* is impressive in its ordering of detail. Karl von Schwartz, however, thought the same details could be found in Luther.[45] A work that I would also cite relative to the beginning, or pre-history, of scientific biblical criticism is Flacius's *Glossa Compendiaria* on the New Testament (1570) with its introductions.[46]

In his introduction to Matthew, Flacius says that questions of language are of no little moment. He also discusses the "occasion of the writing" (pp. 1–3; 1570 ed.). In his introductions to several Epistles, the occasion is one of four things that should be known ("praenoscenda esse" p. 748) or given to the reader before one begins to speak of the writing. The others are author, scope or argument, and status. Method and sequence (*series*), the "order of the parts" (pp. 640, 748, 873–74, 915, 959, 984–85, 1105–7), are important also. Here, then, Flacius is commenting on issues that a *praefatio* or *argumentum* should deal with. On Ephesians and Philippians he is also interested in the situation of the city (pp. 915, 959); on Colossians about the time of writing (p. 985). On Hebrews his argument for Pauline authorship is among the most extensive I have seen, for or against. His responses to two traditional arguments against Pauline authorship are nuanced and unusual, and basically literary. For one, the reason the language of Hebrews is clearer and more splendid is that Paul is not writing to one church or one person, but to the whole Hebrew nation. Is not the Holy Spirit able to vary the style out of "the necessity of things, times, and hearers"? Besides, Cicero and Aristotle altered their style (pp. 1101–3). Among his fifteen reasons for Pauline authorship, some historical or circumstantial "evidence" is used; for example, it had to have been written before the fall of the temple and Jerusalem, and no disciple of the apostles would have dared to write it or would have gotten by with it if he had (pp. 1103–5).

45   K. A. von Schwartz, "Die theologische Hermeneutik des Matthias Flacius Illyricus," *Lutherjahrbuch* 15 (1933): 149.

46   *Glossa compendiaria M. Matthiae Flacii Illyrici Albonensis in novum Testamentum* (Basel: P. Perna and T. Dietrich, 1570).

My perspective is that Flacius is the continuation, albeit also a synthesizer, of trends under way for some decades. I have in mind the literarygrammatical character of the *Clavis* and the concerns of the *Glossa Compendiaria* with author, occasion, argument, and method; and his reflection on the purpose of a preface.

With reference to secondary literature, two conclusions are offered. First, some sloppy work has been done relative to early sixteenth-century exegetica, perhaps due to ignorance of medieval forms. A good example would be the place of Luther, who is often credited with separating Scripture and churchly tradition, using the former to attack the latter; and then singling out Scripture for study (Kümmel, Hendricus Boers).[47] But the same thing happened in the fifteenth century (with Hus, Gerson, D'Ailly, Erasmus) and probably earlier. Without medieval background, sloppy conclusions arise. Second, histories—especially histories of hermeneutics—have been misled by concentrating on seemingly methodological works without checking the theory in practice or finding theory in the actual commentaries.

CONCLUSION

The field is wide open for a specialist in the sixteenth century to write a history of exegetical method. Hemmingsen's *De methodis libri duo* (1555) should be included because of his discussion of exegetical method for philosophy and theology. Certainly Hemmingsen deserves as much attention as others from his time who are credited with beginning modern critical trends in biblical interpretation,. He deserves attention not only for his actual discussion of exegesis and method but also for his explicit discussion of the function of an introduction to a biblical book. The Danes are certainly correct in the assessment of *De methodis* as "en gylden Bog."[48]

Gratefully acknowledged for their research support for 1982 are the following: Herzog-August-Bibliothek, Wolfenbüttel, and its Geschäftsstelle für das Forschungsprogramm; Norges almenvitenskapelige forskningsråd for the Hemmingsen project at the Royal University Library, Oslo; and Marquette University and its sabbatical program.

---

47   Kümmel, *New Testament*, 20; Hendricus Boers, *What is New Testament Theology? The Rise of Criticism and the Problem of a Theology of the New Testament* (Philadelphia: Fortress, 1979), 17.

48   *DBL*.1.

OBSERVING CATHOLICISM

What I observed about the Catholic Church while teaching with the Jesuits for 33 years at Marquette University

For some time I have thought that after thirty-three years I should be able to say something about how Roman Catholicism looked from this set of Lutheran eyes. I think I gained some insights on how Catholics think and behave.

As was my custom at the end of the Luther class (upper division), after grades were set and all requirements completed, I would ask the class what they really thought about Luther. In one class there was a conservative Catholic and a conservative Lutheran from the Evangelical Lutheran Synod (ELS). The Catholic said if he were living in the sixteenth century he would have joined up with Luther; but then he added "of course it [the Lutheran system] doesn't work." The Lutheran responded "it ain't easy." There you have it: the complexities and differences of perspective.

The concept of church is very different in the two communions. When you say "church" to a Lutheran, what comes to mind often is the communion of saints of all ages, and maybe the church back home. When you say "church" to a Catholic, what comes to mind is the Eucharist, the universal institution, the hierarchy (especially the bishop), church as a bedrock of stability and salvation, and maybe the pope (pro or con). For a Catholic, church is home; not only where the heart is, but more importantly where the soul is. The church is there from cradle to grave.

For the Catholic the sense of church is very different. The church defines the Catholic's essence as catholic. There is something almost mystical about Catholicism, "mystical" in the root meaning of the word *silence*. It is inexpressible. At least that is the way it seemed to me from the outside. My time at the university was to me an academic enterprise. While I pursued academic excellence, I always felt I was not on the inside. It seemed to me that MU had an identity, extra academic, that I could never share.

As I look back at MU and the Catholics there, what I remember is that the church is security for them. It really did not matter what one thought or did, the church was always there for them. This sense of security was always a fallback, a safety net. It was also a whole context within which the Catholic lived. I don't know if I dare compare and say that what Christ is for a Lutheran, the church is for the Catholic. An example of the church as security is a Jesuit's comment to me one day: without a context, he declared that he did not have to worry about being saved. I suppose with the Lutheran focus on justification it might well give the impression that we do worry a lot about being saved.

Lutherans will never understand catholic ecclesiology (and vice versa) and Catholics will never understand the Lutheran teaching of justification by faith alone.

Faith for Catholicism is part of a lifelong process, hence the lifelong faithfulness I observed. Faith is never complete, never over until one's life is over. The sacrament of penance and the weekly obligation carries the penitent along the way of faith being fulfilled by acts of love (*fides formata caritate*). Certitude of salvation during the process is impossible except for a special gift of grace given to a (very) few. You might say that what the certitude of salvation is for Lutherans the certitude of the church is for Catholics. Grace perfects nature, said Thomas Aquinas.

Devotion to the church among the Jesuits took and takes the form of saying the daily office, day in and day out. I traveled in Germany and Norway with one of my best friends, and, yes, there he was with book in hand every day.

Catholic theology can in no way accommodate Lutheran *sola fide*. Catholics say justification by faith, yes, but justification by faith alone? No. For Catholics faith is never alone; faith is to be formed by hope and love. Nor is Christ ever without his mother. Nothing is ever "alone."

Much of Catholic theology is predicated on wholeness: the wholeness of creation, redemption, the individual, and the church. It all hangs together. The Lutheran tendency toward dialectics, the "alones," and the doctrine of sin jar Catholic sensitivities. The Lutheran dialectic of sinner/saint for the Catholic comes out both sinful and saintly.

Organic categories abound in Catholic theology: creation, revelation, salvation, church. All is a process of growth: faith formed by works of love, the church as the extension of the incarnation.

A good (Catholic) friend pointed out to me that Catholicism is a culture, social and ethnic. To be Irish is to be Catholic. Catholic culture is a way of life, it weaves and holds everything together. It is not the same for Lutheranism. Lutheranism is a way of faith amidst a variety of cultures—independent, really, of culture. A convert to Catholicism is never truly an insider. One Jesuit who was a convert to Catholicism was to me such an example. When discussing some Catholic practice, another Jesuit said to him that he'd never get it" since he did not have the total Catholic practice (from the cradle). In other words, Catholicism is more than a set of beliefs. It embraces all aspects of life, cradle to grave, centered in the Eucharist.

Living and teaching among Catholics for thirty-three years, I found that Catholics think about Catholicism the way I think about being an American. For Catholics Catholicism is a matter of identity. The fear of John F. Kennedy's becoming president was based on the belief that Catholicism was answerable to a higher authority. I found that Catholics were proud to be Catholic. In class I always asked how many were Catholic; the Catholics always raised their hands very high. Not so the Lutherans. I remember one discussion in the theology department among the faculty about the identity of theology classes. The discussion was going in the direction of Christian identity until one older Jesuit spoke up and pleaded for Catholic identity.

I found that there was a tremendous variety of belief and action among Catholics. This is different for Catholics because the core of Catholic belief is defined as the *depositum fidei*. Outside of the core (Trinity, Christology, sacraments on the eve of the Reformation) freedom of thought was allowed. This is based on the medieval definition of theology as faith seeking understanding. In one seminar that included a liberal Catholic and a conservative Lutheran of the Wisconsin Evangelical Lutheran Synod, as the discussion went back and forth, the Lutheran said to the Catholic "I don't think the Catholic church has ever taught what you say [along the lines of Hans Küng]."

To put it another way. To use the (Aristotelian) categories of substance and accidents, the *depositum fidei* is the substance of Catholic faith defended by the magisterium, and theological explorations are the accidents. The variety of Catholic schools of thought does not change the substance. The substance is "what everywhere, always, and by every one is believed."

A distinguished Jesuit told me that the Lutheran theological challenge during the Reformation was no problem but that the "split" was not acceptable. The key is the papacy, the teaching office of the church. Not to accept the teaching office is to deny Catholic faith. Luther's theology was not the problem; his views of the papacy were. To put it in perspective, Luther's theology could be classified as right-wing Augustinian. His views of the papacy were Hussite, hence the problem.

In my undergraduate classes on Luther the one area of Luther's theology that met consistent (initial) rejection was his teaching on predestination. I always began this discussion with a question: "How many believe in predestination?" Nobody raised his or her hand. The only time I remember someone raising his hand was a fine ELS student. The "p" word raised red flags. Then I would spend most of the hour explaining the teaching (God has chosen us by grace), after which I asked the same question. Then most of the hands went up.

The main problem with predestination was that it seemed to curtail freedom. Anything that smelled of a denial of free will was not given even a fair hearing by the students. Luther's main emphasis was that salvation is entirely in God's hands. The idea of no human cooperation was unthinkable for the Catholic. Lutheran exclusive categories like faith alone were incomprehensible. Human cooperation, I found, was seen by Catholic theologians to be grounded in Jesus Christ; the human nature cooperated with the divine. The first time I caught wind of this, I was shocked.

Human-divine cooperation seemed to be a basic principle, not only in soteriology but also in ecclesiology, Eucharist, penance ....

I must admit that over the course of my years among Catholics I came to appreciate Catholicism. It is a massive structure. It is a coherent whole. Its logic is tight. The teachings of the Catholic Church are sure and clear. It must be a comfort to be Catholic since there is no doubt about what to believe and do. *Ganz anders* with the evangelical Lutheran Church in America (ELCA). From time to time I must have let this appreciation show since one colleague surmised that I wanted to become a Jesuit. He told me that I first had to become Catholic. Another time a Jesuit tried to put a little pressure on me by trying to present the "argument from history," by which I presumed he meant the length and breadth of the "catholic tradition" demonstrates its truthfulness.

"The one and the many" (*Confutatio* to *Confessio Augustana*). The working out of salvation is a collaborative effort by Christ, Mary, and the Saints in Catholic theology. So, any talk abut Christ alone is okay since, in the Catholic mind, Christ alone does not exclude Mary and the Saints. Christ is never without his mother. It's a whole different mindset.

The matter of Mariology never came up in any of my classes. One discussion panel of graduate students did discuss Mary. A few of the students on the panel reported recent literature about squaring the Trinity (can you believe?). The group present did not really discuss the point. For all the discussion on the Lutheran-Catholic dialogue about Mary (including that by a rapid Mariologist), never did the point about increasing the number of the Godhead come up (thanks be!).

Like Mariology, the papacy never came up in any of my classes. Now I must admit that I did not dwell on Luther's view of the papacy. A few times the pope did come up in comments by faculty. The ones I remember were all negative (by a laicised priest).

Whenever the matter of grace and merit, faith and works, came up with graduate students, Augustine's dictum "When God rewards our merits, he crowns his own gifts" seemed to close all discussion. The dictum seemed to head off any Catholic disagreement with Luther. On the face of it, both the dictum and Luther gave priority to God in matters of grace and salvation.

In fact, I found that graduate students were not interested personally in rehearsing the controversies of the sixteenth century: faith alone, grace alone, Christ alone, the papacy, eucharistic presence, predestination, Bible and tradition, biblical canon. The only time I had a real personal discussion, that is, disagreement, was with the Evangelicals present on the matter of free will. I made the mistake on the first day of saying something to the effect "I can't image anyone being so stupid as to believe in free will." The Evangelicals responded forcefully in the affirmative. It ruined my entire semester.

In discussion with graduate students, I found that on a given topic the Catholics spoke on behalf of "the church" whereas Protestants spoke on behalf of Scripture or themselves. Catholicism is a point of departure for Catholics more strongly than is Lutheranism for Lutherans. You might say that Catholics wear their Catholicism on their sleeve. The Lutheran situation is partly due to the fact that

Lutheranism is fractured into many synods. Besides, who cares what Lutherans think; they want to know the truth!

I do not think it too simplistic to say that Catholics need the church whereas Lutherans need Christ. This came to mind from a recent article in the local paper by the Archbishop who spoke of the need for Catholics to remain close to the church. This Lutheran feels the need to "go" to church (often), but that is different from needing the church. For Catholics to remain "close to the church" means to adhere closely to the church's teaching, especially on the moral issues, and to live a sacramental life. The teachings of the ELCA are so loose that there is nothing to adhere to.

For all my admiration of "Catholic," I found it confusing and puzzling when a very good friend of mine (a Jesuit) said one day: "We say we are 'catholic' but we're not," pointing to all the fractured denominations (the separated brethren).

The above are some thoughts about what I experienced at Marquette. It is in no way a comparison of Catholicism and Lutheranism. I must say that during my thirty-three years at Marquette I felt like I was an outsider looking in at Catholicism in practice. I was not a part of Catholic culture even though thirty-three years is a long time and even though our best friends were Catholic (and still are). This is not unlike Luther's view of our relationship with God: the closer we come to God the greater the distance we see between ourselves and God.

THE DECLINE OF CHRISTIANITY IN EUROPE

There is plenty of evidence of the decline of Christianity in Europe. First, I will make some personal observations from living in Germany and Norway about the evidence of the decline. Second, I will discuss some of the reasons why the decline has happened. Third, I will draw out the consequences of the decline.

EVIDENCES OF DECLINE

An example of the decline can be seen in the secularization of *Anrufen* from "calling upon the name of the Lord" to making a telephone call. A commercial for the telephone in Germany, *ruf mich an* (call me up), hit me one day. *Anrufen* sounds like theology. Luther's description of *Beruf* (vocation) has continued to influence modern German language and culture, such that everyone has one; *Beruf* (occupation) is used on all civil documents (name your *Beruf*). The secularization of Luther's vocabulary can also be seen in words that were central to Luther's theology that are now used with reference to the telephone (a friend of mine in Wolfenbüttel who verified my linguistics called this "The Reformation of the Telephone"). *Anrufen*, which meant to call upon the name of the Lord, now means to make a call. *Wählen*, which meant the Lord's choosing, now means to dial. *Vermittlung*, which meant mediator, now means the operator. The word that was a synonym for *Beruf*, namely, *Amt*, now means a line out or extension.

The topic of "The Decline of Christianity in Europe" has more than a passing academic interest for me. When we were going back and forth to Germany and Norway, my wife noticed that new styles in Europe soon made their way to the United States. I knew from my research in Norway that new movements of thought in Germany took about a generation to make inroads into Norway. Romanticism, liberalism, and skepticism (*Vantro* paganism) all found their way north. The main focus will not be on the United States; but if it were, certainly some decline has already set in. The Evangelical Lutheran Church in America (ELCA) and other mainline Protestant groups have increasingly made their existence irrelevant. In abdicating their prophetic role of announcing God's judgment on a godless culture and providing "a light to the nations," they have become a willing partner in the moral decline of the United States. The stream of decline in Europe seems to have moved from denial of Christianity to the irrelevance of religion to life in secular society. It is a movement from active denial to passive (practical) denial.

Secularization, associated with the modern era, has had deep effects. Perhaps no country in Europe is more secularized than Sweden. CNN.com posted this story from Stockholm: "Wanted: churchgoers. Place of work: Landeryd church. Salary: good communion" and free taxi rides.[1]

Weekly church attendance in Norway and Denmark is 5 percent, 4 percent in Sweden and Finland, in Germany 14 percent, and the United States 44 percent.[2]

When we lived in Norway in the 1970s and 80s, the faculties of theology in Sweden changed their name for the study of theology to the study of *livsskådningsvetenskap* (worldviews, value systems). It seems that God and theology are too religious. We also read about "secular baptisms" in Sweden. The ceremony was still deemed important for the family, so some secular ceremony for the baby took place in the town square.

According to an editorial in the *Scottish Bulletin of Evangelical Theology*, "The decline of Christianity in Britain is obvious with only about 8 percent of the population ever attending a service regularly. Churches are being converted into restaurants, bookshops, public houses, and homes. Britain is one of the most secular societies in the western world."[3] If present rates continue in Britain, 8 percent will be down to 2 percent by 2020.[4]

---

1 "Wanted: Churchgoers," n.p. Online: www.cnn.com/2003/WORLD/europe/03/02/offbeat church.ap/index.html.

2 "Percentage of Adult Population That Attends Church at Least Once a Week," n.p. Online: www.hewett.norfolk.sch.uk/curric/soc/religion/attend.htm.

3 Scottish Bulletin of Evangelical Theology 19:1 (2001):1.

4 Patrick Goodenough, "British Churches Face Worst Attendance Decline Ever," n.p. December 7 1999. Online: http://www.conservativenews.org/ViewReligion.asp?Page=/Religion/archive/REL19991207a.html. "Christianity in Britain is generally regarded as being in crisis. Most churches will be virtually empty in twenty

News from Britain: "'Christianity Almost Beaten,' Says Cardinal:"
Christianity has almost been vanquished in Britain, Cardinal
Cormac Murphy-O'Connor told a gathering of priests yesterday.
Christ was being replaced by music, New Age beliefs, the environ-
mental movement, the occult and the free-market economy, the
Archbishop of Westminster said. But the Cardinal, leader of 4.1 mil-
lion Roman Catholics in England and Wales, went much further. The
extent to which Christianity informed modern culture and intellectual
life in Britain today had been hugely diminished, he told the National
Conference of Priests in Leeds. Not just vanquished in Britain, but
throughout the West. Western "culture" is now media culture. And
since the Church now takes its cues from secular society, the Church
is driven by media culture. Christianity is drawing its last breaths, and
the sentimental emotionalism that has replaced it is evolving its own
structures. When priests and ministers recite from the pulpit the stuff
they hear on Oprah, and subscribe to the same junk-psychology that
you can pick up from any TV sitcom, you know that the Church is not
to be looked upon as a leader of anything serious.[5]

Norwegian historian, Oscar Garstein, says that the Reformation
never took hold in Norway and that medieval Catholicism was pagan.
Garstein doubts that Norway ever became Christian. A thought that
has crossed my mind more than once while working on this research
is that for much of Europe to go so completely secular, one wonders
how "Christian" it really was in the first place. Is the topic "The Decline
of Christianity in Europe" really begging the question?

The stream of decline in Europe seems to have moved from denial
of Christianity to the irrelevance of religion to life in secular society.

For Norway, another and more acceptable thesis than Garstein's is
that the Reformation in Norway took 200–300 years to catch on, especially in the countryside. Research for Germany also supports this.

---

years if attendance continues dropping at its present rate, according
to statistics published on Monday."

5   Victoria Combe, "Christianity is 'Nearly Vanquished' in Britain,"
    The Times, 6 September 2001, 1. Online: http://portal. tele-
    graph.co.uk/   and   hit   p://www.thetimes.co.uk/article/0,,2-
    2001310271,00.html.

Government authorities, cities, and universities became "Lutheran" far more quickly than the peasants in the countryside.

Could we say that Lutheranization was a very slow process? People's customs are hard to change. Catholic rituals are slow to change, if they ever do. We have the example of a Lutheran church in Norway where, long after Lutheranism was introduced, people leaving church would genuflect toward a now blank, white wall. When the paint was removed, there was displayed the holy family.

In the Norway we experienced, the church is everywhere. Church buildings are omnipresent. Of course, the country and everyone in it is "Christian." People are married in church (if they are baptized), babies are baptized, and later confirmed. Birth and death records are kept in church, and funerals are held in church. But church attendance seems a non-issue. Sundays are for skiing, the cabins, and family. As far as I could tell, none of our relatives went to church.

My second-cousin Karin asked me one day, "Are you a personal Christian?" I did not take this to mean, "Are you born-again?" There would have been a word for that (*gjennomfødt*) and *gjennomfødt* was common pietistic language. I took it to mean (and her daughter said I am correct in this), "Are you personally involved in the church, or is church an important part of your life?" Since she asked the question, I took it that she was not a "personal" Christian. Christian of course, but not a personal Christian. I wonder if that is not the case elsewhere in Europe. People are decent, law-abiding, Christians who see no need to get involved in or attend a worship service. Society and government, which includes the church, take care of the person from cradle to grave and beyond.

Norway now is all up-in-arms because of the ordination of gays and lesbians. The theological faculty is flooded with students because they, and not the "church faculty" (*Menninghetsfakultet*), accept gays.

The Scandinavian people, as I see it, are no longer out to attack Christian doctrine or deny God's existence, but simply to ignore Christian institutions. This is a passive or practical denial. Life in the world is full of meaning and accomplishment. The fulfilled life in this world seems to have no need for weekly religious observance.

The Germany I came to see up close is similar to Norway and Sweden in being secularized, but also pagan to the core—perhaps neo-pagan is the word. The gods, the values, the *Weltanschauung* are all focused on the natural. Everything natural—earth, body—is sacred. Legends and pagan mythology (*Nibelungenlied*) are prevalent. Paganism is romanticized. Life is mythical. What is now called *New Age* religion by meditation was the norm in the house I lived in. The people exhibited high culture, are highly educated, but are exclusively secular. I remember thinking that the Germany of Luther's day was the Germany of today: non-Christian, suffused with personalized hedonism. Sunday is for sport. It is much better to exercise the natural body than to sit in a pew.

WHY HAS CHRISTIANITY DECLINED?

Let me suggest the big picture since the sixteenth-century reformations. However you want to assess medieval, western Christianity, it is clear that both Lutheran and Catholic reformers in the early sixteenth century deemed that Christianity was in dire straits and in need of thorough reformation. You may not be accustomed to thinking of the Catholic reformation alongside Luther's and Zwingli's efforts, but rather think of it as the "Counter Reformation," responding to Protestant reforms later in the sixteenth century. Protestant and Catholic scholars alike have reconceived that account of reformation history. There were several reformations going in the early sixteenth century. All agreed that the Christian church needed reform badly. Further, it is clear that both Lutheran and Catholic reformations did accomplish their intended reforms. Both reformations led to a revitalization of Christianity in their respective territories. While differences (in the sixteenth and seventeenth centuries) were intense within Protestantism, yes, within Lutheranism, and conflicts between Evangelical and Catholic circles fierce and even bloody, you could say that such vigorous battles reflected strong convictions about faith and life. The big picture is that into the eighteenth century the churches were alive and well, building systems of belief and piety, demanding and receiving commitment and followed by the people.

It is hard to assign the credit or blame for the decline of Christianity. One author credits "the liberation of women along with the sexual emancipation of the 1960s."[6] The more usual is to look to the so-called Industrial Revolution (1830–1870) that brought down the traditional pillars and mores of society in England, then spreading to the

---

6   Callum G. Brown, The Death of Christian Britain, (London and New York: Routledge, zool), cited in "Editorial," Scottish Bulletin of Evangelical Theology 19:1, (2001): 1.

Continent. The rise of what became known as the historical-critical method in the study of Scripture in the eighteenth and nineteenth centuries, first with deism in England, then with greater acceptance in France and Germany, had a devastating effect on the authority of Scripture as the divine Word of God.

Along with others, the decline of Christianity in the west began with the eighteenth-century Enlightenment. Deism, naturalism, and rationalism led to the humanization of everything divine. Out of the eighteenth century came existentialism, where subjectivity is truth, and liberalism, where everything is relative. In the nineteenth century, developments in science led to materialism, determinism, skepticism, and outright hostility to religion. By the end of the nineteenth century, neither Protestant nor Catholic had any "unified reaction to materialism."

Religion appeared to be on the defensive, in a world that was responding more and more to non-religious stimuli. For the first time in more than fifteen hundred years, Western European civilization seemed to be ignoring the Christian heritage to which it had been born and in which it had been nurtured.[7]

The word *Enlightenment* is a translation of the German *Aufklärung*, meaning a clearing up, an enlivening of culture, a revival of Christian humanism, an awakening of human potential from the scientific spirit of the previous age (physics, mechanics, and cosmology). Reaction to the persecution and religious warfare of the previous century led to a tolerance of all religions and a search for natural religion, the common elements in all religion. Enlightened adherents "distrusted all authority and tradition in matters of intellectual inquiry, and believed that truth could be attained only through reason, observation, and experiment."[8]

English deism, while not widely accepted in England, had great impact on France and Germany. The most devastating effect on traditional Christianity was the deist claim that reason is the judge of revelation. The effect of the conviction that reason is the prime authority was that Scripture and the traditions of the church were seen to be human in origin. All supernatural claims of Scripture, virgin birth, miracles, resurrection, and the like were all deemed irrational and

---

7   Carlton Hayes and Charles Cole, History of Europe (New York: Macmillan, 1949) II: 325.

8   The Concise Oxford Dictionary of the Christian Church, 1977 ed., s.v. "Enlightenment, The."

dispensable. Dead people do not rise. H. E. G. Paulus (1761–1851) of Heidelberg in the middle of the Enlightenment held that Jesus' resurrection was recovery from an apparent death. R. R. Niebuhr reported that when he was in divinity school the discussion was whether Jesus simply recovered from a severe illness. Now you have New Testament critic John Dominic Crossin with his theory of the dogs.[9] In all this, religion must he reasonable and natural, not mysterious and supernatural.

The flow of ideas went from English deism, to French naturalism, to German rationalism. The French were fanatically intolerant of the Catholic Church and attacked its supernatural superstitions. My favorite here is the French Encyclopedists—driven by rejection of everything against common sense, they attempted to gather all human sciences, all truth known to humanity, into one grand work—the encyclopedia.

An early German rationalist maintained that truth is demonstrable, producing a logical certainty akin to mathematics (his discipline), and sought to transfer to theology that same logical certainty from "pure reason." An optimistic assessment of the human condition led to a belief in a historical progress toward individual and social perfection. Neither supernatural revelation, nor supernatural rescue from sin, but an originally implanted morality leads to this individual and social completeness.

By the end of the nineteenth century, neither Protestant nor Catholic had any unified reaction to materialism.

What really haunts succeeding centuries after the eighteenth century is the dictum by German rationalist and deist Gotthold Ephraim Lessing. The well-known "Lessing's ditch" asserts that "the accidental truths of history can never provide the proof for the necessary truths of reason." A huge chasm is posited between the accidents of history (read: religion) and the necessities of reason. What emerged from this is "historical consciousness," that religion is a part of human history and cannot escape the relativity of history.

---

9   Crossin, a member of the Jesus Seminar and a laicized Catholic priest, has suggested that the body of Christ was eaten on the cross by scavenging animals.

Many currents of thought in the nineteenth century continued along the lines of Enlightenment Christianity. Two already mentioned, existentialism and liberalism, continue the attack on objective truth, whether in Scripture, dogma, or philosophical metaphysics. Value, religious meaning, and spiritual experience come from within the person not from some outside authority. Truth derives from the subject, not the object.

The turn to the subject against metaphysics and the "great syntheses" resulted in theology's turn to sociology as the basis of theology. The turn to the subject as the basis of doctrine away from objective norms (Scripture, tradition, and metaphysics) is the most diabolical development out of the nineteenth century and casts a long shadow into our century, country, and church. Doctrine by committee—polling the experiences of people—becomes the subjective norm, which changes with the shifting sands of the time. Experience in Luther is the last point of reception — application of the truth — not the determination of the truth. Now, however, the primary filter of truth is human experience, of which sociology gives an account. The demise of metaphysics and the "great systems" is especially destructive to Catholic and Lutheran orthodoxies. When the philosophical base of Christian dogmatics erodes, foundations crumble; sociology and psychology are no substitutes, since they lack ontology (reality in being).

One more factor in the cultural milieu of decline is the influence of theology at the university, where pastors are trained and society leaders are educated. I think that universities have not received the attention they deserve in how the shape and mood of the times are formed. The universities I know in Europe (and the United States) are, almost by definition, left leaning. I have heard it said that no "evangelical" could ever be hired in a European or American university. The media people, the publishing houses, the sources of information, all come out of the universities. Teachers are trained in college; college teachers are trained in university graduate schools.

The demise of metaphysics and the "great systems" is especially destructive to Catholic and Lutheran orthodoxies.

What would the layperson have been thinking during these times: the eighteenth to twentieth centuries. How can one keep the faith when pastor and teacher keep changing the faith? Where is the faith when sermons were devoted to a discussion of current events, scientific discourses, and homespun advice on a variety of subjects, such as stall feeding, vaccinia, coffee drinking, drunkenness, careless bathing, the culture of silkworms, intelligent agriculture, the profitableness of potato raising …?[10]

One major problem with relativism is that when religion is based on the experience of the faithful, the faithful end up defining the faith. Relativism in belief leads and led to relativism in behavior. When rock solid mores, moral absolutes, give way to relativism, you end up with twentieth-century situation ethics, where morality is dictated by the situation and the subject. Also out of relativism came twentieth-century world-come-of-age theology, where the secularity of the world is celebrated. University professors can debate whether relativism is relative, but when wrong becomes right people become confused and disillusioned.

I want to emphasize that, in Germany at least, there is a Zeitgeist and it is secular/pagan. Zeitgeist is not just "spirit of the times" but also the prevailing milieu; the very air that you breathe and water you drink contain and convey the fabric that is life in today's romantic/pagan Germany. It seems to me that the Zeitgeist is a two-way proposition: it derives from the populace and in turn influences the populace. The flow of cultural Zeitgeist is to and from the university, the pulpit, the press, and especially the town square. The laity are sucked into the Zeitgeist without knowing it. So a liberal ethos drives society in a certain direction, which in turn drives the ethos.

In nineteenth-century Scandinavia and Germany there is confessionalism, which is orthodoxy revived, and pietism, strong in commitment and following, alongside the prevailing romanticism and liberalism. In the cultural milieu, in university philosophy and theology, among the literati, "the cultured despisers," conservative orthodoxies and pieties, were first debunked and then ignored. The certainties of mathematics and science were held up as the norms for belief in what was possible in this world, the only world we can see, test, and trust.

New impulses in the twentieth century, situational ethics or new morality, world-come-of-age theology, existential theology, the "new hermeneutics," and process theology all furthered the decline. Radical theology, including the death-of-God literature, was the most logical

10 Walter Forster, *Zion on the Mississippi* (St. Louis: CPH, 1953), 12.

outcome of the nineteenth-century turn to the subject, to the individual's experience. If God is absent in the subject, and there is no object without the subject, God is not.

Efforts at religious revival in the twentieth century, missionary and ecumenical movements, revivalism in America, neo-orthodoxy, and the Luther renaissance, indicate that society at large was on a slippery slope, as the popularity of nihilism showed. This is coupled with the fact that the twentieth century became the most barbaric century on human record.

In England, Germany, and France, the Enlightenment did not have the impact on Roman Catholicism that it did on Protestantism. Liberal, Catholic modernism at the end of the nineteenth century was condemned by the Roman hierarchy (1907), and still is. Thus may we say that the deleterious effects of the Enlightenment had less impact on Catholic countries, except France.

Not everyone drinks the same water, as I have emphasized, with the confluence of liberalism and confessionalism, pietism and romanticism. Also I think we have to say that the 8 percent figure for British church attendance is not nothing. So it goes down to 2 percent; 2 percent is not nothing. One thinks of a theology of remnant. The Lord was willing to go down in count and spare Sodom if he could find ten righteous in Sodom, after all. My point is that while the cultural signs point to the decline of Christianity, Christianity is not dead in these lands. We know that the Christian faith was alive, although underground, during the period of communism in Russia, and perhaps was stronger in East Germany during the time of Russian occupation.

The history of modern Christianity is not only a tale of woe to tell. Not all went in the direction of the rationalists. When we speak of new -isms, movements, and changes in the nineteenth century, we must remember that traditional orthodoxies and pieties continued as well. In fact, opposition to rationalism and relativism spurred on the confessional movements in the nineteenth century that are the background of the Missouri Synod. Confessionalism, called Lutheran Awakening, Theology of Repristination, and Erlangen Theology, sought to recapture the christocentric character of the gospel and the authority of Scripture, along with the Lutheran Confessions.

I have tried to indicate on a philosophical and theological level the major causes of the decline of Christianity in Europe. The future does not look good for Europe or America.

WHAT ARE THE CONSEQUENCES?

The results of these developments out of Enlightenment Christianity, through the nineteenth-century -isms, best summarized as rationalism and relativism, are that all the foundations of traditional Christianity are knocked down and destroyed. The Bible belongs to ancient history. Luther is dead. The confessions were produced by a bygone age. All the great systems, doctrines, and ecclesiastical institutions have run their course. All the standards and authorities are turned upside down. Why would anyone want to associate with a religion that has so run itself into the ground?

One seemingly permanent consequence of these nineteenth-century -isms is toleration. No religion has the corner on truth. Truth is a matter of individual preference. Toleration initially was both the awareness and acceptance of religious pluralism. This is on the level of historical fact—the world is full of religions. Where toleration went beyond acknowledgment was in the ecumenical movement where "celebrate diversity" was the slogan. Diversity means that individuals are different, experiences are different, therefore religious belief and practice are different. If people find meaning in church, good for them; if they find meaning some other way, good for them. The seemingly universal acceptance and practice of toleration is the natural outcome of Enlightenment thinking and a primary factor in the decline of European Christianity. If the church down the road has no claim to objective truth, but is only what the pastor on a given Sunday thinks, and I do not like or agree with what he thinks, I have no reason to go. I have my own views. Who is he to tell me what to think and do? It is far better to go skiing alone in the woods.

A current German professor illustrates the results of Enlightenment thinking. He writes regarding gender roles and the reading of Genesis: just as the Bible is no longer an authoritative guide for the origin of the world (geology is better), so too the Bible has lost its status as a standard for defining gender roles (social studies are better).[11] The primary authority is human experience in today's ELCA discussion of the gay agenda. It is a short step from celebrating diversity in religious

---

11   This by a theologian, Christoph Bultmann, and published by LSTC. Christoph Bultmann, "Luther on Gender Relations—Just One Reading of Genesis?" *Currents in Theology and Mission* 29:6, (2002): 425.

belief to celebrating diversity in all dimensions of human experience. A not too subtle shift has taken place, with the full endorsement of modern philosophy and theology, namely, that everything is historically conditioned, including and especially the Bible and all subsequent church history. Thus the primary authority today is not Scripture but modern science, what modern science teaches us about creation, the evolution of the human race, and the complexities of human sexuality. What utterly dumbfounds me here is that science, and not Scripture, is seen to be the objective arbiter of truth. The critics of divine inspiration used to make fun of those who seemed to think that Scripture floated out of heaven untouched by human hands, but now those same critics who advocate the truth of science over Scripture think of science as untouched by human hands. But science is the creation of scientists, who, given the premise of relativism, are as relative as anyone or anything else. Having lived in the university for thirty-three years, I came to see that mathematics and the various sciences were not absolute. There is no such thing as "pure science." Theories were constantly changing. A real eye opener to me about the scientific value of mathematics came in my conversations with the chair of the Marquette Math Department. "What do numbers prove?" I asked in one conversation. "Nothing," was the reply. Science is based on hypothesis. Scientists themselves readily admit the hypothetical character of their theories. To me it is sad for church leaders to take scientific theory, worse yet sociological theory, at face value while relegating Scripture to the relativity of history. A recent conversation with the professor of theology and science at Marquette University helped me see that, given the rationalist's premise, science is filled with as much uncertainty as religion; and the reverse is also true, that theology has as much certainty as science. Witness the Uncertainty Principle in quantum theory from Werner Heisenberg.[12]

---

12 "In the *Quantum Mechanical world*, the idea that we can measure things exactly breaks down. Let me state this notion more precisely. Suppose a particle has momentum p and a position x. In a *Quantum Mechanical world*, I would not be able to measure p and x precisely. There is an *uncertainty* associated with each measurement, e.g., there is some dp and dx, which I can never get rid of even in a perfect experiment. This is due to the fact that whenever I make a *measurement*, I must disturb the system. (In order for me to know something is there, I must *bump* into it.) ... This *uncertainty* leads to many strange things. For example, in a *Quantum*

What utterly dumbfounds me here is that science, and not Scripture, is seen to be the objective arbiter of truth.

Another way to see the changes that took place before and after the Enlightenment is to look at the concept of "history" itself. Prior to the Enlightenment, history was seen to be the arena of God's activity. History revolved around the divine. After the Enlightenment history was seen to revolve around man. Man is in control of his destiny. Imminence replaced transcendence and the foundations of Christianity became uncertain. History is contingent and everything is historical, including the Bible. Since every book is relative to its historical setting, each book needs an introduction; hence the rise of the discipline of biblical introduction. Then came biblical theology, namely biblical theologies in the plural; every book has its own unique point of view. The Bible is not God's word to man, but man's talk about God.

A more recent result of the decline is the media culture, which by definition is secular to the core. "The Church now takes its cues from secular society," and is driven by media culture.[13] When and where there are no moral absolutes, anything goes—and everything usually does go. When relativism is rampant, there are no standards of decency. The fallout from the Enlightenment is that when absolutes are attacked and dismissed, nothing is put in its place—no foundations, everything is sinking sand. A radical reversal has taken place. In previous times, the church, the guardian of truth, announced the judgment of God against secular immorality; now that the church has lost or abdicated its role as protector of morality, the *seculum* (world) defines morality as it pleases (erotic appetites).

Mechanical world, I cannot predict where a particle will be with 100% certainty. I can only speak in terms of probabilities. For example, I can say that an atom will be at some location with a 99% probability, but there will be a 1% probability it will be somewhere else (in fact, there will be a small but finite probability that it will be found across the Universe). This is strange." James N. Inarnura, "Heisenberg Uncertainty Principle," n.p. Online: http://zebu.uoregon.edu/-imamura/208/ jan27/hup.html

13 See note 5.

Some have hoped that a renaissance would come in the twenty-first century, repeating the every-300-year-trend of a renaissance in the past.

The church has "lost or abdicated" its role as protector of truth. The church, whose pastors and teachers are educated at the university (Europe), was all too willing a partner in the decline. The churches that bemoan miserable church attendance, for example, Sweden, have only themselves to blame. When religion classes are allowed to be taught in school by atheists, as in Norway, it is inevitable.

While Enlightenment thinkers had visions of improving society, freed from the tyrannical and superstitious church, they really reversed the course of history. Skepticism, determinism, fatalism, natural religion, and nihilism were the characteristics of classical paganism. "In the fields of art, literature, music, and architecture, the vogue of the Enlightenment was for the 'classical.' It was felt that the models of ancient times, reintroduced by the Renaissance, were the most rational and the most natural."[14] The Enlightenment was really a throwback to primitive times, one result of which was the loss of freedom. If everything is historically conditioned, we are caught in the web of causality. Fatalism and nihilism were the characteristics of the culture that Christianity arose in and attacked. The Christian gospel provides a way out of the inexorable cycles of nature. God broke into history to break the claws of historical determinism.

History and historical consciousness will never provide freedom from the shackles of paganism. Romanticize paganism all you want, praise "the classical," and you end up with Paul's assessment of a temple on every corner (Acts 17). It turns out that the new is very old and enslaving. There must be something tempting about "classicism," trying to maximize human potential. It did not work in the fifteenth century or in the eighteenth.

I am concerned that the decline in Europe, showing no signs of reversal, will ever increase the decline in America. Leadership coming out of Europe on the Protestant side is going nowhere; it is floundering because confessionalism did not carry the day and liberalism provides no foundation for theological inquiry. Mediational theology (*Vermittlungstheologie*), trying to harmonize the two, fizzled out. Everyone is on his or her own. On the Catholic side, significant

14   History of Europe, 11:107.

theological leadership fed into Vatican II and continues to go forward, but the impact of academic theology on the laity, judging from France and Italy, seems minimal.

I do not see any signs of a reversal of the trend of decline in Europe and the United States. There are pockets of orthodoxy, pietism, and evangelicalism on the Protestant side and movements of Catholic renewal. But I see no major philosophical or theological movement afoot to reverse the trend of decline. There is some interest in metaphysics again. A few years back, the Tübingen Prof. Dr. Eberhard Jüngel was held up as a significant breakthrough out of the logjam of liberalism and neo-orthodoxy. Some, myself included, have hoped that a renaissance would come in the twenty-first century, repeating the every-300-year-trend of a renaissance in the past. We will see.

In the light of the turn to sociology and science, the word "decline" would be a compliment. If the world were not filled with so much violence, the word "assassination" of Christianity might be more appropriate.

One would hope that the deleterious effects of the Enlightenment would have run their course. How much more can you squeeze out of nothingness? Many have hoped that the leadership of the historical-critical method in biblical studies would decline. How many more methods can there possibly be to try in biblical studies? Would the mainline Protestant denominations take a strong position of reversing the sexual revolution instead of contributing to its furtherance?

Since the eighteenth century, Christianity has been in severe decline in Northern Europe and increasingly in America. We have heard for a few decades now that the center of Christianity is shifting from the West to Africa. The percentage of the world's total Christians in North America is projected to go from 15.0 percent in 1975 to 9.3 percent in 2025; compared to Africa 10.2 percent in 1975 to 25.9 percent in 2025.[15]

First, be suspicious, even skeptical, of the "advances" of science and social studies that seek to supplant "the faith of our fathers living still." Two can play the skeptics game. Their theories come and go. Jesus Christ is not a theory; he is God in flesh and blood.

---

15 "Southward shift of Christianity from North to Third World," n.p. Online: http://www.synergos.net/synergos/missions/Mega-tr_01.html

NOTE

KENNETH HAGEN, a Logia contributing editor, is Professor Emeritus of Historical Theology at Marquette University and chief editor of *Luther Digest*, a publication of the Luther Academy. He resides in Lake Mills, Wisconsin. An earlier version of this article was presented at Concordia University Wisconsin, Mequon, April 15, 2003, for their spring program, Christianity and Europe, sponsored by the Cranach Institute.

INDEX